Shooter's Bible

GUIDE TO FIREARMS ASSEMBLY, DISASSEMBLY, AND CLEANING

Shooter's Bible

GUIDE TO FIREARMS ASSEMBLY, DISASSEMBLY, AND CLEANING

ROBERT A. SADOWSKI

Skyhorse Publishing

This book is dedicated to all those tinkerers who have an insatiable urge to understand how firearms work and how parts fit together, and those students of guns who know a firearm is nothing more than a tool that needs cleaning and maintenance to perform best.

Skyhorse Publishing books may be purchased in bulk at special discounts for sales promotion, corporate gifts, fund-raising, or educational purposes. Special editions can also be created to specifications. For details, contact the Special Sales Department, Skyhorse Publishing, 307 West 36th Street, 11th Floor, New York, NY 10018 or info@skyhorsepublishing.com.

Skyhorse® and Skyhorse Publishing® are registered trademarks of Skyhorse Publishing, Inc.®, a Delaware corporation.

Visit our website at www.skyhorsepublishing.com.

14

Library of Congress Cataloging-in-Publication Data

Sadowski, Robert A.
   Shooter's bible guide to firearms assembly, disassembly, and cleaning / Robert A. Sadowski.
      pages cm
   ISBN 978-1-61608-875-0 (pbk. : alk. paper)
   1. Firearms--Maintenance and repair.   I. Title.
   TS535.4.S23 2012
   683.4'03--dc23

                                                         2012033040

Printed in China

CONTENTS

CONTENTS

Acknowledgments

I thank my loving wife Deborah for her mastery with a camera (she took most of the disassembly photos) and her patience as I looked for sprung springs on my hands and knees on the floor. Cooper, too, for sniffing out those pesky springs and tiny oily pins. Bella did not participate in this project, as she soon realized that after the umpteenth long gun was taken out of the case we were not going bird hunting.

To my dad, Robert Anthony Sadowski, who taught me how to use tools and the patience to understand how things come apart and go back together. And to mom, Carol Sadowski, who always believed in my projects, whatever they may have been or will be.

Special thanks to Neal Delmonico, owner of BTP (Brooklyn Trading Post), and his crew in Brooklyn, Connecticut, for help in procuring firearms. Without his help and generosity I would never have been able to write this book. Please buy stuff from BTP. Also, thanks to Stu Stoyanovich for his generosity.

Many manufacturers and manufacturers' representatives helped in creating the book, and in no particular order I'd like to thank: Greg Jenks and Sue Gray of Numrich Gun Parts; Gradient Lens Corporation; Larry Weeks of Brownells; George Dewey of J. Dewey Rods; Greg Cohen of Mil-Comm Products; Scott Baron of PistolGear.com; Matthew O'Donnell of Model & Toolmaking; Daniel Humke of RockYourGlock.com; Dan Wray of We-Deas Inc.; Bill Dermody of Savage Arms; Cara Pebbles of Otis Technologies; Deb Williams and Chad Dyer of Springfield Armory; Mark Malkowski of Stag Arms; Mike Farrel of Ithaca; Mike Leeds of Stoeger, Benelli and Franchi; Laura Burgess of Laura Burgess Marketing for Bersa; Paul Thompson of Browning and Winchester; Nick Ecker and Wayne Oliver of Charter Arms; Beverly Haynes and Joyce Rubino of Colt; Chad Shearer and Dudley McGarity of CVA; Jason Morton of CZ USA; Rick Homme of Legacy Sports International; Anthony Imperato of Henry Repeating Arms, Frank Harris of Kahr Arms; Ryan Williams of Kel Tec; Aaron Cummins of Kimber; Jessica Kallum of Remington and Marlin; Linda Powell of Mossberg; Kenny Barlow of North American Arms; Chris Peterson of PTR Inc.; Lana Prenevost of Media Direct for Taurus, Rossi, and Heritage Arms; Ken Jorgensen and Beth McAllister of Ruger; Matt Rice of Blue Heron Communications for Smith and Wesson; Chris Ballard of Cimarron Firearms Co.; Justin Biddle of Umarex USA; Craig Cushman of Thompson-Center; Allen Forkner of Swanson-Russell and Kathy McQueeney of SIG SAUER; Eric Wood of Steyr Arms; Alison Hall of Traditions Performance Firearms; and Jeff Patterson of Swanson-Russell and Tim Frampton of Weatherby.

Finally thanks to Skyhorse Publishing and my editor, Jay Cassell.

DISCLAIMER

Neither the author nor the publisher is responsible for damage to your firearm while performing these disassembly/assembly and cleaning instructions. These procedures are suggestions and do not supersede manufacturers' recommended instructions and procedures. Refer to the manufacturer with specific questions about your firearm. Also note that firearms with custom modifications void most manufacturers' warranties.

Introduction

I'm obliged to first state, though it should be a given, that you should carefully examine and ensure all firearms are unloaded prior to field stripping, disassembly, and cleaning. The steps that follow assume all firearms have been unloaded. Remember a firearm does not know you are looking down the barrel when you accidently press the trigger with your thumb. Nor does it know that it has fallen off the work bench on a concrete floor hammer first. Be careful. Be safe. Detailed disassembly of a firearm is seldom, if ever, required to clean a firearm. A normal field stripping is enough to thoroughly clean the weapon. But there are those times when weather, canoes, muddy river banks, tree stands, swamps, sand, ice, mice, attics, barns, neighbors, friends, floods, hurricanes, saltwater, vehicle trunks, pickup truck beds, dogs, horses, bird feathers, and other assorted occurrences completely muck up your firearm, requiring a detail disassembly. Disassembling a firearm is relatively simple, and there are only a few models that require real mechanical aptitude. Most disassemblies and cleanings are common sense and the steps that follow are presented in the order they should be performed. There are many ways to skin a cat and to strip down a firearm, but the steps here are presented in a fashion that is easy to understand and accomplish. You can disassemble as much or as little as you are comfortable with. Part numbers from manufacturers' exploded view drawings are also included, and an effort was made to use the manufacturers' nomenclature

If you have never disassembled and cleaned a firearm, first use a well ventilated area that has a large flat surface and good overhead lighting. Best practice is to lay out the parts as they are removed and in the order they were removed. Keep parts from different guns separate, and keep the separated parts in a container with a lid so they can be stored until the broken part is delivered. This way you will have all your parts in one place. Read through the steps completely before starting, and take your time. Remember, if the parts do not fit together easily, then something is amiss. Many of the firearms in this book are from the same family and over the years small details have changed but instructions should generally apply to all model families.

Robert A. Sadowski
East Haddam, Connecticut
May 2012

Tools

"Buggered is as Buggered Be."

Any work to be done on guns—work to be done right—needs specific tools. Use the wrong tool and you can easily "bugger" a perfectly fine firearm. Bugger is the pseudo-technical term describing the aftermath from some idiot who tried to use a crescent wrench to remove the grip screw from a pocket pistol or some other dubious act that caused said firearm to plummet in value according to the Blue Book and/or caused a gunsmith to grimace in disgust.

Screw slots, stripped threads, stretched springs, dinged stocks, scratched receivers—the list of mistakes made from the use of inappropriate tools and handling is long. It is also avoidable by using the proper tools and work space. Some of the mistakes are cosmetic and can reduce the value of your firearm. Others are potentially dangerous and can cause a firearm to jam or malfunction, while other mistakes are interred in a shoebox, a bunch of loose parts. Invest in and use the proper tools for disassembling your firearm. In all the years I have worked on firearms, I strive to leave the weapon in the same condition as I received it after the problem is fixed or work is complete. Here are some suggestions on how you should tool up.

≫ This is a sideplate screw on an S&W 329PD. Too much torque and wrong tool. Don't gorilla screws.

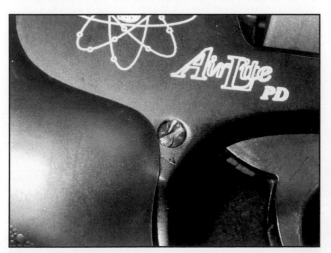

≫ The screw on this Ruger Mini-30 may not look bad, but go to trade this rifle and this slightly mangled screw slot will reduce the firearm's value. It might also cause a potential buyer to wonder what else has been buggered inside the mechanism.

SCREWDRIVERS

There was once a time when a gunsmith used specific screwdrivers for a specific brand of firearm. Smith & Wesson screw slots were different than side-by-side shotgun screw slots, for instance. Today special or unique screw slots are still found on certain types of firearms, such as side-by-side and over-and-under shotguns. A screwdriver set is a good investment. Sets that allow you to swap out tips are convenient, as numerous blade types and sizes allow for a perfect fit for many types of firearms. A set with flat blade tips, Philips tips, hex or Allen tips, and Torx tips should suffice in most situations. The tips are also softer than the screws they are removing, so you bugger the tip rather than the firearm. New tips are inexpensive. A set of small jeweler's screwdrivers is also helpful, especially when you need to manipulate the legs of springs in confined spaces.

≫ Left: example of a poorly fitted screwdriver in a screw slot; Right: some screw with properly fitted screwdriver.

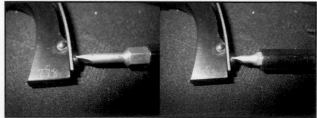

≽ This Pachmayr screwdriver set has an assortment of tips that will work for most jobs; a small jeweler's set allows access to tight places and tiny screws.

PUNCHES

Next on the tool list are punches. Many current semi-automatic pistols and shotguns hold their innards in place with pins. You will most likely come across straight pins, tapered pins, and rolled pins. A set of small diameter flat punches for straight and tapered pins, and a set of small diameter roll pin punches are required. Many new-manufacture pistols have the extractor retained by a roll pin, and if a flat punch is used on a roll pin, the punch can damage the pin. Pins are inexpensive but can be difficult to find at your local or big-box hardware store. Ordering pins online and shipping them takes time. Purchase extra pins if you anticipate frequent disassembly. You may also come across domed pin heads on an old S&W revolver or a double barrel shotgun. Concave punches are required for those pins, as a flat punch will mash—yes, bugger—the pin head.

≽ Note the rolled pin punches (right) have a domed tip.

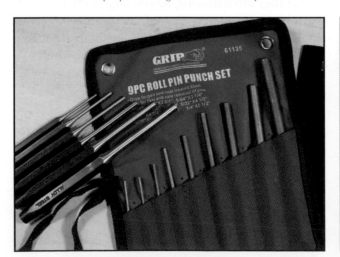

HEX AND TORX WRENCHES

A small set of standard and metric hex or Allen wrenches is invaluable, especially a set that offers numerous sizes. Many grips and rear sights use a hex or Torx-style screw head. Torx head screws can easily shut down a disassembly session fast. Have the right wrenches.

≽ These wrench sets from Gorilla Grip in metric, standard and Torx have up to nine different sized tips that fold out for use.

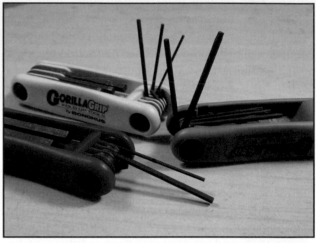

PLIERS

Needle-nose pliers are a must for grabbing spring legs and small parts. A straight as well as an angled pair are even better, as each provides a different way to hold and manipulate a part. A pair of non-marring pliers is smart, since they leave no teeth marks on whatever they take purchase. Also handy, especially in some weapons without a hole in the hammer strut, are a pair of locking pliers. Clamp them onto the strut to restrain the hammer spring, and the spring, hammer strut, and hammer are easy to handle.

≽ Assortment of pliers helps to grasp small parts and manipulate springs.

HAMMERS

I don't abide by the philosophy "If it doesn't fit, get a bigger hammer." In a firearm all pieces have a purpose and a place. I use three hammers: brass, nylon, and rubber. The brass is used to tap on a punch to remove a pin. A nylon head will not mar the finish when tapping home a pin. Knocking a wood stock off a receiver is reserved for the rubber mallet. It is gentle but firm with a nice piece of fine wood.

≽ The Brownells nylon/brass hammer makes short work with stubborn pins, while the large rubber mallet is gentle on wood stocks and metal finishes.

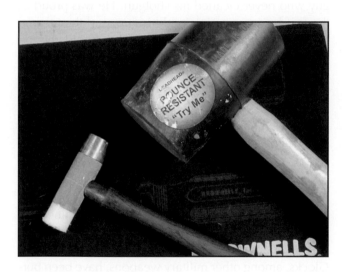

BENCH BLOCK, PADDED BENCH MAT, AND BENCH VISE

Unless you use a New York City phone book, most yellow pages are not thick enough to properly let a drifted pin fall free from a frame. A bench block has holes pre-drilled that allow the pin to fall free yet trap it in the hole. Use the phone book method and you may be on your hands and knees searching the floor for a lost pin. Many bench blocks are nylon and will not mar a firearm's finish. They also have molded grooves, so an oddly shaped part can be secured. A padded bench mat spares not only your firearm from dings and scratches but your table top, too. A work bench is a luxury for some of us, but sometimes a kitchen table or coffee table must make do. An old foam rubber yoga mat works great for those of you who are frugal. A bench vise is a good investment. Remember to pad the jaws so as not to mar a gun's finish.

≽ The nylon bench block allows pins to fall free, helps to keep rear sights free from damage, and helps to keep the firearm secure while working; the padded bench mat helps protect the weapon's finish and stock from scratches and dings. Both are from Brownells.

SMALL FLASHLIGHT OR HEAD LAMP

A weapon should be disassembled in a well-lit area over a flat bench top with plenty of room for arranging parts and maneuvering long guns. Overhead lighting is helpful, but at times you will need a light to see inside the frame or receiver.

EYE PROTECTION

If you are of the age to be wearing drugstore reading glasses, jump to the next section. If you don't make sure you wear safety glasses, accidents can happen. Weapons have springs that are under compression and want to relieve that tension. They will fly out and—God forbid—poke your eye out. Wear protection.

DIGITAL CAMERAS

As you disassemble a firearm, take pictures to show the relationship of parts in the mechanism. When reassembling and in doubt to where or how a part is oriented, refer to the digital images.

SPECIAL TOOLS

Some tools help make work on a specific model easier. Working on AR-15s is a much more pleasant experience when a lower receiver vise block is used. Chuck up the vise block in a bench vise, and insert the lower on the vise block as if it were a magazine. It's great for replacing triggers and hammers. If you work on weapons with coiled mainsprings like Ruger, Taurus, and some S&W revolvers, there will come a time when a mainspring compressor is the required third hand. A bushing wrench for a 1911 is another special tool that makes disassembly easier. Brownells (brownells.com) is a great source for tools. They can also help replace that spring that the carpet ate, too.

⩔   The coil spring compressor (top) and XDm extractor tool (bottom) are special-purpose tools designed for one specific job.

ODDS AND ENDS, WHATNOTS, AND BITS AND PIECES

Invaluable at times is a paperclip to retrain coil springs, or bits of wood to gently pry parts apart or hold a piece in a vise. Carpentry nails make great slave pins, too.

BEST PRACTICES

When I disassemble any firearm I always use a container to hold the parts. A shoe box will work. I use the plastic containers from take-out Chinese food to temporarily store screws, grip panels, gas pistons, pins, etc. In the event you need to relocate your work space, the containers hold all the parts and prevent them from getting lost. I also lay out parts as they come off the weapon in the order they were removed. This is especially helpful if you do not have a schematic for the weapon.

⩔   Here is how I lay out the parts, in this case a Mossberg 930 SPX.

CLEANING TOOLS

Professionals who rely on their weapons on a daily basis know the need to properly and consistently clean and maintain their firearms. Competitive shooters cannot allow a dirty gun to malfunction and cause them to lose a match. Hunters aiming at a trophy buck or facing a charging water buffalo want to be able to pull the trigger and have their rifle go bang. If you carry and store a gun for protection, all the more need to ensure your pistol or shotgun will perform when required.

A clean gun is a happy gun, I've heard said. It is also a sign of an owner's pride in his firearm and a requirement if you shoot. I've hunted pheasants with a guy who never cleaned his shotgun. He was proud of the fact he never maintained his gun, and there came a time when the pheasants flushed, he shouldered the gun, and nothing. No bang. No click. Come to find out you could have ground mushrooms in the barrel and action of that old semi-auto it was so dirty. I needed a large set of adjustable pliers and some gorilla muscle to remove the magazine cap.

Another acquaintance who frequented GSSF shoots equated low maintenance with no maintenance. His Glock jammed during competition and the range officer recommended he have the on-site armorer examine the pistol. The shooter explained the situation to the armorer, who took one look at the G17 and asked, "When was the last time you oiled this?" Glocks, among other military weapons, have been buried, soaked, and frozen, among other assorted torture methods, and come out shooting; that does not mean the pistol does not have to be maintained.

Hunting rifles can be subjected to cold, rain, snow, and other weather events. If caught in a downpour while in a treestand, strip your rifle down and pull the stock from the barrel/receiver assembly and thoroughly dry the components. Wood stocks are notorious for swelling and knocking sights out of zero, so dry your firearm as soon as possible. Shotguns, especially those used by waterfowl hunters, are subjected to wet, cold, and snowy conditions. In a duck blind or on the water there have been numerous occasions where a shotgun was accidently dropped in the water. I have a hunting acquaintance who dropped a beautiful Browning Auto-5 in a swamp. It involved a canoe and a hunting partner overly excited about a pair of mallards.

We all demand that our weapons perform and provide reliable service. Here are some easy and effective procedures to ensure your rifle, pistol, revolver, shotgun, or muzzleloader delivers on demand. Remember eye protection and latex gloves are excellent ideas when using solvents and oils. Also do everything over newspaper, paper bags, or a rag to absorb overspray and spills. It will save your kitchen table from smelling like a machine shop. Always refer to your firearm's manual prior to cleaning, as the manufacturers will have the recommendations on cleaning products and methods.

Always clean the bore from breech to muzzle. By pulling or pushing the patch and brush from breech to muzzle any dirt particles will be expelled out of the muzzle and not pushed into the weapon's action. Be extra cautious at the muzzle. Poor cleaning practices can wear the muzzle and adversely impact accuracy. The inside of your barrel is most important. Without cleaning, fouling from copper jackets and lead can build up and adversely affect accuracy. A poorly maintained barrel can also lead to rust and pitting. Gradient Lens Corporation manufactures borescopes that allow shooters to see the inside of their weapon's barrel. Examples of neglected bores are below.

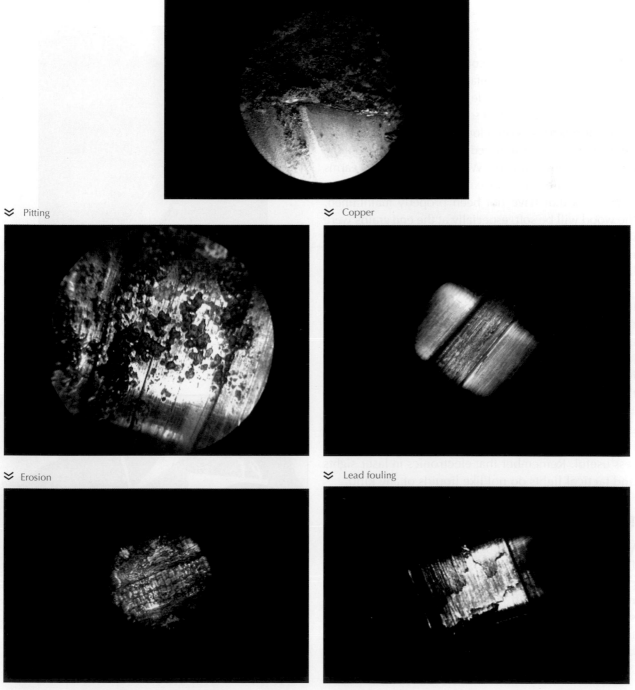

Rust

Pitting

Copper

Erosion

Lead fouling

Courtesy of Gradient Lens Corporation

Never use a wire brush or any type of abrasive to clean the exterior surface of a firearm, as you will scratch the finish. An old toothbrush is better to loosen and remove any dirt or grime buildup. Use a soft cloth to wipe the finish clean. AR uppers, for instance, are made of aluminum and susceptible to scratching and damage from a wire brush. There's also no need to add gouges and scratches to a nicely engraved sideplate on an over-and-under either.

There is a reason gun oil comes in small containers. Only a minimal amount is needed to keep your firearm operating. Too much oil accumulates dirt and debris, can make the gun slippery to hold, and will spit an oil vapor back in the face of the shooter. The oil vapor won't harm you if you are wearing shooting glasses, but you will look like a raccoon when you remove your glasses. Follow the manufacturer's recommendation on lubrication points inside the firearm. Outside the firearm, only a wipe with a soft, oily cloth if required. If the firearm is to be stored long-term, a slightly heavier oil wipe or grease is required depending on the storage length and environment. Wood stocks and forearms can deteriorate when in contact with oil. On some older guns that have not been properly maintained, the wood will be soft, especially at the end grains were the wood absorbed the oil. Most polymer frames will not deteriorate from gun solvents or oils, but check the label to be sure.

Avoid getting cleaning solvents and oils on optics. If the lenses are dirty or become contaminated with oil or solvents, spray the lens with a lens cleaner and use a lens cleaning cloth. Wipe the lens with the cloth in a circular motion. Never clean an optic lens that is dry, since you may scratch the surface coating on the lens.

Lasers and tactical lights on handguns and shotguns should be removed. Oil on a laser's lens will diffuse the laser beam. It will also make a tactical light less useful. Remember that electronics in laser sights and tactical lights do not like liquids of any kind.

RODS

When you think cleaning rods, think push or pull. Dewey Rods are the gold standard in rods and are pushed through the bore from breech to muzzle. The rods are coated with polymer so they do not mar or scratch barrel rifling. Otis Industries kits and Hoppe's Bore Snake use the pull method. Drop the non-marring brass weight of the Bore Snake down the bore and pull

the cord through. Otis rods are made of a flexible cable that is plastic coated to prevent scraping of the rifling. Bore Snakes are easy to use since the patch and brush are all one piece. When it gets dirty it can be cleaned in a dishwasher. Otis and Dewey rods allow users to change patches and brushes to suit their need. Dewey rods are one long straight piece of rod that can be used with a bore guide. A bore guide centers the rod in the barrel to help prevent the rod from flexing and rubbing against the rifling as it is pushed through the bore.

≫ Dewey rods have either a protective plastic coating or are brass so they will not scratch rifling.

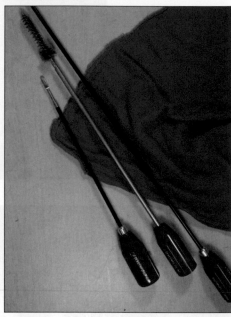

≫ The Hoppe's Bore Snake and Otis flexible cable are pulled through the barrel from the muzzle. The Bore Snake is made of cloth, while the Otis tool is plastic-coated cable.

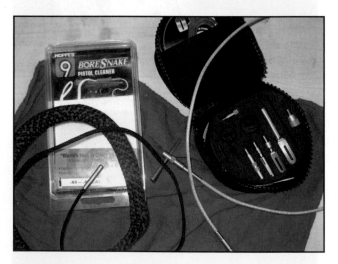

BRONZE AND NYLON BRUSHES

Bronze brushes are softer than steel, so they will not scratch the bore; nylon brushes are also safe to use on rifling and breeches. When using copper-removing bore cleaners, i.e. those that contain ammonia, use a nylon brush. Bronze is made with copper, and copper-removing solvents, if left on bronze bore brushes, will erode the brushes' bristles.

⩔ Bronze and nylon brushes; nylon is better for solvents containing ammonia. Slotted tip and jags push or pull patches through the barrel.

PATCHES AND MOPS

Use 100% cotton patches, which absorb and hold solvents and grime better than synthetic fabric. Mops hold solvents best, allowing solvent to evenly coat the inside of the barrel.

SOLVENTS AND DEGREASERS

Solvents are used to remove burned powder residue, lead, and metal fouling. Solvents come in liquids, aerosol sprays, gels, and paste. There are basically two types: solvents with ammonia and solvents without ammonia. Those with ammonia usually contain about 5% ammonia in the solvent; the ammonia is effective in breaking down and dissolving the copper residue from shooting copper jacketed bullets, such as those from high power centerfire rifles. Ammonia-based solvents attract moisture, so be sure to completely remove the solvent and lightly oil the barrel afterward. Non-ammonia based solvents work fine on fouling from lead bullets. Most solvents are liquid and are used to soak a cleaning patch; some solvents have a foaming action with foam evaporating as the solvent does its job.

⩔ A lineup of some of the usual suspects in solvents. Shooters Choice, Hoppe's, Butch's Bore Shine, and MC50 are liquid; Otis 085 Ultra Bore is a gel; Break Free CLP is an aerosol; and Gunslick is a foaming aerosol.

CLP

There are also CLP (Cleaner Lubricant Preservative) products that are sprayed on the firearm to dissolve carbon and fouling. It then leaves a lubricant for the mechanism and a preservative for the finish.

⩔ CLP products offer an easy one-product solution for cleaning, lubricating, and preserving.

OILS AND GREASE

Lubricants help keep your gun functioning as well as protect against corrosion and wear. A light coating of oil on metal-to-metal surfaces, like slide guides on polymer-framed pistols and base pins on single action revolvers, helps the mechanism work more easily, especially in mechanisms that receive a lot of heat like semi-automatic weapons. On AR-15s or 1911 competition pistols, for example, grease helps the sliding parts, as it does not burn off nor is it shed or flung off the parts as light oil is. Ever feel a fine spray in your face after firing your just-cleaned and just-oiled gun? That's the action flinging off excess oil. Grease is designed to stick to surfaces. Use it sparingly. In cold weather, grease can impede the gun's operating mechanism from working. Duck hunters in below-zero temperatures can attest to grease and oil seizing their guns, retarding the firing pin strike among other issues.

⩔ Slick operators like Rem Oil, MC2500 and others are used in the final cleaning step.

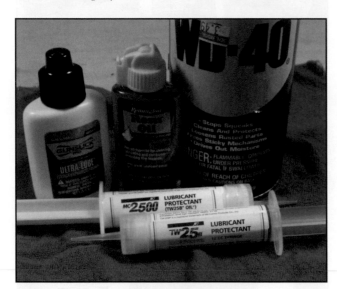

SPECIAL AND NOT SO SPECIAL CLEANING TOOLS

Canned air is extremely helpful, since the blast of air helps dislodge crud. It also makes your job easier as you may not need to detail strip a firearm to clean it. An old toothbrush soaked in solvent can help remove built-up gunk. Dental picks are helpful to clean out hard to reach areas inside a weapon's frame. A bore guide centers the rod in the barrel to help prevent the rod from flexing and rubbing against the rifling as it is pushed through the bore. Penetrating oils are helpful to loosen stubborn screws that are fouled from burnt powder residue or rust. A gun vise holds a rifle steady for cleaning.

Cleaning and Lubricant

Rifles

BOLT ACTIONS

Bolt actions are typically uncomplicated designs and, as the name infers, are turn-bolt mechanisms that are manually cocked by the shooter. The two main types of bolt actions in use today are control-feed and push-feed actions. In a controlled-round action the cartridge is grasped by the bolt's claw-type extractor as soon as the bolt pushes the cartridge forward from the magazine and into the chamber. In a push-feed action the round is not held by the extractor as it exits the magazine and enters the chamber. The controlled-feed actions can be found in current rifles by CZ, Kimber, Ruger, Winchester (current models only), and others. Push-feed actions are used in rifles by Remington, Steyr, Thompson Center, Weatherby, Savage, Browning, Howa, and Mossberg, among others.

⌄ Example of four bolt styles (left to right) Weatherby MK V, Ruger Hawkeye, Thompson Center Icon, and Remington 700; the Ruger Hawkeye is an example of a control-feed, Mauser-style; the other three are push-feeds.

Bolt-action rifles are very easy and simple to clean and maintain. The bolt assembly, barrel/receiver, and trigger are the main components, and each needs specific maintenance. Rimfire bolt action rifles can foul more easily than centerfire bolt actions, since .22 rimfire ammo is coated with a dry lubricant that quickly builds up in the chamber area. Here's how to keep your bolt action cranking and grouping for years to come.

BOLT ACTIONS: BOLT ASSEMBLY

1. Remove the bolt assembly from the barrel receiver and disassemble the bolt assembly enough to remove the firing pin.
2. Use a spray degreaser to remove any oil or grease from the firing pin, mainspring, and firing pin channel in the bolt body.
3. Keep these parts relatively dry and wipe with an oiled cloth. Too much oil can cause the mechanism to misfire, as the oil can collect dirt and in cold weather the oil thickens.
4. The bolt face is the next area to clean, as grit, powder residue, and brass bits and shavings from cartridges can build up. Push-feed actions with their recessed bolt faces seem to accumulate more grime than claw-type extractor actions. Use a solvent to loosen grit, then use a small dental pick or toothpick to clean the recesses. An old toothbrush works well, too, especially on the extractor. On centerfire bolt actions, function test the extractor to ensure the spring works and nothing is causing it to stick or not operate. Use a fired case of the correct caliber and hook the rim of the case under the extractor to compress the ejector spring, Figure 1.

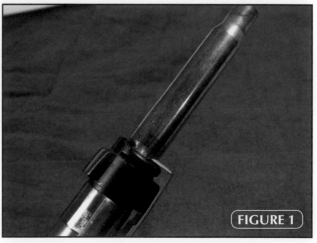

FIGURE 1

5. Place a drop of oil or grease on the lugs. The lugs mate with recesses in the receiver. This a tight metal-against-metal fit. Judicious use of oil and a dab of grease is all that is needed. For a rimfire bolt, lightly oil or grease the bolt body where it contacts the inside of the receiver.

BOLT ACTIONS: BARREL

1. Attach a clean patch to your rod of choice and soak it in a bore solvent.
2. Run the patch from breech to muzzle and let the solvent work for a few minutes, Figure 2.

FIGURE 2

Remember, ammonia based solvents must be completely removed from the bore as they attract moisture, which can lead to rusting and pitting. A bore guide can be used to ensure the cleaning rod stays centered in the bore, Figure 3.

FIGURE 3

3. If the barrel is excessively fouled, run a solvent soaked nylon bristle brush through the bore. Repeat these steps if you see debris.
4. Repeatedly run patches through until the patch is clean, Figure 4.

FIGURE 4

5. Run a clean patch that is lightly oiled through the bore.

BOLT ACTIONS: RECEIVER/STOCK

1. Run a lightly oiled rag of soft cloth over metal surfaces; use a dry cloth on wood or synthetic stocks. If the stock is dirty use some soapy water to clean it. A household cleaner may be too harsh for some stock finishes.

SEMI-AUTOMATIC ACTIONS

AR-15, Remington 740s, Browning BARs, Benelli R1s, PTR-91s, M1As, and others all use the energy of a fired cartridge to manipulate the action. Some actions bleed gas from a fired cartridge from the barrel into a piston that opens the action and ejects an empty cartridge case. A recoil spring closes the action but not before chambering a fresh round. Since the action mechanism is subjected to the burned gas of a fired cartridge, residue builds up on those parts more quickly than other types of actions. Each specific rifle has its own maintenance requirements. The AR-15 is a good example of how a centerfire semi-automatic rifle should be cleaned. Steps following assume the AR is field stripped.

SEMI-AUTOMATIC ACTIONS: UPPER RECEIVER

1. Attach a slotted tip to the end of the rod then snake the rod from muzzle to chamber so the tip emerges from the chamber end, Figure 5.

FIGURE 5

2. Attach a patch to the slotted tip and apply solvent to the patch.
3. Twist the solvent soaked patch so the chamber area is wet then pull the patch through the bore from chamber to muzzle. Allow the solvent to work for three to five minutes.
4. Snake the rod through without a tip attached and when it emerges from the chamber add a brush—nylon for ammonia based solvents—and pull it through, Figure 6.
5. Replace the brush tip with a slotted tip and snake through the bore; at the chamber end add a patch to the slotted tip and pull through. Repeat until patch is clean.
6. Run a lightly oiled patch through the bore.

7. For AR-15s use an AR-specific chamber brush soaked in solvent attached to a small rod; plunge the brush into the chamber several times and rotate the brush when it is fully plunged into the chamber, Figure 7.

FIGURE 7

8. Use an all-purpose brush or and an old toothbrush soaked in solvent to clean around the gas tube, then run a pipe cleaner into the tube.
9. Wipe the inside and outside of the upper dry.
10. Use a lightly oil patch at the end of a rod to lubricate the inside of the upper, the chamber and especially the locking lugs.

SEMI-AUTOMATIC ACTIONS: BOLT COMPONENTS

1. Soak the bolt with solvent and allow it to work. For AR-15s use a cotton swab or pipe cleaner soaked with solvent to clean out the gas key and carrier vent holes on the bolt carrier, then wipe dry, Figure 8. The dry lubricant applied to

FIGURE 6

FIGURE 8

.22 Short/Long/Long Rifle bullets and the lead the bullets most .22 rimfire are loaded with can gunk up the bolt breech face and extractor. Saturate these areas with solvent and allow the solvent to work. Then use a dental pick or toothpick to pick out and scrub away the debris. Wipe clean, then lightly oil.

2. Clean the bolt, firing pin, firing pin retaining pin, and cam pin with solvent then wipe dry. An old toothbrush helps remove carbon built up between the bolt lugs, Figure 9.

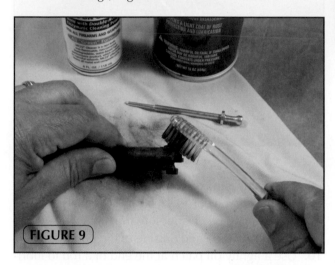

FIGURE 9

3. With the extractor installed in the bolt, place a few drops of solvent around the ejector then take a fired case and place it under the lip of the extractor and use the empty case to rock the extractor back and forth. Wipe off excess solvent, then lightly lubricate.

4. Lightly lube the firing pin and the firing pin hole in the bolt, the charging handle latch, and the inner and outer surfaces of the bolt carrier. Place a drop of lubricant on the inside of the carrier key.

5. Liberally lube the cam pin and bolt as well as the slide rail areas of the bolt carrier where it contacts the inside of the upper.

SEMI-AUTOMATIC ACTIONS: LOWER RECEIVER

1. Clean with solvent all areas of powder fouling. Use an old toothbrush to scrub away stubborn fouling. Do not use a wire brush to clean the lower as it is made of aluminum and will scratch easily.

FIGURE 10

2. Wipe away or use canned air to blow out dirt from the trigger mechanism, Figure 10.

3. Clean the magazine well, magazine release button, and magazine catch recess on the left side of the lower. Also clean the bolt catch mechanism, and make sure the takedown and pivot pins are clean.

4. Clean the buffer, action spring, and inside the receiver extension/buffer tube with a large patch or soft cloth attached to a cleaning rod.

5. Lightly lube the inside of the receiver extension/ buffer tube.

6. Liberally oil the trigger and hammer pivot pin areas, bolt catch, and magazine release button.

RIFLE MAGAZINE

1. Use solvent to clean the follower and the lips of the magazine body.

2. Run a lightly oiled cloth through the magazine body.

LEVER ACTIONS

Lever actions do not lend themselves easily to cleaning since they are more complicated to disassemble. A hunter who infrequently shoots does not need to remove the lever or bolt. Cowboy action shooters the likes of Dirty Deb and The Original Mexican Bob, who shoot frequently and shoot lead, should regularly disassemble their rifle. This is especially true if you use black powder loads. Black powder residue attracts moisture and can cause a rifle to rust as quickly as overnight.

LEVER ACTIONS: BARREL

1. Fully open the finger lever.
2. Using a pull type rod and snake it through the muzzle, then add a patch saturated with solvent and pull it through. Allow solvent to work for a few minutes.
3. If fouled and leaded, pull a brush through. Repeat until no debris comes out of the barrel.
4. Run clean patches through the bore until the patch comes out clean. Then run a lightly oiled patch through the barrel.

LEVER ACTIONS: RECEIVER/BOLT

1. Use a solvent soaked toothbrush to brush the face of the breech bolt and extractor trying to brush the residue out of the action. Canned air can be used to blow out the action. Hold the rifle upside down to brush/blow the grit out of the receiver, Figure 11.

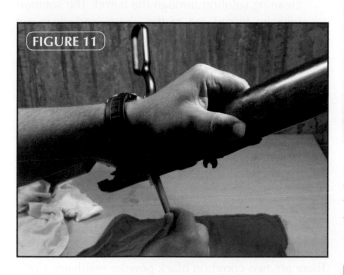

FIGURE 11

2. Use a patch to wipe away the solvent.
3. For Winchester 1866s and 1873s, Marlin 336s and 1894s, and Henrys, place a drop of oil on both sides of the breech block where it slides in the receiver, on lever actions with vertical recoil blocks, like Winchester 1892s, 1886s, and Model 94s and 71s add a drop of oil where the block slides against the inside of the receiver. On Browning BLRs, lube the rotating bolt head.
4. Place less than a drop of oil on the hammer and trigger pivot pins, on the outside edge of the magazine follower, the trunions, and where the lever mates and pivots in the frame.
5. Wipe the outside of the rifle—metal and wood—with a lightly oiled, soft cloth.

SINGLE-SHOT ACTIONS

The actions of single shots vary. There are falling block types—Ruger No. 1, Winchester 1885, Sharps 1874, and others—where the breech block drops vertically to load a cartridge when the lever is moved forward. For rifles like the TC Encore, Rossi Wizard, and CVA Apex, the barrel pivots open to load a cartridge.

SINGLE-SHOT ACTIONS: BARREL

1. Clean the bore as you would a bore for a bolt action rifle.
2A. For falling block actions: Apply solvent in the breech area of falling-block actions and use a brush to scrub clean.
2B. For models with tilting barrels: Apply solvent to the frame where it mates with the breech when the barrel is in the closed position.

Black Powder

Hot soapy water is a good way to clean black powder residue; there are also solvents specifically made for dissolving black powder. With either method remember to oil the entire firearm after cleaning, as black powder residue will attract moisture.

INLINE IGNITION MUZZLELOADERS

Inline ignition muzzle loaders are a breeze to clean compared to side lock rifles. Stainless steel and synthetic stocks easily clean up from black powder residue, and breech plugs make short work of bore cleaning.

1. Remove the breech plug.
2. Run a solvent soaked patch from the breech to the muzzle. Allow the solvent to work.
3. Next pull a bore brush through the bore, Figure 12.
4. Run patches through until they come out clean, then run a lightly oiled patch through.

FIGURE 12

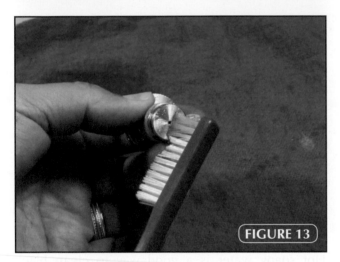

FIGURE 13

5. Use an old toothbrush to scrub the breech plug and the threads inside the breech of the barrel, Figure 13.
6. Apply an anti-seize compound to the threads of the breech plug, Figure 14.
7. Lightly oil the outside metal surfaces.

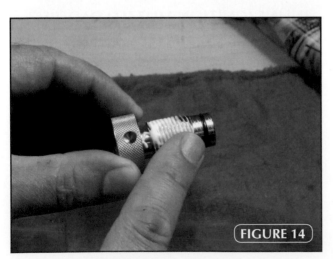

FIGURE 14

SIDE LOCK MUZZLELOADERS

Many modern replicas of Hawken, Pennsylvania, and Kentucky long rifles as well as Brown Bess and other muskets have a hooked breech that allows the barrel to be removed from the stock. Some rifles are still made as they were in the 18th century, and the barrel is not easily removed from the stock. Usually a series of small pins hold the barrel to the stock and removing the pins can easily damage a nice curly maple stock. For a hooked breech model follow the steps for a modern inline muzzleloader. For old-school models, follow these steps.

1. Remove the nipple and clean-out screw from the bolster/drum of a percussion lock gun or the touch hole liner from a flintlock ignition gun.
2. Wrap a patch around a jag tip attached to a ramrod.
3. Pour warm soapy water or solvent down the muzzle and use the patched jag to pump the cleaning solution through the barrel. The solution with be forced out of the nipple and clean-out screw holes on a percussion lock and the touch hole liner for a flintlock.
4. Continue to pump the patch up and down the barrel and change patches as they become dirty. Repeat until patch is clean. Dry parts thoroughly.
5. Run a liberally oil patch through the bore and lightly oil the outside surface.
6. Clean the lock by rubbing it with solvent and scrubbing it with a brush, then dry and lightly oil

REVOLVERS

There are two common black powder revolvers, Colt's with an open-top frame and cylinder base affixed to the frame and Remington 1858 models with a full frame like modern revolvers. The Ruger Old Army is similar to the Remington 1858. All need to be thoroughly cleaned immediately after shooting to avoid rust.

1. Soak the cylinder in solvent or hot soapy water. For the Remington 1858 model, soak the base pin. For the Ruger Old Army, also soak the rammer/loading lever.
2. Remove the nipples from the cylinder and soak the nipples in solvent/soapy water.
3. For Colt style revolvers, run a solvent soaked patch through the barrel and let it work or pour hot soapy water through the barrel. For Remington

1858 models and Ruger Old Army models, run a solvent soaked patch through the barrel and let it work or pour hot soapy water through the barrel from the forcing cone end so water does not flow into the mechanism. Continue with hot soapy water until it turns clear or patches come out clean.

4. Use a bristle brush to scrub the barrel, cylinder, and nipples. Pay attention to the forcing cone and scrub away any leading. For Colt style revolvers, wipe down the loading lever.

5. For Colt style revolvers, wipe down the frame and cylinder pin. For Remington 1858 models and Ruger Old Army models, wipe down the frame and loading lever. Make sure parts are clean and dry.

6. Liberally oil a soft clean cloth and rub all the parts and reassemble.

7. Add a drop of oil in the frame openings—trigger, hammer, pawl, cylinder latch/bolt—and work the mechanism to distribute the oil.

Shotguns

There are three types of shotgun actions pump, semi-auto and break-actions like over-and-unders, side-by-sides and single-shots. Regardless of the action type, the barrel or barrels are cleaned the same.

BARREL BORE

1. Attach a clean patch to a rod of your choice and soak the patch in bore solvent.

2. Run the patch from breech to muzzle and let the solvent works for a few minutes. Remove the choke tube(s) if so equipped.

3. If the barrel is excessively fouled run a solvent soaked bronze bristle brush through the bore. Twist the brush around the choke tube treads inside the barrel. Repeat these steps if you see debris ejected when the brush emerges from the muzzle.

4. Repeatedly run patches through until the patch is clean.

5. Run a clean patch that is lightly oiled through the bore.

6. If your shotgun has a ported barrel liberally swab the ported areas with solvent, allow it to work, then scrub the wad plastic residue from the inside of the barrel with a bronze brush. An old toothbrush works well from the outside,

FIGURE 15

Figure 15. You may need to use a dental pick or toothpick to remove debris from a clogged port hole.

7. Use solvent to clean the choke tube, dry, and lightly oil. Apply an anti-seize compound to the threads of the choke tube and screw the choke tube back into the muzzle.

8. Lightly oil the outside surface of the barrels.

SEMI-AUTOMATIC ACTIONS

There are three basic semi-auto shotgun actions: gas-operated systems like Remington's 1100 and 11-87, Weatherby SA-08, Beretta AL391, and others; re-coil actions like older Browning Auto-5s and Franchi AL48s; and inertia action guns like those manufactured by Benelli.

1. For gas-operated shotguns, use solvent to clean the gas piston and the area where the piston sits

FIGURE 16

in the barrel lug, Figure 16. You may need to use a fine steel wool and solvent to remove carbon build up. Do not oil the gas piston as oil will collect grime and quickly build up. For recoil-action guns, remove the recoil spring and wipe down the magazine tube then lightly oil it. For inertia-action guns, periodically clean the recoil spring, recoil plunger, and recoil spring tube. You will need to remove the stock. Lightly oil the inside of the tube and recoil plunger.

2. For all action types clean the bolt with solvent, allow it to work
3. Use a brush to scrub the extractor area.
4. Wipe the solvent clean then lightly oil the bolt.
5. Use solvent inside the receiver to remove carbon build up, wipe dry, and lightly oil.
6. Clean the action bars and magazine tube, then lightly oil. Work the action to distribute the oil.
7. Spray the trigger group assembly with cleaner and wipe or used canned air to blow crud out of the mechanism.
8. Lightly oil the trigger, hammer, and carrier pivot pins.
9. Lightly oil the outside metal surfaces with a soft cloth.

PUMP ACTIONS

The rails are the key to keeping your pump gun shucking and chambering shells. Clean the barrel, trigger assembly, receiver, and bolt as indicated above. Most pump-action shotguns have two action rails, some guns, like the Ithaca Model 37, have one rail.

1. Use solvent to clean the rail(s), inside of the action slide that rides the outside of the magazine tube, and the magazine tube.
2. Lightly oil the rails and magazine tube, Figure 17. Then work the action to distribute the oil.

BREAK ACTION

On side-by-side, over-and-under and single-shot shotguns, remove the barrels and clean per steps indicated above. The locking lugs and ejectors or extractors are unique for double guns and they need inspection. Many double guns do not need to be disassembled in detail like other shotguns. You

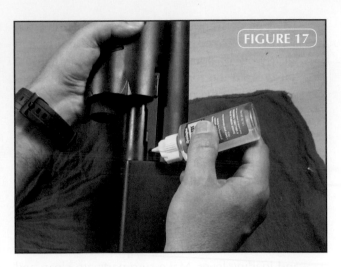

FIGURE 17

may want to pull the stock off the frame and blow out any debris that has accumulated inside the mechanism, but typically the mechanism is sealed with only the firing pin holes receiving residue, Figure 18.

1. Clean the action and locking lugs on the barrels. Place a dab of grease where the barrels pivot in the frame, Figure 19.
2. Clean the ejectors/extractors on the barrels and scrub the breech face using solvent, Figure 20.
3. Brush then wipe dry and lightly oil.
4. Clean the outside surfaces with a clean soft cloth and lightly oil metal surfaces.

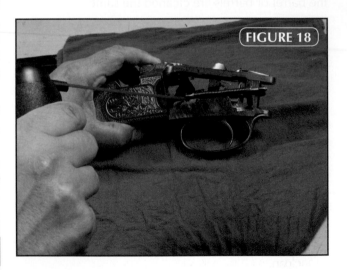

FIGURE 18

Revolvers

Wheelguns come it three basic types. Single-action (SA) models like the Colt Single Action Army; Colt clones by Uberti and Cimarron and others; Ruger

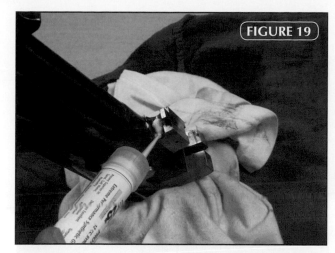

FIGURE 19

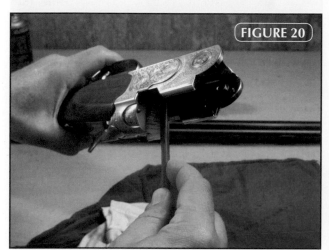

FIGURE 20

process a layer of copper is used prior to the nickel. If there is a scratch or nick in the nickel plate the

≫ Three areas on a revolver that need attention: cylinder face

≫ back of frame

≫ and forcing cone.

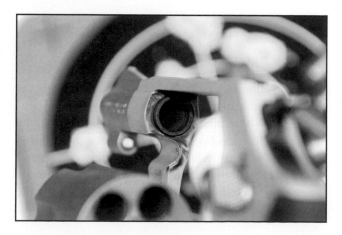

Vaquero, Blackhawk, and Single-Six models with safety transfer bars; Freedom Arms Model 83 and 97; and others. Swing out cylinder models have both single- and double-action triggers though some models are solely double action; and the cylinder is accessed by swinging it out of the frame. All current models from S&W and Taurus, Ruger's Redhawk and GP100, and others are what are referred to as modern, double-action revolvers. The third type is top-break or break-top actions like replicas of S&W's Schofield No. 3 and No. 3 New Model Russian by Uberti and Cimarron, Webley MK VI, H&R Sportsman, and others. Cleaning procedures are basically the same for all revolver types with the difference in how the cylinder is accessed.

Revolvers manufactured with matte stainless steel finish are subject to staining by powder residue. Do not use a solvent with ammonia to clean nickel-plated revolvers. During the nickel plating ammonia-based solution will get under the plate and begin to erode it.

The side plate is not routinely removed, but over years oil and grease can varnish and gum up the mechanism.

⌄ Before with over 50 years of aged lubricant.

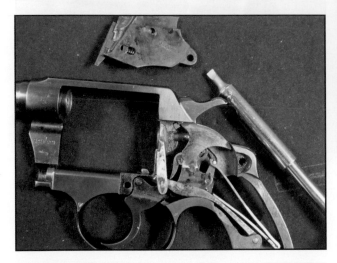

⌄ After a good soaking of CLP.

forcing cone to the muzzle, Figure 21. Allow the solvent to work.

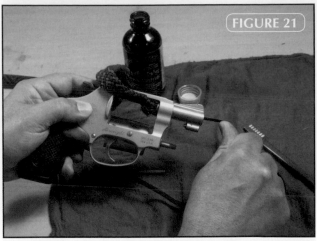

3. Run a bristle brush through the bore until no debris is pushed/pulled through.
4. Use a brush to scrub the forcing cone, Figure 22. Lead can build up in the forcing cone. Also scrub the back of the frame.

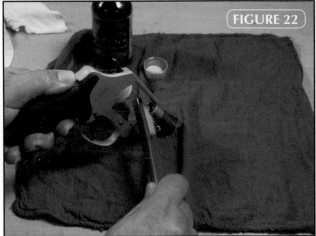

SINGLE ACTION, SWING-OUT CYLINDER & TOP BREAK

1. For swing-out cylinder models, swing open the cylinder from the frame. For single-action models, pull the base pin and remove the cylinder from the frame. For top-break models, remove the cylinder from the barrel via a takedown screw or button.
2. Push a solvent saturated patch from the muzzle to the forcing cone or pull a flexible rod from the

5. Run patches through the bore until they come out clean.
6. Run a lightly oiled patch through the bore.
7. Run a patch saturated in solvent into each chamber/charge hole in the cylinder.
8. Allow the solvent to work and push through a bore brush then clean patches until all patches come out clean.
9. Scrub the front of the cylinder with a nylon brush soaked in solvent, Figure 23. For revolvers with

FIGURE 23

titanium cylinders, do not use abrasive material such as steel wool, sand paper, Scotch Brite pads, and similar to clean the chambers or the front of the cylinder as it will remove a protective outer surface layer and cause the cylinder to excessively wear.

10. For swing-out cylinder models, push in the ejector rod and clean under the ejector with a brush, Figure 24. For top-break models, replace

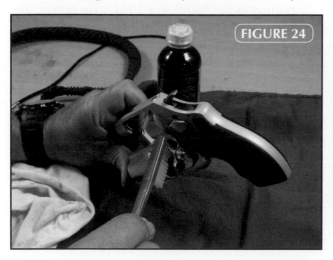

FIGURE 24

the cylinder to the barrel, close the barrel then reopen it so the extractor emerges from the cylinder. Use a brush to clean under the extractor.

11. For swing-out cylinder models, lightly oil the trigger and hammer mechanism and the ejector rod. For single-action models, lightly oil the base pin and bushing. For top-break models, lightly oil the extractor rod, the barrel hinge, and the trigger and hammer mechanism.

12. Wipe the outer metal surfaces with a soft, lightly oiled cloth.

Semi-Automatic Pistols

The most common pistol mechanisms encountered today are striker-fire pistols like all models of Glock, S&W's M&P series, Taurus 24/7 Gen 2, and others; single-action pistols like the 1911 and Browning Hi-Power; single- and double-action pistols like the Beretta 92FS, SIG P220, Walther P1, and others. The types can further be broken down by how the barrel is attached to the frame via a link and pin like the 1911 or cam lock like the Glock and others. Slides also differ: those with a barrel bushing like a 1911 and those without like a SIG P226 and open slide like a Beretta M9. All are cleaned the same way but there certain characteristics for each mechanism that should be noted. The bore can be cleaned quickly without disassembly using a pull-type rod.

≫ At the very least pull a Bore Snake through the pistol immediately after shooting. Here a Gen2 Glock G21 is given a quick cleaning prior to a proper scrubbing.

Best practice is to field strip the pistol for thorough cleaning. Steps below assume the pistol is field stripped and has been wiped with a clean soft cloth. Conceal carry handguns need to be cleaned more frequently. Magazines also need to be maintained. Though not needed routinely, it makes sense to completely strip the magazine every other cleaning.

BARREL

1. Push or pull a solvent soaked patch from the chamber to muzzle, on the feed ramp and wipe the guide rod down. Allow the solvent to work.

≫ The perfect combination of low velocity handloads and a dirty magazine. This Walther P1 choked for two reasons: handloads that were loaded for target shooting and lack of magazine maintenance.

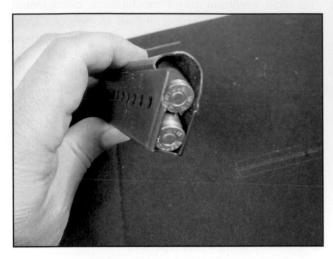

≫ The Walther P1 magazine was completely stripped and wiped clean. Magazines do not need a lot of lubricant; a lightly oiled cloth is sufficient.

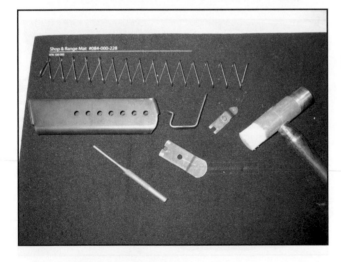

≫ Lint from clothing needs to be wiped clean routinely from conceal carry weapons. Remember to unload before wiping down.

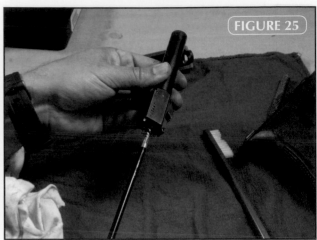

FIGURE 25

2. Run a bristle brush through the barrel, Figure 25.
3. Repeatedly run patches through the barrel until they come out clean. Wipe down the outside of the barrel and guide rod.
4. Run a lightly oiled patch through the bore and over the barrel.
5. Add a drop of oil to the barrel lugs and the front portion of the barrel. For 1911 style pistols, add a drop of oil to the front portion of the barrel where it rides in the barrel bushing and a dab of grease on the barrel locking lugs on the top side of the barrel. Add a drop of lube along the guide rod if so equipped. For Beretta 92FS/M9 pistols, lightly oil the locking block.

FRAME

1. Insert a clean cloth into the magazine well and pull it through, Figure 26.
2. Use a solvent soaked patch to wet the slide rail, trigger bar, and slide stop, allow to work.
3. Scrub the wet areas with a nylon bristle brush and wipe clean, Figure 27.
4. Add a drop of oil to the slide rails in frame and where the rear of trigger bar/transfer bar attaches to the connector, Figure 28. For 1911 style pistols, rub a drop of lube—oil or grease—along both rails. For Beretta 92FS/M9 pistols, lightly oil the disassembly latch, magazine catch, slide stop, trigger system, hammer, and sear.

SLIDE

1. Run a solvent soaked patch along the inside of the slide and allow the solvent to work.

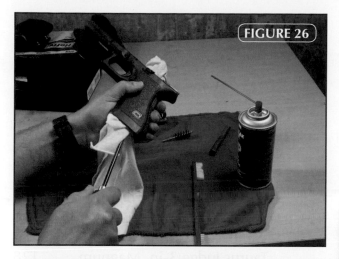

FIGURE 26

2. Use a brush to scrub the frames rails, breech face and extractor.
3. Wipe the inside of the slide clean and then run a lightly oil cloth inside the frame.
4. Add a drop of oil to the recesses in the slide rails and forward of the ejection port where the barrel hood runs against the slide, Figure 29. For 1911 style pistols, add a drop of lube on the disconnector, the recesses in the slide, and the edge of the barrel bushing.

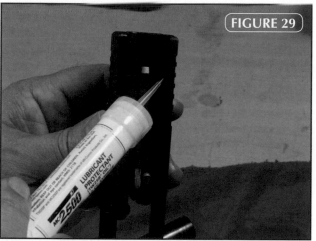

FIGURE 29

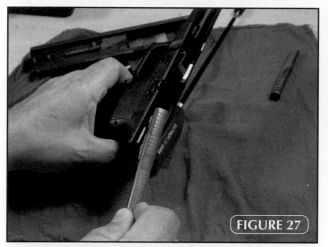

FIGURE 27

5. Reassemble the gun and cycle the action a few times to distribute the lube; wipe off any excess with a clean soft cloth. For Beretta 92FS/M9 pistols, place a few drops of oil around the extractor, firing pin block, and safety.

MAGAZINE

1. Run solvent on the follower and the magazine lips.
2. Wipe clean with a lightly oiled cloth.
3. Push a clean patch or cloth through the magazine body. Typically, magazines need minimal, if any, lubricant. If the follower is sticking to the inside of the magazine body, wipe the follower side with a lightly oiled cloth.

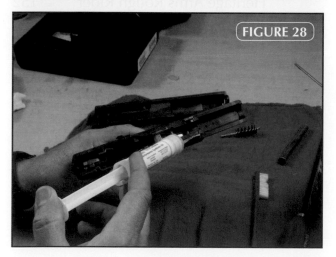

FIGURE 28

Handguns

Centerfire Semi-Automatic Pistols

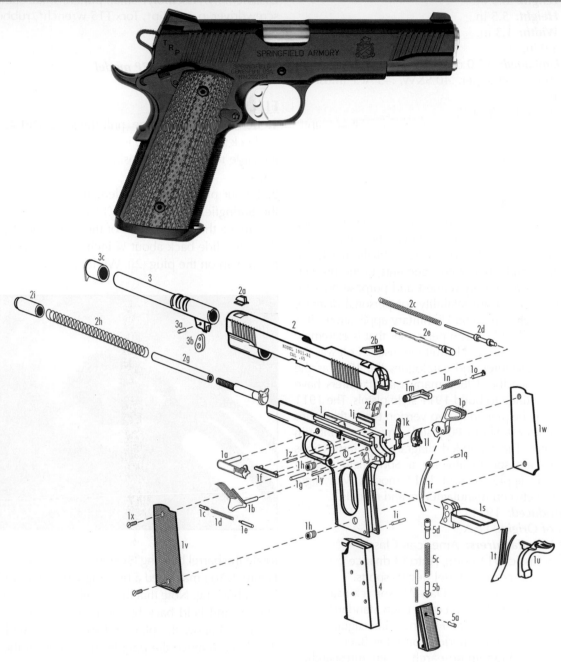

PARTS LIST

1. Frame
1a. Slide Stop
1b. Thumb Safety
1c. Slide Stop Plunger
1d. Thumb Safety Slide Stop Spring
1e. Safety Plunger
1f. Plunger Tube
1g. Hammer Pin
1h. Grip Screw Escutcheon
1i. Mainspring Housing Retainer Pin

1j. Ejector
1k. Disconnector
1l. Sear
1m. Magazine Catch
1n. Magazine Catch Spring
1o. Magazine Catch Lock
1p. Hammer
1q. Hammer Strut Pin
1r. Hammer Strut
1s. Trigger
1t. Sear Spring
1u. Grip Safety
1v. Grip (L.H.)
1w. Grip (R.H.)

1x. Grip Screw
1y. Sear Pin
1z. Ejector Pin
2. Slide
2a. Dovetail Front Sight
2b. Fixed Combat Rear Sight
2c. Extra Power Firing Pin Spring
2d. Titanium Firing Pin
2e. Extractor
2f. Firing Pin Stop
2g. Recoil Spring Guide
2h. Recoil Spring
2i. Guide Plug

3. Barrel
3a. Barrel Link Pin
3b. Barrel Link
3c. Barrel Bushing
4. Magazine
5. Mainspring Housing
5a. Locking Bolt
5b. Mainspring Retainer
5c. Mainspring
5d. Mainspring Cap
5e. Plunger
5f. Plunger Spring

SPECIFICATIONS

Model: TRP (Springfield Armory)
Action: recoil-operated, autoloader, single action
Overall Length: 8.3 in.
Overall Height: 5.5 in.
Overall Width: 1.3 in.
Barrel: 5.0 in.
Weight Unloaded: 37.0 oz.
Caliber: 9mm, .38 Super, .40 S&W, .45 ACP (most common)
Capacity: 8 + 1 (.45 ACP)
Common Features: firing pin block safety (Series 80); lowered/flared ejection port; beaver tail grip safety; ambidextrous thumb safety

BACKGROUND

The 1911 has been in service with the U.S. military since 1911, first as the 1911 during WWI then after a few modifications as the 1911A1 during WWII through Korea and Vietnam and smaller engagements to the present. Today's 1911s are highly refined and purpose built for various scenarios: concealability for personal defense, target/action shooting, and LE/military applications. It is a versatile and field proven performer that is extremely popular with civilian and LE/military users. Colt was the original manufacturer and catalogues the 1911 as the Model O. Since the 1980s many manufacturers have built and continue to build 1911 style pistols. The 1911 can generally be placed in two version types; the Series 70 and Series 80. Series 80 pistols employ a firing pin block system. The exploded diagram and instructions that follow are specifically for a Springfield Armory TRP but will apply to most 1911 models with slight differences between manufacturers and models.

Year Introduced: 1911
Country of Origin: USA
Current Manufacturers: American Classic (americanclassic1911.com), Auto-Ordnance (auto-ordnance.com), Citadel (legacysports.com), Colt (coltsmfg.com), Dan Wesson (cz-usa.com), Ed Brown (edbrown.com), High Standard (highstandard.com), Ithaca Firearms (ithacagun.com), Kimber (kimberamerica.com), Les Baer (lesbaer.com), Magnum Research (magnumresearch.com), Nighthawk Tactical (nighthawktactical.com), Olympic Arms (olyarms.com), Para USA (paraord.com), Remington (remington.com), SIG SAUER (sigsauer.com), Smith & Wesson (smith-wesson.com), Springfield Armory (springfield-armory.com), STI (stiguns.com), Sturm, Ruger & Co. (ruger.com), Taurus (taurususa.com), Wilson Combat (wilsoncombat.com)
Similar Models: Commander (4 in. barrel), Officer/compact (shorter barrel lengths and frame heights)

REQUIRED TOOLS

Field Stripping: bushing wrench, 5/32 hex or Allen wrench*
Disassembly/Assembly: small punch, small standard screwdriver, paperclip*, Torx T15 wrench*, rubber band*, nylon hammer

***Springfield Armory TRP model**

FIELD STRIP

1. Remove the magazine, pull the slide (Part #2) back to check that no cartridge is in the chamber and release the slide to its forward position with the hammer (1p) down.

2. If your pistol uses a full length guide rod (2g), like the Springfield TRP, use a 5/32 hex or Allen wrench to remove the front portion of the guide rod, Figure 1. Push the slide back about ¼ inch and use your thumb to press in on the plug (2i). While depressing the plug,

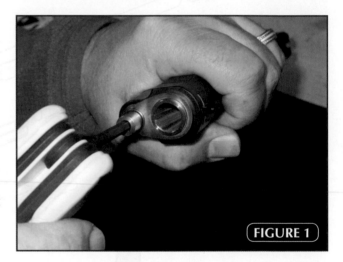

FIGURE 1

rotate the barrel bushing (3c) clockwise about a ¼ turn, Figure 2. You may need a bushing wrench to rotate the barrel bushing. Note that the recoil spring (2h) is under tension and held back by the barrel bushing so control it and allow the plug and spring to extend out of the slide. Remove the plug from the end of the recoil spring.

3. Cock the hammer so you can easily pull the slide back and align the disassembly notch on the left side of the slide with the slide stop (1a), Figure 3.

4. Push the slide stop out from the right side of the frame (1) and pull it out of the left side of the frame. fcente

5. Pull the slide assembly forward and remove it from the frame.

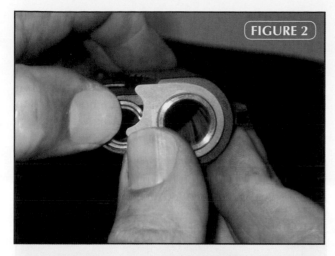

FIGURE 2

FIGURE 3

MODEL 1911-A1
CAL.45

6. Remove the recoil spring and recoil spring guide rearward through the back of the slide.

7. Rotate the barrel bushing counterclockwise and remove it from the slide.

8. Tilt the barrel link forward and remove the barrel (3) from the front of the slide, Figure 4.

At this point the 1911 is field stripped for routine cleaning.

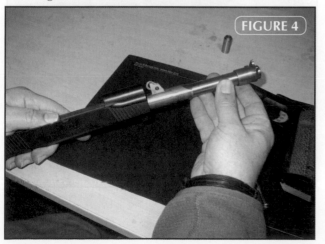

FIGURE 4

FRAME DISASSEMBLY

1. Cock the hammer and rotate the thumb safety (1b) almost to the on safe position.

2. Pull the thumb safety from the frame. Note, depending on your 1911 model, the slide stop plunger (1c), thumb safety/slide stop spring (1d) and safety plunger (1e) will be released when the thumb safety is removed. The plunger is under spring tension and may pop out; with some models you will need to use a small punch to push it out from the tube on the frame. The TRP, like many current 1911s, has an ambidextrous thumb safety with the actual left and right thumb safeties that nest together when assembled on the frame. Remove the thumb safety from the left side as described and the right side thumb safety should fall free once the left is removed.

> **Disassembly Tip:** Avoid prying the left thumb safety since this will bend the pins that extend into the frame. To get more leverage on the thumb safety, slip a zip tie under the thumb safety lever and pull straight up.

3. With thumb safety removed, next remove the mainspring housing (5). The TRP like many Springfield Armory 1911 models has a Integral Locking System (ILS) built into the main spring housing. Deactivate the ILS with the tool provided. The ILS is unlocked/deactivated when the two holes in the ILS switch are vertical. With the hammer down wrap a heavy-duty rubber band around the grip safety (1u) so it is completely depressed. Cock the hammer fully back and then insert the takedown pin or paper clip into the takedown hole, Figure 5. Control the hammer and lower it to the fired position. Use a small punch and hammer to drive out the mainspring housing retaining pin (1i), Figure 6.

4. Remove the mag well, and the mainspring housing will now slide off the frame. Leave the takedown pin/paper clip in the TRP's mainspring housing until reassembly.

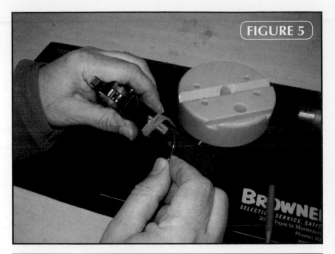

FIGURE 5

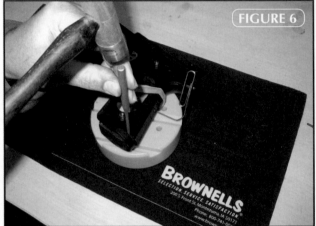

FIGURE 6

5. With main spring housing removed, the grip safety (1u) can easily be removed from the frame and then the leaf spring (1t).

6. Next use a small punch to remove the hammer pin (1g). It should easily fall free from the nudge of a punch from the right side of the frame. The hammer and strut (1r) will now easily be removed from the frame.

7. Next use a punch to push out sear pin (1y) from the right to the left side of the frame. The sear pin should easily be pushed free from the frame.

8. Tip back and the sear (1l) and disconnector (1k) will fall free from the frame.

9. Next use a small flat blade screwdriver on the magazine catch (1m) on the right side of the frame. Depress the magazine catch and rotate the slotted screw to the left. The magazine catch will then fall free from the right side of the frame.

10. After the magazine catch is removed, the trigger (1s) is free to be removed.

11. The left (1v) and right (1w) grips do not need to be removed for field stripping or detail disassembly. To remove the grips use a hex, Torx wrench or flat blade screwdriver to remove the four grip screws (1x); two screws per grip.

SLIDE DISASSEMBLY

1. To disassemble the slide, use a small punch or use the hammer strut is a small punch is not available. Push in on the firing pin (2d) and at the same time use a small flat blade screwdriver or your fingernail to push downward against the top edge of the firing pin stop (2f), Figure 7. Note the firing pin spring (2c) is under tension, control the spring.

FIGURE 7

2. With the firing pin stop removed, the firing pin and firing pin spring can be pulled from the rear of the slide.

3. Remove the extractor (2e) by gently prying it straight, back and out of the rear of the slide with a small flat blade screwdriver, Figure 8.

4. To remove the rear sight (2b) from the slide use a punch and hammer and drift it out of the dovetail from the left side of the slide to the right side of slide.

To reassemble follow the reverse order.

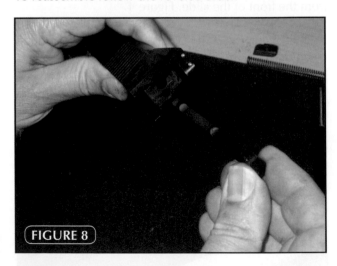

FIGURE 8

Maintenance Tip: To avoid what is commonly known as an "idiot scratch" or a scratch made by the slide stop when inserted back into the frame, make sure the takedown/disassembly notch in the slide is centered above the notch in the frame where the rear portion of the slide stop inserts into the frame. Insert the slide stop pin in the hole on the frame and push it until it is almost home. Ensure the notch in the slide aligns with the notch in the frame and push the slide stop in at about 45 degrees. It should snap back into place without creating a scratch. ISPT (Idiot Scratch Proof Tool, 1911-ispt. com) manufactures a tool out of a thin polymer that fits between the slide stop and frame and protects the frame from being scratched during reassembly. The ISPT lasts for numerous reassembles.

BERETTA 92FS/M9

PARTS LIST

1 Barrel
2 Locking Block
3 Locking Block Plunger
4 Locking Block Plunger Retaining Pin
5 Slide
6 Extractor
7 Extractor Pin
8 Extractor Spring
9 Rear Sight
10 Trigger Bar Release Plunger
11 Trigger Bar Release Plunger Spring

12 Firing Pin
13 Firing Pin Spring
14 Safely
15 Firing Pin Plunger
18 Recoil Spring
19 Recoil Spring Guide
20 Frame
21 Disassembling Latch
22 Slide Catch Spring
23 Slide Catch
24 Trigger
25 Trigger Pin
26 Trigger Spring
27 Trigger Bar
28 Trigger Bar Spring

29 Disassembling Latch Release Button
30 Disassembling Latch Release Button Spring
31 Hammer Release Lever
32 Ejector
33 Hammer Release Lever Pin
34 Ejector Spring Pin
35 Hammer
36 Hammer Pin
37 Hammer Spring Guide
38 Hammer Spring
39 Hammer Spring Cap
40 Sear
41 Sear Spring

42 Sear Pin
43 Magazine Release Button
46 Magazine Release Button Spring
47 Hammer Spring Cap Pin
48/49 Grips Pair
50 Grip Screw
51 Grip Bush
52 Magazine Box
53 Magazine Follower
54 Magazine Bottom
55 Magazine Spring
56 Magazine Lock Plate
57 Firing Pin Catch Spring
58 Firing Pin Catch

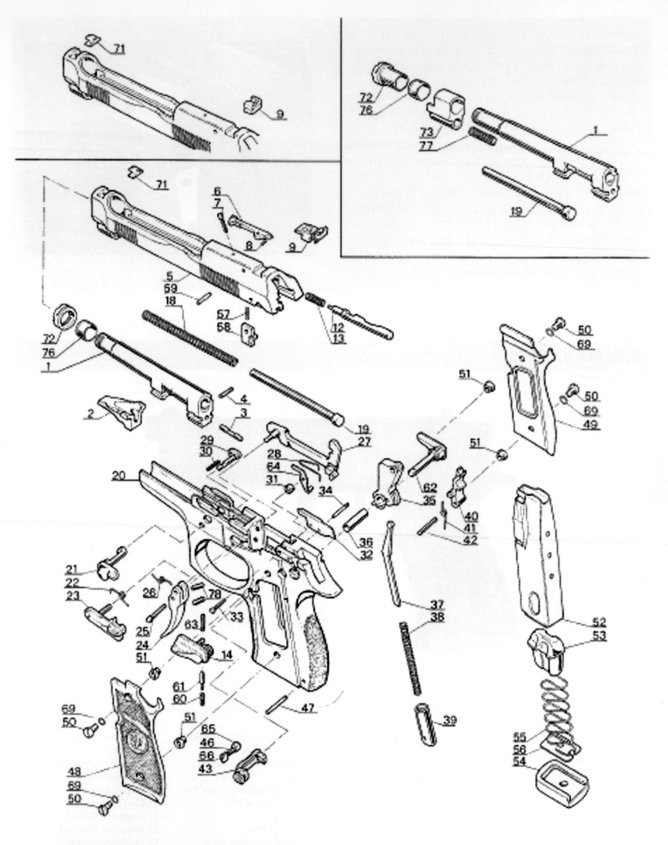

59 Firing Pin Catch Retaining
   Spring Pin
60 Safety Plunger Spring

61 Safety Plunger
62 Right Safety Lever
63 Right Safety Lever Spring Pin

64 Firing Pin Catch Lever
65 Magazine Catch Spring Bush
   (Short)

66 Magazine Catch Spring Bush
   (Long)
69 Spring Washer

SPECIFICATIONS

Model: 92FS/M9
Action: autoloader; locking block barrel; SA/DA
Overall Length: 8.5 in.
Overall Height: 5.4 in.
Overall Width: 1.5 in.
Barrel: 4.9 in.
Weight Unloaded: 33.3 oz.
Caliber: 9mm
Capacity: 15 + 1
Common Features: open slide; aluminum alloy frame; steel slide and barrel, ambidextrous thumb with decocker, firing pin block and half-cock safeties; reversible magazine release; external hammer; loaded chamber indicator; checkered front/back grip frame; lanyard loop; drop-free magazine; beveled magazine well; sand-resistant PVC coated magazine; Picatinny rail; checkered wood or plastic grips; fixed front/dovetail rear, 3-dot sights; Bruniton matte black finish

BACKGROUND

The Beretta 92FS designated the M9 pistol has been in service with the U.S. military since 1985 as a replacement for the M1911A1 and since 2005 as the M9A1 after a spec revision. Many other nations' armed forces use a 92 variant as well as some U.S. LE agencies. The newer M9A1 incorporates enhancements like a Picatinny rail, 3-dot sights, checkering on the front and backstraps, the magazine well is beveled and the magazine is more sand resistant. It also incorporates an open slide, a design which is a characteristic of many previous Berettas. The open slide reduces weight as well as allows users to easily clear a stove pipe jam. What was so novel about the 92FS when it first came out was the single- and double-action trigger and the high-capacity double-stack magazine, features that most shooters today expect in a modern pistol. The instructions that follow will generally work with 92 variants, though there are differences—Taurus models feature a manual thumb safety on the frame, the 92's manual thumb safety is on the slide. It is not unusual for a well-trained operator to field strip and reassemble the 92FS/M9 in under 20 seconds.
Year Introduced: 1975
Country of Origin: Italy
Current Manufactures: Beretta (berettausa.com)
Similar Models: 92A1, 90-two, M9A1 (U.S. Marine Corp. spec M9), 96A1, Model 92B (Taurus), Model 92B-17 (Taurus), Model 92SS (Taurus), Model 92SS-17 (Taurus), Model 100B (Taurus), Model 100B-11 (Taurus), Model 100SS (Taurus), Model 100SS-11 (Taurus), numerous Beretta models including Vertec, Elite I, Elite II, Inox, Centurion among others

REQUIRED TOOLS

Field Stripping: none
Disassembly/Assembly: hex or Allen wrench, small punch, small flat blade screwdriver, needle-nose pliers

FIELD STRIP

1. Engage the safety (part #14) to the "safe" position and remove the magazine.
2. While holding the pistol in your right hand use your left hand to depress the disassembly latch release button (29), Figure 1. Then rotate the disassembly latch (21) clock wise until it stops, Figure 2.

FIGURE 1

FIGURE 2

3. Pull the barrel/slide assembly toward the muzzle and off the frame (20), Figure 3. Note the recoil spring is under tension so control the slide.
4. Place the barrel/slide assembly top side down in the palm of your hand or on a padded surface and slightly

FIGURE 3

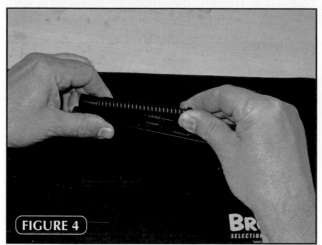

FIGURE 4

compress the recoil spring (18) and recoil spring guide (19) off the barrel (1) and locking block (2) then pull the recoil spring and recoil spring guide up and out, Figure 4. Make sure to control the recoil spring.

5. Depress the locking block plunger (3) and pull the barrel and locking block out of the slide (5) as an assembly, Figure 5.

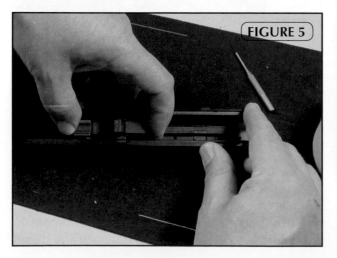

FIGURE 5

At this point the 92FS/M9 is field stripped.

SLIDE DISASSEMBLY

1. Remove the firing pin catch (58) by first placing the slide right side down on a padded surface or bench block then use a small punch to drift out the firing pin catch retaining spring pin (59), Figure 6. Leave

FIGURE 6

the punch in place and flip the slide over, bottom side up, and place your thumb over the firing pin catch through the inside of the slide and remove the punch. Note the firing pin catch spring is under pressure. The firing pin catch and firing pin catch spring can then be removed from the bottom of the slide.

2. Remove the right safety lever (62) by placing the slide on a padded surface or bench block and drifting out the two safety lever pins, Figure 7. Drift the pins

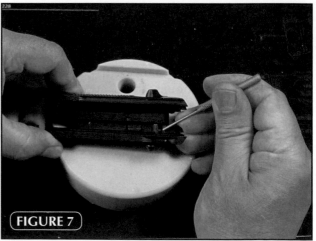

FIGURE 7

from the inside of the slide to the outside. With the pins removed the right safety lever can be pulled from the slide.

3. Next slightly rotate the left side safety upward and use a small punch to push in on the firing pin (12) continue to push up on the safety until it stops. Then pull the safety from the left side of the slide. Note the trigger bar release plunger (10) and trigger bar release plunger spring (11) on the right will come free on the right side of slide when the safety is removed. The firing pin plunger (15), safety plunger (61) and safety plunger spring (60) can then be removed from the safety.

4. Remove the extractor (6) by placing the slide top side down on a padded surface or bench block and using a small punch drift out the extractor pin (7) from the inside of the slide to the outside of the slide. Keep the punch in place and holding the end of the extractor and extractor spring (8) will your thumb pull the punch free and the extractor and extractor spring will fall free. Note the extractor spring is under tension.

5. The firing pin (12) and firing pin spring (13) can then be removed from the rear of the slide.

FRAME DISASSEMBLY

1. Remove the grip panels (48 and 49) by unscrewing the four grip screws (40), two for each grip. Use a flat blade screwdriver or hex or Allen wrench, Figure 8.

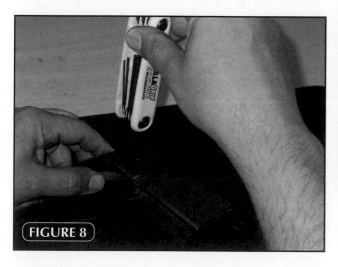

FIGURE 8

2. Rotate the disassembly latch counter clock wise and pull it from the frame, Figure 9.

3. Pull the disassembly latch release button from the right side of the frame. With the disassembly latch release button removed the disassembly latch release button spring (30) will come free from the frame.

4. Remove the slide catch (23) by moving the trigger spring (26) out of the groove in the shaft of the slide catch. Then slightly press upward on the slide catch and pulling it partially from the left side of the frame.

FIGURE 9

With the slide catch partial pulled out of the frame use a small screwdriver to lift the leg of the slide catch spring (22) out of the recess in the frame.

5. The trigger bar (27) is removed by using a small screwdriver to push down on the trigger bar spring (28) and it will fall free, Figure 10. Then pull the trigger bar from the frame. You may need to gently pry the trigger bar free.

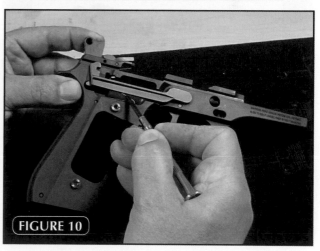

FIGURE 10

6. Next press out the trigger pin (25) using a punch from the right side of the frame. The trigger (24) and the trigger spring (26) can then be removed from the top of the frame.

7. Remove the hammer assembly by first ensuring the hammer is in the fully forward or "fired" position, then press in the hammer spring cap/lanyard loop (39) and the hammer spring cap pin (47) will fall free, Figure 11. Control the hammer spring cap as it is under tension from the hammer spring (38). The hammer spring cap and hammer spring will then fall free from the butt of the frame.

8. With the hammer spring removed, pull out the hammer pin (36) and press reward on the hammer release lever (31) and the hammer (35) can be pulled

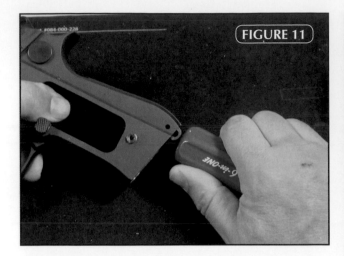

FIGURE 11

Reassembly Tip: Use a pair of needle-nose pliers to replace the trigger bar spring. First put the 90° bend on the spring in the small hole in the frame, ensure the other leg is in the slot of trigger bar, and then the loop of the spring can be fitted into the slot in the frame. The magazine release button can easily be converted from right-hand to left-hand by reinstalling it with the button protruding from the right side of the frame.

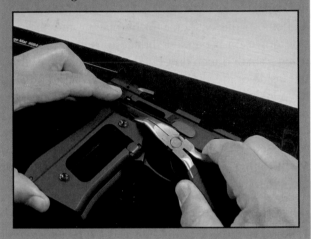

Tuning Tip: The Wolff (gunsprings.com) trigger conversion unit improves trigger staging and smoothes trigger pull. The unit was designed at the request of Immigration and Naturalization Service (INS) to address the problem of trigger spring breakage.

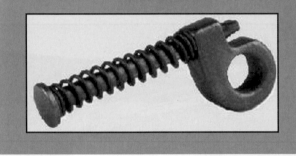

9. The sear (40) is removed by first placing your thumb over the sear spring (41) then using a small punch push the sear pin (42) through the frame. Note the sear spring is under tension and when the sear pin is removed the sear and sear spring will fall free.

10. To remove the magazine release button (43) push it from the right side of frame id set up for a right hand shooter.

Reassemble is reverse order.

from the top of the frame. Tip the frame upside down and the hammer strut, Beretta calls it a hammer spring guide (37), will fall free from the frame.

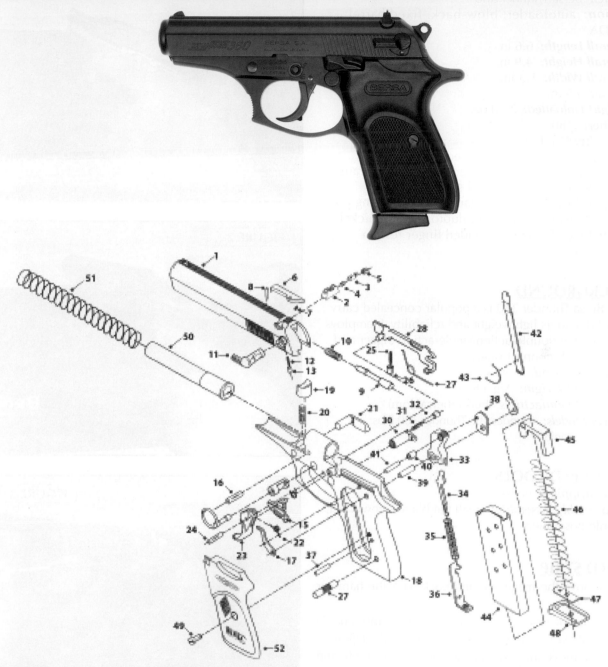

PARTS LIST

1. Slide
2. Rear sight
3. Rear sight blade
4. Rear sight spring
5. Rear sight screw
6. Extractor
7. Extractor spring
8. Extractor pin
9. Firing pin
10. Firing pin spring
11. Safety
12. Safety spring

13. Safety stop
14. Slide catch spring
15. Slide catch
16. Barrel pin
17. Ejector
18. Frame
19. Slide stop
20. Slide stop spring
21. Disassembly bar
22. Trigger spring
23. Trigger
24. Trigger pin
25. Firing pin stop spring

26. Firing pin stop
27. Grip pin
28. Disconnector
29. Disconnector spring
30. Magazine catch
31. Magazine catch spring
32. Magazine catch pin
33. Hammer
34. Hammer spring guide
35. Hammer spring
36. Cocking piece
37. Cocking piece pin
38. Hammer release

39. Hammer pin
40. Hammer release bush
41. Hammer release pin
42. Magazine safety
43. Magazine safety spring
44. Magazine tube
45. Feeder platform
46. Feeder platform spring
47. Magazine bottom holder
48. Magazine bottom
49. Grip screw
50. Barrel
52. Grip Panels

SPECIFICATIONS

Model: Bersa Thunder 380
Action: autoloader; blow-back, fixed barrel; SA/DA
Overall Length: 6.6 in.
Overall Height: 4.9 in.
Overall Width: 1.3 in.
Barrel: 3.5 in.
Weight Unloaded: 20.0 oz.
Caliber: .380
Capacity: 7 + 1
Common Features: checkered polymer grips; fixed front/dovetail rear, 3-dot sights; alloy frame; combat trigger guard; steel slide and barrel; integral locking system, manual thumb, firing pin safeties; external hammer; duotone, satin nickel, matte black finishes; extended finger rest on magazine

BACKGROUND

The Bersa Thunder 380 is a popular concealed carry pistol due to its lightweight and reliability. It employs a traditional double-action/single-action trigger and magazine disconnect safety.
Year Introduced: 1995
Country of Origin: Argentina
Current Manufactures: Bersa (bersa.com)
Similar Models: Thunder .32, Thunder 380 Plus (15 + 1 capacity)

REQUIRED TOOLS

Field Stripping: none
Disassembly/Assembly: small flat blade screwdriver, needle-nose pliers

FIELD STRIP

1. Remove the magazine and cock back the hammer (part #33).
2. Rotate the disassembly bar (21) and pull the slide (1) back until you can lift up the rear of the slide, Figure 1.
3. Then move the slide forward off the barrel (50) and frame (18), Figure 2.

At this point the Thunder 380 is field stripped for cleaning.

SLIDE DISASSEMBLY

1. To remove the firing pin (9) first remove the safety (11) by rotating the safety lever to the middle between "safe" and "fire" and use a small flat blade screw driver to push out the safety lever, Figure 3.

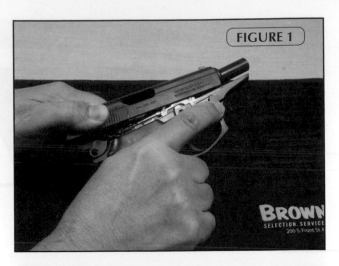

FIGURE 1

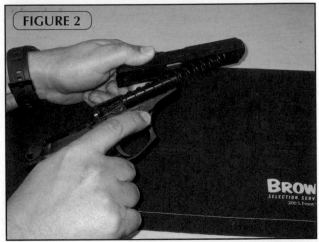

FIGURE 2

FIGURE 3

2. With the safety lever removed the firing pin and firing pin spring (10) can be removed from the rear of the slide.

3. The extractor (6) is removed by drifting out the pin (9) from the inside to the outside of the slide, Figure 4. Note that the extractor spring (7) is under compression.

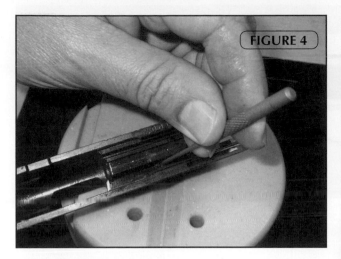

FIGURE 4

Reverse the procedure to reassemble.

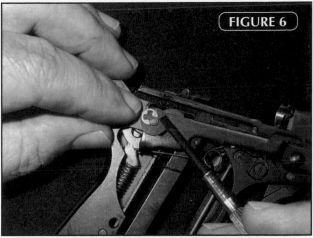

FIGURE 6

FRAME DISASSEMBLY

1. Remove the grip screw (49) and remove the two grip panels (52) from the frame.

2. The trigger bar, Bersa calls it a disconnector (28), is removed by lifting out the leg of the disconnector spring (29) from the notch in the disconnector, Figure 5. Remove the C-clip and shim by using a small

FIGURE 7

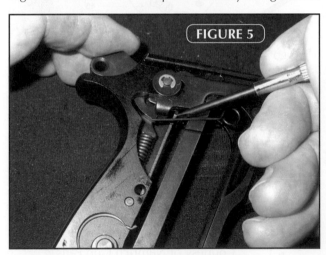

FIGURE 5

screwdriver to push off the C-clip, Figure 6. Slightly pull the trigger (23) and remove the disconnector from the trigger. Leave the disconnector spring as it is staked to the frame, Figure 7.

3. Use a small flat blade screwdriver to push the magazine safety spring (43) from the notch in the frame, Figure 8. The magazine safety spring is under compression so control it. Next slide the magazine safety (42) down toward the butt so it clears the frame and remove.

4. To remove the magazine catch (30) depress the magazine catch and use a small flat blade screwdriver to turn the magazine catch pin (32) clockwise until it stops. Then remove the magazine catch from the right side of the frame.

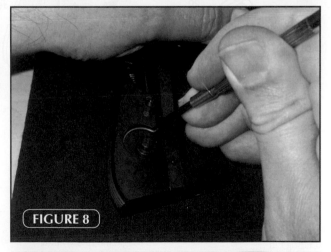

FIGURE 8

Reassembly Tips: You make need to insert an empty magazine into the frame to ensure the forward pin of the disconnecter is inserted fully into the hole in the trigger. Place the small diameter end of the recoil spring on the barrel before replacing the slide.

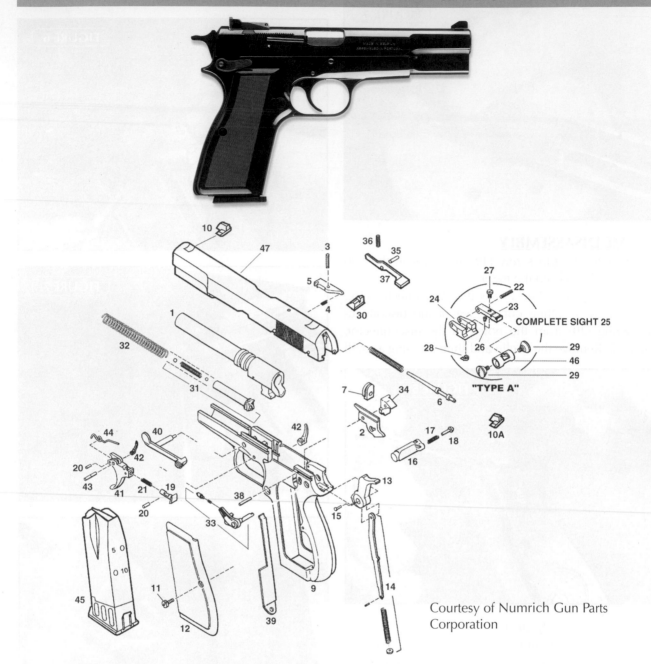

Courtesy of Numrich Gun Parts Corporation

PARTS LIST

1 Barrel
2 Ejector
3 Extractor Pin
4 Extractor Spring
5 Extractor
6 Firing Pin
7 Firing Pin Retaining Plate
8 Firing Pin Spring
9 Frame
10 Front Sight
11 Grip Screw (2 Req'd.)
12 Grips
13 Hammer
14 Hammer Strut Assembly

15 Hammer Strut Pin
16 Magazine Latch
17 Magazine Latch Spring
18 Magazine Latch Spring Guide
19 Magazine Safety
20 Magazine Safety Pin & Trigger Spring Pin
21 Magazine Safety Spring
22 Rear Sight Aperture Housing Pin, Adjustable
23 Rear Sight Aperture Housing, Adjustable
24 Rear Sight Base, Adjustable

25 Rear Sight Complete, Adjustable
26 Rear Sight Elevation Screw Spring, Adjustable
27 Rear Sight Elevation Screw, Adjustable
28 Rear Sight Elevation Spring, Adjustable
29 Rear Sight Adjustment Screw (2 Req'd.)
30 Rear Sight, Blue
31 Recoil Spring Guide Assembly
32 Recoil Spring
33 Safety

34 Sear
35 Sear Lever Pin
36 Sear Lever Spring
37 Sear Lever
38 Sear Pin
39 Sear Spring w/ Button
40 Slide Stop
41 Trigger
42 Trigger Lever
43 Trigger Pin
44 Trigger Spring
45 Magazine
46 Rear Sight Aperture, Adjustable

SPECIFICATIONS
Model: Hi-Power
Action: recoil-operated, autoloader, single action, locked breech
Overall Length: 7.8 in.
Overall Height: 5 in.
Overall Width: 1.4 in.
Barrel: 4.7 in.
Weight Unloaded: 32 oz.
Caliber: 9mm
Capacity: 13 + 1
Common Features: ambidextrous thumb and magazine safeties; blued finish; adjustable rear/fixed front sights; checkered walnut grip

BACKGROUND
The Hi-Power as it is called, also known as the HP or M1935 was John Browning's last pistol design and was actually finished by Dieudonne Saive at FN. It offers a 13-round magazine, accuracy and dependability. Over 50 countries have used the Hi-Power as their sidearm. It is standard issue for Canadian forces, as well as the armies of Belgium, UK, India, Australia, Singapore, and others. The Hi-Power also has the distinction of being used by axis and Allied forces during WWII. Details below are for newer MK II pistols, but the slight differences between old and new manufacture should not impede savvy users.
Year Introduced: 1935
Country of Origin: Belgium
Current Manufacturers: Browning (browning.com)
Similar Models: Mark III (fixed rear sight, checkered composite grip)

REQUIRED TOOLS
Field Stripping: none
Disassembly/Assembly: small roll-pin punch, small punch, small flat blade screwdriver, brass hammer

FIELD STRIP
1. Remove the magazine (Part #45) then lock the slide (47) in its rearward most position by pushing up the safety (33) into the disassembly recess in the slide, Figure 1.
2. Remove the slide stop (40) by pressing on its pin on the right side of the frame (9), Figure 2. At the same time slightly elevating the slide stop on the left side of the frame, Figure 3. Pull the slide stop free from the frame.
3. Press down on the thumb safety while grasping the slide and push the slide forward and off the frame. Note

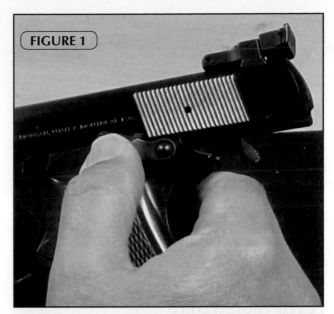

FIGURE 1

FIGURE 2

FIGURE 3

that the slide assembly is under compression from the recoil spring (32).
4. Next remove the recoil spring and recoil spring guide (31).
5. Lift the barrel (1) up and out of the slide, Figure 4.

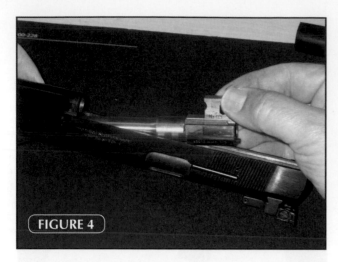

FIGURE 4

At this point the Hi-Power is field stripped for routine cleaning.

FRAME DISASSEMBLY

1. Ensure the hammer (13) is fully forward/in "fired" position then use a small punch or in a pinch the firing pin to push out the sear pin (38), Figure 5.

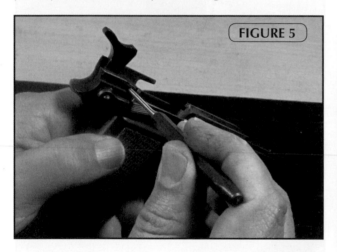

FIGURE 5

2. Remove the sear (34) from the top of the frame.
3. Rotate the ejector (2) forward and down into the frame and the safety can be pulled from the left side of the frame.
4. With the safety catch removed, the ejector can be pulled from the top of the frame and the hammer, hammer strut assembly (14) can be pulled out the top of the fame.
5. Remove the magazine catch (16) by pressing it until it is flush with the frame the use a small flat blade screwdriver to rotate the catch assembly (17 and 18) on the right side of the frame. Remove the magazine catch from the right side of the frame.

6. Remove the trigger (41) using a small punch to drift out trigger pin (43) then rotate the trigger forward into the trigger guard area of the frame to remove. the

SLIDE DISASSEMBLY

1. Use a small screwdriver to press down on the sear lever (37) and at the same time use a small punch—the protrusion on the slide stop will also work in a pinch—to depress the firing pin (6) and slide down the firing pin retaining plate (7) from the slide, Figure 6. The firing pin spring is under compression from the firing pin spring (8) so control it as you remove the firing pin retaining plate.
2. Pull out the firing pin and firing pin retaining plate from the rear of the slide.
3. Use a small roll-pin punch to drift out the sear lever pin (35) and the sear lever (37) and sear lever spring (36) will come free from the bottom of the slide.
4. Remove the extractor (5) by drifting out the extractor pin (3) from the top of the slide. The extractor spring (4) can then be removed from the slide.

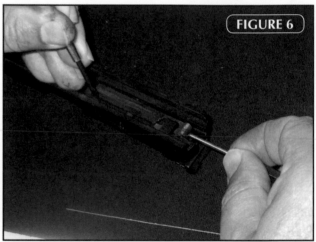

FIGURE 6

To reassemble follow the reverse order.

Reassembly Tip: When reinstalling the sear pin, place the hammer at full cock and keep the hammer in position by holding it against the edge of the work bench with your chest. Next make sure the sear spring is in its notch in the frame and through the frame use your thumb to press the sear spring into the inside of the butt frame. Drop the sear in place and use your free hand to insert the sear pin.

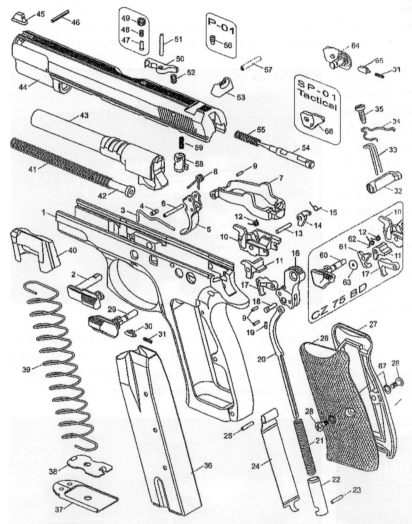

PARTS LIST

1 Frame
2 Slide Stop
3 Slide Stop Spring
4 Slide Stop Spring Pin
5 Trigger
6 Trigger Pin
7 Trigger Bar
8 Trigger Spring

9 Pin (3x)
10 Ejector
11 Sear
12 Sear Spring
13 Sear Pin
14 Firing Pin Block Lever
15 Firing Pin Block lever Spring
16 Hammer
17 Disconnector

18 Hammer Pin
19 Hammer Pin Retaining Peg
20 Main Spring Strut
21 Main Spring
22 Main Spring Plug
23 Main Spring Plug Pin
24 Magazine Guide
25 Magazine Guide Pin
26 Grip Panel – Left

27 Grip Panel - Right
28 Grip Panel Screw (2x)
29 Safety
30 Safety Detent Plunger
31 Safety Detent Plunger Spring
32 Magazine Catch
33 Magazine Catch Spring
34 Trigger Bar Spring
35 Magazine Catch Spring
   Screw
36 Magazine Body
37 Magazine Base
38 Magazine Base Lock
39 Magazine Spring
40 Follower
41 Recoil Spring
42 Recoil Spring Guide
43 Barrel
44 Slide
45 Front Sight
46 Front Sight Pin
47 loaded Chamber Indicator
48 Loaded Chamber Indicator
   Spring
49 Loaded Chamber Indicator
   Nut
50 Extractor
51 Extractor Pin
52 Extractor Spring
53 Rear Sight
54 Firing Pin
55 Firing Pin Spring
56 Securing Screw
57 Firing Pin Coiled Pin
58 Firing Pin Block Stop
59 Firing Pin Block Stop Spring
60 Hammer Decocking Lever
   Controller
61 Decocking Lever
62 Decocking Lever Spring
63 Fixing Insert
64 Safety - Right
65 Safety Detent Plunger - Right
66 Hammer Decocking Lever
   Controller - Right
67 Fan-shaped Washer (2x)

SPECIFICATIONS

Model: CZ 75 D PCR Compact
Action: autoloader; short recoil, tilting barrel; SA/DA
Overall Length: 7.2 in., 8.1 in. (full size model)
Overall Height: 5.0 in., 5.4 in. (full size model)
Overall Width: 1.4 in.
Barrel: 3.8 in., 4.7 in. (full size model)
Weight Unloaded: 16.7 oz., 35.2 oz. (full size model)
Caliber: 9mm, .40 S&W
Capacity: 14 + 1 (9mm), 16 + 1 (9mm full size model)
Common Features: checkered rubber grips; fixed front/ dovetail rear, Tritium 3-dot sights; alloy frame; combat trigger guard; manual thumb, safety stop on hammer, firing pin safeties; external hammer; magazine bumper pad; Picatinny rail; black polycoat, duo tone, satin nickel and matte and bright stainless finishes

BACKGROUND

The CZ 75 uses a linkless cam locking system similar to the Browning Hi-Power. What sets the CZ 75 apart from other semi-automatic pistols is the design feature of the slide rails riding on the inside of the frame instead of the outside, Figure 1. The CZ slide/frame set up provides a tight fit and is one factor why the CZ is accurate. The P-01 and SP-01 variants have a slightly different grip geometry and full dust cover. The CZ 75 has a reputation for reliability and accuracy and is used many Eastern European country militaries and law enforcement agencies including Czech Republic, Lithuania, Poland, Russian Federation and Slovakia. It has spawned many clones. The CZ 97 is a .45 ACP variant. The instructions here are specifically for the CZ 75 D PCR Compact but can be used with slight differences for all CZ 75s.

Year Introduced: 1976
Country of Origin: Czech Republic
Current Manufactures: CZ (cz-usa.com)
Similar Models: CZ 75 B, CZ 75 BD (decocker), CZ 75 Compact, CZ 75 D Compact (decocker), CZ 75 SemiCompact, CZ 75 P-01, 75 SP-01, 75 SP-01 Shadow, 75 SP-01 Phantom, 75 SP-01 Tactical, Tanfoglio TZ-75 (Italy), BUL Cherokee (Israel), Sphinx 2000 (Switzerland), Armalite AR-24 (USA), EAA Witness (USA) among others.

REQUIRED TOOLS

Field Stripping: none
Disassembly/Assembly: nylon hammer; 1/16, 3/32 punch; 1/8 roll pin punch; center punch; vise

FIELD STRIP

1. Grip the pistol in your left hand by placing your left thumb through the trigger guard and use your left index finger to push rearward on the front of the slide assembly. Push the slide back enough to align two index marks; one on the slide (part #44) and one on the frame (1), Figure 2.

FIGURE 2

2. Keeping the index marks aligned rotate the pistol so to the right side and push out the slide stop (2) using your thumb or a nylon hammer, Figure 3. In a pinch you can use the magazine floor plate corner.

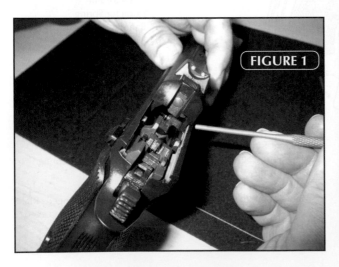

FIGURE 1

FIGURE 3

3. With the slide stop removed, slide the slide assembly off the front of the frame.

4. Place the slide top side down and remove the recoil spring (41) and recoil spring guide (42) by pressing the guide rod forward toward the muzzle and out and away from the barrel (43).

5. The barrel is removed from the slide by slightly moving it forward then up and out rearward of the slide.

At this point the CZ 75 is field stripped for cleaning.

FRAME DISASSEMBLY

1. Remove the grip screw (28) from the left grip (26) and right grip (27).

2. Remove the decocking lever (60) by using a small blade screwdriver to raise the long leg of the sear spring (12) out of the notch of the decocking lever shaft. Then pull the decocking lever out from the left side of the frame.

3. To remove the ejector block/sear assembly, first remove the sear pin retainer insert (63) by sliding toward the front/muzzle.

4. Use a 3/32 punch to drift out the sear pin (13).

5. With the pin driven out do not remove the punch until you have turned the frame rail side down on the work surface. Slowly remove the punch. Note there is spring tension so contain the parts.

6. The main spring plug (22), main spring (21) and magazine brake (24) are removed by first placing the hammer in forward most/fired position and drifting out the magazine brake pin (25) from the frame.

7. Against the work surface, compress the lanyard loop which is part of main spring plug to relieve the tension on the main spring plug pin (23).

8. Push the main spring plug pin from the frame and slowly relieve the tension on the main spring plug, Figure 4.

FIGURE 4

9. The main spring and main spring plug can then be pulled free from the hammer strut (20).

10. Remove the hammer assembly by using a small flat blade screwdriver push the hammer pin retaining peg (19) up into the frame.

11. Then push the hammer pin (18) out of the frame from right to left.

12. Pull the hammer assembly from the top of the frame.

13. The trigger bar (7) is removed by drifting out the trigger pin (6) from the frame from left to right, Figure 5. Note that the trigger pin is flared on both sides of the frame. Drift the pin end with the smallest flaring. Do not remove the punch once the pin is driven through the frame.

FIGURE 5

14. Turn the frame rail side down on the bench top and slowly remove the punch. The trigger return spring (8) is under tension and will drop out when the punch is removed.

15. The trigger assembly can then be lifted out from the top of the frame.

16. The slide stop spring pin (4) is removed by using a 1/16 inch punch and drifting it from the frame right to left.

17. With the pin removed the slide stop spring (3) can be lifted out from the top of the frame.

SLIDE DISASSEMBLY

1. Drift out the firing pin roll pin (57) from the slide using a 1/8 inch roll pin punch, Figure 6.

2. With the firing pin roll pin removed, press on the firing pin block (58) and the firing pin and firing pin spring (55) will come free toward the rear of the slide.

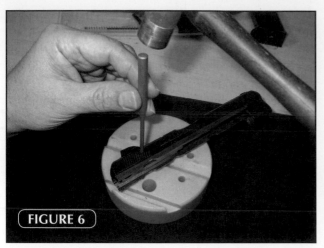

FIGURE 6

4. The extractor (50) is removed by drifting out the extractor pin (51) from the slide from top to bottom with a 1/16 inch punch.

5. After the extractor pin is removed, slide the extractor forward toward the muzzle and remove it from the slide. The extractor spring (52) can then be removed from the slide.

Reassemble is reverse order.

Reassembly Tip: The trigger pin is flared on both ends to keep it in place. Reinstall the pin and ensure it is flush on both sides of the frame. Flare one end of the pin by locking a ¼ inch punch into a vise. Center the ¼ inch punch on the pin and from the opposite side use a center punch to flare the pin.

3. With the firing pin removed, the firing pin block and firing pin block spring (59) will come free from the slide.

GLOCK G17

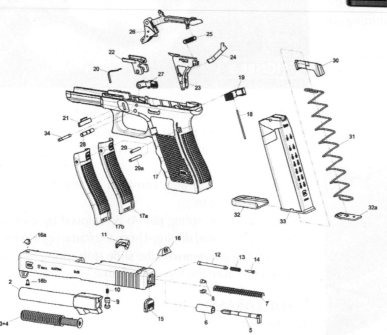

PARTS LIST

01 Slide
02 Barrel
03+04 Recoil spring assembly
05 Firing pin
06 Spacer sleeve
07 Firing pin spring
08 Spring cups
09 Firing pin safety
10 Firing pin safety spring
11 Extractor
12 Extractor depressor plunger
13 Extractor depressor plunger spring
14 Springloaded bearing
15 Slide cover plate
16 Rear sight
16a/b Front sight / Screw

17 Frame
17 a/b Back Straps
18 Magazine catch spring
19 Magazine catch
20 Slide lock spring
21 Slide lock
22 Locking block
23 Trigger mechanism housing with ejector
24 Connector
25 Trigger spring
26 Trigger with trigger bar
27 Slide stop lever
28 Trigger pin
29 Trigger housing pin short
29 a Trigger housing pin long
30 Follower
31 Magazine spring
32 Magazine floor plate
32a Magazine insert
33 Magazine tube
34 Locking block pin

SPECIFICATIONS

Model: G17
Action: autoloader; short recoil, locked breech; striker-fired
Overall Length: 7.3 in.
Overall Height: 5.4 in.
Overall Width: 1.2 in.
Barrel: 4.5 in.
Weight Unloaded: 22.0 oz.
Caliber: 9mm
Capacity: 17 + 1
Common Features: polymer frame; textured polymer with finger groove grips; fixed front/dovetail rear, dot/outline; Picatinny rail; magazine bumper pad; textured front/back grip straps; external extractor; loaded chamber indicator; serrated combat trigger guard; trigger, firing pin, drop safeties; hexagonal rifling; matte black Tenifer finish

BACKGROUND

Glock did not invent the polymer framed pistol but they did create a "plastic pistol" that is durable, reliable, accurate, and turned the firearm industry on its ear. Glock pistols have about 65% market share among U.S. law enforcement agencies. The G17 was the first model produced and similar models followed in compact and subcompact versions in numerous calibers—9mm, .40 S&W, 10mm, .357 SIG, .45 ACP, .45 GAP—a .380 version is not imported to the U.S. Notable design features include: a low slide profile that keeps the barrel axis close to the shooters hand to reduce muzzle flip, a nylon-based polymer frame with steel inserts, a polygonal rifled barrel, and three independent safety mechanisms: the striker-fire action system, a firing pin safety and a drop safety. Glock touts perfection and they are very close. Disassembly of Glocks is just as simple. The instructions are for a G17 but will work for all Glock models, including Gen 4 models which have a modular grip system and enhanced grip texture.

Year Introduced: 1982
Country of Origin: Austria
Current Manufacture: Glock (glock.com)
Similar Models: G17C, G19, G19C, G26, G22, G23, G27, G22C, G23C, G20, G29, G20C, G21, G30, G36, G21C, G31, G32, G33, G31C, G32C, G34, G35, G17 Gen4, 22 Gen4, G19 Gen4, G26 Gen4, G23 Gen4, G27 Gen4, G35 Gen4, G20 SF, G29 SF, G21 SF, G30 SF, G37 Gen4, G13 Gen4

REQUIRED TOOLS

Field Stripping: none
Disassembly/Assembly: small flat blade screwdriver, 3/32 punch or Glock disassembly tool

FIELD STRIP

1. Remove the magazine and press the trigger.

2. Grasp the pistol in one hand so the four fingers of that hand rest over the slide (part #1) and the thumb rests on the rear of the frame (17) at the beavertail, Figure 1. Use your fingers to draw back the slide about 1/16 inch. If you pull back the slide too much, you will need to rack the slide and pull the trigger, then start over. While holding the slide back, use your thumb and forefinger of the opposite hand to pull down on the tabs of the slide lock (21) on either side of the frame. While holding down on the slide lock tabs, ease the grip in your other hand and let the slide move forward.

FIGURE 1

3. The slide can then be moved forward and off the frame, Figure 2.

FIGURE 2

4. Push the recoil spring assembly slightly forward and up with your thumb and remove it from the slide assembly.

5. Grasp the barrel and move it forward slightly and then up and out of the slide.

At this point the pistol can be cleaned.

> **Maintenance Tip:** Do not over lubricate Glocks. There are only six areas that need only a drop of oil: top inside the slide forward of the ejection port, the two slide rails, the forward end of the barrel where it contacts the slide during recoil, the barrel locking lugs where the barrel pivots during recoil, the two rear steel rails in the frame.

SLIDE DISASSEMBLY

1. Place slide muzzle end on the bench top surface and use a small screwdriver or Glock disassembly tool to push down on the spacer sleeve (6) while sliding the slide cover plate (15) toward the bottom of the slide, Figure 3. Note that the firing pin spring (7) is under tension. If the slide cover plate is stubborn, gently pry it out with a small flat blade screwdriver.

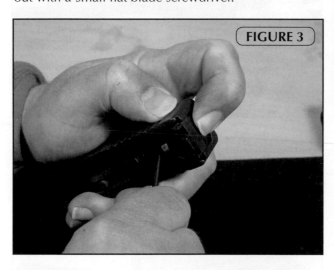

FIGURE 3

2. With the slide cover plate removed the firing pin (5) and firing pin spring can be removed from the rear of the slide. Also remove the extractor depressor plunger assembly which consists of the extractor depressor plunger (12), extractor depressor plunger spring (13) and spring loaded bearing (14).

3. To remove the extractor (11), hold the slide with the bottom facing up and depress the firing din safety (9) with your thumb. Use your Glock disassembly tool in the rear of the extractor and lift it from the slide. Note the firing pin safety is under tension. Remove the firing pin safety and firing pin safety spring (10) from the slide, Figure 4.

4. To disassemble the firing pin assembly, grasp the firing pin spring between your thumb and forefinger and pull down on it to allow the two spring cups (8).

> **Tuning Tip:** The trigger spring and the connector are two parts that can be replaced to either increase the trigger pull, in the case of a conceal carry pistol, or decrease the trigger pull for a competition pistol. Glock offers the New York Trigger spring in 8 pounds that is olive in color; the 11 pound spring is orange. Connectors are available in 4.5 and 8 pounds; a 5.5 pound connector is standard equipment. Aftermarket connectors are available in 2, 3.5, 4.5, and 5 from Ghost Inc. (ghostinc.com), Scherer, Lone Wolf Distributors (lonewolfdist.com) among others. Follow the manufacturer's instructions.

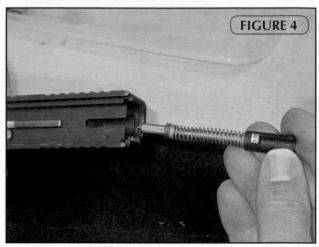

FIGURE 4

FRAME DISASSEMBLY

1. Push out the trigger housing pin (29) with a punch, Figure 5.

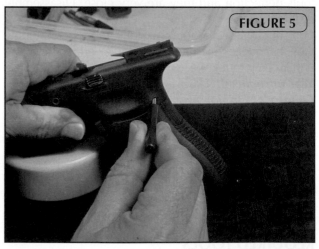

FIGURE 5

2. Gently pry the trigger housing (23) out of the frame. Sometimes you can easily pull up on the ejector using your fingers without any tools. Note that the trigger

housing will be connected to the trigger via the trigger bar (26).

3. With the trigger housing up and out of the frame but still connected to the trigger with trigger bar (26), rotate the trigger housing to the left of the frame to disengage the left tab of the trigger bar from the slot in the trigger housing, Figure 6. At this point the connector (24) can be pried from the trigger housing and the trigger spring (25) can be removed.

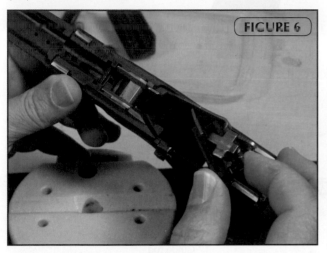

FIGURE 6

4. To remove the trigger with trigger bar assembly and the slide stop lever (27), push out the trigger pin (28). With the pin removed, the slide stop lever can be removed to the rear and out of the frame. The trigger with trigger bar assembly can be moved to the rear and out of the frame.

5. To remove the locking block (22), use a small screwdriver or Glock disassembly tool to depress the side lock spring and pull the slide lock from either side of the frame. The locking block can then be gently pried upward and out of the frame.

6. To remove the magazine catch (19), hold a finger or thumb on the magazine catch on the right side of the frame. Insert a small flat blade screwdriver into the top of the magazine well and push the magazine catch spring (18) out of the magazine catch groove and to the right until it aligns with the notch in the magazine catch then move it out of the notch and let the spring return to the left. The magazine catch can then be removed from the right side of the frame.

MAGAZINE DISASSEMBLY

1. Hold the magazine in your hand magazine floor plate (32) facing up and insert the Glock disassembly tool or a small punch through the hole in the magazine floorplate then push down on the tool/punch while pulling the magazine floor plate toward the front of the magazine tube (33) until it comes off. Note that the magazine spring (31) is under tension so control the spring.

2. The magazine spring, follower (30) and magazine insert (32a) can then be removed.

Reassemble in reverse order.

Pirates and Trucker Girls: Skate board tape can easily give you more grip on 3rd generation an older Glocks. Slip on rubber boots by Hogue (getgrip.com) and Pachmayr (pachmayr.com) or a beaver tail insert by Grip Force (gripforceproducts.com) can help you hang on with sweaty hands. Of course your hands may get sweatier looking at the backside on the back of your slide with Rock Your Glock's (rockyourglock.com) Trucker Girl back slide cover plate of magazine floorplate. For those into screaming skulls, pirates, devils, and biohazards, Rock Your Glock has that covered, too, Figure 7. They'll also customize one to whatever you like.

Latin Translated Here: Some of the magazine floor plates from Rock Your Glock's (rockyourglock.com) require you to learn Latin: Veritas Aequitas (Truth Justice), Molon labe (Come and take them).

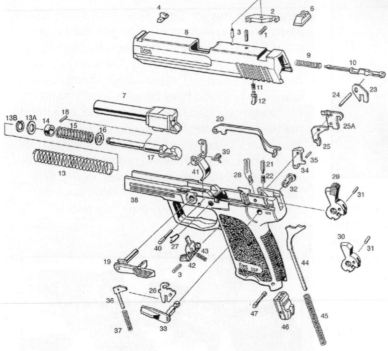

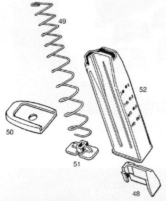

13B Snap ring
14 Buffer spring retainer
15 Buffer spring
16 Rear recoil spring retainer
17 Guide rod
18 Roll pin, buffer spring retainer
19 Slide release
20 Trigger bar, complete
21 Trigger bar detent
22 Trigger bar detent spring
23 Disconnector
24 Sear axle
25 Catch
25A Sear actuator latch
26 Detent plate
27 Shaped spring (slide release)
28 Flat spring
29 Hammer
30 Hammer
31 Cylinder pin, hammer strut pin
32 Hammer axle
33 Control lever
34 Sear
35 Roll pin, sear
36 Detent slide
37 Compression spring
38 Frame
39 Trigger rebound spring
40 Trigger axle
41 Trigger
42 Magazine release
43 Magazine release spring
44 Hammer strut
45 Hammer spring
46 Lanyard loop insert
47 Lanyard loop insert pin
48 Magazine Follower
49 Magazine spring
50 Magazine floorplate
51 Locking plate
52 Magazine housing

PARTS LIST

1 Extractor spring
2 Extractor
3 Roll pin (extractor, firing pin, mag. release)
4 Front sight
6 Rear sight

7 Barrel
8 Slide
9 Firing pin spring
10 Firing pin
11 Firing pin block spring
12 Firing pin block
13 Recoil spring 214843
13A Front recoil spring retainer

SPECIFICATIONS

Model: USP

Action: autoloader; SA/DA; short recoil

Overall Length: 7.6 in. (9mm, .40 S&W); 7.9 in. (.45 ACP)

Overall Height: 5.4 in. (9mm, .40 S&W); 5.6 in. (.45 ACP)

Overall Width: 1.3 in.

Barrel: 4.3 in. (9mm, .40 S&W); 4.4 in. (.45 ACP)

Weight Unloaded: 16.7 oz. (9mm); 16.8 oz. (.40 S&W); 32.0 oz. (.45 ACP)

Caliber: 9mm; .40 S&W; .45 ACP

Capacity: 15 + 1 (9mm); 13 + 1 (.40 S&W); 12 + 1 (.45 ACP)

Features: polymer frame; decocking lever; ambidextrous magazine release; Picatinny rail; magazine bumper pad; checkered front strap; external extractor; loaded chamber indicator; serrated oversized combat trigger guard; external hammer; polygonal rifling; matte black finish; numerous trigger variants; textured polymer grip; dovetail front/rear, luminous 3-dot sights

BACKGROUND

Heckler & Koch (H&K) has a reputation for pushing the design envelope with innovative features and manufacturing techniques like the squeezing-cocking mechanism of the P7 and polymer frame of VP70Z. The USP prototype was entered into the U.S. Special Operations Command (USSOCOM) program for testing of a new combat handgun. The result of those tests was the H&K Mk 23 and the USP when through more design refinement and debuted in .40 S&W. The USP is conventional in design using a type of Browning cam-locking action similar to the 1911. The USP employs a mechanical recoil reduction system which reduces felt recoil by 30%. It also features a modular trigger system that allows up to nine different civilian variants. Controls are also ambidextrous.

Year Introduced: 1993

Country of Origin: Germany

Current Manufacture: Heckler & Koch (hk-usa.com)

Similar Models: USP Compact, USP Tactical (threaded barrel, magazine funnel), USP Compact Tactical

REQUIRED TOOLS

Field Stripping: none

Disassembly/Assembly: small punch, small rollpin punch, nylon hammer

FIELD STRIP

1. Cock the pistol and remove the magazine.

2. Retract and hold the slide (part #8) to the rear so that the pin, H&K calls it an axle, of the slide release (19) is visible through the notch in the left side of the slide, Figure 1.

FIGURE 1

3. Remove the slide release from the left side of the frame by pressing on the axle of the slide release from the right side of the frame (38), Figure 2.

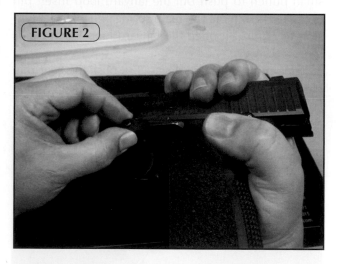

FIGURE 2

4. Remove the slide with barrel (7) and recoil spring assembly by sliding it forward and off of the frame, Figure 3.

5. Next remove the recoil spring assembly from the barrel locking block by lifting up the rear of the recoil spring guide rod (17). Note the recoil spring (13) is under tension. The entire recoil spring assembly can now be lifted out of the slide.

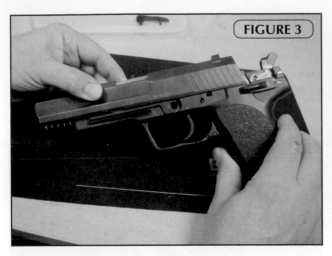

FIGURE 3

6. Lift the rear of the barrel by the locking block and withdraw it from the slide.

At this point the USP is sufficiently disassembled for routine cleaning.

FRAME DISASSEMBLY

1. To remove the main spring (45), hold the hammer (29) and pull the trigger (41) so the hammer rests in the fired position.

2. Press in the lanyard loop insert (46) and use a small punch to push out the lanyard loop insert pin (47), Figure 4. Note the main spring (45) is under tension so control it once the lanyard loop insert pin is removed.

3. To remove the safety lever (33), push the sear pin, H&K calls it a sear axle (24), from the left side of the frame to the right, Figure 5.

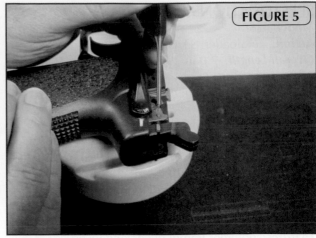

FIGURE 5

4. Remove the detent plate (26) from the left side of the frame by moving it upward, Figure 6.

5. Remove from the top of the frame the disconnector (23), catch (25) and sear actuator latch (25a).

6. Next use a small flat blade screwdriver to push down on the detent slide (36) and compression spring (37), then pull the control lever (33) from the left side of the frame.

7. Flip the frame rail side down and the detent slide and compression spring will fall out the top of the frame.

8. The hammer (29) is removed by using a punch to push out the hammer axle (32) via the control lever frame hole on the left side of the frame. Remove the hammer and hammer strut (44) from the top of the frame.

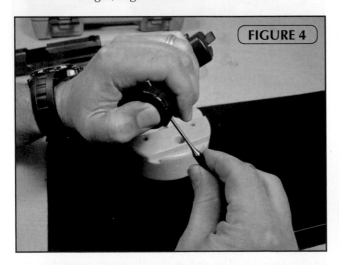

FIGURE 4

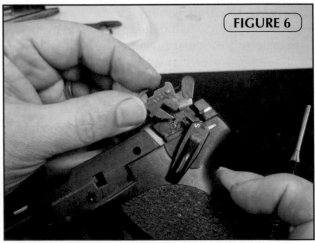

FIGURE 6

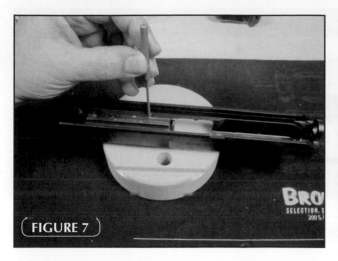

FIGURE 7

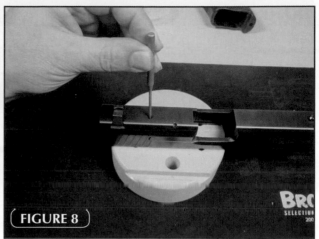

FIGURE 8

9. Remove the trigger bar (20) by rotating the rear portion upward. Pull the trigger slightly to align it with a cut in the frame and pull it free.

SLIDE DISASSEMBLY

1. To remove the extractor (2), drive out the roll pin (3) from bottom of slide to top using a small roll pin punch and hammer, Figure 7. The extractor and extractor spring (1) can now be removed.

2. To remove the firing pin (10) drift out the firing pin roll pin (3) using a small roll pin punch, Figure 8.

3. Depress the firing pin block (12) while holding the slide muzzle end up and the firing pin with partially protrude from the rear of the slide. Remove the firing pin block and firing pin block spring (9).

Reassembly Tip: Make sure the sear axle slightly protrudes on the left side of the frame so it fits into the detent plate.

4. Now the firing pin and firing pin block spring can then be removed from the rear of the slide.

Reassemble in reverse order.

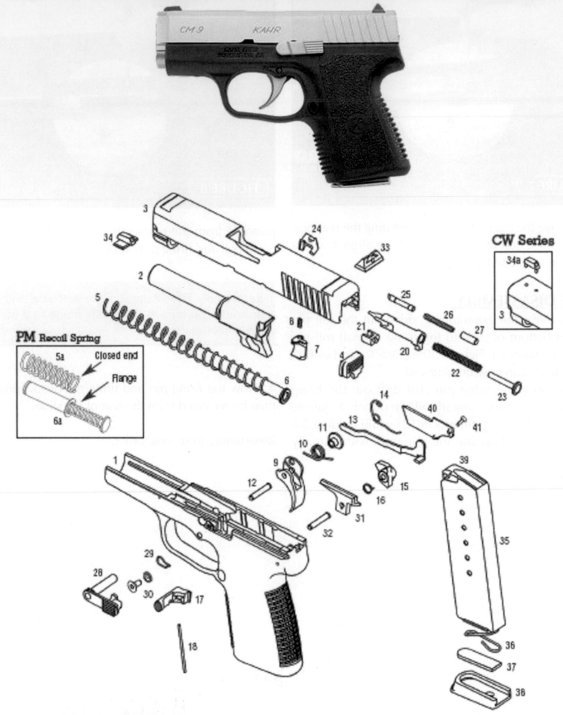

PARTS LIST

1 Frame
2 Barrel
3 Slide
4 Slide Back
5 Recoil Spring
6 Recoil Spring Guide
7 Striker Block
8 Striker Block Spring
9 Trigger

10 Trigger Spring
11 Trigger Spacer
12 Trigger Pivot Pin
13 Trigger Bar
14 Trigger Bar Spring
15 Cocking Cam
16 Cocking Cam Spring
17 Magazine Catch Body
18 Magazine Catch Spring
19 Magazine Catch Lock Pin
20 Striker

21 Striker Spacer
22 Striker Spring
23 Striker Spring Guide
24 Extractor
25 Extractor Pin - Front
26 Extractor Spring
27 Extractor Pin - Back
28 Slide Stop
29 Slide Stop Spring
30 Slide Stop Spring Retaining
  Pin

31 Ejector
32 Cocking Cam Pivot Pin
33 Rear Sight
34 Front Sight
35 Magazine Tube
36 Magazine Spring
37 Magazine Base Lock
38 Magazine Base
39 Magazine Follower

SPECIFICATIONS
Model: CM9
Action: autoloader; locked breech; striker-fired
Overall Length: 5.9 in.
Overall Height: 4.5 in.
Overall Width: 0.9 in.
Barrel: 3.6 in.
Weight Unloaded: 15.8 oz.
Caliber: 9mm
Capacity: 7 + 1
Common Features: polymer frame; serrated front/back straps; textured polymer grips; dovetail front/rear, white bar dot sights; passive striker block safety; magazine bumper pad; two-tone finish

BACKGROUND
Kahr Arms took root in the need for a better small pistol for concealed carry. Justin Moon first designed the compact K9 with stainless steel frame in 1996 and gave the pistol teeth when he chambered in 9mm. Since then, Kahr pistols are produced in both steel and polymer frames. Caliber choice ranges from 9mm to .40 S&W, .45 ACP and .380. The striker firing mechanism of all Kahr pistols operate with a passive firing pin safety. Kahrs are known for their thin girth, lightweight and smooth trigger pull made possible by a double-lobed cocking cam, which is very different from Glock's striker system. The instructions are specifically for the CM9, an economy version of the popular PM9 model, but will generally work for all polymer Kahrs in all calibers.
Year Introduced: 2011
Country of Origin: USA
Current Manufacture: Kahr Arms (kahr.com)
Similar Models: T9, TP9, K9, CW9, P9, MK9, PM9

REQUIRED TOOLS
Field Stripping: nylon hammer (optional)
Disassembly/Assembly: T5 and T6 screwdriver, 1/8 inch punch, brass/nylon hammer, small pointed tool (such as a dental pick), small needle nose pliers

FIELD STRIP
1. Remove the magazine and pull back the slide (part #3) back so that the index marks on the left side of the frame and slide align and the internal tab on the slide stop (28) can be seen through the half-moon cut out in the slide, Figure 1.

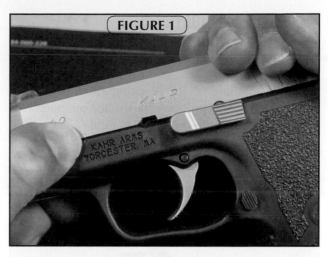

FIGURE 1

2. From the right side of the frame, push out the slide stop. You may need to use a nylon hammer to tap the slide stop out.

3. With the slide stop removed, pull the trigger (9) and keep it pulled as you ease the slide forward and off the frame, Figure 2. Note that the slide assemble is under tension from the recoil spring (5).

FIGURE 2

4. To remove the barrel (2) from the slide, slightly push forward and up on recoil spring guide (6) to clear the recoil lug of the barrel. Note that the recoil spring is under tension.

5. Then grasp the recoil lug of the barrel and slightly push it forward then lift it up and out of the slide.

The pistol is now field stripped for routine cleaning and maintenance.

SLIDE DISASSEMBLY

1. Place the slide muzzle end on the bench surface and use a small flat blade screwdriver to pull down on the striker spring (22) and the striker spring guide (23). While pulling the striker spring and striker spring guide, insert a wooden dowel or use the pin portion of slide stop between the striker spring guide and the slide back (4), Figure 3.

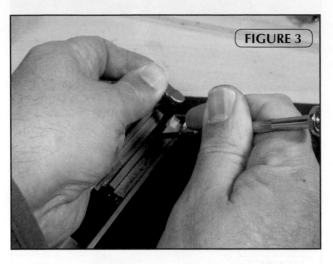

FIGURE 3

2. Next remove the slide back by inserting a small screwdriver into the half circle cutout in the slide back and depress the back extractor pin (27) which locks the slide back into the slide. You only need to depress the pin about 1/16 inch. As you depress the back extractor pin, use your thumb to control and slide the slide back free from the slide, Figure 4. Note that the slide back is under tension from the striker spring. You may need to gently pry the slide back with a flat blade screwdriver if it is tight.

3. With the slide back removed, pull out the striker spring and the striker spring guide from the rear of the slide.

4. To remove the striker (20), press the striker block (7) and the striker will slide out the rear of the slide.

5. With the striker removed, the striker space (21) can easily be removed from the striker. When reinserting the striker spacer it does not matter which side is inserted into the striker.

6. Remove the back extractor pin and use a small screwdriver to push back on the front extractor pin (25) and extractor spring.

7. Place the slide so the extractor (24) faces up then push it down at the front to remove. Insert as small diameter punch in the extractor slot in the slide to punch out the front extractor pin and extractor plunger. Once these parts are removed, the striker block and striker block spring (8) can be removed from the slide.

FRAME DISASSEMBLY

1. Use a T6 screwdriver to remove the slide stop spring screw and washer (30) retaining the slide release spring (29) from the left side of the frame, Figure 5.

2. Next flip the pistol over and with a T5 screwdriver remove the side panel screw (41) located at the rear on the right side of the frame. Gently pry the side panel (41) up and out of the frame.

3. Using a pair of needle nose pliers, grasp the top portion of the trigger bar spring (14) and pull down and outward removing it from the frame.

4. Next, with a 1/8 inch punch push out the trigger pivot pin (12) from the left side of the frame to the right

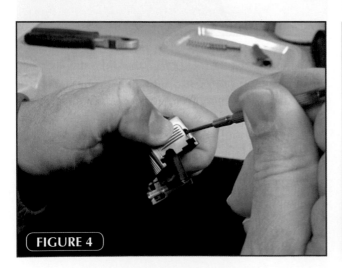

FIGURE 4

FIGURE 5

BROWNE
SELECTION. SER...

side of the frame. Note that the trigger spring (10) is under tension.

5. With the trigger pivot pin removed the trigger (9), trigger spring, trigger spacer (11), and trigger bar (13) can be removed from the frame.

6. Use a small pick, hook the cocking cam pivot pin (32) through the small hole in the head and remove it from the frame.

7. Grasp the ejector (31) and pull it out of the frame along with the cocking cam (15) and cocking cam spring (16).

8. To remove the magazine catch body (17), from the top of the magazine well use a small pick to hook the magazine catch leaf spring (18) and pull it to the side and outward to release it from the magazine catch body.

9. Using a pair of needle nose pliers grab the top of the magazine catch leaf spring and pull it straight and out of the frame.

10. Remove the magazine catch from the right side of the frame.

Reassemble in reverse order.

Reassembly Tip: Note that the front extractor pin needs to engage the extractor is a specific way. The concave end of the front extractor pin must face in when engaging the rear of the extractor. Insert the front extractor pin in the slide then the extractor. Use a piece of masking tape to hold the two pieces in place. After the slide is reassembled, the extractor is installed properly if it freely moves. The two legs of the cocking cam spring (16) align with one hole in the ejector (31) and one hole in the cocking cam (15). The spring can be placed in either way. To reinstall the trigger bar spring attach the hook onto the bar as normal and then use a pair of needle nose pliers to grab the loop in the spring and bend the lower half into the slot in the frame. Do not over tighten the Torx screws as you may strip the screw hole threads.

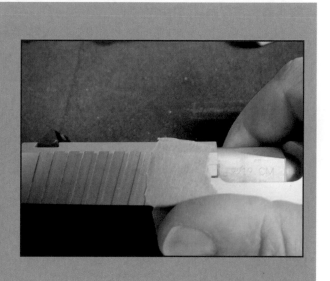

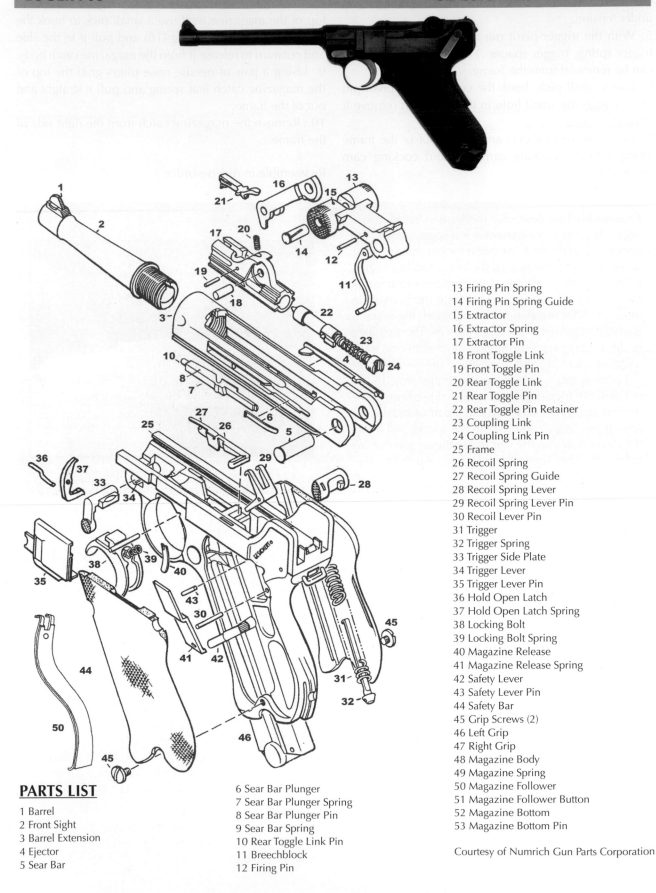

13 Firing Pin Spring
14 Firing Pin Spring Guide
15 Extractor
16 Extractor Spring
17 Extractor Pin
18 Front Toggle Link
19 Front Toggle Pin
20 Rear Toggle Link
21 Rear Toggle Pin
22 Rear Toggle Pin Retainer
23 Coupling Link
24 Coupling Link Pin
25 Frame
26 Recoil Spring
27 Recoil Spring Guide
28 Recoil Spring Lever
29 Recoil Spring Lever Pin
30 Recoil Lever Pin
31 Trigger
32 Trigger Spring
33 Trigger Side Plate
34 Trigger Lever
35 Trigger Lever Pin
36 Hold Open Latch
37 Hold Open Latch Spring
38 Locking Bolt
39 Locking Bolt Spring
40 Magazine Release
41 Magazine Release Spring
42 Safety Lever
43 Safety Lever Pin
44 Safety Bar
45 Grip Screws (2)
46 Left Grip
47 Right Grip
48 Magazine Body
49 Magazine Spring
50 Magazine Follower
51 Magazine Follower Button
52 Magazine Bottom
53 Magazine Bottom Pin

Courtesy of Numrich Gun Parts Corporation

PARTS LIST

1 Barrel
2 Front Sight
3 Barrel Extension
4 Ejector
5 Sear Bar

6 Sear Bar Plunger
7 Sear Bar Plunger Spring
8 Sear Bar Plunger Pin
9 Sear Bar Spring
10 Rear Toggle Link Pin
11 Breechblock
12 Firing Pin

SPECIFICATIONS

Model: Luger P08
Action: autoloader, short recoil-operated, toggle-locked
Overall Length: 10.75 in. (6 in. barrel)
Overall Height: 5.5 in.
Overall Width: 1.37 in.
Barrel: 3.74 to 7.87 in.
Weight Unloaded: 30.72 oz.
Caliber: 9mm
Capacity: 8 + 1
Features: steel frame; loaded chamber indicator; thumb safety; fixed front/rear sight; blue finish; checkered wood grip

BACKGROUND

The Luger P08 is one of the most iconic and unique pistols ever manufactured. It uses a toggle mechanism that was invented by Hugo Borchardt and highly redesigned by George Luger who patented his design in 1898. Originally chambered in .30 Luger (7.62x21mm) caliber, the P08 has the distinction of being the pistol the 9mm (9x19mm Parabellum) was developed. The Swiss Army adopted the Luger in 1900, the Germany Navy in 1904 and the German Army in 1908. It served Germany in both world wars. The P08 was manufactured by Deutche Waffen- und Munitionsfabriken (DWM), Erfurt, Mauser, Simon & Co., Krieghoff and others. These pistols are highly prized by collectors with some variations more rare and coveted. More recently Stoeger and Mitchell Arms sold stainless steel versions of the P08. Disassembly instructions below use a Stoeger American Eagle model and take down will be similar with all Lugers.
Year Introduced: 1900
Country of Origin: Germany

REQUIRED TOOLS

Field Stripping: none
Disassembly/Assembly: small flat blade screwdriver, medium punch

FIELD STRIP

1. Remove magazine and grasp the pistol in your right hand pull back on the barrel/receiver or if tight slightly push the muzzle against a padded surface or push back with your left hand until the barrel/receiver moves about 1/4 inch to the rear.
2. Rotate the locking bolt (part #38) downward clockwise, Figure 1.
3. While still holding the barrel/receiver assembly with your right hand, pull out trigger plate (33) from the frame (25), Figure 2.

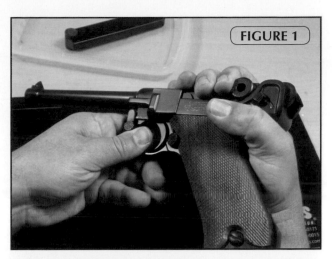

FIGURE 1

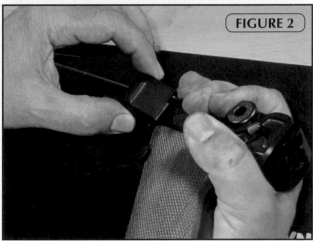

FIGURE 2

4. Slide the barrel/receiver assembly forward and off the frame, Figure 3.

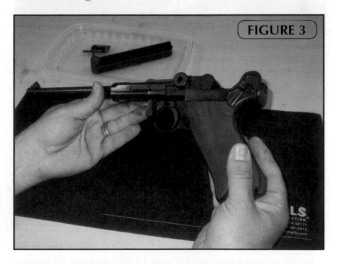

FIGURE 3

5. Slightly pull up on the toggle knobs on the rear toggle link (20) so the rear and front toggle link (18) buckle, then use your finger or a non-marring punch to press out the receiver axle (10) from the right to the left side of the receiver (3), Figure 4. The toggle links and

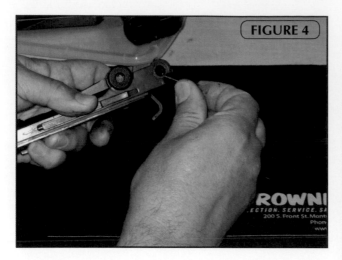

FIGURE 4

breechblock (11) can now be pulled from the receiver as an assembly.

At this stage the Luger is field stripped.

BARREL/RECEIVER DISASSEMBLY

1. Flip the toggle links and breechblock so the bottom faces up and insert a small flat blade screwdriver in the slot in firing pin spring guide (14). Slightly press the in firing pin spring guide with the screwdriver and rotate counterclockwise about a quarter turn, Figure 5. The firing pin spring guide is under tension from the firing pin spring (13) so control it as it comes free.

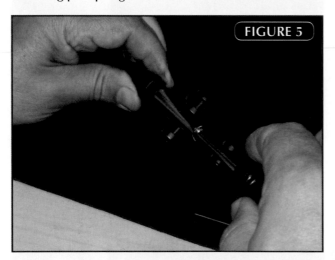

FIGURE 5

2. Remove the firing pin (12) rearward from the breechblock.
3. The ejector (4) is removed by inserting the blade of a small screwdriver under rear of the ejector in recess of the receiver and gently prying up.
4. Pry up forward end of sear bar spring (9) with a small screwdriver and slide the spring forward and out of its slot in the receiver. Then lift the sear bar (5) out of its recess in left side of receiver.

5. Remove the ejector (4) by gently lifting the rear of the ejector with a small screwdriver just enough to free it from its recess in the receiver.

Swiss-Style Grip: During the Luger's regain as a top military pistol the configuration of the pistols changed. Collectors characterize the configuration by year. The straight front grip strap is known as the 1929 Swiss Pattern.

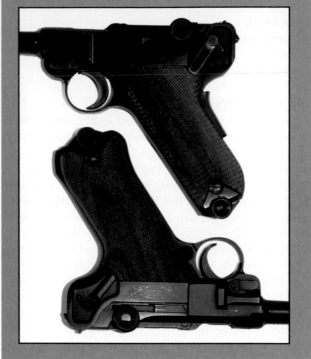

FRAME DISASSEMBLY

1. The trigger (38) and trigger spring (39) can be lifted out of frame as an assembly, Figure 6.
2. Remove the grip panels (46 and 47) by unscrewing the two grip screws (45); one on each side of the frame.

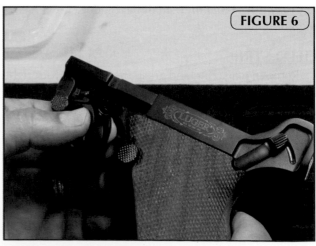

FIGURE 6

3. The magazine release (40) is removed by sliding the magazine release spring (41) out of its recess in the left side of the frame using a small blade screwdriver. The magazine release can then be removed from the right side of the frame.

4. The locking bolt (38) can be pulled from the left side of the frame.

5. Remove the hold open latch (36) and hold open latch spring (37) by lifting rear of latch slightly and pressing down and to the rear on hold open latch, disengaging the hold open latch and hold open latch spring assembly from frame.

6. The safety lever (42) and safety bar (44) are removed by drifting out the safety lever pin (43) from inside of frame.

7. To remove the recoil spring lever (28), recoil spring (26), and recoil spring guide (27) insert a punch to use as a retaining pin into the hole in the recoil spring guide and compress the recoil spring toward the top of the frame to free the recoil spring lever from the recoil spring guide. Then control the recoil spring and recoil spring guide as you allow it to expand toward the right side of the frame.

Reverse these assembly procedures to reassemble.

Reassembly Tip: When reinstalling the barrel/receiver assembly on the frame the coupling link (23), which is "S" shaped and hangs from the bottom of the rear of the toggle assembly, needs to drop in front of the of the upper arm of the recoil spring lever.

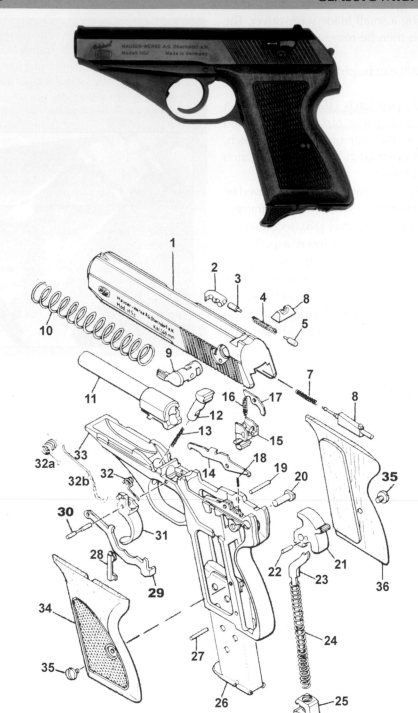

PARTS LIST

1. Slide
2. Extractor
3. Extractor plunger
4. Extractor spring
5. Safety detent plunger
6. Rear sight
7. Firing pin spring
8. Firing pin
9. Safety catch

10. Recoil spring
11. Barrel
12. Takedown latch
13. Takedown latch spring
14. Magazine safety
15. Sear
16. Sear spring
17. Cartridge feed com
18. Magazine safety spring
19. Sear hinge pin
20. Hammer hinge pin

21. Hammer
22. Strut pin
23. Hammer strut
24. Hammer spring
25. Magazine catch
26. Magazine
27. Magazine catch pin
28. Disconnector
29. Trigger bar
30. Trigger pin
31. Trigger

32. Trigger spring
33. Frame
34. Left grip
35. Grip screw
36. Right grip
37. Grip screw

Courtesy of Numrich Gun Parts
    Corporation

SPECIFICATIONS

Model: HSc
Action: autoloader, blowback, SA/DA
Overall Length: 6 in.
Overall Height: 4 in.
Overall Width: 1.06 in.
Barrel: 3.4 in.
Weight Unloaded: 25 oz.
Caliber: .32 ACP; .380
Capacity: 8 + 1 (.32 ACP); 7 +1 (.380)
Features: steel frame/slide, manual thumb and magazine safeties, checkered wood grips, fixed blade front/drift adj. rear sights, blued or nickel finish

FIGURE 1

BACKGROUND

The Mauser HSc was developed for civilian use to compete against Walther and Sauer pistols, but the start of World War II shifted demand to the military. Thousands of pistols were made in Nazi Germany during the war procured mainly by the Navy and Army. The design makes use of stamped metal parts like most modern pistols, yet still retains the renowned Mauser quality with its finish and reliability. The HSc—"HS" stands for Hahn Selbstspanner (self-cocking hammer) and the "c" indicates the third and final design. It has smooth edges, is easy to carry, and has a smooth double-action trigger pull. The slide stays open on the last round fired. The magazine must be slightly withdrawn and replaced then the slide will close automatically.

Year Introduced: 1940
Country of Origin: Germany

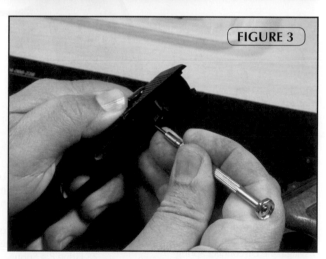

FIGURE 2

REQUIRED TOOLS

Field Stripping: none
Disassembly/Assembly: small flat blade screwdriver

FIELD STRIP

1. Withdraw the magazine, fully cock the hammer (part #21) and rotate the safety catch (9) to the "safe" position.
2. Hold down the notch of the takedown latch (12) inside the front of trigger guard and at the same time pull the slide (1) forward and upward off the frame (33), Figure 1.
3. Remove the barrel (11) and recoil spring (10) by pushing the barrel forward and upward until it clears the slide, Figure 2.

At this point the HSc is sufficiently disassembled for cleaning.

SLIDE DISASSEMBLY

1. To remove the firing pin (8) and safety catch, use a small flat blade screwdriver to push the rear of the firing pinto clear the safety catch, Figure 3.

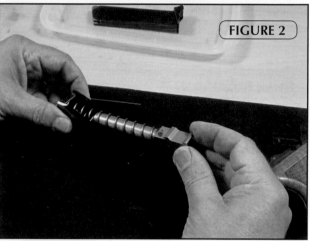

FIGURE 3

2. Turn the safety catch halfway between "fire" and "safe" to move the firing pin out of its recess in the slide. Then use a screwdriver to push the safety catch out from the slide.
3. With the safety catch removed the extractor (2), extractor plunger (3), extractor spring (4), and safety detent plunger (5) can be removed.

FRAME DISASSEMBLY

1. To remove takedown latch use a medium flat blade screwdriver to push down on the takedown latch and rotate it clockwise 180°. The take down latch spring (13) is under compression so control the takedown latch.

2. Remove the grips (34 and 36).

3. With grips removed, the trigger bar (29) can be removed from the left side of the frame, Figure 4.

4. Remove the trigger (31) and trigger spring (32) by drifting out the trigger pin (30) using a small punch.

5. 5. Ensure the hammer is fully forward then remove the magazine catch pin (27) and the magazine catch (25), hammer strut (23), and hammer spring (24) will come free.

Reassemble in reverse order.

FIGURE 4

RUGER P345

PARTS LIST

1 Slide
2 Front Sight
3 Extractor Pivot Pin
4 Loaded Chamber Indicator Spring
5 Loaded Chamber Indicator
6 Magazine Disconnect
7 Magazine Disconnect Spring
8 Firing Pin Block
9 Firing Pin Block Spring
10 Firing Pin Block Plunger
11 Rear Sight Assembly
12 Rear Sight Lock Screw
13 Extractor
14 Extractor Spring
15 Safety Lever Spring
16 Safety Lever Retainer

17 Safety Strut
18 Safety, Right
19 Safety Assembly, Left
20 Safety Detent Plunger Spring
21 Safety Detent Plunger
22 Lock Pin
23 Lock Plunger Detent Spring
24 Lock Detent Plunger
25 Firing Pin Spring
26 Firing Pin
27 Recoil Spring
28 Buffer Spring
29 Camblock
30 Slide Stop Detent
31 Barrel
32 Trigger Bar Spring
33 Trigger Bar
34 Trigger

35 Trigger Plunger Spring
36 Trigger Plunger
37 Hammer Assembly
38 Hammer Pivot Pin
39 Magazine Latch
40 Trigger Pivot Pin
41 Blocker Lever
42 Sear Spring
43 Sear
44 Ejector Spring
45 Ejector Pivot Assembly
46 Ejector
47 Magazine Latch Spring
48 Hammer Spring Seat
49 Hammer Spring Detent
50 Hammer Spring
51 Hammer Strut
52 Hammer Spring Seat Pin

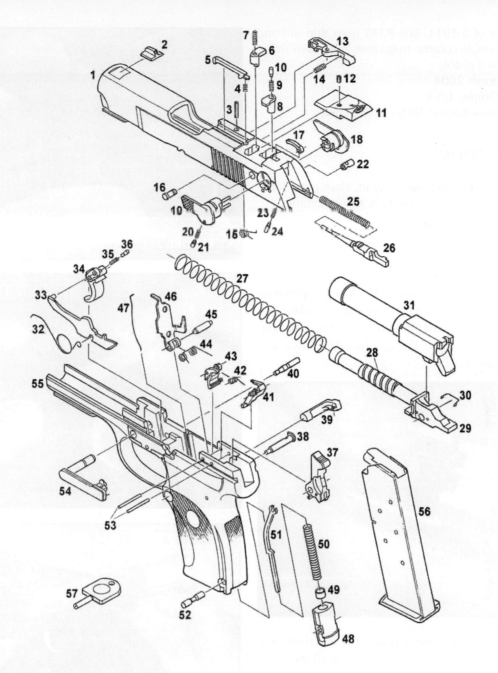

53 Sear Pivot Pin, 2 Req'd.
54 Slide Stop Assembly
55 Frame

56 Magazine, Complete, 8-shot
57 Internal Lock Key

SPECIFICATIONS
Model: P345
Action: autoloader, short recoil-operated, locked breech, SA/DA
Overall Length: 7.5 in.
Overall Height: 5.8 in.
Overall Width: 1.2 in.
Barrel: 4.2 in.
Weight Unloaded: 29.0 oz.
Caliber: .45 ACP

Capacity: 8 + 1
Features: polymer frame; loaded chamber indicator; textured front/rear grip straps; ambidextrous safety; magazine base pad; external hammer, extractor; textured polymer grip; fixed front/adj. rear 3-dot sight; matte or two-tone finish

BACKGROUND
The P345 is a short recoil-operated, locked breech semi-automatic pistol. Like all Ruger P-series pistols it uses a locking system like a SIG P220 and the tilting

barrel system of a 1911. The P345 feels thin in hand because of a single column magazine. It is a well-made work horse of a pistol.

Year Introduced: 2004
Country of Origin: USA
Current Manufacturers: Ruger (ruger.com)

REQUIRED TOOLS

Field Stripping: none
Disassembly/Assembly: two 1/16 in. slave pins, 3/32, 1/8 in. punch, 3/32 roll pin punch, nylon hammer, thin strip of wood or metal, bench block, small hook, flat blade screwdriver

FIELD STRIP

1. Pull slide (part #1) rearward and lock in the open position by pressing upward on the slide stop assembly (54).
2. Through the ejection port, use your finger or non-marring dowel to push the ejector (46) down and forward, Figure 1.

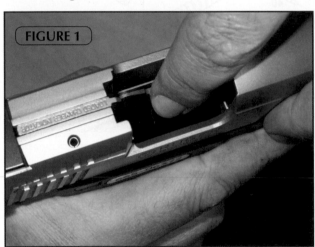

FIGURE 1

3. Next grasp slide, press down on the slide stop and allow the slide to move forward until the vertical disassembly line on the frame (55) is aligned with the vertical disassembly line on the slide, Figure 2.
4. From the left side of the frame, press in on the end of the slide stop assembly. Pull slide stop out of frame, Figure 3.
5. Push the slide forward and off the frame, Figure 4.
6. Disengage the rear of the camblock/recoil spring assembly from the barrel (31) lug. Withdraw the camblock/recoil spring assembly to the rear of the slide, Figure 5. Note that the recoil spring (27) is under tension.
7. Pull the barrel upward and out of the slide to the rear.

The P345 is now field stripped for routine cleaning.

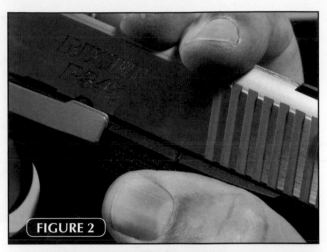

FIGURE 2

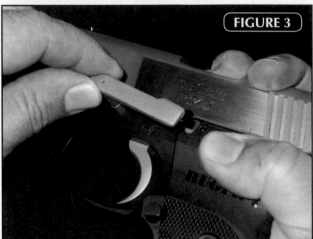

FIGURE 3

FIGURE 4

SLIDE DISASSEMBLY

1. With a 2mm hex or Allen wrench loosen the rear sight lock screw (12), Figure 6.
2. Rest the left side of the slide on the bench block then use a nylon hammer to gently drift the rear sight assembly (11) from right to left. Note there are three springs under tension—the firing pin block spring (9) with firing pin block plunger (10), loaded

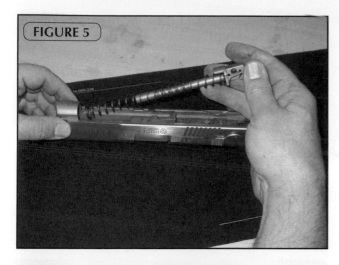

FIGURE 5

FIGURE 6

4. Next place the slide top down so the bottom faces up. With one hand use a small punch or small flat blade screwdriver to push down on the leg of the safety lever spring (15) then with your other hand use a small pick or small screwdriver to push out the safety lever retainer (16) from the inside to outside of the slide. With the safety lever retainer removed, remove the safety lever spring.

5. Remove the safety assembly, left (19) by pulling it from the slide. Note the safety detent plunger (21) and safety detent plunger spring (20) are under tension so control them as you remove safety assembly, left.

6. With safety assembly, left removed, the safety strut (17) can now be removed from the slide.

7. Next push the safety lever, right (18) downward until it can be pulled from the right side of the slide.

8. The firing pin (26) and firing pin spring (25) can now be pulled out from the rear of the slide. 9. Remove the extractor (13) by drifting out the extractor pivot pin (3) with a small roll pin punch. The extractor spring (14) will come off with the extractor.

FRAME DISASSEMBLY

1. Ensure the hammer is in the "fired" or forward most position and use your thumb to press in on the hammer spring seat (48) then push the hammer spring seat pin (52) from left to right, Figure 8. Then pull the hammer spring seat from the butt of the frame along with hammer spring detent (49), hammer spring (50) and the hammer spring strut (51) will fall free from the butt, Figure 9.

2. Use a small punch to drive out the trigger pivot pin (40) from the left to the right, Figure 10. Note the trigger plunger (36) and trigger plunger spring (35) are under tension. Place your finger over the top of the trigger to control the trigger plunger and

chamber indicator spring (4) and magazine disconnect spring (7). As the rear sight assembly is drifted right to left the spring will be revealed in this order. Hold your thumb over the springs to control them, Figure 7.

3. With the rear sight assembly removed, the loaded chamber indicator (5) will fall free. Lift out the firing-pin block (8) and the magazine disconnect (6).

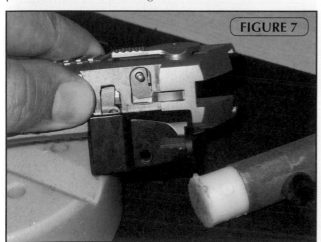

FIGURE 7

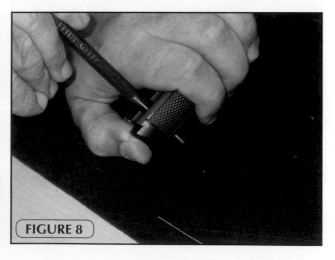

FIGURE 8

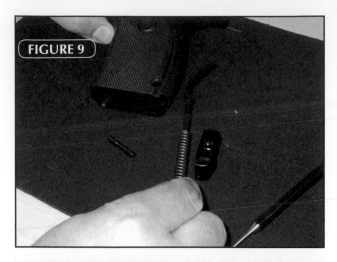

FIGURE 9

the sear spring (42) and then lay the frame on the right side and push out the first or forward most sear pin. The sear spring will fall free from the frame. Push out the rear most sear pivot pin and the blocker lever (41), sear (43), and sear spring (42) can easily be removed from the frame as an assembly.

5. The hammer pivot pin (38) should fall free from the right side of the frame and then the hammer can be pulled out from the top of the frame.

6. Remove the trigger transfer bar by prying up the forward most leg of the trigger bar spring (32) with a small flat blade screwdriver. The trigger transfer bar and trigger bar spring will come out the top of the frame as an assembly.

7. Next remove the ejector (46) by first pushing in on one end of ejector pivot assembly (45) from either side of the frame with a small punch. Pull the ejector forward and angle it in the frame the ejector pivot assembly does snap back into place in the frame. Depress the other end of the ejector pivot assembly from the opposite side of the frame and pull the ejector, ejector pivot assembly, and ejector spring as one assembly from the top of the frame.

Reverse these assembly procedures to reassemble the P345.

FIGURE 10

trigger plunger spring as you drift out the trigger pivot pin.

3. Push up on the trigger toward the top of the frame, Figure 11. Remove the trigger from the trigger bar (33).

Reassembly Tip: Use a small flat blade screw driver to hold down the firing pin block spring with firing pin block plunger, loaded chamber indicator spring and extractor, and magazine disconnect spring when tapping the rear sight assembly back in place, Figure 12. Remember to reinsert an empty magazine into the P345 after reassembly. The empty magazine pushes the ejector back into position.

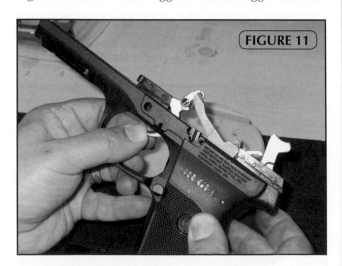

FIGURE 11

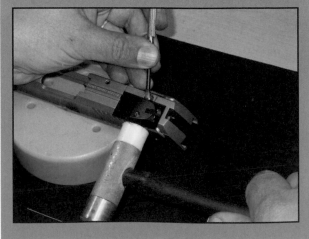

4. Next remove the two sear pivot pins (53) by placing a finger over the top of the frame to control

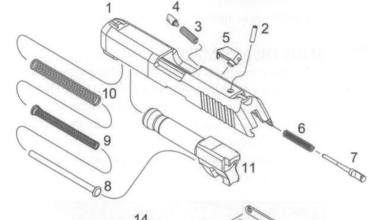

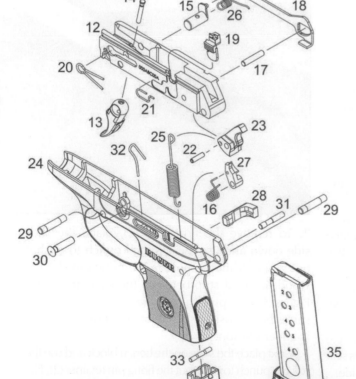

PARTS LIST

1 Slide
2 Firing Pin Retainer
3 Extractor Spring
4 Extractor Plunger
5 Extractor
6 Firing Pin Spring
7 Firing Pin
8 Guide Rod
9 Recoil Spring, Inner
10 Recoil Spring, Outer
11 Barrel
12 Frame Insert
13 Trigger
14 Trigger Pin
15 Trigger Pivot
16 Hammer Catch Spring
17 Hammer Pivot Pin
18 Trigger Bar
19 Hold Open
20 Takedown Pin Detent
21 Hold Open Detent
22 Hammer Spring Retainer Pin
23 Hammer
24 Frame
25 Hammer Spring
26 Trigger Spring
27 Hammer Catch
28 Magazine Latch Catch
29 Frame Insert Pin, 2 Req'd.
30 Takedown Pin
31 Hammer Catch Pin
32 Magazine Latch Spring
33 Hammer Spring Seat Pin
34 Hammer Spring Seat
35 Magazine, Complete

SPECIFICATIONS
Model: LCP-LM
Action: short recoil-operated, autoloader
Overall Length: 5.2 in.
Overall Height: 3.6 in.
Overall Width: 0.8 in.
Barrel: 2.75 in.
Weight Unloaded: 9.4 oz.
Caliber: .380
Capacity: 6 + 1
Features: glass-filled nylon frame; alloy steel slide and barrel; external extractor; fixed front/ rear sights; black finish; checkered polymer grip; some models fitted with LaserMax Centerfire laser sight

BACKGROUND
Ruger's LCP (Lightweight Compact Pistol) is slim, lightweight and compact. It is a locked-breech design where the barrel and slide are locked together upon firing and as the slide/barrel move rearward the barrel unlocks from the slide, spits out the empty and scraps a fresh round out of the magazine. A design similar to large, full-size pistols. The Ruger also takes some design cues from the Kel-Tec P-3AT which has been in production since 2003.
Year Introduced: 2008
Country of Origin: USA
Current Manufacturers: Ruger (ruger.com)
Similar Models: Standard (fixed sights only, no laser sights), Coyote Special

REQUIRED TOOLS
Field Stripping: small flat blade screwdriver
Disassembly/Assembly: two 1/16 in. slave pins, 3/32, 1/8 in. punch, 3/32 roll pin punch, nylon hammer, thin strip of wood or metal, bench block, small hook, flat blade screwdriver

FIELD STRIP
1. Remove the magazine from the pistol. Rack the slide (part #1) to cock the LCP.
2. Push the slide slightly backward—about 1/16 inch—and using a small flat blade screw driver place it in the slide cut out to pry up the takedown pin (30), Figure 1.
3. Remove the takedown pin from the frame (24).
4. Next move the slide assembly forward and off the frame.
5. Remove the recoil spring assembly—guide rod (8), recoil spring inner (9), recoil spring outer (10) —from the slide by slightly compressing the recoil spring from its seat against the barrel (11) lug and pull it out from the slide.

FIGURE 1

6. Remove the barrel by slightly moving it forward and then down and back. Extract the barrel from the slide.

The LCP is now field stripped for routine cleaning.

SLIDE DISASSEMBLY
1. Remove the extractor (5) by slight flexing the extractor out from the slide then place the .059 inch slave pin in the hole just aft of the extractor, Figure 2. Apply slight pressure toward the muzzle with the pin and use a small screwdriver to flip out the extractor from the rear. Do not remove the slave pin as the extractor spring (3) is under pressure.

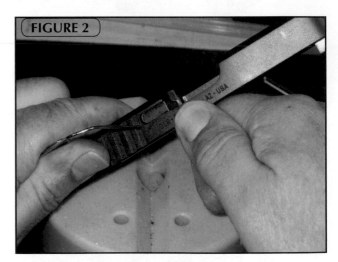
FIGURE 2

2. To remove the firing pin (7), place the slide top side down and use the 1/8 inch punch to push in the firing pin. While pushing in the firing pin slip the thin wood or metal strip between the slide and firing pin, Figure 3. In a pinch use a piece of a wooden painter stirrer or a popsicle stick. Note the firing pin spring (6) is under tension.
3. Next place the slide on the bench block and use the 3/32 roll pin punch to drive out the firing pin retainer (2), Figure 4.

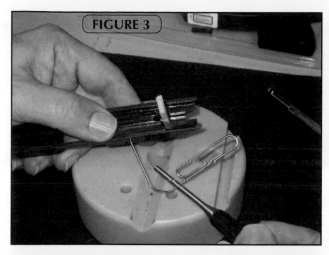

FIGURE 3

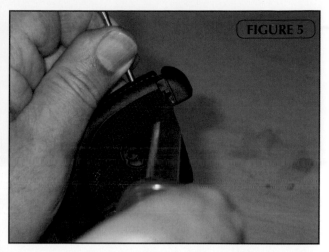

FIGURE 5

FIGURE 4

10. Then drive out the two frame insert pins (29) from the right side to left side of the LCP. The frame insert can now be lifted out from the top of the frame.

11. Place the frame insert on its left side and hold down the trigger spring (26) and then lift the trigger bar (18) from the frame insert. Note the trigger spring is under tension.

12. When the trigger bar is removed control the spring as it releases tension.

13. Next remove the hammer (23) by easily pushing out the hammer spring retainer pin (22) from the frame insert. The hammer and hammer spring will then fall free from the frame insert.

LASER SIGHT DISASSEMBLY

1. To replace the battery in the laser sight, unscrew the two Phillips screws and then gently pry the laser sight apart with a thin flat blade screwdriver, Figure 6. The LCP uses one 3N lithium battery or two 357 silver oxide batteries, Figure 7.

4. With the pin removed, place your finger at the rear of the slide and remove the thin wood/metal strip. The firing pin and firing pin spring will easily fall out the rear of the slide.

5. To remove the frame insert (12), first remove the hammer spring seat (34) using a 3/32 punch via the hole in the rear grip.

6. With the muzzle on a padded surface, slightly depress the tab on the hammer spring seat and use a flat blade screwdriver to gently pry the hammer spring seat from the bottom of the frame, Figure 5.

7. Next remove the hammer spring (25) and hammer spring seat pin (33) using a small hook.

8. Grasp the frame in one hand, hook the hammer spring and hammer spring seat pin and pull them out of the frame until the hammer spring seat pin clears the notches in the frame. Control the spring and gently let it retract.

9. Next place the left side of pistol on the bench block and insert a 1/16 slave pin in the access hole on the right side of the frame.

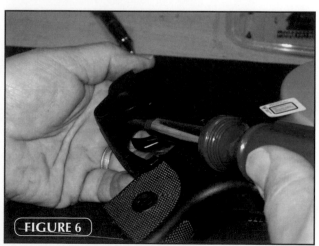

FIGURE 6

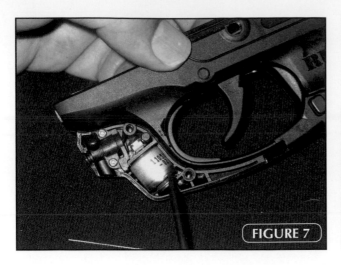

FIGURE 7

2. The laser sight can be removed by gently snapping it off the trigger guard.

Reassemble in reverse order.

Reassembly Tip: The hammer spring retainer pin should extent slightly out of the frame insert just enough to holds the loop in the rear of the trigger bar. Frame insert pins are tapered so insert the tapered end of the pin into the hole on the left side of the pistol. Drive them from left to right. Insert the pin closest to the trigger first.

SIG SAUER P226

PARTS LIST

1 Barrel
2 Recoil Spring Guide
3 Recoil Spring
4 Slide
5 Front Sight
6 Rear Sight
7 Firing Pin Positioning Pin
8 Extractor Spring
9 Extractor Pin
10 Extractor
11 Firing Pin
12 Firing Pin Spring

13 Safety Lock
14 Safety Lock Spring
15 Frame
16 Takedown Lever
17 Locking Insert
18 Slide Catch Lever
19 Slide Catch Lever Spring
20 Trigger
21 Trigger Pivot Pin
22 Trigger Bar
23 Trigger Bar Spring
24 Sear
25 Sear Spring
26 Sear Pivot Pin

27 Sear Spring Pin
28 Safety Lever
29 Hammer
30 Hammer Pin
31 Hammer Pivot Pin
32 Ejector
33 Hammer Strut
34 Mainspring
36 Mainspring Seat
37 Hammer Stop
38 Hammer Reset Spring
39 Hammer Stop Pin
40 Decocking Lever
41 Decocking Lever Bearing

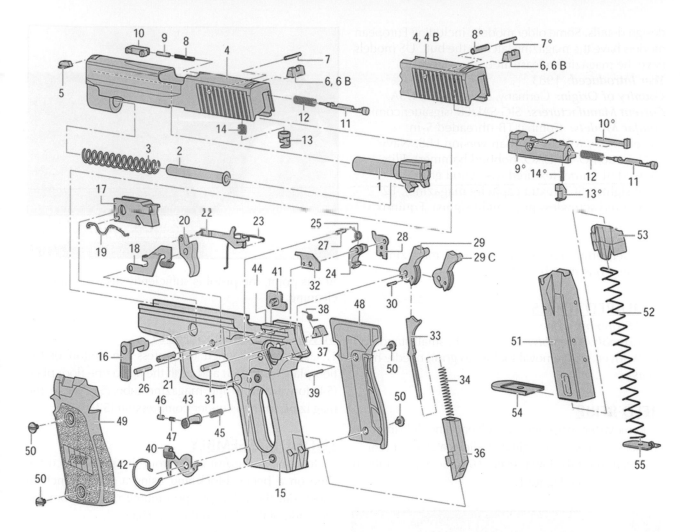

42 Decocking Lever Spring
43 Magazine Catch
44 Support Plate
45 Magazine Catch Spring
46 Magazine Catch Stop

47 Catch Stop Spring
48 Grip Plate, Right
49 Grip Plate, Left
50 Grip Plate Screw
51 Magazine Tube

52 Magazine Spring
53 Magazine Follower
54 Magazine Floorplate
55 Floorplate Insert

SPECIFICATIONS

Model: P226
Action: locked breech, short-recoil, autoloader, DA/SA trigger
Overall Length: 7.7 in.
Overall Height: 5.5 in.
Overall Width: 1.5 in.
Barrel: 4.4 in.
Weight Unloaded: 34.0 oz.
Caliber: .22 LR, 9mm, .357 SIG, .40 S&W
Capacity: 10 + 1 (.22 LR); 5 + 1 (9mm); 12 + 1 (.357 SIG, .40 S&W)
Common Features: textured polymer grips; alloy frame; Picatinny rail; serrated combat trigger guard; textured front/rear grip staps; decocking lever safety; various finishes (matte Nitron, digital camo, Two-Tone)

BACKGROUND

The P226 is a popular combat handgun used by numerous nations—Canada, UK, Spain, Netherlands, Malaysia, Luxembourg, Germany, Finland—and others. In the US, the Navy SEALs use a modified P226 and other US agencies—Coast Guard, Dept. of Homeland Security, Federal Air Marshals, FBI, DEA, Secret Service, Texas Rangers—as well as state police departments in CT, FL, NY, TN, NJ and TX. Notable features include an enlarged breech section that's locks the barrel and slide together, and a decocking lever that allows shooters a safe way to lower the hammer. As the decocker lever is depressed the automatic firing pin lock is engaged. The P226 can also be converted to other calibers with factory kits. The instructions that follow are similar to other Sig pistol variants like the P220, P225, P228, and P229 with slight differences in design details. Some older models, including European models have the magazine latch in the butt. US models have the magazine release aft of the trigger.

Year Introduced: 1983
Country of Origin: Germany, Switzerland, USA
Current Manufacturers: SIG SAUER (sigsauer.com)
Similar Models: Combat TB (threaded 5-in. barrel), Navy/MK 25 (civilian version U.S. Navy SEAL issue), DAK (DAO, bobbed hammer), Elite (beavertail frame, textured rosewood grips, night sights), SCT (extra capacity magazine), E2 (contoured screwless grip, night sights), Equinox (two-tone slide/matte black frame, checkered wood grips), X-Five models (5 in. barrel, magazine well, beavertail frame, extra capacity magazine, ambidextrous thumb safety)

REQUIRED TOOLS

Field Stripping: none
Disassembly/Assembly: small punch, small standard screwdriver, grip removal tool (ergo grip), needle nose pliers

FIELD STRIP

1. Remove the magazine and pull back the slide (part #4) and lock it back by engaging the slide catch lever (18).
2. Rotate the takedown lever (16) clockwise to the 6 o'clock position, Figure 1.

FIGURE 1

3. Retract the slide slightly to disengage the slide catch lever and then let the slide move forward off the frame (15). Warning, the recoil spring (3) within the slide assembly is under compression.
4. With the slide assembly removed from the frame, push the recoil spring guide (2) forward and up.
5. Remove the barrel (1) from the slide by pulling it up and to the rear, Figure 2.

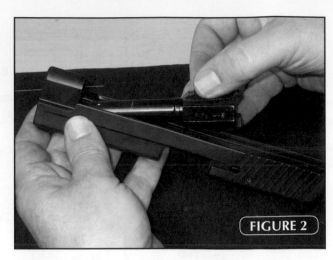

FIGURE 2

At this point, the pistol is sufficiently disassembled for cleaning.

MAGAZINE DISASSEMBLY

1. Use a small punch to depress the button of the floorplate insert (55) and push the magazine floor plate (54) forward from the magazine tube (51). Note the magazine spring is under compression (52).

SLIDE DISASSEMBLY

1. To remove the firing pin from the slide, place the slide on a bench block and using a small punch to knock out the firing pin positioning pin (7) from the right side of the slide to the left, Figure 3.

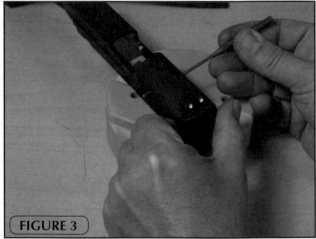

FIGURE 3

2. Depress the safety lock (13) with a small punch and holding the slide muzzle end up, the firing pin (11) and firing pin spring (12) can then be removed from the rear of the slide.
3. Once the firing pin is removed, the safety lock and safety lock spring will easily fall free for the slide.

FRAME DISASSEMBLY

1. To remove the mainspring from the frame, remove the grip plate left (49) and grip plate right (48) by removing the four grip plate screws (50).

2. Remove the modular one-piece ergo grip using the Sig-supplied tool by inserting it into the magazine well of the frame and rotating the tool a quarter turn. Keep the rod end of the tool centered in the magazine well and the grip will snap out then remove it rearward from the frame, Figure 4.

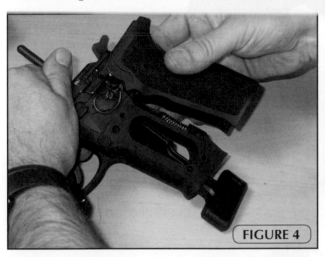

FIGURE 4

3. With the hammer (29) at rest, push up on the mainspring seat (36) using a small flat blade screwdriver inserted into the slot, Figure 5.

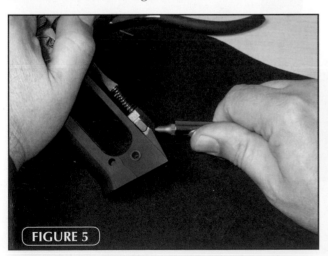

FIGURE 5

Tuning Tip: At this point an aftermarket spring kit can be installed like those from SIG SAUER or Wolff. Follow the manufacturer's instructions and reinstall in reverse order.

4. To remove the trigger (20), rotate the takedown lever so it points toward the muzzle end of the frame. Use a punch to push it through the frame.

5. The locking insert (17) can now be removed from the frame by pulling it up and forward.

6. The slide catch lever spring (19) is attached to the locking insert. Lay the frame on the left side of the frame and using your fingers or needle nose pliers remove the trigger bar spring (23) by unhooking the end of the spring closet to the hammer.

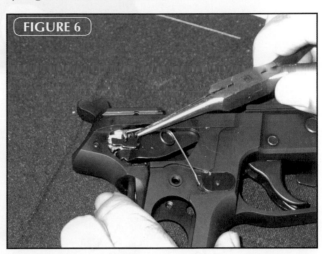

FIGURE 6

7. Push out the trigger pivot pin (21) from the right side to left side of the frame, Figure 6. Note it looks like a screw as it has a slot.

8. The trigger pivot pin also secures the slide catch lever; remove it from the top of the frame.

9. The trigger and trigger bar (23) are connected; remove diagonally out of the top of the frame.

Reassemble in reverse order.

Tuning Tip: At this point the SIG SAUER short trigger can be swapped for the stock trigger. The short trigger is thinner than the stock trigger to reduce the distance from the face of the trigger to back edge of the grip. It is designed to reduce trigger reach for shooters with small hands.

26 Sear Pivot Pin
27 Sear Spring Pin
28 Safety Lever
29 Hammer
30 Hammer Pin
31 Hammer Pivot Pin
32 Ejector
33 Hammer Strut
34 Mainspring
36 Mainspring Seat
37 Hammer Stop
38 Hammer Reset Spring
39 Hammer Stop Pin
40 Decocking Lever
41 Decocking Lever Bearing
42 Decocking Lever Spring
43 Magazine Catch
44 Support Plate
45 Magazine Catch Spring
46 Magazine Catch Stop
47 Catch Stop Spring
48 Grip Plate, Right
49 Grip Plate, Left
50 Grip Plate Screw
51 Magazine Tube
52 Magazine Spring
53 Magazine Follower
54 Magazine Floorplate
55 Floorplate Insert

PARTS LIST

1 Barrel
2 Recoil Spring Guide
3 Recoil Spring
4 Slide
5 Front Sight
6 Rear Sight
7 Firing Pin Positioning Pin

8 Extractor Spring
9 Extractor Pin
10 Extractor
11 Firing Pin
12 Firing Pin Spring
13 Safety Lock
14 Safety Lock Spring
15 Frame
16 Takedown Lever

17 Locking Insert
18 Slide Catch Lever
19 Slide Catch Lever Spring
20 Trigger
21 Trigger Pivot Pin
22 Trigger Bar
23 Trigger Bar Spring
24 Sear
25 Sear Spring

SPECIFICATIONS

Model: P238 Tactical Laser
Action: locked breech, short-recoil, autoloader, SA trigger
Overall Length: 5.5 in.
Overall Height: 3.9 in.
Overall Width: 1.1 in.
Barrel: 2.7 in.
Weight Unloaded: 34.0 oz.
Caliber: .380
Capacity: 6 + 1
Common Features: alloy beavertail frame; steel slide; serrated front grip strap; thumb safety; matte Nitron, digital camo, Two-Tone finishes; textured polymer, wood, aluminum grips, integrated laser

BACKGROUND

The P238 is subcompact pistol that appears to be a shrunken 1911. It does share similarities with the 1911: a single action trigger, thumb safety, and slide release. The magazine release is pure 1911, but the pistol's pedigree is definitely SIG SAUER. The slide and barrel lock up similar to other SIG pistols. The Tactical Laser model seamless attaches a laser sight that can quickly and easily be removed to go laserless.
Year Introduced: 2009
Country of Origin: Switzerland, USA
Current Manufacturers: SIG SAUER (sigsauer.com)
Similar Models: Two Tone (matte frame, stainless slide), Nitron (matte Nitron finish), Rosewood (checkered rosewood grips, blue finish), Blackwood (matte frame, stainless slide, blackwood grips), Rainbow (rainbow titanium finish, rosewood grips), Equinox (two-tone slide/matte black frame, checkered wood grips), HD (stainless finish, G10 grips), SAS (two-tone, wood grips), Lady (red Cerakote frame, scroll engraving), Extreme (extended magazine, G10 grips), Gambler (engraved slide), Diamond Plate (diamond plate finished slide, matte frame), HDW (stainless finish, rosewood grips), Desert (light tan finish, Hogue wraparound grip), Scorpion (Hogue Piranha G-10 grips, flat dark earth finish), Black Diamond Plate (black diamond plate finish)

REQUIRED TOOLS

Field Stripping: none
Disassembly/Assembly: small punch, 1.5mm and 3/32 hex or Allen wrenches, small flat blade screwdriver, needle-nose pliers

FIELD STRIP

1. Lay the P238 with the slide stop and safety facing up and use a 1.5mm hex or Allen wrench to remove the two laser guard sight screws.
2. Remove the left side of the laser guard sight, Figure 1.

Disassembly Tip: Best practice is to remove laser sights before cleaning the firearm. Oil and cleaning solvents are not good for the laser electronics. Oil on the laser lens can also distort the laser dot.

FIGURE 1

3. Manually retract the slide (part #5) until the slide disassembly notch is aligned with the slide stop tab, Figure 2.

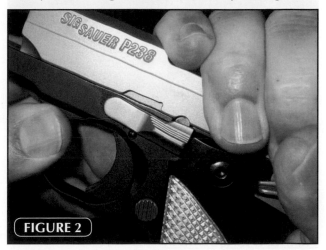

FIGURE 2

4. Remove the slide stop (2) by pushing it through from the right side of the frame (1), Figure 3.
5. Move the slide assembly forward on the frame until it can be removed.
6. Push the recoil guide (21) forward slightly and lift from the rear to remove the recoil spring (35) and recoil guide from the slide.
7. Remove the barrel (4) from the slide by pulling upward slightly and to the rear.

At this stage the pistol is sufficiently disassembled for cleaning.

SLIDE DISASSEMBLY

1. Use a small punch to push in the firing pin (12) from the rear of the slide and slide down on the firing

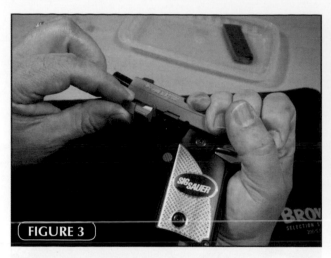

FIGURE 3

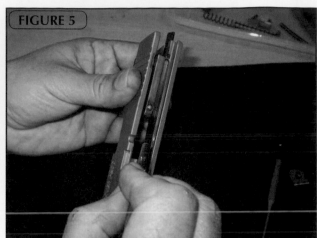

FIGURE 5

pin stop (7), Figure 4. Note the firing pin spring (39) is under tension so control the firing pin block as it is removed. Remove the firing pin and firing pin spring.

2. Next use a small flat blade screwdriver to push out the extractor (16) from the slide, Figure 5.

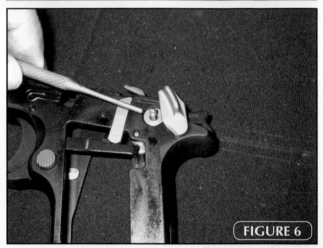

FIGURE 6

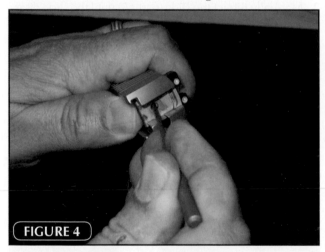

FIGURE 4

FRAME DISASSEMBLY

1. Remove the grips, left grip panel (27) and right grip panel (26), by removing two grip screws (28) two per grip panel with a 3/32 hex or Allen wrench.

2. Lay the frame right side down with the thumb safety (3) facing up and rotate the thumb safety clockwise. Note the plunger (29) and safety plunger spring (38) are under tension so as the thumb safety is rotated capture the plunger and safety plunger spring, Figure 6.Remove the plunger and plunger spring from the hammer pin (14), Figure 7.

3. Ensure the hammer (6) is fully forward in the fired position then remove the safety by rotating it clockwise and pulling it from the frame, Figure 8.

4. Remove the hammer by drifting out the main spring housing pin (41) from left to right, Figure 9. Slightly pull out the main spring housing (19) from the frame to relieve mainspring tension. Drift out the hammer pin from the

FIGURE 7

right side of the frame to the left, Figure 10. With the hammer pin removed, the hammer, hammer strut (15), mainspring (25) and mainspring housing pin lock (33).

5. To remove the sear (34) and ejector (20) use a small punch to drift out the trigger bar pin (32) from the left to right side of the frame. The sear and ejector will fall free from the frame once the pin is removed.

6. Remove the mainspring housing and sear spring (24) using a small punch or flat blade screwdriver to

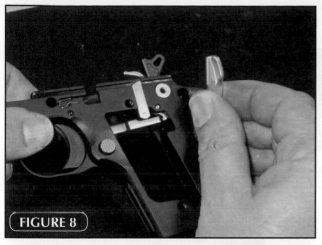

FIGURE 8

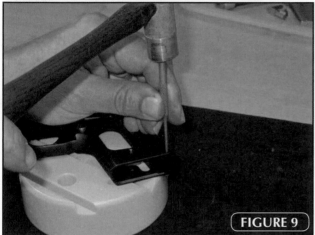

FIGURE 9

FIGURE 10

move the sear spring away from the trigger bar (11). Pull the mainspring housing and sear spring from the bottom of the frame.

7. The magazine catch (8) is removed by pressing the magazine catch on the left side of the frame and from the right side of the frame use a small flat blade screwdriver to rotate the magazine catch lock clockwise about a quarter turn. The magazine catch will fall free from the right side of the frame.

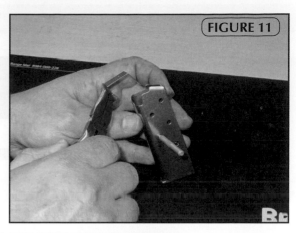

FIGURE 11

MAGAZINE DISASSEMBLY

1. Depress the magazine follower and using a small punch or nail pin through one of the cartridge witness holes in the magazine tube restrain the magazine spring, Figure 11.

2. Lift and rotate the magazine follower to remove it from the magazine tube.

3. Remove the magazine spring from the magazine tube.

Reassemble in reverse order.

Reassembly Tips: The firing pin spring has a small end and large end, Figure 12. The small end goes onto the firing pin. Depress the ejector to clear slide as the slide assembly is mated back to the frame, Figure 13.

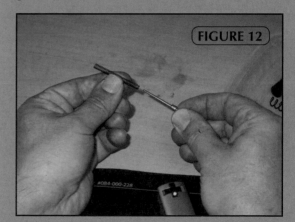

FIGURE 12

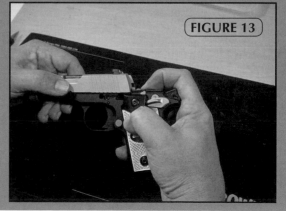

FIGURE 13

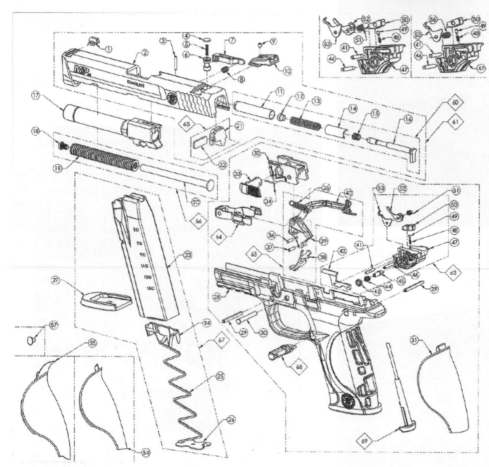

32 Locking Block
33 Takedown Lever
34 Retaining Wire for
Takedown Lever
35 Spring, Trigger Return
36 Pin, Trigger Bar
37 Pin, Trigger Assembly
38 Trigger, Lower
39 Trigger, Upper
40 Trigger Bar
41 Pin, Sear
42 Ejector
43 Sleeve, Lock
44 Spring, Lock
45 Cam, Lock
46 Pin, Sear Deactivation
Lever
47 Sear Housing Block
48 Spring, Sear
49 Plunger, Sear Return
50 Sear
51 Spring, Mag. Safety Lever
52 Safety Lever, Mag.
53 Deactivation Lever, Sear
54 Grip Strap, Small
55 Grip Strap, Large
56 Spring, Spacer
57 Plug. Frame Key
60 Assembly. Striker
61 Assembly. Slide
62 Assembly, Sear Housing
Block
63 Assembly, Trigger Bar
64 Assembly, Slide Stop
65 Assembly, End Cap
66 Assembly, Recoil Guide Rod
67 Assembly, Magazine
68 Assembly, Magazine Catch
69 Assembly Frame Tool

PARTS LIST

1 Sight, Front
2 Slide
3 Pin, Extractor
4 F/P Plunger Spacer
5 Spring, Striker Block
6 Striker Block
7 Extractor
8 Spring, Extractor
9 Set Screw, Rear Sight

10 Sight, Rear
11 Guide, Striker Spring
12 Keeper, Striker Spring
13 Spring, Striker
14 Bushing, Striker
15 Spring, Striker Return
16 Striker
17 Barrel
18 Cap, Recoil Guide Rod
19 Spring, Recoil
20 Guide Rod, Recoil

21 End Cap, Slide
22 Plate, Slide End Cap
23 Magazine Tube
24 Follower, Mag. Tube
25 Magazine Spring
26 Butt Plate Catch, Mag.
27 Butt Plate, Mag.
28 Frame
29 Coil Pin, Locking Block
30 Headed Pin, Trigger
31 Grip Strap, Med.

SPECIFICATIONS

Model: M&P40
Action: autoloader; striker-fired, short-recoil, locked breech
Overall Length: 6.7 in. (Compact); 8.5 in.
Overall Height: 4.3 in. (Compact); 5.5 in.
Overall Width: 1.2 in.
Barrel: 3.5 in. (Compact); 5.0 in.
Weight Unloaded: 21.7 oz. (Compact); 25.2 oz.
Caliber: .40 S&W
Capacity: 10 + 1 (Compact); 15 + 1
Features: polymer frame; 3 interchangeable grip sizes; ambidextrous thumb safety, slide release; external extractor; Picatinny rail; available in various frame/barrel configurations

BACKGROUND

S&W debuted the M&P (Military & Police) in .40 S&W and has since offered the pistol in 9mm, .357 SIG and .45 ACP. The design is well-thought out with grip inserts for different size hands, a simple takedown procedure, steel magazines and excellent pointability. The design borrows a few cues from other pistols—the takedown in similar to SIG and a small lever inside the magazine well needs to be pushed down similar to the ejector in a Ruger P345.
Year Introduced: 2005
Country of Origin: USA
Current Manufacturers: Smith & Wesson (smith-wesson.com)
Similar Models: M&P9, M&P357, M&P45

REQUIRED TOOLS

Field Stripping: none
Disassembly/Assembly: small flat blade screwdriver, 1/8 in. roll pin punch, small punch

FIELD STRIP

1. Remove magazine then pull the slide (part #2) fully to the rear and press upward on the slide stop (64)
2. Remove the frame tool (69) from the butt of the frame (28) by rotating it a 1/4 turn in either direction and pulling it out of the frame, Figure 1.
3. Using the frame tool, small screwdriver or your finger to push down and lower the sear deactivation lever (53) into the magazine well of the frame, Figure 2.
4. Next rotate the take down lever (33) clockwise. Then grasp the slide and slightly pull it rearward then forward and off the frame, Figure 3.
5. Remove the recoil spring (19) and guide rod (20), Figure 4.
6. Remove the barrel (17) from the bottom of the slide.

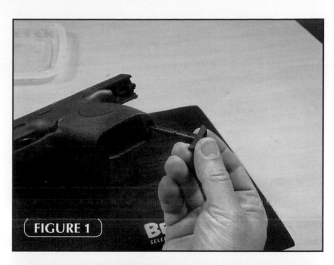

FIGURE 1

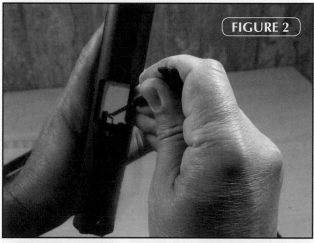

FIGURE 2

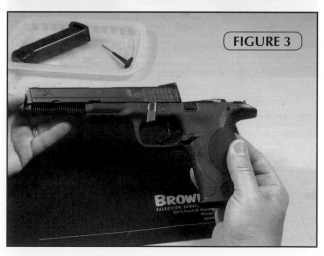

FIGURE 3

At this point the M&P is field stripped for routine cleaning.

Maintenance Tip: There are seven lubrication points on the M&P. Place a drop of lubricant on the four rail insert in the frame, outside muzzle end of the barrel, top front corners of the barrel hood, and rear of trigger bar.

FIGURE 4

SLIDE DISASSEMBLY

1. Use a small flat blade screwdriver or the frame tool to push down on striker spring guide (11) and slide end cap (21) out of slide, Figure 5.

FIGURE 5

2. Push down on the striker block (6) and remove the striker assembly—striker (16), striker return spring (15), striker bushing (14), striker spring (13) and two halves of the striker spring keepers (12)—rearward.

3. Remove the extractor (7) using a small punch to drift out extractor pin (3) from the top side of the slide.

4. Remove extractor and extractor spring (8).

FRAME DISASSEMBLY

1. Rotate takedown lever counterclockwise until it stops the pull takedown lever out of frame.

2. Remove locking block pin (29) by drifting it from right to left of frame using a 1/8 inch roll pin punch, Figure 6.

FIGURE 6

3. Drift out trigger pin (30) right to left with a punch.

4. Remove locking block out from the top of frame.

5. Next remove the slide stop and trigger assembly (63) from the top of frame.

6. The sear housing assembly (62) is removed by drifting out the sear housing assembly pin (29) and gently prying up on the sear housing assembly from the top of the frame.

7. Remove ejector (42) from sear housing assembly.

Reassemble in reverse order.

PARTS LIST

1 Receiver
4 Locking Block
5 Locking Block Pin/Trigger pin-2
6 Locking Block Pin/Trigger Pin Retainer-2

7 Trigger with Safety
8 Trigger Bar
9 Trigger Bar Spring
10 Sear
11 Sear Pin
12 Ejector Pin

13 Sear Spring
14 Ejector
15 Grip Safety
16 Grip Safety Pin
17 Grip Safety Spring
18 Slide Stop Lever

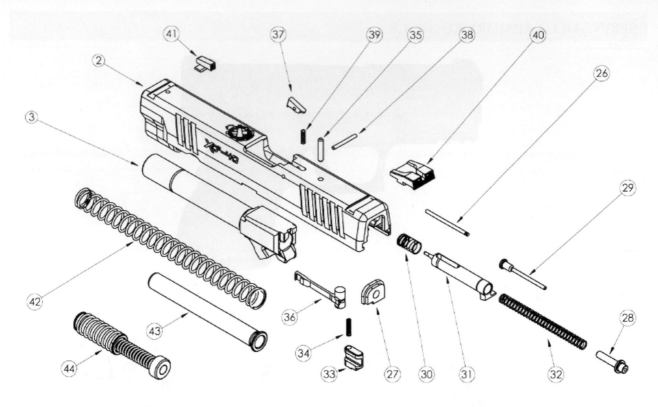

19 Slide Stop Lever Spring	43 Magazine Body	50 Backstrap - 3
20 Disassembly Lever	44 Magazine Spring	51 Backstrap/Lanyard Loop Roll Pin
21 Magazine Catch	45 Magazine Follower	52 Disassembly Bar
22 Magazine Catch Pin	46 Magazine Locking Plate	53 Disassembler
23 Magazine Catch Spring	47 Magazine Base	54 Disassembly Lever Spring
24 Magazine Release Button	48 Backstrap - 1	55 Striker Safety Lever Spring
25 Striker Safety Lever	49 Backstrap - 2	

SPECIFICATIONS

Model: XD(M) 3.8

Action: autoloader; SA; short recoil-operated locked breech striker fired

Overall Length: 7.0 in.

Overall Height: 4.6 in. (Compact); 5.6 in.

Overall Width: 1.3 in.

Barrel: 3.8 in.

Weight Unloaded: 27.5 oz. (9mm); 28.0 oz. (.40 S&W)

Caliber: 9mm; .40 S&W

Capacity: 13 + 1 (Compact 9mm); 19 + 1 (9mm); 11 + 1 (Compact .40 S&W); 16 + 1 (.40 S&W)

Common Features: polymer frame; grip, trigger safeties; ambidextrous magazine release; loaded chamber, striker status indicators; textured front/rear grip straps; combat trigger guard; Picatinny rail; textured polymer, 3 backstrap size modular grip; dovetail front/rear, 3-dot sights

BACKGROUND

The XD(M) evolved from the XD pistol which itself was derived from the HS2000, which was designed in Croatia in 1998 and became that country's first polymer frame service pistol. Springfield Armory licensed and sells the pistol as the Springfield XD (eXtreme Duty). The XD(M)—short for eXtreme Duty More—is the latest evolution of the pistols and delivers on the promise of more. The XD(M) features interchangeable backstraps, a match grade barrel, and a revised grip angle. Compact models accept the magazines from their larger model siblings. Some magazines also feature a grip extension giving compact models the grip of a full size, Figure 1. It also sports aggressive slide serrations and grip texture. Notable design features include a trigger safety, similar to Glock, a grip safety, similar to a 1911, and a drop safety that prevents the striker from releasing if dropped. Some models also feature a thumb safety. The two-stage trigger is renowned for it short, crisp pull. When the trigger is pulled the sear slides down and disengages the firing pin. There are major differences in the mechanisms between the XD and XD(M). These instructions are for the XD(M) 3.8.

Year Introduced: 2008

Country of Origin: Croatia

Current Manufacturers: Springfield Armory (springfield-armory.com)

Similar Models: XD(M) 45, XD(M)

FIGURE 1

REQUIRED TOOLS
Field Stripping: none
Disassembly/Assembly: 1/16, 3/32, 1/8, and 3/16 punches; hammer; small flat blade screwdriver; extractor tool

FIELD STRIP
1. Remove the magazine and pull back the slide (part #2) fully to the rear and lock it into position by pushing up on the slide stop lever (18).
2. Rotate the disassembly lever clockwise to the 12 o'clock position, Figure 2.

FIGURE 2

3. Pull the slide back to release the slide stop lever and while maintaining a grip on the slide, allow the slide to move forward. Note that the recoil spring assembly (44) is under tension. Continue to pull the slide assembly forward from the frame.
4. From the slide assembly, remove the recoil spring assembly. Note that the compact, 3.8 models use a captive style recoil assembly and longer barrel models use a recoil spring (42) and recoil spring rod guide (43). Remove the barrel (3) from the slide by moving slightly forward and out. The field stripping procedure is the same for XD(M) regardless of caliber.

At this point the pistol is ready to be cleaned.

FRAME DISASSEMBLY
1. To remove the locking block (4), rotate the disassembly lever counterclockwise until you hear a click. Then gently pull the disassembly lever out from the frame and rotate it back and forth past the slide stop lever spring (19) which is attached to the locking block.
2. With the disassembly lever clear from the frame, use a 3/16 inch punch to remove the two locking block/trigger pins (5) drifting the pins from the left side of the frame out the right side of the frame, Figure 3.
3. Lift the locking block from the frame. Next remove the slide stop lever.

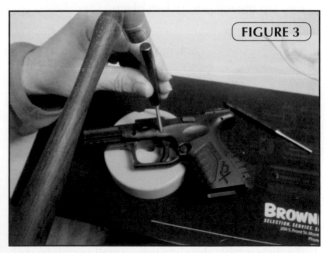

FIGURE 3

4. Next remove the trigger with safety (7) and trigger bar (8).
5. Finally remove the disassembly bar (52).
6. To remove the sear (10), use a small, flat blade screwdriver to push the ejector pin (12) to the left side of the frame flush with the ejector. The ejector pin cannot be driven through the frame via a punch. Note the orientation of striker safety lever spring (55) and the sear spring (13) with the ejector pin, Figure 4.

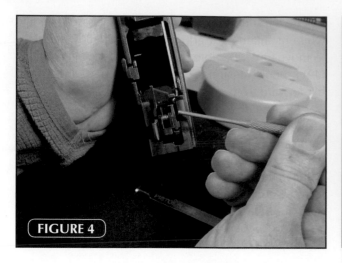

FIGURE 4

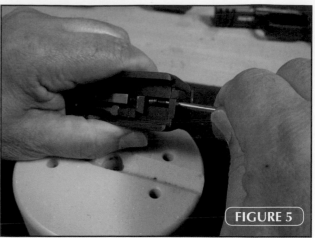

FIGURE 5

7. Next use a 1/8 inch punch to remove the sear pin. Note that the striker safety lever spring and the sear spring are under tension. The sear, ejector, striker safety lever (25), striker safety lever spring and the sear spring can now be removed.

8. To remove the back strap (48, 49 or 50), use a 3/32 roll pin punch to drift out back strap/lanyard roll pin (51) from the left side to right side. Lift up on the bottom of the back strap and pull it away from the frame (1).

9. To reinstall a back strap, insert the upper portion of a back strap into the frame and rotate it down so the pin hole in the back strap aligns with the holes in the frame. Tap the roll pin back in place.

Tuning Tip: To smooth out the trigger pull, try installing a pair of stainless steel sear pivot shims. The shims fit on the pivot pin, one on each side of the sear. The shims eliminate side to side movement of the sear and produce a smoother trigger pull.

SLIDE DISASSEMBLY

1. To disassemble the slide use a small punch to push in the striker spring guide (28) through the striker locking plate (27) and slide the striker locking plate from the slide, Figure 5. Note the striker spring guide is under tension from striker spring (32).

2. Tip the slide muzzle end up so the striker status indicator (29) slides out.

3. Next lay the slide topside down and using a punch drift out the striker retainer pin (35) from the inside of the slide to outside of the slide.

4. With the striker retainer pin removed the striker (31) and striker dampening spring (30) will fall out the rear of the slide.

5. Pry out the striker safety pin (26) from the rear of the slide using a small flat blade screwdriver. Note that the striker safety (33) and striker safety spring (34) are held in place by striker safety pin. There is tension from striker safety spring, so place down on the striker safety with your thumb as you pry out the striker safety pin.

6. When the striker safety pin is removed the striker safety and striker safety spring will fall free from the slide. At this point the extractor (36) can be removed using a special tool.

7. Hook the tool under the extractor where it is press fit into the slide and pry it up and out of the slide, Figure 6.

MAGAZINE DISASSEMBLY

1. Magazines are slightly different between calibers and models. For all .40 S&W, .45 ACP and compact models, depress the magazine locking plate (46) using a small screwdriver or punch and slide the magazine base forward and off the magazine body (43).

2. For 9mm and full size models there is no magazine locking plate, so depress the magazine spring (44) and

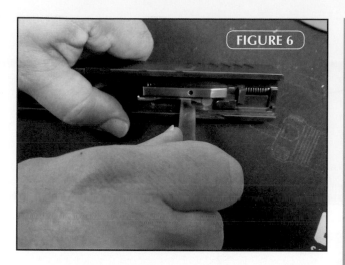

FIGURE 6

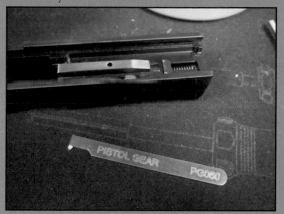

Tool Tip: The PistolGear Xtractor Tool (PistolGear.com) makes removing the extractor easier. In fact Springfield Armory gunsmiths use the PistolGear Xtractor Tool. It's produced by Matthew ODonnell of Model & Toolmaking in Andover, Ohio, exclusively for Pistol Gear.

slide off the magazine base. Note that in both instances the magazine spring is under pressure.

To reassemble reverse the order.

TAURUS 24/7 G2

PARTS LIST

1 Slide assembly
1.1 Slide
1.2 Sight screw
1.3 Front sight
1.4 Rear sight
1.5 Extractor
1.6 Extractor spring
1.7 Extractor pin
1.8 Loaded chamber indicator

1.9 Loaded chamber indicator spring
1.10 Firing pin guide
1.11 Firing pin return spring
1.12 Firing pin
1.13 Captive firing pin spring assembly
1.14 Firing pin retaining spring
1.15 Slide cap
1.16 Firing pin lock

1.17 Firing pin lock spring
1.18 Firing pin block cover
1.19 Cocking indicator
1.20 Rear sight screw
1.21 Key lock
1.22 Key lock spring
1.23 Key lock ball
1.24 Key lock pin
2 Barrel
3.1 Recoil spring

3.2 Recoil spring guide
3.3 Recoil spring loop
4.1 Frame
4.2 Frame bushing
4.3 Disassembly latch
4.4 Trigger bar ramp
4.5 Trigger bar ramp
4.6 Firing pin block lever
4.7 Ejector
4.9 Manual safety spring

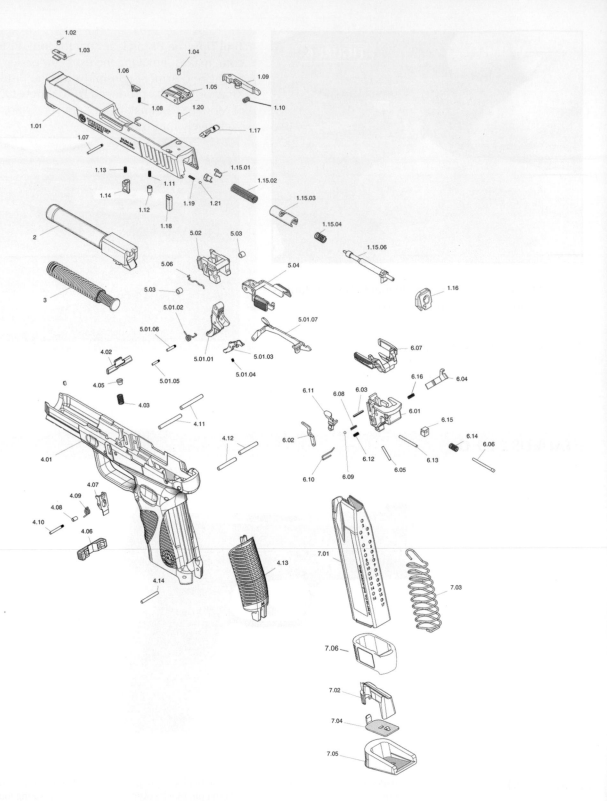

4.10 Trigger bar
4.11 Trigger support pin
4.12 Slide catch
4.13 Slide catch spring
4.14 Trigger
4.15 Trigger safety
4.16 Trigger spring
4.17 Trigger pin

4.18 Trigger safety
4.19 Trigger safety axle
4.20 Trigger safety spring
4.21 Manual safety - right
4.22 Link
4.23 Manual safety - left
4.24 Manual safety ball spring
4.25 Manual safety ball

4.26 Central safety
4.27 Link pivot
4.28 Sear pin
4.30 Sear
4.31 Sear spring
4.32 Safety lever
5.1 Grip
5.2 Grip pin

5.3 Magazine release
5.4 Magazine release spring
5.5 Lanyard loop
6.1 Magazine body
6.2 Follower
6.3 Magazine spring
6.4 Magazine spring plate
6.5 Magazine bottom

SPECIFICATIONS

Model: 24/7 G2
Action: recoil-operated, autoloader, hybrid striker-fired
Overall Length: 6.6 in. (Compact); 7.3 in. (Standard)
Overall Height: 5.2 in.
Overall Width: 1.2 in.
Barrel: 3.5 in. (Compact); 4.2 in. (Standard)
Weight Unloaded: 27.0 oz. (Compact); 28.0 oz. (Standard)
Caliber: 9mm; .40 S&W; .45 ACP
Capacity: 17 + 1 (9mm); 15 + 1 (.40 S&W); 12 + 1 (.45 ACP)
Features: ambidextrous magazine release, thumb safety; polymer frame; external extractor; loaded chamber indicator; Picatinny accessory rail; 3 backstrap configurations; cocked indicator; strike-two trigger allows second pull of trigger without resetting; black finish; textured polymer, modular grips; dovetail front/adj. rear sights

BACKGROUND

The 24/7 G2 combines features from the Taurus 800 Series, 24/7 Series and 24/7 OSS. The 24/7 G2 offers the "Strike Two" capability. If a round misfires the trigger can be pulled again in double action mode in an attempt to fire the cartridge.
Year Introduced: 2010
Country of Origin: Brazil
Current Manufacturers: Taurus (taurususa.com)
Similar Models: Compact (3.5 in. barrel)

REQUIRED TOOLS

Field Stripping: none
Disassembly/Assembly: punch, needle-nose pliers

FIELD STRIP

1. Remove the magazine by pressing the magazine release button (part #40.6) and make sure the pistol is by checking that the chamber is empty.
2. Hold the pistol in your so that your four fingers rest over the slide and your thumb rests on the rear of the grip. Use your fingers to draw back the slide about 1/8 inch and with your other hand pull disassembly latch (40.2) down, Figure 1.
3. Release the slide assembly and then release the disassembly latch. The slide assembly will move forward toward the muzzle and off the frame, Taurus calls it a grip (40.1).

FIGURE 1

4. Remove the recoil spring assembly (3) by pushing it toward the muzzle and up. Warning the recoil spring assembly is under compression.
5. Remove the barrel (2) from the slide by lifting it up and to the rear.

MAGAZINE DISASSEMBLY

1. Use a small punch to press in the magazine spring plate (7.04) and slide the magazine floor plate, magazine bottom (7.06) forward. Warning the magazine spring (7.03) is under compression.
2. With the floor plate removed you can remove the magazine spring and follower (7.02).

SLIDE DISASSEMBLY

1. To remove the firing pin assembly, use a small flat-blade screw driver to pull back on the firing pin sleeve (1.15.03) and push up on the slide cap (1.16), Figure 2. The firing pin assembly can then be removed.

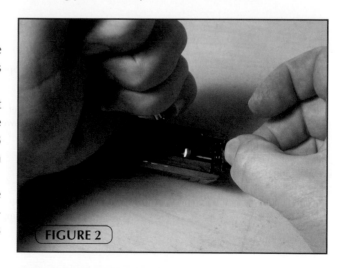

FIGURE 2

GRIP DISASSEMBLY

1. To change the grip inserts, use a small punch to drive out backstrap pin (4.14) and pull off the backstrap (4.13).
2. When inserted the backstrap remember the tab at the top of the backstrap needs to be inserted into the grip first, Figure 3.

Reassemble in reverse order.

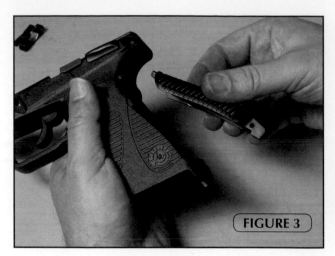

FIGURE 3

Maintenance Tip: After cleaning and before reassembling the 24/7 G2, place a drop of oil on the contact areas: the mechanism housing (6.01), trigger bar (5.01.07), trigger bar block (6.11), the metals rails in the grip (4.01) and disconnector (6.04).

WALTHER P38
CLASSIC MILITARY FIREARM

PARTS LIST

A Slide
B Firing Pin Spring
C Firing Pin & Indicator Cover
D Rear Sight
E Automatic Firing Pin Lock Spring
F Automatic Firing Pin Lock
G Firing Pin Retainer Pin
H Cartridge Indicator Pin
I Cartridge Indicator Spring
J Firing Pin
K Extractor
L Extractor Plunger

M Extractor Plunger Spring
N Safety Catch
O Ejector
P Firing Pin Lock Lifter
Q Safety Hammer Lowering Lever
R Trigger Bar Spring
S Trigger Bar
T Sear
U Sear Pin
V Hammer Strut
W Hammer Assembly
X Hammer Lever Spring
Y Strut Axle Pin
Z Hammer Lever Pin

AA Hammer Lever
BB Hammer Spring
CC Magazine Catch
DD & FF Grips
EE Magazine
GG Grip Screw
HH Hammer Pin
II Slide Stop Return Spring
JJ Trigger
KK Slide Stop
LL Trigger Bushing
MM Frame
NN Trigger Spring
OO Barrel Retaining Latch

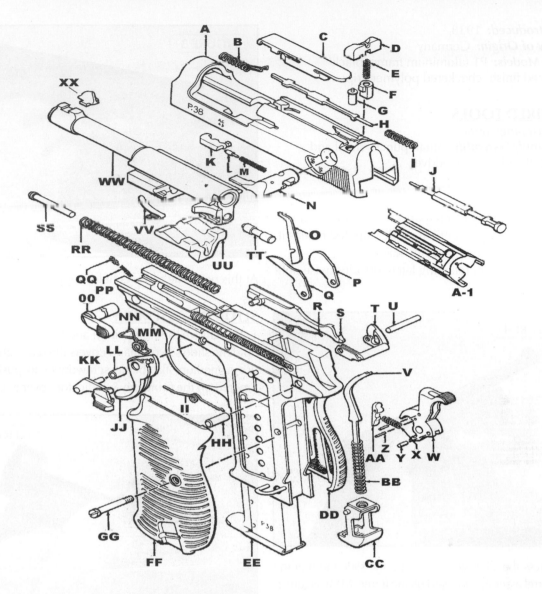

PP Retainer Latch Plunger Spring
QQ Retainer Latch Plunger
RR Recoil Spring
SS Recoil Spring Guide

TT Locking Block Operating Pin
UU Locking Block
VV Locking Block Retainer Spring

WW Barrel
XX Front Sight

Courtesy of Numrich Gun Parts Corporation

SPECIFICATIONS

Model: P38
Action: autoloader, short recoil, locked breech, SA/DA
Overall Length: 8.4 in.
Overall Height: 5.3 in.
Overall Width: 1.43 in.
Barrel: 5 in.
Weight Unloaded: 33.7 oz.
Caliber: 9mm
Capacity: 8 + 1
Features: steel frame/slide, decocking safety, external hammer, grooved Bakerlite grips, fixed blade front/drift adj. rear sights, blued finish

BACKGROUND

The P38 was developed as replacement for the Luger P08 and was designed with ease of production in mind. The Wehrmacht adopted the P38 as their service pistol in 1938 at the start of WWII. The design was high-tech when it debuted and to this day design aspects of the P38 are still in use. The P38 was the first locked breech pistol to use a double-/single-action trigger mechanism, a loaded chamber indicator, and an open slide design. The current Beretta 92FS/M9 utilizes many of these design characteristics. Postwar P38 pistols differ from war time specimens— an aluminum frame replaced the WWII-built steel frame models—and are marked P1. The P1 was in service with the German military through the 1990s. A P1 is use to demonstrate the disassembly steps.

Year Introduced: 1938
Country of Origin: Germany
Similar Models: P1 (aluminum frame, black/parkerized finish, checkered polymer grip)

REQUIRED TOOLS
Field Stripping: none
Disassembly/Assembly: small punch, small and medium flat blade screwdriver

FIELD STRIP
1. Rotate the safety catch (part #N) to "safe" position, pull back the slide (A) until the slide stop (KK) retains it, and then remove the magazine (EE).
2. Rotate the barrel retaining latch (OO) clockwise until it stops, Figure 1.

FIGURE 1

3. Depress the slide stop to release the slide the pull the slide/barrel assembly forward off the frame (MM), Figure 2.

FIGURE 2

4. Remove the barrel (WW) by pushing in locking block operating pin (TT) to separate the barrel from the slide, Figure 3.

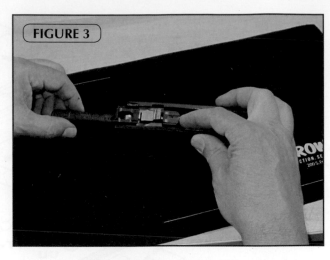

FIGURE 3

At this point the pistol is field stripped for cleaning.

SLIDE DISASSEMBLY
1. To remove the firing pin (J) and the indicator pin (H), hold the slide so your hand covers the rear sight (D) then use a medium flat blade screwdriver to push up and forward on the firing pin & indicator cover (C), Figure 4.

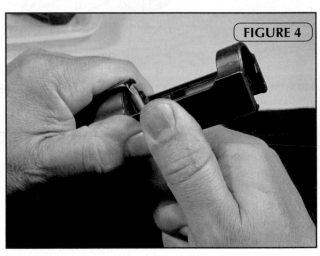

FIGURE 4

2. With the firing pin & indicator cover removed from the slide, the rear sight (D) with fall free from the slide.
3. Remove automatic firing pin lock spring (E), automatic firing pin lock (F) and firing pin retainer pin (G) from the top of the slide.
4. Remove the cartridge indicator (H) and cartridge indicator spring (I) from the top of the slide.
5. Push the safety catch to the "safe" position and the firing pin (J) can be pulled from the rear of the slide, then the firing pin spring (B) and can be removed from the top of the slide.
6. Rotate the safety catch between "safe" and "fire" then use a small flat blade screwdriver to nudge the safety catch out from the slide.

7. With the safety catch removed, the extractor plunger spring (M), which also places tension on the safety catch, and the extractor (K) can be removed.

8. Remove the locking block (UU) by rotating down from the barrel.

FRAME DISASSEMBLY

1. Unscrew the grip screw (GG) and remove the two grip halves (DD and FF).

2. Remove the trigger bar (S) by first using a small screwdriver to push the rear most leg of the trigger bar spring (R) out of its slot in the trigger bar, Figure 5. Then lift the loop of the trigger spring (NN) to disengage it from the trigger bar. Uncouple the rear of the trigger bar from the sear (T) and remove the trigger bar.

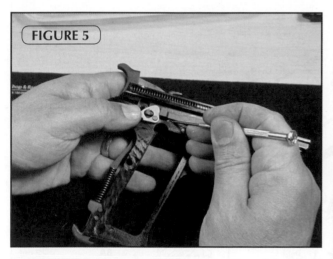

FIGURE 5

3. Remove the slide stop latch spring (II) and then pull the slide stop from the frame.

4. With the slide stop removed the trigger (JJ), trigger spring and trigger bushing (LL) can be pulled from the top of the frame.

5. Push the magazine catch (CC) so the pin on the magazine catch is freed from the frame, Figure 6. The hammer spring (BB) is under compression so control it. Remove the magazine catch, hammer spring and hammer strut (V).

6. Push out the hammer pin (HH) and pull the hammer (W) from the top of the frame.

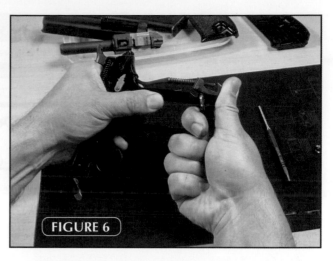

FIGURE 6

7. With the hammer removed the firing pin lock lifter (P) and safety hammer lowering lever (Q) can be removed via the top of the frame.

8. The two recoil springs (RR) are removed by inserting a small flat blade screwdriver a few coils back from the front of the recoil spring guide (SS) and compressing the recoil spring until you can remove the guide. The recoil springs are under pressure.

Reassemble reversing the process.

Reassembly Tip: When replacing the barrel/slide assembly on the frame, make sure the hammer in fully forward/"fired" position and the ejector is pushed down into the frame so it clears the barrel/slide assembly.

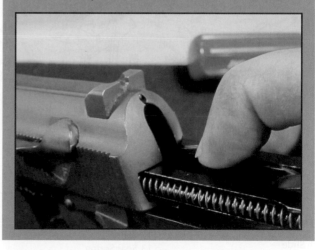

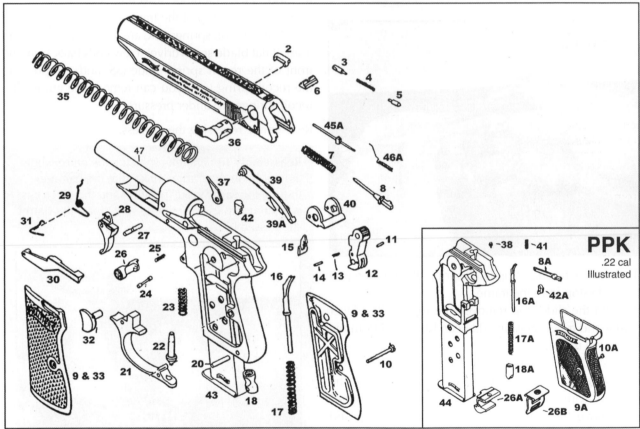

PARTS LIST

1 Slide
2 Extractor
3 Extractor Plunger
4 Extractor Spring
5 Safety Catch Plunger
6 Rear Sight
7 Firing Pin Spring
8 Firing Pin, Flat
9 & 33 Grips & Escutcheons
10 Grip Screw

11 Sear Pin
12 Hammer
13 Sear Spring
14 Hammer Strut Pin
15 Sear
16 Hammer Strut
17 Hammer Spring
18 Hammer Plug
20 Spring Plug Pin
21 Trigger Guard
22 Trigger Guard Plunger
23 Trigger Guard Spring

24 Trigger Guard Pin
25 Magazine Catch Spring
26 Magazine Catch
27 Trigger Pin
28 Trigger
29 Trigger Spring
30 Ejector
31 Ejector Spring
32 Hammer Pin
35 Recoil Spring
36 Safety Catch
37 Hammer Release

38 Hammer Block Plunger
39 Trigger Bar
40 Cocking Piece
41 Hammer Block Spring
42 Hammer Block
43 Magazine
45 Cartridge Indicator Pin
46 Cartridge Indicator Spring
47 Barrel

Courtesy of Numrich Gun Parts
   Corporation

SPECIFICATIONS

Model: PPK/S
Action: autoloader, blowback, SA/DA
Overall Length: 6.1 in.
Overall Height: 3.8 in.
Overall Width: 0.98 in.
Barrel: 3.35 in.
Weight Unloaded: 20.8 oz.
Caliber: .32 ACP; .380
Capacity: 8 + 1 (.32 ACP); 7 +1 (.380)
Features: steel frame/slide, decocking and firing pin safeties, extended beaver tail, checkered polymer grips, fixed blade front/adj. rear sights, blued or stainless finish

BACKGROUND

The PP, PPK and PPK/S family of pistols are some of the most popular and successful small pistols ever designed. Since the 1930s Walther's PP and PPK have been known for their reliability and concealability. The PP (*Polizeipistole*) is the largest of the trio with the PKK (*Polizeipistole Kriminalmodel*) having a shorter grip frame and barrel. The main design difference between the two is the PPK uses the grip halves to form the pistol's backstrap. PPK/S models mate a PP frame to a PPK slide to meet U.S. firearms importation guidelines set down by the Gun Control Act of 1968. During WWII the PPK was issued to numerous German military and police forces. The PPK inspired other small pistol designs like the Soviet Makarov, Bersa Thunder 380 from Argentina, the Hungarian FEG PA-63, and others. Though smaller and lighter polymer-frame pistols have taken away market share, the PPK's influence and notoriety was sealed when Ian Fleming issued the PPK to his secret agent character, James Bond, in his series of spy novels. It is currently manufactured in the U.S. under license by Smith & Wesson.
Year Introduced: 1929 (1978 manufactured in USA)
Country of Origin: Germany
Current Manufacturer: Walther (smith-wesson.com) currently manufactured by Smith & Wesson in USA
Similar Models: PPK (shorter frame, one less cartridge capacity), PP (long barrel/frame)

REQUIRED TOOLS

Field Stripping: none
Disassembly/Assembly: punch, needle-nose pliers

FIELD STRIP

1. Rotate the safety catch (part #36) into the down or "safe" position and remove the magazine.
2. With one hand hold the grip and with your other hand, pull down on the front of the trigger guard (21), Figure 1. When the front of the trigger guard comes out of the frame, slightly move it sideways to keep it from

FIGURE 1

springing back up into the frame or place your finger between the trigger guard and frame, Figure 2.

FIGURE 2

3. Next grasp the slide (1) and pull it rearward until you can lift the back end up and off the frame, Figure 3. Control the slide and ease it forward, toward the muzzle, and off the barrel (47). Note the recoil spring (35) is under tension.

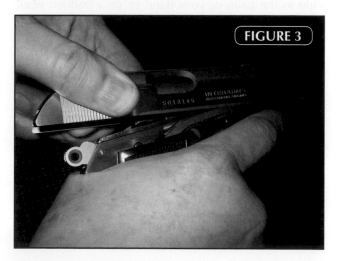

FIGURE 3

4. Pull the recoil spring off the front of the barrel.

At this point no further disassembly is required.

SLIDE DISASSEMBLY

1. Remove the safety catch by rotating the safety catch forward to the "fire" position and then pushing down on the firing pin (8) with a small punch to compress the firing pin spring (7), Figure 4.

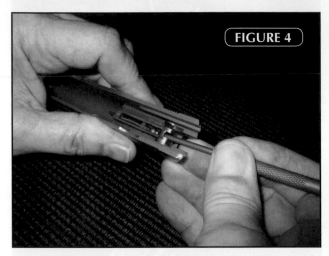

FIGURE 4

2. While pushing in on the firing and the safety catch can be removed from the left side of the slide. You may need to gently pry the safety catch out from the slide. Note the firing pin spring is under tension so control it until tension is relieved and then the firing pin and spring will pull free from the slide. You may want to use a pair of needle nose pliers.

3. The cartridge indicator (45A) is removed by pushing in the indicator spring with a small flat blade screw driver toward the rear of the slide.

4. Next the extractor plunger (3) and extractor plunger spring (4) can be removed by tapping the rear of the slide in the palm of your hand or on a padded work surface. You may need a pair of needle nose pliers to pull them free.

5. Next tip the slide so the ejection port faces down and the extractor will fall free.

FRAME DISASSEMBLY

1. Remove the grips (9 & 33) by unscrewing the grip screw (10), Figure 5.

2. On the left side of the frame remove the ejector (30) by depressing the ejector spring (31) with a small flat

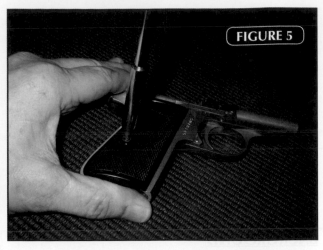

FIGURE 5

blade screwdriver then the ejector and ejector spring can be pulled out of the frame, Figure 6.

FIGURE 6

3. Next remove the hammer spring (17) by first carefully lowering the hammer to the fired position.

4. Then push in on the hammer spring plug (18) with your thumb and with a small punch push out the hammer spring plug pin (20), Figure 7. The hammer spring plug and hammer spring can then be withdrawn from the bottom of the frame. Note that with the tension relieved from the hammer spring, the hammer spring plug pin may easily fall free from the left side of the frame.

5. Flip the frame over so the left side faces up and then use a small screwdriver to easily remove the hammer release (37) and hammer (12).

6. Then tip the frame top side down to allow the hammer strut (16) to fall free from the frame.

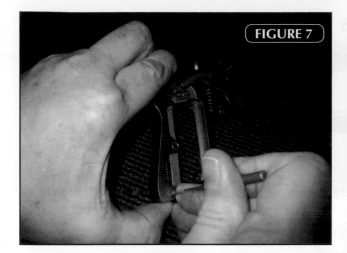

FIGURE 7

7. Next push out the trigger pin (27) out using a small punch while slightly pulling back on the trigger.

8. Next remove the trigger bar (39) by using a small flat blade screwdriver to push the forward tab out of the frame while pulling the trigger (28) as far back. Use the screwdriver to lift the bar out of the frame. The trigger and trigger spring will fall free from the frame once the trigger bar is removed.

Reassemble reversing the process.

Reassembly Tip: Install the small end of the recoil spring on the barrel first. Note that the trigger pin has a groove in it that is off center. When reinstalling it, the groove end is on the left side of the frame.

Centerfire Single-Shot Pistols

THOMPSON/CENTER ENCORE PRO HUNTER

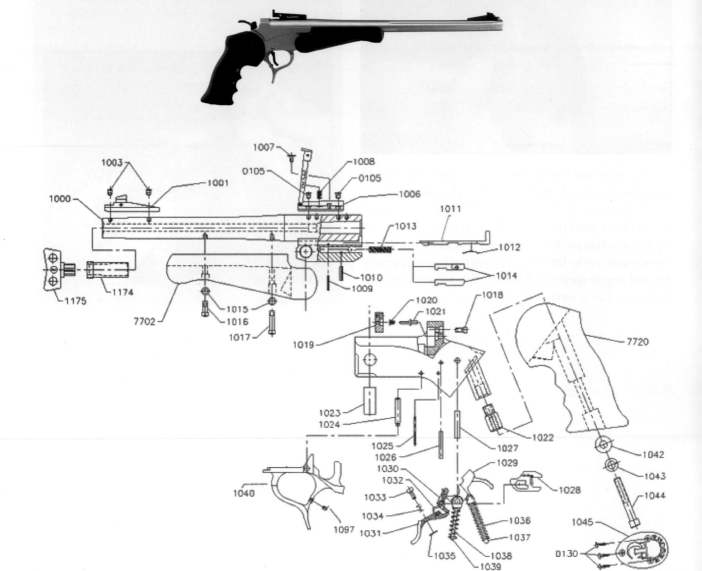

PARTS LIST

0105 Rear Sight Screw (2 Req'd)
0130 Grip Cap Screw (3 Req'd)
1000 Barrel
1001 Front Sight
1003 Front Sight Screw (2 Req'd)
1006 Rear Sight
1007 Rear Sight Elevation Screw
1008 Rear Sight Elevation Spring
1009 Extractor Stop Pin
1010 Bolt Stop Pin

1011 Extractor
1013 Bolt Spring
1014 Bolt Set, 2 Piece
1015 Forend Washer (2 Req'd)
1016 Forend Screw, Front
1017 Forend Screw, Rear
1018 Firing Pin Bushing Screw
1019 Firing Pin Bushing
1020 Firing Pin Spring
1021 Firing Pin
1022 Grip Adapter
1023 Barrel & Frame Hinge Pin
1024 Trigger Guard Pin
1025 Trigger Pin
1026 Sear Pin

1027 Hammer Pin
1028 Interlock
1029 Hammer
1030 Sear
1031 Trigger
1032 Trigger & Sear Spring
1033 Trigger Plunger
1034 Trigger Plunger Spring
1035 Trigger Plunger Retaining Ring
1036 Hammer Spring
1037 Hammer Strut
1038 Trigger Guard Spring
1039 Trigger Guard Strut
1040 Trigger Guard

1042 Grip Screw Washer
1043 Grip Screw Lock Washer
1044 Grip Screw
1045 Grip Cap
1097 Trigger Stop Screw
1174 Choke Tube
1175 Choke Tube Wrench
7654 Forend Complete, Rubber
7702 Forend Complete, Walnut
7720 Grip

Courtesy of Numrich Gun Parts Corporation

SPECIFICATIONS
Model: Encore Pro Hunter
Action: break action
Barrel: 15 in. fluted barrel
Caliber: .17 HMR, .22 LR, .204 Ruger, .22-250, .223 Rem, .243 Win, .25-06 Rem, .270 Win, 7mm-08, .30 TC, .30-06, .308 Win, .338 Federal
Capacity: 1
Common Features: stainless frame; adjustable swing hammer; open sights on some barrels; numerous wood or synthetic stock configurations.

BACKGROUND
The Encore evolved from T/C's very popular Contender pistol and true to its heritage the Encore Pro can be configured into a pistol, rifle, shotgun or muzzleloader. Numerous caliber options are available making the Encore unique and suitable for hunting many species. There is typically no need to disassembly the mechanism for routine cleaning.
Year Introduced: 2006
Current Manufacturer: Thompson/Center (tcarms.com)
Country of Origin: USA
Similar Models: rimfire and centerfire configurations for pistols and rifles, muzzleloaders, shotguns

REQUIRED TOOLS
Field Stripping: medium flat blade screwdriver, large punch, nylon/brass hammer
Disassembly/Assembly: small Phillips screwdriver, 3/16 hex or Allen wrench

FIELD STRIP
1. Remove the two forend screws—forend front (1016) and foreend rear (1017)—using a medium flat blade screwdriver, Figure 1.
2. Pull the forend (7702) off the barrel (1000).
3. Open the action by pulling back on the trigger guard (1040) then use a large punch to drift out the barrel & hinge pin (1023) from the frame, Figure 2.
4. With the barrel & hinge pin removed the barrel will come free from the frame.

At this point the Encore Pro Hunter is sufficiently disassembled for cleaning.

DETAILED DISASSEMBLY
1. Remove the three grip cap screws (0130) using a small Phillips screwdriver, Figure 3.

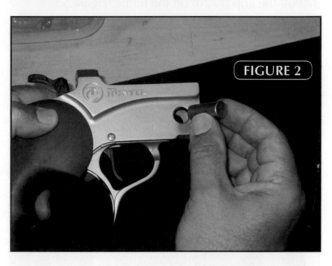

FIGURE 1

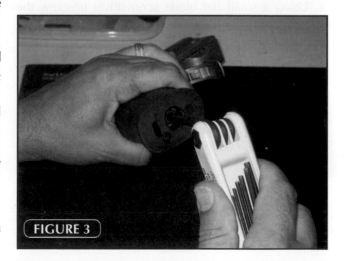

FIGURE 2

2. Use a 3/16 hex or Allen wrench to remove the grip bolt (1044) along with the grip screw washer (1043), grip screw lock washer (1042) and grip adapter (1022), Figure 4.

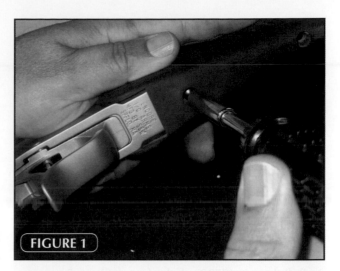

FIGURE 3

FIGURE 4

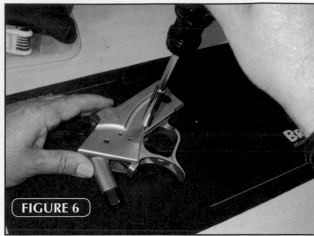

FIGURE 6

3. Pull the grip (7720) off the frame, Figure 5.

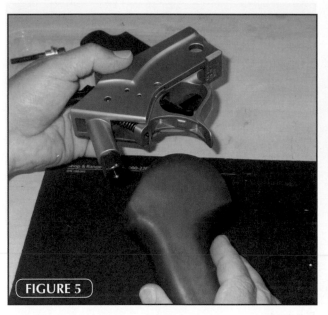

FIGURE 5

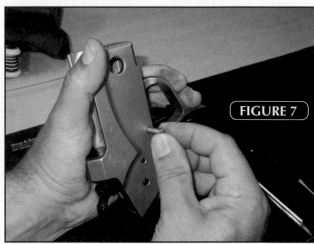

FIGURE 7

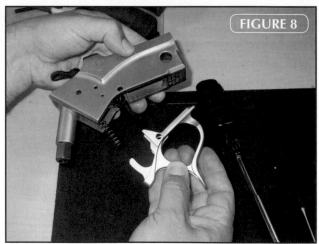

FIGURE 8

4. Using a small flat blade screwdriver unscrew the trigger guard pin (1024) on the right side of the frame, Figure 6. With the head of the trigger guard pin protruding from the frame slightly use a non-marring punch to push the pin through the frame, then pull up on the trigger guard while you pull the trigger guard pin free from the frame, Figure 7.

5. Pull the trigger guard and trigger guard return spring (1038) from the bottom of the frame, Figure 8.

Reassemble reversing the above procedures.

Reassembly Tip: Reinstall the trigger guard by first aligning the trigger in its slot in the trigger guard while lining up the hammer strut with its opening at the rear of the trigger guard. Squeeze the trigger guard into the frame to slightly compress the hammer spring and partially insert the trigger guard pin until its movement is stopped by the trigger plunger (1033) on the trigger. Looking inside the frame push down on trigger plunger using a small punch then press the trigger guard pin in over the top of the trigger plunger until the threaded end of the threads of the trigger guard pin engage the opposite side of the frame.

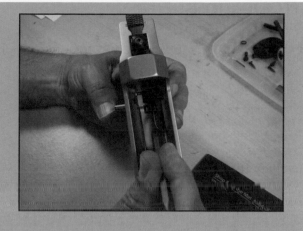

Cleaning Tip: With the trigger guard removed use canned air to blow out any debris.

Centerfire Revolvers

COLT 1851 NAVY CONVERSION

PARTS LIST

1 Frame Assembly
2 Hammer Assembly
3 Barrel
4 Wedge
5 Cylinder
7 Hand
8 Backstrap
10 Trigger
11 Rough Grip
11 Polished Grip
12 Bolt
15 Sight
18 Hand Spring
19 Trigger Bolt Spring
20 Main Spring
21 Base Pin
23 Barrel Pin

25 Roller
26 Triggerguard
30 Hammer Pin
31 Front Triggerguard Screw
32 Backstrap & Triggerguard Screw
33 Wedge Screw
35 Trigger Bolt Spring Screw

36 Main Spring Screw
37 Hammer Screw
38 Trigger Screw
40 Bolt Screw
91 Hammer Safety Bar
98 Firing Pin
135 Ejector Spring
136 Gate Spring
142 Gate
143 Ejector Rod Tube
144 Ejector Rod Tube Screw
145 Gate Spring Screw
147 Hammer Safety Spring
149 Safety Pin
152 Hammer Safety Stop Screw
164 Ejector Nut Assembly
492 Breech
455 Connect Screw

SPECIFICATIONS

Model: 1851 Navy Conversion
Action: revolver; SA
Overall Length: 13 in.
Overall Height: 4.9 in.
Overall Width: 1.54 in.
Barrel: 7.5 in.
Weight Unloaded: 42.3 oz.
Caliber: .38 Special
Capacity: 6
Common Features: case colored frame, blued octagon barrel, brass backstrap/trigger guard, notched hammer rear/brass front sight, smooth walnut grip

BACKGROUND

Colt in the 1870s fitted their revolvers to use the latest technology—metallic cartridges, Figure 1. Previously

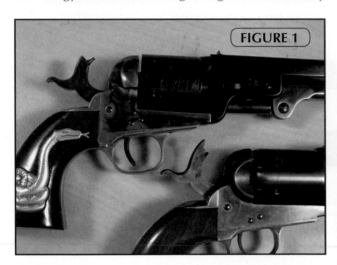

FIGURE 1

all revolvers were cap-and-ball designs were powder, ball and cap were each loaded separately. Colt began converting their percussion revolvers to use metallic cartridges, Figure 1. Conversion revolvers are known by two types, the Richard Conversion and the Richards-Mason Conversion, where ejection rods were added to barrels and the back of cylinders cut off. Back plates with loading gates were installed to the frames or frames were newly made with a loading gate. The Cimarron "Man With No Name" revolver is a hybrid of percussion revolver and cartridge revolver that deviates from original Colt conversions. The revolver is the poetic license that comes from an Italian director with a cast of American actors on a movie set in Spain. The prop man on the set of "The Good, The Bad and The Ugly" has Clint Eastwood wielding a Colt Model 1851 Navy Conversion about 10 years before the Colt conversion was available. The Civil War occurred from 1861-65; Colt's conversions were introduced in the 1870s. Though not a fully factual representation of an original Colt conversion, this spaghetti western six-

shooter has a wicked-cool silver rattle snake inlay in the grip and that soundtrack. Wah-Wah-Wah.

Year Produced: circa 1870
Country of Origin: USA
Original Manufacturer: Colt (coltsmfg.com)
Current Manufacturers: Cimarron (cimarron-firearms.com), Uberti (uberti.com)
Similar Models: 1872 Early Model Open-Top (Uberti)

REQUIRED TOOLS

Field Stripping: nylon hammer
Disassembly/Assembly: small flat blade screwdriver, nipple wrench

FIELD STRIP

1. Pull back the hammer (part #2) to half cock.
2. Rotate the wedge screw (part #38) so the flat edge of the screw is against the wedge pin (4). Then grasp the wedge pin and pull it free, Figure 2.

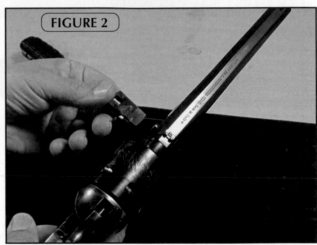

FIGURE 2

3. Pull the barrel forward from the frame (1), Figure 3.

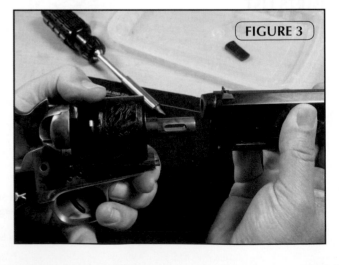

FIGURE 3

4. Pull the cylinder (5) from the frame, Figure 4.

FIGURE 4

At this point the conversion revolver is field stripped.

FRAME DISASSEMBLY

1. Use a small flat blade screwdriver to remove the two backstrap screws (32). Remove the trigger guard & butt screw (31). The backstrap (8) and grip (11) will come free from the frame.

2. Remove the mainspring screw (36). Then pull the mainspring (20) free from the hammer.

3. Next remove the two trigger guard screws (32) and one trigger guard & Butt screw (31). The trigger guard (26) will fall free.

4. Unscrew the bolt spring screw (35) and remove the sear and bolt spring (19).

5. Remove the trigger screw (38) and pull the trigger (10) from the bottom of the frame.

6. Unscrew the bolt screw (40) and remove the bolt (12) from the bottom of the frame.

7. Take out the hammer screw (37) and the hammer, hand (7) and hand spring assembly (18) will come free from the hammer.

8. Remove the gate (142) by taking out the gate screw, Figure 5.

9. The gate spring (136) is removed by unscrewing the gate spring screw (145), Figure 5.

FIGURE 5

BARREL DISASSEMBLY

1. For the "Man With No Name" revolver use a medium flat blade screwdriver to remove the plunger screw (20) and the loading lever assembly—loading lever (12), loading lever latch (11), loading plunger (17)—will come free from the barrel. For other conversion revolvers with an ejector rod use a small flat blade screwdriver to remove the ejector rod tube screw (144) and the ejector rod tube assembly— ejector rod tube (143), ejector rod (164), ejector spring (135)—will come free from the barrel.

Reassemble in reverse order.

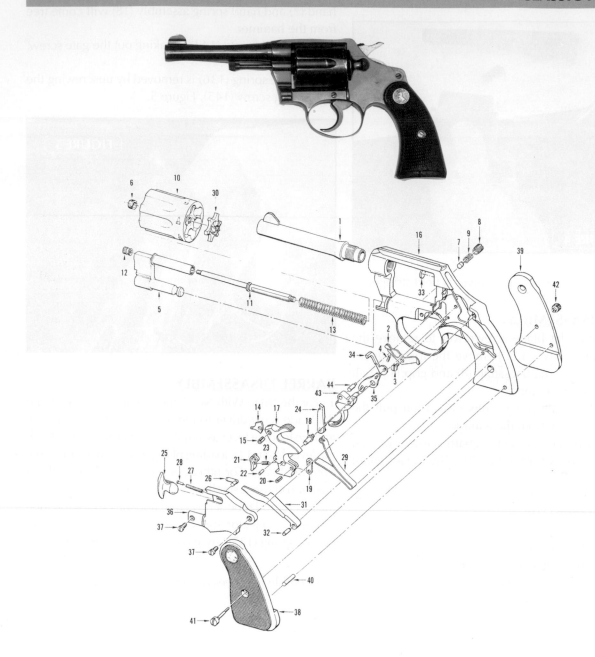

PARTS LIST

1 Barrel
2 Bolt
3 Bolt Screw
4 Bolt Spring
5 Crane
6 Crane Bushing
7 Crane Lock Detent
8 Screw, Spring Retaining
9 Crane Lock Spring
10 Cylinder
11 Ejector Rod
12 Ejector Rod Head
13 Ejector Spring
14 Firing Pin

15 Roll Pin
16 Frame
17 Hammer Assembly
18 Hammer Pin
19 Hammer Stirrup
20 Stirrup Pin
21 Hammer Strut
22 Hammer Strut Pin
23 Hammer Strut Spring
24 Hand
25 Latch
26 Latch Pin
27 Latch Spring
28 Latch Spring Guide
29 Mainspring
30 Ejector Ratchet

31 Rebound Lever
32 Rebound Lever Pin
33 Recoil Plate
34 Safety Assembly
35 Safety Lever
36 Side Plate
37 Side Plate Screw (2 Req'd.)
38 Stock Assy. L.H.
39 Stock Assy. R.H.
40 Stock Pin
41 Stock Screw
42 Stock Screw Nut
43 Trigger Assembly
43 Trigger
44 Pin

SPECIFICATIONS
Model: Police Positive Special
Action: revolver; DA/SA
Overall Length: 8.62 in.
Overall Height: 4.75 in.
Overall Width: 1.37 in.
Barrel: 4 in.
Weight Unloaded: 23 oz.
Caliber: .38 Special
Capacity: 6
Common Features: steel frame/barrel, blued finish, V-notch rear/fixed blade front sight, checkered walnut grip, various barrel lengths

BACKGROUND
The Police Positive Special evolved from the Colt Police Positive both of which share Colt's slim D-frame. Whereas the Police Positive was chambered in the smaller length Colt .38 rounds as well as .32, the Police Positive Special was lengthened and strengthened to accept the .38 Special cartridge. Over 750,000 Police Positive Special revolvers were produced between 1908 and 1995. It was very popular with law enforcement agencies as well as civilians. Colt's "Positive Lock" safety prevents the firing of the weapon if the hammer is struck from being dropped.
Years Produced: 1908-1995, 1907-47 (Police Positive)
Country of Origin: USA
Original Manufacturer: Colt (coltsmfg.com)
Similar Models: Police Positive (.32 Long/Short, .32 S&W Long, .38 S&W)

REQUIRED TOOLS
Disassembly/Assembly: small flat blade screwdriver, nylon hammer, needle-nose pliers

CYLINDER DISASSEMBLY
1. Remove the spring retaining screw (part #8), crane lock spring (9) and crane lock detent (7), Figure 1.
2. Pull back latch (25) and swing out cylinder (10) then pull cylinder and crane assembly out from the front of the frame (16), Figure 2.
3. Use a padded pair of pliers to grasp the ejector rod head (12) and unscrew in counterclockwise looking at the front.
4. Remove ejector ratchet (30) using a Colt ejector/ratchet tool and unscrew counterclockwise looking from the rear.
5. With the ejector ratchet removed, the crane (5) and ejector rod assembly from the cylinder. Then remove

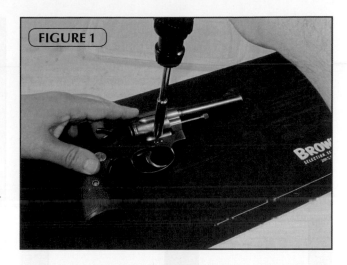

FIGURE 1

FIGURE 2

the crane bushing (6) using a Colt crane bushing tool to unscrew it.
6. With the crane bushing removed the ejector rod (11) and ejector spring (13) can be removed from the crane.

FRAME DISASSEMBLY
1. Remove the stock (38) by unscrewing the stock screw (41).
2. Unscrew the two side plate screws (37) using a small flat blade screwdriver, Figure 5. Then cup the revolver in your hand with side plate (36) facing your palm and tap the grip portion of the frame with a nylon hammer. The side plate and latch assembly will fall free from the frame and into your palm, Figure 6.
3. Remove the latch (25) and latch spring (27) and latch spring guide (28) from the side plate.
4. To remove the mainspring (29) by grasping and compressing it with a pair of non-marring needle-nose

Tool Tip: Two special tools are required to strip down some Colt cylinders and are available from Brownells (brownells.com). A combination Colt 1911 bushing wrench and ejector/ratchet tool; the hexagonal cutout is used to remove the cylinder ratchet, Figure 3. The Colt crane bushing tool to used to remove the crane bushing, Figure 4.

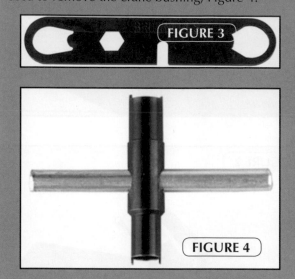

FIGURE 3

FIGURE 4

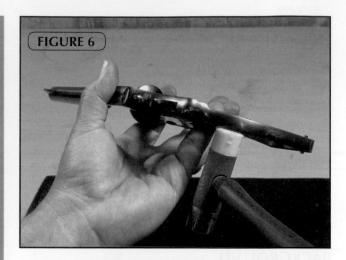

FIGURE 6

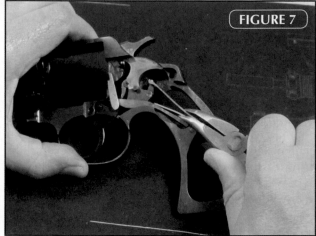

FIGURE 7

FIGURE 5

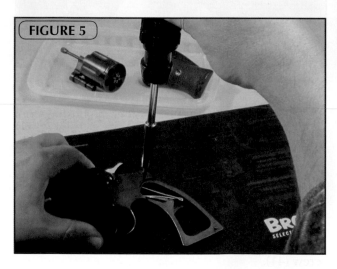
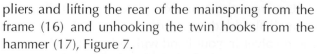

strut spring (23), hammer strut pin (22), hammer stirup (19) and stirup pin (20).

8. Next remove the trigger and hammer block/safety assembly.

9. Remove the bolt screw (3) and the bolt (2) and bolt spring (4) can be taken out from the frame. Note that the bolt spring is under compression.

10. The latch pin (26) can be dropped out of its recess in the frame.

The revolver is reassembled in reverse order.

pliers and lifting the rear of the mainspring from the frame (16) and unhooking the twin hooks from the hammer (17), Figure 7.

5. Next remove the hand (24) from the trigger (43).

6. Use a small punch to drift out the rebound lever pin (32) and pull the rebound lever (31) out of its notch in the frame and then out from the frame.

7. Pull back the hammer to its rear most/full cock position and pull the hammer off the hammer pin (18). The hammer will come out as an assembly with the firing pin (14), roll pin (15), hammer strut (21), hammer

Criminal Provenance: Al Capone the notorious Chicago mobster from the Prohibition Era and architect of the St. Valentines Massacre carried a nickel plated Police Positive. Christie's auction house sold Capone's piece for $109,080 in June 2011.

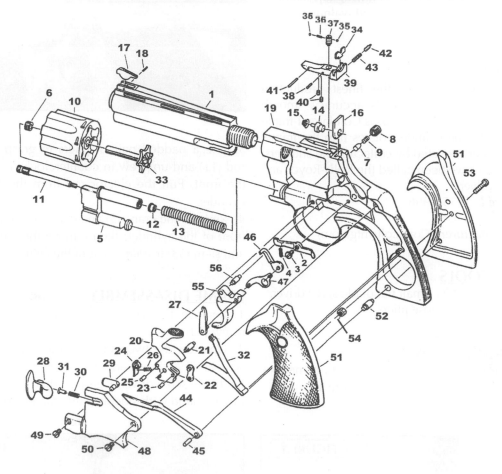

PARTS LIST

1 Barrel
2 Bolt
3 Bolt Screw
4 Bolt Spring
5 Crane
6 Crane Bushing
7 Crane Lock Detent
8 Crane Lock Screw
9 Crane Lock Spring
10 Cylinder Assembly
11 Ejector Rod
12 Ejector Rod Bushing
13 Ejector Spring
14 Firing Pin

15 Firing Pin Spring
16 Firing Pin Stop
17 Front Sight Blade
18 Front Sight Blade Pin (2 Req'd.)
19 Frame Detail Assembly
20 Hammer Assembly
21 Hammer Pin
22 Hammer Stirrup Assembly
23 Roll Pin
24 Hammer Strut
25 Hammer Strut Pin
26 Hammer Strut Spring
27 Hand Assembly
28 Cylinder Latch
29 Latch Pin Detail Assembly

30 Latch Spring
31 Latch Spring Guide
32 Mainspring
33 Ejector Ratchet And Stem
34 Rear Sight Blade
35 Rear Sight Detent Ball
36 Rear Sight Detent Spring
37 Rear Sight Elevation Screw
38 Rear Sight Elevation Screw Pin
39 Rear Sight Leaf
40 Rear Sight Elevation Spring
41 Rear Sight Leaf Pin
42 Rear Sight Windage Screw
43 Rear Sight Windage Spring
44 Rebound Lever

45 Rebound Lever Pin
46 Safety Assembly
47 Safety Lever
47 Safety Lever
48 Sideplate
49 Sideplate Screw, Front
50 Sideplate Screw, Rear
51 Grips
52 Stock
53 Stock Screw
54 Stock Screw Nut
55 Trigger Assembly
56 Trigger Pin

Courtesy of Numrich Gun Parts Corporation

SPECIFICATIONS

Model: Python
Action: revolver; DA/SA
Overall Length: 9.7 in. (4 in. barrel)
Overall Height: 5.5 in.
Overall Width: 1.4 in.
Barrel: 2.4 in., 3 in., 4 in., 6 in., or 8 in.
Weight Unloaded: 42 oz. (4 in. barrel)
Caliber: .357 Magnum
Capacity: 6
Common Features: steel frame, under lug barrel with vent-rib, blued, stainless or nickel finish, adjustable rear/fixed blade front sight, checkered walnut or rubber grip, various barrel lengths

BACKGROUND

The Colt Python is one of the finest production revolvers ever built known for its accuracy, smooth trigger pull and tight lock-up. It uses Colt large I-frame and like all Colts the cylinder rotates into the frame. These revolvers are coveted by collector and shooters. No wonder they have been called the Rolls-Royce and Cadillac of revolvers.
Years Produced: 1955-1996
Country of Origin: USA
Original Manufacturer: Colt (coltsmfg.com)

REQUIRED TOOLS

Disassembly/Assembly: small flat blade screwdriver, nylon hammer, needle-nose pliers

CYLINDER DISASSEMBLY

1. Remove the crane lock screw (part #8), crane lock spring (9) and crane lock detent (7), Figure 1.

2. Pull back the cylinder latch (28) and swing out cylinder (10) then pull cylinder and crane assembly out from the front of the frame (19), Figure 2.

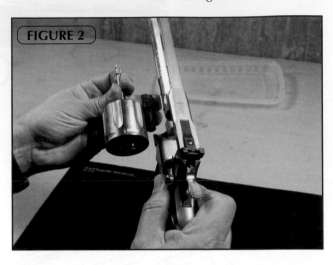

FIGURE 2

3. Use a padded pair of pliers to grasp the ejector rod (11) and unscrew in counterclockwise looking at the front. Pull the ejector rod from the front of the cylinder.

4. Remove the crane (5) and crane bushing () from the front of the cylinder; then remove the ejector ratchet and stem (33) from the rear of the cylinder.

FRAME DISASSEMBLY

1. Remove the stock (51) by unscrewing the stock screw (53).

2. Unscrew the two side plate screws, front sideplate screw (49) and rear sideplate screw (50) using a small flat blade screwdriver, Figure 3. Then cup the revolver in your hand with sideplate (48) facing your palm and

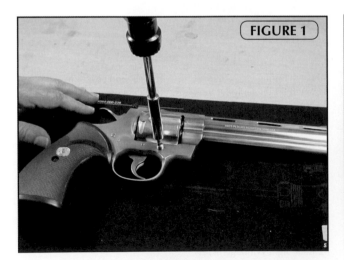

FIGURE 1

FIGURE 3

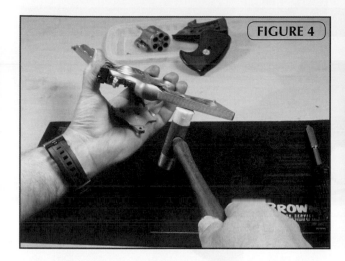

FIGURE 4

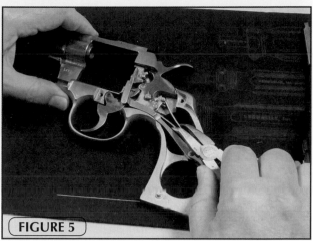

FIGURE 5

tap the grip portion of the frame with a nylon hammer. The side plate and latch assembly will fall free from the frame and into your palm, Figure 4.

3. Remove the cylinder latch and latch spring (30) and latch spring guide (31) from the side plate.

4. To remove the mainspring (32) by grasping and compressing it with a pair of non-marring needle-nose pliers and lifting the rear of the mainspring from the frame and unhooking the twin hooks from the hammer (20), Figure 5.

5. Next remove the hand assembly (27) from the trigger assembly (55).

6. Use a small punch to drift out the rebound lever pin (45) and pull the rebound lever (44) out of its notch in the frame and then out from the frame.

7. Pull back the hammer and lift the hammer off the hammer pin (21).

8. Remove the cylinder latch pin detail assembly (29) toward the rear and pull it from the frame.

9. Next remove the trigger and safety lever (47) and safety assembly (46).

The revolver is reassembled in reverse order.

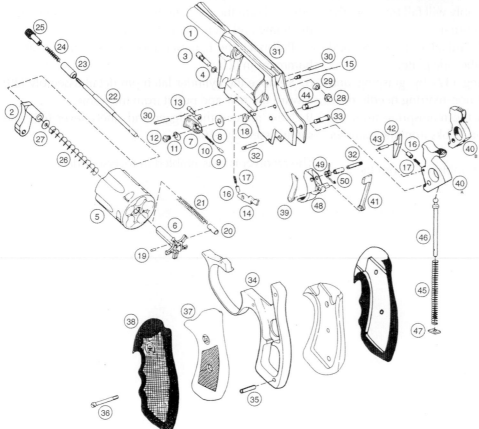

23 Ejector Rod Collar
24 Ejector Rod Collar Spring
25 Ejector Rod Head
26 Ejector Rod Return Spring
27 Ejector Rod Washer
28 Firing Pin
29 Firing Pin Spring
30 Firing Pin Retaining Pin
30 Cylinder Retaining Pin
31 Frame Assembly
32 Frame Assembly Pin
32 Trigger Pin
33 Frame Assembly Screw
34 Grip Frame & Trigger Guard
35 Grip Locating Pin
36 Grip Screw
37 Grips, Bulldog Style
38 Grips, Neoprene
39 Hand
40A Hammer
40B Hammer - Pocket
41 Hammer Block
42 Hammer Pawl
43 Hammer Pawl Pin
44 Hammer Screw
45 Main Spring
46 Main Spring Guide Rod
47 Main Spring Seat
48 Trigger
49 Trigger Spring
50 Trigger Spring Bushing

PARTS LIST

1 Barrel Assembly
2 Crane
3 Crane Screw
4 Crane Screw Washer
5 Cylinder
6 Ejector
7 Cylinder Latch
8 Cylinder Latch Washer
9 Cylinder Latch Plunger
10 Cylinder Latch Plunger Spring
11 Cylinder Latch Cover Plate

12 Cylinder Latch Retaining Screw
13 Cylinder Latch Release Screw
14 Cylinder Stop
15 Cylinder Stop Bushing
16 Cylinder Plunger
16 Hammer Plunger
17 Cylinder Plunger Spring
17 Hammer Plunger Spring
18 Cylinder Stud/Retaining Ring
19 Ejector Rod Assembly Pin
20 Ejector Rod Bushing
21 Ejector Rod Lock Spring
22 Ejector Rod

SPECIFICATIONS

Action: revolver, SA/DA
Overall Length: 7.4 in.
Overall Height: 4.9 in.
Overall Width: 1.5 in.
Barrel: 2.5 in.
Weight Unloaded: 21.0 oz.
Caliber: .44 SPL
Capacity: 5
Features: hammer block safety; 3-point cylinder lock-up; protected ejector rod; steel frame; external hammer; fixed front ramp/rear groove sights; checkered black rubber grips; custom finishes (black, tiger and black), stainless or blue finishes

BACKGROUND

Though the company name has changed over the years, Charter Arms is known for producing inexpensive yet functional and reliable lightweight, snubnose revolvers. The design of the Bulldog like all Charter Arms revolvers has fewer moving parts than other revolvers and utilizes a one piece frame unlike other revolver manufacturers' designs which employ a side plate in the frame. The one-piece frame is stronger and strength is required especially in the Bulldog which is chambered in .44 Special. The Bulldog was extremely popular in the 1970's and '80s and has evolved from the Son of Sam era with tapered barrel with exposed ejector rod and bulbous walnut grip to a full shrouded barrel and checkered rubber grips. Charter Arms revolvers are known for their light trigger pull in both single and double action.

Year Introduced: 1978
Country of Origin: USA
Current Manufacturers: Charter Arms (charterfirearms.com)
Similar Models: Target Bulldog (4 in. and 5 in. barrel models), Crimson Bulldog (Crimson Trace laser grip), Bulldog DAO, Bulldog On Duty, Bulldog Classic (hi-luster blue finish)

REQUIRED TOOLS

Disassembly/Assembly: paperclip or small nail, small and medium flat blade screwdrivers, small punch, brass mallet, pliers

FRAME DISASSEMBLY

1. First remove the grips (part #37 Bulldog style or 38 neoprene style) by unscrewing the grip screw (36) and popping apart the grip panels, Figure 1.
2. Cock back the hammer (40) and hold it while inserting a paperclip or nail into the hole in the main spring rod guide (46). Pull the hammer fully back and the main spring rod guide, main spring (45) and main

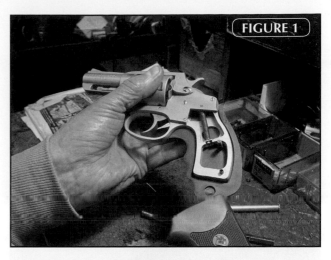

FIGURE 1

spring seat (47) with the paperclip/nail will fall free from the frame, Figure 2.

FIGURE 2

3. Next remove the grip frame & trigger guard (34) by unscrewing the frame assembly screw (33) and drifting out the two pins, the cylinder retaining pin (30) and the frame assembly pin (33), using a small punch and hammer, Figure 3. The grip frame & trigger guard

FIGURE 3

can then be pulled out from the bottom of the frame assembly, Figure 4.

FIGURE 4

4. Remove the hammer by unscrewing the hammer screw (44) from the left side of the frame assembly, and pull it out from the top of the frame assembly, Figure 5.

FIGURE 5

5. Remove the trigger by drifting out the trigger pin (32) and pulling the trigger assembly—trigger, hand (39), trigger spring (49), trigger spring bushing (50), hammer block (41)—from the frame assembly, Figure 6.

Maintenance Tip: Every 200 rounds or so make sure three screws are tight—the cylinder latch screw (12), crane screw (3) and hammer screw. The recoil from full power .44 Special rounds is not dainty.

FIGURE 6

CYLINDER DISASSEMBLY

1. The cylinder assembly is removed by unscrewing and removing the crane screw using a medium flat blade screwdriver. The cylinder assembly can then be removed from the frame assembly, Figure 7.

FIGURE 7

2. The cylinder can be disassembled by grasping the ejector rod (22) close to the crane (2) with a pair of pliers while unscrewing the ejector rod head (25). The ejector rod collar (23) and ejector rod collar spring (24) will fall free once the ejector rod head is removed.

Reassemble in reverse order.

Reassembly Tip: When replacing the trigger assembly, make sure the straight part of the trigger spring bears tension on the inside of the frame assembly. Push the trigger assembly up into the frame assembly and use a nail or drift punch as a slave pin to hold the assembly in place before tapping in the trigger pin.

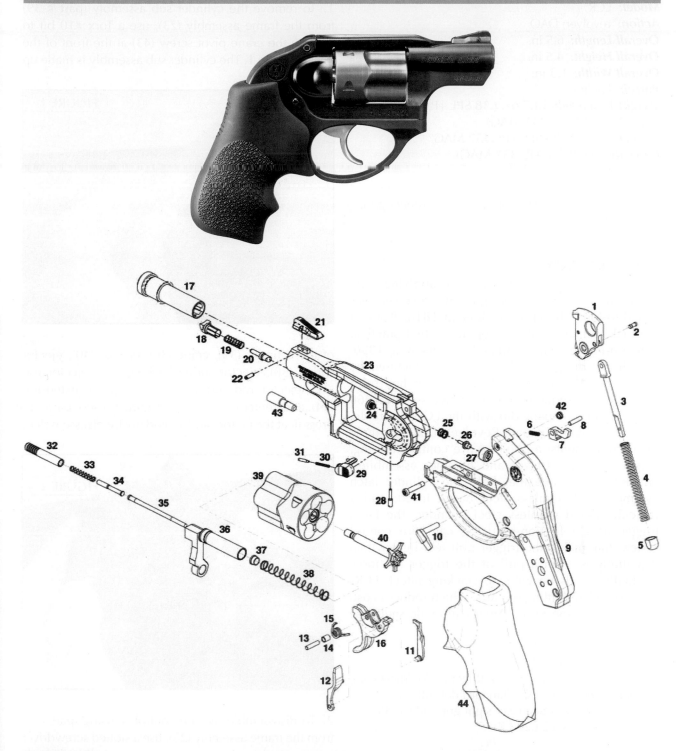

PARTS LIST

1 Hammer Sub-Assembly
2 Hammer Strut Pin
3 Hammer Strut
4 Mainspring
5 Mainspring Seat
6 Cylinder Latch Spring
7 Cylinder Latch

8 Trigger/Latch Pivot Pin
9 Fire Control Housing/Lock Sub-Assembly
10 Hammer Pivot Pin
11 Pawl
12 Transfer Bar
13 Trigger/Latch Pivot Pin
14 Trigger Spring Bushing
15 Trigger Return Spring
16 Trigger

17 Barrel
18 Front Latch Cap
19 Front Latch Spring
20 Front Latch Pin
21 Front Sight
22 Front Sight Cross Pin
23 Frame Assembly

SPECIFICATIONS
Model: LCR
Action: revolver; DAO
Overall Length: 6.5 in.
Overall Height: 4.5 in.
Overall Width: 1.3 in.
Barrel: 1.9 in.
Weight Unloaded: 13.5 oz. (.38 SPL +P); 14.9 oz. (.22 LR), 17.10 oz (.357 MAG)
Caliber: .22 LR, .38 SPL +P; .357 MAG
Capacity: 5 (38 SPL +P, .357 MAG), 8 (.22 LR)
Common Features: matte black aluminum frame; stainless fluted cylinder; Hogue textured rubber grip; fixed front/rear sights

BACKGROUND
The LCR is a great example of applying new technology to an old design. The revolver was first developed by Elisha Collier in 1818. It was a flintlock. Samuel Colt developed the first practical percussion cap revolver, the Colt Paterson, in 1836. The first cartridge revolver was manufactured by Smith and Wesson in 1856. Bill Ruger had been manufacturing double action revolvers since 1968 and what his company did with the LCR is notable. The Lightweight Compact Revolver (LCR) has three main components: a polymer fire control housing, which holds the trigger and hammer assemblies; an aluminum frame that hold the cylinder latch assembly and stainless steel barrel insert; and a radically fluted stainless steel cylinder. The DOA trigger uses a friction-reducing cam fire control system that makes the trigger pull feel lighter than it actually is, with a pull of the trigger the force gradually builds up with no stacking effect. LCRs require no hand fitting of parts, which reduces cost. It is the evolution of the American-made snubnose revolver.
Year Introduced: 2009
Country of Origin: USA
Current Manufacturer: Sturm, Ruger & Co. (ruger.com)
Similar Models: LCR-XS (standard dot tritium), LCR-LG (Crimson Trace laser sight grip), KLCR-357 (.357 MAG), LCR-22 (.22 LR)

REQUIRED TOOLS
Disassembly/Assembly: small standard screwdriver, Torx #10 bit, small roll pin punch, 1/8 inch punch, torque wrench

DISASSEMBLY
1. To remove the cylinder sub assembly (part # 39) from the frame assembly (23), use a Torx #10 bit to remove the crane pivot screw (43) at the front of the frame, Figure 1. The cylinder sub assembly is made up

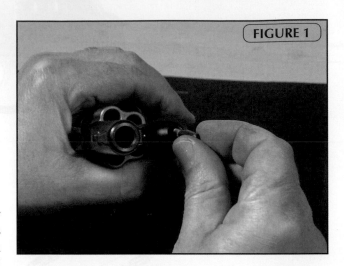

FIGURE 1

of the cylinder (39), crane (36), ejector (40), ejector spring (38), ejector spring bushing (37), ejector rod (32), ejector rod spring (33), locking pin extension (34), and center lock pin (35), Figure 2. These parts are press fit at the factory and should not be disassembled.

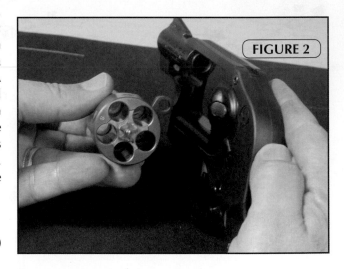

FIGURE 2

2. To disassemble the fire control housing (part # 9) from the frame assembly (23), use a slotted screwdriver to remove the grip retaining screw and slide the grip (44) off the fire control housing.
3. Use a Torx #10 bit to remove the fire control housing screw (41) at the top, left side of the frame, Figure 3. The fire control housing screw mates with

FIGURE 3

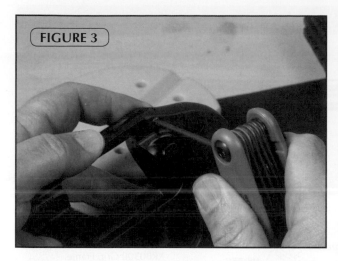

a fire control housing nut (42) on the top right of the frame. Note there is spring tension on the fire control housing.

4. Once the fire control housing nut is off, use a small punch to push through the fire control housing screw.

5. The frame can then be pulled away from the fire control housing, Figure 4. Note that the pawl (11) and

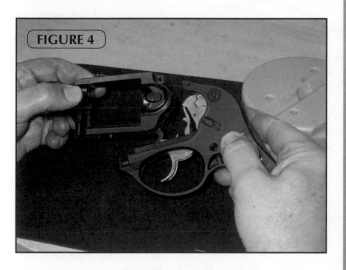

FIGURE 4

transfer bar (12) may fall free when taking the two pieces apart.

6. To remove the front sight (21), use a small roll pin punch to drift out the front sight cross pin (22) and pull out the front sight.

Reassemble in reverse order.

Maintenance Tip: The internal components of the LCR are coated to minimize the need for lubricant. It is, however, recommended that the hammer (1) and hammer pivot pin (10) be lubricated after 1,000 rounds of live fire or dry fire. With the grip removed lay the revolver so the right side faces up and use a 1/8 inch punch to slightly push out the hammer pivot pin. No need to push the pin all the way out of the fire control housing. From the right side, add two to three drops of oil in the hammer pivot pin hole, Figure 3. Rotate the hammer pivot pin a few times to work the oil into the mechanism then from the left side of the fire control housing align the hammer pivot pin in the recess and fully seat the pin. Dry fire the revolver five to 10 times to fully work the oil in the mechanism.

Reassembly Tip: The fire control housing nuts fits into the fire control housing with smooth edge facing up. When reassembling the fire housing unit screw and nut tighten to six to nine lb./in. Torque the crane pivot screw to 23 to 27 lb./in. A dab of Loctite on the crane pivot screw is a good practice.

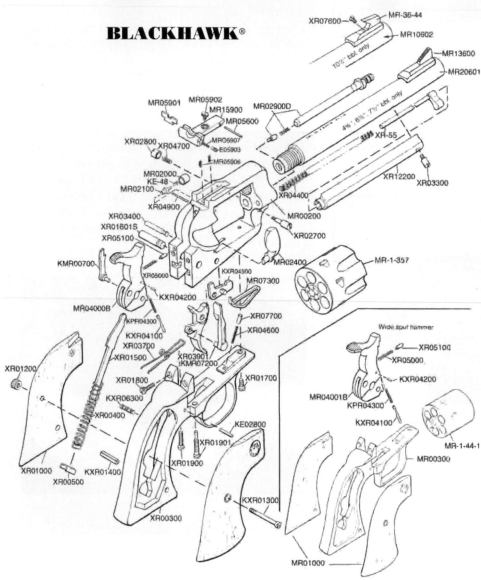

BLACKHAWK®

SUPER BLACKHAWK®

KMR13601 Front Sight Base
MR03600 Front Sight Blade
MR05700 Front Sight Locating Pin
MR02400 Gate
MR07300 Gate Detent Spring
XR00300 Grip Frame
XR01700 Grip Frame Screw - A - Front
XR01800 Grip Frame Screw - B - Back (2 Req'd.)
XR01900 Grip Frame Screw - C - Bottom
XR01901 Grip Frame Screw & Pivot Lock
KXR01400 Grip Panel Dowel
XR01200 Grip Panel Ferrule - Left
XR01100 Grip Panel Ferrule - Right
KXR01300 Grip Panel Screw
XR01000 Grip Panels
MR04000B Hammer Assembly
XR01601S Hammer Pivot Pin
KXR04100 Hammer Plunger
KXR04200 Hammer Plunger Cross Pin
KPR04300 Hammer Plunger Spring
XR01500 Hammer Strut
XR00400 Mainspring
XR00500 Mainspring Seat
XR05200 Medallion (2 Req'd.)
KMR00700 Pawl
XR05000 Pawl Spring
XR05100 Pawl Spring Plunger
MR15900 Rear Sight Base Assembly
MR05901 Rear Sight
MR05902 Rear Sight Elevation Screw
MR05906 Rear Sight Elevation Spring (2 Req'd.)
MR05600 Rear Sight Pivot Pin
E05903 Rear Sight Windage Adjustment Screw
MR05907 Rear Sight Windage Spring
MR02000 Recoil Plate
XR04900 Recoil Plate Cross Pin
KMR07200 Transfer Bar
XR03901 Trigger
XR03400 Trigger Pivot Pin
XR03700 Trigger Spring
KE02800 Trigger Spring Pivot Pin

PARTS LIST

MR50602 Barrel
MR02900D Base Pin Assembly

XR02700 Base Pin Latch Body
XR02800 Base Pin Latch Nut
XR04700 Base Pin Latch Spring
MR-1-45C Cylinder

SPECIFICATIONS

Model: New Model Blackhawk
Action: revolver; SA
Overall Length: 10.5 in.
Overall Height: 5.4 in.
Overall Width: 1.7 in.
Barrel: 4.6 in.
Weight Unloaded: 36 oz.
Caliber: .30 Carbine, .327 FED MAG, .357 MAG, .41 MAG, .44 SPL, .45 Colt
Capacity: 6
Common Features: aluminum grip frame; alloy steel cylinder frame; fluted cylinder; checkered hard rubber grip or smooth rosewood; fixed front/adjustable rear sights; transfer bar safety

BACKGROUND

The Blackhawk rode into town when "Gunsmoke," "The Lone Ranger," "Bonanza," and other TV westerns were on prime time. The Blackhawks were originally referred to as Flattops models because the frame strap along the top of the cylinder was flat. The design was tweaked so the top strap helps protect the rear sight. These single-actions then evolved into "three screw" models and in 1973 the New Model Blackhawk debuted with a transfer bar that prevents the hammer from firing a round if the revolver is dropped on its hammer. It is a robust revolver perfect for cowboy action shooting, hunting and protecting the ranch. Part numbers vary depending on finish and model type (Bisley, Hunter, Super Blackhawk, etc.); part numbers below are for a blued Blackhawk. Disassembly for the Vaquero is similar to New Model Blackhawk but the mechanism are different and they do not share many parts.
Year Introduced: 1955
Country of Origin: USA
Current Manufacturer: Sturm, Ruger & Co. (ruger.com)
Similar Models: Blackhawk Bisley (Bisley grip), Super Blackhawk (.44 MAG), Super Blackhawk Hunter (.44 MAG), Super Blackhawk Bisley(.44 MAG, Bisley grip), convertible models with spare cylinder (.357 MAG/9mm, .45 Colt/.45 Auto Cylinder)

REQUIRED TOOLS

Field Strip: none
Disassembly/Assembly: small standard screwdriver, retaining pin

FIELD STRIP

1. Open the gate (part # MR02400) and press in the base pin latch nut (XR02800) on the left side of the cylinder frame (MR00200) while withdrawing the base pin assembly (MR02900D), Figure 1.
2. Remove the cylinder from the right side/gate side of frame, Figure 2.

FIGURE 1

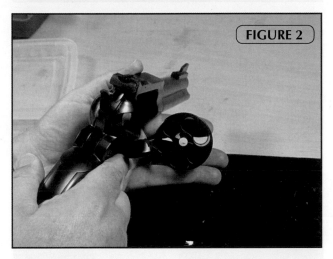

FIGURE 2

At this point the Blackhawk is field stripped for routine cleaning.

DETAILED DISASSEMBLY

1. Remove grip panel screw (KXR01300) and grip panels (XR0100).
2. Pull the hammer (KMR00700) back to full cock position then insert a retaining pin—either a nail or small punch—into the hole at the bottom of the hammer strut (XR01500). Hold the hammer and pull the trigger (XR03901) to ease the hammer forward.
3. Next remove the five screws—two grip frame screw – B – back (XR01800), grip frame screw – C – bottom (XR01900), grip frame screw & pivot lock (XR01901),

grip frame screw - A - front (XR01700)—that fasten the grip frame (XR00300) to the cylinder frame (XR05000), Figure 3.

4. Disengage the grip frame rearward and downward to separate it from the cylinder frame, Figure 4.

FIGURE 3

FIGURE 4

5. Remove the hammer strut with the retaining pin holding the mainspring (XR00400) and mainspring seat (XR00500) as an assembly from the grip frame. Leave the retaining pin.

6. Remove the cylinder latch spring (XR04600) and cylinder latch plunger (XR07700) from its hole in the Grip frame just above the trigger guard.

7. Next disengage the rear legs of the trigger spring (XR03700) from the trigger spring pivot pin (KXR06300) in the grip frame, and remove the trigger spring.

8. Pull out the pawl spring (XR05000) and pawl spring plunger (XR05100) from the rear of the cylinder frame.

9. Use a small screwdriver to free the gate detent spring (MR07300) from its groove in the trigger pivot (XR.0400). Then using a punch, drift out the trigger pivot out of the cylinder frame. Remove the gate detent spring, cylinder latch assembly (KXR04500), and trigger some the bottom of the cylinder frame. The gate can now be removed by pulling it forward from the cylinder frame.

10. Use a punch to push out the hammer pivot (XR01601S) and pull the hammer from the rear of the cylinder frame. The pawl (KMR00700) will be attached to the hammer.

11. With the hammer removed the transfer bar (KMR07200) can be easily removed from the bottom of the cylinder frame.

12. The ejector housing (XR12200) is removed by grasping the barrel and housing while removing the ejector housing screw (XR03300). The ejector housing spring (XR04400) is under compression so control it as you remove the ejector housing from the barrel. The ejector rod assembly (XR-55) will come free once the ejector housing is removed.

13. To remove the base pin latch nut (XR02800), use two flat blade screwdrivers. Hold the base pin latch nut with the screwdriver from the left side of the cylinder frame and use the other screwdriver to hold the base pin latch body (XR02700) then unscrew them. The base pin latch spring (XR04700) will come free with the base pin latch nut.

14. The rear sight is removed from the cylinder frame by drifting out the pivot pin (MR05600) and removing the elevation screw (MR05902). The rear sight will come off as an assembly.

Reassemble in reverse order.

Cleaning Tip: Cartridges with lead bullets can leave metal fouling in the chamber throats, forcing cone, and bore. A Lewis Lead Remover uses special woven brass patches that scrap away lead without scratching rifling.

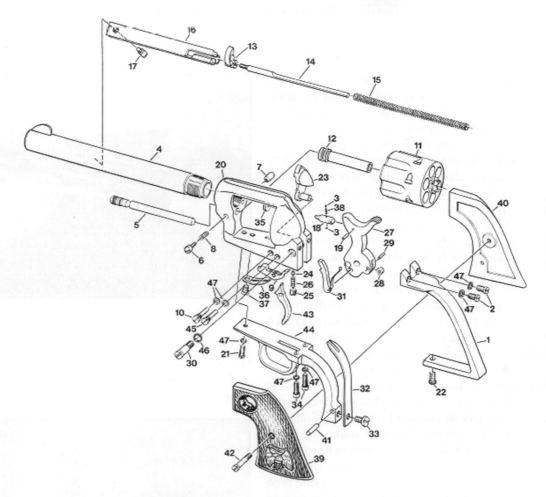

PARTS LIST

1 Back strap
2 Back strap Screw (12)
3 Ball (2)
4 Barrel
5 Base Pin
6 Base Pin Screw
7 Base Pin Screw Nut
8 Base Pin spring
9 Bolt
10 Bolt Screw
11 Cylinder
12 Base Pin Bushing
13 Ejector Rod Head
14 Ejector Rod

15 Ejector Spring
16 Ejector Tube
17 Ejector Tube Screw
18 Firing Pin
19 Firing Pin Rivet
20 Frame
21 Front Guard Screw
22 Front Strap Screw
23 Gate
24 Gate Catch
25 Gate Catch Screw
26 Gate Spring
27 Hammer Assembly
28 Hammer Roll
29 Hammer Roll Pin
30 Hammer Screw

31 Hand Assembly
32 Main Spring
33 Main Spring Screw
34 Rear Guard Screw (2)
35 Recoil Plate
36 Bolt Spring
37 Bolt Spring Screw
38 Spring
41 Stock Pin
42 Stock screw
43 Trigger
44 Trigger Guard
41 Trigger Scrow
46 Washer
47 Washer No. 8 (7)
50 Stock Assembly

SPECIFICATIONS

Model: U.S. Fire Arms SAA
Action: revolver; SA
Overall Length: 11 in. (5.5 in. barrel)
Overall Height: 5.5 in.
Overall Width: 1.6 in.
Barrel: 4.75 in., 5.5 in., 7.5 in.
Weight Unloaded: 36.8 oz. (.45 LC, 5.5 in. barrel)
Caliber: .32 WCF, .38 WCF, .38 SPL/.357 MAG, .44 WCF, .44 SPL., .45 LC
Capacity: 6
Common Features: steel frame, fluted cylinder; checker polymer or smooth wood grip; fixed front/rear sights

BACKGROUND

Most Single Action Army (SAA) revolvers of late have pedigrees that are not exactly authentic. In the good old days, the SAA was a Colt Model P. The Colt SAA has gone through three generations of model refinements—Colt purists might debate the number of generations—and it has been in continuous production since 1873 save a few years when production was mothballed during World War II. This revolver is the stuff of legends and probably the most recognized revolver every produced. What other pistol has been used to protect life and limb as well as be an engraver's canvas? Thumb back the hammer and the four distinct clicks are music to some ears. It was Colt's first revolver specifically designed for the then new metallic cartridge. The design is simple, the balance superb and the power from a .45 Long Colt knocks down bad guys. Known as the Peacemaker, hog leg, six-shooter among other nicknames, westerners were also fond of saying "God did not make men equal, Colonel Colt did." What Colt did to make men equal the Italian reproduction SAAs and Spaghetti westerns did to cowboy movies. Clones like those from Uberti are dead ringers for Colt SAA revolvers though subtle differences make the parts incompatible. The SAA is an easy revolver to work on. A U.S. Firearms SAA is shown and unlike its Italian brethrens it is 100% American made and at one time was actually produced under the original blue-domed Colt factory in Hartford, Connecticut. USFA hog legs are historically correct to early Colt SAAs.
Year Introduced: 1873
Country of Origin: USA
Original manufacturer: CoH
Current Manufacturers: Beretta (berettausa.com), Cimarron (cimarron-firearms.com), Colt (coltsmfg.com), European American Armory (eaacorp.com), Taylor's & Company (taylorsfirearms.com), Uberti (uberti.com), U.S. Fire Arms Mfg. Co. (usfirearms.com)
Similar Models: Sheriff (3.5 in. barrel, with or without ejector rod), Birdshead (birdshead grip), Bisley (longer grip strap, wide spur hammer), Buntline (12-16 in. barrel)

REQUIRED TOOLS

Field Stripping: none
Disassembly/Assembly: small, medium standard screwdrivers

FIELD STRIP

1. Thumb back the hammer (part #27) to half cock and loosen the catch screw on black powder frame models or depress the bolt (9) on newer generation models.
2. Pull out the base pin (5) toward the front/muzzle, Figure 1.

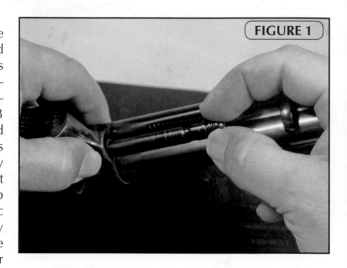

3. Open the loading gate (23) and remove the cylinder (11) from the right side of the frame (20).
4. Remove the base pin bushing (12) from the cylinder, Figure 2.

At this point the revolver is field stripped for routine cleaning and maintenance.

DETAILED DISASSEMBLY

1. To further disassemble the revolver, unscrew the stock screw (42) and remove the left and right stock (39 and 40). If the revolver has a one-piece grip stock, remove the front strap screw (22) at the flat bottom of the back strap (1) and the two back strap screws (2) and washers (47) near the base of the hammer then pull the back strap to the rear, Figure 3. Remove the one-piece grip.

2. Next remove the mainspring screw (33) and the mainspring (23) will drop out of the frame, Figure 4.

3. To remove the trigger guard (44), remove the front guard screw (21) and washer (47) and the two rear guard screws (34) and washers (47) using a flat blade screwdriver that fits properly.

4. Then remove the trigger guard from the frame, Figure 5.

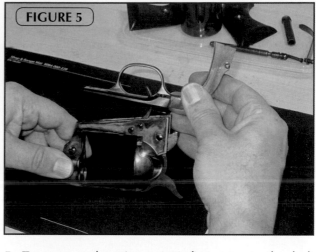

FIGURE 5

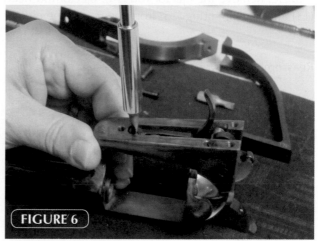

5. To remove the trigger (43) first remove the bolt spring screw (37) and remove the bolt spring (36) from frame, Figure 6.

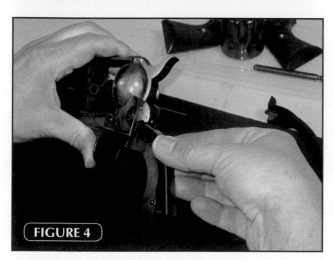

FIGURE 3

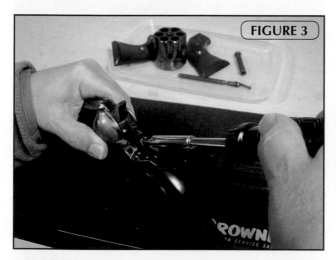

FIGURE 4

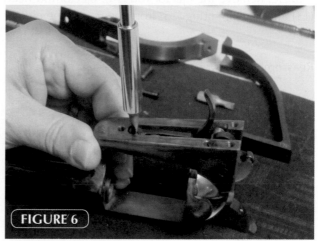

FIGURE 6

6. Remove the trigger screw (45) and washer (47) and pull the trigger from the frame.

7. Remove the bolt screw (10) and washer (47) and remove the bolt (9) from the frame.

8. Finally remove the hammer screw (30) and washer (46) and move the hammer with the attached hand and spring or hand assembly (31) down and out of the frame.

9. To remove the loading gate, unscrew the gate catch screw (25) from the underside of the frame. The gate spring (26) and gate catch (24) will fall free. Note the gate catch spring is under tension.

10. The base pin screw is removed by unscrewing the base pin screw from base pin screw nut (7). Hold the base pin screw nut with another flat blade screwdriver, Figure 7. Note the base pin spring (8) is under tension.

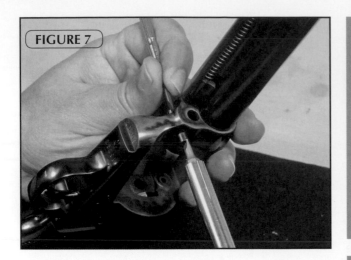

FIGURE 7

Tuning Tip: To give your SAA a poor man's trigger job shim the mainspring. This can be done to any SAA clone no matter who the manufacturer. The shim increases the bend in the mainspring and changes the trigger pull and hammer spring tension. In the old days, shims were made of leather but today shims are made of polymers or metal. Place the shim between the inside of the grip frame and the mainspring. A drop of Loctite on the screw head is advised. Brownells sells polymer shims .187 inches thick. You will need to trim the shim so the grip fits on the grip frame. Follow the manufacturer's instructions.

11. To remove the ejector assembly, unscrew the ejector tube screw (17) from the barrel (4) and lift the ejector tube (16) from the frame toward the front/ muzzle. Remove the ejector rod (14), ejector rod head (13) and ejector spring (15) from the rear of the ejector tube.

Reassemble in reverse order.

Jigged or Stag: Hollywood's B-movie cowboys made jigged bone grips famous. According to NC Ordnance (gungrip.com), the jigged grip style is "double cut" or "twice cut." This referred to:
1. Cutting the stag slab to fit the revolver and
2. Cutting the "jig" pattern. The grip was then said to be "Jigged." Stag horn grips are made from a number of natural horn types including American elk. Sambar horn from India is very popular. Eagle Grips (eaglegrips.com) produces a nice sambar stag horn grip.

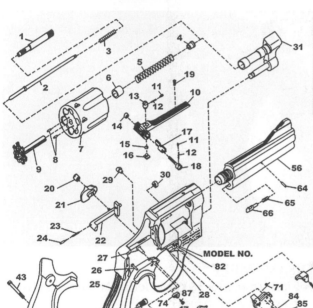

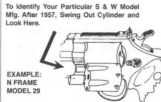

To Identify Your Particular S & W Model Mfg. After 1957, Swing Out Cylinder and Look Here.

EXAMPLE:
N FRAME
MODEL 29

35 Stock Pin
36 Firing Pin Bushing
37 Firing Pin Spring
38 Firing Pin
39 Firing Pin Bushing Pin
40 Front Sight
41 & 45 Grips / Stocks
42 Escutcheon
43 Stock Screw
44 Escutcheon Nut
46 Hammer Assembly
47 Hammer Nose Spring
48 Hammer Nose
49 Sear
50 Sear Spring
51 Hammer Nose Rivet
52 Sear Pin
53 Stirrup
54 Stirrup Pin
55 Strain Screw
56 Barrel
57 Front Sight Elevation Screw
58 Front Sight Leaf
59 Front Sight Leaf Spring
60 Front Sight Base
61 Front Sight Pivot Pin
62 Front Sight Cam
63 Front Sight Pin
64 Locking Bolt Pin
65 Locking Bolt Spring
66 Locking Bolt
67 Cylinder Stop
68 Cylinder Stop Spring
69 Trigger Assembly
70 Trigger Lever
71 Hand Torsion Spring
72 Hand
73 Hand Pin
74 Hand Stop
75 Rebound Slide
76 Rebound Slide Pin
77 Rebound Slide Spring
78 Hammer Block
79 Mainspring
80 Mainspring Stirrup
81 Mainspring Rod Swivel
82 Cylinder Stop Stud
84 Hand Spring Pin
85 Hand Spring Torsion Pin
86 Trigger Lever Pin
87 Trigger Stop Screw
88 Mainspring
90 Front Sight
91 Front Sight Pin

Courtesy of Numrich Gun Parts
Corporation

PARTS LIST

1 Extractor Rod
2 Center Pin
3 Center Pin Spring
4 Extractor Rod Collar
5 Extractor Spring
6 Gas Ring
7 Cylinder Assembly
8 Extractor Pin (2 Req'd.)
9 Extractor
10 Rear Sight Leaf

11 Rear Sight Plunger
12 Rear Sight Plunger Spring
13 Rear Sight Elevation Nut
14 Rear Sight Windage Nut
15 Rear Sight Spring Clip
16 Rear Sight Elevation Stud
17 Rear Sight Slide
18 Rear Sight Windage Screw
19 Rear Sight Leaf Screw
20 Thumbpiece Nut
21 Thumbpiece
22 Bolt

23 Bolt Plunger Spring
24 Bolt Plunger
25 Frame
26 Rebound Slide Stud
27 Hammer Stud
28 Trigger Stud
29 Frame Lug
30 Hammer Nose Bushing
31 Yoke
32 Sideplate (2 Req'd.)
33 Plate Screw
34 Yoke Screw

SPECIFICATIONS

Model: Model 329PD
Action: revolver; SA/DA
Overall Length: 7.6 in.
Overall Height: 5.6 in.
Overall Width: 1.7 in.
Barrel: 2.5 in.
Weight Unloaded: 25.1 oz.
Caliber: .44 Spl/.44 Mag
Capacity: 6
Features: scandium N-frame, titanium cylinder; large exposed hammer; matte finish; fixed Tritium front/Cylinder & Slide notched rear sights; textured synthetic or smooth wood grip

BACKGROUND

S&W manufactures the 329PD using scandium and titanium. Carbon steel and stainless steel are the most common materials used to manufacture revolvers. The frame of 329PD is machined from scandium, a rare earth metal with strength similar to steel but with less weight. The cylinder is titanium which offers strength and lightweight with elasticity. The barrel consists of a rifled steel tube surrounded by an aluminum sleeve. The result is the 329PD scandium revolvers weighs 40% less than the Model 629 steel revolver with the same barrel length. No special disassembly procedures need to be followed to strip down a scandium frame revolver, follow the procedures from that size frame, but it should be noted that the 329PD and other magnum revolvers like the 340PD, 360PD and some Night Guard models will differ slightly from similar models with carbon steel or stainless steel frames. The 329PD uses steel pivot pin studs that are press fit into the scandium frame and are obvious when compared to a steel frame model, Figure 1. Do not attempt to remove the pins as they are press fit and not designed to be removed. Also note that the 329PD has a heat shield between the frame and forcing cone which should also not be removed, Figure 2.

Year Introduced: 2003
Country of Origin: USA
Current Manufacturers: Smith & Wesson (smith-wesson.com)
Similar Models: Model 329 Night Guard (.44 Mag/.44 Spl, scandium frame/stainless steel cylinder), Model 357 Night Guard (.41 Mag, scandium frame/stainless steel cylinder), Model 325 Night Guard (.45 ACP, scandium frame/stainless steel cylinder), Model 310 Night Guard (10mm/.40 S&W, scandium frame/stainless steel cylinder), Model 327 Night Guard (.357 Mag/.38 Spl, 8 round capacity, scandium frame/stainless steel cylinder)

REQUIRED TOOLS

Disassembly/Assembly: small and medium flat blade screwdriver, rubber/nylon mallet, padded pliers

FIGURE 1

FIGURE 2

DISASSEMBLY

See instructions for S&W Model 57 (N-frame revolvers).

Maintenance Tip: When replacing the side plate screws add a drop of Loctite to the screw threads.

Inertia Ammo Test: Before using any lightweight framed revolver, like the scandium framed models test the ammo you intend to use for bullets jumping their crimp or otherwise known as "prairie-dogging." Because of the inertia from the violent recoil in these lightweight revolvers with magnum loads the bullets can be pulled out from the cases and protrude from the cylinder preventing rotation. Effectively jamming the revolver. To test fully load the revolver with ammo and fire all but the last round. Inspect the last round to see if the bullet has unseated from the case. If the ammo is prairie-dogging, test another brand of ammo until you find ammo that does not unseat. Also note that magnum cartridges loaded with bullet weights of less than 120 grains could possibility prematurely erode titanium alloy cylinders.

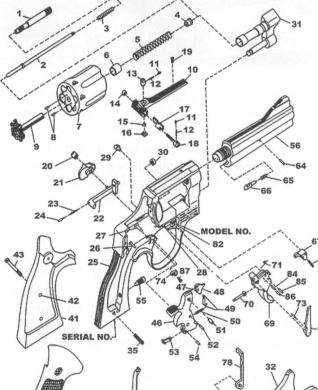

SMALL
"J" FRAME
REVOLVERS

32 Sideplate (2 Req'd.)
33 Plate Screw
34 Yoke Screw
35 Stock Pin
36 Firing Pin Bushing
37 Firing Pin Spring
38 Firing Pin
39 Firing Pin Bushing Pin
40 Front Sight
41 & 45 Grips / Stocks
42 Escutcheon
43 Stock Screw
44 Escutcheon Nut
46 Hammer Assembly
47 Hammer Nose Spring
48 Hammer Nose
49 Sear
50 Sear Spring
51 Hammer Nose Rivet
52 Sear Pin
53 Stirrup
54 Stirrup Pin
55 Strain Screw
56 Barrel
57 Front Sight Elevation Screw
58 Front Sight Leaf
59 Front Sight Leaf Spring
60 Front Sight Base
61 Front Sight Pivot Pin
62 Front Sight Cam
63 Front Sight Pin
64 Locking Bolt Pin
65 Locking Bolt Spring
66 Locking Bolt
67 Cylinder Stop
68 Cylinder Stop Spring
69 Trigger Assembly
70 Trigger Lever
71 Hand Torsion Spring
72 Hand
73 Hand Pin
74 Hand Stop
75 Rebound Slide
76 Rebound Slide Pin
77 Rebound Slide Spring
78 Hammer Block
79 Mainspring
80 Mainspring Stirrup
81 Mainspring Rod Swivel
82 Cylinder Stop Stud
84 Hand Spring Pin
85 Hand Spring Torsion Pin
86 Trigger Lever Pin
87 Trigger Stop Screw
88 Mainspring
90 Front Sight
91 Front Sight Pin

Courtesy of Numrich Gun Parts
   Corporation

PARTS LIST

1 Extractor Rod
2 Center Pin
3 Center Pin Spring
4 Extractor Rod Collar
5 Extractor Spring
6 Gas Ring
7 Cylinder Assembly
8 Extractor Pin (2 Req'd.)
9 Extractor

10 Rear Sight Leaf
11 Rear Sight Plunger
12 Rear Sight Plunger Spring
13 Rear Sight Elevation Nut
14 Rear Sight Windage Nut
15 Rear Sight Spring Clip
16 Rear Sight Elevation Stud
17 Rear Sight Slide
18 Rear Sight Windage Screw
19 Rear Sight Leaf Screw
20 Thumbpiece Nut

21 Thumbpiece
22 Bolt
23 Bolt Plunger Spring
24 Bolt Plunger
25 Frame
26 Rebound Slide Stud
27 Hammer Stud
28 Trigger Stud
29 Frame Lug
30 Hammer Nose Bushing
31 Yoke

SPECIFICATIONS

Model: Model 42 Classic Centennial
Action: revolver; DAO
Overall Length: 6.5 in.
Overall Height: 4.4 in.
Overall Width: 1.3 in.
Barrel: 1.9 in.
Weight Unloaded: 11.4 oz. (scandium frame), 14.4 oz. (aluminum frame); 19.5 oz. (steel frame)
Caliber: .38 SPL +P, .357 Mag
Capacity: 5
Common Features aluminum or steel J-frame; internal hammer; steel barrel, cylinder; checkered wood Crimson Trace laser or textured rubber grips; fixed front/ rear sights; grip safety (Centennial, Model 40 and 42)

BACKGROUND

Smith & Wesson has been producing "hammerless" revolvers with grip safeties since 1888. The official model name was New Departure but they and subsequent models are commonly known as "lemon squeezers." They are not truly hammerless as the hammer is enclosed with the frame and is DOA only. In 1952 S&W debut the Model 40 Centennial which coincided with S&W 100th anniversary. In 1953 a lightweight alloy frame Model 42 Centennial Airweight was produced. Today the hammerless design lives on in various models—340PD, 351, 43, 442, 640 and 642—albeit without the grip safety. In 2008 S&W reintroduced the Model 42 in it Classic Firearms series. Instructions that follow show a reintroduced Model 42 with grip safety, but will work with models without grip safeties.
Year Introduced: 1952
Country of Origin: USA
Current Manufacturers: Smith & Wesson (smith-wesson.com)
Similar Models: Model 40 Centennial (steel frame), Model 42 Centennial Airweight, Model 340PD (scandium frame/titanium cylinder), Model 351 C (.22 Mag), Model 43 C (.22 LR), Model 442 (aluminum frame/steel cylinder), Model 640 (stainless steel frame/cylinder), Model 642 (aluminum frame/stainless steel cylinder)

REQUIRED TOOLS

Disassembly/Assembly: small flat blade screwdriver, rubber/nylon mallet, hex or Allen wrench (non-grip safety models), small nail or paper clip, padded pliers

CYLINDER DISASSEMBLY

1. The cylinder assembly is removed by unscrewing the most forward screw, yoke screw (34), on the frame (25) using a small standard screwdriver.

2. Push the cylinder latch, S&W calls it a thumb piece (21), forward and swing out the cylinder (7).

3. Align one of the cylinder flutes with the flange at the front of the frame. Pull the yoke (31) and cylinder assembly out toward the muzzle, Figure 1.

FIGURE 1

4. With a pair of padded pliers grasp the end of the ejector rod, extractor rod (1) turning clockwise—these are left-hand threads—looking at the front of the cylinder. If the extractor rod is stubborn place the extractor rod in a padded vise and unscrew the cylinder. The extractor rod can then be removed from the front of the cylinder.

FRAME DISASSEMBLY

1. Remove the rubber grip (part #41) by unscrewing the grip screw (43) at the butt of the grip using a hex or Allen wrench. Slide the grip off the frame. For models with the grip safety, remove the grip screw then use a rubber mallet to gently tap off the wood grips.

2. To remove the side plate (32), unscrew the small head side plate screw (33) and the flat head side plate screw (33), Figure 2. Cup the revolver in your hand with side plate facing your palm and tap the grip portion of the frame with a nylon hammer. The side plate will fall out into your palm.

3. To remove the mainspring (79) pull back on the trigger (69) until the small hole at the base of the mainspring rod (80) clears the mainspring swivel (81) then insert a paperclip through the hole from either side of the frame. The paperclip with hold the mainspring compressed. The mainspring assembly can then be removed. Note that the mainspring in under tension, Figure 3.

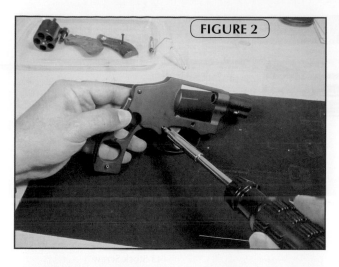

FIGURE 2

FIGURE 3

4. To remove the hammer (54) pull back on the cylinder latch, S&W calls it a thumbpiece (21), and pull the trigger back.

5. Rotate the hammer back and pull it up and out of the frame, Figure 4.

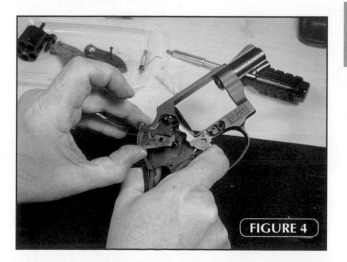

FIGURE 4

6. Remove the rebound slide (75) and rebound slide spring (77) by slightly compressing the rebound slide spring with a small flat blade screwdriver and lifting free from the retainer pin in the frame. Note that the rebound slide spring in under tension.

7. To remove the trigger assembly, slightly move the cylinder hand (72) rearward so it clears the slot in the frame and pull the trigger up and off the pin in the frame.

8. Remove the thumbpiece by unscrewing the thumbpiece screw (20).

9. To remove the safety lever in models with the grip safety, use a small punch to drive out the safety lever pin and remove the safety lever and safety lever spring from the rear of the grip. Note the safety lever spring in under tension.

Reassemble is reverse order. Note relationship of hammer to trigger and grip safety, Figure 5.

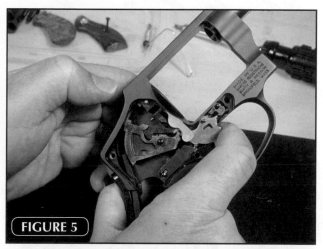

FIGURE 5

Maintenance Tip: When replacing the side plate screws add a drop of Loctite to the screw threads.

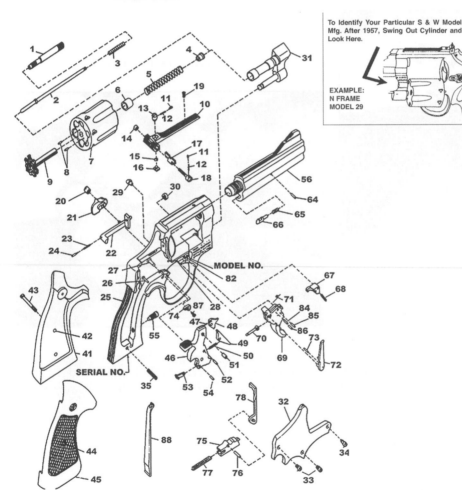

To Identify Your Particular S & W Model Mfg. After 1957, Swing Out Cylinder and Look Here.

EXAMPLE:
N FRAME
MODEL 29

32 Sideplate (2 Req'd.)
33 Plate Screw
34 Yoke Screw
35 Stock Pin
36 Firing Pin Bushing
37 Firing Pin Spring
38 Firing Pin
39 Firing Pin Bushing Pin
40 Front Sight
41 & 45 Grips / Stocks
42 Escutcheon
43 Stock Screw
44 Escutcheon Nut
46 Hammer Assembly
47 Hammer Nose Spring
48 Hammer Nose
49 Sear
50 Sear Spring
51 Hammer Nose Rivet
52 Sear Pin
53 Stirrup
54 Stirrup Pin
55 Strain Screw
56 Barrel
57 Front Sight Elevation Screw
58 Front Sight Leaf
59 Front Sight Leaf Spring
60 Front Sight Base
61 Front Sight Pivot Pin
62 Front Sight Cam
63 Front Sight Pin
64 Locking Bolt Pin
65 Locking Bolt Spring
66 Locking Bolt
67 Cylinder Stop
68 Cylinder Stop Spring
69 Trigger Assembly
70 Trigger Lever
71 Hand Torsion Spring
72 Hand
73 Hand Pin
74 Hand Stop
75 Rebound Slide
76 Rebound Slide Pin
77 Rebound Slide Spring
78 Hammer Block
79 Mainspring
80 Mainspring Stirrup
81 Mainspring Rod Swivel
82 Cylinder Stop Stud
84 Hand Spring Pin
85 Hand Spring Torsion Pin
86 Trigger Lever Pin
87 Trigger Stop Screw
88 Mainspring
90 Front Sight
91 Front Sight Pin

Courtesy of Numrich Gun Parts
Corporation

PARTS LIST

1 Extractor Rod
2 Center Pin
3 Center Pin Spring
4 Extractor Rod Collar
5 Extractor Spring
6 Gas Ring
7 Cylinder Assembly
8 Extractor Pin (2 Req'd.)
9 Extractor

10 Rear Sight Leaf
11 Rear Sight Plunger
12 Rear Sight Plunger Spring
13 Rear Sight Elevation Nut
14 Rear Sight Windage Nut
15 Rear Sight Spring Clip
16 Rear Sight Elevation Stud
17 Rear Sight Slide
18 Rear Sight Windage Screw
19 Rear Sight Leaf Screw
20 Thumbpiece Nut

21 Thumbpiece
22 Bolt
23 Bolt Plunger Spring
24 Bolt Plunger
25 Frame
26 Rebound Slide Stud
27 Hammer Stud
28 Trigger Stud
29 Frame Lug
30 Hammer Nose Bushing
31 Yoke

SPECIFICATIONS

Model: Model 57
Action: revolver; SA/DA
Overall Length: 9.5 in.
Overall Height: 6 in.
Overall Width: 1.7 in.
Barrel: 4 in.
Weight Unloaded: 41 oz.
Caliber: .41Mag
Capacity: 6
Features: steel N-frame/cylinder; wide spur hammer; wide serrated target rigger; transfer bar safety; bright blue finish; pinned red ramp front/micro adj. rear sights; checkered walnut grip

BACKGROUND

The Model 57 uses S&W's second largest frame, the N-frame, which was introduced in 1908 with the .44 Hand Ejector First Model "New Century." It is a heavy, robust revolver frame capable of handling large calibers and magnum cartridges. Notable N-frame revolvers include: the Model 1917, the first revolver chambered for .45 ACP and used in WWI and WWII and the Model 27, the first revolver chambered in .357 Magnum. The most illustrious of all N-frames is the Model 29 chambered for .44 Magnum which was championed by big-bore revolver aficionado Elmer Keith and was made famous in the Dirty Harry films. Jerry Miculek used an N-frame Model 625 in .45 ACP to the set the world record for 12 rounds on target in 2.99 seconds with one reload. N-frame revolvers have gone through numerous design changes over the years that S&W fans can cite engineering modifications like catechism. Instruction are for the current models with a transfer bar firing system and to some extent can be used for revolvers that still wear a firing pin in the hammer.
Year Introduced: 1908 first N-frame (1964 Model 57)
Country of Origin: USA
Current Manufacturers: Smith & Wesson (smith-wesson.com)
Similar Models: Model 22 (.45 ACP, blue finish), Model 24 (.44 Spl, blue finish), Model 25 (.45 LC, blue finish), Model 27 (.38 Spl/.357 Mag, adj. rear/fixed front sights), Model 29 (.44 Mag, blue finish), Model 58 (.41 Mag, fixed sights), Model 325 Thunder Ranch (.45 ACP, adj. rear/fixed front sights, matte finish), Model 327 TRR8 (.38 Spl/.357 Mag, adj. rear/fixed front sights, 8-round capacity, matte finish), Model 329 (.44Spl/.44 Mag, matte finish), Model 625 (.45 ACP, stainless, adj. rear/fixed front sights), Model 627 (.357 Mag, adj. rear/fixed front sights, stainless, 8-round capacity), Model 629 (.44 Mag/.44 Spl, stainless frame/cylinder), Model M&P R8 (.38 Spl/.357 Mag, adj. rear/fixed front sights, 8-round capacity, matte finish), Model 657 (.41 Mag, stainless frame/cylinder)

REQUIRED TOOLS

Disassembly/Assembly: small and medium flat blade screwdriver, rubber/nylon mallet, padded pliers

CYLINDER DISASSEMBLY

1. The cylinder assembly is removed from the frame (part #25) by removing the yoke screw (34), using a small flat blade screwdriver, Figure 1.

2. Push the cylinder latch, S&W calls it a thumb piece (21), forward and swing out the cylinder then align a flute in the cylinder (7) with the frame and pull the yoke (31) and cylinder assembly out of the frame toward the muzzle, Figure 2.

3. With a pair of padded or non marring pliers grasp the end of the ejector rod, extractor rod (1) and turn it clockwise looking at the front of the cylinder, Figure 3 (see next page). Note these are left-hand threads. If the extractor rod is stubborn place the extractor rod in a padded vise and unscrew the cyl-

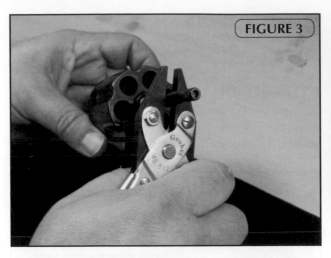

FIGURE 3

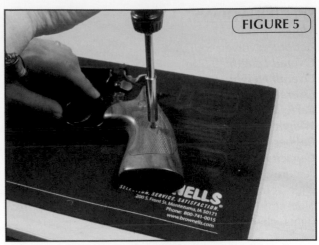

FIGURE 5

inder. The extractor rod can then be removed from the front of the cylinder along with the center pin (2) and ejector spring (3), Figure 4.

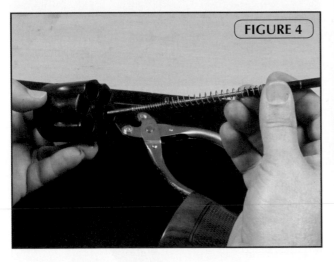

FIGURE 4

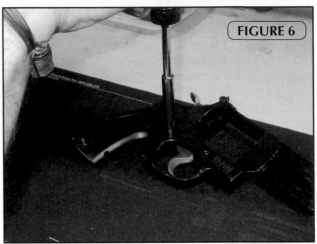

FIGURE 6

4. The ejector/ratchet (9) will fall from the front of the cylinder.

FRAME DISASSEMBLY

1. Remove the two grip panels (42) by unscrewing the grip screw (43) using a small flat blade screwdriver, Figure 5. For models with one-piece rubber grips, remove the grip screw located at the butt and slide the rubber off the frame.

2. The side plate (32) is removed by unscrewing the last three side plate screws—two near the grip (33) and one screw near the rear sight with a small flat blade screwdriver, Figure 6. Cup the revolver in your hand with side plate facing your palm and tap the grip portion of the frame with a nylon hammer. The side plate will fall out into your palm, Figure 7. Note that the hammer block (78) may fall free from the side plate.

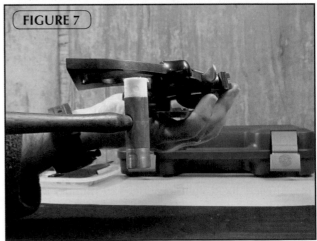

FIGURE 7

3. Remove the mainspring strain screw (55) in the front of the grip frame, or back off the mainspring strain screw enough to relieve tension the mainspring (88), Figure 8. Slide the butt end of the mainspring from the slot in the frame then unhook the top of the mainspring from the hammer (46) by pushing it forward, Figure 9.

FIGURE 8

FIGURE 9

4. The hammer is removed by pulling back on the cylinder latch and pulling the trigger back. Rotate the hammer back and pull it up and out of the frame, Figure 10.

FIGURE 10

5. To remove the trigger assembly, slightly move the hand (72) rearward so it clears the slot in the frame

and pull the trigger (69) up and off the pin in the frame, Figure 11.

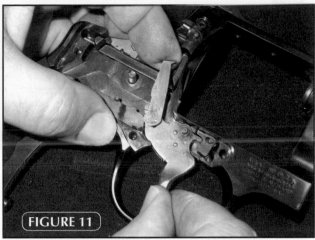

FIGURE 11

6. Remove the thumbpiece by unscrewing the thumbpiece screw (20).

Reassemble is reverse order.

Reassembly Tip: Place the transfer bar in the mechanism prior to replacing the sideplate in the frame.

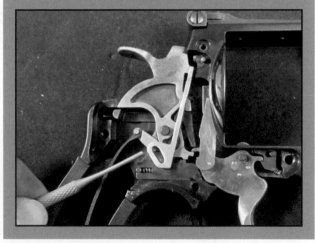

Make My Day: Coke Bottle-style grips on N-frame S&Ws are classic. From the rear the checkered walnut grips with a pronounced palm swell look like an old Coca-Cola bottle. These grips are highly sought after by collectors since they only appeared on early Model 29s, 27s and 57s. Nills Grip (nill-grips.com) in Germany makes an excellent replica grip that can order from Mactec Enterprises (mactec-militaryarms.com).

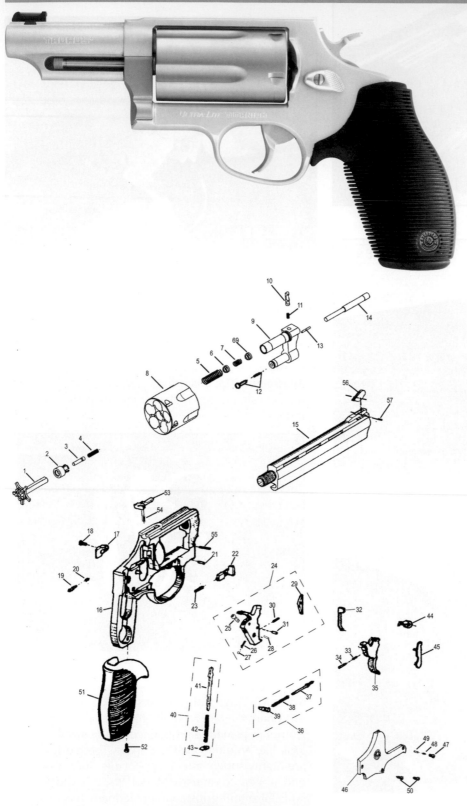

13 Front latch pin
14 Extractor rod
15 Barrel
16 Frame
17 Thumb piece
18 Thumb piece screw
19 Firing pin
20 Firing pin spring
21 Firing pin retaining pin
22 Bolt
23 Bolt spring
24 Hammer assembly
25 Keylock
26 Keylock spring
27 Keylock ball
28 Keylock pin
29 Sear
30 Sear spring
31 Sear pin
32 Transfer bar
33 Hand spring
34 Hand pin
35 Trigger assembly
36 Trigger spring assembly
37 Trigger spring center pin
38 Trigger spring
39 Trigger spring swivel
40 Main spring assembly
41 Main spring center pin
42 Main spring
43 Main spring plate
44 Cylinder stop
45 Hand
46 Side plate
47 Yoke screw
48 Yoke retaining pin spring
49 Yoke retaining pin
50 Side plate screw
51 Rubber grip
52 Grip screw
53 Rear sight assembly
54 Rear sight spring
55 Rear sight pin
56 Front sight
57 Front sight pin
58 Stock pin
60 Firing pin bushing
61 Center pin bushing
63 Rear sight screw
69 Cylinder distance bushing
70 Stellar clip
71 Barrel retaining pin
72 Yoke blocking pin
73 Cylinder assembly catch
    hook
74 Cylinder assembly catch
    spring
75 Cylinder assembly catch
76 Cylinder stop spring
77 Cylinder stop spring
78 Cylinder stop spring pin
79 Side plate screw front
80 Cylinder stop spring bushing
    pin

PARTS LIST

1 Extractor
2 Cylinder retaining bushing
3 Center pin

4 Center pin spring
5 Extractor spring
6 Extractor rod collar
7 Extractor rod spring
8 Cylinder

9 Yoke
10 Front latch
11 Front latch spring
12 Cylinder stop plunder with
    spring

SPECIFICATIONS
Model: 4510TKR-3SSMAG
Action: revolver; SA/DA
Overall Length: 9.5 in. (3 in. barrel)
Overall Height: 6.2 in.
Overall Width: 1.5 in.
Barrel: 2.5 in. (Public Defender model), 3 in.
Weight Unloaded: 20.7 oz
Caliber: .45 LC/.410 Gauge
Capacity: 5
Common Features: matte stainless steel frame, barrel, cylinder; ribbed rubber grips; fiber optic dovetail front/fixed rear; 2.5 in. or 3-in. chamber, some models with ported barrels; some models with blued finish

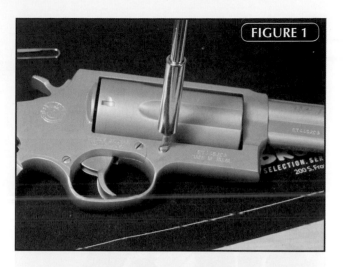

FIGURE 1

BACKGROUND
The Taurus Judge innovatively chambers the .45 Long Colt cartridge and the .410 shot shell in a revolver offering a versatile option for self defense. The design is similar to other Taurus revolvers, but by no means are parts interchangeable. The distinctive stretched frame and cylinder accommodates the .410 shot shell.
Year Introduced: 2007
Country of Origin: Brazil
Current Manufacturers: Taurus (taurususa.com)
Similar Models: Public Defender

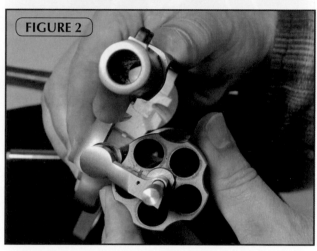

FIGURE 2

REQUIRED TOOLS
Field Stripping: none
Disassembly/Assembly: small standard screwdriver, pliers, small punch, rubber/nylon mallet, hex or Allen wrench, small nail or paper clip

CYLINDER DISASSEMBLY
1. Remove the rubber grip (part #51) by unscrewing the grip screw (52) at the butt of the grip using a hex or Allen wrench. Slide the grip off the frame (16).

2. Remove the most forward screw, yoke screw (47), on the frame using a small standard screwdriver, Figure 1.

3. Push the cylinder latch, thumb piece (17), forward and swing out the cylinder assembly. Align one of the cylinder flutes with the flange at the front of the frame.

4. Pull the yoke (19) and cylinder assembly out toward the muzzle, Figure 2.

5. To remove the ejector rod, extractor rod (14), use your fingers or a pair of padded pliers and grip the end

of the ejector rod and turn clockwise—these are left-hand threads—looking at the front of the cylinder (8). If the extractor rod is stubborn place the extractor rod in a padded vise and unscrew the cylinder. The extractor rod can then be removed from the front of the cylinder, Figure 3.

FIGURE 3

FRAME DISASSEMBLY

1. To remove the main spring assembly (40), remove the three side plate screws (50) and flip the frame in your hand so the thumb piece faces up. Using a nylon or rubber mallet, tap the frame to release the side plate (46) in your hand, Figure 4. Do not pry the side plate off

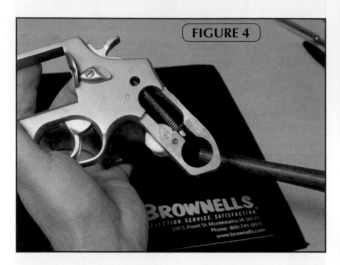

FIGURE 4

as you can mar and damage the side plate and frame. The firing pin retaining pin (21) may fall out when the side plate falls free.

2. Move the thumb piece rearward and cock the hammer assembly (24) and insert a small nail or paper clip in the main spring center pin (41), Figure 5. Ease

FIGURE 5

the hammer assembly forward and remove the main spring assembly, which consists of the main spring center pin, main spring and main spring plate (43). Warning the main spring assembly is under spring compression.

Disassemble Tip: With Taurus and Smith and Wesson revolvers, if the side plate is rusted in place or stuck from oil and debris, cock the revolver and place a small wedge of hardwood between the frame and side plate and gently tap the wedge until the side plate breaks free while gently and evenly prying the side plate near the trigger and main spring.

To reassemble follow the disassembly instructions in reverse order.

Reassembly Tip: The side plate has a small flange at the top which must be inserted into the frame first, then use a rubber mallet or nylon hammer to seat the side plate into the frame.

Rimfire Semi-Automatic Pistols

BROWNING BUCK MARK

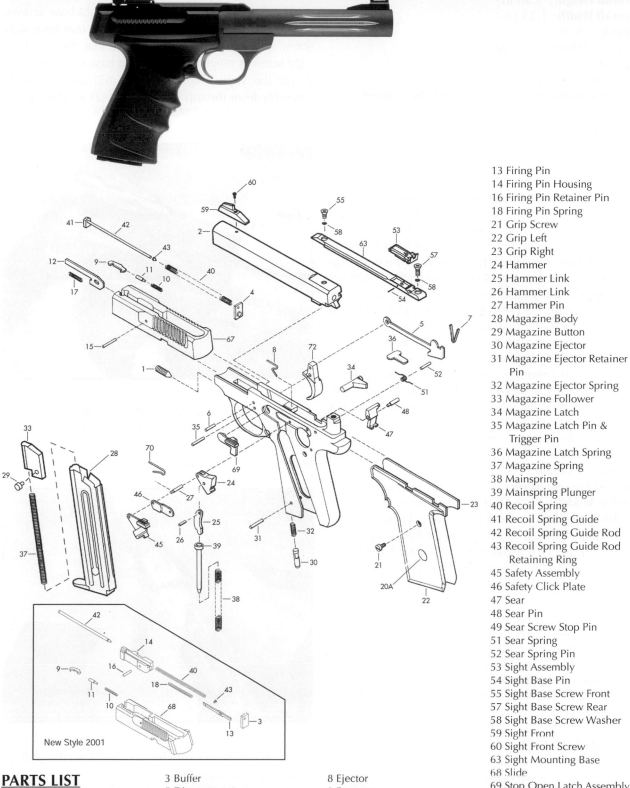

13 Firing Pin
14 Firing Pin Housing
16 Firing Pin Retainer Pin
18 Firing Pin Spring
21 Grip Screw
22 Grip Left
23 Grip Right
24 Hammer
25 Hammer Link
26 Hammer Link
27 Hammer Pin
28 Magazine Body
29 Magazine Button
30 Magazine Ejector
31 Magazine Ejector Retainer
   Pin
32 Magazine Ejector Spring
33 Magazine Follower
34 Magazine Latch
35 Magazine Latch Pin &
   Trigger Pin
36 Magazine Latch Spring
37 Magazine Spring
38 Mainspring
39 Mainspring Plunger
40 Recoil Spring
41 Recoil Spring Guide
42 Recoil Spring Guide Rod
43 Recoil Spring Guide Rod
   Retaining Ring
45 Safety Assembly
46 Safety Click Plate
47 Sear
48 Sear Pin
49 Sear Screw Stop Pin
51 Sear Spring
52 Sear Spring Pin
53 Sight Assembly
54 Sight Base Pin
55 Sight Base Screw Front
57 Sight Base Screw Rear
58 Sight Base Screw Washer
59 Sight Front
60 Sight Front Screw
63 Sight Mounting Base
68 Slide
69 Stop Open Latch Assembly
70 Stop Open Latch Spring
72 Trigger

New Style 2001

PARTS LIST

1 Barrel Mount Screw
2 Barrel
3 Buffer
5 Disconnector
6 Disconnector Pin
7 Disconnector Spring
8 Ejector
9 Extractor
10 Extractor Spring
11 Extractor Spring Plunger

SPECIFICATIONS

Model: Buck Mark Lite Gray 5.5
Action: blowback-operated, autoloader, SA
Overall Length: 9.5 in.
Overall Height: 5.38 in.
Overall Width: 1.25 in.
Barrel: 5.5 in.
Weight Unloaded: 28 oz.
Caliber: .22 LR
Capacity: 10 + 1
Common Features: alloy frame and fluted barrel sleeve; manual thumb and magazine disconnect safeties; Ultragrip RX ambidextrous grip; fixed fiber-optic front/adj. rear sights; gold plated trigger

BACKGROUND

Buck Mark rimfire pistols started out with a distinct slab-side barrel. The popularity and the desire to customize these smallbore pistols now includes models with round and round fluted barrels. Some are Picatinny equipped for optics. A nice design feature is the spring loaded magazine ejector that propels the magazine from the butt when the magazine button is pressed. The grips play a role in keeping some parts in place so be aware that what is a simple grip swap on some pistols requires slightly more time and finesse with the Buck Mark. The pistol went through a redesign in 2001 and the instructions below are for the newer models though will work with older models with some differences. Newer model have a different firing pin assembly and a magazine disconnect safety.
Year Introduced: 1985
Country of Origin: USA
Current Manufacturer: Browning (browning.com)
Similar Models: Buck Mark Camper (matte or stainless finish), Buck Mark Contour (5.5-in or 7.25-in, bull barrel, adj. sights), Buck Mark Hunter (heavy tapered barrel, adj. sights, integral scope base), Buck Mark Lite Green (fluted barrel, adj. sights, matte green finish), Buck Mark Micro Standard URX (4-in. slabside barrel, adj. sights), Buck Mark Plus Rosewood UDX (slabside barrel, adj. sights, matte blue finish, textured rosewood grip), Buck Mark Plus Stainless UDX (slabside barrel, adj. sights, stainless finish, Ultragrip RX ambidextrous grip), Buck Mark Plus UDX (slabside barrel, adj. sights, matte blue finish, textured wood grip), Buck Mark Standard URX (slabside barrel, adj. sights, matte blue or stainless finish, Ultragrip RX ambidextrous grip)

REQUIRED TOOLS

Field Strip: medium flat blade screwdriver, 3/32 and 7/64 hex or Allen wrenches
Disassembly/Assembly: medium flat blade screwdriver, slave pin, small punch

FIELD STRIP

1. With the slide (part #67) fully forward, use a 3/32 hex or Allen wrench to remove the two sight base screws, the front base sight screw (55) and the rear base sight screw (57) and washers (58). Note that the rear base sight screw is longer than the front base sight screw.
2. Lift the sight mounting base (63) and rear sight assembly from the top of the barrel (2) and the frame, Figure 1.

FIGURE 1

3. Pull the slide back just enough to grasp the recoil spring guide rod (42) and recoil spring (40) and pull up and away from the barrel face, Figure 2. The firing pin housing (14), recoil spring guide rod, recoil spring and

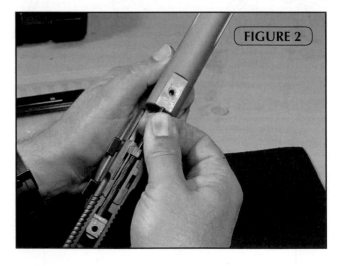

FIGURE 2

buffer (3) will then easily lift out the top of the slide as an assembly, Figure 3.
4. Next pull the slide up and off the frame.

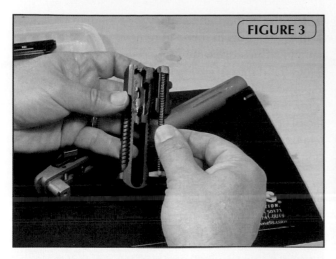

FIGURE 3

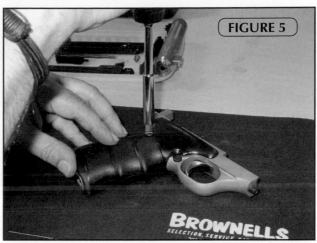

FIGURE 5

5. Use a 7/64 hex or Allen wrench to remove the barrel from the frame by backing out the barrel mount screw (1) until the barrel is free from the frame, Figure 4.

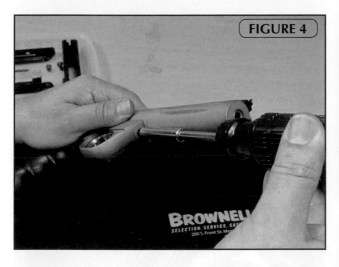

FIGURE 4

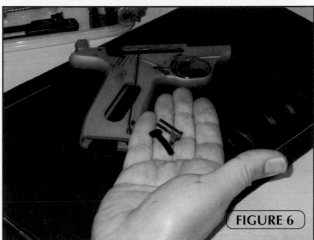

FIGURE 6

FRAME DISASSEMBLY

1. The grip, either two panels (22 and 23) or one-piece wrap around, is removed by unscrewing the two grips screws (21), one on each side. Use a medium size flat blade screwdriver, Figure 5. Note that the stop open latch on the left side of the frame and the magazine latch (34) and magazine latch spring (36) on the right side of the frame may fall free once the grip is removed, Figure 6.

2. Remove the disconnector (5) by laying the frame left side down on a padded surface and using a pair of needle-nose pliers pull out the v-shaped connector spring (7) and then pull the disconnector out of the frame, Figure 7.

3. The magazine disconnector is removed by first inserting the magazine button into the frame and inserting an empty magazine into the frame. With the empty magazine inserted the top of the magazine disconnec-

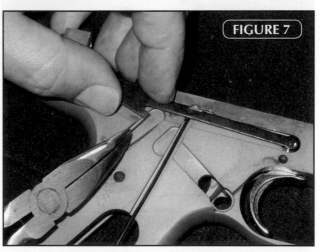

FIGURE 7

tor will pop out of place. Then unhook the bottom end of the magazine disconnector from the magazine ejector in the frame's butt, Figure 8.

4. To remove the trigger (72), drift out the disconnector pin (6) then drift out the magazine latch pin (35). Both pins are drifted out from the left to the right side of the frame.

Handguns • **133**

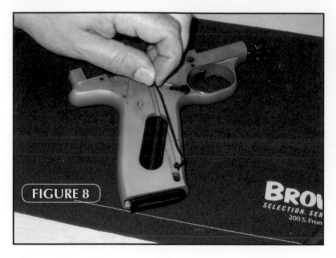

FIGURE 8

9. Lay the frame right side down and align the safety with the cut outs in frame to remove the safety.

10. Next push out the sear spring pin (52) from the left to the right.

11. The mainspring is removed by inserting a small screwdriver or punch in the top of the frame to depress the mainspring plunger freeing the slave pin/punch that retains the mainspring. Note the mainspring is under tension so control it once the slave pin/punch is removed.

Reassemble in reverse order.

5. For the safety (45), sear (47) and hammer (24) to be removed the mainspring (38) must be compressed by pressing down on the hammer and inserting a slave pin or punch through the frame to capture the mainspring plunger (39), Figure 9.

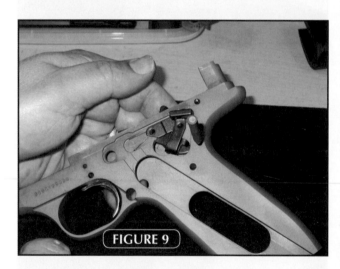

FIGURE 9

6. Using a small punch, slightly push in the sear pin (48) from left to right until it clears the safety click plate (46). Note that the smaller diameter end of the sear pin fits into the safety click plate.

7. Next lift the safety click plate off the hammer pin (27) then move it forward and out from between the frame and safety.

8. Remove the hammer pin by drifting it from the right side of the frame to the left side of the frame. The stop open latch spring (70) is connected to hammer pin. With the hammer pin removed, the hammer and the hammer link (25), which are connected via the hammer link pin (26) can be removed from the top of the frame. Note the safety will fall into the frame once the hammer pin is removed.

Reassembly Tip: Inserting an empty magazine in the frame can help keep the parts in place. Position the stop open latch in the left side of frame, Figure 10. Then replace the grip panel. Do the same for the right side of the frame with the magazine latch and magazine latch spring, Figure 11. If the grip is one-piece place the stop open latch in the left side of frame and pull the grip over it to secure it. Then place the magazine spring in place and secure the grip.

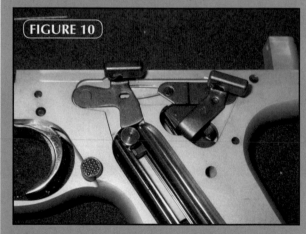

FIGURE 10

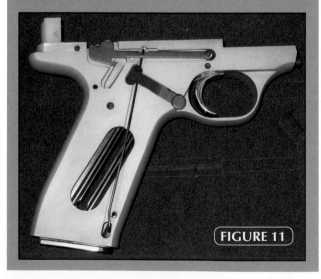

FIGURE 11

Tactical Buck: Tactical Solutions (tacticalsol.com) manufactures drop-in barrels for Buck Mark pistols manufactured with an aluminum sleeve surrounding a steel barrel liner. The feed ramp and barrel block are stainless. Optional threaded barrels accept Tactical Solutions compensator with 360° gas ports or their Cascade series suppressors.

KEL-TEC PMR-30

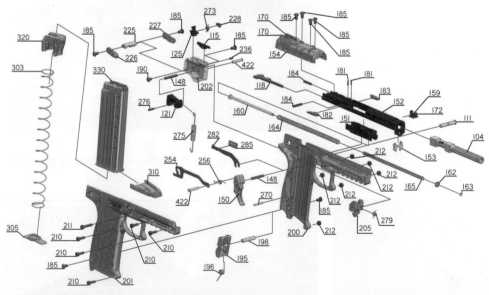

PARTS LIST

104 Barrel
111 Assembly Pin
115 Ejector
118 Firing Pin
121 Hammer
125 Sear
148 Trigger Axis
150 Trigger

151 Barrel Block
152 Slide
153 Buffer
154 Slide Cover
159 Fiber Front Sight
160 Recoil Spring Guide
162 Recoil Spring Catch
163 Recoil Spring Guide
    Locking Ring
164 Outer Recoil Spring

165 Inner Recoil Spring
170 Rear Sight Fiber
172 Front Sight Fiber
181 Extractor Axis
182 Extractor Right
183 Extractor Left
184 Extractor Spring
185 Slide Cover Screw
190 Receiver Screw
195 Magazine Catch

196 Magazine Catch Spring
198 Magazine Catch Axis
200 Grip Left
201 Grip Right
202 Receiver
205 Feedramp
210 M3-10 Socket Head
211 M3-16 Socket Head
212 M3 Nut
225 Safety
226 Safety Lever Right
227 Safety Lever Left
228 Safety Snap
236 Ejector Pin
254 Trigger Bar
256 Trigger Spring
270 Hammer Spring Catch
273 Sear Spring
275 Hammer Spring
276 Hammer Spring Pin
279 Slide Stop Spring
282 Slide Stop Brazement
285 Slide Stop Button
303 Magazine Spring
305 Magazine Spring Plate
310 Magazine Bottom Plate
320 Magazine Follower
330 Magazine Body
422 Sear Axis

SPECIFICATIONS

Model: PMR-30
Action: semiautomatic, blowback operated
Action: blowback-operated, autoloader, SA
Overall Length: 7.9 in.
Overall Height: 5.8 in.
Overall Width: 1.3 in.
Barrel: 4.3 in.
Caliber: .22 Mag
Capacity: 30 + 1
Common Features: adj. rear/fixed front sights; manual safety; matte finish; aluminum frame; steel slide and barrel; polymer grip, slide cover, trigger, magazine release and safety levers; Picatinny rail

BACKGROUND

The PMR-30 is full size, polymer-framed pistol chambered in .22 Magnum with a magazine capacity of 30 rounds. It is light weight even with a fully loaded magazine. The mechanism is a hybrid of blow back and locked-breech systems. The mechanism works with a variety ammunition with different cartridge pressures.
Year Introduced: 2011
Country of Origin: USA
Current Manufacturer: Kel-Tec CNC Industries, Inc. (keltecweapons.com)

REQUIRED TOOLS

Field Strip: small punch

FIELD STRIP

1. Remove the magazine, cycle the slide (part #152) to cock the hammer (121) and engage the safety lever (226 right, 227, left).

2. Use a small punch—in a pinch the tip of a cartridge will do—to push out and remove the assembly pin (111), Figure 1.

3. Move the slide assembly forward and off of the grip assembly, Figure 2.

FIGURE 2

4. Turn the slide assembly topside down then grasp the recoil spring assembly—recoil spring guide (160), outer recoil spring (164) and inner recoil spring (165)—near the barrel block (151) to slightly compress the springs and free them, Figure 3. Lift the recoil spring assembly up controlling the tension on the springs.

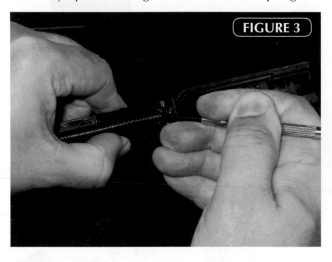

FIGURE 3

5. Remove the buffer (153) from the front of the slide (152), Figure 4.

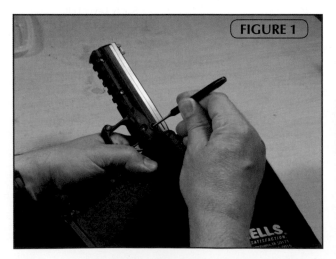

FIGURE 1

FIGURE 4

6. Slide the barrel block fully forward and lift it out of the slide, Figure 5.

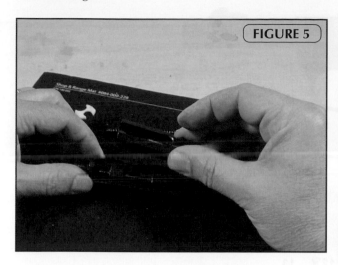

FIGURE 5

The PMR-30 is now fully field stripped for cleaning.

Reassemble is reverse order.

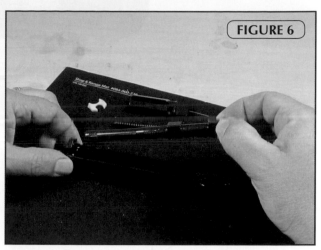

FIGURE 6

7. Flip the slide over and the barrel (104) will fall free, Figure 6.

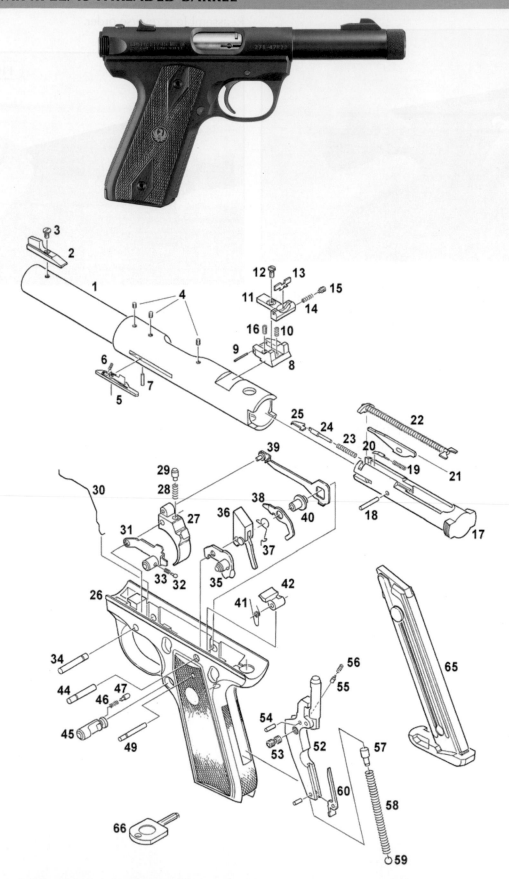

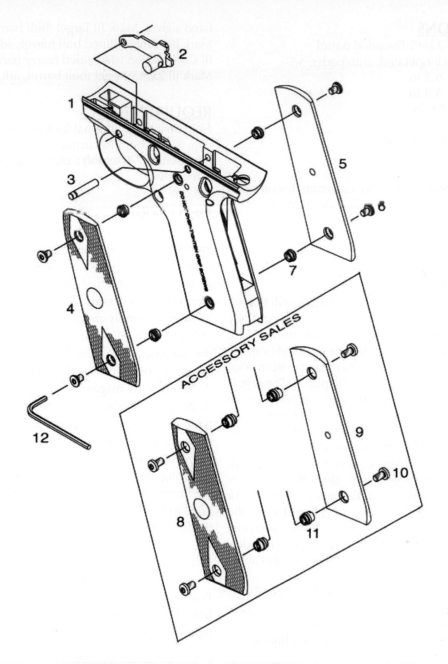

PARTS LIST

1 Barrel/Receiver Assembly
2 Front Sight
3 Front Sight Screw
4 Barrel/Receiver Filler Screws, 3 Req'd.
5 Loaded Chamber Indicator
6 Loaded Chamber Indicator Spring
7 Loaded Chamber Indicator Pin
8 Rear Sight Body
9 Rear Sight Pivot Pin
10 Rear Sight Elevation Spring
11 Rear Sight Base
12 Rear Sight Elevation Screw
13 Rear Sight Blade
14 Rear Sight Windage Spring
15 Rear Sight Windage Adjustment Screw

16 Rear Sight Base Set Screw
17 Bolt
18 Firing Pin Stop
19 Rebound Spring
20 Rebound Spring Support
21 Firing Pin
22 Recoil Spring Assembly
23 Extractor Spring
24 Extractor Plunger
25 Extractor
26 Grip Frame with Trigger Guard
27 Trigger
28 Trigger Spring
29 Trigger Spring Plunger
30 Trigger Pivot Retainer
31 Bolt Stop Assembly
32 Bolt Stop Plunger
33 Bolt Stop Plunger Spring
34 Trigger Pivot Pin

35 Safety Assembly, Complete
36 Hammer Assembly, Complete
37 Magazine Disconnector Spring
38 Magazine Disconnector
39 Disconnector Assembly
40 Hammer Bushing
41 Sear Spring
42 Sear
43 Bolt Stop Thumbpiece
44 Hammer Pivot Pin
45 Magazine Latch
46 Magazine Latch Spring
47 Magazine Latch Spring Plunger
48 Magazine Latch Screw
49 Sear Pivot Pin
50 Sear Spring Stop Pin

51 Magazine Latch Pin, 2 Req'd.
52 Mainspring Housing Assembly
53 Lock Pin
54 Spring Back-up Pin
55 Lock Detent Plunger
56 Lock Detent Plunger Spring
57 Hammer Spring Plunger
58 Hammer Spring
59 Mainspring Housing Detent Ball
60 Mainspring Housing Latch
61 Mainspring Housing Latch Pin
62 Grip Frame Filler
63 Grip Panels
64 Grip Panel Screw, 2 Req'd.
65 Magazine, Complete (10-round)
66 Internal Lock Key

SPECIFICATIONS

Model: Mark III 22/45 Threaded Barrel
Action: blowback-operated, autoloader, SA
Overall Length: 8.5 in.
Overall Height: 5.4 in.
Overall Width: 1.0 in.
Barrel: 4.5 in.
Weight Unloaded: 32.0 oz.
Caliber: .22 LR
Capacity: 10 + 1
Common Features: thumb and magazine disconnect safeties; Zytel polymer frame; alloy steel barrel; checkered polymer grips; fixed front/dovetail rear sights; frame tapped for Picatinny rail; blue finish; barrel threaded

BACKGROUND

The MK III 22/45 can trace its lineage back to Bill Ruger's garage in 1949 when he duplicated a Japanese Baby Nambu pistol that was a WWII souvenir from a U.S. Marine. Ruger took the bolt system he tweaked from the Nambu, got together some venture capital from Alex Sturm and started building .22 rimfire pistols. The pistols were inexpensive to manufacture and shooters like the nostalgic style that was similar to the Luger P08. Since that time the Standard pistol evolved to the MK II in 1982 and the MK III which features a loaded chamber indicator, magazine release behind the trigger guard, magazine disconnect safety and other details. These instructions are for a MK III 22/45 model and will work on a MK II models but with the exception that on the MK II models you will not have to insert the magazine. The 22/45 frame is polymer and MK III standard models have a steel frame. Each has its own distinct grip angle but is disassembled similarly, Figure 1.

Year Introduced: 1949 (Mark III introduced 2006)
Country of Origin: USA
Current Manufacturer: Ruger (ruger.com)
Similar Models: Mark III Standard (tapered barrel, fixed sights), Mark III Target (bull barrel, adj. sights), Mark III Hunter (fluted bull barrel, adj. sights), Mark III Competition (slab sided heavy barrel, adj. sights), Mark III 22/45 Target (bull barrel, adj. sights)

REQUIRED TOOLS

Field Stripping: internal lock key, nylon mallet, paper clip, 1/8 inch non-marring
Disassembly/Assembly: punch, small flat blade screwdriver

FIELD STRIP

1. Verify the pistol and the magazine is unloaded. Since the magazine is needed during disassembly, make sure it is unloaded.
2. Unlock the internal lock with the internal lock key (Part #66), if necessary.
3. With an empty magazine inserted, push the safety (35) in the "fire" position and pull the trigger to drop the hammer. Note the hammer must be uncocked before the pistol can be disassembled.
4. Remove the magazine.
5. Next use the loop of a paperclip to pry open the mainspring housing latch (66) located in the oval recess of the back of the grip, Figure 2. A small flat blade screwdriver will also work in lieu of the paperclip.
6. Swing the mainspring housing assembly out from the frame (26) and pull it downward, Figure 3. You may need to gently tap the bolt stop pin from the topside of the barrel/receiver assembly (1) if the mainspring housing assembly is tight. Use a non-marring punch and hammer.
7. Next insert the empty magazine into the frame. Point the muzzle upward and pull the trigger (27). The bolt (17) can then be easily removed from the barrel/receiver assembly.

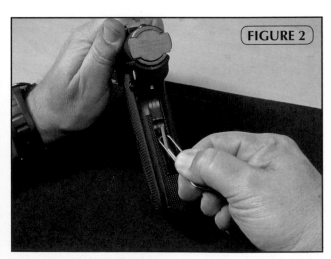

FIGURE 1

FIGURE 2

FIGURE 3

8. Remove the magazine.

9. To disengage the barrel/receiver assembly from the frame, use a nylon hammer to tap the rear of barrel/receiver assembly forward.

At this point the pistol can be cleaned.

FRAME DISASSEMBLY

1. To remove the trigger and bolt stop (31), use a small flat blade screwdriver to press down on the trigger pivot retainer (30) sandwiched between the trigger and frame. While keeping pressure on the trigger pivot retainer push it down and out of the groove in the trigger pivot pin (34).

> **Reassembly Tip:** The trigger pivot retainer is grooved on one end. Insert the non-grooved end first on the right side of the frame. The retainer will click into place with finger pressure.

2. Rotate the trigger and disconnector assembly up and out of the trigger guard, Figure 4. The trigger, trigger spring (28) and trigger plunger (29) can now easily be removed from the disconnector.

FIGURE 4

3. Rotate the bolt stop assembly down so the trigger pin hole of the bolt stop is sticking out of the trigger slot in the frame and the opposite end of the bolt stop is free from the notch in the frame. Be careful to capture the bolt stop plunger (32) and bolt stop plunger spring (33).

4. To remove the hammer (36) and safety (35), first remove the grip panels to access the hammer pin. Next use a small flat blade screw driver to push the sear spring (41) out of the groove in the hammer pivot pin (44) and then push the hammer pivot pin out of the frame, Figure 5. The disconnector assembly (39), hammer bushing (40), hammer assembly (36), magazine disconnector spring (37) and safety assembly (35)

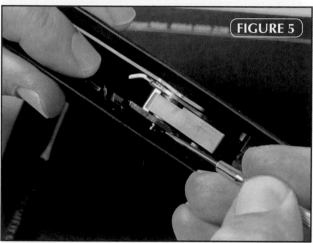

FIGURE 5

can now be easily removed from the top of the frame. Note it is not necessary to remove the trigger to remove the hammer and safety.

> **Tuning Tip:** It's easy to trick out a Ruger rimfire pistol. Numerous aftermarket triggers and accurizing kits for the Mark III and 22/45 from manufacturers like Volquartsen (volquartsen.com) and Majestic Arms (majesticarms.com) make it simple and easy. Remember to follow the manufacturers' instruction to ensure it's simple, easy and safe.

5. With the hammer removed, the sear (42) can be removed by pushing out the sear pivot pin (49) from the frame. Remove the sear and sear spring (41).

BOLT DISASSEMBLY

1. Remove the recoil spring assembly (22). Next remove the firing pin (21) by pushing out the firing pin stop (18) with a punch, Figure 6.

2. To remove the extractor (25) use a small screwdriver to push down and hold the extractor plunger (24) and extractor spring (23) while rotating the claw of the

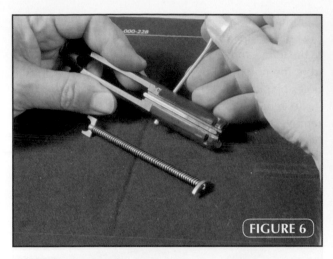

FIGURE 6

FIGURE 7

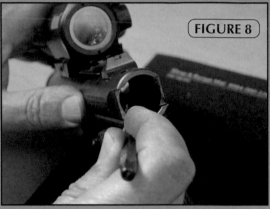

FIGURE 8

extractor toward the bolt face then slide it out from the bolt. Ease off on the extractor spring and it and the extractor plunger can be removed.

Reassemble sub assemblies in reverse order.

Reassembly Tip: The hammer and the magazine are two critical pieces with Mark III models. At certain points in the reassembly procedure the hammer must be in the correct position when parts are reassembled and the magazine must be in place so the trigger can be pulled as Mark III models have a magazine disconnect safety.

When reassembling after field strip, first make sure the safe in on the "fire" position and the hammer is cocked. Make sure the hammer strut rests on the outside of the cross pin.

When reassembling the barrel/receiver to the frame make sure the loaded chamber indicator pin is flush in the receiver. Line up the lug of the grip frame with the notch in the barrel/receiver. Note that the grip frame with slightly over hang the barrel receiver, Figure 7. With muzzle on a padded bench surface, use a nylon mallet to tap the rear of the grip frame so it slides along the barrel receiver. Next insert an empty magazine and point the muzzle up and pull the trigger so the hammer will fall to the rear of the receiver. Look through the rear of the receiver to be sure the hammer lays flat. If not use a small punch to push the hammer down flat, Figure 8. Remove the magazine and make sure the slide stop lever is in the down position.

Before sliding the bolt into the receiver be certain that the firing pin stop pin is in the bolt. Insert the bolt assembly with the recoil spring assembly facing upward into the receiver. Insert and empty magazine. Point the muzzle downward and pull the trigger. The hammer should fall fully forward. If it does not use a small punch to push it forward, Figure 9. Remove the magazine. Install the mainspring housing strut assembly into the

rear of the frame by first inserting the large pin so in protrudes from the top of the receiver. Point the muzzle up and swing the mainspring housing strut assembly into the rear of the frame. Note you will feel spring tension. Push the mainspring housing strut assembly until it is flush with the frame and push the latch forward so it locks into place.

When the mainspring housing strut assembly is locked into place check to be sure the pistols is assembled correctly by pulling back the bolt fully and locking it back. If you cannot fully retract the bolt that means the hammer was in the incorrect position during reassembly. Remove the mainspring housing strut assembly and make sure the hammer is fully forward.

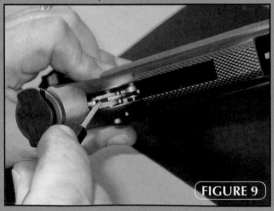

FIGURE 9

PARTS LIST

1a Barrel
1b Barrel
1c Barrel
2 Recoil spring guide
3a Recoil spring, white (standard)
3b Recoil spring (high velocity)
4 Slide
5a Front sight
5b Front sight
5c Front sight
6 Rear Sight
7 Slide breech block pin
8 Trigger bar spring
9 Breech block
10 Extractor
11 Firing pin

12 Firing pin spring
13 Safety lock
14 Safety lock spring
15 Frame
16 Takedown lever
17 Striker pin for integral safety lock
18 Slide catch lever
19 Slide catch lever spring
20 Trigger
21 Trigger pivot
22 Trigger bar
23 Lock
24 Sear
25 Takedown lever insert
27 Spring for integral safety lock
28 Safety lever
29 Hammer
30 Spring for safety lever
31 Ball for safety lever
32 Ejector
33 Hammer strut
34 Mainspring
35 Action casing half (left)
36 Ball centering
37 Action casing half (right)
38 Extractor spring
39 Magazine safety
40 Decocking lever
41 Decocking lever bearing
42 Decocking lever spring
43 Magazine catch
44 Safety lever (Manual safety), right
45 Magazine catch spring
46 Safety lever (Manual safety), left
47 Feeder axle
48 Grip plate, right
49 Grip plate, left
50 Grip plate screws
51 Magazine tube
52 Magazine spring
53 Feeder
54 Magazine floor plate
55 Floorplate insert
56 Threaded socket for grip plates
57 Retainer
58 Screw for grip
59 Hammer reset spring
60 Hammer pivot pin
61 Hammer strut pin
62 Trigger bar pin
63 Spring for magazine safety
64 Safety lever pin
65 Magazine safety pivot pin
66 Screw for decocking lever
67 Screw for safety lever

68 Adjusting screw
69 Key
70 Main spring washer
71 Main spring washer
72 Key ring

73 Extractor guide
74 Extractor pivot pin
75 Breech block pin
76 Breech block spring
77 Counterweight

78 Cap
79 Threaded pin
80 Allen wrench
81 Threaded cap
82 Assembly wrench

SPECIFICATIONS

Model: Mosquito
Action: blowback-operated, autoloader, DA/SA trigger
Overall Length: 7.2 in., 8.3 in. (threaded barrel model)
Overall Height: 5.3 in.
Overall Width: 1.5 in.
Barrel: 3.9 in., 4.9 in. (threaded barrel)
Weight Unloaded: 24.6 oz.
Caliber: .22 LR
Capacity: 10 + 1
Common Features: ambidextrous thumb and magazine safeties; polymer frame and grips; adjustable front/rear sights; Picatinny rail; various finishes (matte Nitron, digital camo, Two-Tone)

BACKGROUND

The Mosquito is a scaled down rimfire version of SIG's P226 centerfire pistol chambered in 9mm, .357 SIG or .40 S&W. The Mosquito's controls—take down lever, slide stop and decocker lever—are similar to the P226's. Differences in the Mosquito include an ambidextrous thumb safety located on the slide, polymer frame and integral safety lock that once engaged prevents the firing of the pistol.
Year Introduced: 2005
Country of Origin: Germany, Switzerland, USA
Current Manufacturers: SIG SAUER (sigsauer.com)
Similar Models: Threaded barrel (4.9 in. barrel), counter weight slide

REQUIRED TOOLS

Field Stripping: none
Disassembly/Assembly: punch, small standard screwdriver, Loctite

FIELD STRIP

1. Remove the magazine and pull back on the slide (part #4) to ensure no cartridges are in the chamber.
2. Rotate the take down lever (16) clockwise until it points forward.
3. Retract the slide assemble fully and lift up on the rear of the slide, Figure 1. The slide will disengage from the frame (15). Take caution to control the slide as the recoil (3a or 3b) is compressed. Move the slide forward toward the muzzle and remove the slide assembly, Figure 2.
4. Remove the recoil spring and recoil spring guide (2) and lock (23).
At this point no further disassembly is needed to clean the Mosquito.

FIGURE 1

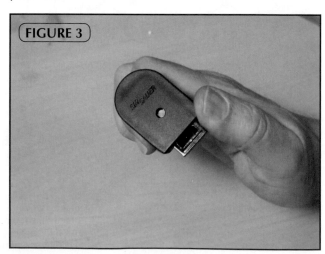
FIGURE 2

MAGAZINE DISASSEMBLY

1. To disassemble the magazine assembly, depress the floorplate insert (55) with a small punch or screwdriver so it clears the magazine floorplate (54) and slide the magazine floorplate off the magazine tube (51), Figure 3. Take caution as the magazine spring (52) is under compression.

FIGURE 3

FRAME DISASSEMBLY

1. To remove the barrel (1a standard barrel, 1b counter weight slide or 1c threaded barrel) use a small standard screwdriver to unscrew the take down lever screw (66) and remove the take down lever.

2. Unscrew the barrel screw (58) and using a screwdriver gently pry the barrel up from the frame (15), Figure 4.

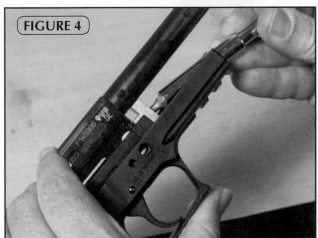

FIGURE 4

It is not recommended to further disassemble the pistol as complete maintenance and cleaning can be performed following the previous steps. Within the frame is the action casing sandwiched between the left action casing (35) and the right action casing (37). The entire assembly is under pressure from the main spring (34). Caution is advised when removing this assembly.

To reassemble follow the disassembly instructions in reverse order starting with the barrel.

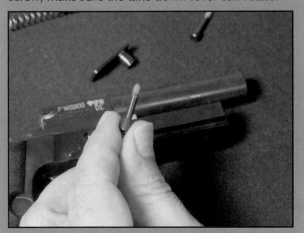

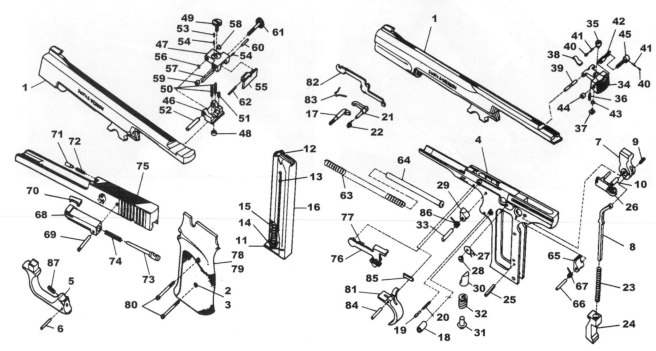

PARTS LIST

01 Barrel
02 Escutcheon
03 Escutcheon Nut
05 Guard
06 Trigger Guard Pin
07 Hammer Assembly
08 Stirrup
09 Stirrup Pin
10 Hammer Pin
11 Magazine Buttplate
12 Magazine Assembly
13 Magazine Pin
14 Magazine Spring Plunger
15 Magazine Spring
16 Magazine Tube
17 Magazine Catch
18 Magazine Catch Nut

19 Magazine Catch Plunger
20 Magazine Catch Spring
21 Magazine Disconnector
22 Magazine Disconnector Spring
23 Mainspring
24 Mainspring Retainer
25 Mainspring Retainer Pin
26 Safety, Manual
27 Safety Spring Plate, Manual
28 Safety Spring Plate Screw, Manual
29 Pawl
30 Pawl Cam
31 Pawl Cam Plunger
32 Pawl Cam Spring
33 Pawl Pin
34 Rear Sight Body, For 7" Barrel
35 Rear Sight Elevation Nut, For 7" Barrel
36 Rear Sight Elevation Spring, For 7" Barrel

37 Rear Sight Elevation Stud, For 7" Barrel
38 Rear Sight Pivot Clip, For 7" Barrel
39 Rear Sight Pivot Pin, For 7" Barrel
40 Rear Sight Plunger, For 7" Barrel (2 Req'd.)
41 Rear Sight Plunger Spring, For 7" Barrel (2 Req'd.)
42 Rear Sight Slide, .213, For 7" Barrel
43 Rear Sight Spring Clip, For 7" Barrel
44 Rear Sight Windage Nut, For 7" Barrel
45 Rear Sight Windage Screw, For 7" Barrel
46 60320 Rear Sight Base, For 5-1/2" Barrel
47 Rear Sight Body, For 5-1/2" Barrel
48 Rear Sight Elevation Nut, For 5-1/2" Barrel
49 Rear Sight Elevation Screw, For 5-1/2" Barrel
50 Rear Sight Elevation Spring, For 5-1/2" Barrel, (2 Req'd.)

51 Rear Sight Lock Screw, For 5-1/2" Barrel	62 Rear Sight Windage Spring, For 5-1/2" Barrel	74 Firing Pin Spring
52 Rear Sight Pivot Pin, For 5-1/2" Barrel	63 Recoil Spring	75 Slide Assembly
53 Rear Sight Plunger, For 5-1/2" Barrel	64 Recoil Spring Guide	76 Slide Stop & Ejector Assembly
54 Rear Sight Plunger Spring, For 5-1/2" Barrel	65 Sear	77 Slide Stop Spring
55 Rear Sight Slide, For 5-1/2" Barrel	66 Sear Pin	78 & 79 Stocks, Checkered Walnut
56 Rear Sight Spring Clip, For 5-1/2" Barrel	67 Sear Spring	80 Stock Screw (2 Req'd.)
57 Rear Sight Traverse/Pin, For 5-1/2" Barrel	68 Bolt	81 Trigger
58 Rear Sight Wavy Washer, For 5-1/2" Barrel	69 Bolt Pin	82 Trigger Bar
59 Rear Sight Windage Nut, For 5-1/2" Barrel	70 Extractor	83 Trigger Bar Spring
60 Rear Sight Windage Plunger, For 5-1/2" Barrel	71 Extractor Plunger	84 Trigger Pin
61 Rear Sight Windage Screw, For 5-1/2" Barrel	72 Extractor Spring	85 Trigger Pull Adjusting Lever
	73 Firing Pin	86 Trigger Spring
		87 Trigger Stop Screw

SPECIFICATIONS

Model: Model 41
Action: blowback-operated, autoloader, SA
Overall Length: 10.5 in. (5.5 in. barrel)
Overall Height: 5 in.
Overall Width: 1.73 in.
Barrel: 5.5 in. or 7 in.
Weight Unloaded: 41 oz. (5.5 in. barrel)
Caliber: .22 LR
Capacity: 12 + 1
Common Features: thumb safety; micrometer click adj. target rear/undercut partridge front sights; checkered wood target grips, target trigger with adj. trigger stop; blued finish

BACKGROUND

The Model 41 is a top of the line rimfire pistol used in national level competition. It is considered one of the best .22 target pistols ever manufactured. The design is simple and it has the feature of easily swapping barrels. Life is too short to shoot an inaccurate .22 pistol.
Year Introduced: 1957
Country of Origin: USA
Current Manufacturers: Smith & Wesson (smith-wesson.com)

REQUIRED TOOLS

Field Stripping: none
Disassembly/Assembly: small flat blade screwdriver, small punch, brass hammer, needle-nose pliers

FIELD STRIP

1. Remove the magazine (part #12) then retracted the slide (75) rearward locking it back by pressing up on the slide stop lever (76).
2. Rotate the trigger guard (5) down, Figure 1. Lift off the barrel (1) from the frame (4), Figure 2.
3. Grasp the slide and pull it back and up, Figure 3. Control it forward and off the frame, Figure 4. The recoil spring (63) is under compression.
4. Remove recoil spring and recoil spring guide (64) from slide.

At this point the Model 41 is sufficiently disassembled for routine cleaning.

FIGURE 1

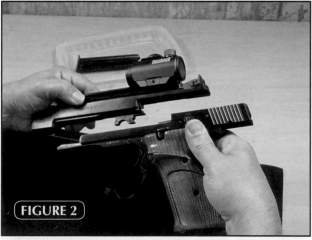

FIGURE 2

Maintenance Tip: There are two lubrication points on the left and right slide grooves of the frame. Apply a single drop of oil after cleaning.

SLIDE DISASSEMBLY

1. Use a small punch to drift out the bolt pin (69) from the right to the left side of the slide, Figure 5.
2. With the bolt pin removed, use a non-marring punch to drift the bolt (68) forward in the slide. Once the extractor (70) claw the slot in the slide the bolt assembly can be removed from the slide.
3. Remove from the bolt the extractor, firing pin (73) and firing pin spring (74).

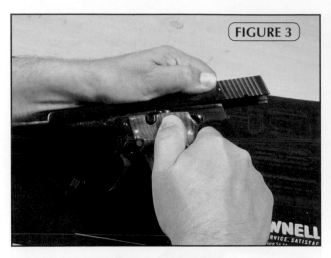
FIGURE 3

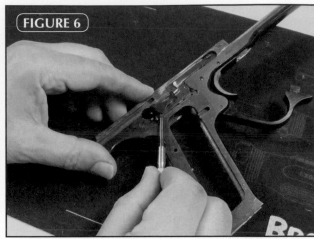
FIGURE 6

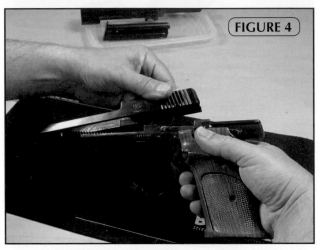
FIGURE 4

3. Remove the trigger bar spring (83) and then pull and rotate the trigger bar (82) from the frame.

4. Make sure the hammer is in the forward/"fired" position and drift out the mainspring retainer pin (25). The mainspring (23) and mainspring retainer (24) will fall free from the butt of the frame. Note the mainspring is under tension.

To reassemble follow the disassembly instructions in reverse order.

Tuning Tip: The Model 41 allows the user to adjust the trigger pull between two and three pounds by moving the adjustment lever forward or backward. Each notch in the adjustment lever is about ¼ pound. With the pistol field stripped, use a small punch to partially drift out the trigger pivot pin (84) from the right to the left side of the frame. Drift out the trigger pivot pin about half way and clear of the adjustment lever (85). Move the adjustment lever toward the muzzle to increase trigger pull or to the rear to decrease trigger pull. Once the adjustment lever is at the desired position drift the trigger pivot pin back in place.

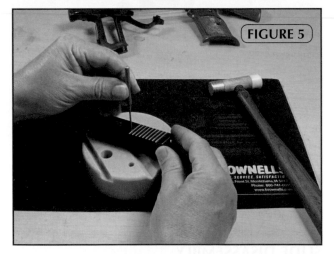
FIGURE 5

4. Pull forward to remove the extractor plunger (71) and extractor spring (72) from the slide.

FRAME DISASSEMBLY

1. Remove left and right stock (78 & 79) using a small flat blade screwdriver.

2. The magazine disconnector (21) is removed by pulling up and off the frame, Figure 6.

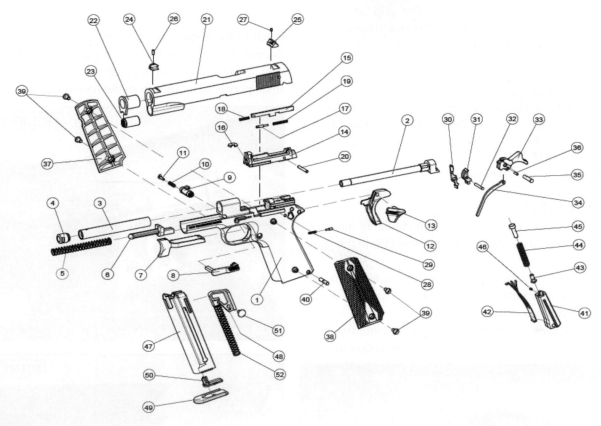

PARTS LIST

1 Receiver
2 Barrel
3 Barrel Sleeve
4 Barrel nut
5 Recoil Spring
6 Recoil Spring Guide
7 Trigger
8 Slide Stop
9 Magazine Catch
10 Spring
11 Magazine Catch Lock
12 Grip Safety

13 Safety Lever
14 Breech Block
15 Firing Pin
16 Extractor
17 Pin for Extractor
18 Spring
19 Spring
20 Dowel Pin
21 Slide
22 Barrel Bushing
23 Recoil Spring Plug
24 Front Sight
25 Rear Sight
26 Grub Screw

27 Grub Screw
28 Spring
29 Safety Lever Plunger
30 Disconnector
31 Sear
32 Pin
33 Hammer
34 Hammer Strut
35 Pin
36 Pin
37 Grip Panel, Right
38 Grip Panel, Left
39 Grip Panel Screw
40 Pin

41 Main Housing
42 Sear Spring
43 Pin Retainer
44 Main Spring
45 Mainspring Cap
46 Dowel Pin
47 Magazine Body
48 Magazine Follower
49 Magazine Butt Plate
50 Butt Plate Holder
51 Magazine Button
52 Magazine Spring

SPECIFICATIONS

Model: Colt 1911 Rail
Action: blowback-operated, autoloader, SA
Overall Length: 8.6 in.
Overall Height: 5.3 in.
Overall Width: 1.5 in.
Barrel: 4.9 in.
Weight Unloaded: 36 oz.
Caliber: .22 LR
Capacity: 12 + 1
Common Features: thumb and grip safeties; drift adj. front/rear sights; Picatinny rail; matte finish

BACKGROUND

The Umarex is a full size replica of a 1911 pistol chambered in .22 Long Rifle. The grip and thumb safeties function like centerfire 1911s and the grips and sights can be interchanged with 1911 after-markets parts. Take down is totally different from the 1911.
Year Introduced: 2010
Country of Origin: Germany
Current Manufacturers: Umarex (umarexusa.com)
Similar Models: Government 1911, 1911 Gold Cup

REQUIRED TOOLS

Field Stripping: small punch

FIELD STRIP

1. Remove the magazine, cock the hammer (part #33) and then push up on the thumb safety (13) in the "safe" position.

2. Set the pistol on a padded work surface with muzzle pointing up, Figure 1. Push the recoil spring plug (23) down with your finger and rotate the barrel bushing (22) clockwise until the recoil is free. Note the recoil spring (5) is under tension. Remove the recoil spring.

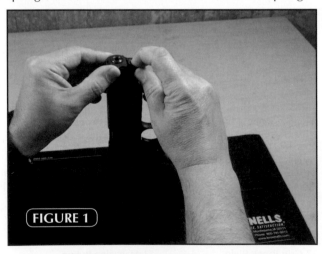

FIGURE 1

3. Rotate the barrel bushing counterclockwise until it can be pulled free from the muzzle, Figure 2.

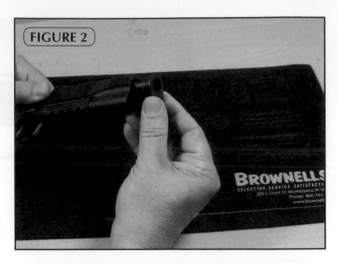

FIGURE 2

4. Disengage the thumb safety and align the disassembly notch in the frame, Umarex calls it a receiver (1), with disassembly notch in the slide, Figure 3. Push the slide stop (8) out from the right to left side of receiver using a small punch then pull it from the receiver, Figure 4.

FIGURE 3

FIGURE 4

5. Pull the slide all the way to the rear and lift the rear portion of the slide off the receiver, Figure 5. Then slide it forward along the barrel (2) and off the receiver, Figure 6.

FIGURE 5

FIGURE 6

6. Tilt the receiver muzzle down to remove the recoil spring guide (6) from the frame under the barrel.

At this point no further disassembly is needed to clean the Umarex 1911.

MAGAZINE DISASSEMBLY

1. To disassemble the magazine assembly, depress the floorplate insert (50) with a small punch or screwdriver so it clears the magazine floorplate (49) and slide the magazine floorplate off the magazine tube (47), Figure 7. Take caution as the magazine spring (52) is under compression.

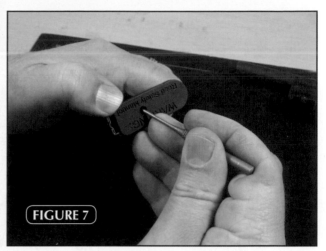

FIGURE 7

2. Slide the follower (48) and magazine spring toward the bottom of the magazine body to align the magazine button (51) with the hole in the magazine body. Pull out the magazine button from the follower.

3. Remove the magazine spring and follower from the bottom of the magazine body.

To reassemble follow the disassembly instructions in reverse order.

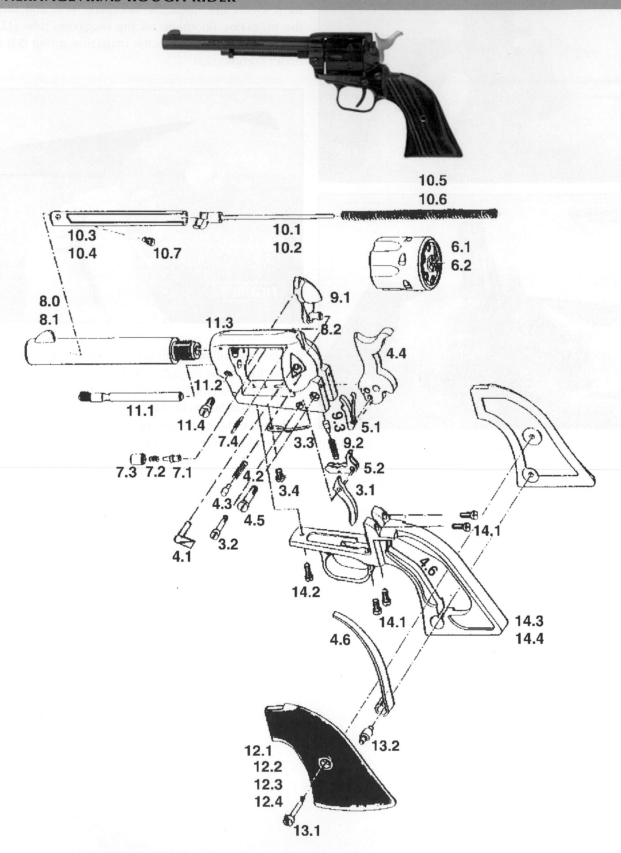

PARTS LIST

3.1 Trigger
3.2 Trigger Screw
3.3 Trigger Spring
3.4 Trigger Spring Screw
4.1 Hammer Block
4.2 Hammer Block Spring
4.3 Hammer Block Detent
4.4 Hammer
4.5 Hammer Screw
4.6 Hammer Spring
5.1 Cylinder Hand
5.2 Cylinder Bolt
6.1 Cylinder 22 LR
6.2 Cylinder 22 WMR

7.1 Firing Pin
7.2 Firing Pin Spring
7.3 Firing Pin Cup
7.4 Firing Pin Pin
8.1 Front Sight Blade
8.2 Rear Adj. Sight
9.1 Loading Gate
9.2 Loading Gate Spring
9.3 Loading Gate Detent
10.1 Ejector Rod & Lever 2 & 3"
10.2 Ejector Rod & Lever 4.75-9"
10.3 Ejector Tube 2 & 3"
10.4 Ejector Tube 4.75-9"
10.5 Ejector Spring 2 & 3"
10.6 Ejector Spring 4.75-9"
10.7 Ejector Tube Screw

11.1 Base Pin
11.2 Base Pin Lock Spring
11.3 Base Pin Lock Nut
11.4 Base Pin Lock Screw
12.1 Grips-Cocobolo Regular
12.2 Grips-Cocobolo Bird Head
12.3 Grips- See Internet or Mother of Pearl-Regular
12.4 Grips- See Internet or Mother of Pearl-Bird Head
13.1 Grip Screw
13.2 Grip Pin
14.1 Back Strap Screws (4 Req'd.)
14.2 Back Strap-Front Screw
14.3 Back Strap-Regular
14.4 Back Strap-Bird Head

SPECIFICATIONS

Model: Rough Rider SA Small Bore Combo
Action: revolver; SA
Overall Length: 11.875 in. (6.5 in. barrel)
Overall Height: 5.1 in.
Overall Width: 1.5 in.
Barrel: 3.5 in., 4.75 in., 6.5 in. or 9 in.
Weight Unloaded: 33.4 oz. (6.5 in. barrel)
Caliber: .22 LR/.22 Magnum
Capacity: 6
Features: alloy or steel frame; combo models with extra .22 Mag, cylinder; blued, matte, silver, simulated case hardened finishes; smooth cocobolo, simulated ivory or simulated mother or pearl grips; fixed front/rear or fixed front/adj. rear sights

BACKGROUND

This Heritage Rough Rider revolver is very similar to Colt-style single action revolvers but with a manual safety, Figure 1. Unlike old-time six-shooters the firing

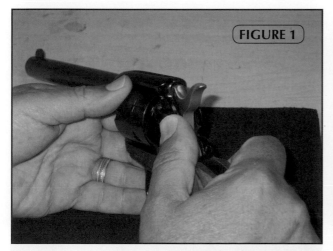

pin of the Rough Rider is not located in the hammer but in the frame. Other than that and a few other minor differences the Rough Rider is a scaled down version of a Peacemaker chambered in .22 Long Rifle. Those four clicks are a classic sound upon cocking back the hammer. Some revolvers also come with a combo .22 Magnum cylinder.

Year Introduced: 1993
Country of Origin: USA
Current Manufacturer: Heritage Manufacturing, Inc. (heritagemfg.com)
Similar Models: Bird Head grip frame

REQUIRED TOOLS

Field Stripping: none
Disassembly/Assembly: small flat blade screwdriver

FIELD STRIP

1. Pull back the hammer (part #4.4) to the second notch or click and open the loading gate (9.1).
2. Rotate the safety, Heritage Arms calls it a hammer block (4.1), to the up or "safe" position.
3. Press the base pin lock nut (11.3) and pull the base pin (11.1) toward the muzzle and out of the frame, Figure 2.

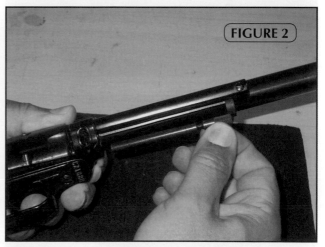

4. Remove the cylinder (6.1) from the right side of the frame, Figure 3.

At this point the revolver is sufficiently disassembled for cleaning.

FIGURE 3

DETAILED DISASSEMBLY

1. Use a small flat blade screwdriver to remove the grip screw (13.1) and remove the grips (12.1) from the back strap (14.3).

2. Next remove the five back strap screws (14.1); two near the hammer and two behind the trigger (3.1), Figure 4. For easier removal of the fifth screw, the front back strap screw (14.2), use your hand to squeeze the back strap/trigger guard to the frame, Figure 5. The hammer spring/mainspring (4.6) is applying tension to the hammer and will push the back strap away from the frame.

With the five screws removed the back strap with hammer spring/mainspring (4.6) and grip pin (13.2) will come free from the frame, Figure 6.

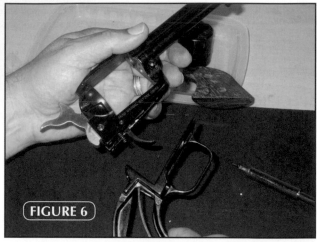

FIGURE 6

3. Remove the loading gate, loading gate spring (9.2) and loading gate detent (9.3) from the bottom of the frame, Figure 7.

4. Unscrew and remove the trigger spring screw (3.4) and the trigger spring (3.3) should fall free from the bottom of the frame, Figure 8.

5. Remove the trigger screw (3.2) from the left side of the frame and pull the trigger (3.1) and cylinder bolt (5.2) from the bottom of the frame.

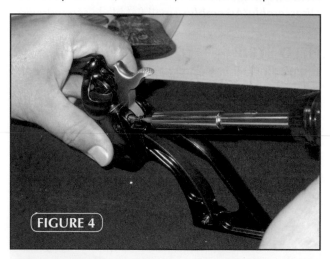

FIGURE 4

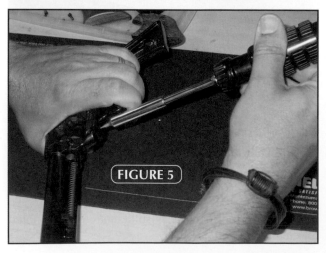

FIGURE 5

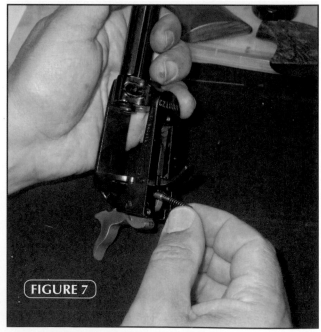

FIGURE 7

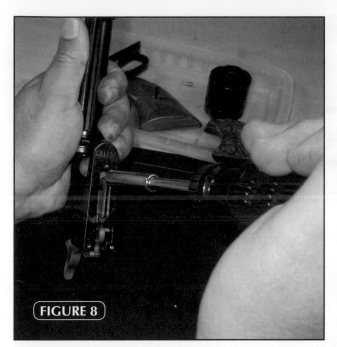

FIGURE 8

6. Remove the hammer screw (4.5) from the left side of the frame and push the hammer down and out the bottom of the frame. The cylinder hand (5.1) will be attached to the hammer.

7. Remove the ejector assembly by unscrewing the ejector tube screw (10.7) from the barrel (8.1) and lifting the ejector tube (10.3) from the frame toward the front/muzzle. Remove the ejector rod (10.1) and ejector spring (10.5) from the rear of the ejector tube. Note the ejector spring in under compression.

Reassemble in reverse order.

Reassembly Tip: Use one hand to squeeze the back strap into the frame and screw in the back strap screws closest to the hammer first.

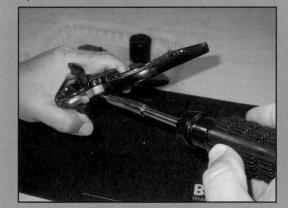

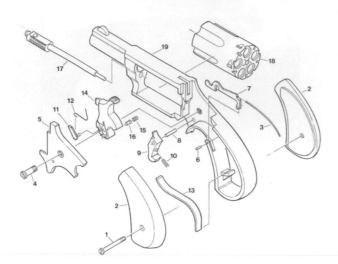

PARTS LIST

1 Grip Screw
2 Grip Rosewood
3 Bolt Spring
4 Main Screw
5 Sideplate
6 Bolt Pin
7 Cylinder Bolt
8 Trigger Pin
9 Trigger
10 Trigger Spring
11 Hand Aft
12 Hand Spring
13 Main Spring
14 Hammer
15 Index Spring
16 Index Pin
17 Cylinder Pin Assembly
18 Cylinder
19 Frame

SPECIFICATIONS

Model: .22 Long Rifle Mini-Revolver
Action: revolver; SA
Overall Length: 4.0 in. (1.1 in. barrel); 4.5 in. (1.6 in. barrel)
Overall Height: 2.4 in.
Overall Width: 0.8 in.
Barrel: 1.1 in.; 1.6 in.
Weight Unloaded: 4.5 oz. (1.1 in. barrel); 4.6 oz. (1.6 in. barrel);
Caliber: .22 LR
Capacity: 5
Features: stainless frame; spur trigger; matte stainless finish; smooth wood grips; fixed front/rear sights

BACKGROUND

This diminutive revolver is probably one of the most easily concealable firearms in production. It can even be carried in a belt buckle without much notice, Figure 1. The small stature of this revolver requires small tools. Its single action mechanism is tiny and caution be given to those who crack open

FIGURE 1

this little five shooter's sideplate as springs are tiny and yearn to be at rest. The sideplate screw is reverse threaded.

Year Introduced: 1975
Country of Origin: USA
Current Manufacturer: North American Arms (naaminis.com)
Similar Models: 22 Short, 22 Magnum, 22 Magnum Ported (ported barrel), 22 Magnum Wasp (vent rib barrel), 22 Magnum Pug (white-dot sights, rubber grip), 22 Mini Master (4-in. vent-rib barrel, adj. sights, rubber grip), Black Widow

REQUIRED TOOLS
Field Stripping: none

FIELD STRIP
1. Place the hammer (part #14) in the half-cock position.
2. Grasp the knurled portion of the cylinder pin assembly (17) between your thumb and middle finger, and depress the release button with the forefinger and withdraw the cylinder pin assembly from the frame (19), Figure 2.
3. Remove the cylinder (18) from either side of the frame, Figure 3.

At this point the mini revolver is sufficiently disassembled for cleaning.

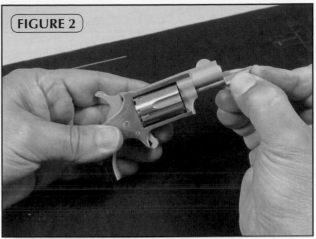

FIGURE 2

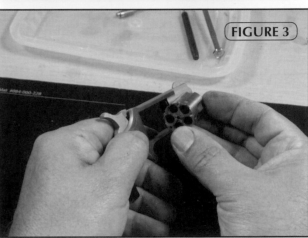

FIGURE 3

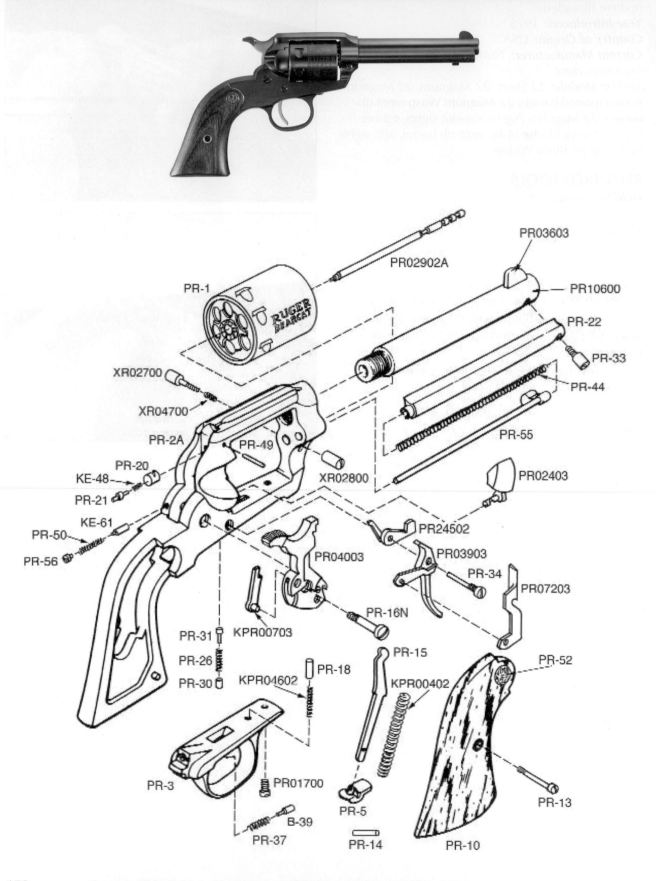

PARTS LIST

PR10600 Barrel
PR-2A Frame
PR02902A Base Pin Assembly
XR02700 Base Pin Latch Body
XR02800 Base Pin Latch Nut
XR04700 Base Pin Latch Spring
PR-1 Cylinder
PR24502 Cylinder Latch Assembly
KPR04602 Cylinder Latch Spring
PR-18 Cylinder Latch Spring Plunger
PR-22 Ejector Housing
PR-33 Ejector Housing Screw
PR-55 Ejector Rod Assembly
PR-44 Ejector Rod Spring
PR-21 Firing Pin
KE-48 Firing Pin Rebound Spring
PR03603 Front Sight
PR02403 Gate
PR-31 Gate Plunger
PR-26 Gate Plunger Spring
PR-30 Gate Spring Retaining Screw
PR-10 Grip Panels, Left and Right
PR-14 Grip Panel Dowel

XR01100 Grip Panel Ferrule, Right
XR01200 Grip Panel Ferrule, Left
PR-52 Grip Panel Medallion, 2 Req'd.
PR-13 Grip Panel Screw
PR04003 Hammer
PR-16N Hammer Pivot Pin
PR-15 Hammer Strut
KPR00402 Mainspring
PR-5 Mainspring Seat
KPR20402 Mainspring/Strut Assembly
KPR00703 Pawl
KE-61 Pawl Plunger
PR-50 Pawl Plunger Spring
PR-56 Pawl Spring Retaining Screw
PR-20 Recoil Plate
PR-49 Recoil Plate Cross Pin
PR07203 Transfer Bar
PR03903 Trigger
PR-3 Trigger Guard
PR01700 Trigger Guard Screw
PR-34 Trigger Pivot Screw
PR-37A Trigger Return Plunger/Spring Assembly
PR-37 Trigger Spring
B-39 Trigger Spring Plunger

SPECIFICATIONS

Model: New Bearcat
Action: revolver; SA
Overall Length: 9 in.
Overall Height: 4.25 in.
Overall Width: 1.18 in.
Barrel: 4.2 in.
Weight Unloaded: 24 oz.
Caliber: .22 LR
Capacity: 6
Common Features: matte stainless or blued finish, transfer bar/loading gate safety, fixed rear/front sights, smooth rosewood grip

BACKGROUND

Bill Ruger loved old guns and it is evident in the design of the Bearcat which uses a one piece grip and cylinder frame construction like the Remington 1861 and 1858 cap and ball revolvers. The similarities end there as the mechanism is all Ruger. The Bearcat is a favorite with those who frequent the outdoors. The scaled-down size makes it an easy carrying belt gun. A cougar and bear are engraved on the non-fluted cylinder.
Year Introduced: 1958 (New Bearcat introduced 1994)
Country of Origin: USA
Current Manufacturer: Ruger (ruger.com)

REQUIRED TOOLS

Field Stripping: none
Disassembly/Assembly: small flat blade screwdriver, paper clip or small nail, 1/16 hex or Allen wrench, non-marring pliers

FIELD STRIP

1. Open the gate (part # PR02403) and pull the hammer (PR04003) back one click to half cock.
2. While depressing the base pin latch body (XR02700) on the left side of the frame (PR-2A), withdraw the base pin assembly (PR02902A) toward the muzzle, Figure 1.

FIGURE 1

3. Remove the cylinder (PR-1) from the right side of the frame, Figure 2.
At this point the Bearcat is field stripped for routine cleaning.

DISASSEMBLY

1. Unscrew the grip panel screw (PR-13) and remove grip panels from the frame.
2. Fully cock the hammer (PR04003) and insert a nail or paperclip into the small hole at the lower end of

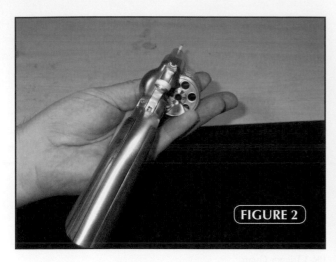

FIGURE 2

the hammer strut (PR-15), Figure 3. Pull the trigger (PR03903) so the hammer falls forward in the fired position. Remove the hammer strut (), mainspring and mainspring seat (PR-5).

FIGURE 3

3. Remove the trigger guard screw (PR01700) and pull the trigger guard (PR-3) from the bottom of the frame, Figure 4. The cylinder latch plunger (PR-18) and

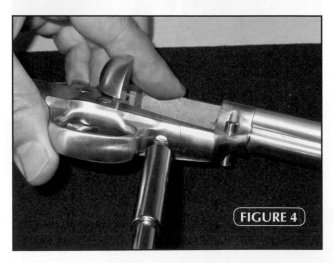

FIGURE 4

cylinder latch plunger spring (KPR04602), and the trigger spring (PR-37) and trigger spring plunger (B-39) will come free once the trigger guard is removed. Figure 5.

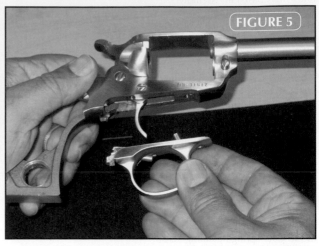

FIGURE 5

4. Next use a 1/16 hex or Allen wrench to remove the pawl plunger spring (PR-50) and pawl plunger (KE-61), Figure 6.

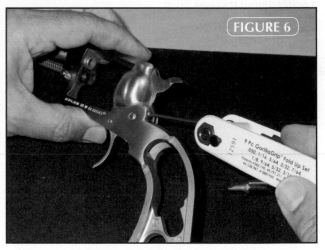

FIGURE 6

5. Remove the hammer pivot screw (PR-16N) and the trigger pivot screw (PR-34) using a flat blade screwdriver, Figure 7. Then slightly move the hammer downward so the trigger (PR03903), cylinder latch assembly (PR24502) and transfer bar (PR07203) can be removed from the bottom of the frame, Figure 8.

6. Next push the hammer into the frame so the bottom portion protrudes out the bottom of the frame and remove the cylinder had, Ruger calls it a pawl (KPR00703), from the hammer. The hammer can now be pulled free from the top of the frame.

7. Remove the gate by unscrewing the gate spring retaining screw (PR-30) and remove the gate plunger (PR-31) and gate plunger spring (PR-26) from the bottom of the frame. Then pull the gate free from the frame.

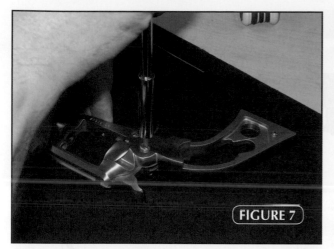

FIGURE 7

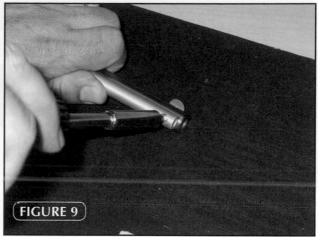

FIGURE 9

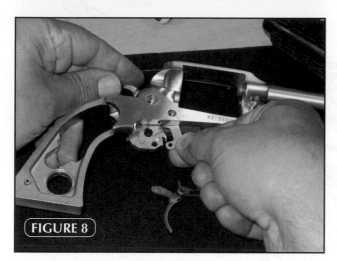

FIGURE 8

8. Remove the ejector assembly by holding the ejector housing (PR-22) to the barrel (PR10600) and removing the ejector housing screw (PR-33), Figure 9. The ejector housing spring (PR-44) is under compression so control it as you lift the ejector housing from the barrel. The ejector housing spring and ejector rod assembly (PR-55) will come free once the ejector housing is removed.

9. Hold the base pin latch nut (XR02800) with non-marring pliers on the left side of the frame and unscrew the base pin latch body using a flat blade screwdriver. The base pin latch spring is under compression so control it once the base pin latch body is free from the base pin latch nut.

Reverse order to reassemble.

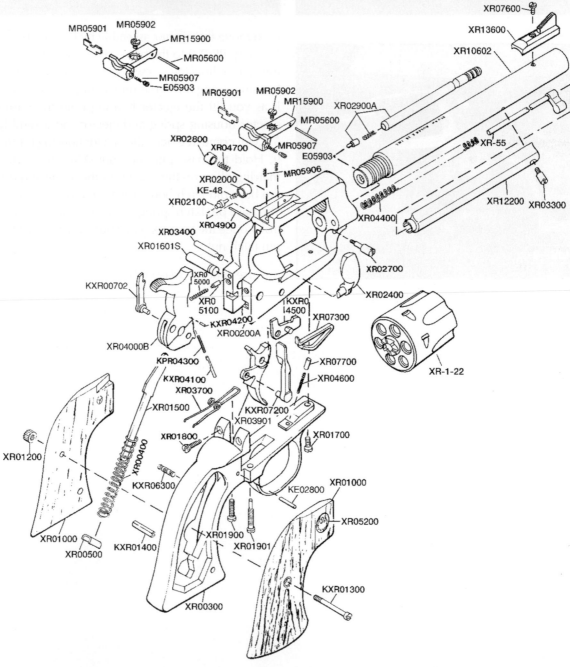

MR05901
MR05902
MR15900
MR05600
MR05907
E05903
MR05901
MR05902
MR15900
MR05600
MR05907
E05903
MR05906
XR02800
XR04700
XR02000
KE-48
XR02100
XR04900
XR03400
XR01601S
XR05000
XR05100
KXR00702
KXR04200
XR00200A
XR04000B
KPR04300
KXR04100
XR03700
XR01500
XR01800
KXR07200
XR03901
XR01200
XR00400
KXR06300
XR01000
XR00500
KXR01400
XR01900
XR01901
XR00300
XR07600
XR13600
XR10602
XR02900A
XR-55
XR04400
XR12200
XR03300
XR02700
XR02400
KXR04500
XR07300
XR07700
XR04600
XR-1-22
XR01700
KE02800
XR01000
XR05200
KXR01300

PARTS LIST

XR10602 Barrel
XR02900A Base Pin Assembly
XR02700 Base Pin Latch Body
XR02800 Base Pin Latch Nut
XR04700 Base Pin Latch Spring
XR-1-22 Cylinder
XR00210 Cylinder Frame
KXR04500 Cylinder Latch
XR04600 Cylinder Latch Spring
XR07700 Cylinder Latch Spring Plunger
XR12200 Ejector Housing
XR03300 Ejector Housing Screw
XR-55 Ejector Rod Assembly
XR04400 Ejector Rod
XR02100 Firing Pin
KE-48 Firing Pin Rebound Spring
XR13600Front Sight, Adjustable
XR03611 Front Sight Blade, Fixed
XR07600 Front Sight Screw
XR02400 Gate
XR07300 Gate Detent Spring
XR00300 Grip Frame
XR01700 Grip Frame Screw-A-Front
XR01800Grip Frame Screw-B-Back (2 Req'd.)
XR01900 Grip Frame Screw-C-Bottom
XR01901 Grip Frame Screw & Pivot Lock
XR01000 Grip Panels
KXR01400 Grip Panel Dowel

XR01200 Grip Panel Ferrule, Left
XR01100 Grip Panel Ferrule, Right
KXR01300 Grip Panel Screw
XR04000B Hammer Assembly
XR01601S Hammer Pivot Pin
KXR04100 Hammer Plunger
KPR04300 Hammer Plunger Spring
XR01500 Hammer Strut
XR00400 Mainspring
XR00500 Mainspring
XR05200 Medallion (2 Req'd.)
KXR00702 Pawl
XR05100 Pawl Plunger
XR05000 Pawl Plunger Spring
MR15900 Rear Sight Base Assembly Complete
MR05908 Rear Sight Detent Ball - Adjustable
MR05901 Rear Sight Blade
MR05902 Rear Sight Elevation Screw
MR05906 Rear Sight Elevation Spring (2 Req'd.) - Adjustable
MR05600 Rear Sight Pivot Pin
E05903 Rear Sight Windage Adjusting Screw
MR05907 Rear Sight Windage Spring Single
XR02000 Recoil Plate
XR04900 Recoil Plate Cross Pin
KXR07200 Transfer Bar
XR03901 Trigger
XR03400 Trigger Pivot
XR03700 Trigger Spring
KE02800 Trigger Pivot Pin
KXR06300 Trigger Spring Retaining Pin

SPECIFICATIONS

Model: New Model Single-Six Convertible
Action: revolver; SA
Overall Length: 11 in. (5.5 in. barrel)
Overall Height: 4.0 in.
Overall Width: 1.4 in.
Barrel: 4.62 in., 5.5 in., 6.5 in.
Weight Unloaded: 42 oz. (5.5 in. barrel)
Caliber: .22 LR/.22 Mag
Capacity: 6
Common Features: matte stainless or blued finish, extra cylinder, transfer bar/loading gate safety, adjustable rear/fixed front sights, smooth wood or checkered polymer grip

BACKGROUND

Back in the 1950s cowboys were a staple of movies and TV. America was enamored with the old west and Bill Ruger thought a single action .22 was a good idea. The Single-Six is a scaled down version of the Colt SAA but used coiled springs throughout. The New Model Single-Six employ a hammer transfer bar safety system which allows the revolver to be fully loaded without the risk of an accidental discharge if it is dropped on its hammer. The instructions here are for the New Model Single-Six and the parts numbers are for the blued finish models.
Year Introduced: 1953 (New Model Single Six introduced 1984)

Country of Origin: USA
Current Manufacturer: Ruger (ruger.com)
Similar Models: Single-Ten (10 shot cylinder), Hunter (7.5 in. barrel with integral scope mounts), .17 HMR (.17 HMR caliber)

REQUIRED TOOLS

Field Stripping: none
Disassembly/Assembly: small flat blade screwdriver, paper clip or small nail, punch, brass hammer

FIELD STRIP

1. Open the gate (part #XR02400) and press in the base pin latch nut (XR02800) on the left side of the cylinder frame (XR00200A) while withdrawing the base pin assembly (XR02900A), Figure 1.
2. Remove the cylinder from the right side/gate side of frame, Figure 2.

At this point the Single-Six is field stripped for routine cleaning.

DISASSEMBLY

1. Unscrew the grip panel screw (KXR01300) and remove the two grip panels (XR01000).
2. Pull the hammer (XR04000B) back to its full cock position and insert a nail or paperclip in into the hole

FIGURE 1

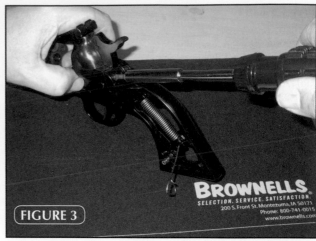

FIGURE 3

FIGURE 2

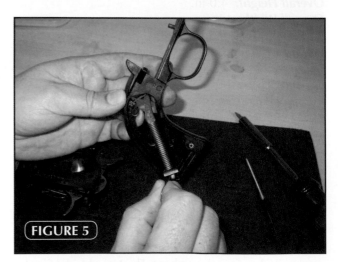

FIGURE 4

at the lower end of the hammer strut (XR01500). Control the hammer and squeeze the trigger to ease the hammer down to its full forward position.

3. Remove the five screws that fasten the grip frame (XR00300) to the cylinder frame; two at the base of the hammer (XR01800), two rear of the trigger guard (XR01900 and XR01901) and one forward of the trigger guard (XR01700), Figure 3. Note that these screws are all slightly different.

4. Pull the grip frame to the rear and down separating it from the cylinder frame, Figure 4. If the grip frame does not easily separate from the cylinder frame, slightly cock back the hammer or gently tap the grip frame with a rubber mallet.

5. Remove the mainspring assembly—mainspring (XR00400) and hammer strut—from the grip frame. Keep the nail/paperclip retaining in place, Figure 5.

6. With the grip frame removed, the pawl plunger spring (XR05000) and pawl plunger (XR05100) in the rear of the left side of the cylinder frame will

FIGURE 5

easily pull free, Figure 6. The cylinder latch spring (XR04600) and cylinder latch spring plunger (XR07700) in the inside of the grip frame will also easily pull free.

7. Next remove the trigger pivot (XR03400) by using a small flat blade screwdriver to depress the

FIGURE 6

11. To remove the ejector housing (XR12200) grasp the ejector housing and barrel (XR10602) in one hand and control it while removing the ejector housing screw (XR03300). Note the ejector housing is under spring tension from the ejector spring (XR04400).

Reassemble in reverse order.

FIGURE 7

gate detent spring (XR07300) so that the end of the spring is moved out of the groove in the trigger pivot, Figure 7.

8. Then use a punch and hammer to drift out the trigger pivot out of the cylinder frame.

9. Next remove the cylinder latch (KXR04500), gate detent spring (XR07300), and gate (XR02400).

10. Remove the hammer pivot (XR01601S) then remove the hammer/pawl assembly and the trigger/transfer bar assembly.

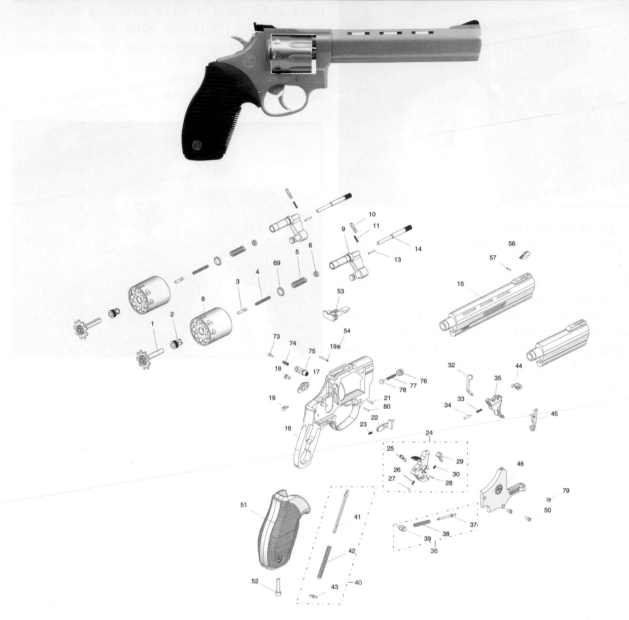

PARTS LIST

1 Extractor
2 Cylinder retaining bushing
3 Center pin
4 Center pin spring
5 Extractor spring
6 Extractor rod collar
7 Extractor rod spring
8 Cylinder
9 Yoke
10 Front latch
11 Front latch spring
12 Cylinder stop plunder with spring
13 Front latch pin
14 Extractor rod
15 Barrel

16 Frame
17 Thumb piece
18 Thumb piece screw
19 Firing pin
20 Firing pin spring
21 Firing pin retaining pin
22 Bolt
23 Bolt spring
24 Hammer assembly
25 Keylock
26 Keylock spring
27 Keylock ball
28 Keylock pin
29 Sear
30 Sear spring
31 Sear pin
32 Transfer bar
33 Hand spring
34 Hand pin
35 Trigger assembly

36 Trigger spring assembly
37 Trigger spring center pin
38 Trigger spring
39 Trigger spring swivel
40 Main spring assembly
41 Main spring center pin
42 Main spring
43 Main spring plate
44 Cylinder stop
45 Hand
46 Side plate
47 Yoke screw
48 Yoke retaining pin spring
49 Yoke retaining pin
50 Side plate screw
51 Rubber grip
52 Grip screw
53 Rear sight assembly
54 Rear sight spring
55 Rear sight pin

56 Front sight
57 Front sight pin
58 Stock pin
60 Firing pin bushing
61 Center pin bushing
63 Rear sight screw
69 Cylinder distance bushing
70 Stellar clip
71 Barrel retaining pin
72 Yoke blocking pin
73 Cylinder assembly catch hook
74 Cylinder assembly catch spring
75 Cylinder assembly catch
76 Cylinder stop spring
77 Cylinder stop spring
78 Cylinder stop spring pin
79 Side plate screw front
80 Cylinder stop spring bushing pin

SPECIFICATIONS
Model: 990SS6
Action: revolver; SA/DA
Overall Length: 11.5 in.
Overall Height: 5.5 in.
Overall Width: 1.5 in.
Barrel: 6.5 in.
Weight Unloaded: 44 oz
Caliber: .22 LR
Capacity: 9
Common Features: matte stainless steel frame, barrel, cylinder; ribbed rubber grips; fixed front/adj. rear sights; vent-rib barrel drilled and tapped for optics

BACKGROUND
The Taurus Tracker rimfire revolver series includes calibers ranging from .17 HRM (Model 17SS6), .22 LR and .22 Magnum (Model 991). There are slight differences between the models but the instructions for the Model 990 can generally be followed.
Year Introduced: 2008
Country of Origin: Brazil
Current Manufacturers: Taurus (taurususa.com)
Similar Models: 4 in. barrel models

REQUIRED TOOLS
Field Stripping: none
Disassembly/Assembly: small flat blade screwdriver, pliers, small punch, rubber/nylon mallet, hex or Allen wrench, poper clip or small nail

CYLINDER DISASSEMBLY
1. To remove the cylinder, first remove the rubber grip (part #51) by unscrewing the grip screw (52) at the butt of the grip using a hex or Allen wrench. Slide the grip off the frame (16).
2. Remove the most forward sideplate screw, yoke screw (47), using a small standard screwdriver.
3. Push the cylinder latch, thumb piece (17), forward and swing out the cylinder assembly. Align one of the cylinder flutes with the flange at the front of the frame.
4. Pull the yoke (19) and cylinder assembly out toward the muzzle.
5. To remove the ejector rod, extractor rod (14), use your fingers or a pair of padded pliers and grip the end of the ejector rod and turn clockwise—these are left-hand threads—looking at the front of the cylinder (8), Figure 1. If the extractor rod is stubborn place the extractor rod in a padded vise and unscrew the cylinder. The extractor rod can then be removed from the front of the cylinder.

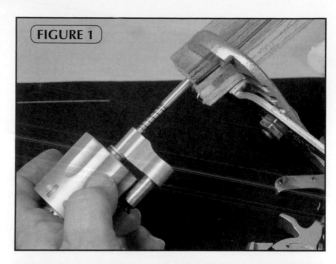

FIGURE 1

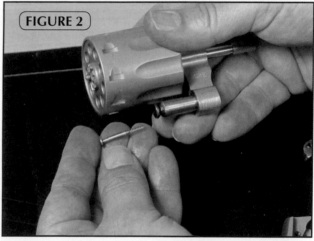

FIGURE 2

6. Tip the yoke upwards and the cylinder stop plunger with spring (12) will fall free, Figure 2.

FRAME DISASSEMBLY
1. To remove the main spring assembly (40), remove the three side plate screws (50) and flip the frame in your hand so the thumb piece faces up. Using a nylon or rubber mallet, tap the frame to release the side plate (46) in your hand. Do not pry the side plate off as you can mar and damage the side plate and frame. The firing pin retaining pin (21) may fall out when the side plate falls free.
2. Move the thumb piece rearward and cock the hammer assembly (24) and insert a small nail or paper clip in the main spring center pin (41), Figure 3. Ease the hammer assembly forward and remove the main spring assembly, which consists of the main spring center pin, main spring and main spring plate (43). Warning the main spring assembly is under spring compression.

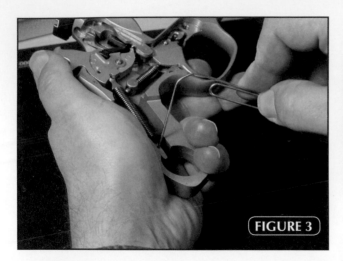

FIGURE 3

on the hammer assembly clears the hand (45) on the trigger assembly, Figure 4.

> **Disassembly Tip:** With Taurus and Smith and Wesson revolvers, if the side plate is rusted in place or stuck from oil and debris, cock the revolver and place a small wedge of hardwood between the frame and side plate and gently tap the wedge until the side plate breaks free while gently and evenly prying the side plate near the trigger and main spring.

To reassemble follow the disassembly instructions in reverse order.

> **Reassembly Tip:** Note the side plate has a small flange at the top which must be inserted into the frame first, then use a rubber mallet or nylon hammer to seat the side plate into the frame.

FIGURE 4

3. The hammer assembly can easily be removed by pulling back on the thumb release and then cocking back the hammer and pulling the trigger so the sear (29)

Rifles

Centerfire Semi–Automatic Action

AR-15

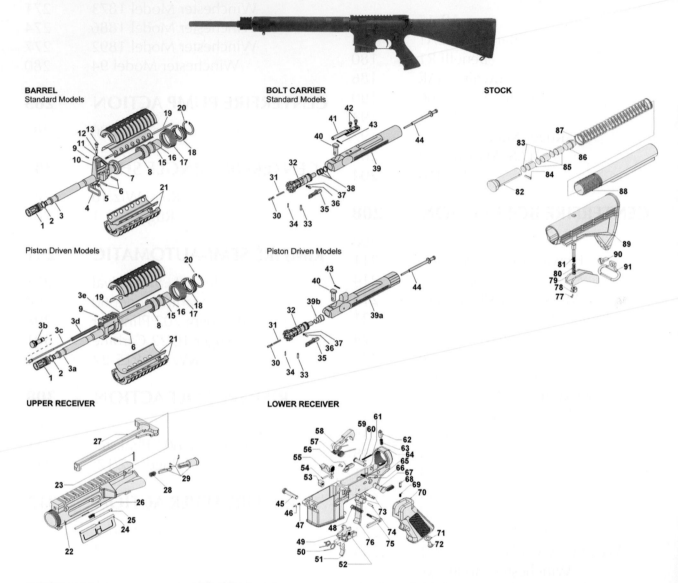

BARREL
Standard Models

BOLT CARRIER
Standard Models

STOCK

Piston Driven Models

Piston Driven Models

UPPER RECEIVER

LOWER RECEIVER

PARTS LIST

1 Flash Suppressor
2 Crush Washer
3 Barrel (Standard Models)
3a Barrel (Piston Driven Models)
3b Gas Plug (Piston Driven Models)
3c Gas Piston (Piston Driven Models)
3d Piston Spring (Piston Driven Models)
3e Gas Block (Piston Driven Models)
4 Front Sling Swivel
5 Front Sling Swivel Rivet
6 Front Sight Taper Pin (2)

7 Side Sling Swivel Assembly
8 Handguard Cap
9 Gas Tube Roll Pin
10 Front Sight
11 Front Sight Detent Spring
12 Front Sight Detent
13 Front Sight Post
14 Barrel Nut
15 AMBI Barrel Extension
16 Barrel Indexing Pin
17 Delta Ring
18 Weld Spring
19 Gas Tube
20 Handguard Snap Ring
21 Thermoset Hand Guard With Heat Shield (2)

22 Left-Handed A3 Upper Receiver
23 Forward Assist Spring Pin
24 Left-Handed Ejection Port Cover
25 Ejection Port Cover Pin
26 Ejection Port Cover Spring
27 Charging Handle Assembly
28 Forward Assist Spring
29 Forward Assist Assembly
30 Ejector
31 Ejector Spring
32 Left-Handed Bolt
33 Extractor Pin
34 Ejector Roll Pin
35 Extractor
36 Extractor Spring

37 Extractor Insert
38 Gas Rings (3)
39 Left-Handed Bolt Carrier (Standard Models)
39a Bolt Carrier (Piston Driven Models)
39b Bolt Carrier Spring (Piston Driven Models)
40 Cam Pin
41 Bolt Carrier Key (Standard Models)
42 Bolt Carrier Key Screws (Standard Models)
43 Firing Pin Retaining Pin
44 Firing Pin
45 Pivot Pin
46 Pivot Pin Detent

47 Pivot Pin Spring Assembly	59 Takedown Pin
48 Magazine Catch Spring	60 Takedown Pin Detent
49 Disconnector	61 Takedown Pin Spring
50 Trigger Spring	62 Buffer Retainer
51 Trigger	63 Buffer Retainer Spring
52 Disconnector Spring	64 Lower Receiver
53 Magazine Release Button	65 Bolt Catch Spring
54 Bolt Catch Roll Pin	66 Bolt Catch Plunger
55 Bolt Catch	67 AMBI Selector Assembly (1)
56 AMBI Selector Assembly (2)	68 Safety Detent
57 Hammer Spring	69 Safety Detent Spring
58 Hammer With J Pin	70 Pistol Grip

71 Lock Washer	83 Buffer Rubber Spacer
72 Pistol Grip Screw	84 Buffer Roll Pin
73 Hammer And Trigger Pins	85 Spacer Weight
74 Trigger Guard Roll Pin	86 Buffer Plug
75 Magazine Catch	87 Action Spring
76 Trigger Guard	88 Receiver Extension
77 Receiver Nut Roll Pin	89 Buttstock
78 Receiver End Nut	90 Rear Sling Loop Bolt
79 Lock Lever	91 Rear Sling Loop
80 Pin Stock Spring	
81 Shoulder Headle Pin	
82 Buffer Body	

SPECIFICATIONS

Model: Stag Arms Model 7 (Hunter)
Action: semi-automatic, gas impingement system
Overall Length: 39 in.
Barrel: 20.77 in.
Weight Unloaded: 10 lbs
Caliber: 6.8 SPC
Capacity: 5 + 1
Common Features: forged aluminum lower/upper receiver, stainless barrel, parkerized finish, manual safety, A2 buttstock, Hogue pistol grip/free-float handguard

BACKGROUND

Full automatic AR-15s have been in U.S. military service since 1958, civilian sales of semi-automatic AR-15 rifles began in 1963. Today the rifle is perhaps the most copied rifle in the U.S. with dozens of manufacturers building all sorts of variants from highly accurate competitions rifles and tactical models to varmint and big-game hunting rifles. The rifle's operating system is direct gas impingement where gas from a fired round travels from the barrel through a gas port, down a gas tube and into a bolt carrier. The bolt carrier acts like a piston to eject and chamber a cartridge. The action is renowned for minimal recoil especially when chambered for 5.56 NATO/.223 Remington ammo; the rifle's most common caliber. The rifle is modular so upper and lower receivers can be easily swapped depending on the shooting scenario. ARs are also easily customized with the only limits being the builder's imagination.

Year Introduced: 1957 (ArmaLite)
Country of Origin: USA
Current Manufacturers: Alexander Arms (alexanderarrns.com), American Spirit Arms (americanspiritarms.com), Anderson Manufacturing (atdrnachineshop.com), Armalite (armalite.com), Armscor (armscor.com), Barrett (barrettrifles.com), Blackheart International (bhigear.com), Bravo Company USA, Inc. (bravocompanymfg.com), Bushmaster (bushrnaster.com), Christensen Arms (christensenarms.com), CMMG (cmmginc.com), Colt (coltsmfg.com), Daniel Defense (danieldefense.com), Defensive Edge SLR15 Rifles (slr15.com), Del-Ton (del-ton.com), Double Star (star15.com), DPMS (dprnsinc.com), DSA (dsarms.com), E.D.M. Arms (edmarms.com), E.M.F. (emf-company.com), Fulton Armory (fulton-armory.com), Heckler & Koch (hk-usa.com), High Standard (highstandard.com), JP Enterprises (jprifles.com), Knight's Manufacturing (knightarmco.com), Les Baer (lesbaer.com), Lewis Machine & Tool (lewismachine.net), LWRC International (lwrci.corn), MGI (mgimilitary.com), Mossberg (rnossberg.com), Noveske Rifleworks (noveskerifleworks.com), Olympic Arms (olyarrns.com), Para (para-usa.com), Patriot Ordinance Factory (pof-usa.com), Primary Weapons Systems (primaryweapons.com), Remington (rernington.com), RND Manufacturing (rndedge.com), Rock River Arms (rockriverarms.com), Ruger (ruger.com), SI Defense (si-defense.corn), SIG SAUER (sigsauer.com), Smith & Wesson (srnith-wesson.com), Sog Armory (sogarmory.com), Spike's Tactical (spikestactical.com), Stag Arms (stagarms.com), Superior Arms (superiorarms.com), Tactical Rifles (tacticalrifles.net), Tactical Weapons Solutions (tacticalweapon.com), TNW Firearms (tnwfirearrns.corn), Vigilance Rifles (vigilancerifles.com), Vulcan Arms (vulcanarms.com), Wilson Combat (wilsoncombat.com), Yankee Hill Machine (yhm.net), Xtreme Machining (xtrernemaching.com), Z-M Weapons (zmweapons.com)

REQUIRED TOOLS

Field Strip: non-marring punch
Disassembly/Assembly: nylon/brass hammer, armorer's wrench, lower receiver vise block, small/medium punches, handguard removal tool

FIELD STRIP

1. Ensure the bolt carrier is in the forward position.
2. From the left side of the lower receiver (part #64) push in the takedown pin (59) with a punch or the bullet point from a cartridge will do in the field, Figure 1 (see next page). Then pull out the takedown pin from the right side of the lower receiver until it stops, Figure 2 (see next page).

FIGURE 1

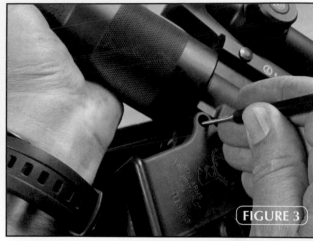

FIGURE 3

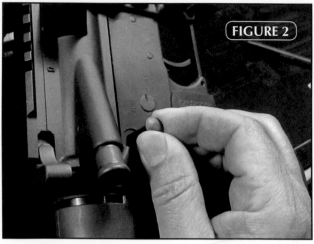

FIGURE 2

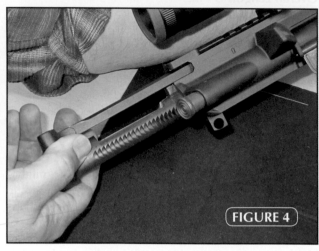

FIGURE 4

3. Pivot the lower receiver away from the upper receiver (22) and push the pivot pin (45) with a punch/cartridge point, Figure 3. Pull the pivot pin until it stops and separate the upper and lower receivers.

4. Pull back on the charging handle assembly (27) to remove charging handle assembly and bolt carrier assembly from upper receiver, Figure 4. The charging handle will easily fall free from the bolt carrier assembly.

BOLT DISASSEMBLY

1. Remove the firing pin retaining pin (43), Figure 5.
2. Push the bolt assembly (32) into the bolt carrier (39), Figure 6.
3. Remove the firing pin (44) by pulling it rearward through the rear of the bolt carrier assembly, Figure 7.
4. Turn the cam pin (40) 90°, Figure 8. Pull the cam pin from the bolt carrier assembly, Figure 9. Then pull the bolt assembly from bolt carrier assembly, Figure 10.

5. Push in on the rear of the extractor (35) and use a small punch to push through the extractor pin (33), Figure 11. The extractor and extractor spring (36) and extractor inset (37) will then fall free from the bolt carrier, Figure 12.

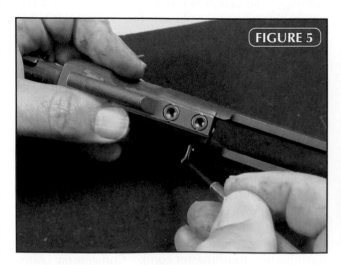

FIGURE 5

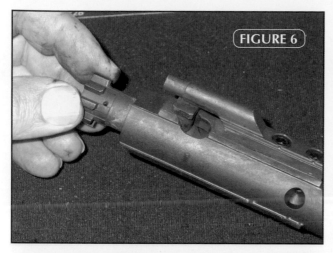

FIGURE 6

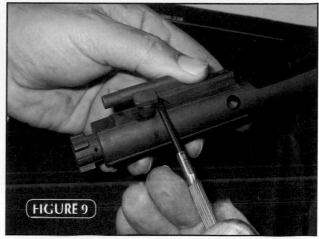

FIGURE 9

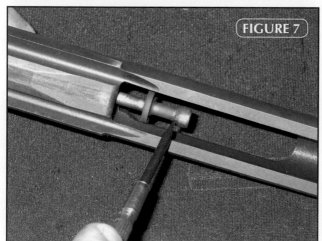

FIGURE 7

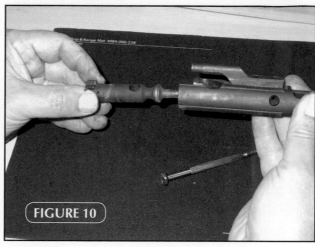

FIGURE 10

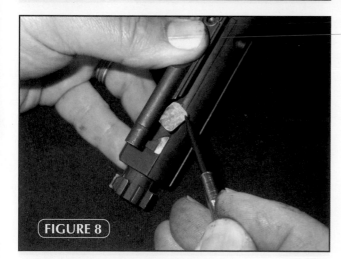

FIGURE 8

2. Hold the hammer (58) and pull the trigger (51) to allow the hammer to move fully forward in the fired position. Then push out the trigger pin (73) with a punch, Figure 14. The hammer and hammer spring (50), which is under compression, can be removed from the top of the lower receiver.

3. Remove the safety (61) by rotating halfway between "safe" and "fire" and drift it out of the lower receiver using a punch. Then pull the safety from the lower receiver, Figure 15.

4. Use a punch to push out the trigger pin (73), Figure 16. Pull the trigger and trigger spring (51, 50) out from the top of the lower receiver, Figure 17.

5. Buttstocks vary widely on AR-15s, but most are removed by unscrewing one screw. To remove an A2 buttstock (89) unscrew the top buttstock screw and pull the buttstock off the receiver extension (88). Note the takedown detent spring (60) will come free once the buttstock is removed.

6. Remove the pistol grip (70) by unscrewing the pistol grip screw (72) and removing it and the lock washer (71).

LOWER RECEIVER DISASSEMBLY

1. To remove the buffer assembly and action spring (87), hold the buffer body in place and press down on the buffer retainer (62) with a small punch, Figure 13. The action spring is under compression so control it as it expands.

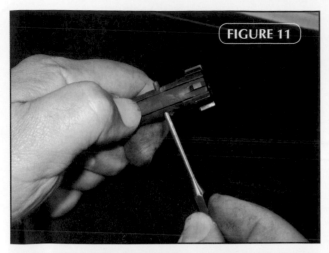

FIGURE 11

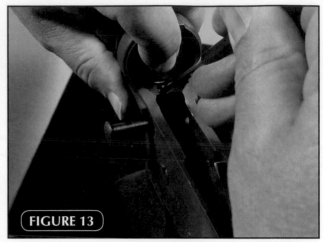

FIGURE 13

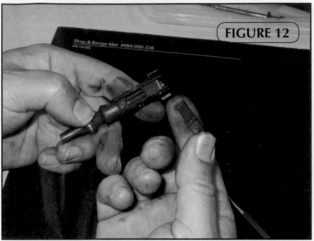

FIGURE 12

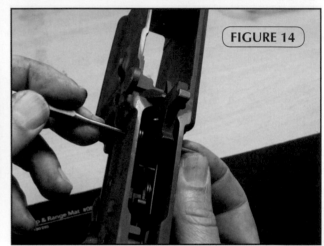

FIGURE 14

UPPER RECEIVER DISASSEMBLY

1. Hand guards (21) also vary widely and mainly come in two types—one-piece free float or two-piece. For standard two-piece hand guards, stand the rifle on the buttstock and use an AR hand guard tool to press down on the delta ring (17) which compresses down on the weld spring (18).

Free Float: Free-float hand guards do not contact the barrel and help improve accuracy. Depending on how your rifle is set up, the front sights assembly/gas block (10) and gas tube (19) will need to be removed before installing a free-float hand guard. For rifles with low-profile gas blocks, the free-float hand guard may slide over the gas block. Yankee Hill Machine (yhm. net) manufactures a number of different hand guards from smooth to Diamond Series with a cheese grater texture. Follow the manufacturers' instructions.

FIGURE 15

2. While pressing down on the delta ring, tip out the ends of the hand guards from the ring.

3. Flash suppressors (1) also know as comps/brakes/flash hiders are all removed from the barrel (3) using a wrench of the appropriate size. A crush washer (2) will come free from the muzzle when the flash suppressor is removed.

4. Some rifles have a front sight/gas port others have a gas block without a sight. To remove the front sight/gas port drift out the two front sight taper pins (6) using a 1/8" diameter punch. The pins are tapered so be sure to drive the pin out from the small end. Then pull front sight/gas port assembly and gas tube from the barrel.

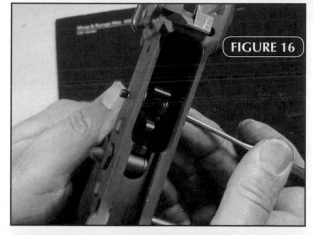

FIGURE 16

FIGURE 17

5. Remove the gas tube using a 1/16" roll pin punch to drift out the gas tube roll pin (9).

6. The ejection port cover (24) is removed by using a small screwdriver to remove the c-clip on the forward end of ejection port cover pin (25), then pull the ejection port cover pin toward the buttstock. The ejection port cover spring (26) is under tension so control it as you remove the pin.

MAGAZINE DISASSEMBLY

1. Use a punch or the bullet point of a cartridge to pry up on bottom of baseplate and push the indentations of the baseplate past the magazine body, Figure 19. Then slide the baseplate from the magazine body. The magazine spring is under compression so control it.

2. Gentle shake the magazine body and the magazine spring and follower will come out as an assembly.

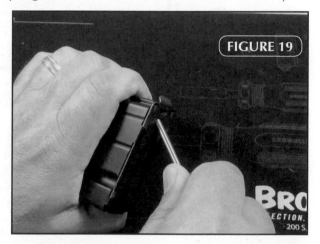

FIGURE 19

Reassemble in reverse order.

Cleaning Tip: After wiping the carbon and powder residue from the bolt make sure gaps in the gas rings do not line up; rotate and position them 120° apart, Figure 18.

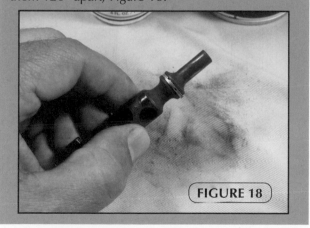

FIGURE 18

Tooling Up: ARs are easy rifles to work on especially if you have the right tools. A multi-use wrench (top), handguard removal tool (middle), lower receiver vise block (bottom) and upper receiver action block are value assets in an AR tool kit.

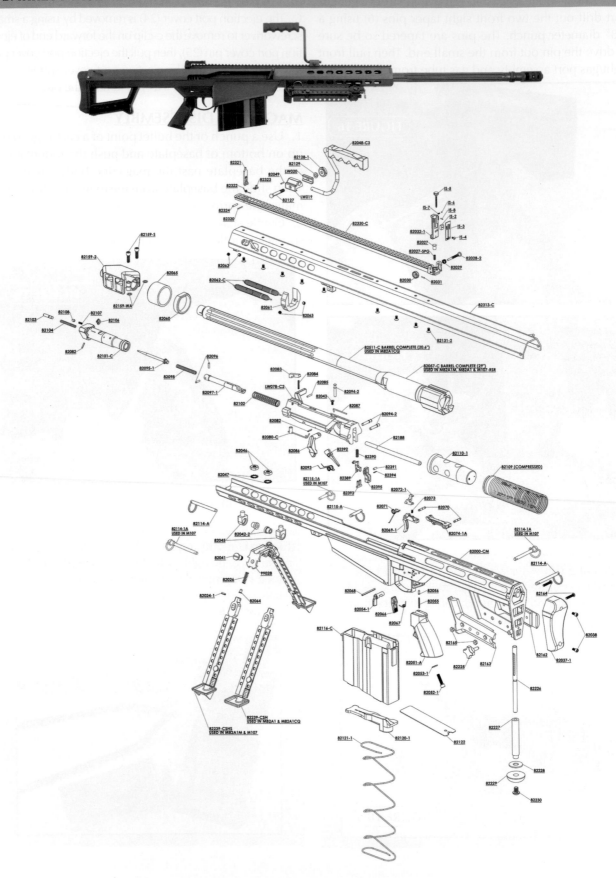

PARTS LIST

82000C Lower Receiver Complete
82013-C2 Upper Receiver Complete
82021 Front Sight
82022 Front Sight Spring
82023 Front Sight Detent
82024 Front Sight/Bipod Pin (3 Req'd.)
82026 Bipod Spring (2 Req'd.)
82027 Rear Sight Base Detent
82027-SPG Rear Sight Base Spring
82028-1 Windage Screw
82029 Windage Screw Spring
82030 Windage Knob
82031 Windage Knob Pin
82032 Rear Sight Body
82033 Rear Sight Post
82033-S Rear Sight Post Screw
82034-2 Rear Sight Scale
82034-S Rear Sight Scale Screw
82035 Elevation Indicator
82037-1 Recoil Pad
82038 Recoil Pad Screw (2 Req'd.)
82041 Bipod Screw (2 Req'd.)

82042-2 Bipod Shim Bushing (2 Req'd.)
82043 Accelerator Spring Screw
82045 Yoke Mount (2 Req'd.)
82046 Yoke Mount Nut (2 Req'd.)
82047 Yoke Mount Washer (2 Req'd.)
82048 Carrying Handle Stock
82049 Carrying Handle Pin
82050 Carrying Handle
82051-A Pistol Grip Stock Assembly
82052-1 Pistol Grip Screw
82053-1 Pistol Grip Washer
82054-1 Safety
82055 Safety Spring
82056 Safety Detent
82057-C Barrel Complete
82060 Battery Bumper
82061 Barrel Key
82062-C Barrel Spring Assembly (2 Req'd.)
82063 Barrel Spring Screw (4 Req'd.)
82064 Bipod Detent (2 Req'd.)
82065 Impact Barrel Bumper
82066 Magazine Catch
82067 Magazine Catch Spring
82068 Magazine Catch Pin
82069-1 Trigger

82070 Trigger Housing Pin (2 Req'd.)
82071 Trigger Spring
82072 Disconnector
82073 Disconnector Spring
82074-A Transfer Bar Assembly
82080-C Cam Pin Assembly
82082 Cam Pin Pin/Ejector Pin (2 Req'd.)
82083 Bolt Latch
82084 Bolt Latch Spring
82085 Bolt Latch Pin
82086 Accelerator
82087 Accelerator Spring
82089 Sear
82090 Sear Spring
82092 Cocking Lever
82093 Cocking Lever Spring
82094 Bolt Carrier Pin (3 Req'd.)
82095-1 Firing Pin
82096 Firing Pin Pin (2 Req'd.)
82097-1 Firing Pin Extension
82098 Firing Pin Extension Spring
82101-8,9,10 Bolt
82102 Bolt Spring
82103 Ejector
82104 Ejector Spring
82106 Extractor
82107 Extractor Spring

82108 Extractor Plunger
82109 Main Spring
82110 Main Spring Buffer
82114-A Rear Lock Pin Assembly (2 Req'd.)
82115-A Midlock Pin Assembly
82116-C Magazine Complete
82120 Magazine Follower
82121 Magazine Spring
82122 Magazine Floor Plate
82130-12 Scope Base
82131-2 Scope Base Screw (8 Req'd.)
82145-KIT Muzzle Brake Shim Kit
82159-2 Muzzle Brake
82159-S Muzzle Brake Screw (2 Req'd.)
82159-WA Muzzle Brake Washer (2 Req'd.)
82188 Accelerator Rod
82239CSH Bipod Leg Complete (2 Req'd.)
99028 Bipod Yoke
LW019 Carrying Handle Mount
LW020 Carrying Handle Mount Clamp
LW078C Bolt Carrier Complete

SPECIFICATIONS

Model: M82A1
Action: semi-automatic, recoil-operated
Overall Length: 57 in. (29-in. barrel)
Barrel: 29 in.
Weight Unloaded: 30.9 lbs (29-in. barrel)
Caliber: .50 BMG, .416 Barrett
Capacity: 10 + 1
Common Features: sheet steel lower/upper receiver, fluted barrel with muzzle brake, matte black finish, manual thumb safety, pistol grip, flip-up open sights and scope mount, carry handle, folding bipod, detachable box magazine

BACKGROUND

The name Barrett is synonymous with .50 caliber rifles and in particular semi-automatic .50-caliber rifles. For over two decades the M82A1 design has been refined so that it is reliable and accurate in whatever environmental hell it is required to perform. Military agencies around the globe use this light recoiling rifle which has a maximum effective range of 1,800 meters (1,869 yards). In 1990 the U.S. government employed M82A1s in operations Desert Shield and Desert Storm in Kuwait and Iraq using it as an anti-material weapon able to effectively disable vehicles, parked aircraft, radar installations among other high-value targets. In the hands of snipers the Barrett can defeat enemy personnel at ranges conventional shoulders weapons are ineffective. In operation the barrel recoils slightly backward then the rotating bolt takes over and spits out the empty cartridge shell and scraps a fresh round from the magazine. Like the AR platform the M82A1 has and upper and lower receivers.

Year Introduced: 1980
Country of Origin: USA
Current Manufacturer: Barrett (barrett.net)
Similar Models: M82A1 CQ (20-in. barrel)

REQUIRED TOOLS

Field Strip: non-marring punch
Disassembly/Assembly: nylon/brass hammer, armorer's wrench, lower receiver vise block, small/medium punches, handguard removal tool

FIELD STRIP

1. Pull out and rotate the bipods legs (part #82239CSH) until they lock into place and are fully extended.

2. Rotate the safety lever (82054-1) to the "safe" position the press the magazine catch (82066) forward, towards the magazine (82116-C), and remove the magazine.

3. Remove the rear lock pin assembly (82114-A) from the rear of the buttstock, Figure 1.

FIGURE 3

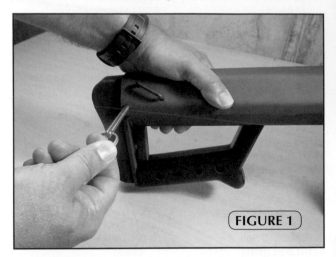

FIGURE 1

4. Remove the midlock pin assembly (82115-A) from the hole near center bottom of the lower receiver (82000C), Figure 2.

FIGURE 4

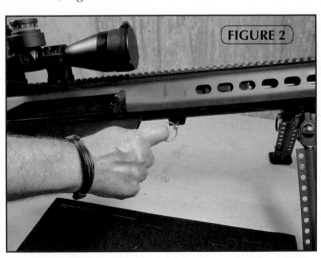

FIGURE 2

metal sleeve of the lower receiver; lift the bolt carrier out of the lower receiver, Figure 5.

5. Position yourself behind the rifle and retract the charging handle on the bolt carrier (LW078C) until the bolt carrier withdraws from and clears the barrel (82057-C), Figure 3.

6. Lift the upper receiver (82013-C2) at the rear, far enough to clear the bolt carrier, then slowly release the charging handle to allow the bolt carrier to move forward, Figure 4.

7. Continue to lift and pivot the upper receiver until it can be unhinged from the lower receiver.

8. Remove the bolt carrier from the lower receiver by sliding bolt carrier forward until it is free of the sheet

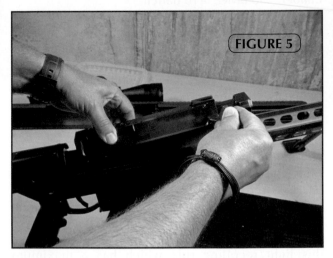

FIGURE 5

9. Use the rear lock pin or your finger to depress the bolt catch (82083) this allows the bolt (82101) to rotate into the bolt carrier, Figure 6.

FIGURE 6

10. While depressing the bolt catch with your finger use the rear lock pin to pull back on the cam pin assembly (82080), Figure 7.

FIGURE 7

11. Continue to depress the bolt latch using your finger or rear lock pin and pull the bolt from the bolt carrier, Figure 8.

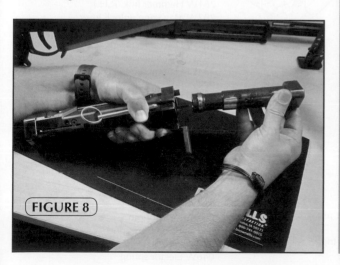

FIGURE 8

Reassemble in reverse order.

Reassembly Tip: The M82A1 is transported in a hard Pelican case so the rifle needs to be put into transport position. For the lower receiver, hold down and pull back the charging handle of the bolt carrier until the hole in the bolt carrier aligns with the first slot in the lower receiver and insert the midlock pin to retain the bolt assembly in the lower receiver, Figure 9. For the upper receiver,

FIGURE 9

place it top side down and press up on the barrel key (82061) through the air vent slots in the handguard until you hear the spring is sprung or the barrel key can be grasped with your fingers, Figure 10. Control the barrel key as the two barrel

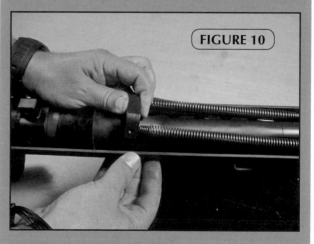

FIGURE 10

spring assemblies (82062-C) are under tension. Allow the barrel spring assemblies to contract then slide the impact barrel buffer (82065) forward, Figure 11. Then carefully slide the barrel backward into the upper receiver, Figure 12.

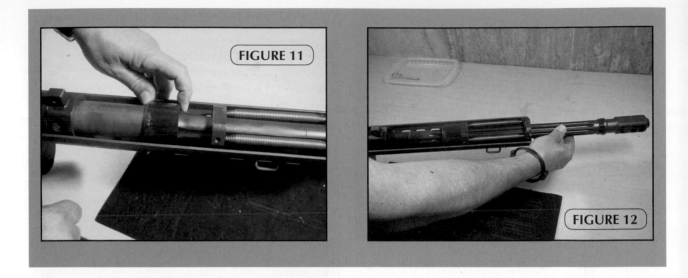

FIGURE 11

FIGURE 12

Cleaning Tip: Barrett recommends cleaning the bore of the .50 caliber rifle every 50-60 rounds using a copper solvent and allowing the solvents to set for two or three minutes.

BENELLI R1

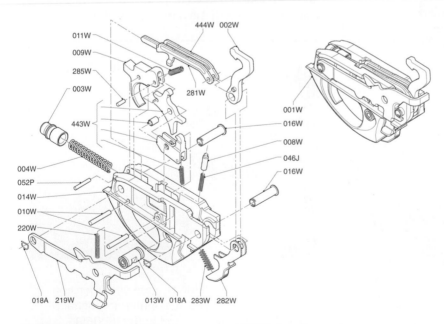

014W Trigger guard
016W Trigger pin bush
018A Trigger guard pin spring
046J Safety spring
052P Roller
219W No-load indicator lever
220W No-load indicator spring
281W Hammer link (R.H.)
282W Magazine unlock lever
283W Magazine lock spring
285W Disconnector trigger roller
443W Disconnector assembly
444W Hammer link (L.H.)
024W Bolt group
025W Firing pin
027W Link
028A Firing pin retaining pin
029W Link pin
030W Bolt handle
031W Locking head pin
032W Locking head
033W Extractor spring
034W Extractor
035A Extractor pin
037W Firing pin spring
045W Ejector
046W Ejector spring
074C Extractor castor

PARTS LIST
001W Trigger group assembly
002W Hammer
003W Hammer link spring cap
004W Hammer spring

008W Safety plunger pin
009W Trigger
010W Disconnector trigger roller
011W Trigger spring
013W Silenced safety button

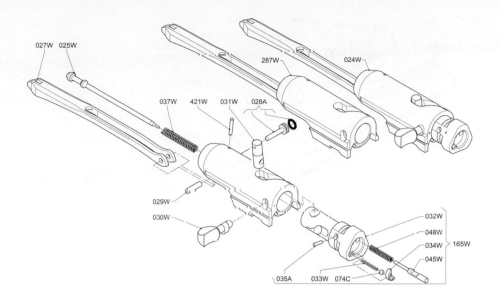

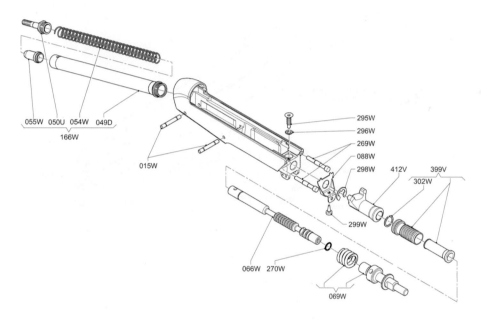

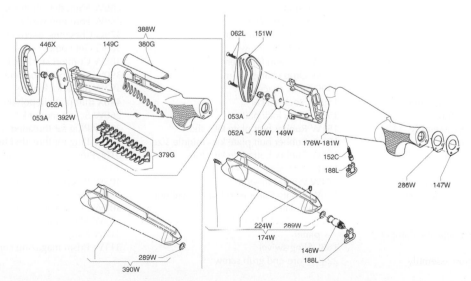

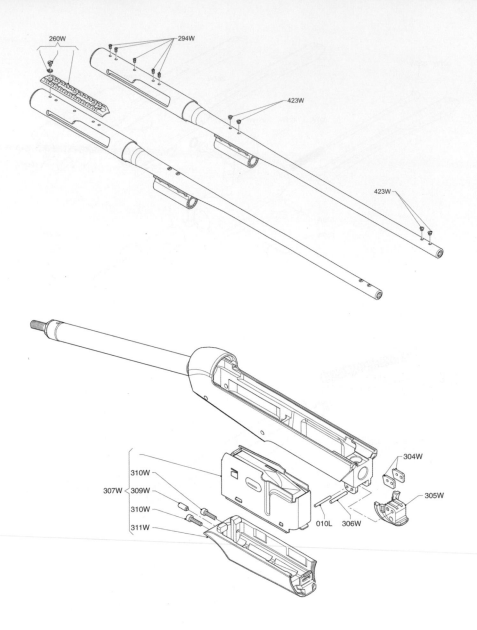

165W Locking head assembly
287W Bolt, partial
421W Extractor pin
015W Trigger guard pin
049D Recoil spring tube
050U Stock retaining nut screw
054W Recoil spring
055W Recoil spring plunger pin
066W Cylinder plunger pin
069W Barrel lock cap assembly
088W Pin shoulder-plate
166W Recoil spring tube assembly
269W Bolt follower pin
270W O-ring, cylinder plunger-pin
295W Cylinder plunger-pin screw
296W Conical-toothed washer
298W Piston plunger-pin
299W Break-action magazine damper
302W Piston
399V Piston extension assembly

412V Piston
052A Spring washer
053A Stock retaining nut
062L Butt plate screw
146W Fore-end follower
147W Drop change shim
149C Stock spacer
149W Stock spacer
150W Shim lock plate
151W Rubber butt plate kit - short
151W Rubber butt plate kit - middle-size
151W Rubber butt plate kit - long
152C Stock sling swivel pin
174W Wood fore-end
176W Monte Carlo wood stock (without butt plate)
181W Pig-backed wood stock (without plate)
188L Sling swivel
224W Fore-end grub screw

286W Shim deviation spacer
289W Fore-end washer
379G Chevrons assembly
380G Gel comb
388W Comfort stock (R.H.)
390W Soft Touch fore-end
392W Stock lock plate
446X Butt plate in polyurethane (R.H.)
260W Scope mount kit
294W Plug for threaded holes, cover
423W Plug for threaded holes, barrel
010L Pin
304W Magazine boss insert
305W Prism magazine boss
306W Pin
307W Prism magazine assembly
309W Magazine presser
310W Magazine fixing screw
311W Prism magazine carrier

SPECIFICATIONS

Model: R1
Action: semi-automatic, auto regulating gas-operated piston, rotating 3-lug bolt
Overall Length: 22.8 in.
Barrel: 44 in. (22-in. barrel)
Weight Unloaded: 7.2 lbs
Caliber: .30-06, 300 Win Mag, 338 Win Mag
Capacity: 3 + 1 (300 Win Mag, 338 Win Mag), 4 + 1 (.30-06)
Common Features: adj. adj. rear/front sight (depending on model), drilled/tapped for optic mounting, detachable magazine, manual safety, wood or synthetic stock, matte finish, detachable magazine

BACKGROUND

The R1 uses an adapted version of Benelli's proven and reliable Auto Regulating Gas Operated (A.R.G.O.) system used in the M1014 military shotgun. The R1 also allows shooters to easily swap barrels and calibers. The R1 like all Benelli firearms is simple to disassemble and reassemble. The design is clean and simple.
Year Introduced: 2002
Country of Origin: Italy
Current Manufacturer: Benelli (benelliusa.com)

REQUIRED TOOLS

Field Strip: none
Disassembly/Assembly: small punch

FIELD STRIP

1. Pull open the bolt group (Part #024W) locking it in the rearward most position.
2. Unscrew fore-end follower (146W) and slide off the fore-end (174W/wood or 390W/polymer), Figure 1.
3. Next unscrew the barrel lock cap assembly (069W) using the sling-swivel pin on the fore-end follower on the fore-end, Figure 2. Pull the barrel lock cap assembly from the cylinder plunger pin (066W), Figure 3.
4. Press the bolt lever, Benelli calls it a no-load lever (219W), to close the bolt.
5. Remove the barrel assembly by pulling off the stock-receiver assembly, Figure 4.

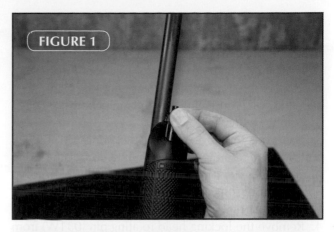

FIGURE 1

FIGURE 2

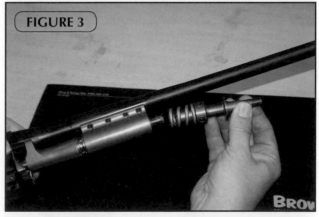

FIGURE 3

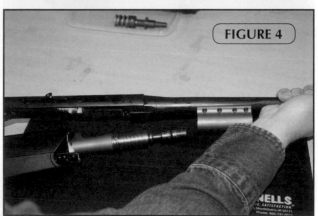

FIGURE 4

BARREL/BOLT DISASSEMBLY

1. Slide the bolt group rearward and pull out the bolt handle (030W) from the bolt (287W), Figure 5.

2. Use your finger to push forward on the locking head assembly (165W) and rotate it to the right. Then slide the bolt group rearward and out of barrel-receiver assembly, Figure 6.

3. Use your thumb to control the firing pin (025W) and firing pin spring (037W) then slide out the firing pin retaining pin (028A), Figure 7. Tip the bolt group and the firing pin and firing pin spring will fall free from the rear of the bolt.

4. Remove the locking head rotating pin (031W) from the bolt, Figure 8. Then slide the bolt locking head from the bolt, Figure 9.

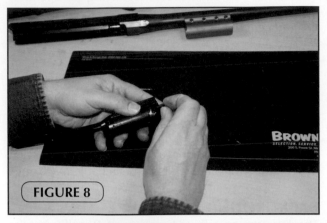

FIGURE 8

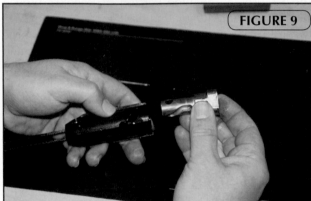

FIGURE 9

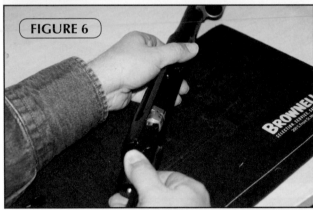

FIGURE 5

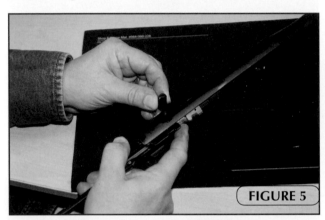

FIGURE 6

FIGURE 10

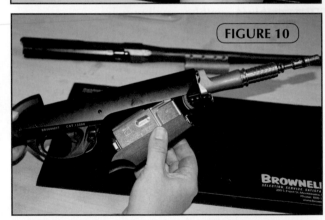

FIGURE 7

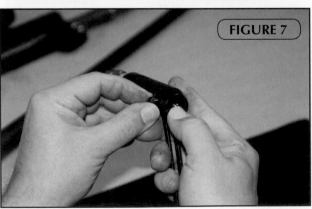

FIGURE 11

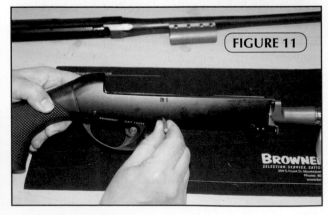

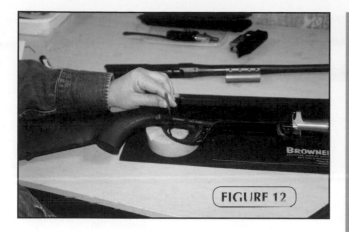

FIGURE 12

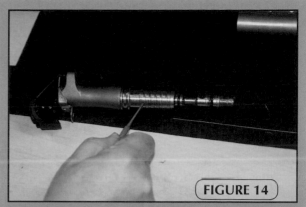

FIGURE 14

STOCK-RECEIVER DISASSEMBLY

1. Remove the magazine (307W), Figure 10.
2. Use a punch to push out the two trigger guard pins (015W) from the stock-receiver assembly. One pin forward of the trigger guard, Figure 11. One aft of the trigger guard, Figure 12.

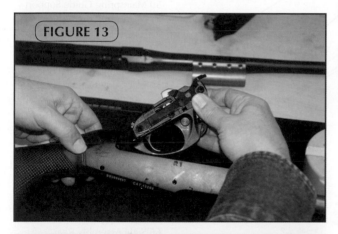

FIGURE 13

FIGURE 15

3. The remove the trigger guard assembly (001W) by rotating it upwards and out the top of the stock-receiver assembly, Figure 13.

Reassemble is reverse order

Reassembly Tip: Ensure the hammer is cocked in the trigger group assembly before reinstalling.

Tuning Tip: The drop and cast of the R1 stock can be adjusted for a customized fit. For wood stocks, unscrew the two butt plate screws (062L) and remove the butt plate (151W). For synthetic stocks use your thumbs to press out the butt plate (446X). Then for either style stock unscrew the stock retaining nut (053A) using a 13 mm hex or Allen wrench and remove the stock retaining nut, spring washer (052A), stock locking plate (392W), stock (388W/synthetic or 176W-181W/wood), shim deviation spacer (286W) and drop change shim (147W) off the recoil spring tube (049D). Reassemble in reverse order following factory instructions on what shim to install to achieve the desired fit. Make sure the stock is correctly fitted into the receiver before tightening up the stock retaining nut. After firing a first few rounds, check the stock retaining nut to see if it needs retightening.

Maintenance Tip: Do not lubricate the piston (412V), Figure 14. Nor lubricate the inside of the gas collector cylinder under the barrel, Figure 15. Oil can lead to the accumulation of combustion residue. Clean the piston assembly and the inside of the gas collector cylinder with a brush and make sure that the piston slides freely.

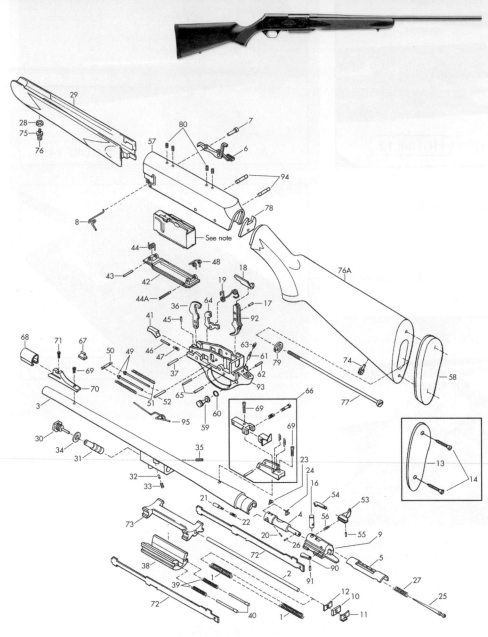

43 Magazine Floorplate
   Retainer Pin
44 Magazine Floorplate Spring
44A Magazine Floorplate
   Spring Pin
45 Magazine Latch Pin
46 Magazine Latch Spring
   Guide
47 Magazine Latch Spring
48 Magazine Retaining Spring
49 Mainspring Guide
50 Mainspring Guide Support
51 Mainspring Right or Left
52 Mainspring Support
53 Operating Handle Bar
54 Operating Handle Lock
55 Operating Handle Lock Pin
56 Operating Handle Lock
   Spring
57 Receiver
58 Recoil Pad
59 Safety
60 Safety O-Ring
61 Safety Plunger
62 Safety Spring Retaining Pin
63 Safety Spring
64 Sear
65 Sear/Trigger Pin
66 Sight Assembly Rear
67 Sight Front
68 Sight Hood
69 Sight Mount Screw
70 Sight Ramp Front
71 Sight Ramp Screw Front
   Long
72 Slide Bar Right & Left
73 Slide Head
74 Slide Eye Rear
75 Sling Eye Washer Front
76 Sling Eyelet Front
77 Stock Bolt
78 Stock Bolt Plate
79 Stock Bolt Washer
80 Telescope Mount Fill Screw
90 Timing Latch
91 Timing Latch Retaining Pin
92 Trigger
93 Trigger Guard
94 Trigger Guard Retaining Pin
95 Trigger Guard Retaining Pin
   Spring

PARTS LIST

1 Action Spring
2 Action Spring Guide
3 Barrel
4 Bolt
5 Bolt Cover
6 Bolt Release
7 Bolt Release Pin
8 Bolt Release POS Spring
9 Bolt Sleeve
10 Buffer
11 Buffer Plate Front
12 Buffer Plate Rear
13 Butt Plate
14 Butt Plate Screws

16 Cam Pin
17 Disconnector Pin
18 Disconnector
19 Disconnector Spring
20 Ejector Retainer Pin
21 Ejector
22 Ejector Spring
23 Extractor
24 Extractor Spring
25 Firing Pin
26 Firing Pin Retainer Pin
27 Firing Pin Spring
28 Forearm Escutcheon
29 Forearm
30 Gas Cylinder Cap

31 Gas Piston
32 Gas Regulator Screw Lock
   Plunger
33 Gas Regulator Screw Lock
   Screw
34 Gas Regulator Gasket
35 Gas Regulator Screw
36 Hammer
37 Hammer Pin
38 Inertia Piece
39 Inertia Piece Spring
40 Inertia Piece Spring Rod
41 Magazine Floorplate
   Latch
42 Magazine Floorplate

SPECIFICATIONS
Model: BAR MK II Safari
Action: semi-automatic, gas-operated piston with rotating bolt
Barrel: 20 to 24 in.
Caliber: .243 Win, .308 Win, .25-06 Rem, .270 Win, .270 WSM, .30-06, 7mm Rem Mag, 7mm WSM, 300 Win Mag, 300 WSM, 338 Win Mag
Capacity: 4-round (magnum calibers) or 5-round (standard calibers) detachable magazines
Common Features: adj. rear/fixed front sight (depending on model), drilled/tapped for optics mount, detachable magazine, crossbolt safety, wood or synthetic stock, blued, matte or camo finish, BOSS muzzle brake (depending on model)

BACKGROUND
Not to be confused with the military weapon M1918 Browning Automatic Rifle, the BAR is a dedicated hunting rifle with a semi-automatic action that allows use of high power hunting cartridges like the 7mm Remington Magnum and the .300 and .338 Winchester Magnums. The design has changed over the years and these procedures are for the newer MK II models with an improved action and removable trigger assembly.
Year Introduced: 1967
Country of Origin: USA
Current Manufacturer: Browning (browning.com)
Similar Models: Lightweight Stalker (alloy receiver, matte finish, polymer stock), White Gold Medallion (gloss nickel, engraved receiver; grade II/III walnut stock)

REQUIRED TOOLS
Field Strip: none
Disassembly/Assembly: small punch

FIELD STRIP
1. Ensure the bolt assembly is in the forward most position and swing open the magazine floorplate (part #42).
2. Push out the two trigger guard retaining pins (94) from either side of the receiver (57) using a small punch, Figure 1.
3. Pull the trigger assembly out from the bottom of the receiver, Figure 2.

At this point the BAR is sufficiently disassembled for cleaning.

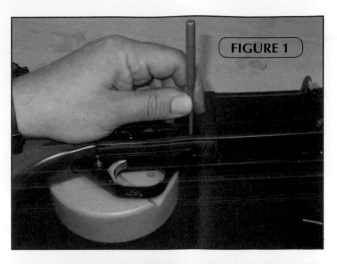

FIGURE 1

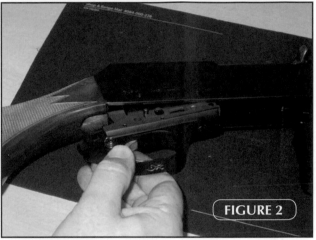

FIGURE 2

DISASSEMBLY
1. Lay the BAR top side down and unscrew the front sling eyelet (76) from the bottom of the forearm (29) using a punch or small screwdriver through the eyelet, Figure 3.
2. Slide the forearm toward the muzzle along the barrel until it comes free, Figure 4.

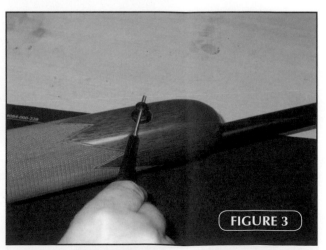

FIGURE 3

FIGURE 4

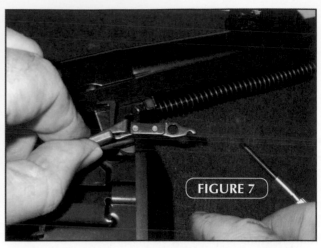

FIGURE 7

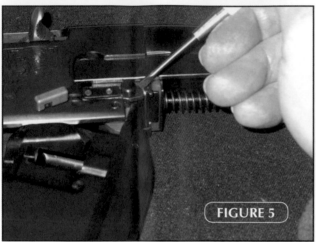

FIGURE 5

FIGURE 8

3. Remove the bolt release (6) from the right side of the receiver by first moving the bolt release spring (8) out of the way to remove tension on the bolt release, Figure 5. Then use a small flat blade screwdriver to gently pry up the bolt release pin (7), Figure 6. The bolt release can then easily be pulled free toward the front/muzzle, Figure 7.

4. Next remove the muzzle end of right slide bar (72) by disconnecting it from the slide head (73) and then pulling the rear tabs of slide bar free from the bolt sleeve (9). Then remove the slide bar by pulling it forward and out from the receiver. Do the same with the left slide bar (72), Figure 8.

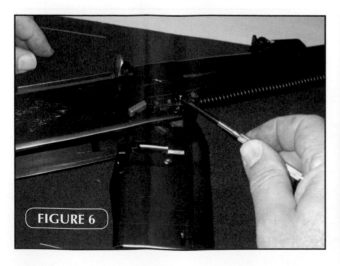

FIGURE 6

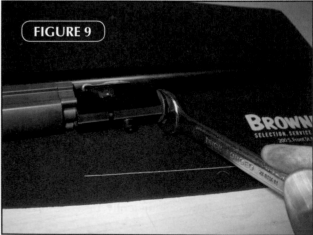

FIGURE 9

5. Unscrew the gas cylinder cap (30) using an 11/16 inch open end wrench, Figure 9. Remove the gas cylinder cap and gas regulator gasket (34).

6. Tip the rifle muzzle end down and tap the muzzle on a padded work surface to dislodge the gas piston (31). It should fall free into your hand, Figure 10.

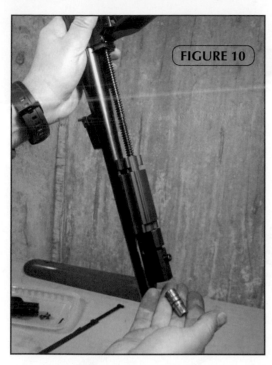

FIGURE 10

7. Next remove the action spring (1) and action spring guide (2) by grasping them and compressing the spring toward the muzzle until it is free from the receiver, Figure 11. Note the guide spring is under tension.

8. To remove the bolt assembly from the receiver, first slide the bolt cover (5) rearward with a small flat blade screwdriver to expose the operating handle lock bar (54). Remove the operating handle (53) by lifting operating handle lock bar with a small flat blade screwdriver, Figure 12. Then slide the operating handle forward and out from the bolt. Move the bolt slightly

rearward and it will come free through the bottom of the receiver.

Reassemble in reverse order.

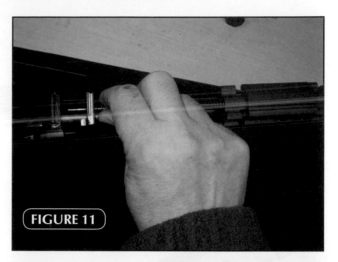

FIGURE 11

FIGURE 12

Cleaning Tip: Do not oil the gas piston. Oil will break down under the intense heat from fired rounds and gung up the piston. Just wipe it clean. Place anti seize compound on the threads of the gas cylinder cap.

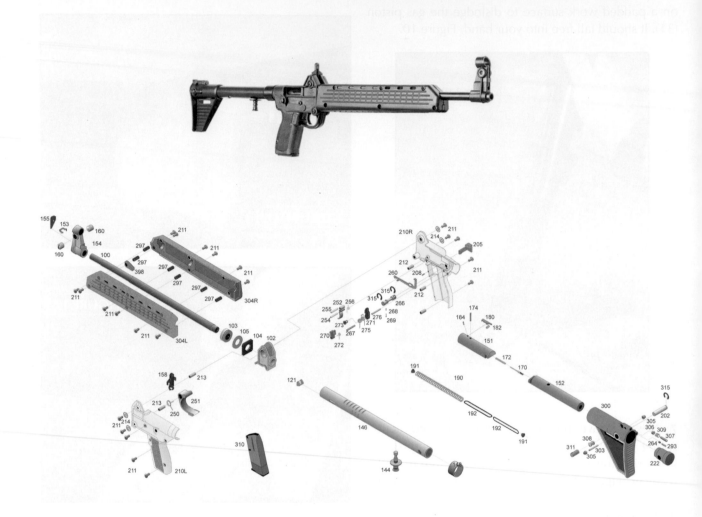

PARTS LIST

100 Barrel
102 Hinge
103 Lock Nut
104 Lock Nut Washer
105 Washer
121 Feed Ramp
144 Operating Handle
146 Bolt Tube
148 Collar
149 Stock Collar
151 Bolt Head
152 Bolt
153 Front Sight Clip
154 Front Sight Body
155 Front Sight Post
158 Rear Sight

160 Windage Screws
170 Firing Pin
172 Firing Pin Spring
174 Firing Pin Pin
180 Extractor
182 Extractor Spring
184 Extractor Pin
190 Recoil Spring
191 Recoil Spring Plug
192 Recoil Spring Guide
202 Stock Pin
205 Magazine Catches
208 Magazine Catch Spring
210L Receiver Left
210R Receiver Right
211 Receiver Screws
212 Receiver Nut 16
213 Receiver Nut 27

214 Washer
222 Buffer
250 Trigger Guard Spring
251 Trigger Guard
252 Trigger
254 Trigger Axis
255 Trigger Bar Pin
256 Trigger Spring
260 Trigger Bar
264 Stock Pin Spring
266 Safety
267 Sear Axis
268 Safety Spring
269 Safety Pin
270 Sear
271 Hammer
272 Sear Spring
273 Hammer Bushing

275 Hammer Spring
276 Hammer Axis
293 Stock Pin Pin
297 Forend Nuts
300 Butt Stock
303 Button Shaft
304 Forend L/R
305 Button
306 Sleeve
307 Pin Lock
308 Lock Shaft
309 Lock Spring
310 Magazines
311 Key
315 Safety E-rings
398 Forend Insert

SPECIFICATIONS

Model: SUB 2000
Action: semiautomatic, blowback operated
Barrel: 16.1 in.
Caliber: 9mm or .40 S&W
Capacity: can be conFigured to accept detachable pistol magazines
Common Features: adj. rear/hooded post front sights, manual safety, blued finish, polymer stock

BACKGROUND

The SUB-2000 is unique because the barrel can be folded making a compact package for storage, Figure 1. Another unique feature of this weapon is that it is compatible with magazines from Glock, S&W, Beretta or SIG. The use of polymers and stamped steel parts make the weapon economical to manufacture and in this case economical to manufacture is not a detriment as the SUB-2000 is a sturdy, accurate weapon. Paired with a pistol that's magazine is compatible makes a formidable home defense system.
Year Introduced: 2001
Country of Origin: USA
Current Manufacturer: Kel-Tec CNC Industries, Inc. (keltecweapons.com)

REQUIRED TOOLS

Field Strip: small punch
Disassembly/Assembly: Philips screwdriver, small flat blade screwdriver, hammer, wood dowel or non-marring rod

FIELD STRIP

1. Place the bolt (part #151) in the forward position with the hammer (271) cocked and the safety (266) on.
2. Use a small punch—or the nose of a cartridge will do in a pinch—to push in the stock pin () from the left to the right side of the stock (202), Figure 2. Pull the stock pin from the right side of the frame enough

FIGURE 1

to remove the buffer (222) from the rear of butt stock (300), Figure 3.
3. Next pull back on the operating handle (144) to move the bolt rearward. The recoil spring (190) will fall free from the butt stock, Figure 4.
4. Pull down on the operating handle and remove it from the bolt tube (146), Figure 5. Point the muzzle upward and the bolt will fall free from the butt stock or use your finger to slide it free, Figure 6.

At this point the SUB-2000 is sufficiently disassembled for routine cleaning. Since the SUB-2000 is manufactured

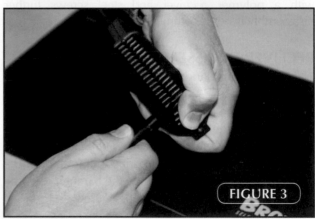

FIGURE 2

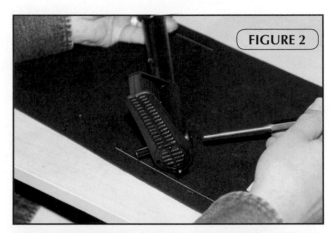

FIGURE 3

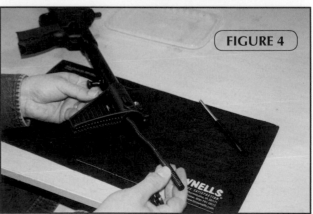

FIGURE 4

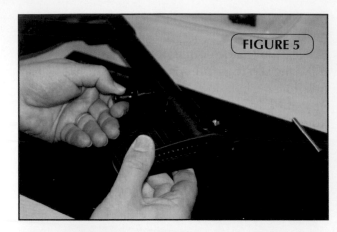

FIGURE 5

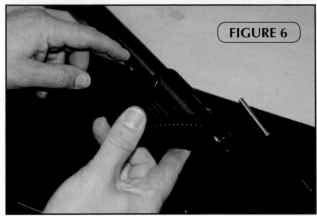

FIGURE 6

with a polymer receiver and steel screws further disassembly is not recommended.

RECEIVER DISASSEMBLY

1. Fold the barrel and place the rifle right side facing up.
2. Insert a piece of small wood dowel or non-marring rod—I use a large Sharpie pen or toothbrush handle—into the front of the receiver to control the hammer. While using the wood/non-marring tool to control the hammer, pull the trigger to allow the hammer to come fully forward in the fired position, Figure 7.

FIGURE 7

3. Next use a punch and hammer to remove the stock collar (143) by rotating it counterclockwise. Place the punch in the notches of the stock collar for leverage, Figure 8.
4. Remove the safety E-ring (315) off the safety (266) using a small flat blade screwdriver, Figure 9.

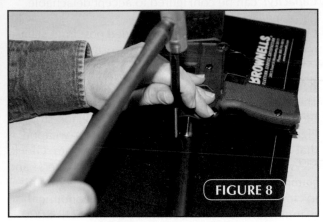

FIGURE 8

5. Using a Phillips screwdriver, remove five receiver screws (211). Note that the two forward most screws have a washer (214).
6. Insert a wooden dowel or wooden hammer handle into the magazine well and/or barrel area to gently pry apart the two halves of the receiver—receiver right (210R) and receiver left (210L). The receiver halves are made of polymer and can be easily marred or ruined with too much force. Do not gorilla-arm the receiver. Note that the receiver halves contain the inner mechanism in place. The magazine catch spring (208) will come free with the receiver right.
7. With the receiver right removed, the barrel assembly can be pulled off the receiver nut (213). With the barrel removed the rear sight (158) will fall free.
8. Remove the trigger bar (260) and trigger (252) as an assembly.

Reassemble in reverse order.

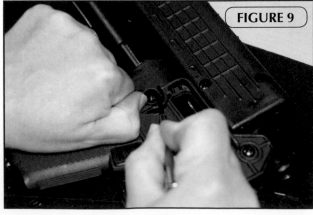

FIGURE 9

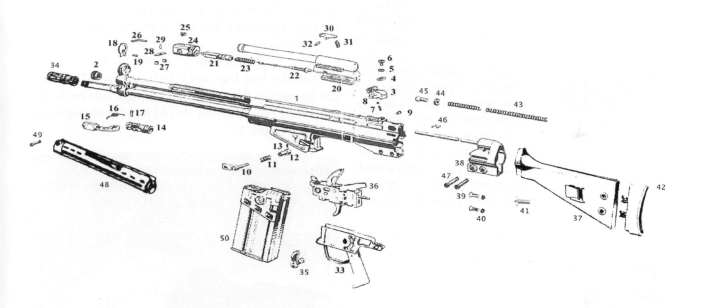

PARTS LIST

1 Receiver with barrel and cocking lever housing
2 Cap complete
3 Rotary rear sight
4 Washer
5 Toothed lock washer
6 Clamping screw
7 Compression springs for ball catch (2 Req'd.)
8 Balls (2 Req'd.)
9 Windage adjusting screw
10 Magazine catch complete
11 Compression spring for magazine catch

12 Push button for magazine catch
13 Clamping sleeve
14 Support for cocking lever
15 Cocking lever
16 Elbow spring for cocking lever
17 Cocking lever axle
18 Front sight
19 Clamping sleeve
20 Bolt head carrier
21 Locking piece
22 Firing pin
23 Firing pin spring
24 Bolt head, complete

25 Extractor
26 Extractor spring
27 Locking roller
28 Holder for cocking rollers
29 Clamping sleeve 2 x 6.9
30 Bolt head locking lever
31 Compression spring for bolt head locking lever
32 Cylindrical pin
33 Pistol grip
34 Flash hider
35 Safety, complete
36 Trigger housing, complete
37 Butt stock
38 Back plate, complete

39 Countersunk screw for buffer
40 Lock washer
41 Recoil Buffer
42 Butt plate
43 Recoil spring
44 Recoil spring guide ring
45 Recoil spring stop pin
46 2 riveted pins
47 Butt stock locking pin
42 Butt plate
41 Recoil buffer
48 Handguard
49 Handguard locking pin
50 Magazine 20 rounds

SPECIFICATIONS

Model: PTR91KC
Action: semiautomatic, roller-delayed blowback
Barrel: 16.0 in.
Caliber: 7.62x51mm NATO/.308 Win
Capacity: 5-, 10-, 20-round detachable magazines
Common Features: rotary drum rear/hooded post front sights, flash suppressor, grooved receiver for clamp optics mount, sling swivels, manual safety, blued finish, polymer stock, ventilated stamped steel handguard

BACKGROUND

The PTR91 is a design variation of the battle-proven Heckler & Koch G3 rifle. CETME helped refine the design. It came into service in the late 1950s and derivations are still in service with many militaries in Africa, South America, Asia and Europe. The PTR91 is a semi-automatic civilian version that is made in the U.S. It uses a roller-delayed blowback action that compared to gas or recoil operated mechanisms is simple and effective, Figure 1. When a cartridge is fired the bolt is driven rearward as rollers on the sides of the bolt are pushed inward against a tapered bolt carrier. The energy is transferred to the locking piece and bolt carrier as energy pressure drops the mechanism ejects the case, scraps a fresh round out of the magazine and pushes it into the chambers. All in an instant. It can also be instantly disassembled.

Year Introduced: 2000 (H&K G3 debuted in the 1959)
Country of Origin: USA (H&K, West Germany)
Current Manufacturer: PTR91 (ptr91.com)
Similar Models: PTR91F, PTR91C, PTR91KF, PTR91KFM4, PTR91KCM4, PTR91KFM4R, PTR91KCM4R, PTR91KPF, PTR91KPFR, PTR91SC, PTR91SCC, PTR MSG91, PTR MSG91C, PTR MSG91SS, PTR G.I., PTR-91 PDW

REQUIRED TOOLS

Field Strip: none
Disassembly/Assembly: small punch

FIELD STRIP

1. Remove the magazine and place the safety lever (part #35) on "safe" or "S."
2. Unfold the cocking handle (15) on the left side of the barreled receiver (1) at the front of the handguard (48). Pull the cocking handle fully rearward to cock the rifle and release the cocking handle allowing it to return to forward most position.

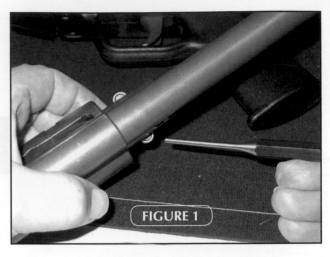
FIGURE 1

3. Rotate the selector lever to "fire" or "F" and press the trigger to allow the bolt to return to its closed or fired position.
4. Rotate the selector back to "safe" or "S."
5. Push the two butt stock locking pins (47) located just forward of the stock from the right side to the left side of the rifle. The pins should move with just finger pressure, Figure 3.

Disassembly Tip: It is best practice to place the butt stock locking pins into the pin holders in the butt stock so they do not get lost, Figure 2.

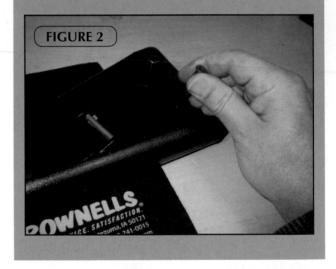
FIGURE 2

6. Next the butt stock assembly consisting of butt stock (37), butt plate (42), back plate (38) and recoil spring (43) can now be pulled from the rear of the barreled receiver, Figure 4. If it is snug, use the palm of your hand to hit the stock comb.
7. With the butt stock assembly removed, remove the trigger group—pistol grip (33) and complete trigger

FIGURE 3

FIGURE 5

housing (36)—by pulling downward on the pistol grip, Figure 5.

8. Next the bolt assembly will easily slide out of the rear of the barreled receiver by tipping the muzzle upward. Place your hand at the rear of barreled receiver to catch the bolt assembly, Figure 6. If the bolt assembly is snug, unfold the cocking handle and pull it rearward. This will free up the bolt assembly so it can be pulled out of the barreled receiver.

At this point the PTR-91 is field stripped.

FIGURE 4

FIGURE 6

4. The extractor (25) is removed with a small flat blade screwdriver by lifting the extractor spring (26) to clear the edge of the extractor and then pull the extractor spring out to the front of the bolt head. The extractor can then be lifted out of the bolt head.

BOLT DISASSEMBLY

1. To disassemble to bolt assembly, first turn the bolt head (24) one half turn—about 90°—clockwise and pull it forward out of the bolt head carrier (20) toward the front/muzzle, Figure 7.

2. Then rotate the locking piece (21) counterclockwise until its lug clears the carrier.

3. The firing pin (21) and firing pin spring (23) can now be removed.

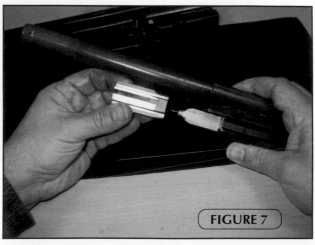

FIGURE 7

TRIGGER HOUSING DISASSEMBLY

1. The trigger assembly can be further disassembled by first ensuring the hammer is in the fired position, then turn the safety lever up to a vertical position and remove it from the pistol grip, Figure 8.

2. The trigger housing can then be pulled out from the top of the pistol grip, Figure 9.

3. The ejector is removed by first holding the ejector and pushing the ejector pin from the inside of the trigger housing to the outside of the trigger housing. Pull the ejector out of the housing.

4. Remove the hammer spring by restraining the hammer spring and hammer strut with your thumb.

5. Then through a cut out hole in the right side of the trigger housing use a small screwdriver

Reassembly Tip: When inserting the bolt head on the locking piece make sure the slot on the bolt head is at the top. Then turn the bolt head clockwise until the angled relief cut at the base of the bolt is aligned with the bolt head locking piece. The bolt head is correctly installed if the bolt rollers can be squeezed into each other.

FIGURE 8

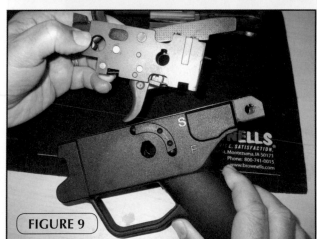

FIGURE 9

to push the hammer strut out of its notch in the hammer.

Reassemble is reverse order.

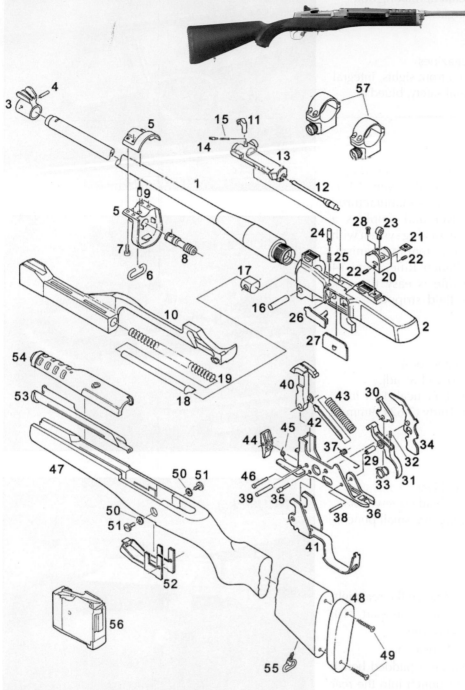

PARTS LIST

1 Barrel
2 Receiver
3 Front Sight
4 Front Sight Cross Pin
5 Gas Block, Top & Bottom, 2 pieces
6 Sling Swivel, Front
7 Gas Block Screw (4 Req'd.)
8 Gas Pipe
9 Gas Port Bushing

10 Slide Assembly
11 Extractor
12 Firing Pin
13 Bolt
14 Extractor Plunger
15 Extractor Spring
16 Buffer Cross Pin
17 Buffer Bushing
18 Buffer Guide Rod
19 Slide Spring
20 Rear Sight Base

21 Rear Sight Dovetail Slide
22 Rear Sight Windage Screw (2 Req'd.)
23 Rear Sight Aperture
24 Bolt Lock Plunger
25 Bolt Lock Plunger Spring
26 Ejector Bolt Lock
27 Cover Plate
28 Rear Sight Attachment Screw
29 Trigger Bushing
30 Secondary Sear

31 Trigger M
32 Secondary Sear Spring
33 Trigger Spring
34 Safety Assembly
35 Safety Spring Retainer Pin
36 Trigger Housing
37 Safety Detent Spring
38 Trigger Pivot Pin
39 Hammer Pivot Pin
40 Hammer
41 Trigger Guard
42 Hammer Strut
43 Hammer Spring
44 Rear Magazine Latch
45 Magazine Latch Spring
46 Magazine Latch Pivot Pin
47 Stock, Wood
48 Butt Pad
49 Butt Pad Screw (2 Req'd.)
50 Stock Reinforcement Lock Washer (2 Req'd.)
51 Stock Reinforcement Screw (2 Req'd.)
52 Stock Reinforcement
53 Forearm Liner & Stock Cap Assembly
54 Handguard Assembly
55 Sling Swivel, Rear
56 Magazine, Complete

SPECIFICATIONS

Model: Mini-14 Ranch
Action: semiautomatic, gas-operated, rotating bolt
Stock: wood or polymer w/ fiberglass handguard
Barrel: 18.5 in.
Caliber: 5.56mm NATO/.223
Capacity: 5-, 10-, 20-round magazines
Common Features: adj. rear/fixed front sights, integral scope bases, sling swivels, manual safety, blued or stainless finish

BACKGROUND

The Mini-14 was the first in a series of compact, high capacity, semi-automatic rifles produced by Ruger. Based on the U.S. Military M14, the Mini-14 is smaller in size, hence the name. It is manufactured with an investment cast receiver and employs a version of the M1 rifle breechbolt locking system with a self-cleaning, fixed-piston gas system mechanism. Current variants include the Ranch Rifle, Mini-14 Tactical and Mini Thirty. The rifle is easy to work on and with practice can be field stripped rather quickly.

Year Introduced: 1974
Country of Origin: USA
Current Manufacturer: Ruger (ruger.com)
Similar Models: Target (22.0 in. barrel w/ adj. harmonic dampener, .223 caliber), Tactical (16.1 in. barrel w/ flash suppressor), Mini Thirty (7.62x39mm caliber)

REQUIRED TOOLS

Field Strip: small punch or screwdriver
Disassembly/Assembly: small flat blade screwdriver; paperclip or small nail for retaining pin, small punch, hammer

FIELD STRIP

1. Remove the magazine and fold down the rear sight then cycle the action by pulling the slide (part #10) fully to the rear so the hammer is cocked.
2. Put the safety (34) in the "safe" position.
3. Place the rifle top side down on a padded bench and insert a small screwdriver or punch into the rear hole in the trigger guard (41) and push forward and up to unlatch the trigger guard tab from the slot in the trigger housing (36), Figure 1.
4. Next pull the trigger assembly straight upward, out of the bottom of the stock (47), Figure 2.
5. Gently pull up on the rear of the receiver and the barreled receiver will come free from the stock, Figure 3.
6. Remove the fiberglass handguard (54) from the receiver/barrel assembly using both thumbs to pop off

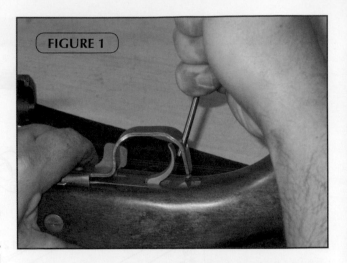

FIGURE 1

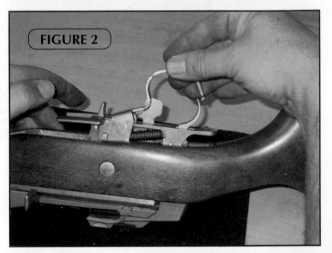

FIGURE 2

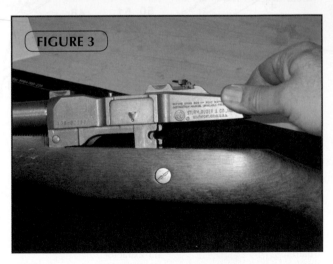

FIGURE 3

the spring clip retainer on the underside of the handguard from the barrel. Apply pressure to raise the rear portion of the handguard first then pull it back out from the gas block top.

7. Next grasp the guide rod (18) and recoil spring (19) and pull them to slightly compress the recoil spring and clear the retaining recess in the front of the

receiver (2), Figure 4. Note the recoil spring is under tension so control it as it relieves tension and pull the recoil spring and guide rod to the rear until it is free from the slide.

8. The buffer bushing (17) and buffer cross pin (17) may fall out of the receiver once the recoil spring is removed.

9. Next pull the slide rearward so that its rear lug aligns with the notch in the receiver and then pull it out from the receiver, Figure 5.

10. Next move the bolt (13) forward and remove it by pivoting up and to the right, Figure 6.

At this point the Mini-14 and its variants is field stripped for routine cleaning.

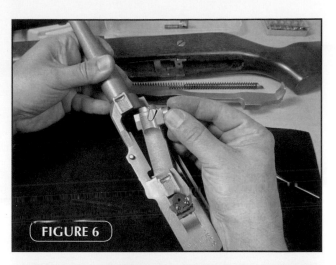

FIGURE 6

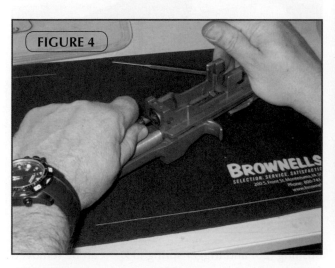

FIGURE 4

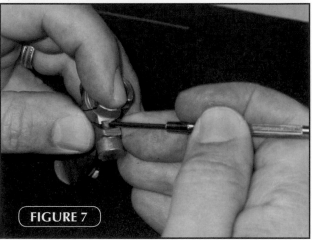

FIGURE 7

bolt. Note that the extractor plunger is under tension from the extractor spring (15) make sure to control it.

2. With the extractor removed the firing pin (12) can be removed from the rear of the bolt.

RECEIVER DISASSEMBLY

1. To remove the bolt latch (26) and bolt lock plunger (24) from the receiver, first slide the cover plate (27) down and out from the receiver. You may need a punch to start the cover plate.

2. Depress the bolt lock plunger with one hand and cup your hand over bolt lock plunger, Figure 8. Flip the barrel/receiver assembly to the left and the bolt latch will fall out. Note the bolt lock plunger is under tension from the bolt lock plunger spring (25) so control it as you release pressure and remove it from the receiver.

3. To remove the hammer, pull back on the hammer as if cocking it and insert a paperclip, small nail or small punch through the hole in the hammer strut (42) to restrain the hammer spring (43), Figure 9.

4. Then push the safety to "fire" position, pull the trigger and control the hammer to relieve tension. You can then lift the front of the hammer strut from the hammer

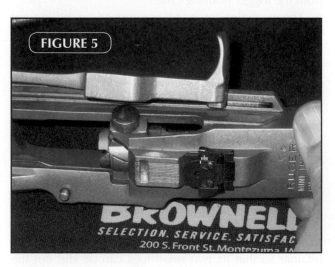

FIGURE 5

BOLT DISASSEMBLY

1. To further disassemble the bolt, insert a small flat blade screwdriver between the extractor (11) and extractor plunger (14), Figure 7. While depressing the extractor plunger you will be able to move the extractor from the

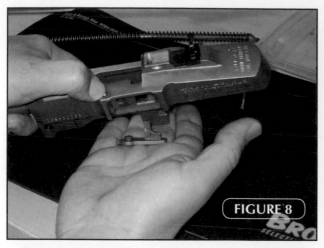

FIGURE 8

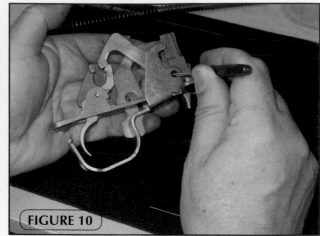

FIGURE 10

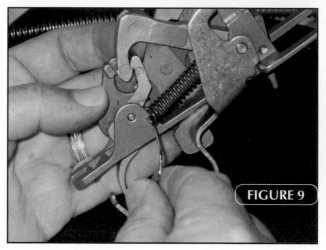

FIGURE 9

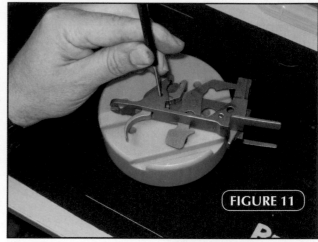

FIGURE 11

and the rear from the trigger housing. Note the hammer spring is under pressure, do not remove the nail.

5. Next push out the hammer pivot pin (39) with a punch and the hammer and the trigger guard will come free, Figure 10.

Disassembly Tip: Note that the gas block should not be removed and the four gas block screws are staked at the factory. The gas block assembly is removed from the barrel (1) by unscrewing the four gas block screws (7) with a 9/64 hex or Allen wrench. With screws removed the gas block assembly—gas block top & bottom (5), gas port bushing (9), gas pipe (8)—can easily be removed from the barrel. If you do remove the gas block, be sure to tighten all four screws evenly. Use a feeler gauge to ensure the gap is the same all around and torque to 30 in-lbs.

6. To remove the trigger assembly, use a small punch to push out the trigger pivot pin (38). The pin should push easily out, Figure 11.

7. With the pin removed, the trigger assembly—trigger, secondary sear (30), secondary sear spring (32), trigger

bushing (29) and trigger spring (33) —can be removed from the trigger housing (36).

8. The magazine latch (44) is removed by drifting out the magazine latch pin (46) from the right side of the trigger housing to left side. Note the magazine latch is under tension from the magazine latch spring (45).

MAGAZINE DISASSEMBLY

1. Disassemble the magazine by inserting a mall screwdriver into the hole located in the magazine bottom and depressing the magazine bottom retainer.

2. Push the magazine bottom rearward as you push down on the spring-loaded bottom retainer with the screwdriver.

3. With the magazine bottom removed from the magazine shell, raise the rear of the magazine bottom retainer so that its two small lugs can be slid out the rear of the magazine shell. Note the magazine spring is under tension. With the magazine bottom retainer removed the magazine spring and magazine follower extracted from the magazine shell.

Reassemble in reverse order.

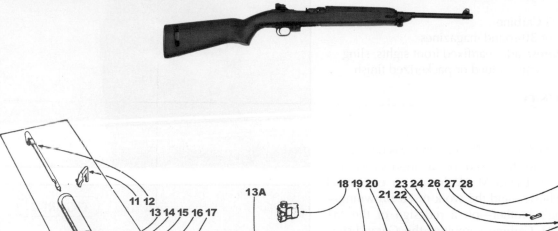

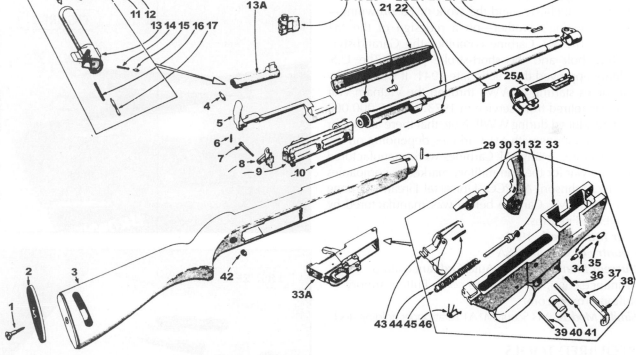

Courtesy of Numrich Gun Parts Corporation

PARTS LIST

1. Buttplate Screw
2. Buttplate
3. Stock
4. Slide Lock
5. Slide
6. Slide Lock Spring
7. Recoil Plate Screw
8. Recoil Plate
9. Receiver
10. Operating Slide Spring
11. Extractor

12. Firing Pin
13. Bolt
14. Extractor Spring
15. Extractor Spring Plunger
16. Ejector Spring
17. Ejector
18. Rear Sight
19. Gas Piston Nut
20. Gas Piston
21. Handguard
22. Barrel
23. Recoil Spring Guide

24. Band Spring
25. Barrel Band
26. Front Sight
27. Front Sight Key
28. Front Sight Pin
29. Trigger Housing Pin
30. Sear
31. Hammer
32. Hammer Spring Plunger
33. Trigger Housing
34. Safety Spring
35. Safety Spring Plunger

36. Magazine Catch Spring
37. Magazine Catch Spring
38. Magazine Catch Plunger
39. Magazine Catch
40. Trigger Pin
41. Safety
42. Hammer Pin
43. Stock Escutcheon
44. Trigger
45. Sear Spring
46. Hammer Spring
47. Trigger Spring

SPECIFICATIONS
Model: M1 Carbine
Action: semiautomatic, gas-operated, rotating bolt
Stock: wood
Barrel: 18 in.
Caliber: .30 US Carbine
Capacity: 15- or 30-round magazines
Common Features: adj. rear/fixed front sights, sling swivels, manual safety, blued or packerized finish

BACKGROUND
In military parlance it's called the United States Carbine, Caliber .30, M1, but to most everyone else it's known as the M1 Carbine. The carbine was developed from 1938-41 mostly based on a short-stroke gas piston design by David M. Williams, an ex-convict hired by Winchester, and the work of Ed Browning—John Browning's brother—on a redesign of the M1 Garand. The M1 Carbine combines the Garand-style rotating bolt and the short-stroke piston. The U.S. military approved the rifle in late 1941. It was used by our forces starting in WWII through the Vietnam War and was retired from service in 1973. Over 6,000,000 were produced during WWII. Note that there are minor design variations with M1 Carbines depending on the manufacturer. Many M1 Carbines were manufactured after the war for the non-military market by companies like Iver Johnson, AMPCO, Universal Firearms among others. The M1 Carbine below was manufactured by Universal Firearms.
Year Introduced: 1941
Country of Origin: USA
Current Manufacturers: Auto Ordnance (auto-ordnance.com), CMP (odcmp.com), Fulton Armory (fulton-armory.com)
Similar Models: M3 Scout, M1A1 Paratrooper (folding stock)

REQUIRED TOOLS
Field Strip: medium flat blade screwdriver
Disassembly/Assembly: bolt assembly-disassembly tool (optional), two small flat blade screwdrivers, vise (optional)

FIELD STRIP
1. Remove magazine.
2. Loosen barrel band (25) and depress the band spring (24) using a medium flat blade screwdriver, Figure 1.
3. Slide barrel band forward toward muzzle and off barrel (22) or side it as far as the front sight. Some models have a collar attached to the band.
4. Slide the handguard (21) forward until its metal liner or the tab of the handguard disengages from the front of receiver (9) and lift handguard off barrel, Figure 2.

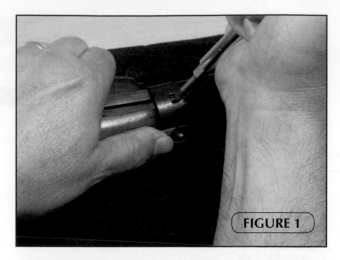

FIGURE 1

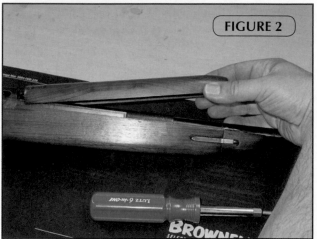

FIGURE 2

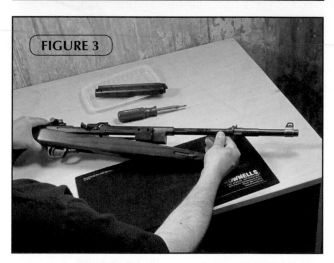

FIGURE 3

5. Lift muzzle of barrel to separate barrel/receiver assembly from stock (3), Figure 3.
6. Push the trigger housing retaining pin (29) out of receiver and trigger housing (33) from left to right, Figure 4.
7. Slide the trigger housing forward until it clears the grooves at rear of receiver and remove it from receiver, Figure 5.

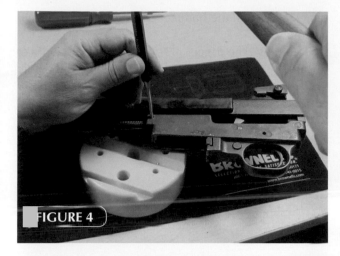

FIGURE 4

FIGURE 5

8. Next grasp the recoil spring guide (23) and operating slide spring (10) and pull them to slightly compress the recoil spring and clear the retaining seat in the receiver. Note the operating slide spring is under tension so control it. On some variations there are a pair of recoil spring guides and operating slide springs

9. Slide the slide (5) toward the muzzle until the projection on the operating slide aligns with the notch in the receiver, then pull the slide away from the receiver.

10. Rotate and pivot the bolt assembly (13A) to remove it from the receiver.

At this point the M1 Carbine and its variants is field stripped for routine cleaning.

BOLT DISASSEMBLY

1. To remove the extractor (11) use two small screwdrivers; one screwdriver holds down the extractor spring plunger (15) and the other screwdriver gently pries out the extractor. The extractor spring (14) in under compression so control it and the extractor plunger once the extractor is removed from the bolt

(13). If you use the two screwdriver method it is easier if you hold the bolt in a padded vise.

2. With the extractor removed the firing pin (12) can be removed from the rear of the bolt.

Tool Tip: Numrich Gun Parts Corp. (gunpartscorp.com) has original, GI issue, bolt tools that make extractor removal easy, Figure 6. It's like having a third hand.

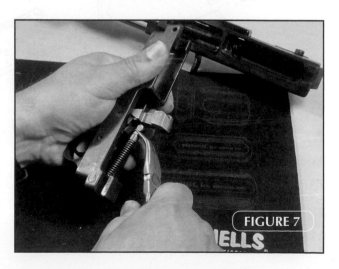

FIGURE 6

RECEIVER DISASSEMBLY

1. To remove the hammer (31), restrain the hammer and pull the trigger (43) to allow the hammer to move to its forward/"fire" position. Next insert a medium punch into the hole of the hammer spring plunger (32) to restrain the hammer spring (45). Then pull the hammer spring plunger and the hammer spring out from the back of the hammer. Or on some variations use a pair of needle-nose pliers to pull back on the hammer spring plunger and hammer spring to remove it from the hammer, Figure 7. Next remove the hammer

FIGURE 7

FIGURE 8

pin (41) and pull the hammer out the top of the trigger assembly.

2. To remove the trigger (43), use a small screwdriver to partially pull out the trigger spring (46) from the hole in the rear of the trigger housing (33) as far as it will come. Next hold down the sear (30) and use a punch to push out the trigger pin (39). Then remove the sear, sear spring (44) and trigger from the top of the trigger housing, Figure 8.

Reassemble in reverse order.

U.S. M14　　　　　　　　　　　　**CLASSIC MILITARY FIREARM**

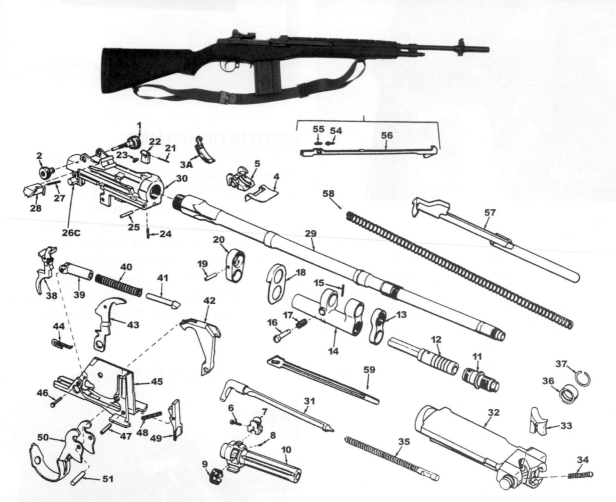

Courtesy of Numrich Gun Parts Corporation

PARTS LIST

1 Rear Sight Elevation Pinion	6 Front Sight Screw	12 Gas Piston	18 Front Band
2 Windage Knob	7 Front Sight	13 Gas Cylinder Lock	19 Operating Rod Guide Spring
3A Aperture	8 Flash Suppressor Set Screw	14 Gas Cylinder	Pin
4 Rear Sight Cover	9 Flash Suppressor Nut	15 Gas Cylinder Pin	20 Operating Rod Guide
5 Rear Sight Base	10 Flashhider/Flash Suppressor	16 Gas Cylinder Valve Spindle	21 Bolt Lock Pin
	11 Gas Cylinder Plug	17 Gas Cylinder Valve Spring	22 Bolt Lock

23 Bolt Lock Spring	33 Extractor	43 Safety	53 Connector Rod Pin
24 Connector Lock Pin	34 Extractor Plunger & Spring	44 Safety Spring	54 Connector Spring
25 Connector Lock	35 Ejector & Spring	45 Trigger Housing	55 Connector Plunger
26C Selector	36 Bolt Roller	46 Trigger Pin	56 Connector Rod Body
27 Clip Guide Pin	37 Bolt Roller Retainer	47 Magazine Latch Pin	57 Operating Rod
28 Cartridge Clip Guide	38 Trigger & Sear Assembly	48 Magazine Latch Spring	58 Operating Rod Spring
29 Barrel	39 Hammer Spring Housing	49 Magazine Latch	59 Operating Rod Spring Guide
30 Receiver	40 Hammer Spring	50 Trigger Guard	
31 Firing Pin	41 Hammer Plunger	51 Trigger Guard Pin	
32 Bolt	42 Hammer	52 Connector Rod Assembly	

SPECIFICATIONS

Model: M14
Action: semiautomatic, gas-operated, rotating bolt
Stock: wood or polymer
Barrel: 22 in.
Caliber: .308 (7.62x51mm)
Capacity: 20-round magazines
Common Features: adj. rear/fixed front sights, sling swivels, manual safety, blued or packerized finish

BACKGROUND

Known officially as the United States Rifle, 7.62mm, M14, this combat rifle featured selective fire. It was delivered to the U.S. Army in 1959 and deployed to troops in 1961. Though it served in Vietnam, jungle warfare did not suit this rifle. It was long and heavy, and the wood stock deteriorated in the humid jungle environment. Troops liked the knockdown power of the 7.62x51mm (.308 Winchester) cartridge, but the rifle was very hard to control on full automatic. Fiberglass stocks fixed the rot problem and the M14 was replaced with M16 in 1970. In Afghanistan and Iraq M14s served as designated marksman and sniper rifles being highly effective to ranges beyond 300 meters. The M14 easily disassembles.

Year Introduced: 1959
Country of Origin: USA
Current Manufacturers: Fulton Armory (fulton-armory.com), Springfield Armory (springfield-armory.com)
Similar Models: SOCOM (16-in. barrel), Scout Squad (18-in. barrel), Match (target barrel)

REQUIRED TOOLS

Field Strip: small punch or screwdriver
Disassembly/Assembly: 1/16 inch hex or Allen wrench, a gas block wrench, castle nut pliers

FIELD STRIP

1. Remove the magazine, close the bolt assembly and place the safety (part #43) on "safe."
2. Remove the trigger housing group by placing the rifle upside down with top of receiver (30) resting on a bench block to protect the rear sight. Insert a punch or small screwdriver into the hole in the rear of the trigger guard (50) and pull upward and outward until the trigger guard is released from the trigger housing (45), Figure 1.
3. Lift out the trigger housing group from the bottom of the stock, Figure 2.
4. Next separate the barrel/receiver assembly from the stock by gasping the top of the receiver and gently tapping the stock away from the barrel/receiver assembly, Figure 3.

At this point the M14 is sufficiently disassembled for cleaning.

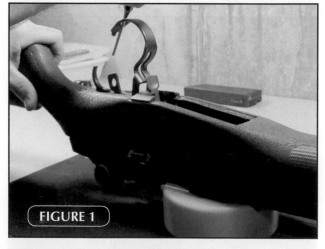

FIGURE 1

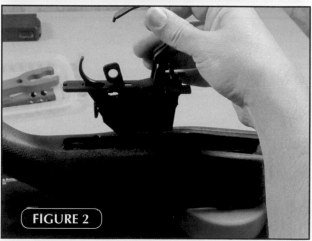

FIGURE 2

BARREL/RECEIVER DISASSEMBLY

1. Place the barrel/receiver assembly sights down on a bench top then pull the operating rod spring (58) and operating rod spring guide (59) toward the muzzle and pull out the connector lock (25) as far as it will go to disengage the operating spring guide and the receiver, Figure 4.

The operating rod spring is under tension so control it as it expands.

2. Flip the barrel/receiver assembly so the sights are facing up and pull back on the operating rod (57) until the lug in its inside surface is aligned with the disassembly notch on the right side of the receiver. Then rotate the operating rod upward and outward to disengage it from the barrel/receiver assembly, Figure 5.

3. Grasp the bolt roller (36) and while sliding it forward lift it upward and outward to the right front of the barrel/receiver assembly, Figure 6.

4. To remove the flashhider/flash suppressor (10) use a 1/16 hex or Allen wrench to unscrew and remove the flash suppressor set screw (8) then using a gas block wrench to hold the gas cylinder (14) use castle

FIGURE 3

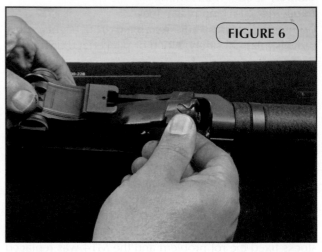

FIGURE 6

FIGURE 4

nut pliers to loosen the flash suppressor nut (9) and remove the flashhider/flash suppressor from the muzzle.

5. The gas cylinder plug (11) is removed by using a gas block wrench to hold the gas cylinder then use a GI multi-tool or a 3/8 inch box end wrench to remove the gas cylinder plug, Figure 7.

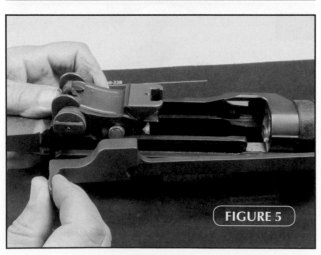

FIGURE 5

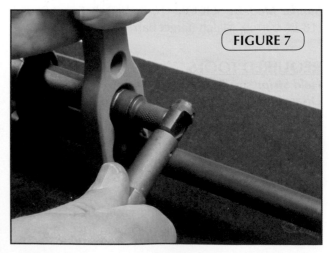

FIGURE 7

Disassembly Tip: Place a witness mark with a pencil on the gas cylinder plug and gas cylinder so you know how much to tighten gas cylinder plug during reassembly.

BOLT DISASSEMBLY

1. Place the cutout portion of a GI multi tool over the ejector (35) and the flat blade screwdriver portion of the tool under the extractor (33), Figure 8.

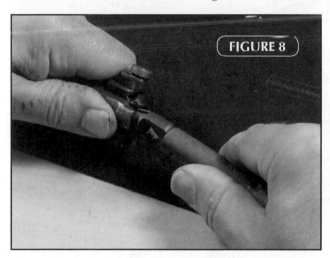

FIGURE 8

2. Push the tool into the bolt face and rotate the tool clockwise. The extractor and ejector can then be removed from the front of the bolt and the firing pin (31) can be removed from the rear of the bolt.

Reassemble in reverse order.

Tool Tip: Use a gas block wrench (top) to hold the gas block without damaging it, then use the GI multi tool (botto m) to unscrew the gas cylinder plug, Figure 9. Castle nut pliers are invaluable when removing flash suppressors, Figure 10.

SADLAK INDUSTRIES LLC

FIGURE 9

FIGURE 10

Cleaning Tip: Use a 3M Scotch Brite pad to remove carbon build-up on the outside of the gas piston (12).

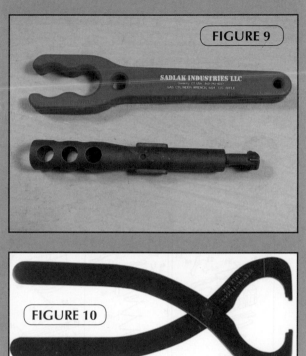

Centerfire Bolt Action

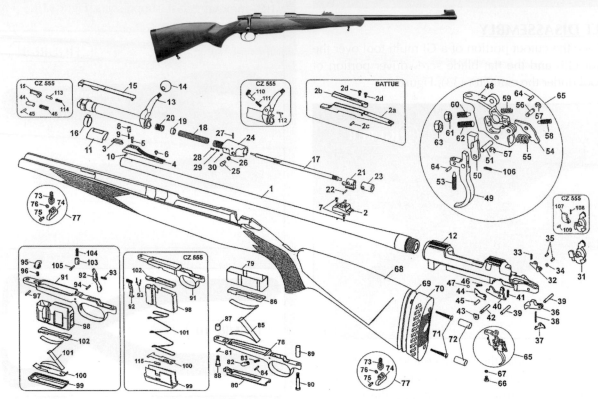

PARTS LIST

1 Barrel
2 Rear Sight
3 Front Sight
4 Front Sight Base
5 Front Sight Base Screw
6 Front Sight Base Screw
7 Rear Sight Base Screw
8 Front Sight Detent
9 Detent Spring
10 Pin, Front Sight Detent
11 Front Sight Cover
12 Receiver
13 Bolt
14 Bolt Handle Knob
15 Extractor
16 Extractor Collar
17 Firing Pin
18 Firing Pin Spring
19 Support, Firing Pin Spring
20 Nut, Firing Pin Spring
21 Cocking Piece
22 Pin, Firing Pin Nut
23 Cap
24 Bolt Sleeve
25 Disassembly Catch
26 Disassembly Catch Spring
27 Disassembly Catch Pin
28 Disassembly Catch Plunger
29 Plunger Spring
30 Plunger Pin

31 Safety
32 Safety Pawl (A)
33 Safety Pawl Spring (A)
34 Roller
35 Safety Pawl Pin (2x)
36 Sear
37 Sear Stop
38 Sear Spring
39 Sear Pin (2x)
40 Bolt Stop
41 Bolt Stop Spring
42 Safety Pin
43 Retaining Plate
44 Ejector
45 Ejector Pin
46 Ejector Spring
47 Ball
48 Trigger Housing
49 Trigger
50 Trigger Lever
51 Trigger Lever Pin
53 Adjusting Screw, Set Trigger
54 Set Trigger Lever
55 Spring, Set Trigger Lever
56 Pin
57 Retaining Ring (2x)
58 Adjusting Screw (B)
59 Spring, Trigger Pull
60 Adjusting Screw, Trigger
   Pull (A)
61 Locking Nut

62 Adjusting Screw, Trigger
   Overtravel (C)
63 Locking Nut M4
64 Nylon Pin (2x)
65 Trigger Mechanism
66 Screw
67 Spring Washer
68 Stock
69 Butt Plate Spacer
70 Butt Plate
71 Screw, Butt Plate (2x)
72 Butt Plate Plug (2x)
73 Swivel Wood Screw
74 Sling Swivel
75 Swivel Screw
76 Swivel Screw Washer
77 Swivel Assembly (2x)
78 Trigger Guard - Box Version
79 Box Shell
80 Floor Plate
81 Floor Plate Pin
82 Floor Plate Latch
83 Spring, Floor Plate Latch
84 Pin, Floor Plate Latch
85 Magazine Box Spring
86 Magazine Follower
87 Front Spacer
88 Frame Screw, Front
89 Rear Spacer
90 Frame Screw, Rear
91 Trigger Guard - Magazine

   Version
92 Magazine Latch
93 Magazine Latch Spring
94 Magazine Latch Pin
95 Magazine Catch
96 Magazine Catch Spring
97 Magazine Catch Pin
98 Magazine Shell
99 Magazine Floor Plate
100 Floor Plate Lock
101 Magazine Spring
102 Follower
103 Magazine Ejector
104 Magazine Ejector Spring
105 Magazine Ejector Pin
106 Trigger Spring
107 Safety Pawl (B)
108 Safety Pawl Spring (B)
109 Safety Pawl Pin
110 Bolt Pawl
111 Bolt Pawl Spring
112 Bolt Pawl Pin
113 Extractor Pin
114 Extractor Pin Spring
115 Magazine Floor Plate Insert
116 Fore End Band
117 Fore End Band Screw
118 Fore End Band Nut

SPECIFICATIONS

Model: CZ 550 FS
Action: bolt, control feed, two lug
Stock: Turkish walnut, fiberglass or Kevlar; some models with aluminum bedding
Barrel: 16 in. (Urban Sniper), 20 in. (FS, Medium Battue Lux, Kevlar Carbine), 24 in., 26 in. (Varmint), 28 in. (Magnum H.E.T.)
Weight Unloaded: 8 lb., 9.4 lb. (Safari Magnum), up to 10.9 lb. (Safari Express), 13 lb. (Magnum H.E.T.)
Caliber: .22-250, .243 Win, 6.5x55, .270 Win, 7mm Rem Mag, .308 Win, .30-06, .300 Win Mag, 9.3x62 (standard models); .300 H&H Mag, .338 Win Mag, .338 Lapua, .375 H&H Mag, .404 Jeffery, .416 Rigby, .416 Rem, .450 Rigby, .458 Win Mag, .500 Jeffery, .505 Gibbs (Safari Express models)
Capacity: 3 to 5 (depending on caliber)
Common Features: two position safety, open sights (some models), box or detachable magazine, square bridge receiver with a 19mm dovetail for mounting optics, single set trigger (some models), cocking indicator

BACKGROUND

The DNA of the CZ 550 action is clearly Mauser: a claw extractor for positive, controlled feeding and a two lug bolt with a 90-degree bolt lift. The trigger is adjustable for trigger pull, trigger travel prior to discharge and trigger travel after discharge. Some models including a set trigger. The CZ 550 used in the following instructions has a set-trigger. Push the trigger forward and the trigger will break with a light touch of about 2-1/2 pounds. To unset the trigger, point the rifle in a safe direction, engage the safety rearward in the safety-on position and pull the trigger. This will unset the trigger and place the trigger in unset mode. The bolt can only be cranked when the safety is forward in the fire position. Models range in caliber suitable from gophers to elephants. Tactical models offer polymer stocks and the 750 Sniper uses a 550 action.
Year Introduced: imported since 1995
Country of Origin: Czech Republic
Current Importer: CZ-USA (cz-usa.com)
Similar Models: Medium Lux, Varmint, Medium Battue, American, FS (full stock/mannlicher), Ultimate Hunting, Kevlar (rifle and carbine), Urban Counter Sniper

REQUIRED TOOLS

Field Stripping: none
Disassembly/Assembly: small and large standard screwdrivers, 1/8 in. punch, rubber mallet, block of wood

FIELD STRIP

1. Ensure the rifle is unloaded by opening the magazine floor plate (part #80) by pressing the floor plate latch (82) located on the outside, forward end of the trigger guard (78).
2. To remove the bolt assembly push the safety (31) in the fire position, lift the bolt handle up and partially pull it rearward, Figure 1.
3. The bolt stop (40) is located on the left side of the receiver (12). Push the bolt stop forward and continue to remove the bolt assembly from the receiver.

At this point, no further disassembly is needed for routine maintenance. After numerous cartridges have been fired, the bolt should be disassembled for a detailed cleaning.

BOLT DISASSEMBLY

1. To remove the firing pin assembly from the bolt assembly insert the bolt assembly back into the receiver and cock the firing mechanism. Note that the end of firing pin (17) is protruding from the cap (23) in the bolt sleeve indicating the rifle is cocked.
2. Press the disassembly catch (25) located on the left side of the bolt sleeve and while depressing the disassembly catch open the bolt and move it partially rearward.
3. Unscrew the bolt sleeve and firing pin assembly and remove, Figure 2.
4. Then pull the rest of the bolt assembly rearward out of the receiver.
5. Using a small flat blade screw driver, gently pry the support, firing pin spring (19).
6. Using your fingers, unscrew the nut, firing pin spring (20), Figure 3. Be careful as the firing pin spring (18) is under tension.

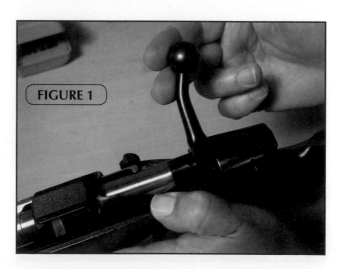

FIGURE 1

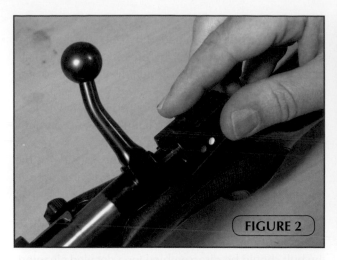

FIGURE 2

FIGURE 5

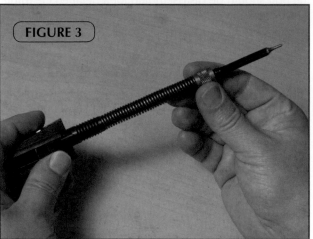

FIGURE 3

2. To remove the trigger assembly (65), place the barreled action on a padded bench with the trigger (49)

> **Tuning Tip:** At this point an aftermarket trigger like those from Timney can be installed. Follow the aftermarket manufacturer's instructions and reinstall in reverse order. Be sure to check that the trigger and safety work properly before reassembly the rifle.

facing up, Figure 5. Using a flat blade screw driver remove the screw (66) and spring washer (67).

3. Using a 1/8 in. punch, push out the safety pin (42) and retaining plate (43) from the safety (31) side.

4. Remove the bolt stop (40) and be careful to retain the bolt stop spring (41) which pushes against the rear arm of the bolt stop.

5. Remove the safety pawl (32) while leaving the dent arm of the safety in place.

6. Push out the pin (35) behind the front detent arm of the safety.

7. Remove the trigger.

BARREL/RECEIVER DISASSEMBLY

1. To remove the barrel and action from the stock, remove the front frame screw (88) and rear frame screw (90) using a larger flat blade screw driver, Figure 4. The stock should fall free. If not use a rubber mallet to gently knock the barreled action from the stock.

To reassemble follow the disassembly instructions in reverse.

> **Reassembly Tip:** When reassembling the firing pin and bolt sleeve assembly, press the firing pin (17) down on a block of wood to compress the firing pin spring until the disassembly catch (25) can be depressed. Then screw the firing pin and bolt sleeve assembly back into the bolt (13).

FIGURE 4

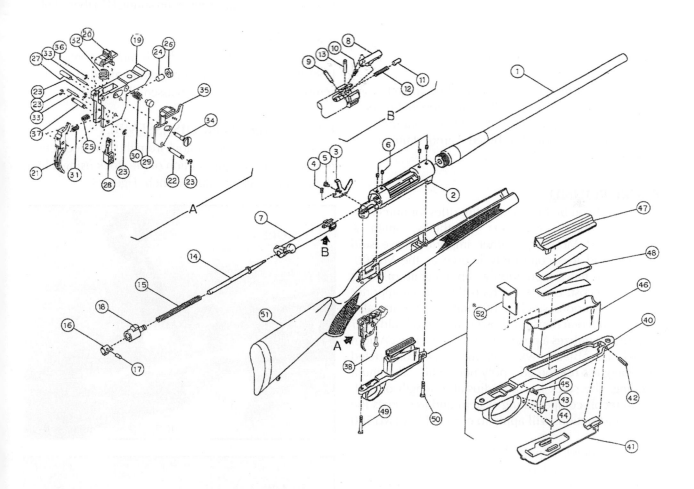

PARTS LIST

1 Barrel
2 Receiver
3 Bolt stop
4 Bolt stop spring
5 Bolt stop screw
6 Receiver plug screw
7 Bolt body
8 Extractor
9 Extractor pin
10 Extractor spring
11 Ejector
12 Ejector spring

13 Ejector pin
14/16 Firing pin
15 Main spring
17 Firing pin retaining pin
18 Bolt sleeve
19 Trigger housing
20 Sear
21 Trigger
22 Actuator pin
23 Retaining ring
24 Trigger adjusting screw
25 Actuator spring
26 Lock nut 27 Sear pin

28 Actuator
29 Safety
30 Safety spring
31 Trigger spring
32 Sear spring
33 Sear stopper pin
34 Safety lever screw
35 3Safety lever
36 Retaining hinge, safety lever
37 3Trigger pin
38 Trigger housing screw
40 Trigger guard
41 Floor plate

42 Floor plate pin
43 Floor plate catch
44 Floor plate catch pin
45 Floor plate catch spring
46 359-07-321-01 Magazine
47 Magazine follower
48 Magazine spring
49 Rear guard screw
50 Front guard screw
52 Magazine spacer

SPECIFICATIONS
Model: Axiom Varminter (M1500)
Action: bolt, push feed
Stock: Blackhawk Axiom synthetic, Blackhawk Talon synthetic, Hogue Overmolded synthetic, laminate
Barrel: 20 in., 22 in., 24 in.
Weight Unloaded: 6.9 lb. (youth), 7.1 lb. (compact), 7.7 lb. (standard, .375 Ruger), 8.5 lb. (compact varminter) 9.7 lb. (varminter)
Caliber: .204 Ruger, .223 Rem, .22-250 Rem, .243 Win, 6.5x55 Swede, .25-06, .270 Win, 7mm-08, 7mm Rem Mag, .308 Win, .30-06, .300 Win Mag, .338 Win Mag, .375 Ruger
Capacity: 3 + 1 (magnum calibers), 5 + 1 (standard calibers)
Common Features: three position safety; forged steel flat bottom receiver, drilled and tapped; box or detachable magazine; heavy fluted barrel (varmint models); cocking indicator; blued, camo, stainless finishes

BACKGROUND
Howa has been building centerfire rifles for numerous American brands, including Weatherby, Smith & Wesson and Mossberg. Other importers have sold the rifle and it is commonly known as the M1500. The M1500 has a reputation as an accurate rifle at a reasonable cost. Legacy Sports is the current importer and offers various stock configurations. Legacy also offers barreled actions for those wanting to build their own rifle. It utilizes a push-feed bolt. The Howa/Axiom model uses Blackhawk's Axiom stock constructed of fiberglass-reinforced polymer with aluminum bedding. The stock has an adjustable length of pull, a dual recoil compensating system and free floats the barrel. Instructions will apply to current Howa M1500 models.
Year Introduced: imported since 1988
Country of Origin: Japan
Current Importer: Legacy Sports (legacysports.com)
Similar Models: Howa/Hogue, Howa/Hogue .375 Ruger, Howa/Hogue Ranchland Compact, Howa/Hogue 20" Heavy Barrel Varminter, Howa/Hogue Youth, Talon Thumbhole, Howa Laminate Ambivarminter, Howa Laminate Thumbhole Varminter

REQUIRED TOOLS
Field Strip: none
Disassembly/Assembly: large Torx wrench, long shaft ¼ in. hex or Allen wrench, medium Philips screwdriver

FIELD STRIP
1. To remove the bolt assembly, lift the bolt handle (part # 7) partially withdraw the bolt from the receiver (2) while depressing the bolt stop (3), Figure 1.
2. Pull the bolt assembly from the receiver. At this point the M1500 can be cleaned.

BOLT DISASSEMBLY
1. To disassemble the bolt assembly, hook the edge of the cocking piece (16) on the edge of the workbench and pull down to compress the main spring (15) then slightly rotate the bolt sleeve/firing pin assembly clockwise until it is released from the bolt body, Figure 2. Warning the bolt sleeve/firing pin assembly is under compression from the main spring. It is not recommended to disassemble bolt sleeve/firing pin assembly further.

BARREL/RECEIVER DISASSEMBLY
1. To remove the Axiom stock from the barreled action, remove the pistol grip portion of the stock using a long shaft ¼ inch hex or Allen wrench, Figure 3.

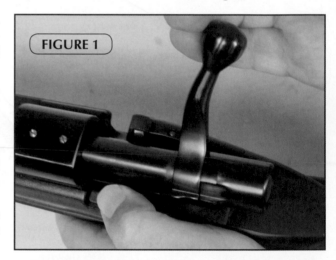

FIGURE 1

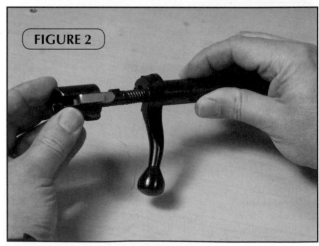

FIGURE 2

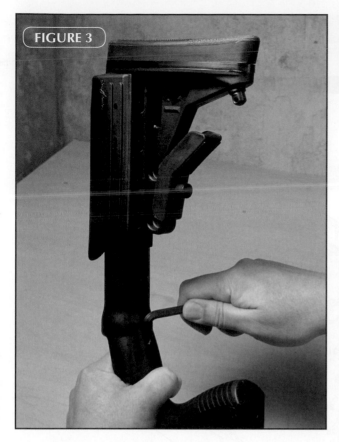

FIGURE 3

Tuning Tip: With the trigger assembly removed a Jared or Timney aftermarket rigger can be installed. Refer to the trigger manufacturer's instructions on how to install the aftermarket trigger.

To reassemble follow the disassemble instructions in reverse.

Reassembly Tip: When reassembling the bolt assembly align the bolt sleeve/firing pin assembly so that the small lug on the bolt sleeve aligns with the slot in the end of the bolt body. You will need to compress the main spring until the bolt sleeve/firing pin assembly bottoms out against the rear of the bolt body. While holding the bolt sleeve/firing pin assembly in place slightly rotate the bolt sleeve/firing pin assembly counter-clockwise until the cocking piece in the bolt sleeve engages a shallow v-notch on the rear of the bolt body. Note that the firing pin (14) will be retracted inside the

2. To remove the remainder of the Axiom stock, place it on a padded surface with the receiver facing down. Remove the front guard screw (50) and rear guard screw (49) using a large Torx wrench.

3. Remove the trigger guard assembly. The barreled action can now be removed from the stock.

4. To remove the trigger assembly, place the barreled action on a padded surface with trigger (21) pointing upward. Using a medium Philips screw driver, unscrew the trigger hosing screw (38), Figure 4.

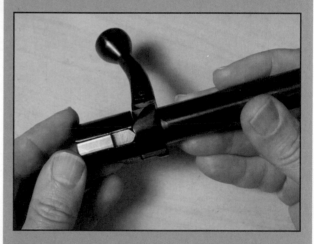

bolt face of the bolt body. The firing pin is in the cocked position. If the firing pin protrudes from the bolt face when the firing pin is in uncocked position and the cocking piece must be pushed down on the edge of a your workbench or piece of wood. Then rotate the bolt sleeve/firing pin assembly clockwise until the cocking piece engages the shallow notch. Alternate the tightness of the front and rear guard screws until they are both snug. Then tighten both screws firmly.

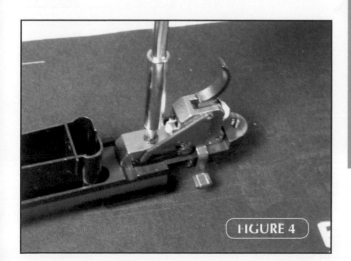

FIGURE 4

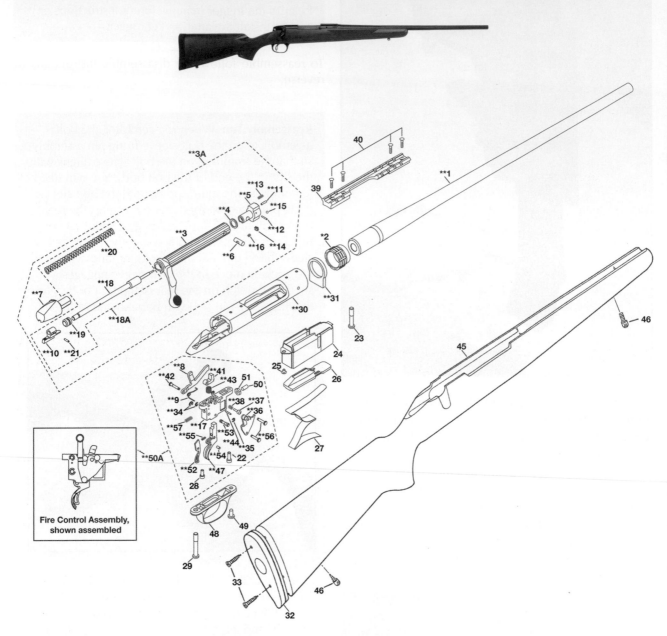

PARTS LIST

1 Barrel
2 Barrel Nut
3A Breech Bolt Assembly
3 Bolt Assembly
4 Bolt Friction Washer
5 Bolt Head
6 Bolt Head Retaining Pin
7 Bolt Sleeve
8 Bolt Stop
9 Bolt Stop Spring
10 Cocking Piece
11 Ejector
12 Ejector Retaining Pin
13 Ejector Spring
14 Extractor

15 Extractor Ball
16 Extractor Spring
17 Fire Control Housing
18A Firing Pin Assembly
18 Firing Pin
19 Firing Pin Sleeve
20 Firing Pin Spring
21 Firing Pin, Cocking Piece Pin
22 Front Fire Control Mt Screw
23 Front Takedown Screw
24 Magazine Box
25 Magazine Box Screw
26 Magazine Follower
27 Magazine Spring
28 Rear Fire Control Mt Screw
29 Rear Takedown Screw

30 Receiver
31 Recoil Lug
32 Recoil Pad
33 Recoil Pad Screw
34 Retaining Ring
35 Retaining Ring
36 Safety
37 Safety Plunger
38 Safety Plunger Spring
39 Scope Mount Base
40 Scope Mount Base Screw
41 Sear
42 Sear Bolt Stop Pin
43 Sear Spring
44 Sear Stop Pin
45 Stock

46 Swivel Studs
47 Trigger
48 Trigger Guard
49 Trigger Guard Screw
50A Fire Control Assembly
50 Trigger Pull Adj. Screw
51 Trigger Pull Jam Nut
52 Trigger Release
53 Trigger Release Pin
54 Trigger Release Pivot Pin
55 Trigger Release Spring
56 Trigger Safety Lever Pin
57 Trigger Spring

SPECIFICATIONS

Model: X7
Action: bolt, push feed, two lug
Stock: synthetic
Barrel: 20 in., 22 in., 24 in.
Weight Unloaded: 6.5 lb., 7.8 lb. (X7VH)
Caliber: .22-250 Rem, .243 Win, .25-06, .270 Win, 7mm-08, .308 Win,.30-06
Capacity: 4 + 1
Common Features: two position safety; Picatinny rail; box magazine; crowned barrel; cocking indicator; blued finish

BACKGROUND

A bolt-action from one of America's best lever-action rifles makers seems a bit odd but Marlin's proprietary X7 rifles series is serious business at a reasonable cost. The rifles feature a two-lug bolt with a 90-degree lift. The bolt head is pinned into the bolt body via a bolt head retaining pin silimar to the Savage 110. Sandwiched between the bolt body and bolt head is a bolt friction washer which gives a slight amount of play to allow the lugs to center in the receiver lug recesses. The barrel is also attached to the receiver similar to Savage by a nut. This set makes for cost-effective production and consistent accuracy. Marlin passes both the cost saving to users along with the X7 series excellent accuracy.

Year Introduced: 2008
Country of Origin: USA
Current Manufacturer: Marlin Firearms (marlinfirearms.com)
Similar Models: X7C (Realtree APG HD camo stock finish), X7S (stainless barrel/receiver, black synthetic stock), X7Y (shorter youth-size stock), X7VH (heavy varmint barrel)

REQUIRED TOOLS

Field Strip: none
Disassembly/Assembly: small diameter nail/punch as retaining pin, 9/64 hex or Allen wrench, medium Philips screwdriver

FIELD STRIP

1. Put the safety (part #36) in the "safe" or fully rearward position.
2. Lift the bolt handle and pull rearward while depressing the bolt-release latch (8), Figure 1. Pull the breech bolt assembly (3A) free from the action.

At this point the X7 is sufficiently disassembled for cleaning.

FIGURE 1

BOLT DISASSEMBLY

1. Insert the bolt assembly fully into the action and close the bolt.
2. Using a small diameter punch, nail or hex or Allen wrench as a retaining pin, insert the pin into the notch in the bolt sleeve (7), Figure 2. Only insert the pin far enough so the pin can be viewed in the notch on the other side of the bolt sleeve. If inserted to far it will interfere with the safety.
3. Lift the bolt handle and depress the bolt-release latch then withdraw the bolt assembly from the action, Figure 3.

FIGURE 2

FIGURE 3

4. Looking at the rear of the bolt assembly, rotate the bolt sleeve clockwise until the firing pin assembly (18A) is free from the bolt assembly (3), Figure 4.

5. Push out the bolt head retaining pin (6) using a small punch, Figure 5. Pull the bolt head (5) from the bolt assembly. The bolt friction washer (4) will fall free once the bolt head is removed, Figure 6.

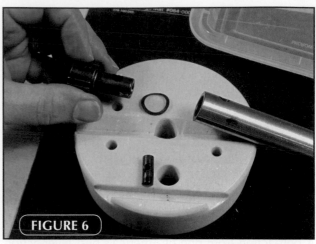

FIGURE 6

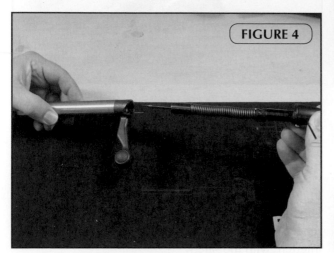

FIGURE 4

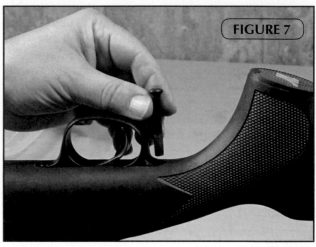

FIGURE 7

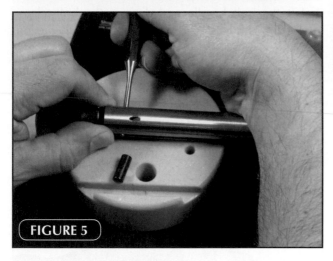

FIGURE 5

2. Pull the stock up and off the barreled action.

3. The magazine box (24) is removed by using a Phillips screwdriver to unscrew the magazine box screw (25), Figure 8. The magazine box, along with the magazine follower (26) and magazine spring (27) can then be lifted up and off from the receiver (30).

BARREL/RECEIVER DISASSEMBLY

1. To remove the barreled action from the stock (45), lay the rifle top side down on a padded surface and remove the rear takedown screw (29) and the front takedown screw (23), Figure 7. Use a medium flat blade screwdriver or 9/64 inch hex or Allen wrench. The front trigger guard screw (49) does not need to be removed.

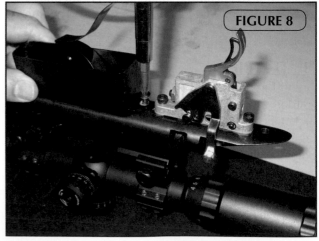

FIGURE 8

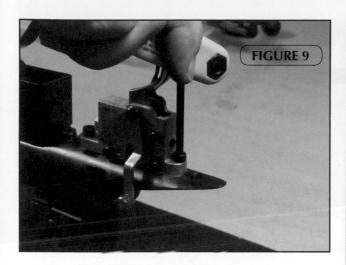

FIGURE 9

4. Remove the trigger assembly (50A) by removing the rear fire control mounting screw (28) and front fire control mounting screw (22) using a 9/64 hex or Allen wrench, Figure 9.

Reassemble in reverse order.

Reassembly Tip: Align the magazine spring with the stock inletting notch. Use a drop of Loctite on the magazine box screw. Replace the front takedown screw first then follow with the rear takedown screw.

Tuning Tip: To adjust the trigger, first remove the stock. Using a 3/8 open end wrench or non-marring pliers, loosen the trigger pull jam nut (51). Use a 3/32 hex or Allen wrench to turn the trigger pull adjusting screw. To increase the trigger pull, turn the hex or Allen wrench clockwise; to decrease the trigger pull, turn the hex or Allen wrench counter-clockwise.

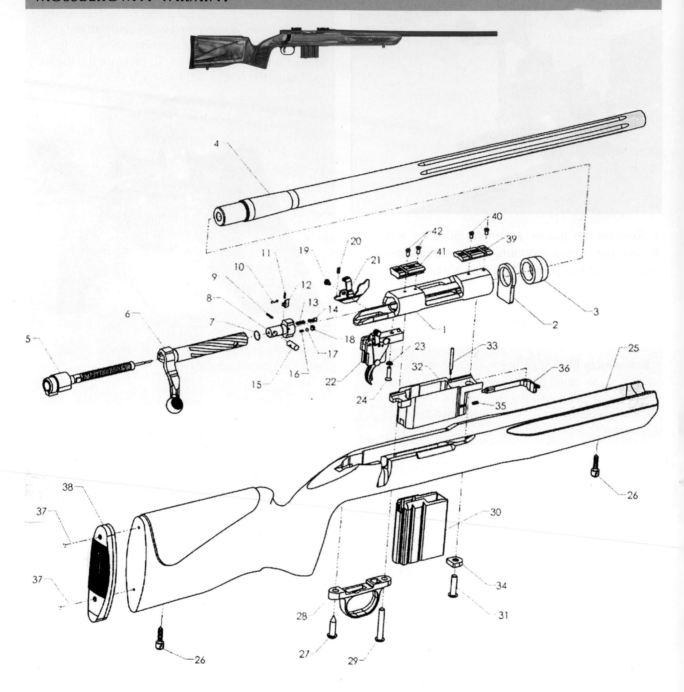

PARTS LIST

1 Receiver
2 Recoil Lug
3 Barrel Lock Nut
4 Barrel
5 Striker Assembly
6 Bolt Body Assembly
7 O-Ring
8 Bolt Head
9 Ejector Retaining Pin
10 Cartridge Pusher Spring

11 Cartridge Pusher Pin
12 Cartridge Pusher
13 Ejector Spring
14 Ejector
15 Bolt Head Assembly Pin
16 Extractor Spring
17 Detent Ball
18 Extractor
19 Bolt Stop Screw
20 Bolt Stop Spring
21 Bolt Stop

22 Trigger Housing Assembly
23 Trigger Housing Washer
24 Trigger Housing Screw
25 Stock
26 Swivel Stud
27 Trigger Guard Screw
28 Trigger Guard
29 Rear Action Screw
30 Magazine Assembly
31 Front Action Screw
32 Magazine Guide

33 Magazine Latch Pin
34 Escutcheon
35 Magazine Latch Spring
36 Magazine Latch
37 Recoil Pad Screw
38 Recoil Pad
39 Front Scope Base
40 Front Scope Base Screws
41 Rear Scope Base
42 Rear Scope Base Screws

SPECIFICATIONS

Model: MVP Varmint
Action: bolt, drop-push feed, two lug
Stock: grey-black laminate
Barrel: 24 in.
Weight Unloaded: 7.5 lb.
Caliber: 5.56mm NATO (.223)
Capacity: 5-, 10-
Common Features: two position safety; weaver-style bases; accepts AR-15 style magazines; crowned barrel; cocking indicator; matte finish; benchrest style stock; LBA adjustable trigger

BACKGROUND

The Mossberg MVP (Mossberg Predator Varmint) rifle was purpose-built with prairie dog and coyote hunting in mind. The rifle is chambered in 5.56mm/.223 Remington and uses AR-15 style magazines. The two-lug bolt has a drop-down cartridge-pusher that drops down from the bottom of the bolt to scrap a cartridge out of the AR-15 magazine and into the chamber, Figure 1. The barrel is attached to the receiver via nut. The stock takes a cue from a benchrest rifle with a wide flat bottom forend and a high comb stock for easy use of optics.

Year Introduced: 2011
Country of Origin: USA
Current Manufacturer: O.F. Mossberg & Sons (mossbergs.com)
Similar Models: MVP Varmint Scoped Combo (factory installed scope and bipod), MVP Predator (18- or 20-in. barrel, sporter stock)

REQUIRED TOOLS

Field Strip: none
Disassembly/Assembly: medium flat blade screwdriver, 5/32 hex or Allen wrench

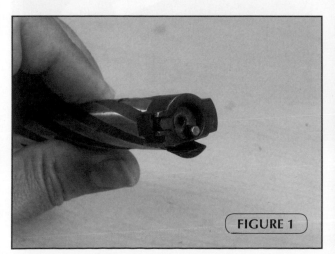

FIGURE 1

FIELD STRIP

1. Push the safety lever in the "safe" or fully rearward position and remove the magazine (part #30).
2. Lift the bolt handle and pull rearward while depressing the bolt stop (21), Figure 2. Pull the bolt assembly free from the receiver (1).

At this point the MVP is sufficiently disassembled for cleaning.

BOLT DISASSEMBLY

1. Hold the bolt assembly and rotate the striker assembly (5) clockwise from the rear to disengage the striker assembly from the bolt assembly.
2. Remove the striker assembly rearward from the bolt body assembly (6), Figure 3. With the striker assembly removed, the bolt head pin assembly pin (15) will fall free from the bolt body assembly. The bolt head (8) can then be pulled out of the front of the bolt body assembly along with the O-ring (7).

FIGURE 2

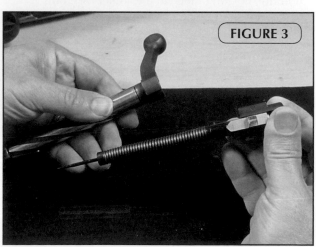

FIGURE 3

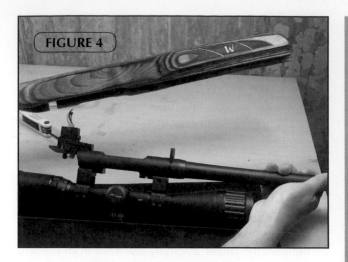

FIGURE 4

Tuning Tip: To adjust the trigger first remove the stock then turn the trigger pull adjusting screw clockwise to increase trigger pull or counterclockwise to decrease trigger pull. Reinstall the barrel/receiver assembly in the stock and tighten the trigger guard screw first then tighten the rear action screw. Dry fire to test trigger pull.

BARREL/RECEIVER DISASSEMBLY

1. Remove the barrel/receiver assembly from the stock (25) by removing the trigger guard screw (27) and the rear action screw (29) using a 5/32 hex or Allen wrench. Pull the stock from the barrel/receiver assembly, Figure 4. The magazine guide (32) will stay in the stock.

2. The trigger housing assembly (22) is removed by unscrewing and removing the trigger housing screw (24) and trigger housing washer (23).

Reassemble in reverse order.

Reassembly Tip: Insert the striker into the bolt assembly then push the striker assembly into the bolt assembly while turning it counter-clockwise until the cocking piece in the striker assembly engages a shallow notch on the rear of the bolt assembly.

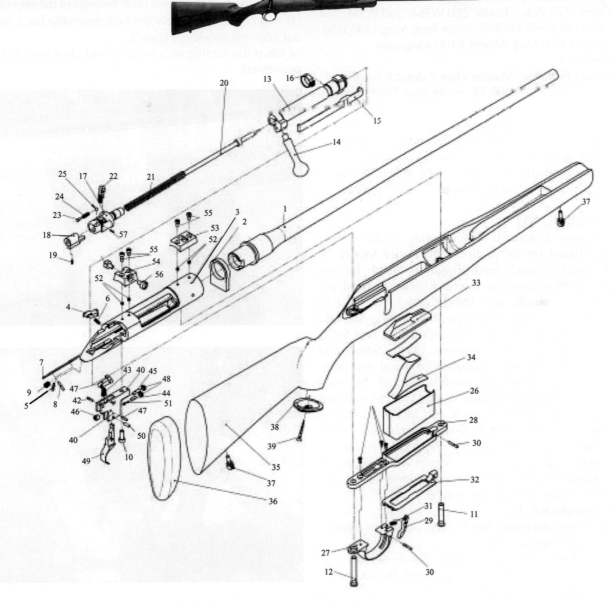

PARTS LIST

1 Barrel
2 Recoil Lug
3 Receiver
4 Bolt Stop
5 Bolt Stop Screw
6 Bolt Stop Spring
7 Ejector
8 Ejector Pin
9 Ejector Spring
10 Trigger Fixing Screw
11 Takedown Screw - Front
12 Takedown Screw - Rear
13 Bolt
14 Bolt Handle
15 Extractor

16 Extractor Clip
17 Cocking Piece Housing
18 Cocking Piece
19 Cocking Piece Screw
20 Firing Pin
21 Firing Pin Safety
22 Safety
23 Cocking Piece Housing
   Plunger
24 Safety Plunger Spring
25 Cocking Piece Housing
   Plunger
26 Magazine Well
27 Trigger Guard
28 Floor Plate
29 Latch

30 Trap Door Pin
31 Latch Spring
32 Trap Door
33 Magazine Follower
34 Magazine Spring
35 Stock
36 Butt Plate
37 Sling Swivel (2)
38 Grip Cap
39 Grip Cap Screw
40 Trigger Housing
41 Sear
42 Sear Pivot Pin
43 Sear Spring
44 Trigger Pressure Spring
45 Trigger Overtravel Screw

46 Sear Contact Adjustment
   Screw
47 Securing Pin
48 Trigger Adjustment Nut
49 Trigger
50 Trigger Pivot Pin
51 Trigger Spring
52 Scope Base Plug (4)
53 Scope Base, Front
54 Scope Base, Rear
55 Scope Base Screw (4)
56 Scope Clamping Screw (2)
57 Safety Fixing Pin
58 Trigger Guard Screw (3)

SPECIFICATIONS

Model: 8400 Classic
Action: bolt, control feed
Barrel: 24 in.
Weight Unloaded: 6.2 lb.
Caliber: .270 Win, .30-06; 270 WSM, 300 WSM, 325 WSM (Model 8400 WSM); 7mm Rem Mag, .300 Win Mag, .338 Win Mag (Model 8400 Magnum)
Capacity: 5
Common Features: Mauser claw extractor two-lug bolt with 90-degree bolt lift, matte blue finish, glass/pillar bedding, Pachmayr Decelerator recoil pad, cocking indicator, three-position Winchester Model 70-type safety, adjustable trigger, American walnut (Classic), French walnut with ebony cap (Classic Select) or synthetic (Montana, Patrol, Police Tactical, Tactical, Advanced Tactical) stock

BACKGROUND

The Kimber Classic is exactly that, a classic rifle design based on the famed Winchester Model 70 with control-round feed/extraction, dual locking lugs and three-position safety. Kimber married the design with aesthetics—hand-rubbed oil finished stock with hand-cut 20 line-per-inch checkering and a matte blue finish—in a balanced rifle that looks beautiful and performs superbly. Classic Select and Super America models feature fine wood and deep blue finishes. Montana models are all business with a Kevlar/carbon fiber stock. Tactical versions feature heavy contour barrels and McMillan stocks. Police and Patrol models feature laminated wood. The instructions here are for the Model 8400 but will generally apply to the Model 84L and 84M, too; Kimber's signature lightweight long action and medium action rifles, respectively.
Year Introduced: 2003
Current Manufacturer: Kimber (kimberamerica.com)
Country of Origin: USA
Similar Models: Classic Stainless, Classic Select Grade, Super America, Montana, Patrol, Police Tactical, Tactical, Advanced Tactical

REQUIRED TOOLS

Field Stripping: none
Disassembly/Assembly: 5/32 hex or Allen wrench, 3/32 punch, brass hammer

FIELD STRIP

1. Place the safety lever (part #22) to Position 2, Figure 1.
2. Lift bolt handle (14) and retract it to the rear.
3. Press the bolt stop lever (4) at the rear of the receiver (3) and continue to draw the bolt assemble back and out from the receiver, Figure 2.
At this point routine maintenance and cleaning can be performed.

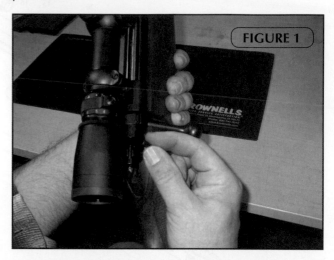

FIGURE 1

FIGURE 2

BOLT DISASSEMBLY

1. To disassemble the bolt (13), use your hand to unscrew the cocking piece housing (18) counterclockwise and remove it from the bolt assembly, Figure 3.

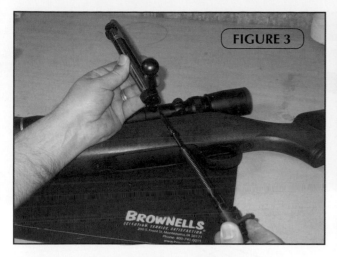

FIGURE 3

FIGURE 4

BARREL/RECEIVER DISASSEMBLY

1. To remove the barreled action from the stock (35), place the rifle so the underside of the stock faces up and using a 5/32 hex or Allen wrench remove the two takedown screws, takedown screw, front (11) and takedown screw, rear (12) from the floor plate (28), Figure 4.

2. Flip over the rifle and lift the barreled action out from the stock.

3. Remove the magazine well (26) by lifting the forward section up slightly and then pull the magazine well from the action.

To reassemble reverse the order.

Reassembly Tip: When reassembling the magazine well, fit the rear portion of the magazine well into the action and then push the front portion down until it is seated into the action. The trigger guard and floor plate need to be replaced before the barreled action is placed back into the stock.

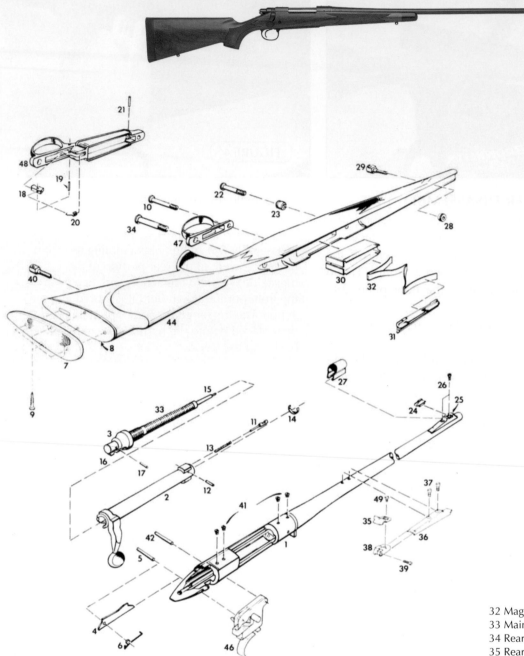

PARTS LIST

1 Barrel Assembly
2 Bolt Assembly
3 Bolt Plug
4 Bolt Stop (Restricted)
5 Bolt Stop Pin (Restricted)
6 Bolt Stop Spring (Restricted)
7 Butt Plate
8 Butt Plate Spacer
9 Butt Plate Screw
10 Center Guard Screw ADL
   Grade

11 Ejector
12 Ejector Pin
13 Ejector Spring
14 Extractor
16 Firing Pin Assembly
17 Firing Pin Cross Pin
18 Floor Plate Latch, BDL
   Grade
19 Floor Plate Latch Pin, BDL
   Grade
20 Floor Plate Latch Spring,
   BDL Grade

21 Floor Plate Pivot Pin, BDL
   Grade
22 Front Guard Screw
23 Front Guard Screw Bushing,
   ADL Grade
24 Front Sight
25 Front Sight Ramp BDL
26 Front Sight Ramp Screw
27 Front Sight Hood
29 Front Swivel Screw
30 Magazine, ADL Grade
31 Magazine Follower

32 Magazine Spring
33 Main Spring
34 Rear Guard Screw
35 Rear Sight Aperture
36 Rear Sight Base
37 Rear Sight Base Screw (2)
38 Rear Sight Slide
39 Elevation Screw
40 Rear Swivel Screw
41 Receiver Plug Screw
42 Sear Pin (Restricted)
44 Stock Assembly, ADL Grade
46 Trigger Assembly (Restricted)
47 Trigger Guard
48 Trigger Guard Assembly,
   BDL Grade
49 Windage Screw

SPECIFICATIONS

Model: 700 BDL
Action: bolt, push feed
Barrel: 20 in., 22 in., 24 in., or 26 in.
Weight Unloaded: 6.75 lb. to 8.5 lb. (depending on model)
Caliber: .17 Rem Fireball, .204 Ruger, .220 Swift, .22-250, .243 Win, .25-06, .257 Wby Mag, .260 Rem, .264 Win Mag, .270 Win, .270 WSM, .280 Rem, 7mm-08, 7mm Rem Mag, 7mm Rem Ultra Mag, .30-06, .300 Win Mag, .300 WSM, .308 Win, .300 Rem Ultra Mag, .338 Win Mag, .338 Rem Ultra Mag, .35 Whelan, .375 H&H, .375 Rem Ultra Mag
Capacity: 3, 4, or 5 (depending on caliber)
Common Features: two-lug bolt with 90-degree lift; bedded stock (some models); cocking indicator; two-position safety; externally adjustable trigger; walnut, laminated wood, thumbhole or synthetic stock; open sights (some models); various round or triangular barrel contours; detachable, box or blind magazine

BACKGROUND

When tailfins on cars were still common, Remington came out with a bolt-action rifle in the new 7mm Remington Magnum caliber and—as they say—the rest is history. The Model 700 is a benchmark in rifle design with more than 5 million different Model 700s built in 40 calibers—from .17 Rem to the .458 Win Mag—over the years. The goal with the Model 700 was to design a rifle that was more economical to manufacture than previous Remingtons. Not only is it easier to manufacture it is exceptionally strong with "three rings of steel." The first ring is the bolt face which is recessed to enclose the base of the cartridge. The second ring is the chamber end of the barrel that surrounds the bolt face. The third is the front receiver ring which in turn surrounds the chamber end of the barrel. A Model 700 BDL complete with white spacers, skip-line checkering and a stock so glossy you can shave in the reflection is used in the following instructions though the steps will apply to all grades of Model 700 and generally to the Model Seven.
Year Introduced: 1962
Current Manufacturer: Remington (remington.com)
Country of Origin: USA
Similar Models: CDL, CDL SF, Target Tactical, SPS, SPS Stainless, SPS DM, SPS Tactical, SPS Varmint, VLSS Thumbhole, Mountain LSS, Varmint SF, VLS, VS SF II, Sendero SF II, XCR II, XHR, VTR, XCR Tactical, XCR LR Tactical

REQUIRED TOOLS

Field Stripping: none
Disassembly/Assembly: coin or thin strip of metal, medium flat blade screwdriver, 5/32 hex or Allen wrench, 3/32 punch, brass hammer, vise (optional)

FIELD STRIP

1. To remove the bolt assembly (part #2), place the safety lever in the "safe" or "S" position.
2. Raise the bolt handle and pull the bolt handle all the way back, then push bolt stop release located in the trigger guard (47), Figure 1.
3. The bolt assembly can now be slid from the receiver, Remington calls it the barrel assembly (1).

BOLT DISASSEMBLY

1. To disassemble the bolt assembly, put a thin piece of metal in a vise so the edge is exposed and hook the notch on the firing pin head over the metal edge and pull the bolt assembly to compress the firing pin spring, main spring (33). Or if a vise is not handy, insert a medium flat blade screwdriver in the notch of the firing pin assembly.

FIGURE 1

Tuning Tip: To adjust the trigger pull on some grades of the Model 700 there is no need to field strip or disassemble the rifle. Use a 1/16 hex or Allen wrench to access the adjustment screw via the trigger, Figure 2.

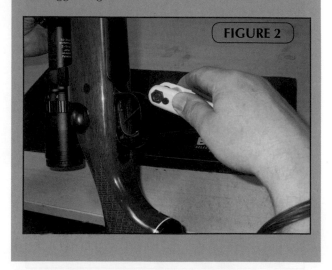

FIGURE 2

With the screwdriver handle tucked into your hip pull back on the bolt with one hand. If you think pennies are useless here's an example where they are not. While pulling back and compressing the firing pin spring put a coin into the slot near the back edge of the firing pin head, Figure 3. If you use this alternative method make sure the screwdriver fits nicely in the notch of the firing pin and in the slot of the bolt plug, Figure 4.

2. With the coin in place, hold the bolt assembly and turn the bolt plug counter-clockwise until the firing pin assembly (16) can be removed from the bolt assembly, Figure 5.

BARREL/RECEIVER DISASSEMBLY

1. To remove the barreled action from the stock (44), turn the rifle upside down and depress the floor plate latch (18) to relieve the magazine spring (32) tension then remove the two floor plate screws—front guard screw (22) and rear guard screw (34)—using a 5/32 hex or Allen wrench.

2. Remove the trigger guard assembly (48). Lift the stock away from the barreled receiver.

3. To remove the trigger assembly (46) from the receiver, place the safety in the rearward or "safe"/"S" position.

4. Lay the barreled receiver on its left side. Use a 3/32 punch to drift out the bolt stop pin (5) from the right side of the receiver to the left side. Note the bolt stop spring is under tension.

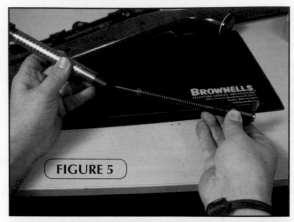

FIGURE 5

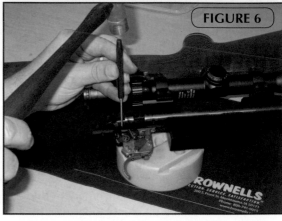

FIGURE 6

5. Remove the bolt stop (4) and bolt stop spring (6).

6. With the bolt stop removed next drift out the sear pin (42) from right to left as with the bolt stop pin, Figure 6.

Reassemble in reverse order.

Reassembly Tip: The bolt must be cocked to reassemble the rifle. To put the bolt assembly back together, insert the firing pin assembly into the rear of the bolt body and screw it to tighten the bolt plug into the bolt assembly. Pull the coin from the slot in the firing pin head. Turn the bolt plug until the firing pin head goes into the small notch on the rear rim of the bolt, Figure 7. The bolt is now cocked.

FIGURE 3

FIGURE 4

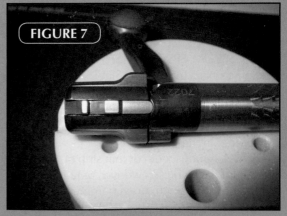

FIGURE 7

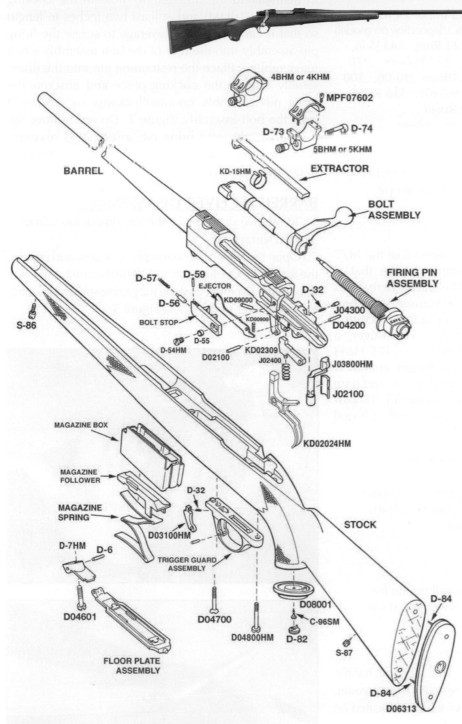

BARREL

4BHM or 4KHM

MPF07602

D-73

D-74

5BHM or 5KHM

KD-15HM

EXTRACTOR

BOLT ASSEMBLY

FIRING PIN ASSEMBLY

D-57
D-59
EJECTOR
D-56
KD09000
D-32
BOLT STOP
KD00900
S-86
D-55
J04300
D04200
D-54HM
D02100
KD02309
J02400
J03800HM
J02100
KD02024HM

MAGAZINE BOX

MAGAZINE FOLLOWER

MAGAZINE SPRING

D-32

D-7HM
D-6
D03100HM
TRIGGER GUARD ASSEMBLY

STOCK

D-84

D04601
D04700
D04800HM
D08001
C-96SM
D-82
S-87

FLOOR PLATE ASSEMBLY

D-84
D06313

D06713 Front Sight Blade
D-69 Front Sight Plunger Spring
D-68 Front Sight Retainer Plunger
S-86B Front Sling Swivel Screw
D22707 Magazine Box - Long Action
KD03023 Magazine Follower, with tab - Long Action
D-32 Magazine Latch Spring All Models
D-148 Magazine Spring
D08001 Pistol Grip Cap - Plastic "
D-82 Pistol Grip Cap Medallion
C-96SM Pistol Grip Cap Screw
D04800HM Rear Mounting Screw
D-151HM Rear Sight Base
D-62HM Rear Sight Base Screw
D07725HM Rear Sight Blade
D-64HM Rear Sight Clamp Screw
D-83 Rear Sight Williams Gib Lock Clamp
S-87 Rear Sling Swivel Stud
D06313 Recoil Pad
D-84 Recoil Pad Screw, 2 Req'd.
J03800HM Safety Selector
J04300 Safety Selector Detent
D-32 Safety Selector Detent Spring
J02100 Safety Selector Retainer
KD02309 Sear
D04200 Sear Pivot Pin
Stock
KD02024HM Trigger
D20202HM Trigger Guard Assembly
D02100 Trigger Pivot Pin
J02400 Trigger/Sear Spring

PARTS LIST

Barrel
D-53HM Bolt Stop
D-56 Bolt Stop Plunger
D-57 Bolt Stop Plunger Spring
D-59 Bolt Stop Plunger Spring Retaining Pin
D-55 Bolt Stop Stud Bushing

D-54HM Bolt Stop Screw Stud - Blued Models
D04700 Center Mounting Screw
D01810HM Cocking Piece Ejector Contact
KD00900 Ejector Spring Extractor Contact
KD-15HM Extractor Band

D-19 Firing Pin Cross Pin
D01202 Firing Pin Spring
KD20511 Floor Plate Assembly
D-7HM Floor Plate Hinge
D03100HM Floor Plate
D-6 Floor Plate Pivot Pin
D04601 Front Mounting Screw
KS06500 Front Sight Base
D-70 Front Sight Base Set Screw

SPECIFICATIONS

Model: M77 Hawkeye
Action: bolt, control feed
Barrel: 16.5 in., 20 in., 22 in., 23 in., or 24 in.
Weight Unloaded: 6.5 lb. to 8.75 lb. (depending on model)
Caliber: .204 Ruger, .22-250, .223 Rem, .243 Win, .25-06, 6.5 Creedmoor, 6.8 SPC, .257 Roberts, .270 Win, 7mm-08, 7mm Mag, 7.62x39mm, .30-06, .300 RCM, .300 Win Mag, .308 Win, 9.3x62, .338 RCM, .338 Win Mag, .375 Ruger, .416 Ruger
Capacity: 3, 4, or 5 (depending on caliber)
Common Features: two-lug bolt with 90-degree lift; cocking indicator; three-position safety; walnut, laminated wood, or synthetic stock; open sights (some models); box magazine; integral scope mounts

BACKGROUND

The Ruger M77 Hawkeye is a refinement of the M77 MKII with a rounded and slimmer profile that is svelte compared to past M77s. The Hawkeye features the LC6 (Light, Crisp) trigger, a Mauser style bolt with controlled feed/extraction and a three-position safety. The rifle debuted with the .375 Ruger, a cartridge that provides the power of the .375 H&H Magnum in the size of a .30-06 length action. A Ruger M77 Hawkeye African is used below and note that part numbers vary depending on model, the part numbers indicated here are for rifles with a blued finish.

Year Introduced: 2007
Current Manufacturer: Ruger (ruger.com)
Country of Origin: USA
Similar Models: Standard, All-Weather, Compact, Laminate Compact, Compact Magnum, African, Alaskan, Sporter, Tactical, Predator

REQUIRED TOOLS

Field Stripping: none
Disassembly/Assembly: nail or small punch for restraining pin, large standard screwdriver, small punch, brass hammer

FIELD STRIP

1. To remove the bolt assembly, lift the bolt handle and pull it to the rear while at the same time pivoting open the bolt stop (part #D-53HM) which is located on the left side of the receiver, Figure 1.
At this point the rifle is sufficiently dismantled for routine cleaning.

BOLT DISASSEMBLY

1. To disassemble the bolt assembly, the firing pin must be cocked.

2. Use a small punch or nail as a restraining pin. The restraining pin should be as close as possible in diameter to the disassembly hole in the cocking piece (D01810HM) and at least two inches in length so that it can be used as leverage to screw the firing pin assembly into the rear of the bolt assembly when reassembling. Place the restraining pin into the disassembly hole in the cocking piece and unscrew the firing pin assembly counterclockwise to remove it from the bolt assembly, Figure 2. Do not remove the restraining pin until firing pin assembly is reassembled into the bolt. Note that the firing pin assembly is under spring pressure.

BARREL/RECEIVER DISASSEMBLY

1. To remove stock, place the top side of the rifle on a padded surface.
2. Open the floor plate assembly to access and remove the forward mounting screw (D04601) which holds the floor plate assembly and the magazine spring and magazine follower to the stock, Figure 3.

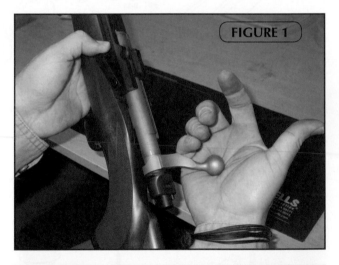

FIGURE 1

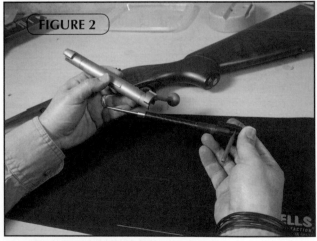

FIGURE 2

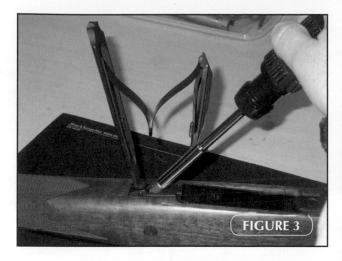

FIGURE 3

3. Remove the center mounting screw (D04700) and the rear mounting screw (D04800HM) from the trigger guard assembly.

4. Lift the trigger guard assembly up from the stock.

5. Remove magazine box. If magazine box does not come out easily, it can be lifted out with the stock.

6. Lift the stock straight up from barreled action.

7. To remove the trigger (KD02024HM), place the safety selector (J03800HM) in the "Fire" position.

8. Hold the trigger assembly in place, and use a small punch to drift out the trigger pivot pin (D02100). The trigger is under spring pressure.

9. To remove the sear (KD02309) press out the sear pivot pin (D04200), Figure 4. Turn the receiver upside down and slide the sear forward. The sear will drop out of the top slot in the receiver.

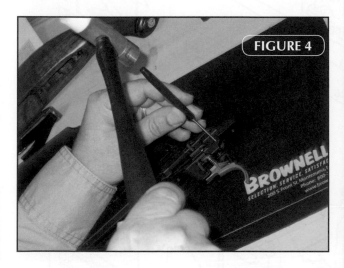

FIGURE 4

10. To remove the safety assembly, rotate the safety selector so that the upper section is positioned fully over the center of the receiver tang. While holding the safety selector in place with your thumb and forefinger, slide the retainer up out of receiver. The safety selector is under spring tension from the Safety Selector Detent Spring (D-32) and Safety Selector Detent (J04300) take caution to contain these parts as you lift out the safety selector.

To reassemble reverse the procedure.

Reassembly Tip: When replacing the safety assembly apply downward pressure and slide the safety selector into the dovetail from the top and align the notch is the safety selector retainer with the rear pivot pin hole. When replacing the sear, place the end with the hole in it into the slot from the top of the receiver and align the hole in the sear with the holes in the receiver, then insert the sear pivot pin. When reinstalling the trigger make sure the trigger/sear spring (J02400) is over the dimple in the trigger. Align the trigger/sear spring on the dimple on the sear then replace the trigger pivot pin.

When reassembling the firing pin assembly into bolt, screw the firing pin assembly fully into the bolt. The assembly is properly positioned in the bolt when the flat on the bottom right side of the bolt sleeve (front of bolt facing you) is aligned with the flat on the bottom end of the bolt handle. The cocking piece fits in a shallow notch at the rearward end of the bolt body, Figure 5. When the firing pin assembly is being turned into the bolt body, it may be necessary to use the restraining pin as a lever to slightly retract the cocking piece nose so it can be moved into the notch. When the firing pin assembly is correctly positioned in the bolt body, the restraining pin can be removed.

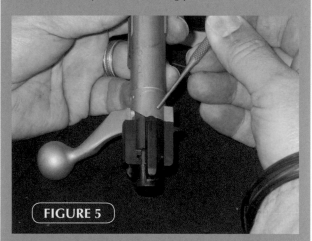

FIGURE 5

When reattaching the stock to the barreled action, place the box magazine so the tab in the box magazine fits into the notch in the receiver, Figure 6. Alternate tightening of the center and rear mounting screws so that the screws are tightened equally. The dome head screw is the rear mounting screw and flat head screw is the center mounting screw.

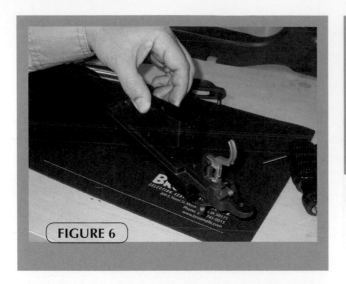

FIGURE 6

Reassembly Tip: With Mauser-type bolt actions such as the Ruger M77 Hawkeye make sure the extractor is aligned correctly. Replace the bolt assembly into the receiver by positioning the bolt handle in an upward position and align the extractor with the right hand locking lug. Align the locking lugs with the channels in each side of the rear of the receiver and partially insert the bolt, then push the bolt fully forward.

SAVAGE MODEL 10

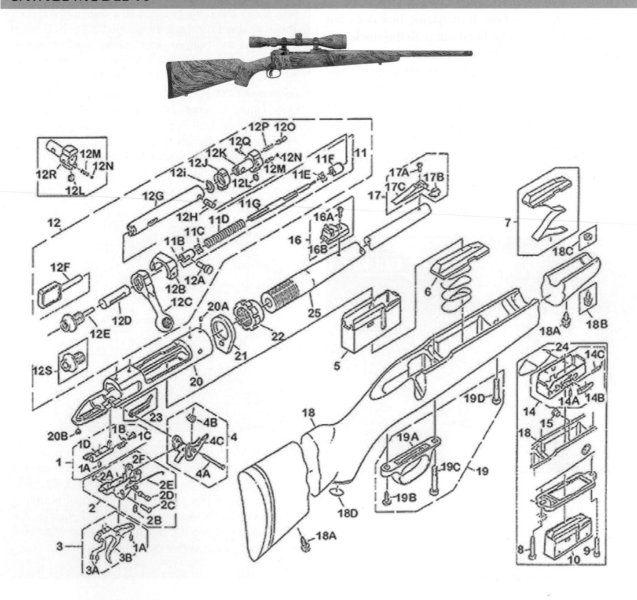

PARTS LIST

1 Safety Assembly
1A Socket Screw
1B Safety Detent Spring
1C Pan Head Screw
1D Safety
2A Safety Retaining Ring
2B Trigger Pull Adjustment Screw
2C Trigger Pin
2D Safety Bearing Pin
2E Trigger Pull Adjustment Spring
2F Trigger Bracket
3 Trigger Assembly
3A Socket Screw
3B Trigger
4A Sear Pin
4B Sear Spring
4C Sear
5 Magazine Box
6 Magazine Follower Assembly
7 Magazine Follower Assembly
8 Action Screw, Rear
9 Action Screw, Front
10 Magazine Box Assembly
11 Firing Pin Assembly
11B Cocking Piece
11C Cocking Piece Lock Washer
11D Mainspring
11E Firing Pin Stop Nut Washer
11F Firing Pin Stop Nut
11G Firing Pin
12 Bolt Assembly
12A Cocking Piece Pin
12B Baffle Assembly, Rear
12C Bolt Handle
12D Cocking Piece Sleeve
12G Bolt Body
12H Bolt Head Retaining Pin
12I Baffle Washer, Front
12J Baffle, Front
12K Bolt Head
12L Extractor
12M Extractor Spring
12M Extractor Spring
12N Steel Ball
12O Ejector
12P Ejector Spring
12Q Ejector Retaining Pin
12R Bolt Head
12S Bolt Assembly Screw
14 Magazine Guide Assembly
14A Magazine Latch Pin
14B Magazine Latch
14C Magazine Latch Spring
15 Magazine Latch Button
17A Front Sight Screw
17B Front Sight Blade
17C Front Sight Base
18 Stock Assembly
18A Swivel Stud
18B Swivel Stud
18C Lock Nut
18D Medallion
19A Trigger Guard
19B Trigger Guard Screw, Rear
19C Action Screw, Rear
19D Action Screw, Front
20 Receiver
20A Dummy Screw
20B Safety Insert
21 Recoil Lug
22 Barrel Lock Nut
23 Ejector
24 Magazine Ejector Spring
25 Barrel

SPECIFICATIONS

Model: Model 10
Action: bolt, push feed, two lug
Barrel: 22 in.
Weight Unloaded: 8.5 lb. (with scope)
Caliber: .204 Ruger, .22-250 Rem., .223 Rem, .243 Win
Capacity: 4
Common Features: two-lug bolt; Accu stock (some models); three-position safety; Accu or standard trigger; wood or synthetic stock; cocking indicator; drilled and tapped for optics; internal or detachable box magazine

BACKGROUND

The Savage Model 10, a short action rifle, is based on the Model 110, a long action rifle. The Model 10 and series family are known for extreme accuracy and inexpensive cost. Something that tickles the frugal Yankee in me. The rifles were designed for ease of manufacturing and assembly. The floating bolt head has a few thousands of an inch of movement to adjust itself when locked into battery. This floating bolt head and the barrel, which is attached to the receiver via a large nut, contribute to the rifles excellent accuracy. The AccuTrigger introduced in 2003 is fully adjustable. Model 10/110 LE Series and Model 12/112 Target/Varmint Series rifles though similar in appearance have slightly different bolts and receivers. Numerous models from the Model 10/110, 11/111, 14/114 and 16/116 series employ the same bolt style, though finish, stock and magazine types differ.
Year Introduced: 1958
Current Manufacturer: Savage Arms (savagearms.com)
Country of Origin: U.S.
Similar Models: 10 Predator Hunter Brush, 10/110 Predator Hunter Max 1, 10 XP Predator Hunter Package, 10/110 International Trophy Hunter XP, 10/110 Trophy Hunter XP, 11 Trophy Hunter XP, 11/111 BTH, 11/111 FCNS, 11/11 FHNS, 11/111 Hog Hunter, 11/111 Lady Hunter, 11/111 Lightweight Hunter, 11/111 Long Range Hunter, 11/111 Hunter XP, 11/111 International Trophy Hunter XP, 11/111 Trophy Hunter XP, 14/114 American Classic, 14/114 American Classic Stainless, 16/116 Bear Hunter, 16/116 International Trophy Hunter XP, 16/116 Trophy Hunter XP, 116 Alaskan Brush Hunter

REQUIRED TOOLS

Field Stripping: none
Disassembly/Assembly: 5/32 and 6mm hex or Allen wrench, small punch, padded vise

FIELD STRIP

1. Remove detachable box magazine assembly (part #10) if so equipped.
2. Lift the bolt handle (12C) and pull it fully rearward.
3. Pull back on the trigger (38) while pressing down on the cocking indicator on the right side of the receiver (20), Figure 1.
4. Withdraw the bolt out of the rear of the receiver.

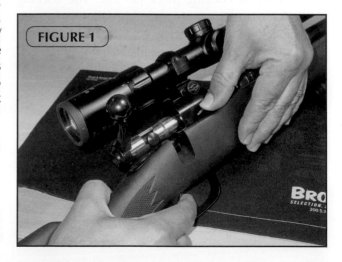

FIGURE 1

At this point the rifle is sufficiently dismantled for routine cleaning.

BOLT DISASSEMBLY

1. Reinstall the bolt assembly back into the receiver and insert a 6mm hex or Allen wrench, or if an older model a large flat blade screwdriver, into the bolt assembly screw (12S). Use the bolt handle as leverage and unscrew the bolt assembly screw with the hex or Allen wrench counterclockwise, Figure 2. If the bolt has never been previously disassembled place the bolt

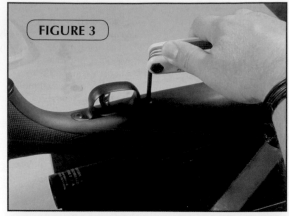

FIGURE 3

FIGURE 2

FIGURE 4

assembly in a padded vise and use the hex or Allen wrench/ large flat blade screwdriver to unscrew the bolt assembly screw. The bolt assembly screw can be stubborn and if you try to gorilla it in the receiver you can damage the receiver and/or bolt assembly.

2. With the bolt assembly screw started, remove the bolt assembly from the receiver and remove the bolt assembly screw from the rear of the bolt assembly.

3. Pull the bolt from the rear of the bolt assembly then the rear baffle assembly (12B).

4. Rotate the cocking piece pin (12A) so it aligns with the slot in the cocking piece sleeve (12D) in the bolt body then pull cocking piece pin free. The cocking piece sleeve and firing pin assembly will then fall free from the rear of the bolt body.

5. Next push out the bolt head retaining pin (12H) with a small punch. The baffle (12J), bolt head assembly (12K) and front baffle washer (12I).

BARREL/RECEIVER DISASSEMBLY

1. Use a 5/32 hex or Allen wrench to remove the front action screw (19D) and the rear action screw (19C) securing the stock (18), Figure 3. For models with a hinged floor plate the front action screw is located under floor plate. Open the floor plate and remove the front action screw.

2. Pull the stock from the barrel/receiver assembly, Figure 4.

Tuning Tip: Use the factory supplied AccuTrigger tool to adjust the pull weight of the trigger. Insert the tool into the bottom of the trigger return spring to engage the spring-tail with the slot on the tool. Turn clockwise for maximum trigger pull. The spring will click when adjusted to maximum trigger pull. Turn counterclockwise for minimum trigger pull.

Reassembly Tip: When reassembling the bolt the bearing inside the rear baffle assembly aligns with a groove in the bolt body.

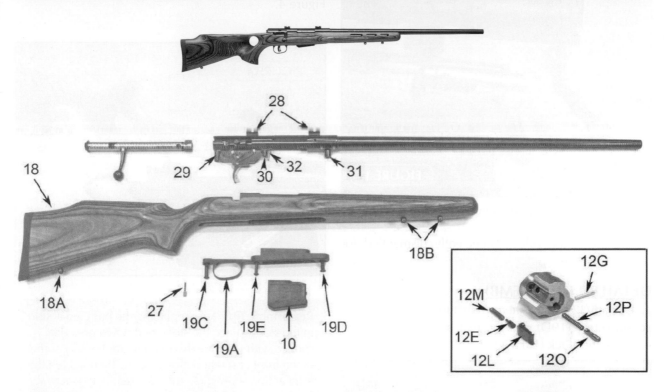

PARTS LIST

10 detachable box magazine
   assembly
12E extractor plunger
12G ejector retaining pin

12L extractor
12M extractor spring
12O ejector
12P ejector spring
18 stock assembly
18A swivel stud rear

18B swivel stud front
19A trigger guard
19C rear action screw
19D front action screw
19E middle support screw
27 tension adjustment tool

28 scope base (2) with screws
29 rear stud
30 middle stud
31 front stud
32 magazine ejector spring

SPECIFICATIONS

Model: Model 25 Lightweight Varminter
Action: bolt, push feed, three lug, short action
Barrel: 24 in.
Weight Unloaded: 8.25 lb.
Caliber: .17 Hornet, .204 Ruger, .22 Hornet, .222 Rem, .223 Rem
Capacity: 4
Common Features: three-lug bolt with 60° lift; free-floated barrel; two-position safety; AccuTrigger; standard or thumbhole laminated wood or standard synthetic with triple pillar bedded stock; cocking indicator; Weaver bases installed for optics; detachable box magazine

BACKGROUND

Savage Model 25 varmint rifles offer a short action with a 60-degree bolt lift and are chambered in a variety of popular small bore calibers. The barrels sport a medium contour and the bolt head is similar to the floating bolt head found in Savage's Model 10/110 and variants. The combination of barrel, floating bolt head and adjustable AccuTrigger is very accurate on gophers, woodchucks, prairie dogs or whatever you call them in your part of the country.

Year Introduced: 2008
Current Manufacturer: Savage Arms (savagearms.com)
Country of Origin: U.S.
Similar Models: 25 Lightweight Varminter (standard laminated wood stock), 25 Walking Varminter (standard synthetic stock)

REQUIRED TOOLS

Field Stripping: none
Disassembly/Assembly: 5/32 hex or Allen wrench

FIELD STRIP

1. Remove detachable box magazine assembly (part #10).
2. Lift the bolt handle and pull it fully rearward while pulling back on the trigger, Figure 1.

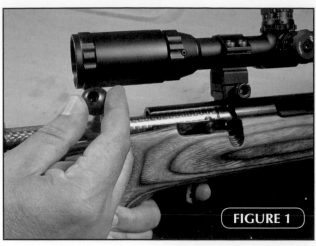

FIGURE 1

3. Withdraw the bolt out of the rear of the receiver.

At this point the rifle is sufficiently dismantled for routine cleaning.

DETAILED DISASSEMBLY

1. Use a 5/32 hex or Allen wrench to remove the front action screw (19D) and the rear action screw (19C) securing the stock (18), Figure 2.

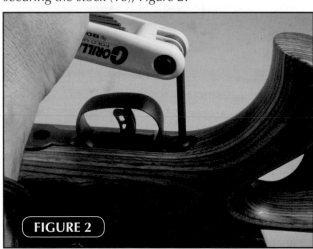

FIGURE 2

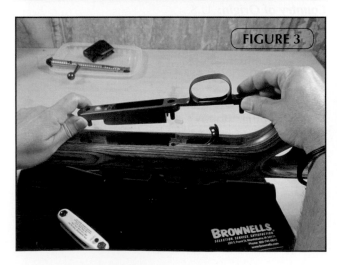

FIGURE 3

2. Pull the trigger guard (19A) from the stock, Figure 3. stock from the barrel/receiver assembly, Figure 4.

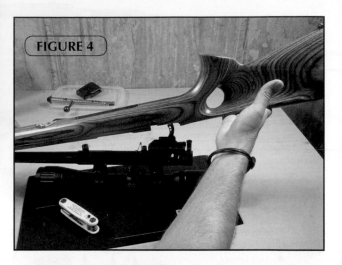

FIGURE 4

Reassembly Tip: After replacing the barreled action in the stock, place the stock butt down on a flat surface with the muzzle pointing up. Loosely screw in the front and rear action screws. Then tighten the front action screw first, then the rear action screw. Function check by cycling the bolt.

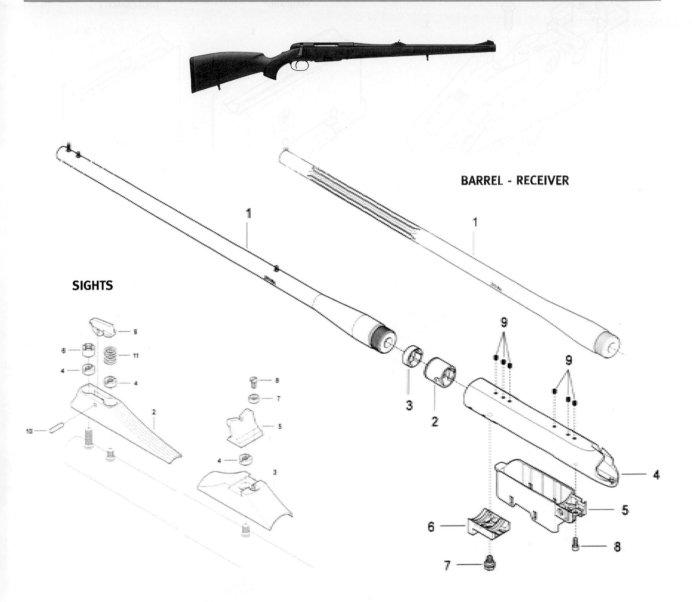

BARREL - RECEIVER

SIGHTS

PARTS LIST

Barrel
1 Barrel
2 Locking Bushing
3 Safety Bushing
4 Receiver
5 Magazine Well
6 Bedding Block
7 Bedding Block Screw
8 Socket Head Cap Screw
9 Headless Set Screw (6 Req'd.)

Sights
2 Front Sight Base
3 Rear Sight Base
4 Slotted Round Nut

5 Rear Sight
6 Set Nut
7 Clamping Sleeve
8 Screw
9 Front Sight
10 Parallel Pin
11 Spring

Bolt
1 Bolt
2 Bolt Handle
2a Bolt Handle Grip
3 Headless Set Screw
4 Firing Pin
5 Bolt Cap
6 Firing Pin Lug
7 Extractor

8 Spring
9 Ejector
10 Ratchet Lever
11 Cam Sleeve
12 Pressure Spring
13 Ratchet Lever Spring
14 Firing Pin Spring
15 Headless Set Screw
16 Lock Washer
17 Spiral Pin
18 Spiral Pin
19 Handle Grip (Scout)
20 Handle

Stock
1 Stock
2 Screw Support

3 Trigger Guard
4 Sling Swivel
8 System Screw Front
9 System Screw Rear
10 Insert Front
11 Insert Rear
12 Fore-End Nose Cap
13 Screw Fore-End Nose Cap
14 Nut Fore-End Nose Cap
Trigger Group
1 Direct Trigger
1 Set Trigger

Magazine Group
1 Magazine (standard)
2 Magazine (high capacity)

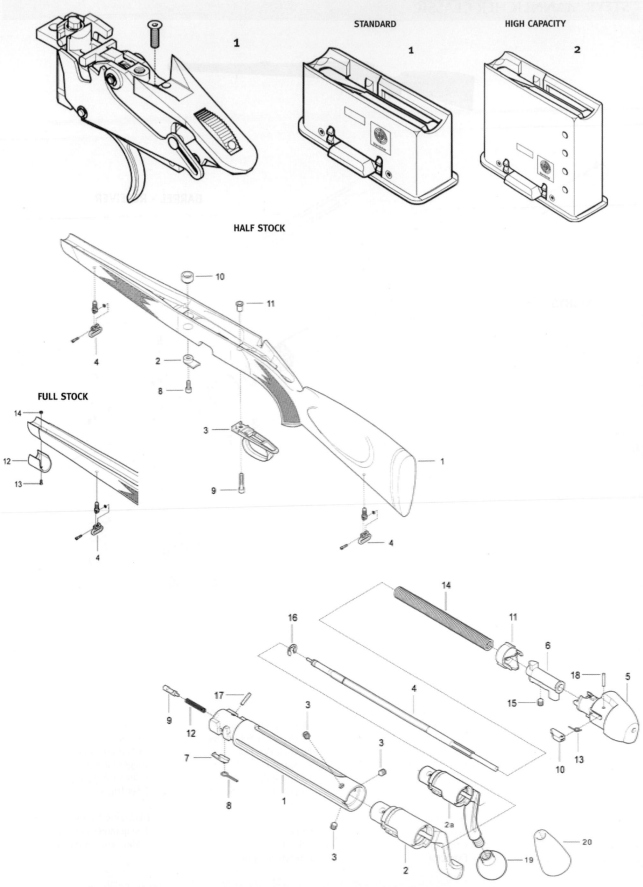

STANDARD

HIGH CAPACITY

HALF STOCK

FULL STOCK

SPECIFICATIONS

Model: Mannlicher Classic
Action: bolt, push feed, 70° bolt lift
Barrel: 20 in., 23 in., 25.6 in. (magnum calibers)
Weight Unloaded: 7.3 lb. to 7.9 lb. (depending on model)
Caliber: .222 Rem, .223 Rem, .243 Win, 6.5x55 SE, 6.5x57, 6.5x68, .270 Win, .270 WSM, 7x64, .25-06 Rem, 7mm-08, 7mm Rem Mag, .30-06, .300 Win Mag, .300 WSM, .308 Win, 8x57, 8x68 S, 9.3x62
Capacity: 3 (magnum calibers) , 4 (standard calibers)
Common Features: two-lug bolt with 70° bolt lift; bedded stock (some models); cocking indicator; three-position safety; set trigger (some models); walnut or synthetic stock; open sights (some models); detachable box magazine; butter-knife bolt handle

BACKGROUND

The Steyr Arms Mannlicher Classic is a direct descendant of the iconic Mannlicher-Schoenauer rifles of the early 20th century. The Steyr is an updated version with the full Mannlicher-style stock and butter-knife bolt handle. As much as the Mannlicher Classic exudes the characteristics of a traditional Teutonic hunting rifle it shares the same action as Steyr's Pro Hunter model which offers the latest innovations in a bolt-action hunting rifle. The bolt is slick on these rifles like a hot framing nail through a stick of butter.
Year Introduced: 1997 (Mannlicher Pro Hunter), 2000 (Mannlicher Full Stock), 2009 (Mannlicher Pro Varminter)
Current Manufacturer: Steyr Arms (steyrarms.com)
Country of Origin: Austria
Similar Models: Mannlicher Pro Hunter, Mannlicher Pro Varminter, Mannlicher Classic Light, Big Bore, Pro Alaskan, Pro African

REQUIRED TOOLS

Field Stripping: none
Disassembly/Assembly: 5mm hex or Allen wrench

FIELD STRIP

1. Remove magazine.
2. Lift bolt handle (part #2) and move safety to rearward/"lock" position so the gray lock snaps out, Figure 1.
3. Pull bolt assembly from the receiver (4).

At this point the rifle is sufficiently dismantled for routine cleaning.

BOLT DISASSEMBLY

1. Grip the bolt and push in the bolt catch, Steyr calls it a ratchet lever (10) then rotate the bolt sleeve, Steyr

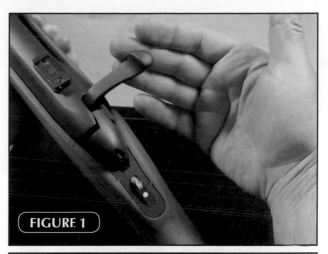

FIGURE 1

FIGURE 2

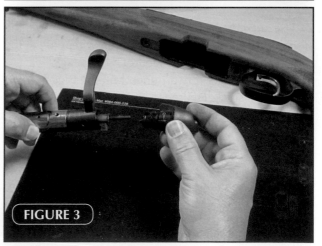

FIGURE 3

calls it a bolt cap (5), clockwise until it unlocks with a "click." Figure 2.
2. Remove the bolt cap, Figure 3.
3. Extract the firing pin assembly from the rear of the bolt (1), Figure 4.

BARREL/RECEIVER DISASSEMBLY

1. Remove the two plastic caps from the stock screws, Steyr calls them system screw front (8) and

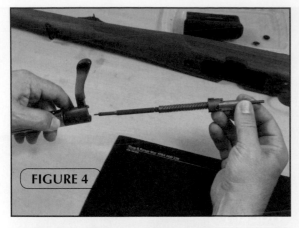

FIGURE 4

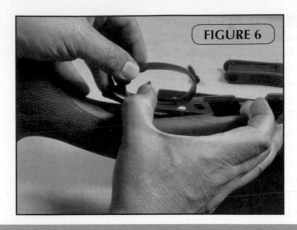

FIGURE 6

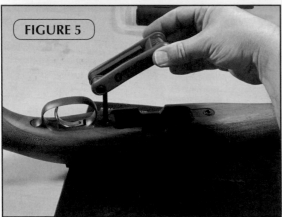

FIGURE 5

Cleaning Tip: For models with wood stocks only use special stock oil with silicone; synthetic stocks should be cleaned with mild soapy water.

Reassembly Tip: The two stocks screws need to be retightened to 5.16 ft lb. If you reassemble the bolt and turn the bolt cap too far, place the bolt on a flat bench surface with the bolt handle in contact with the surface and the bolt cap hanging over the edge of the bench. Press the ratchet lever and rotate the shroud back into position. The square projection of the bolt cap lines up with the bolt handle.

system screw rear (9), at the underside of the stock (1).

2. Use a 5mm hex or Allen wrench to remove the system screw front (8) and system screw rear (9), at the underside of the stock (1), Figure 5.

3. Push the trigger forward then pull the trigger guard (3) from the stock, Figure 6.

4. Separate the barrel/receiver assembly from the stock.

Reassemble in reverse order.

THOMPSON/CENTER ICON

SPECIFICATIONS
Model: Icon
Action: bolt, push feed
Barrel: 22 in. heavy barrel (Precision Hunter, Warlord), 24 in.

Weight Unloaded: 7.5 lb., 7.75 lb. (Precision Hunter), 12.75 lb. (Warlord)
Caliber: .204 Ruger, .22-250, .243 Win, .30 TC, .308 Win, .338 LAPUA
Capacity: 3, 5 or 10 removable magazine (Warlord)

Common Features: three-lug, jeweled bolt with 60-degree lift; integral weaver base; interlock bedding system; modular bolt knob; detachable magazine; cocking indicator; two-position safety; adjustable trigger; Ultra Wood, walnut, laminated hardwood (Precision Hunter) or synthetic (Warlord) stock

BACKGROUND

The Icon is T/C's first bolt-action rifle. They machined the receiver out of bar stock and included an integral Picatinny rail which makes the action rigid and stable. They added a barrel with 5R rifling which uses five lands and five grooves instead of the traditional six lands/grooves. The sides of the lands in a 5R barrel are cut at a 65-degree angle, instead of the conventional 90-degree for less bullet deformation during firing. They also threw in aluminum bedding, an externally adjustable trigger, a three lug bolt with a 60-degree bolt lift and butter-knife bolt handle. The result is a rifle that is MOA Certified—a three shot group is less than one inch at 100 yards. The Precision Hunter and Warlord models shoot even tighter groups with Certified Sub-MOA and Certified Half-MOA, respectively. Sweet. Some of the design reminds me of Tikka rifles from Finland.

Year Introduced: 2007
Current Manufacturer: Thompson/Center (tcarms.com)
Country of Origin: USA
Similar Models: Precision Hunter, Warlord

REQUIRED TOOLS

Field Stripping: none
Disassembly/Assembly: T/C bolt takedown tool, 1/8 inch hex or Allen wrench

FIELD STRIP

1. To field strip, remove the magazine, lift bolt handle and pull it fully to the rear.
2. Place the safety lever in the SAFE position.
3. Press the bolt stop and continue to draw the bolt assembly from the receiver, Figure 1.
At this point routine maintenance and cleaning can be performed.

BOLT DISASSEMBLY

1. To remove the firing pin assembly from the bolt assembly, use the T/C bolt takedown tool. Grasp the bolt body and insert the rear portion of the bolt assembly into the bolt takedown tool and rotate the tool counterclockwise, Figure 3. This uncocks the firing pin, Figure 4.

FIGURE 1

Tuning Tip: With the bolt removed, the trigger weight can be adjusted using the T/C trigger adjustment tool or a hex or Allen wrench, Figure 2. Looking down into the receiver, turn the trigger weight adjustment screw clockwise to increase the pull, turn the screw counterclockwise to decrease the trigger pull.

FIGURE 2

2. With the bolt assembly still in the bolt takedown tool, place the tool and bolt on the bench top and apply downward pressure on the firing pin spring while pulling the bolt handle out from the bolt body.

3. The firing pin assembly can now be removed from the bolt body.

BARREL/RECEIVER DISASSEMBLY

1. To remove the barreled action from the stock, remove the three floor plate screws using a 1/8 inch hex or Allen wrench and gently pull up on the trigger guard and magazine housing, Figure 5.

2. Remove the trigger assembly from the barreled receiver by pushing out two pins and lifting the trigger assembly up and off the receiver.

Reassemble reversing the above procedures.

FIGURE 5

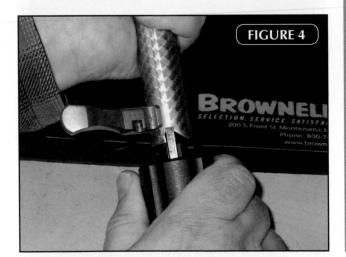

FIGURE 3

FIGURE 4

Reassembly Tip: To reassemble the bolt assembly, put the firing pin assembly back into the bolt body and keep the striker/firing pin in the uncocked position. Insert the bolt handle into the bolt body and then compress the firing pin spring by pushing down on the bolt on the bench top surface. When the firing pin spring is completely compressed continue to insert the bolt handle into the bolt body and then release the tension on the bolt body. After the bolt handle is reinstalled, the striker must be cocked so the bolt assembly can be reinserted into the receiver. Use the T/C bolt takedown tool and rotate the striker clockwise. You will hear the firing pin click when it is cocked.

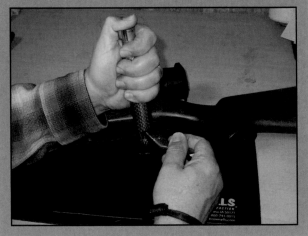

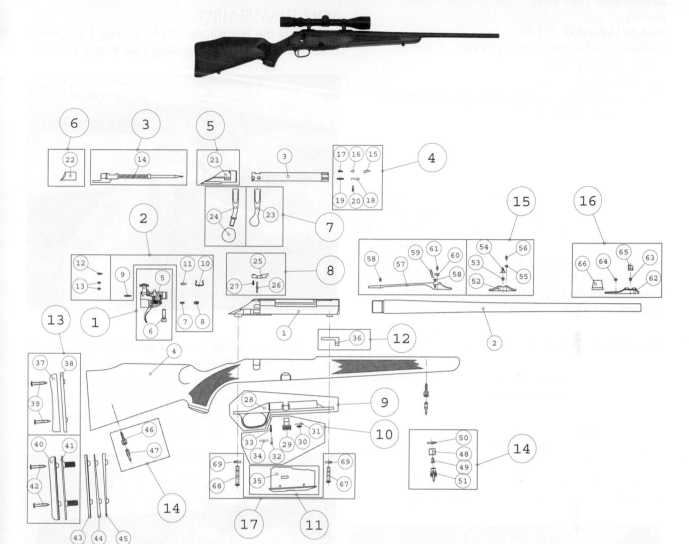

PARTS LIST

1 Receiver
2 Barrel
3 Bolt Body
4 Stock
5 Trigger Mechanism
6 Fastening Screw
7 Trigger Spring
8 Trigger Spring Set Screw
9 Trigger Sear Spring
10 Safety Lever Spring
11 Safety Silencer
12 Set Trigger Spring
13 Set Trigger Set Screw
14 Firing Pin Assembly
15 Extractor
16 Extractor Plunger
17 Extractor Spring
18 Ejector
19 Ejector Spring

20 Pin
21 Bolt Guide Bushing
22 Bolt Shroud
23 Bolt Handle with Steel Knob
24 Bolt Handle with Plastic
   Knob
25 Bolt Release
26 Bolt Release Pin
27 Bolt Release Spring
28 Trigger Guard Assembly
29 Magazine Catch
30 Magazine Catch Spring
31 Pin
32 Magazine Ejector
33 Magazine Ejector Spring
34 Pin
35 Magazine
36 Recoil Block
37 Recoil Pad
38 Recoil Pad Base

39 Mounting Screw
40 Recoil Pad
41 Recoil Pad Base
42 Mounting Screw
43 Straight Butt Spacer
44 Upwards Angled Butt Spacer
45 Downwards Angled Butt
   Spacer
46 Swivel Screw
47 Swivel
48 Swivel Socket
49 Socket Mounting Screw
50 Socket Mounting Plate
51 Front Swivel
52 Rear Sight Base
53 Mounting Screw
54 Blade
55 Blade Mounting Washer
56 Blade Mounting Screw
57 Rear Sight Base

58 Mounting Screw
59 Blade
60 Blade Mounting Washer
61 Blade Mounting Screw
62 Front Sight Base
63 Base Front Mounting Screw
64 Base Rear Mounting Screw
65 Bead
66 Front Sight Hood
62 Front Sight Base
63 Base Front mounting Screw
64 Base Rear mounting Screw
65 Fluorescent Bead
66 Front Sight Hood with Holes
67 Front Fastening Screw
68 Rear Fastening Screw
69 Fastening Screw Washer

SPECIFICATIONS
Model: M658
Action: bolt, push feed
Barrel: 22 in.
Weight Unloaded: 7.3 lb.
Caliber: .25-06 Rem, 6.5x55 Swede, .270 Win., 7x64, .30-06, 9.3x62
Capacity: 3 + 1
Common Features: two-lug bolt; cocking indicator; two-position safety; checkered wood stock with palm swell; drilled and tapped for optics; detachable 3-round magazine; free-floated barrel

BACKGROUND
Tikka is the economy brand for Sako. The M658 is an older model that has since been replaced with the T3 family of rifles. The action of the M658 is super smooth, the stock is ergonomic, the trigger is crisp and it is very accurate. Very Sako-esque.
Year Introduced: 1989
Current Manufacturer: Tikka (tikka.fi)
Country of Origin: Finland

REQUIRED TOOLS
Field Stripping: none
Disassembly/Assembly: 2mm hex or Allen wrench, medium flat blade screwdriver

FIELD STRIP
1. Remove magazine (part #35) and move safety to forward/"fire" position.
2. Lift bolt handle (23) and draw back the bolt assembly while pressing in the bolt release (25), Figure 1.

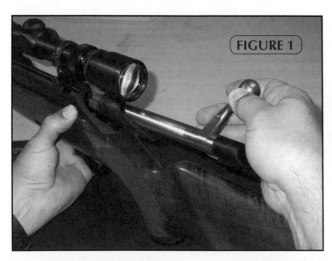
FIGURE 1

3. Pull bolt assembly with bolt guide bushing (21) from the receiver (1).

At this point the rifle is sufficiently dismantled for routine cleaning.

BOLT DISASSEMBLY
1. Remove the bolt shroud (22) by turning it clockwise as far as it will go and then pulling it backward, Figure 2.

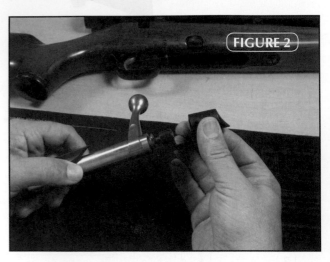
FIGURE 2

2. Next use a screwdriver as a retaining pin by insert the tip of a flat blade screwdriver into the gap between the cocking piece of the firing pin assembly and the bolt handle retainer bushing. Use the screwdriver as a lever and turn it counterclockwise to disengage the firing pin assembly (14), Figure 3.

FIGURE 3

3. Pull the bolt handle out of the bolt body, Figure 4.
4. Remove the firing pin assembly and bolt guide bushing from the bolt body. Leave the screwdriver in place between the cocking piece of the firing pin assembly and the bolt handle retainer bushing.

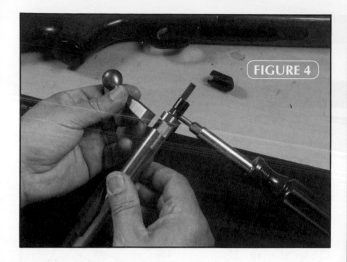

FIGURE 4

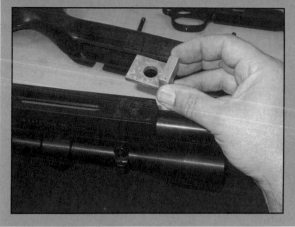

Reassembly Tip: Remember to position the aluminum recoil block (36) on the receiver prior to placing the stock back on the barrel/receiver assembly.

BARREL/RECEIVER DISASSEMBLY

1. Remove the front fastening screw (67) and rear fastening screw (68) at the underside of the stock (4).
2. Pull the trigger guard assembly (28) from the stock.
3. Next pull the barrel/receiver assembly from the stock, Figure 5.

Reassemble in reverse order.

Tuning Tip: The trigger pull on the M658 is adjustable from two to four pounds via the trigger adjustment screw located at the front of the trigger assembly. First loosen the locking nut then turning the screw clockwise will increase trigger pull, turning it counterclockwise will reduce it.

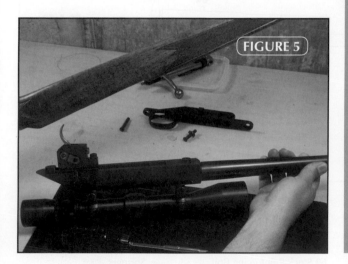

FIGURE 5

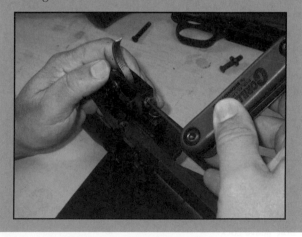

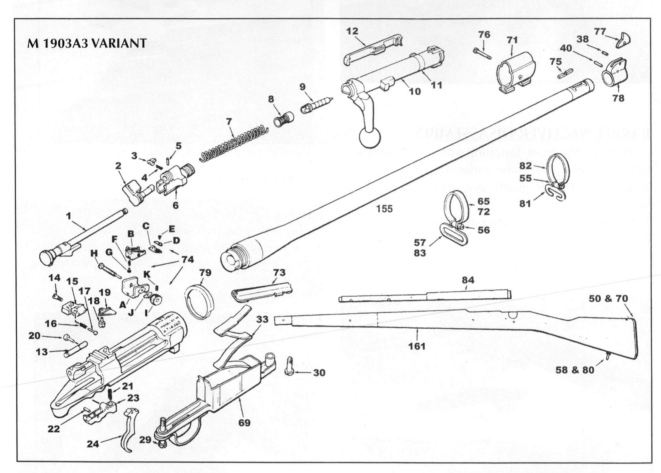

M 1903A3 VARIANT

PARTS LIST

1 Firing Pin Rod
2 Safety Lock Assembly
3 Bolt Sleeve Lock
4 Bolt Sleeve Lock Spring
5 Bolt Sleeve Lock Pin
6 Bolt Sleeve
7 Mainspring
8 Striker Sleeve
9 Striker
10 Bolt
11 Extractor Collar
12 Extractor
13 Cut-Off Spindle
14 Cut-Off Screw
15 Cut-Off
16 Cut-Off Plunger Spring
17 Cut-Off Plunger
18 Ejector Pin

19 Ejector
20 Sear Pin
21 Sear Spring
22 Trigger Pin
23 Sear
24 Trigger
26 Floorplate Catch
27 Floorplate Catch Spring
28 Floorplate Catch Pin
29 Guard Screw, Rear
29A Guard Screw Bushing, Rear
30 Guard Screw, Front
32 Floor Plate
33 Magazine Spring
41 Front Sight Cover
41A Front Sight Cover
52 Buttplate Trapdoor Spring
53 Butt Swivel Screw
53 Butt Swivel Screw

54 Buttplate Screw, Large
55A Stacking Swivel Screw
56A Sling Swivel Screw
61 Stock Reinforcing Nut
62 Stock Reinforcing Bolt
67A Handguard Clip
69 Trigger Guard
70 Buttplate
71 Upper Band
72 Lower Band
72A Lower Band Spring
73 Follower
74 Rear Sight Assembly
74A Rear Sight Base
74B Windage Yoke
74C Slide Aperture
74D Slide Aperture Spring
74E Slide Aperture Screw
74F Windage Yoke Spring
74G Windage Yoke Spring

Plunger
74H Windage Yoke Screw
74I Windage Index Knob
74J Windage Index Knob Click Spring
74K Windage Index Knob Screw
74L Windage Yoke Assembly
75 Front Sight Key
76 Upper Band Screw
77 Front Sight Blade
78 Front Sight Base
79 Handguard Ring
80 Butt Swivel
81 Stacking Swivel
82 Stacking Swivel Band
83 Sling Swivel
84 Handguard
155 Barrel
161 Stock

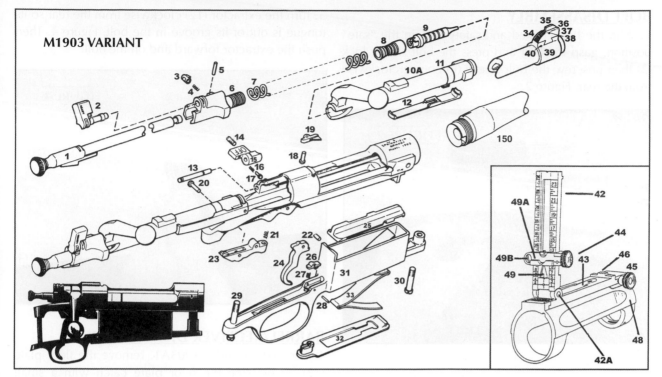

M1903 VARIANT

Courtesy of Numrich Gun Parts Corporation

SPECIFICATIONS
Model: M1903A3 Springfield
Action: bolt, control feed
Barrel: 26 in.
Weight Unloaded: 8 lb. 11 oz.
Caliber: .30-06
Capacity: 5-round fixed magazine
Common Features: two-lug bolt, adjustable aperture rear/fixed front sights, three-position safety, wood stock

BACKGROUND
The United States Rifle, caliber .30-06, Model 1903 was in service with the US military from WWI through WWII. As the M1903A4, a sniper variant, it saw service in WWII as well as the Korean War and limited service during the Vietnam War. It is still used today with many military drill teams. After the war, hunters soon de-militarized the Springfields to use big game hunting. Ernest Hemingway hunted with a sporterized Springfield. The rifle uses a five-shot stripper clip to load the internal magazine. Shown is a M1903A3.
Year Introduced: 1903-57
Manufacturer: Springfield Armory, Rock Island Arsenal, Remington Arms, Smith-Corona
Country of Origin: US
Similar Models: M1903, M1903A1, M1903A4 (sniper model)

REQUIRED TOOLS
Field Stripping: none

Disassembly/Assembly: medium flat blade screwdriver, small punch, rubber mallet

FIELD STRIP
1. Cycle the bolt (part #10) to cock the action and place the magazine cut-off (15) at middle position, then set the safety lock (2) in the vertical position, Figure 1.

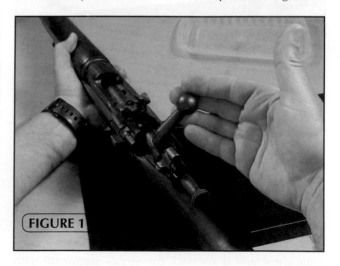

FIGURE 1

2. Lift the bolt and pull it rearward removing it from the receiver.

At this point the rifle is sufficiently disassembled for routine cleaning.

BOLT DISASSEMBLY

1. With the bolt cocked and safety lock in the "safe" position, gasp the bolt and press the bolt sleeve lock (3) then unscrew the bolt sleeve (6) counterclockwise from the rear, Figure 2.

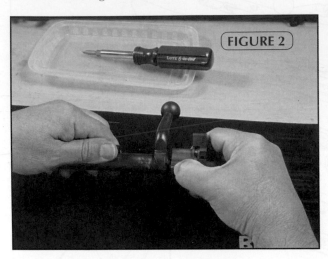

FIGURE 2

2. Remove the firing pin assembly from the rear of the bolt, Figure 3.

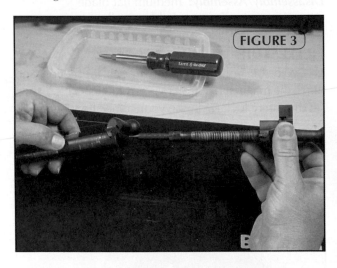

FIGURE 3

3. Gasp the bolt sleeve with one hand and with the other hand pull back on cocking piece on the firing pin rod (1) and turn the safety lock to the "fire"/"ready" position.

4. Brace the cocking piece against the bench top or your chest and draw back the striker sleeve (8) with one hand and while holding it in place remove the striker (9) with your other hand. The mainspring (7) is under compression so control it.

5. Turn the extractor (12) clockwise from the rear so its tongue is out of its groove in the bolt, Figure 4. Then push the extractor forward and off the bolt.

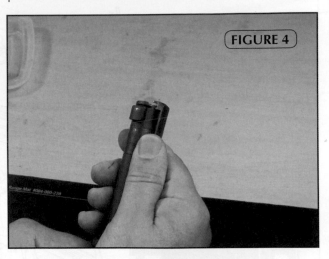

FIGURE 4

BARREL/RECEIVER DISASSEMBLY

1. For M1903 and M1903A1, remove the floor plate (32) by pressing the floor plate catch with a small punch—the US Army Service Manual instructs to use the bullet end of a cartridge—and at the same time pulling rearward. For M1903A3 and M1903A4 models the front trigger guard screw (30) and rear trigger guard screw (29) are removed, Figure 5. The floor plate, magazine spring (33) and follower (73) can then be removed.

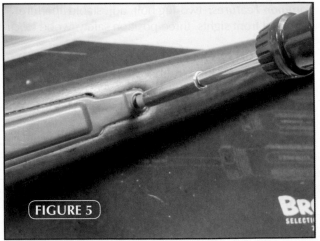

FIGURE 5

2. Remove the upper band screw (76), Figure 6. Then slide upper band (71) toward the muzzle. You may need to tap the upper band with a rubber mallet.

3. Unscrew the lower band screw (56) and remove the lower band (72) by pressing in the rear of the lower

band spring, Figure 7. Slide the lower band forward toward the muzzle.

FIGURE 6

4. Draw the hand guard (84) toward the muzzle and off the barrel.

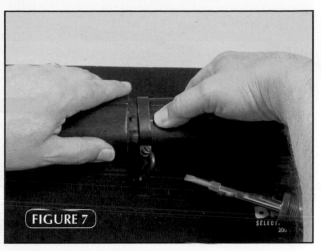

FIGURE 7

5. Remove the front trigger guard screw (30) and rear trigger guard screw (29) and the trigger guard (69) can be pulled from the bottom of the stock (161).

6. The stock can now be removed from the barrel/receiver assembly.

Reassembly is accomplished in reverse order.

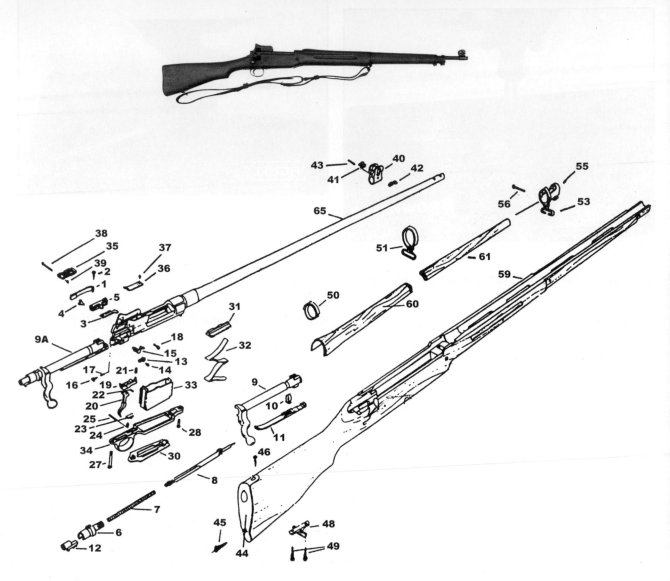

Courtesy of Numrich Gun Parts Corporation

PARTS LIST

1 Bolt Stop Spring
2 Bolt Stop Screw
3 Ejector
4 Bolt Stop Spring Rest
5 Bolt Stop
6 Bolt Sleeve
7 Mainspring
8 Firing Pin
9 Bolt
9A Bolt assembly
10 Extractor Collar
11 Extractor
12 Cocking Piece
13 Safety Lock Holder

14 Safety Lock Holder Screw
15 Safety
16 Safety Lock Plunger
17 Safety Lock Plunger Spring
18 Sear Pin
19 Sear
20 Trigger
21 Sear Spring
22 Trigger Pin
23 Floorplate Catch
24 Floorplate Catch Spring
25 Floorplate Catch Pin
26 Guard Screw Bushing, Rear
27 Guard Screw, Rear
28 Guard Screw, Front
29 Guard Screw Bushing, Front,

30 Floorplate
31 Follower
32 Magazine Spring
33 Magazine Box
34 Trigger Guard
35 Rear Sight Assembly
36 Rear Sight Base Spring
37 Rear Sight Base Screw
38 Rear Sight Axis Screw
39 Rear Sight Axis Nut
40 Front Sight Carrier Base
41 Front Sight Blade
42 Front Sight Spline
43 Front Sight Pin
44 Buttplate w/ Trapdoor
    Assembly

45 Buttplate Screw, Large
46 Buttplate Screw, Small
47 Rear Swivel Base
48 Rear Swivel Assembly
49 Rear Swivel Base Screw
    (2 Req'd.)
50 Handguard Ring
51 Lower Band Assembly
52 Lower Band Screw
53 Stacking Swivel
55 Upper Band
56 Upper Band Screw
60 Handguard, Lower
61 Handguard, Upper
65 Barrel

SPECIFICATIONS
Model: M1917 Enfield
Action: bolt, control feed
Barrel: 26 in.
Weight Unloaded: 9 lb. 3 oz.
Caliber: .30-06
Capacity: 6-round fixed magazine
Common Features: two-lug bolt, adjustable aperture rear/fixed front sights, two-position safety, wood stock

BACKGROUND
The United States Rifle, cal .30, Model 1917 was a U.S. modified and produced version of the British P14. When Great Britain entered WWI they lacked sufficient stockpiles of rifles and contracted three U.S. manufacturers: Winchester, Remington and Eddystone. When the U.S. entered the Great War we, too, needed rifles and it was soon realized that it would be easier and faster for gun factories to build the Enfield instead of retooling for the M1903 Springfield. The design was changed to accommodate the .30-06 cartridge and over 2,000,000 M1917s were produced. Sergeant Alvin York, one of the most decorated soldiers in WWI, used a M1917 to kill 28 German soldiers and capture 132 others during the Meuse-Argonne Offensive in France.
In Service: 1917-53
Manufacturer: Eddystone, Remington, Winchester
Country of Origin: UK

REQUIRED TOOLS
Field Stripping: none
Disassembly/Assembly: medium flat blade screwdriver, small punch, coin or thin strip of metal

FIELD STRIP
1. Hold the bolt stop (part #5) out from receiver and pull bolt assembly (9A) out to the rear, Figure 1.

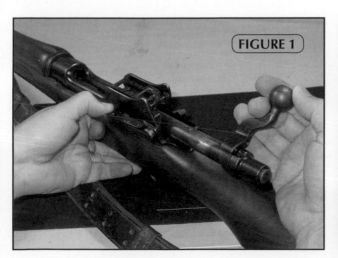

FIGURE 1

At this point the rifle is sufficiently disassembled for routine cleaning.

BOLT DISASSEMBLY
1. With the bolt inserted into the receiver, lift the bolt handle about half way up and slight push it forward then insert a coin between the cocking piece (12) and bolt sleeve (6).
2. Remove bolt assembly from receiver.
3. With bolt assembly removed, unscrew the striker assembly from the bolt body.
4. The extractor (11) is removed by rotating it clockwise from rear to cover the gas port holes and until its front lug is out of the groove in the bolt (9). Then push it forward, Figure 2.

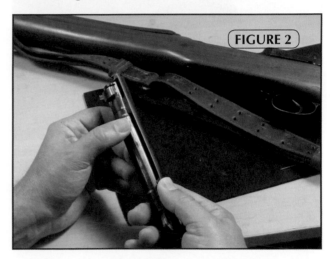

FIGURE 2

BARREL/RECEIVER DISASSEMBLY
1. Remove the magazine assembly by pressing a punch or in a pinch the bullet tip of a cartridge into the hole at bottom rear of floorplate (30) and pulling rearward on the floorplate. The floorplate, magazine spring (32) and follower (31) will come free, Figure 3.

FIGURE 3

2. To remove the barrel/receiver assembly from the buttstock (59) first remove the upper band screw (59), Figure 4. Then slide the upper band (55) toward the muzzle and off the barrel. The upper handguard (61) can now be removed.

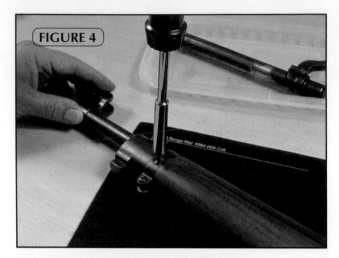

FIGURE 4

3. Next loosen the screw on the lower band assembly (51) and slide it off toward the muzzle.

4. Remove the front guard screw (28) and rear guard screw (27) then pull trigger guard (34) and magazine (33) out from the bottom of buttstock.

Reassembly is accomplished in reverse order.

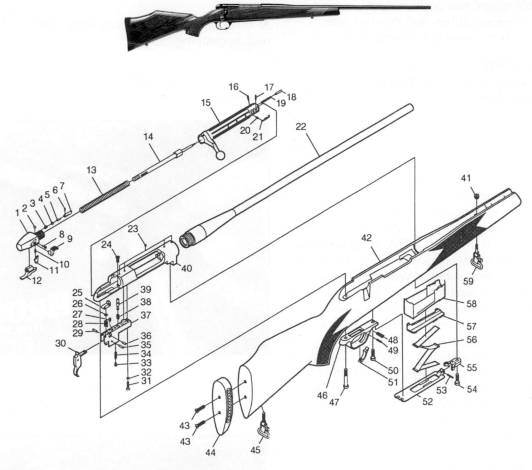

PARTS LIST

1 Bolt sleeve
2 Ball, retaining
3 Spring, plunger
4 Plunger, bolt sleeve lock
5 Retainer leaf, bolt sleeve lock
6 Pin, retainer leaf
7 Bolt sleeve lock
8 Screw, safety lever
9 Safety lever
10 Spring, safety hook
11 Safety hook
12 Cocking piece
13 Spring, firing pin
14 Firing pin
15 Bolt body

16 Pin, ejector
17 Pin, extractor
18 Ejector
19 Spring, ejector
20 Spring, extractor
21 Extractor
22 Barrel
23 Screw, plug, receiver
24 Screw, top trigger housing
25 Sear
26 Washer, sear spring
27 Screw, creep adjustment
28 Spring, sear
29 Pin, sear
30 Trigger
31 Screw, bottom trigger

  housing
33 Screw, weight adjustment
34 Spring, trigger
35 Pin, trigger
36 Pin, sear lock
37 Trigger housing
38 Spring, bolt stop
39 Bolt stop
40 Receiver
41 Nut, swivel stud front
42 Stock
43 Screw, recoil pad
44 Recoil pad
45 Swivel stud, rear
46 Trigger guard
47 Screw, trigger guard rear

48 Spring, floorplate catch
49 Pin, floorplate catch
50 Post, floorplate
51 Latch, floorplate
52 Floorplate
53 Pin, floorplate
54 Screw, trigger guard front
55 Spring, post
56 Spring, follower
57 Follower
58 Magazine box
59 Swivel stud, front
60 Shim
61 Insert, magazine box
62 Accubrake
63 Screw, bolt sleeve lock

SPECIFICATIONS

Model: Mark V Deluxe
Action: bolt, push feed
Barrel: 24 in. (non-Weatherby calibers), 26 in. (Weatherby Magnum calibers), 28 in. (.378 Wby Mag, .416 Wby Mag, .460 Wby Mag)

Weight Unloaded: 6.75 lb. to 10 lb. (depending on caliber)
Caliber: .270 Win, .308 Win, .30-06, .257 Wby Mag, .270 Wby Mag, 7mm Wby Mag, .300 Wby Mag, .340 Wby Mag, .378 Wby Mag, .416 Wby Mag, .460 Wby Mag

Capacity: 2+1 (.378 Wby Mag, .416 Wby Mag, .460 Wby Mag), 3+1 (.257 through . .340 Wby Mag), 5+1(non-Weatherby calibers)

Common Features: nine-lug bolt with 54-degree lift, adjustable trigger, two-position safety, numerous Weatherby Magnum calibers and standard non-Weatherby calibers, wood or synthetic stock

BACKGROUND

Weatherby Mark V rifles can be defined as iconic, luxurious and high performance. It was the late 1940s when Roy Weatherby began building rifles in his California shop. These rifles used what was then Weatherby's wildcat cartridges based on his design philosophy that lightweight bullets traveling at high speed provided the best terminal performance. Those cartridges with their unique double radius venturi shoulder design became a line of proprietary cartridges with calibers ranging from the diminutive .224 up through the colossal .460. The .257 Weatherby Magnum is said to have been Roy's personal favorite. In 1957 the hot rod cartridges were mated to Weatherby's proprietary action, the Mark V, built to be stronger, safer and to withstand the tremendous pressure of Weatherby's high velocity cartridges. The action features nine locking lugs and a 54-degree bolt lift. If the cartridges and action were not unique enough, Weatherby's stock has a distinct Monte Carlo comb sculpted from either fancy wood or hand-laminated with composites or synthetics. Initial production of the Mark V started in California, European and Asian manufacturers have also built the Mark V. It is currently produced in the USA.

Year Introduced: 1957

Current Manufacturer: Weatherby (weatherby.com)

Country of Origin: USA

Similar Models: Accumark (composite stock, fluted barrel), Accumark .338 Lapua, Deluxe (AA fancy walnut stock), Euromark (matte wood stock/barrel finish), Fibermark Composite (fiberglass stock), Lazermark (fancy laser engraved wood stock), Sporter (wood stock), Synthetic (synthetic stock), Ultra Lightweight (composite stock, designed for reduced weight), Ultramark (AAA exhibition grade walnut stock)

REQUIRED TOOLS

Field Stripping: none

Disassembly/Assembly: flat blade screwdriver, torque wrench

FIELD STRIP

1. Unload the rifle and move the safety lever (part #9) to the "Off"/"Safe" position.

2. Raise the bolt handle and draw the bolt assembly to the rear until it stops.

3. Next pull the trigger (30) and continue pull the bolt assembly so it clears the receiver (40).

At this point the rifle is sufficiently disassembled for routine cleaning.

BOLT DISASSEMBLY

1. Disassemble the bolt assembly by using a flat blade

FIGURE 1

screwdriver to push the cocking piece (12) to the rear so its shoulder engages the bolt sleeve (1), Figure 1.

FIGURE 2

2. Push in the bolt sleeve lock (7) using your thumb, Figure 2.

3. Unscrew the bolt body (15) from the bolt sleeve/firing pin assembly keeping the sleeve facing up so the retaining ball (2) will not fall out of its recess in the bolt sleeve, Figure 3.

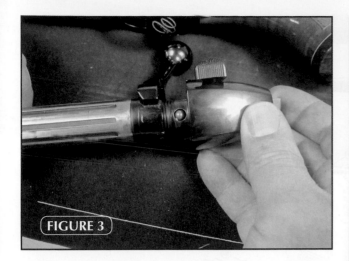

FIGURE 3

4. Remove the retaining ball as soon as it freed.

BARREL/RECEIVER DISASSEMBLY

1. To remove the trigger guard assembly from the stock (42), press the floor plate latch (51) to open the floor plate.
2. Next use a flat blade screwdriver to remove the front (54) and rear (47) trigger guard screws, Figure 4.

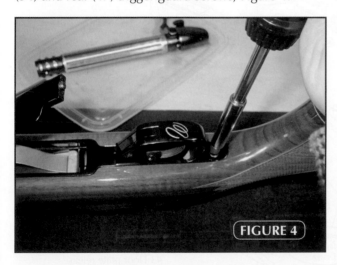

FIGURE 4

3. Next gently remove the trigger guard assembly from the stock. The stock can now be removed from the barreled action.

Reassembly Tip: Make sure that the rear of the firing pin (14) is flush with the rear of the cocking piece then rotate the cocking piece off the engaging shoulder of the bolt sleeve allowing the firing pin assembly to move forward, . When reattaching the stock and trigger guard assembly to the barreled action, first lightly seat the trigger guard screws then position the rifle so it is vertical and the butt rests on the bench top. Pull down on the barrel to help seat the receiver recoil lug with

the stock. The screws must be tightened in proper sequence and to proper torque. First tighten the rear screw to a torque of 30-35 in.-lbs. then torque the front screw to 30-35 in.-lbs. for wood and synthetic stocks. For composite stocks with aluminum bedding blocks, such as the stocks for Fibermark and Accumark models, apply 50-55 in.-lbs. to the rear screw followed by 50-55 in.-lbs. to the front screw.

Reassemble in reverse order.

Tuning Tip: The trigger assembly has two adjustment screws. The stock must be removed to access the adjustment screws. The weight adjustment screw (33) on the bottom of the trigger assembly adjusts the weight of the trigger pull. Use a 5/64 hex or Allen wrench and turn clockwise to increase weight, turn counterclockwise to decrease weight. The adjusting screw on the top of the trigger assembly accessed via a hole in the receiver adjusts sear engagement and is set at the factory. Note that trigger pull cannot be adjusted below approximately 2-3/4 pounds. After adjusting the trigger, engage the safety and pull the trigger to its limit then release the trigger slowly to ensure it returns to the forward position. If the trigger does not return to its position, you have adjusted the trigger pull too lightly.

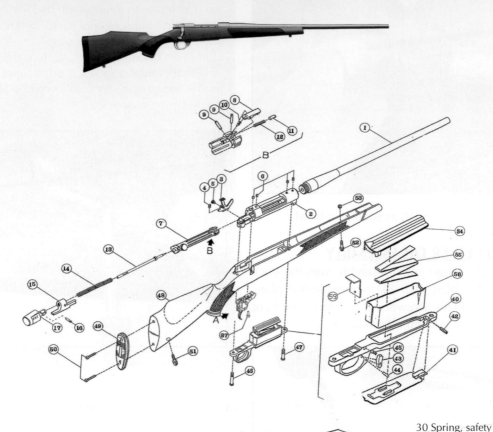

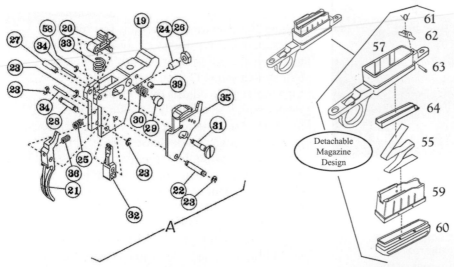

PARTS LIST

1 Barrel
2 Receiver
3 Bolt stop
4 Spring, bolt stop
5 Screw, bolt stop guide
6 Screw, plug
7 Bolt
8 Extractor
9 Pin, extractor (2)

10 Spring, extractor
11 Ejector
12 Spring, ejector
13 Firing pin
14 Spring, firing pin
15 Cocking piece
16 Pin, firing pin retaining
17 Bolt sleeve
19 Trigger housing
20 Sear

21 Trigger
22 Pin, trigger
23 Retaining C-clip (2)
24 Screw, trigger adjusting (front)
25 Spring, trigger
26 Nut, lock (2)
27 Pin, sear
28 Pin, Trigger
29 Safety plunger

30 Spring, safety
31 Screw, safety lever
32 Actuator
33 Spring, sear
34 Pin, sear stopping
35 Safety lever
36 Spring, trigger
37 Screw, trigger housing
39 Screw, slotted set
40 Trigger guard
41 Floor plate
42 Pin, floor plate
43 Floor plate release
44 Pin, floor plate release
45 Spring, floor plate release
46 Screw, trigger guard (rear)
47 Screw, trigger guard (front)
48 Stock
49 Recoil pad
50 Screw, recoil pad (2)
51 Sling swivel stud (rear)
52 Sling swivel stud (front)
54 Magazine follower
55 Spring magazine follower
56 Magazine box
57 Trigger guard
59 Magazine box top
60 Magazine box bottom
61 Spring release
62 Magazine release
63 Pin, magazine release
64 Magazine follower

SPECIFICATIONS

Model: Vanguard Series 2 Synthetic
Action: bolt, push feed
Barrel: 24 in.
Weight Unloaded: 7.5 lb.
Caliber: .223 Rem, .22-250 Rem, .240 Wby Mag, .243 Win, .25-06 Rem, .270 Win, 7mm-08 Rem, .308 Win, .30-06, .257 Wby Mag, .270 WSM, 7mm Rem Mag, .300 Win Mag, .300 WSM, .300 Wby Mag, .338 Win Mag
Capacity: 3+1 (.257 through .338 Win Mag), 5+1 (.223 through .30-06)
Common Features: two-lug bolt with 90-degree lift, Monte Carlo stock, two-stage adjustable trigger, three-position safety

BACKGROUND

Weatherby's Vanguard Series 2 rifles are excellent low-cost rifles manufactured by Howa of Japan to Weatherby specifications. They offer 16 caliber options and guarantee Sub-MOA accuracy—three-shot groups of .99 inches or less with Weatherby factory or premium ammunition. Vanguard Series 2 rifles also feature a two-stage trigger that is adjustable down to 2.5 pounds and a distinctive stock with a raised Monte Carlo-style comb.
Year Introduced: 1970 (Vanguard Series 2 debuted 2011)
Current Manufacturer: Weatherby (weatherby.com)
Country of Origin: USA
Similar Models: Synthetic Stainless (stainless barrel/receiver), Synthetic Youth (adjustable length of pull on stock), Synthetic Combo (optic included), Carbine (20 in. barrel), Varmint Special (22 in. heavy barrel), Sporter (wood stock), Deluxe (fancy wood stock), Synthetic DBM (detachable box magazine), Sporter DBM (detachable box magazine), Range Certified (24 in. barrel), Range Certified Varmint (22 in. heavy barrel, hand-laminated beavertail forearm stock)

REQUIRED TOOLS

Field Stripping: none
Disassembly/Assembly: large flat blade screwdriver

FIELD STRIP

1. Move the safety lever (part #35) to the middle "Safe" position then rotate the bolt handle upward until the bolt rotation stops and move the bolt rearward until it stops.
2. Push down on the bolt release lever (3) and continue to pull the bolt straight rearward until the bolt clears the receiver (2), Figure 1.

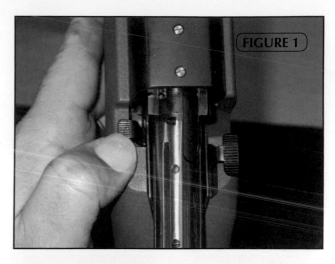

BOLT DISASSEMBLY

1. Hold the bolt body (7) while rotating the bolt sleeve (17) clockwise approximately 170° or until firing pin (13)/bolt sleeve assembly separates from the bolt body.
2. Then withdraw the firing pin/bolt sleeve assembly completely from the bolt body.

BARREL/RECEIVER DISASSEMBLY

1. To remove the trigger guard assembly and stock (48) first lay the rifle top side down on a padded surface and press the floor plate release (43) to open the floor plate (41). Use a flat blade screwdriver to remove the front trigger guard screw (47) and rear trigger guard screw (46).
2. Pull up on the trigger guard assembly to remove it from the stock, Figure 2.
3. Then pull the stock from the barreled action.

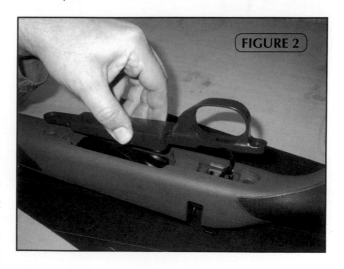

Reassemble in reverse order.

Tuning Tip: The Vanguard Series 2 has one trigger adjustment screw (24) on the front of the trigger assembly that adjusts for the weight of the trigger pull. To increase or decrease trigger pull weight, first remove the trigger guard and stock. Next loosen the lock nut (26) on the front adjusting screw. From the front use a small screwdriver to increase weight of the trigger pull by turning adjusting screw clockwise. To decrease weight of trigger pull, turn the front adjusting screw counter-clockwise. When desired weight of trigger pull is established, tighten the lock nut on front adjusting screw and replace the stock and trigger guard assembly.

Reassembly Tip: Line up the notch on the firing pin assembly with the bolt, Figure 3. Then push the bolt sleeve/firing pin assembly all the way into

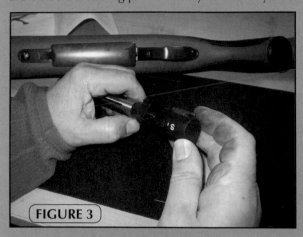

FIGURE 3

the bolt. Note the spring tension. Now rotate the bolt sleeve/firing pin assemble counterclockwise until the triangular tab of the cocking piece (15) fits into the notch of the bolt, Figure 4.

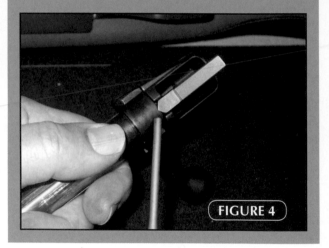

FIGURE 4

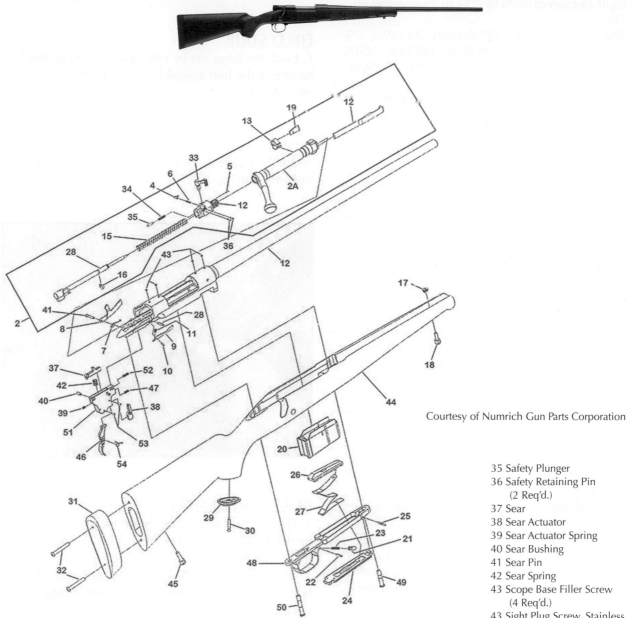

Courtesy of Numrich Gun Parts Corporation

35 Safety Plunger
36 Safety Retaining Pin
   (2 Req'd.)
37 Sear
38 Sear Actuator
39 Sear Actuator Spring
40 Sear Bushing
41 Sear Pin
42 Sear Spring
43 Scope Base Filler Screw
   (4 Req'd.)
43 Sight Plug Screw, Stainless
   (4 Req'd.)
44 Stock
45 Stock Swivel Stud, Rear
46 Trigger
47 Trigger Adjusting Set Screw
48 Trigger Guard
49 Trigger Guard Screw, Front
50 Trigger Guard Screw, Rear
51 Trigger Housing
52 Trigger Overtravel Set Screw
53 Trigger Pin
54 Trigger Spring

PARTS LIST

1 Barrel/Receiver Assembly
2 Bolt Assembly
3 Bolt Sleeve
4 Bolt Sleeve Lock
5 Bolt Sleeve Lock Pin
6 Bolt Sleeve Lock Spring
7 Bolt Stop Spring
8 Breech Bolt
9 Ejector
10 Ejector Pin
11 Ejector Spring
12 Extractor

13 Extractor Ring
14 Firing Pin Assembly
15 Firing Pin Spring
16 Firing Pin Spring Retainer
17 Forearm Swivel Screw Eye
   Escutcheon, Front
18 Forearm Swivel Screw Eye,
   Front
19 Gas Block
20 Magazine
21 Magazine Floorplate Catch
22 Magazine Floorplate Catch
   Pin
23 Magazine Floorplate Catch

Spring
24 Magazine Floorplate
24 Magazine Floorplate
25 Magazine Floorplate Hinge
   Pin
26 Magazine Follower
27 Magazine Spring
28 Mounting Pin
29 Pistol Grip Cap
30 Pistol Grip Cap Screw
31 Recoil Pad
32 Recoil Pad Screw (2 Req'd.)
33 Safety Lever
34 Safety Lock Plunger Spring

SPECIFICATIONS

Model: Model 70 Featherweight
Action: bolt, control feed, two-lug
Barrel: 22 in. or 24 in. (depending on caliber)
Weight Unloaded: 6.75 to 7.25 lb. (depending on caliber)
Caliber: .22-250 Rem, .257 Roberts, .243 Win, .25-06 Rem, .270 Win, 7mm-08 Rem, .308 Win, .30-06, .264 Win. Mag., .270 WSM, 7mm WSM, .300 Win Mag, .300 WSM, .338 WSM
Capacity: 3+1 or 5+1 (depending on caliber)
Common Features: two-lug bolt with 90-degree lift, checkered wood stock, adjustable MOA trigger, three-position safety, free-floated barrel

BACKGROUND

The Model 70 is known as the "rifleman's rifle" and has been chambered in .22 Hornet to .458 Winchester Magnum. It was produced in Connecticut for some 70 years with production stopping in 2006—a bad day in New Haven—but recommenced in North Carolina in 2008. The rifle has gone through numerous design changes and can be categorized by the control feed models from 1936 to 1963, known as pre '64s. From there changes to the design rubbed the fur of Model 70 buffs the wrong way especially with the cost-cutting push feed design change. Jack O'Connor toted a Model 70 in .270 Winchester over numerous continents. Deer and elk hunters are just happy the Model 70 is back with control feed as originally designed. Instructions below are for the "Made in North Carolina" models.

Year Introduced: 1936-1963 (Pre '64), 1964-2006 (push feed/classic), 2008 (North Carolina production)
Current Manufacturer: Winchester Repeating Arms (winchesterguns.com)
Country of Origin: USA
Similar Models: Model 70 Alaskan (Monte Carlo wood stock, open sights), Model 70 Alaskan Stainless Laminate (stainless barrel/receiver, laminated stock), Model 70 Coyote Light (synthetic stock, stainless barrel), Model 70 Coyote Varmint Stainless (stainless barrel/receiver, laminated stock, threaded barrel), Model 70 Coyote Varmint (Thumbhole stock, laminated stock, threaded barrel), Model 70 Extreme Weather SS (stainless barrel/receiver, synthetic stock), Model 70 Featherweight Compact (wood stock, 20-in. barrel), Model 70 Safari Express (open sights, .416 Rem. Mag. or 458 Win. Mag. or 375 H&H Mag. calibers), Model 70 Sporter (walnut stock, blued finish), Model 70 Super Grade (wood stock w/ ebony fore-end tip, blued finish), Model 70 Ultimate Shadow (blued finish, synthetic stock), Model 70 Ultimate Shadow SS (stainless receiver/barrel, synthetic stock)

REQUIRED TOOLS

Field Stripping: none
Disassembly/Assembly: 5/32 inch hex or Allen wrench, small flat blade screwdriver

FIELD STRIP

1. Cock the firing pin by raising and lowering the bolt handle of the bolt assembly (part #2) and rotating the safety lever (33) in the "safe"/middle position.
2. Next lift the bolt handle and draw the bolt assembly fully rearward while depressing the breech bolt stop (8) at the left rear of the receiver and remove the bolt assembly, Figure 1. At this point the rifle is ready for routine cleaning.

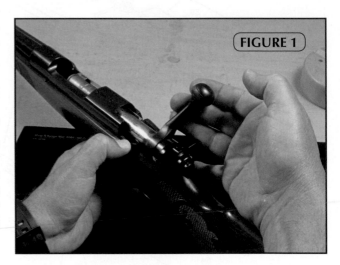

FIGURE 1

BOLT DISASSEMBLY

1. Depress the breech bolt sleeve lock (4) and turn the breech bolt sleeve (3) counterclockwise from the rear of the bolt, Figure 2.
2. Pull the firing pin assembly (14) out of the breech bolt. Leave the safety lever in the "safe"/middle position.

BARREL/RECEIVER DISASSEMBLY

1. Remove the two action screws—the front trigger guard screw (49) and rear trigger guard screw (50)—using a 5/32 inch Hex or Allen wrench.
2. Lift the trigger guard (48) and floorplate assembly (24) from the bottom of the stock (44). The magazine (20) may stay in the stock, Figure 3.
3. Flip the rifle top side up and lift the barrel/receiver assembly (1) out of the stock, Figure 4.

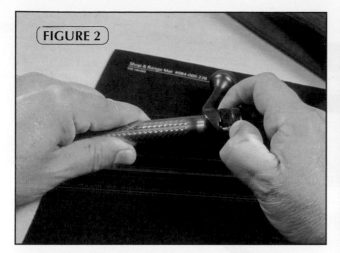

FIGURE 2

FIGURE 4

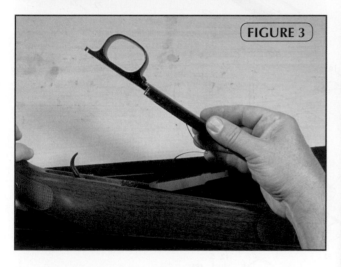

FIGURE 3

Reassemble in reverse order.

Reassembly Tip: Torque the two action screws to 35 inch pounds.

Tuning Tip: The two screws in front of the trigger housing adjust pull weight and overtravel. Looking at the barrel/receiver assembly upside down, the top screw—the trigger adjusting set screw (47)—adjusts trigger pull weight. The bottom screw adjusts overtravel. To decrease trigger pull weight turn the adjustment screw counterclockwise using a 1/16 inch hex or Allen wrench; to increase pull weight turn it clockwise. Do not turn the trigger pull weight adjustment screw too far. Doing so will limit trigger and render the trigger inoperative. Reassemble the rifle and test the trigger. After the desired pull weight is achieved, place a drop of Loctite on the adjustment screw. To increase the amount of overtravel, turn the trigger overtravel set screw (52) counterclockwise using a 1/16 inch hex or Allen wrench; to decrease the amount of overtravel turn the adjustment screw clockwise. If the overtravel screw is turned in too far, the trigger cannot be pulled to release the sear and fire the rifle. Place a drop of Loctite once the desired amount of over travel is achieved.

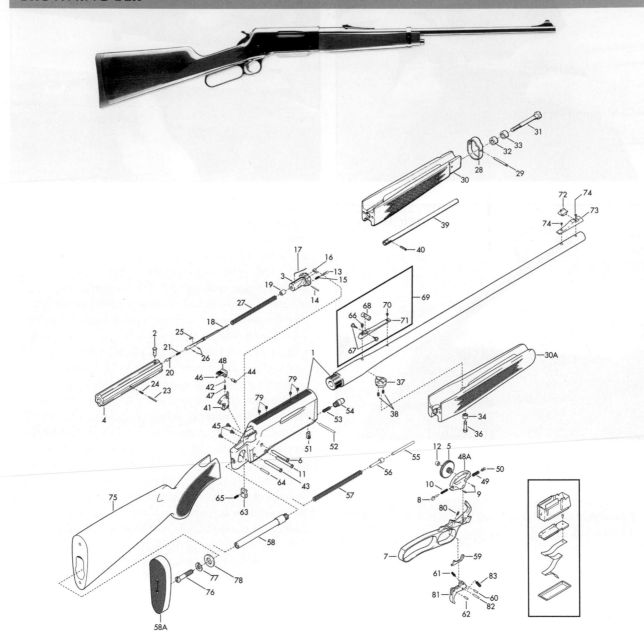

PARTS LIST

1 Barrel/Receiver
2 Bolt Lock Key Pin
3 Breech Bolt Lock
4 Breech Bolt Slide
5 Cocking Gear Assembly
6 Cocking Gear Pin
7 Cocking Lever
8 Cocking Lever Latch
9 Cocking Lever Latch Pin
10 Cocking Lever Latch Spring
11 Cocking Lever Pin
12 Cocking Lever Stop
13 Ejector
14 Ejector Pin

15 Ejector Spring
16 Extractor
17 Extractor Spring
18 Firing Pin
19 Firing Pin Bushing
20 Firing Pin Inertia Slide
21 Firing Pin Inertia Slide Spring
23 Firing Pin Retaining Pin
   Inner
24 Firing Pin Retaining Pin
   Outer
25 Firing Pin Safety Lock
26 Firing Pin Safety Lock Pin
27 Firing Pin Spring
28 Forearm Band

29 Forearm Band Pin
30 Forearm
31 Forearm Bolt
32 Forearm Bolt Spacer Inner
33 Forearm Bolt Spacer Outer
34 Forearm Escutcheon
36 Forearm Screw
37 Forearm Stud
38 Forearm Stud Screw
39 Forearm Tube
40 Forearm Tube Pin
41 Hammer
42 Hammer Detent Ball
43 Hammer Pin
44 Hammer Pin

45 Hammer Pin Screw
46 Hammer Pin Set Screws
47 Hammer Spring
48 Hammer Thumb Piece
48A Lever Gear Rack
49 Lever Gear Rack Spring
50 Lever Gear Rack Spring
   Plunger
51 Magazine Latch
52 Magazine Latch Pin
53 Magazine Latch Spring
54 Magazine Latch Spring
   Retaining Screw
55 Mainspring Follower
56 Mainspring Guide

57 Mainspring	64 Sear Pin
58 Mainspring Tube	65 Sear Spring
58A Recoil Pad	66 Sight Adjusting Screw Rear
59 Sear Link	Elevation
60 Sear Link Pin	67 Sight Adjusting Screw Rear
61 Sear Link Spring	Windage
62 Sear Link Stop Pin	68 Sight Aperture Rear
63 Sear	69 Sight Assembly Rear

70 Sight Base Mounting Screw	77 Stock Bolt Lock Washer
Rear	78 Stock Bolt Washer
71 Sight Base Rear	79 Telescope Mount Base Filler
72 Sight Front	Screw
73 Sight Ramp Front	80 Trigger Adjusting Screw
74 Sight Ramp Screw	81 Trigger
75 Stock	82 Trigger Pin
76 Stock Bolt	83 Trigger Spring

SPECIFICATIONS

Model: BLR Lightweight '81
Action: Lever, rotating bolt
Barrel: 20 in., 22 in., or 24 in. (magnum calibers)
Weight Unloaded: 6.5 lb. to 8.8 lb. (depending on caliber)
Caliber: .223 Rem., .22-250 Rem., .243 Win, .270 Win., .270 WSM, 7mm-08, 7mm WSM, 7mm Mag, .308 Win, .30-06, .300 Win Mag, .300 WSM, .358 Win., .325 WSM, .450 Marlin
Capacity: 3, 4, or 5 (depending on caliber)
Common Features: open sights; aluminum receiver tapped for optics; half-cock safety; folding hammer; stainless or blued finish; straight or pistol grip stock of walnut or laminate

BACKGROUND

The BLR (Browning Lever action Rifle) is notable for numerous design characteristics that set it apart from other lever action rifles. The lever uses what Browning calls a cocking gear that meshes into the teeth of the bottom of the breech bolt slide. It works like a rack and pinion and offers smooth operation. The bolt head rotates and locks its six lugs into the receiver when the lever is closed. The lever itself houses the trigger assembly which moves with the lever when cycled. Finally the rifles use a detachable box magazine, which allows the use of pointed bullets. The BLR is currently offered in standard and long action sizes depending on caliber. Disassembly of the BLR for cleaning is not required and the factory does not recommend disassembly. The BLR is more complicated to disassemble than other lever action rifles.
Year Introduced: 1970
Country of Origin: USA
Current Manufacturer: Browning (browning. com),
Similar Models: Lightweight with pistol or straight grip, Lightweight take-down with pistol or straight grip

REQUIRED TOOLS

Disassembly/Assembly: long shafted standard screwdriver, medium Philips screwdriver, 3/16 inch concave punch, 3/32 inch punch, brass hammer, needle nose pliers, vise

DISASSEMBLY

1. To remove the cocking lever assembly and breech bolt slide, lay the BLR on its right side on a padded work surface and drive out the cocking lever pin (part #11) and the cocking gear pin (6) to the right using the 3/16 inch concave punch, Figure 1. These pins are splined and domed. You will ruin the pin and frame if you drift them out in the wrong direction. The pins are also domed so use a concave punch to drift them out. If you do not you will mar the pins.
2. The lever assembly along with the cocking gear and cocking lever stop can then be removed from the bottom of the receiver.
3. To remove the stock (75), use a medium Philips screwdriver to remove the two screws holding the recoil pad (58A).
4. With the recoil pad removed, insert a long shaft screwdriver into the stock and unscrew the stock bolt (76), Figure 3.

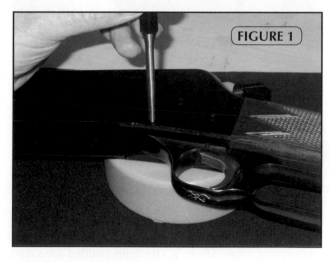

FIGURE 1

5. To remove a banded style forearm (30), drive out the forearm band pin (29) to the right and pull the forearm band (28) toward the muzzle end of the rifle. To remove the schnabel style forearm (30A) remove the forearm screw (36).
6. Pull the forearm to the front.
7. The stock will need to be removed to remove the main spring follower (55), which will relieve tension on the hammer. Method 1: With a pair of needle nose pliers grasp the main spring follower through the access hole in the right side of the frame. Pull the main spring follower rearward and up sliding it along the groove in the bottom of the hammer (41) and pop it out of the cut out at the base of hammer, Figure 4. Note the main

Disassembly Tip: When removing the recoil pad on the BLR and many other rifles and shotguns, look closely for the slit in the rubber to insert the screwdriver, Figure 2. A dab of liquid soap helps the screwdriver turn easily against the rubber.

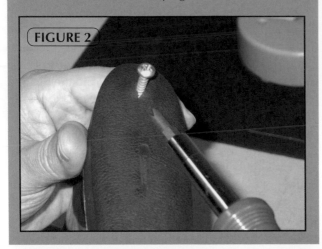

FIGURE 2

FIGURE 4

10. Disassemble the bolt assembly by rotating the breech bolt (3) about 90° clockwise and withdraw from the breech block slide (4).

11. The firing pin (18) will drop out of the breech bolt slide.

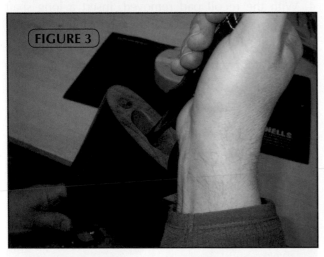

FIGURE 3

Reassembly Tip: Remember to drive all pins from right to left. The splined heads of the pins are on the right side. The timing of the action is critical. Before reinstalling the cocking lever assembly, ensure the bolt assembly is in place and hammer is fully forward in the fired position. Install the cocking lever in the lever-open position with the cocking gear and cocking lever stop positioned at the forward end of the gear rack and place it in the barrel/receiver. Push in the cocking lever pin from the right to left and close the lever. Use the 3/32 punch as slave pin in the cocking gear pin hole in the barrel/receiver then push in the cocking gear pin. Do not tap the pins home yet. To check the timing, cock the hammer which will allow the breech bolt slide to move to the rear between .001 inch and .015 inch. This can be verified with a feeler gauge placed between the forward end of the breech bolt slide and the head of the breech bolt lock.

spring follower is under tension. Method 2: Place the hammer in the fired/fully forward position. Grip the mainspring tube (58) in a vise with padded jaws and unscrew it from the receiver. Note the mainspring (57) is under tension so control the receiver when it is free from the mainspring tube. The mainspring and mainspring guide (56) will come free with the mainspring tube. Then use a pair of needle nose pliers to remove the mainspring follower. Method 2 is the easier of the two methods but it requires a vise.

8. To withdraw the bolt assembly, place the hammer in the full cock position and pull the bolt assembly to the rear of the barrel/receiver (1).

9. Use a 3/16 inch concave punch to drift out the hammer pin (43). The hammer pin is splined and must be driven out from the left side of the receiver (1) to the right side of the receiver.

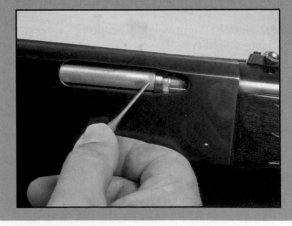

To reassemble follow in reverse order.

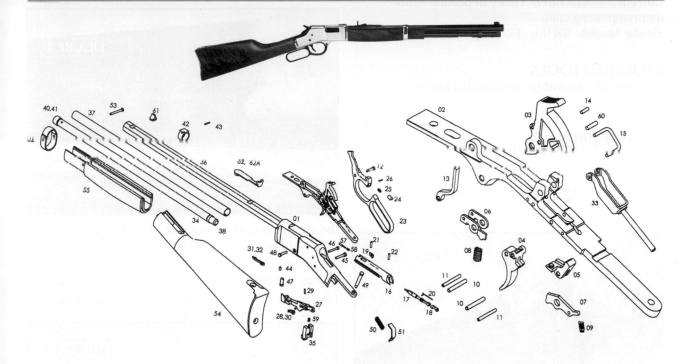

PARTS LIST

01 Receiver
02 Trigger Guard Plate
03 Hammer
04 Trigger
05 Sear
06 Rocker
07 Trigger Lock
08 Sear/Rocker Spring
09 Trigger Lock Spring
10 Sear/Trigger Spring
11 Lever Detent/Trigger Lock Pin
12 Lever Screw
13 Transfer Bar
14 Transfer Bar Pin
15 Trigger/Rocker Link
16 Bolt
17 Firing Pin-Front
18 Firing Pin-Rear
19 Extractor
20 Firing Pin Spring

21 Firing Pin Ret. Pin-Front
22 Firing Pin Ret. Pin-Rear
23 Lever
24 Lever Plunger
25 Lever Plunger Spring
26 Lever Plunger Pin
27 Carrier
28 Carrier Dog
29 Carrier Dog Pin
30 Carrier Dog Spring
31 Ejector
32 Ejector Spring
33 Mainspring Yoke Assembly
34 Inner Mag. Tube
35 Locking Bolt
36 Barrel
37 Outer Mag. Tube
38 Mag. Tube Follower
39 Mag. Tube Spring
40 Mag. Tube Knob
41 Mag. Tube Knob Pin
42 Mag. Tube Support

43 Mag. Tube Support Pin
44 Mag. Tube Ret. Screw
45 Hammer Screw
46 Carrier Screw
47 Trig. Guard Plate Screw
48 Trig. Guard Plate
Support Screw
49 Tang Screw
50 Mainspring
51 Mainspring Seat
52 Barrel Band
53 Barrel Band Screw
54 Buttstock Assembly
55 Forearm
57 Extractor Plunger
58 Extractor Spring
59 Locking Bolt Spring
60 Mainspring Yoke Pin
61 Front Sight
62 Rear Sight
62A Rear Sight Elevator

SPECIFICATIONS

Model: Henry Big Boy .44 Magnum
Action: Lever
Barrel: 20 in.
Caliber: .44 Mag
Capacity: 10
Common Features: brass receiver, butt plate and barrel band; straight-grip American walnut stock; blued barrel and lever; adjustable Marble semi-buckhorn rear/fixed brass bead front sight; removable tube magazine; drilled/tapped for mounting optics

BACKGROUND

It is true what Henry Repeating Arms says about the Big Boy—it's big, brutal and beautiful. The Big Boy is the bigger centerfire counterpart to Henry's rimfire rifles, it is chambered in the powerful .44 Magnum and it is comely with the bright brass receiver. The action is silky smooth and cowboy action shooters have a modern choice for knocking down steel desperados.

Year Introduced: 2003
Country of Origin: USA
Current Manufacturer: Henry Repeating Arms
(henryrepeating.com)
Similar Models: Big Boy .357 Magnum, Big Boy .45 Colt

REQUIRED TOOLS

Disassembly/Assembly: medium flat blade screwdriver

DISASSEMBLY

1. Remove inner magazine tube and fully open the action by swinging the lever (part #23) down.
2. Lay the rifle left side down on a padded surface and remove the lever screw (12), Figure 1.

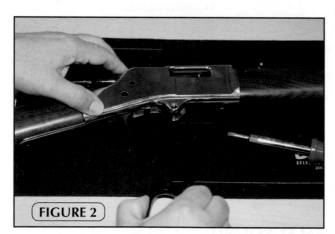

FIGURE 1

3. Pull the lever out from the bottom of the receiver (01), Figure 2.

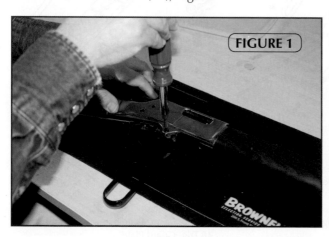

FIGURE 2

4. Next, slide the bolt (16) and remove it from the rear of the receiver, Figure 3 With the bolt removed

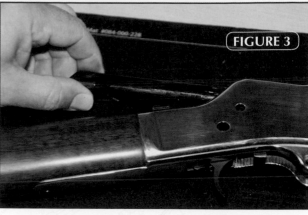

FIGURE 3

the ejector assembly—ejector (31) and ejector spring (32)—will fall free inside the receiver. Remove it from the receiver via the ejector port, Figure 4.
5. The buttstock (54) is removed by unscrewing the tang screw (49). Remove the tang screw from the tang

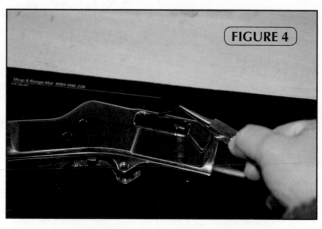

FIGURE 4

of the receiver and pull the buttstock off the receiver.
6. Remove the forearm (55) by unscrewing the barrel band screw (53) and sliding the barrel band (52) toward the muzzle. Pull the forearm toward the muzzle to disengage it from the receiver and pull it off the outer magazine tube (37).

Reassembly Tip: Do not over-tighten the lever screw.

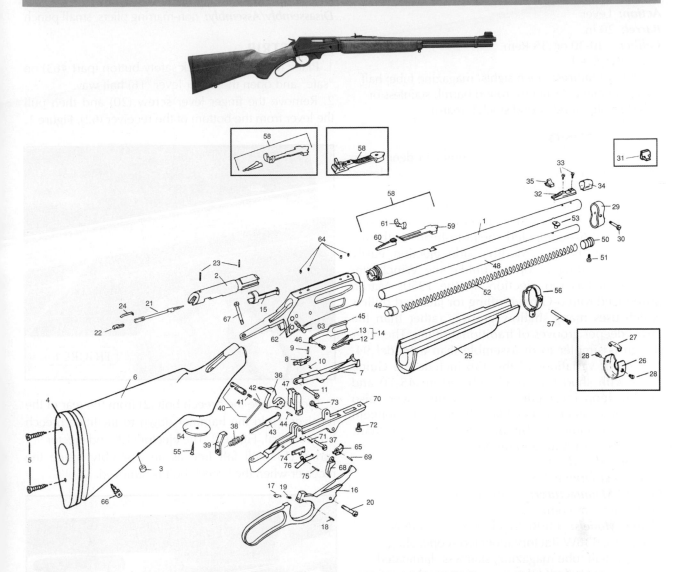

PARTS LIST

1 Barrel
2 Breech Bolt
3 Bullseye
4 Buttplate/Buttpad
5 Buttplate Screw (2 Req'd.)
6 Buttstock
7 Carrier
8 Carrier Rocker
9 Carrier Rocker Pin
10 Carrier Rocker Spring
11 Carrier Screw
12 Ejector
13 Ejector Spring
14 Ejector w/Spring
15 Extractor
16 Finger Lever
17 Finger Lever Plunger
18 Finger Lever Plunger Pin
19 Finger Lever Plunger Spring
20 Finger Lever Screw

21 Firing Pin, Front
22 Firing Pin, Rear
23 Firing Pin Retaining Pin
   (2 Req'd.)
24 Firing Pin Spring
25 Forearm
26 Forearm Tip
27 Forearm Tip Tenon
28 Forearm Tip Tenon Screw
   (2 Req'd.)
29 Front Band
30 Front Band Screw
31 Front Sight
32 Front Sight Base
33 Front Sight Base Screw
   (2 Req'd.)
34 Front Sight Hood
35 Front Sight Insert
36 Hammer
37 Hammer Screw
38 Hammer Spring

39 Hammer Spring Adjusting
   Plate
40 Hammer Spur Complete
41 Hammer Spur Screw
42 Hammer Spur Wrench
43 Hammer Strut
44 Hammer Strut Pin
45 Loading Spring
46 Loading Spring Screw
47 Locking Bolt
48 Magazine Tube
49 Magazine Tube Follower
50 Magazine Tube Plug
51 Magazine Tube Plug Screw
52 Magazine Tube Spring
53 Magazine Tube Stud
54 Pistol Grip Cap
55 Pistol Grip Cap Screw
56 Rear Band
57 Rear Band Screw
58 Rear Sight Assembly

59 Rear Sight Base
60 Rear Sight Elevator
61 Rear Sight Folding Leaf
62 Receiver
63 Safety Button
64 Scope Mount Dummy Screw
   (4 Req'd.)
65 Sear
66 Swivel Stud, Rear
67 Tang Screw
68 Trigger
69 Trigger and Sear Pin
70 Trigger Guard Plate
71 Trigger Guard Plate Latch
   Pin
72 Trigger Guard Plate Screw
73 Trigger Guard Plate Support
   Screw
74 Trigger Safety Block
75 Trigger Safety Block Pin
76 Trigger Safety Block Spring

SPECIFICATIONS

Model: Model 336
Action: Lever
Barrel: 20 in.
Caliber: .30-30 or .35 Rem.
Capacity: 6 + 1
Common Features: open sights, magazine tube; half cock and manual safeties; round barrel; stainless or blued finish; barrel; wood stock/forearm

BACKGROUND

One rite of passage for young hunter in deer camp is the ability to silently cock the hammer on a lever-action rifle. More often than not it's a Marlin. The Marlin 336 descended from the Model 1893 then the Model 36. Marlin's lever-action rifles—the 36 and 336—competed head-to-head with the Winchester 94. The Marlin's side ejection easily allows mounting of optics unlike the Winchester 94, which has top ejection. In the 1950s Marlin introduced Mirco-Groove rifling for jacketed bullets which uses many shallow grooves rather than the fewer deeper grooves of traditional rifling. The lever design is simpler to disassemble than a Model 94. Numerous variations of the 336 include the Guide Guns with short barrels chambered in .45-70 and the big loop lever guns. The 336 rifles were also built under other names like Glenfield or Glenfield Marlin for numerous big-box stores like Wal-Mart, Sears, Western Auto and others.

Year Introduced: 1948
Country of Origin: USA
Current Manufacturer: Marlin Firearms
(marlinfirearms.com)
Similar Models: 336BL (big loop lever), 336SS (stainless), 336W (factory mounted scope, sling), 336XLR (half tube magazine, stainless, laminated stock), 444XLR (half tube magazine, stainless, laminated stock), 444 (.444 Marlin caliber), 1895 (.45-70 caliber), 1895XLR (half tube magazine, stainless, laminated stock), 1895G "Guide Gun" (.45-70 caliber, straight stock), 1895GS "Guide Gun" (.45-70 caliber, straight stock, stainless), 1895SBL (.45-70 caliber, stainless, big loop lever, laminated stock, scout scope mount), 1895M (.450 Marlin caliber, straight stock), 1895MXLR (.450 Marlin caliber, half tube magazine, stainless, laminated stock), 1895GBL (big loop lever, laminated stock), 1895 Cowboy (straight stock, 26-in. barrel), 308MX (.308 Marlin Express caliber, half tube magazine), 308MXLR (.308 Marlin Express caliber, half tube magazine, stainless, laminated stock), 338MXLR (.338 Marlin Express caliber, half tube magazine, stainless, laminated stock), 308MX (.338 Marlin Express caliber, half tube magazine)

REQUIRED TOOLS

Field Strip: medium flat blade screwdriver
Disassembly/Assembly: non-marring pliers, small punch

FIELD STRIP

1. Place the hammer block safety button (part #63) on "safe" and open the finger lever (16) half way.
2. Remove the finger lever screw (20) and then pull the lever from the bottom of the receiver (62), Figure 1.

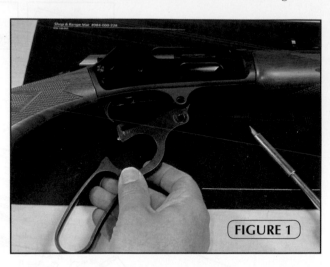

FIGURE 1

3. Then remove the breech bolt (2) from the rear of the receiver. Hold the hammer down to facilitate breech bolt removal, Figure 2. The ejector (12) and ejector spring (13) will fall free as an assembly inside the receiver when the breech bolt is removed.

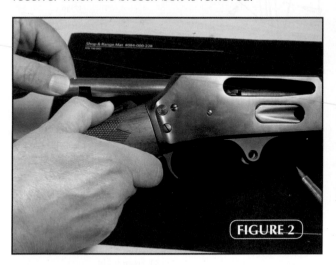

FIGURE 2

BOLT DISASSEMBLY

1. Remove the firing pin (21) and firing pin spring (24) by drifting out the firing pin retaining pin (23) at the rear of the breech bolt, Figure 3. The firing pin and firing pin spring will then come free from the rear of the breech bolt.

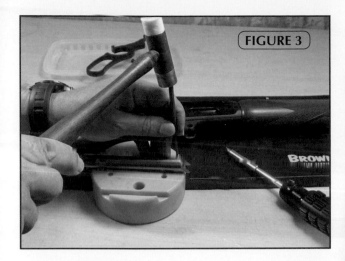

FIGURE 3

2. The extractor (15) is removed by gently prying it with a small flat blade screwdriver out of its groove in the breech bolt, Figure 4.

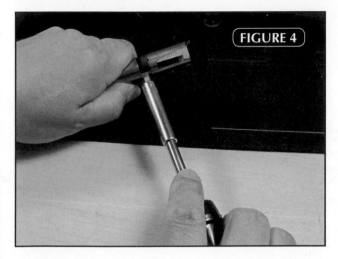

FIGURE 4

BARREL/RECEIVER/MAGAZINE TUBE DISASSEMBLY

1. Remove the buttstock (6) by unscrewing and removing the tang screw (67).

2. Lower the hammer (36) by depressing the trigger safety block (74) and pressing the trigger (68). Control the hammer as it moves forward.

3. Use a pair of non-marring pliers to grasp the hammer spring adjusting plate (39) and remove it from the receiver and trigger guard plate (70) by sliding the hammer spring adjusting plate out of the groove in the trigger guard plate out the side, Figure 5. Control the hammer spring as it is under compression.

4. Next remove the hammer screw (37) using a medium flat blade screw driver, then pull the hammer out from the top of the receiver.

5. Remove the trigger guard plate screw (72) from the bottom of the receiver and the trigger guard plate

support screw (73) from the left side of the receiver. Pull the trigger guard plate from the bottom of the receiver.

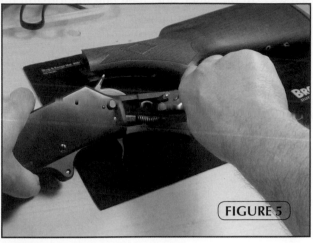

FIGURE 5

6. The trigger is removed by drifting out the trigger and sear pin (69) and the trigger and sear (65) will come free from the trigger guard plate.

7. With the trigger guard plate removed, the locking bolt (47) can be removed from the bottom of the receiver.

8. The carrier (7) is removed by unscrewing and removing the carrier screw (11) on the right side of the receiver. The carrier is then removed through the bottom of the receiver.

9. Remove the magazine tube spring (52), magazine tube follower (49) and magazine tube plug (50) by removing the magazine tube plug screw (51). Control the magazine tube spring as it is under compression.

10. Slide the front sight hood (34) off the front sight then remove the two front sight base screws (33) and remove the front sight.

11. Remove the front band screw (30) and leave the front band (29) on the barrel (1), Figure 6.

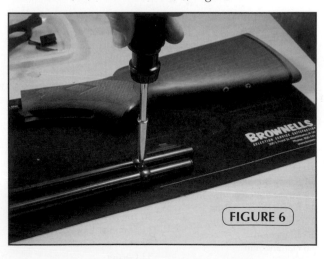

FIGURE 6

12. Remove the rear band screw (57) and slide the rear band forward and off the barrel. If your rifle has a forearm tip (26), remove the two forearm tip tenon screws (28) on either side, then pull the forearm tip and forearm tip tenon off the front of the forearm (25).
13. Next slide the forearm, magazine tube (48) and front barrel band toward the muzzle.
To reassemble, reverse the disassembly steps.

Reassembly Tip: Make sure the ejector is in the slot on the inside of the receiver before inserting the breech bolt. Then slide the breech bolt into the receiver and verify via the ejection port that the ejector and breech bolt are aligned. With the breech bolt pushed into the receiver within about one inch of being fully closed position insert the lever into the bottom of the receiver.

MOSSBERG 464 LEVER-ACTION

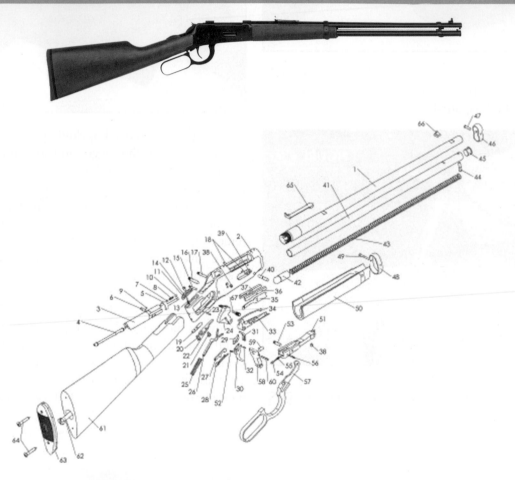

PARTS LIST

1 Barrel
2 Receiver
3 Bolt
4 Firing Pin
5 Extractor
6 Lever Bolt Pin
7 Lever Pin Detent
8 Ejector Spring
9 Ejector Retaining Pin
10 Ejector
11 Safety Button
12 Safety Button Screw
13 Safety Detent Spring
14 Safety Detent Ball
15 Trigger Pin
16 Hammer Pin

17 Carrier Pin
18 Cartridge Guide Screw
   (2 Req'd.)
19 Safety Detent Plate
20 Safety Arm Actuator
21 Safety Pivot Screw
22 Safety Arm
23 Trigger Stop Pin
24 Hammer
25 Hammer Spring
26 Hammer Spring Strut
27 Trigger Stop
28 Trigger Stop/Sear Spring
29 Sear
30 Trigger
31 Hammer Block
32 Hammer Block Pin
33 Carrier

34 Carrier Spring
35 Loading Port Spring Cover
36 Cartridge Guide, Right Hand
37 Cartridge Guide, Left Hand
38 Loading Port Spring Cover
   Screw (2 Req'd.)
39 Carrier Spring Screw
40 Link Pivot Pin
41 Magazine Tube
42 Magazine Follower
43 Magazine Spring
44 Magazine Plug Screw
45 Magazine Plug
46 Front Barrel Band
47 Front Barrel Band Screw
48 Rear Barrel Band
49 Rear Barrel Band Screw
50 Forearm

51 Link
52 Trigger Return Spring
53 Lever Link Pin
54 Link Plunger
55 Link Plunger Spring
56 Link Plunger Retaining Pin
57 Lever
58 Locking Bolt
59 Firing Pin Striker
60 Striker Retaining Pin
61 Stock
62 Stock Bolt
63 Recoil Pad
64 Recoil Pad Retaining Screw
   (2 Req'd.)
65 Rear Sight
66 Front Sight
67 Hammer Extension

SPECIFICATIONS

Model: 464 Lever-Action
Action: Lever
Barrel: 20 in.
Caliber: .30-30 Win.
Capacity: 7 + 1
Common Features: open sights, magazine tube; manual safety; rebounding hammer; round barrel; stainless or blued finish; wood pistol-grip stock/forearm

BACKGROUND

Mossberg's response to shooters interest in lever-action rifles in 2008 was the debut of 464 Lever-Action. The old west meets the 21st century with Mossberg's ZMB and SPX series rifles which mate an adjustable AR stock and Picatinny forearm to the 464. It ain't your grandpa's "thurty-thurty."
Year Introduced: 2008
Country of Origin: USA
Current Manufacturer: O.F. Mossberg & Sons (mossbergs.com)
Similar Models: 464 Straight Grip (straight grip stock, blued or marinecote finish), ZMB Series (16-7/8 in. barrel w/ flash suppressor, AR stock/ Picatinny forearm), 464 SPX (16-7/8 in. barrel w/ or w/o flash suppressor, AR stock/Picatinny forearm)

REQUIRED TOOLS

Disassembly/Assembly: small and medium flat blade screwdriver, small punch, brass hammer

DISASSEMBLY

1. Use a medium flat blade screwdriver to unscrew and remove the lever bolt pin stop screw from the left side of the receiver (part #2), Figure 1.
2. Use a 1/8 inch punch to drift out the lever bolt pin (6) from the right to left side of the receiver, Figure 2.

FIGURE 2

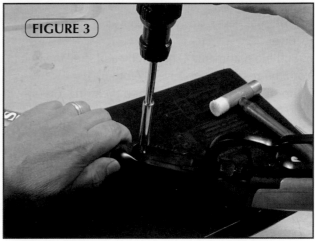

FIGURE 3

3. Next remove the link pin stop screw from the bottom of the link (51), Figure 3. Then push though the lever link pin (53) from either side with a small punch, Figure 4.
4. Slightly move the lever (57) down then link forward to disengage the lever from the locking bolt (58), Figure 5.

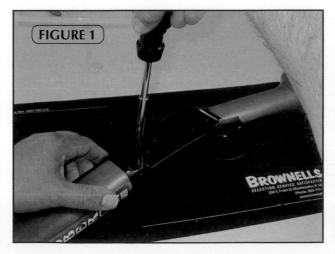

FIGURE 1

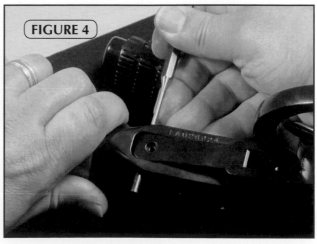

FIGURE 4

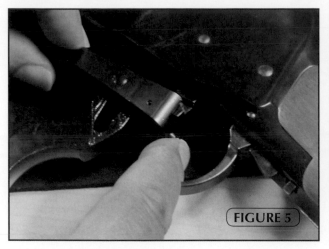

FIGURE 5

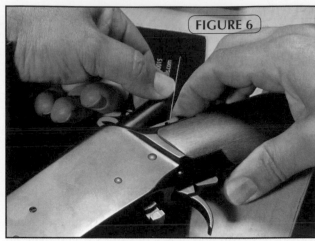

FIGURE 6

5. Pull the lever and link from the bottom of the receiver.

6. Pull the hammer (24) back fully and slide the bolt (3) from the rear of the receiver, Figure 6.

7. Tip the front of the bolt up and the firing pin (4) will drop from the rear of the bolt.

8. Use a small flat blade screwdriver to gently pry the extractor (5) from the bolt.

At this point the 464 is sufficiently disassembled for cleaning.

Reassemble in reverse order.

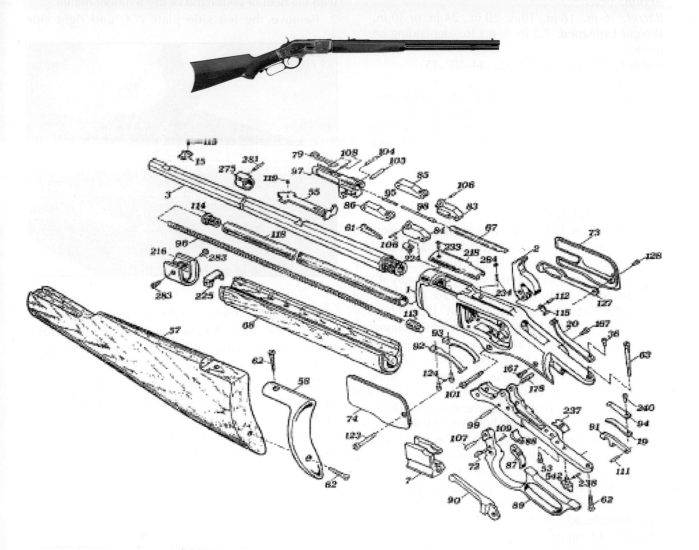

PARTS LIST

2 Breech Bolt w/ Extractor
3 Buttplate
4 Buttplate Screw
5 Stock
6 Carrier
7 Carrier Link
8 Carrier Spring Assembly
9 Carrier Spring Screw
10 Cartridge Guide
11 Cartridge Guide Screw
12 Cartridge Stop
13 Cartridge Stop/Spring Cover
   Screw
14 Ejector
15 Ejector Collar
16 Ejector Spring

18 Extractor
19 Extractor Pin
20 Finger Lever Connecting Pin
21 Finger Lever
22 Firing Pin Assembly
23 Firing Pin Spring
24 Forearm
25 Forearm Tip (Cap)
26 Forearm Tip (Cap) Screw
27 Forearm Tip Tenon
28 Friction Stud
29 Friction Stud Spring
30 Friction Stud Stop Pin
31 Hammer
32 Hammer Screw
33 Hammer Strut
34 Locking Bolt, Left

35 Locking Bolt, Right
36 Locking Bolt Stop Pin
37 Locking Bolt Stop Pin Stop
   Screw
38 Lower Tang
39 Magazine Follower
40 Magazine Plug
41 Magazine Plug Screw
41 Magazine Plug Screw
42 Magazine Ring
43 Magazine Spring
44 Magazine Tube
45 Mainspring
46 Safety Button
47 Safety Lever
48 Safety Lever Screw
49 Safety Lever Spring

50 Sear
51 Sear Spring
52 Rear Sight Elevator
54 Rear Sight
55 Spring Cover
56 Spring Cover Base Assembly
57 Spring Cover Base
59 Spring Cover Spring
60 Spring Cover Stop Pin
61 Strut Support
62 Strut Support Pin
64 Trigger
65 Trigger Block
66 Trigger Block Spring
67 Trigger Block Spring Pin
68 Trigger Pin
69 Upper Tang Screw

SPECIFICATIONS

Model: Uberti Model 1873
Action: Lever
Barrel: 16 in., 18 in., 19in., 20 in., 24 in. or 30 in.
Weight Unloaded: 7.2 lb. to 8.2 lb. (depending on model)
Caliber: .38 Spec./.357 Mag., .44-40, .45 Long Colt
Capacity: 9, 10 or 13 (depending on barrel length)
Common Features: open sights, half or full magazine tube; half cock safety; round or octagon barrel; blued or casehardened finish; barrel bands or forend caps; straight or pistol-grip wood stock/forearm

BACKGROUND

The Winchester factory in New Haven, Connecticut, manufactured over 720,000 Model 1873 repeating rifles between 1873 and 1919. This is the rifle that coined the saying "The gun that won the west." Originally it was chambered in .44-40, .38-40 and 32-20. Modern steel allows the '73 to now be chambered in .38 Special/.357 Magnum and .45 Colt. With a lot of shooters channeling their inner cowboy the 1873 has seen a resurgence with some clones like the Uberti frothy with casehardened colors and real walnut. Instructions and part numbers are for the Uberti version of the Model 1873 and differ slightly from original Winchesters. The 1873 is a relatively easy to disassemble but if you think otherwise, chew on this: In 1879 Texas Ranger George Lloyd was involved a gun fight with Apaches and, as the story goes, Lloyd accidently loaded a .45 Long Colt cartridge in his .44-40 Winchester 1873 rifle jamming it. He removed the side plates to clear the jam and continued the fight.
Year Introduced: 1873
Country of Origin: USA
Current Manufacturers/Importers: Beretta (berettausa.com), Cimarron (cimarron-firearms.com), EMF Company (emf-company.com), Navy Arms (navyarms.com)
Similar Models: rifle, carbine, short rifle, trapper

REQUIRED TOOLS

Disassembly/Assembly: small and medium blade standard screwdrivers, 1/8 in. punch, rubber mallet, brass hammer

DETAILED DISASSEMBLY

1. To disassemble the action, first remove the butt stock (part #57) by unscrewing the upper tang screw (63) and the lower tang screw (62) and pulling the butt stock to the rear. If the butt stock is tightly fitted tap the comb with the heel of your hand or use a rubber mallet.

2. Remove the left side plate (74) and right side

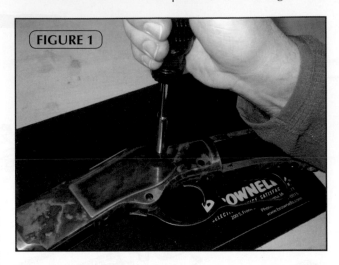

FIGURE 1

plate from the frame (1) by unscrewing the side plate screw (123), Figure 1. If the side plates stick, lightly tap the frame with a nylon hammer or rubber mallet.

3. The loading gate, Uberti calls it a ladle (127), will be attached to the right side plate via the ladle screw (128).

4. Remove right link assembly—right front link (85), right rear link (83) and link pin (106)—and the left link assembly—left front link (86), left rear link (84) and link pin (106), Figure 2. The lever pin (107) should fall free from the lever when the two link assemblies are removed.

FIGURE 2

5. From the underside of the frame, remove the two lever spring screws (124), Figure 3.

6. Unscrew the lever screw (101) and remove the lever (89) from the frame, Figure 4.

7. Cock the hammer (2) so you can move the breech block (97) fully rearward.

8. Now you can remove the carrier lever, Uberti calls it a lifter arm (90). Remove the carrier block (7) from the bottom of the frame.

9. To remove the firing pin (98), drift out the firing pin stop (104) from the breech block (38) using a small punch.

10. With the firing pin stop removed, the firing pin extension can be moved to the rear after the hammer is cocked.

11. The firing pin and firing pin spring (95) can be removed from the rear of the breech block.

12. Removing the lower tang is accomplished by first depressing the safety catch (91), pulling the trigger (87) and setting the hammer at half cock.

13. Remove the two side tang screws (167) on each side of the frame. Pull the lower tang down and out from the frame. The hammer, main spring (20) and trigger assembly will be attached to the lower tang.

14. To disassemble the magazine tube (118) unscrew the magazine tube plug using a standard screwdriver controlling the magazine spring (96) and magazine follower (113), Figure 5.

Reassemble in reverse order

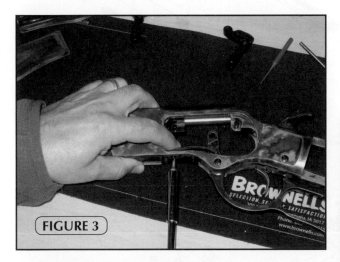

FIGURE 3

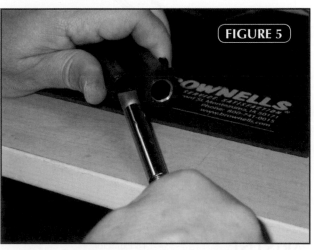

FIGURE 5

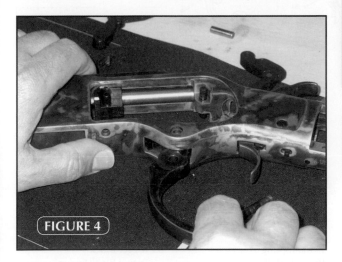

FIGURE 4

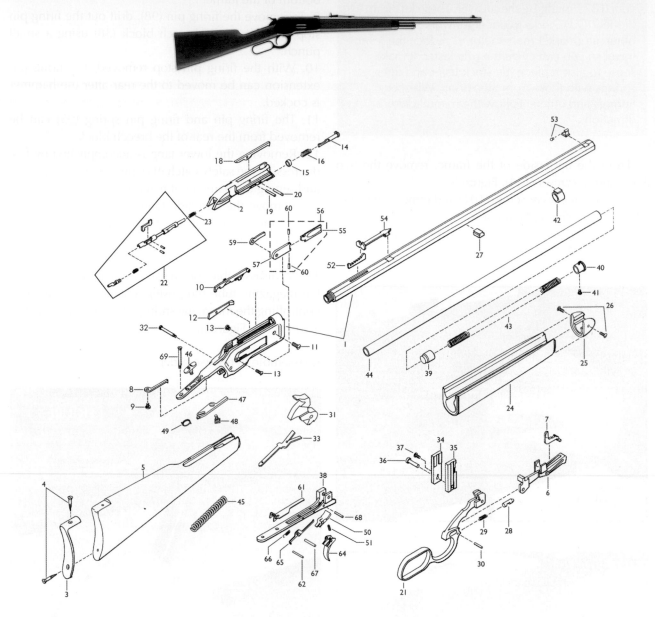

PARTS LIST

2 Breech Bolt w/ Extractor
3 Buttplate
4 Buttplate Screw
5 Stock
6 Carrier
7 Carrier Link
8 Carrier Spring Assembly
9 Carrier Spring Screw
10 Cartridge Guide
11 Cartridge Guide Screw
12 Cartridge Stop
13 Cartridge Stop/Spring Cover
   Screw
14 Ejector
15 Ejector Collar
16 Ejector Spring

18 Extractor
19 Extractor Pin
20 Finger Lever Connecting Pin
21 Finger Lever
22 Firing Pin Assembly
23 Firing Pin Spring
24 Forearm
25 Forearm Tip (Cap)
26 Forearm Tip (Cap) Screw
27 Forearm Tip Tenon
28 Friction Stud
29 Friction Stud Spring
30 Friction Stud Stop Pin
31 Hammer
32 Hammer Screw
33 Hammer Strut
34 Locking Bolt, Left

35 Locking Bolt, Right
36 Locking Bolt Stop Pin
37 Locking Bolt Stop Pin Stop
   Screw
38 Lower Tang
39 Magazine Follower
40 Magazine Plug
41 Magazine Plug Screw
41 Magazine Plug Screw
42 Magazine Ring
43 Magazine Spring
44 Magazine Tube
45 Mainspring
46 Safety Button
47 Safety Lever
48 Safety Lever Screw
49 Safety Lever Spring

50 Sear
51 Sear Spring
52 Rear Sight Elevator
54 Rear Sight
55 Spring Cover
56 Spring Cover Base Assembly
57 Spring Cover Base
59 Spring Cover Spring
60 Spring Cover Stop Pin
61 Strut Support
62 Strut Support Pin
64 Trigger
65 Trigger Block
66 Trigger Block Spring
67 Trigger Block Spring Pin
68 Trigger Pin
69 Upper Tang Screw

SPECIFICATIONS

Model: Model 1886 Extra Light Rifle
Action: Lever
Barrel: 22 in.
Weight Unloaded: 7.4 lb.
Caliber: .45-70
Capacity:
Common Features: open sights, half or full magazine tube; manual safety; round or octagon barrel; blued or casehardened finish; barrel bands or forearm caps; straight or pistol-grip wood stock/forearm; rebounding hammer

BACKGROUND

The Winchester 1886 was designed to handle large, powerful black powder cartridges and was initially chambered for .40-82 WCF, .45-70 Government, and .45-90 WCF. The strong action easily transitioned to smokeless powders. It was the high power rifle of its day. The Model 1886 was the first lever action rifle to feature a sliding vertical bolt. The action is renowned for being fast and smooth. Browning reacquainted America to the big bore lever guns in 1986 in rifle and carbine models. Since 1997 Winchester has produced runs of the 1886 in takedown versions, standard 26-inch octagonal barrel models and Extra Light models with a half magazine and 22-inch round barrel. Current production model have rebounding hammers and manual thumb safeties. Shown is a new production Extra Light model.

Year Introduced: 1886
Country of Origin: USA
Original Manufacturer: Winchester
Current Manufacturers/Importers: Puma (legacysports.com), Winchester Repeating Arms (winchesterguns.com), Cimarron (cimarron-firearms.com), EMF Company (emf-company.com)
Similar Models: 1886 Short Rifle (20-in. round barrel, .45-70 or .45-90 caliber), 1886 Rifle (24-in. barrel), 1886 Carbine (22-in. barrel)

REQUIRED TOOLS

Disassembly/Assembly: small and medium blade standard screwdrivers, 1/8 in. punch, rubber mallet, brass hammer, 2.5mm hex or Allen wrench

DISASSEMBLY

1. Remove the upper tang screw (part #69) and lower tang screw, Figure 1. Then pull the stock (5) rearward off the receiver. You may need to gently rap the comb of the stock with your palm to remove the stock from the receiver.

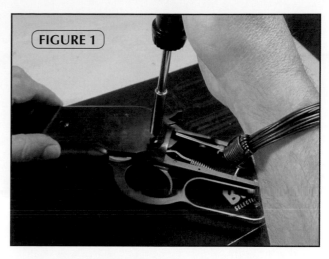

FIGURE 1

2. With the action closed thumb back the hammer (31) to its rear most position. Insert a restraining pin—paperclip, small nail or small punch—into the hole of the hammer strut (33) to restrain the mainspring (45), Figure 2.

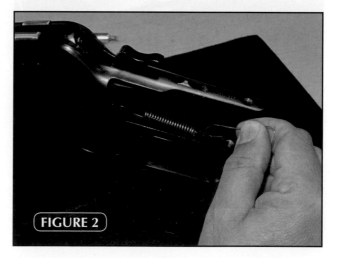

FIGURE 2

3. Use a medium flat blade screwdriver to remove the hammer screw (32), Figure 3.

4. Open the finger lever (21) and slide the lower tang (38) rearward out of the receiver. The trigger mechanism will come out with the lower tang as an assembly. The hammer will come free.

5. Next remove the spring cover screw (13) from the right hand side of the receiver. The spring cover base assembly (56)—spring cover base (57), spring cover (55), spring cover spring (59), spring cover stop pin (60)—will all come free from the right side of the receiver.

6. Position the receiver so the bottom faces up and from the underside of the upper tang remove the carrier spring screw (9), Figure 4. Remove the carrier spring assembly (8).

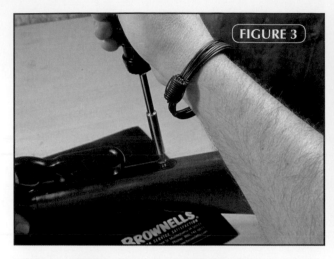

FIGURE 3

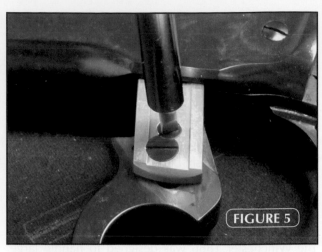

FIGURE 5

FIGURE 4

7. With the finger lever slightly forward, remove the locking bolt stop pin screw (37) from the left locking bolt (34), Figure 5.

8. With the locking bolt stop pin screw removed, push out the locking bolt stop pin (36).

9. Pull the left locking bolt and the right locking bolt (35) out from the bottom of the receiver.

10. Lower the finger lever to slide the breech bolt rearward and out of the receiver and use a medium punch to drift out finger lever connecting pin (20). Then pull finger lever out from the bottom of the receiver.

11. Slide the breech bolt rearward out of the receiver. The ejector (14), ejector spring (16), and ejector collar (15) will come free from the front of the breech bolt.

12. Remove the firing pin assembly (22) by using a punch to drift out the extractor pin (19) and removing the extractor (18) then pull the firing pin assembly from the rear of the breech bolt.

Reassemble in reverse order.

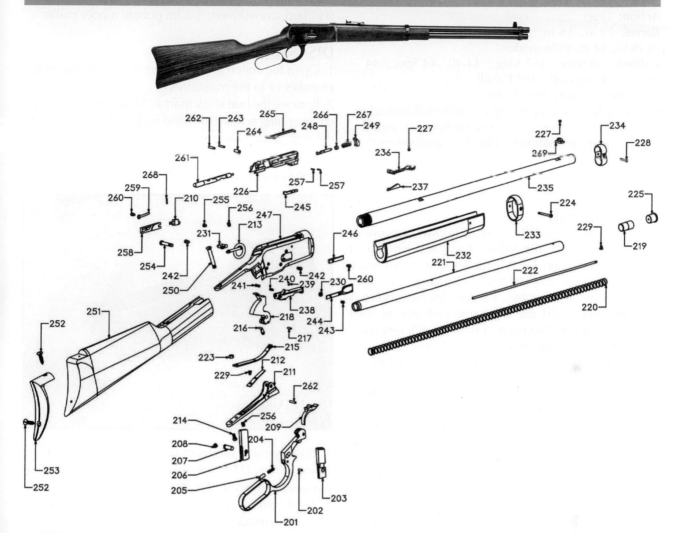

PARTS LIST

201 Lever
202 friction stud stop pin
203 Locking bolt, right
204 Friction stud spring
205 friction stud
206 Locking bolt, left
207 Locking bolt pin
208 Locking bolt pin screw
209 Trigger
210 Cartridge stop
211 Trigger plate
212 Trigger spring
213 Saddle ring
214 Main spring screw
215 Main spring
216 Stirrup
217 Stirrup pin
218 Hammer
219 Magazine follower
220 Magazine spring
221 Loading tube
222 Magazine reduction rod

223 Nut
224 Rear band screw
225 Magazine plug
226 Breech bolt
227 Front sight screw
228 Front band screw
229 Trigger screw
230 Loading gate nut
231 Saddle ring holder
232 Forend
233 Rear band
234 Front band
235 Barrel
236 Rear sight
237 Rear sight leaf
238 Carrier
239 Carrier stop pin
240 Carrier stop spring
241 Carrier stop
242 Carrier screw (2)
243 Spring cover screw
244 Loading gate assembly
245 Ejector lever stop

246 Cartridge guide right
247 Receiver/frame
248 Ejector pin
249 Ejector
250 Receiver tang screw
251 Butt stock
252 Butt plate screw
253 Butt plate
254 Hammer screw
255 Lever- breech bolt hole screw
256 Diopter base hole screw
257 Cartridge stop joint pin
258 Cartridge guide left
259 Cartridge stop spring
260 Cartridge guide screw
261 Firing pin
262 Firing-pin pin / trigger pin
263 Extractor - breech bolt pin
264 Ejector - lever pin
265 Extractor
266 Ejector collar
267 Ejector spring
268 Cartridge stop pin

SPECIFICATIONS

Model: 1892
Action: Lever
Barrel: 12 in., 16 in. (trapper models), 20 in. (carbine models), 24 in. (rifle models)
Caliber: .38 Spec./.357 Mag., .44-40, .44 Spec./.44 Mag, .45 Long Colt, .454 Casull
Capacity: 9 (16 in. barrel), 10
Common Features: open sights, half or full magazine tube; half cock safety or rebounding hammer; round or octagon barrel; stainless, blued or casehardened finish; barrel bands or forend caps; straight wood stock/forearm

BACKGROUND

The 1892 is essentially a scaled-down version of Winchester's 1886 rifle. When it was first introduced over 100 years ago by Winchester it was extremely popular because the 1892 was chambered in pistol calibers. Cowboys, settlers, hunters, lawmen, outlaws and ranchers could use the same cartridge in their pistol as their rifle. No need to buy two different types of cartridges. Winchester manufactured the 1892 until 1941 and it could be had as a trapper's model with a short barrel, a carbine, rifle and musket version with full length military forearm. It could also be ordered from the factory with numerous custom options. Some 1,000,000 rifle models were manufactured. Hollywood helped bolster the '92's reputation, not that it needed it. John Wayne's big loop lever action was an 1892. The 'Rifleman' himself, Chuck Conners had, a modified '92 allowing him to shoot rapid fire. And in "Wanted: Dead or Alive," Steve McQueen used a '92 chopped to pistol size called a "Mare's Leg." Winchester Repeating Arms reintroduced the 1892 in 1995 but other manufacturers like Rossi and Puma were already copying the 1892 design. With today's cowboy action shooters the 1892 has taken its place in the "New West" just like the original did in the Old West. The instructions that follow are specifically for a Puma M-92 Carbine but can generally be used with other 1892 models from various manufacturers. Some models have a manual safety (Rossi, Winchester Repeating Arms). The Puma is traditional with a half-cock hammer safety.

Year Introduced: 1892
Country of Origin: USA
Current Manufacturers/Importers: Cimarron (cimarron-firearms.com), EMF Company (emf-company.com), Legacy Sports (legacysports.com), Rossi (rossiusa.com), Winchester Repeating Arms (winchesterguns.com)
Similar Models: take-down models, Ranch Hand pistol (Rossi)

REQUIRED TOOLS

Disassembly/Assembly: small and medium blade standard screwdrivers, 1/8 in. punch, rubber mallet

DISASSEMBLY

1. Open the action to check there is no cartridge in the chamber or in the magazine.
2. Remove the butt stock (part #251) by unscrewing the receiver tang screw (250) and pulling the butt stock to the rear. If the butt stock is tightly fitted tap the comb with the heel of your hand or use a rubber mallet, Figure 1.

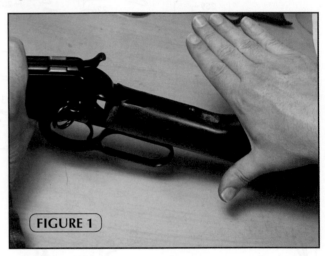

FIGURE 1

3. Slightly open the lever (201) to unscrew the main spring screw (214) and main spring nut (223) then remove the main spring (215).
4. Next remove the hammer screw (254) on the left side of the receiver (247).
5. Remove the hammer (218) upward through the top of the receiver, Figure 2. Pull back on the trigger (209) to ease hammer removal.
6. The trigger plate (211), Winchester calls the part lower tang, fits into grooves inside the receiver and

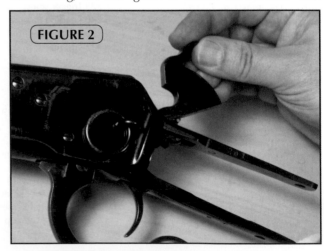

FIGURE 2

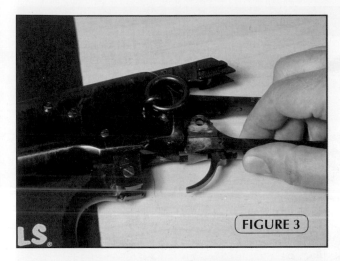

FIGURE 3

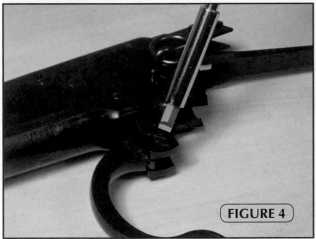

FIGURE 4

13. To disassemble the breech bolt, remove the ejector assembly. It should easily fall free from the front of the breech bolt.

14. Using a small punch, drift out the extractor-breech bolt pin (263). Pull the extractor (265) forward from the face of the breech bolt.

15. To disassemble the magazine tube (221), remove the magazine plug screw (223) and pull the magazine plug (225) out of the loading tube (221), Winchester calls it a magazine tube. Warning the magazine spring (220) is under compression.

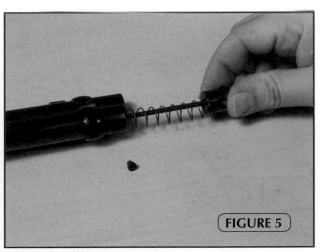

FIGURE 5

must be removed by sliding it to the rear, Figure 3. If the trigger plate is tight a light glancing tap rearward with a rubber mallet eases extraction. Alternate sides of the triggers plate as you tap.

7. The trigger spring (212) and trigger can be accessed once the trigger plate is removed.

8. Next open the lever and from the left side remove the locking bolt pin screw (208), Figure 4.

9. Drift out the locking bolt pin (207) toward the left of the receiver.

10. Pull down from the receiver the locking bolt left (206) and locking bolt right (203).

11. Close the lever and remove the lever-breech bolt pin (255) on the left side of the receiver.

12. Using a small punch drift out the ejector-lever pin (264), Winchester calls the part lever and breech bolt pin, from the right side of the receiver to the left side. The lever can now be removed down from the receiver and the breech bolt (226) assembly rearward.

16. Draw out the magazine spring and magazine follower (219), Figure 5.

17. Some models may have a magazine plug, Puma calls it a magazine reduction rod (222) this limits only five cartridges in the magazine tube. The magazine reduction rod can be removed by unscrewing it from the magazine plug then the magazine can fully loaded.

To reassemble follow the disassemble instructions in reverse.

Tuning Tip: The force of the hammer can be adjusted by using a small screwdriver to main spring strain screw (256). Tightening the screw will make the main spring stronger, loosening the screw will make it less stout. If you loosening the screw too much the hammer may not have the power to drive the firing pin into the cartridge and fire the bullet.

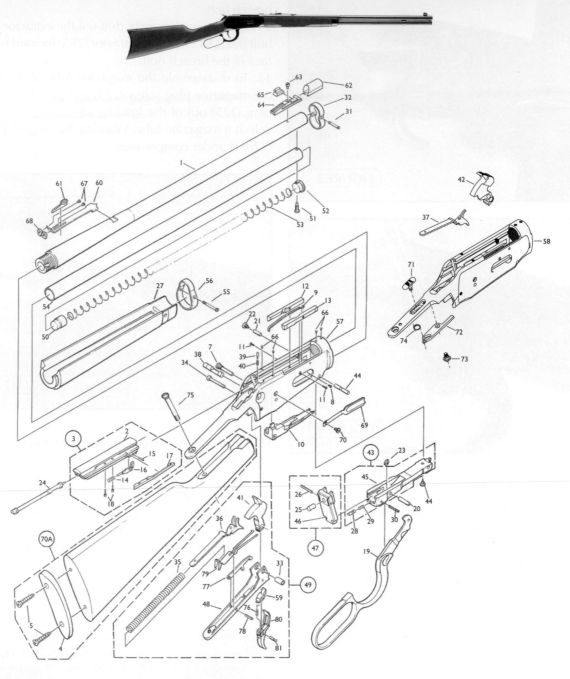

PARTS LIST

1 Barrel
2 Breech Bolt
3 Breech Bolt Complete
4 Buttplate
5 Butt Plate /Pad Screw
   (2 Req'd.)
7 Carrier Screw
8 Carrier Spring Screw
9 Carrier Spring
10 Carrier
11 Cartridge Guide Screw
   (2 Req'd.)

12 Cartridge Guide Left
13 Cartridge Guide Right
14 Ejector Spring
15 Ejector Stop Pin
16 Ejector
17 Extractor
18 Extractor Retaining Screw
   (2 Req'd.)
19 Finger Lever
20 Finger Lever Link Pin
21 Finger Lever Pin
22 Finger Lever Pin Stop Screw
23 Finger Lever/Link Washer

24 Firing Pin
25 Firing Pin Striker
26 Firing Pin Striker Stop Pin
27 Forearm
28 Friction Stud
29 Friction Stud Spring
30 Friction Stud Stop Pin
31 Front Band Screw
32 Front Band
33 Hammer Bushing
34 Hammer Screw
35 Hammer Spring
36 Hammer Spring Guide Rod

37 Hammer Spring Guide Rod
   Tang Safety
38 Hammer Stop
39 Hammer Stop Plunger
40 Hammer Stop Plunger
   Spring
41 Hammer
42 Hammer Tang Safety
43 Link Complete
44 Link Pin
45 Link
46 Locking Bolt
47 Locking Bolt Complete

48 Lower Tang	57 Receiver	66 Sight Plug Screw (4 Req'd.)	73 Tang Safety Lever Screw
49 Lower Tang Complete	58 Receiver Tang Safety	67 Sight Rear Binding Screw (2 Req'd.)	74 Tang Safety Lever Spring
50 Magazine Follower	59 Sear		75 Tang Screw Upper
51 Magazine Plug Screw	60 Sight Rear	68 Sight Rear Blade	76 Trigger Spring
52 Magazine Plug	61 Sight Elevator Rear	69 Spring Cover	77 Trigger Stop
53 Magazine Spring	62 Sight Front Hood	70 Spring Cover Screw	78 Trigger Stop Pin
54 Magazine Tube	63 Sight Front Ramp Screw	70A Stock	79 Trigger Stop Spring
55 Rear Band Screw	64 Sight Front Ramp	71 Tang Safety Button	80 Trigger
56 Rear Band	65 Sight Front	72 Tang Safety Lever	81 Trigger/Sear Pin

SPECIFICATIONS

Model: Winchester Model 94 Short Rifle
Action: Lever
Barrel: 20 in.
Weight Unloaded: 6.75 lb.
Caliber: .30-30 Win, .38-55 Win
Capacity: 8
Common Features: open sights, full-length magazine tube, rebounding hammer, thumb safety, blued finish, wood stock/forearm

BACKGROUND

The Winchester factory churned out over 5,000,000 Model 94s from 1894 through 2006. It is the consummate deer rifle for still hunting in the big woods of the east and carried in many a saddle scabbard out west. I still know an old timer who hunts with a '94 chambered in .38-55 that was manufactured in the 1920s. The lever rattles from years of use. The rifle was reintroduced in 2010. Disassembly is shown for the current production with rebounding hammer and thumb safety, but purists can still follow along for their Pre '64 and pre cross bolt safety models made from 1992-2006. Winchester manufactured Model 94s for Sears, Roebuck and Co.'s private label. The Sears crossbrand models for the Model 94s include Sears 100 and Sears 54.
Year Introduced: 1894 (reintroduced 2011)
Country of Origin: USA
Current Manufacturer: Winchester Repeating Arms (winchesterguns.com)
Similar Models: Sporter (24 in. barrel, checkered wood stock), Takedown (disassembles, .450 Marlin, .30-30Win calibers)

REQUIRED TOOLS

Disassembly/Assembly: small and medium blade standard screwdrivers, 1/8 in. punch

DISASSEMBLY

1. Use a medium flat blade screwdriver to unscrew and remove the finger lever pin stop screw (part #22) from the left side of the receiver (57), Figure 1.
2. Use a 1/8 inch punch to drift out the finger lever pin (21) from the right to left side of the receiver, Figure 2.

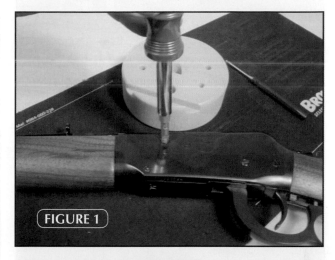

FIGURE 1

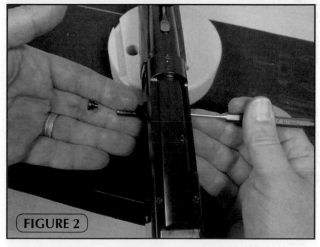

FIGURE 2

3. Next push though the link pin (44) from either side with a concave punch, Figure 3. On older Model 94s there is a link pin screw that needs to be removed before the drifting out the link pin from either side.
4. Slightly move the finger lever (19) down and it and the link (43) can be detached from the locking bolt (46) and removed from the bottom of the receiver, Figure 4.
5. Next remove the carrier screw (7) from the left side of the receiver. On older model 94s, remove the two carrier screws one on each side of the receiver, Figure 5.
6. Remove the carrier (10) from the bottom of the receiver, Figure 6.

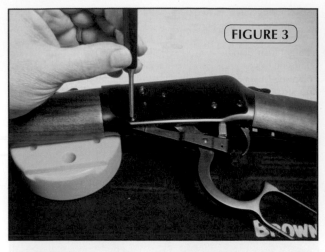

FIGURE 3

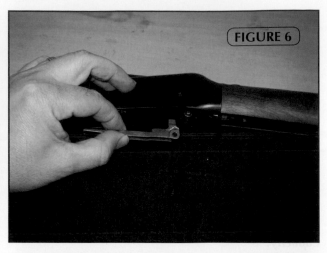

FIGURE 6

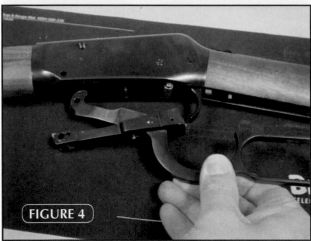

FIGURE 4

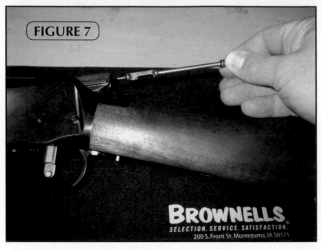

FIGURE 7

BROWNELLS.
SELECTION. SERVICE. SATISFACTION.
200 S. Front St. Montezuma, IA 50171

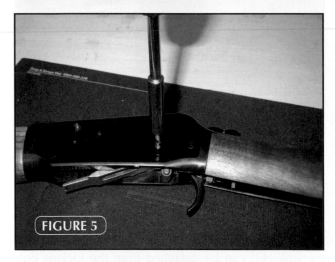

FIGURE 5

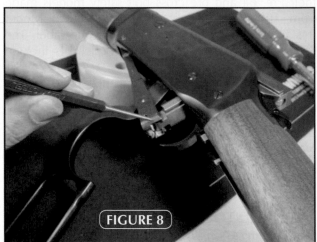

FIGURE 8

7. With the locking bolt pulled down from the bottom of the receiver the firing pin (24) can be removed from the breech bolt assembly (3), Figure 7.

Reassemble in reverse order.

Reassembly Tip: You will need to open the finger lever to pull down on the locking holt so they align.

Centerfire Pump Action

REMINGTON MODEL 7600

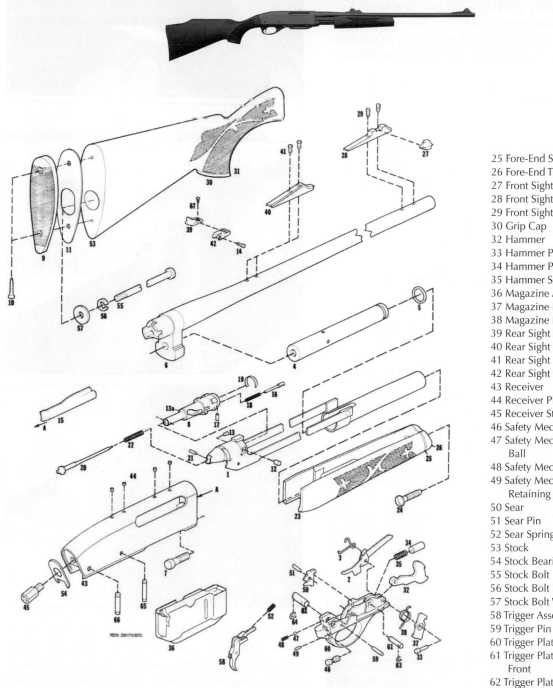

RON SMITHSON

25 Fore-End Spacer
26 Fore-End Tip
27 Front Sight
28 Front Sight Ramp
29 Front Sight Ramp Screw
30 Grip Cap
32 Hammer
33 Hammer Pin
34 Hammer Plunger
35 Hammer Spring
36 Magazine Assembly
37 Magazine Latch
38 Magazine Latch Spring
39 Rear Sight Aperture
40 Rear Sight Base
41 Rear Sight Base Screw
42 Rear Sight Slide
43 Receiver
44 Receiver Plug Screw
45 Receiver Stud
46 Safety Mechanism
47 Safety Mechanism Detent
   Ball
48 Safety Mechanism Spring
49 Safety Mechanism Spring
   Retaining Pin
50 Sear
51 Sear Pin
52 Sear Spring
53 Stock
54 Stock Bearing Plate
55 Stock Bolt
56 Stock Bolt Lock Washer
57 Stock Bolt Washer
58 Trigger Assembly
59 Trigger Pin
60 Trigger Plate
61 Trigger Plate Pin Bushing,
   Front
62 Trigger Plate Pin Bushing,
   Rear
63 Trigger Plate Pin Detent
   Spring, Front
64 Trigger Plate Pin Detent
   Spring, Rear
65 Trigger Plate Pin, Front
66 Trigger Plate Pin, Rear
67 Windage Screw

PARTS LIST

1 Action Bar Assembly
2 Action Bar Lock
3 Action Bar Lock Spring
4 Action Tube Assembly
5 Action Tube Ring
6 Barrel Assembly
7 Barrel Extension Bolt

8 Breech Bolt
9 Butt Plate Frame
10 Butt Plate Frame Screw
12 Cam Pin (Large)
13 Cam Pin (Small)
14 Elevation Screw
15 Ejector Port Cover
16 Ejector

17 Ejector Retaining Pin
18 Ejector Spring
19 Extractor
20 Firing Pin
21 Firing Pin Retaining Pin
22 Firing Pin Retracting Spring
23 Fore-End Assembly
24 Fore-End Screw

SPECIFICATIONS

Model: Model 7600
Action: pump
Barrel: 18.5 in., 22 in.
Weight Unloaded: 7.5 lb. (22 in. barrel)
Caliber: .243 Win, .270 Win, .30-06, .308 Win,
Capacity: 4-round magazine
Common Features: manual safety; walnut or synthetic stock; open sights; detachable box magazine; blued or matte finish

BACKGROUND

The Model 7600 is the latest design refinement of the Model 760 which debuted in 1952. Production of the 7600 began in 1981. The rifle is similar in size and operation as Remington's Model 870 shotgun. The Benoit clan in Vermont prefers short-barreled 7600s in .30-06 to stalk big bucks.
Year Introduced: 1952 (Model 760)
Current Manufacturer: Remington (remington.com)
Country of Origin: USA
Similar Models: Carbine (18.5 in. barrel)

REQUIRED TOOLS

Disassembly/Assembly: small punch, medium flat blade screwdriver

DISASSEMBLY

1. Push the safety mechanism (part #46) in the "safe" position and slide the fore-end assembly (23) forward to close the action. Ensure the hammer (32) is cocked.
2. Use a small punch to tap out the front trigger plate pin (65) and rear trigger plate pin (66), Figure 1.
3. Lift rear of the trigger plate assembly (60) and remove it from the bottom of the receiver (43), Figure 2.
4. Remove the fore-end by unscrewing and removing the fore-end screw (24), Figure 3. Then pull the fore-end toward the muzzle and off the action bar assembly (1). The fore-end screw can be stubborn.

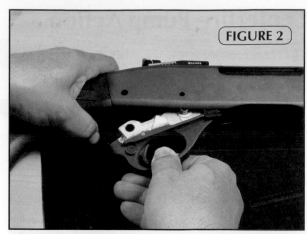

FIGURE 2

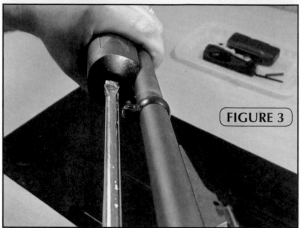

FIGURE 3

FIGURE 4

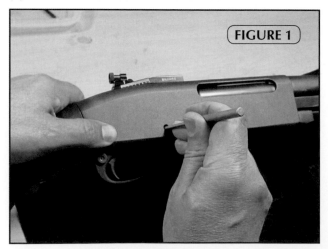

FIGURE 1

5. Slide the action bar assembly forward/toward the muzzle and insert a punch in the opposing pair of holes on the action tube assembly (4), Figure 4. Use the punch to unscrew and remove the action tube assembly from the receiver. Pull the action tube assembly off the front of the receiver stud.
6. The barrel assembly (6) and breech bolt (8) can then be slid out as an assembly from the front of the receiver.
7. Slide the ejection port cover (15) out of its slot in the receiver.

Reassemble in reverse order.

Centerfire Single Shot

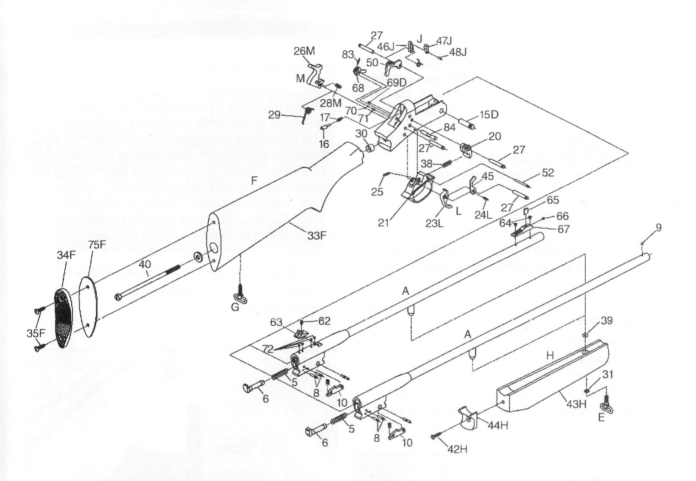

PARTS LIST

A Barrel
E Forearm Assembly Screw
F Stock Assembly
G Lower Swivel
H Forearm Assembly
J Transfer Bar Assembly
L Trigger Assembly
M Hammer Assembly
5 Extractor Spring
6 Extractor
8 Extractor Stop Pin
9 Front Sight
10 Extractor Lever

15D Barrel Pin
16 Firing Pin
17 Firing Pin Spring
20 Locking Plate
21 Trigger Guard
23L Trigger
24L Trigger Lever Pin
25 Trigger Spring
26M Hammer
27 Receiver Assembly Pin
28M Hammer Spring Pin
29 Hammer Spring
30 Stock Assembly Bushing
31 Forearm Assembly Nut
33F Stock

34F Butt Plate
35F Butt Plate Screw
38 Locking Plate Spring
39 O-Ring
40 Stock/Receiver Screw
42H Cap Locking Screw
43H Forearm
44H Forearm Cap
45 Trigger Lever
46J Transfer Bar Lever
47J Transfer Bar
48J Transfer Bar Pin
50 Opening Lever
52 Trigger Guard Pin
62 Rear Sight Screw

63 Rear Sight
64 Front Sight Base Screw
65 Front Sight
66 Front Sight Screw
67 Front Sight Base
68 Safety Lever
69D Safety Stop Pin
70 Safety Locking Ball
71 Safety Locking Spring
72 Cap Screw
75F White Spacer
83 Safety Pin
84 Safety Rod

SPECIFICATIONS

Model: Wizard
Action: Single shot, single action
Barrel: 23 in.
Caliber: .17 HMR, .22LR, .22 Mag, .22-250, .223, .243, .270 Win, .30-06, .308 Win, .35 Whelan, .38 Spec/357 Mag, .44 Mag, .454 Casull, .45-70, 7.62x39; muzzleloader calibers: .45, .50; shotgun gauges .410 bore, 28, 20, 12 gauge
Capacity: 1
Common Features: open sights with scope mount attached; manual safety; blued or stainless finish; wood stock

BACKGROUND

The Wizard is a versatile rifle that enables users to shoot rimfire and centerfire cartridges, shotgun shells, and black powder projectiles, all with the quick change of a barrel. At last count, the Wizard is capable of 23 caliber options.
Year Introduced: 2010
Country of Origin: Brazil
Current Manufacturers/Importers: Rossi/Taurus

REQUIRED TOOLS

Field Strip: none
Disassembly/Assembly: 1/8 in. punch, brass hammer, slave pin, 1/4 in. hex or Allen wrench, small Philips screwdriver

FIELD STRIP

1. To remove the barrel from the receiver, unscrew the forward assembly screw or sling swivel (part #E) until it is free from the barrel (A), Figure 1.
2. Pull the forearm (H) down and off the barrel.
3. Press the opening lever (50) down and pull the barrel down and out of the receiver.

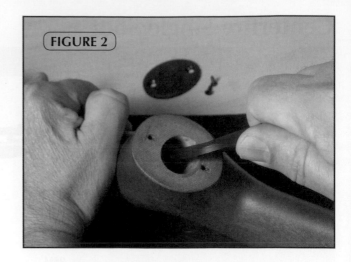

FIGURE 2

At this point the Wizard is field stripped.

Disassembly Tip: Under normal circumstances no further disassembly is required. Note that the pins that secure the trigger assembly, hammer and safety are tapered pins with the larger end of the pins ribbed. This ribbed end press fits into the pin holes. Constant disassembly/reassembly of these parts may mean the pins and/or pin holes will wear. Also be aware the pins need to be driven out so the ribbed portion comes out first.

3. To remove the trigger assembly, use a 1/8 inch punch and drive out the trigger guard pin (52) from the left to the right side of the receiver.
4. Do the same with the receiver assembly pin (27)

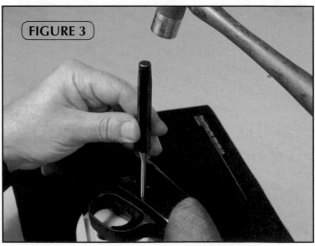

FIGURE 3

knocking it out from left to right, Figure 3.
5. Pull down on the front part of the trigger guard (21). Note that the trigger assembly is comprised of the trigger guard, trigger (23L), trigger spring (25), locking plate spring (38) and trigger lever (45). These parts may fall free when you remove the trigger assembly.

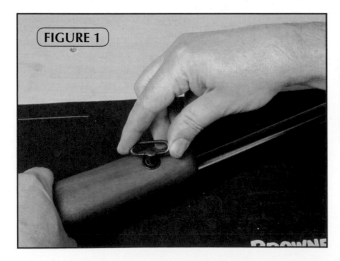

FIGURE 1

To reassemble follow the disassemble instructions in reverse.

Reassembly Tip: Use a slave pin in the trigger guard assembly to align the trigger guard, trigger and trigger lever. As you tap in the receiver assembly pin, the slave pin will fall free. You can make a slave pin from a nail, plastic rod or wood dowel. Insert the front of the trigger guard assembly first so the locking plate spring (38) is against the locking plate (20). Make sure the hammer spring (29) is placed to the rear of the trigger guard assembly. You will feel the hammer spring tension as you push the trigger guard assembly into the receiver. Tap in the receiver assembly pin first from left to right of the receiver. The slave pin will drop free when the pin is in place. Then replace the trigger guard pin from the left to the right of the receiver.

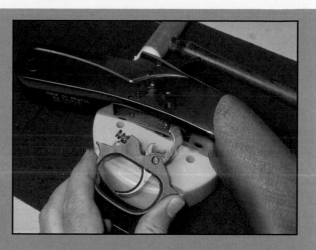

RUGER NO. 1

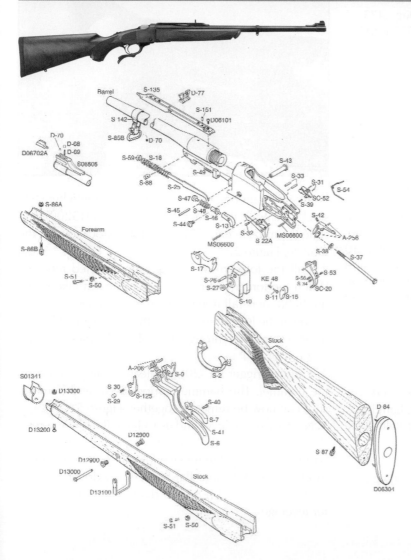

PARTS LIST

Barrel
S-135 Barrel Rib, with Dovetail
S-151 Barrel Rib Dowel, Front
S-151 Barrel Rib Dowel, Rear
S-139 Barrel Rib Screws, Front (2 Req'd.)
D06101 Barrel Rib Screws, Rear (2 Req'd.)
S-10 Breech Block
S-9 Breech Block Arm
A-214 Breech Block Assembly
S-125 Ejector
S-13 Ejector Cam
S-45 Ejector Cam Pivot Pin
S-29 Ejector Plunger
S-30 Ejector Plunger Spring
S-27 Ejector Roller
S-46 Ejector Strut
S-49 Ejector Strut Adjustment Screw
S-48 Ejector Strut Spring
S-47 Ejector Strut Swivel
S-11 Firing Pin
KE-48 Firing Pin Spring
70054 Forearm, With Escutcheon
S-50 Forearm Escutcheon
S-88 Forearm Take Down Nut
S-51 Forearm Take Down Screw
S06505 Front Sight Base
D-70 Front Sight Base Set Screw
D06702A Front Sight Blade Assembly
D-69 Front Sight Plunger Spring
D-68 Front Sight Retaining Plunger
S-17 Hammer
S-18 Hammer Spring
S-59 Hammer Spring Retaining Washer
S-25 Hammer Strut
A-212 Hammer Strut Assembly
S-15 Hammer Transfer Block
S-26 Hammer Transfer Block Pivot Pin

S-6 Lever
S-6B Lever Assembly
S-7 Lever Latch
S-40 Lever Latch Pivot Pin
S-41 Lever Latch Spring
A-206 Lever Link and Pin
   Assembly
S-43 Lever Pivot Pin
S-44 Lever Pivot Screw
S01341 Muzzle Cap
D13300 Muzzle Cap
   Escutcheon
D13200 Muzzle Cap Screw
S-97 Pistol Grip Cap
S-61 Pistol Grip Cap Medallion

S-36 Pistol Grip Cap Screw
D-77 Rear Sight
C-83 Receiver Filler Screws
   (2 Req'd.)
D06304 Recoil Pad
D-84 Recoil Pad Screws,
   (2 Req'd.)
SC-52 Safety
S-16 Safety Arm
S-32 Safety Arm Pivot Pin
S-22 Safety Bar
S-22A Safety Bar Arm Assembly
S-58 Safety Bar Pivot Pin
S-54 Safety Detent Spring
S-39 Safety Detent Spring Pin

S-31 Safety Retaining Pin,
   (2 Req'd.)
S-56 Sear Adjustment Screw
A-256 Sear & Trigger Assembly
S-33 Sear Pivot Pin
S-42 Sear Spring
S-85B Sling Swivel
S-142 Sling Swivel Band
D-70 Sling Swivel Band Set
   Screw
D12900 Sling Swivel
   Escutcheon, (2 Req'd.)
D13100 Sling Swivel, Front
S-87 Sling Swivel Mounting
   Screw, Rear

S-86A Sling Swivel Nut, Front
D13000 Sling Swivel Screw
S-37 Stock Bolt
S-38 Stock Bolt Washer
70052 Stock, Butt, Complete
   With Cap & Pad
SC-20 Trigger
A-254 Trigger Assembly
S-53 Trigger Adjustment Spring
S-2 Trigger Guard
MS06600 Trigger Guard
   Retaining Pin, (2 Req'd.)
S-33 Trigger Pivot Pin
S-34 Trigger Spring Adjustment
   Screw

SPECIFICATIONS

Model: No. 1International
Action: Single shot, single action
Barrel: 20.0 in. (International)
Caliber: .243, 6.5 Creedmoor, .270 Win, .30-06, .300 RCM, .303 British, .308 Win (Light Sporter); .22-250, .223, .25-06, 6.5 Creedmoor (Varminter); .270 Win, 7x57mm, .30-06, (International); .308 Win, .300 H&H, .300 Win Mag, .45-70, .460 S&W Mag, .475 Linebaugh/.480 Ruger (Medium Sporter); .375 H&H, 450/400 Nitro Express, .458 Lott (Tropical)
Capacity: 1
Common Features: open sights (except on Varminter), integral scope base, manual safety, blued finish, wood stock

BACKGROUND

The falling block action of the Ruger No. 1 is a modified version of the Farqharson-style action with internal hammer. A lever that locks into the trigger guard is pressed down to drop the stainless steel block, load the rifle, and cock the hammer. It is an exceptionally strong action that Ruger has chambered in some 50 different calibers over the years. They are unique and sophisticated rifles for a country that cut its teeth on Sharps, Remington, Ballard, Maynard, Stevens and Winchester 1885 single-shot rifles.
Year Introduced: 1966
Country of Origin: USA
Current Manufacturer: Ruger (ruger.com)
Similar Models: Light Sporter (22.0 in. barrel), Varminter (24.0 in. barrel, no sights), Tropical (24.0 in. barrel), Medium Sporter (22.0 in.-26.0 in. barrel), International (22.0 in. barrel, full mannlicher-style stock)

REQUIRED TOOLS

Disassembly/Assembly: small nail for retaining pin; small, medium and two large flat blade screwdrivers; socket with long extension

FIELD STRIP

1. Remove the forearm by unscrewing the forearm takedown screw (part #S-51), Figure 1. If your No. 1

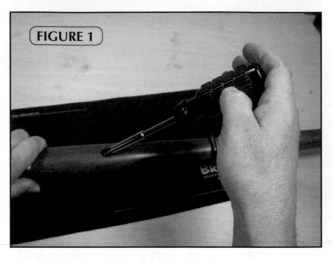

FIGURE 1

is an International model with full mannlicher-style stocks, remove the muzzle cap screw (D13200) and slide the muzzle cap (S01341) off the stock toward the muzzle, Figure 2.

2. Pull the forearm away from the barreled receiver. When the forearm is removed the forearm take down nut (S-88) may fall free from the receiver, Figure 3.

3. Lower the lever (S-6) to cock the hammer (S-17) then insert a small nail through the hole in the hammer strut (S-25), Figure 4.

4. Pull the trigger (SC-20) to release spring tension on the hammer. The hammer spring (S-18) and hammer strut can now be removed together, Figure 5.

5. Next lower the lever and use a large flat blade screwdriver to unscrew the lever pivot screw (S-44) located on the left side of the receiver, Figure 6. You will need to place another large flat blade screwdriver into the lever pivot pin (S-44) on the right side of the receiver for leverage.

FIGURE 2

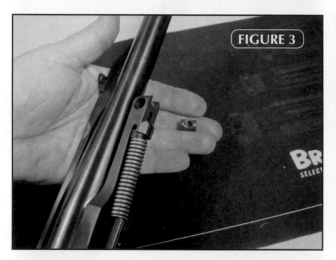

FIGURE 3

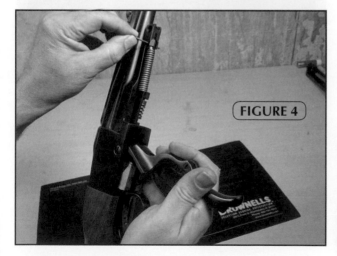

FIGURE 4

6. The hammer can now be removed from the bottom of the receiver, Figure 7.

7. Next raise the lever to close breech, then lower the lever about halfway and pull downward, removing the lever, breech block (S-10), breech block arm (S-9) and the linkage from the bottom of the receiver, Figure 8.

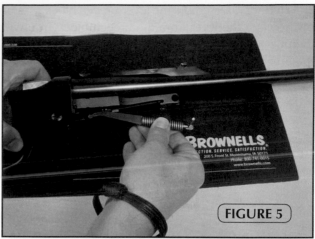

FIGURE 5

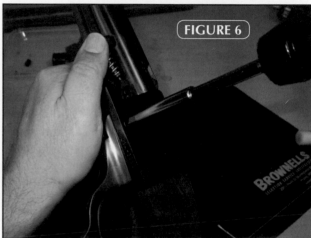

FIGURE 6

This is the extent of disassembly required for routine inspection, cleaning and lubrication.

DETAILED DISASSEMBLY

1. The ejector (S-125), ejector plunger (S-29), and ejector plunger spring (S-30) are removed from the bottom of the receiver. The ejector cam (S-13) is removed by tipping the rear portion downward.

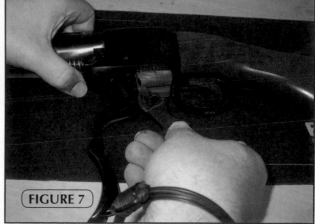

FIGURE 7

2. To further disassemble the lever/breech block assembly, remove the lever from the breech block. You will then be able to remove the ejector roller (S-27) from the breech block.

FIGURE 8

3. Next access the hammer transfer block from the underside of the breech block and work the hammer transfer block back and forth until the hammer transfer block pivot pin protrudes from the right side of the breech bolt. Note the end of the hammer transfer block pivot pin (S-26) has a groove that can be used to pry it out with a small screwdriver. The hammer transfer block can now be removed from the bottom of the breech block.

4. You can now access the firing pin (S-11) and firing pin spring (KE-48) from inside the breech block.

5. To remove the stock first remove the two recoil pad screws (D-84) then the recoil pad (D06304). Using a socket with along extension unscrew the stock bolt (S-37).

6. The stock will then pull free from the receiver.

Reassemble in reverse order.

Tool Tip: The main spring for the No. 1 is a stout coil spring. If you should remove the nail retaining pin your life will be easier with a main spring compressor. This tool allows you to easily compress a coiled mainspring along its strut. If you work on revolvers with coil main springs— Colt, S&W, Ruger, Taurus, et al—you will find this tool invaluable.

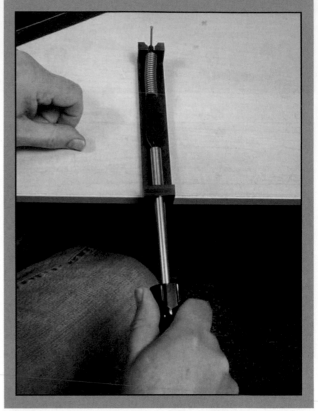

Rimfire Semi-Automatic

HENRY U.S. SURVIVAL

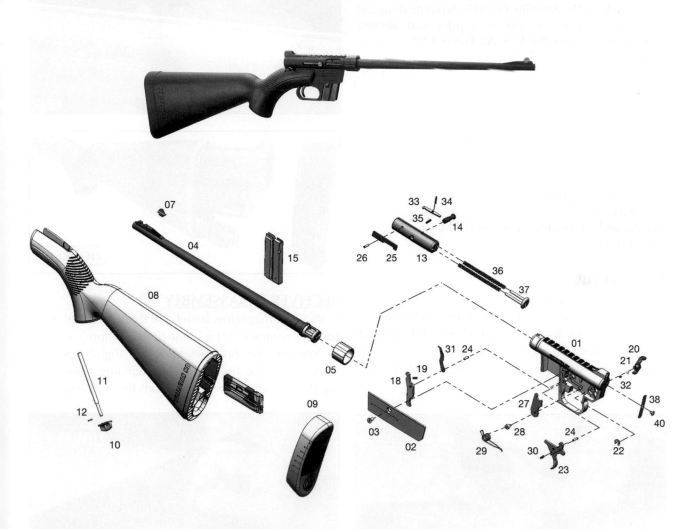

PARTS LIST

1 Receiver
2 Sideplate
3 Sideplate screw
4 Barrel assembly
5 Barrel nut
7 Front sight
8 Stock w/ cap
9 Stock cap only

10 Stock takedown nut
11 Stock takedown screw
12 Stock takedown rollpin
13 Bolt
14 Charging handle
15 Magazine complete
18 Magazine latch
19 Magazine latch spring
20 Safety plate/shaft
21 Safety detent ball

22 Safety snap ring
23 Trigger
24 Trigger pivot pin
25 Firing pin
26 Firing pin assembly pin
27 Hammer
28 Hammer pivot pin
29 Hammer/trigger spring
30 Hammer/trigger safety pin
31 Ejector

32 Ball Spring
33 Extractor
34 Extractor assembly pin
35 Extractor spring
36 Action springs (2)
37 Action spring guide
38 Rear sight only
40 Rear sight screw

SPECIFICATIONS

Model: U.S. Survival
Action: semi-automatic, blowback
Barrel: 16 in.
Weight Unloaded: 3.5 lb.

Caliber: .22 LR
Capacity: 8 + 1
Common Features: textured polymer stock, adjustable rear/front sight, Teflon coated receiver, manual safety

BACKGROUND

There's an irony in disassembling the U.S. Survival rifle since it is typically already disassembled. All components store in the rifle's hollow stock that even floats. Hikers, survivalists, and those who venture into the wild have relied on these rifles ever since the AR-7 was introduced by Armalite in 1959. Armalite designed a similar weapon for use as a pilot and aircrew survival weapon for the U.S. Air Force. Other firearm manufacturers have built versions of the AR-7 and now Henry currently builds this incredibly lightweight, portable rifle.

Year Introduced: 1997
Country of Origin: USA
Current Manufacturer: Henry Repeating Arms (henryrepeating.com)

REQUIRED TOOLS

Field Strip: none
Disassembly/Assembly: medium flat blade screwdriver

FIELD STRIP

1. Remove the magazine (part #15).
2. Unscrew the barrel nut (05) counterclockwise until it is free from the threads from the barrel (04) and pull the barrel from the receiver (01), Figure 1. Hold the receiver right side up as the charging handle (14) will fall free once the barrel is removed.

FIGURE 2

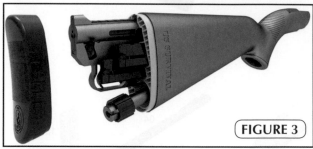

FIGURE 3

FIGURE 1

3. Remove the receiver from the stock (08) by unscrewing the stock takedown nut (10) counterclockwise until it is loose and the receiver can be separated from the stock, Figure 2. At this point the AR-7 is sufficiently disassembled for cleaning. Components can also now be stored in the hollow stock by removing the stock cap (09) and stowing the barrel, receiver and magazine inside the stock, Figure 3. Then replace the stock cap on stock.

RECEIVER DISASSEMBLY

1. With the magazine, barrel and stock removed make sure the hammer (27) is in the fired position.
2. Remove the bolt assembly by slightly pushing rearward on the bolt (13) with your finger and pulling the charging handle free from the bolt, Figure 4.

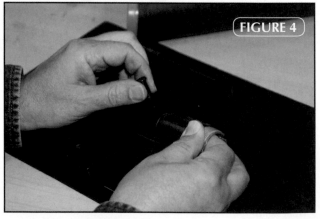

FIGURE 4

The bolt assembly will then slide out the front of the receiver. The action spring guide (37) may stay inside the receiver, Figure 5.
3. Place the receiver left side facing up and unscrew and remove the sideplate screw (03), Figure 6. Pull the sideplate (02) from the receiver. You may need to place your thumb or a piece of wood in the magazine well and gently pry up on the sideplate, Figure 7. Note that the sideplate helps secure internal components.

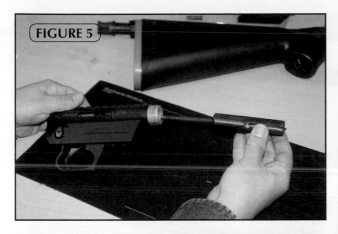

FIGURE 5

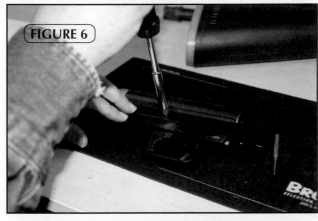

FIGURE 6

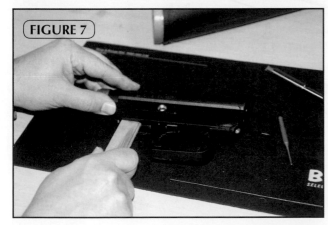

FIGURE 7

4. Move closest leg of the hammer/trigger spring (29) out of the groove in the trigger pivot pin (24)

in the trigger (23), then pull the trigger free from the hammer/trigger safety pin (30) in the receiver, Figure 8.

FIGURE 8

4. Place your finger on the magazine latch spring (19) and pull the magazine latch (18) up and off the receiver pin.
5. Pull out the trigger pivot pin (24) and the ejector (31) can be removed from the receiver.

BOLT DISASSEMBLY

1. Remove the two actions spring (36) and action spring guide.
2. Drift out the firing pin assembly pin (26) to remove the firing pin (25).

Reassemble by first reassembling the bolt assembly and installing the bolt assembly in the receiver. Then follow the procedures in reverse order.

Reassembly Tip: The lower pin in the sideplate should be inserted first into the hole in the trigger. Next ensure the hammer pivot pin (28) fits into the small hole in the sideplate. You may need to move the hammer with a small punch through the ejection port so the hammer pivot pin (28) aligns with the hole in the sideplate. Then screw down the sideplate screw. Do not over tighten the sideplate screw. If the magazine latch does not move freely then the screw is too tight.

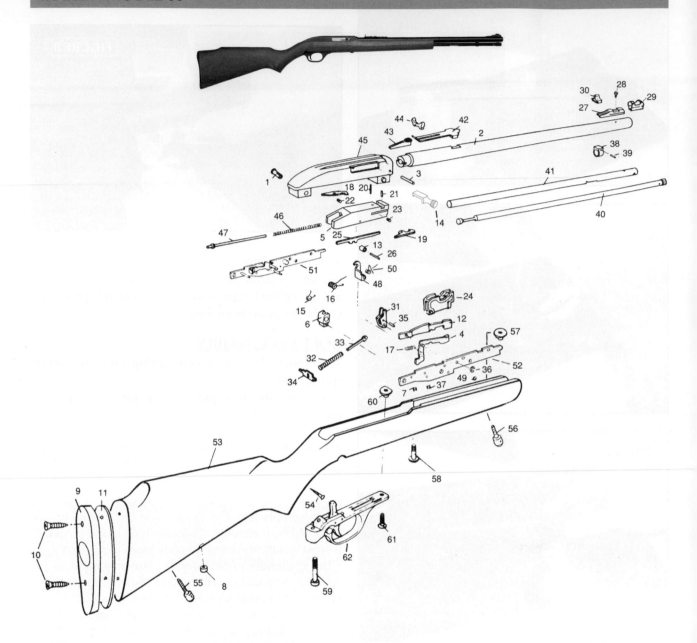

PARTS LIST

1 Assembly Post
2 Barrel
3 Barrel Retaining Pin
4 Bolt Release Lever
5 Breech Bolt
6 Buffer
7 Buffer Pin Ring
8 Bullseye
9 Buttpad
10 Buttpad Screw (2)
11 Buttpad Spacer
12 Cartridge Lifter
13 Cartridge Lifter Roller
14 Charging Handle
15 Disconnector Spring

16 Ejector Lifter Spring
17 Extension Spring
18 Extractor, Left Hand
19 Extractor, Right Hand
20 Extractor Pin, Left Hand
21 Extractor Pin, Right Hand
22 Extractor Spring, Left Hand
23 Extractor Spring, Right Hand
24 Feedthroat
25 Firing Pin
26 Firing Pin Retaining Pin
27 Front Sight Ramp Base
28 Front Sight Ramp Base Screw
29 Front Sight Ramp Hood
30 Front Sight Ramp Insert
31 Hammer

32 Hammer Spring
33 Hammer Strut
34 Hammer Strut Bridge
35 Hammer Strut Pin
36 Hammer Lifter Pin Ring
37 Lever Retaining Ring
38 Magazine Tube Band
39 Magazine Tube Band Pin
40 Magazine Tube Inside
    Complete
41 Magazine Tube Outside
42 Rear Sight Base
43 Rear Sight Elevator
44 Rear Sight Folding Leaf
45 Receiver
46 Recoil Spring

47 Recoil Spring Guide
48 Sear
49 Sear Pin Ring
50 Sear Spring
51 Sideplate, Left Hand
52 Sideplate, Right Hand
53 Stock
54 Stock Reinforcement Screw
55 Swivel Stud, Rear
56 Swivel Stud, Front
57 Swivel Stud Nut
58 Takedown Screw, Front
59 Takedown Screw, Rear
60 Trigger Guard Nut, Front
61 Trigger Guard Screw, Front
62 Trigger Guard Complete

SPECIFICATIONS

Model: Model 60
Action: semi-automatic, blowback
Stock: laminated hardwood
Barrel: 19 in.
Weight Unloaded: 5.5 lb.
Caliber: .22 LR
Capacity: 14
Common Features: two position safety, open sights, tubular magazine, receiver grooved for optic mounts, sling swivels, blued finish

BACKGROUND

The Model 60 is an iconic American rimfire rifle featuring micro-groove barrel rifling that uses 16 small lands and grooves to increase accuracy by decreasing the deformation of bullets as they travel down the barrel. Typical rifling employs four, six or eight grooves. Economically priced, easily allows for mounting optics, and with a Monte Carlo hardwood stock it is no wonder many young shooters started out on the Model 60. The action assembly is housed between two sideplates that are held together with pins and C-clips, Figure 1. It is not advised nor is it required for

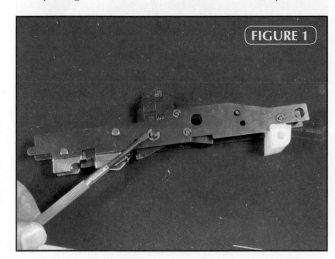

FIGURE 1

thorough cleaning to disassemble the action assembly. The instructions below are specifically for the Model 60 tube magazine rifle, but can be also be loosely used for disassembly the action on Marlin's 795 series with detachable box magazine rifles.

Year Introduced: 1960
Country of Origin: USA
Current Manufacturer: Marlin Firearms
(marlinfirearms.com)
Similar Models: 60C (camo finish stock), 60SB (stainless steel barrel/receiver, laminated wood stock), 60SN (synthetic stock, blue finish), 60SS (stainless steel barrel/receiver, laminated two-tone wood stock)

REQUIRED TOOLS

Disassembly/Assembly: 9/64 hex or Allen wrench, small punch

DISASSEMBLY

1. Place the safety in the "safe" position and remove the inside magazine tube (part #40).
2. Place the rifle top side down and unscrew the front takedown screw (58) and rear takedown screw (59)

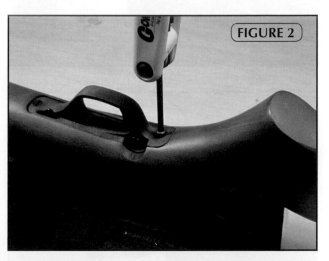

FIGURE 2

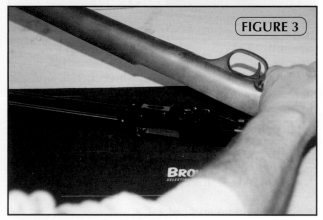

FIGURE 3

using a 9/64 hex or Allen wrench, Figure 2.
3. Separate the stock (53) from the barreled receiver. The trigger assembly (62) will be attached to the stock, Figure 3.
4. Next squeeze the slotted end of the assembly post (1) and push it out from the hole in the receiver (45), Figure 4.
5. Remove action assembly by grasping the left sideplate (51) and right sideplate (52) and sliding the action assembly to the rear and up, Figure 5.
6. Next remove the breech bolt (5), charging handle (14), recoil spring (46) and recoil spring guide (47) by slightly pulling back the charging handle while

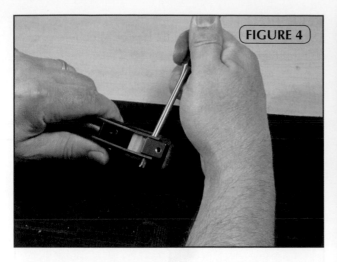

FIGURE 4

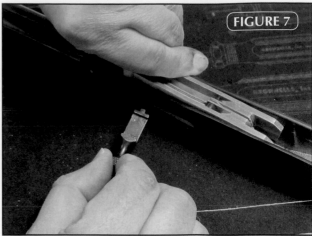

FIGURE 7

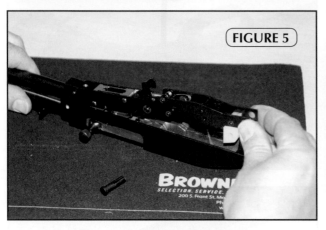

FIGURE 5

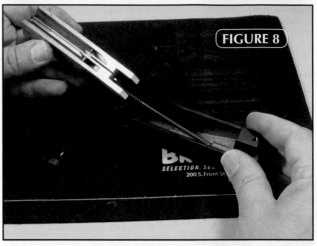

FIGURE 8

inserting a thumb between the breech bolt and the barrel (2), Figure 6. Use your thumb to lift the front of the breech bolt from the receiver. As the breech bolt is lifted free from the receiver the charging handle will come free, Figure 7. Grasp the breech bolt, recoil spring, and recoil spring guide and control them as they are removed from the receiver, Figure 8.

Reassemble in reverse order.

Maintenance Tip: Marlin recommends cleaning the inside of the receiver, bolt face, extractors, and chamber after every 250 rounds. Depending on the brand of ammunition, cleaning may need to be performed more frequently.

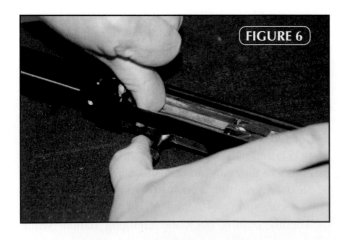

FIGURE 6

Reassembly Tip: Hold breech bolt and recoil spring in one hand and use your other hand to support the spring while compressing the spring until guide enters breech bolt, Figure 9. Replace the action assembly by first hooking the notched front of the action assembly under the two posts in the receiver, Figure 10. Then pull back on the charging handle and squeeze down on the action assembly into the receiver, Figure 11. Then replace the assembly pin.

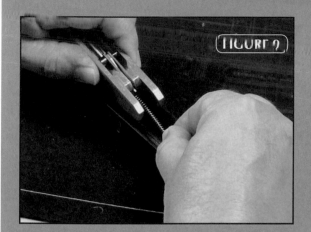

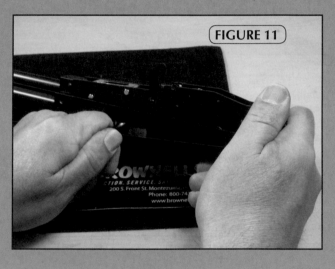

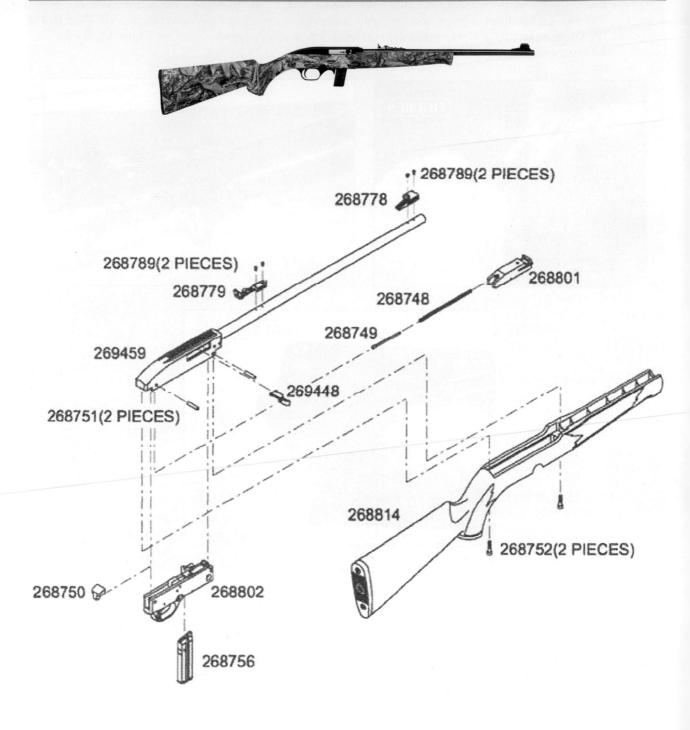

268789(2 PIECES)

268778

268789(2 PIECES)

268779

269459

268751(2 PIECES)

269448

268748

268749

268801

268814

268752(2 PIECES)

268750

268802

268756

PARTS LIST
268814 Stock Assembly
268752 Take Down Screw (2 Req'd.)
269459 Receiver and Barrel Assembly
269448 Operating Handle

268801 Bolt Assembly
268748 Bolt Recoil Spring
268749 Bolt Recoil Spring Guide
268750 Bolt Plastic Buffer
268751 Pin (2 Req'd.)

268779 Rear Sight Assembly
268789 Rear Sight Screw (2 Req'd.)
268778 Front Sight Assembly
268802 Trigger Guard Assembly
268756 Magazine Assembly

SPECIFICATIONS
Model: 702 Plinkster
Action: semi-automatic, blowback
Barrel: 18 in. or 20 in.
Weight Unloaded: 4.0 lb.
Caliber: .22 LR
Capacity: 10- and 25-round magazine
Common Features: two position safety, open sights, detachable magazine, receiver drilled and tapped for mounting optics, wood or synthetic stock, blued or brushed chrome finish

BACKGROUND
The 702 Plinkster is a semi-automatic rifle suited for small game hunting, holding back marauding soda cans and teaching youngsters to shoot. The 702 models are manufactured in Brazil and imported into the U.S. by Mossberg International.
Year Introduced: 2006
Country of Origin: Brazil
Current Importer: O.F. Mossberg & Sons (mossbergs.com)
Similar Models: 702 Bantam Plinkster (12-1/4 in. LOP), 702 Thumbhole Tipdown (thumbhole stock with tipdown forend)

REQUIRED TOOLS
Disassembly/Assembly: Phillips screwdriver, 1/8 inch punch, brass hammer

DISASSEMBLY
1. Remove the magazine (part #268756).
2. Pull back the operating handle (269448) fully rearward and lock the bolt assembly (268801) in the open position by push the operating handle inward, Figure 1.
3. Push the safety button to the "safe" position.
4. Use a Phillips screwdriver two remove the two take down screws (268752) in the front and rear of the trigger guard assembly (268802).

FIGURE 2

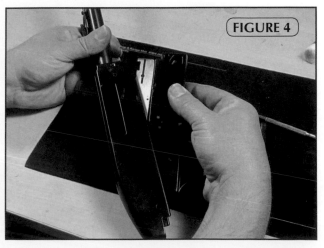
FIGURE 3

5. Pull the receiver and barrel assembly (269459) from the stock assembly (268814), Figure 2.
6. Next use a small punch to push out the two pins (268751) from the trigger guard assembly and receiver and barrel assembly, Figure 3.
7. Pull the trigger guard assembly from the bottom of the receiver and barrel assembly, Figure 4.

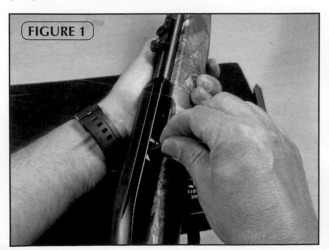
FIGURE 1

FIGURE 4

8. Pull the operating handle outward and control the forward movement of the bolt assembly. The bolt plastic buffer (268750) may fall free from the receiver and barrel assembly.

9. Lay the receiver and barrel assembly top side down and pull back the operating handle backward until you can insert a finger between the bolt assembly and receiver. Then slightly lift the bolt assembly and remove the operating handle. The bolt assembly can then be removed through the bottom of the receiver and barrel assembly.

10. Remove the bolt recoil spring (268748) and bolt recoil spring guide (268749) from the bolt assembly.

11. Slide the bolt assembly off the trigger guard assembly.

Reassemble reversing the order.

Reassembly Tip: Reattached the bolt assembly to the trigger guard assembly. Next insert the bolt recoil spring guide end of the bolt recoil spring into the hole in the inside of the receiver first then insert the other end of the bolt recoil spring into the hole in the back of the bolt assembly. As you compress the bolt recoil spring by pushing back on the bolt assembly/trigger guard assembly pushing rear of the bolt assembly/trigger guard assembly into the receiver. Continue to compress and pivot the front into place. Before fully inserting bolt assembly/trigger guard assembly into the receiver insert the operating handle.

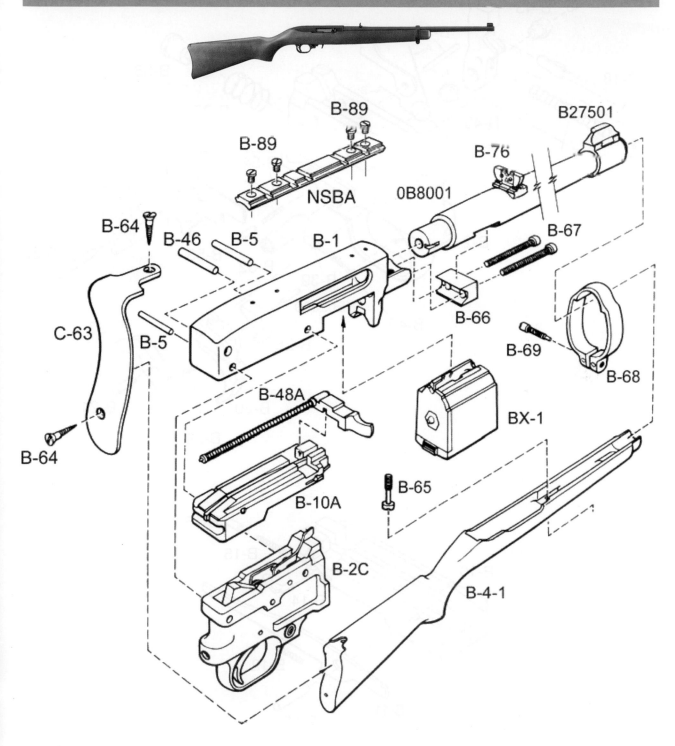

B-89

B-89

B27501

B-76

NSBA

0B8001

B-64

B-46

B-5

B-1

B-67

C-63

B-5

B-66

B-69

B-68

B-64

B-48A

BX-1

B-10A

B-65

B-2C

B-4-1

PARTS LIST

0B8001 Barrel
B-68 Barrel Band
B-69 Barrel Band Screw
B-66 Barrel Retainer, V-Block
B-67 Barrel Retainer Screw, 2 Req'd.
B-10 Bolt

B-41 Bolt Lock
B-42 Bolt Lock Spring
B-18 Hammer Strut
B-45 Hammer Strut Washer
BX-1 Magazine, Complete, 10-Shot
   Capacity
B00034 Magazine Latch

B-35 Magazine Latch Pivot & Ejector Pin,
   2 Req'd.
B-36 Magazine Latch Plunger
B-37 Magazine Latch Plunger Spring
B-76 Rear Sight, Open
B-5 Receiver Cross Pin, 2 Req'd.
C-83 Receiver Filler Screws, 4 Req'd.

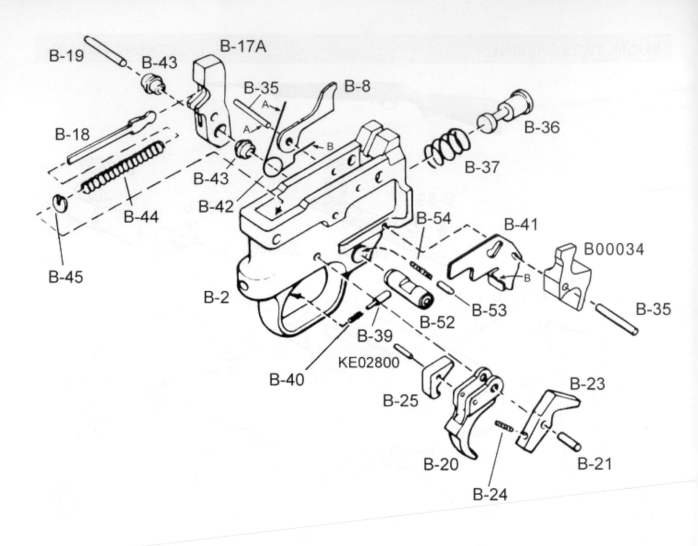

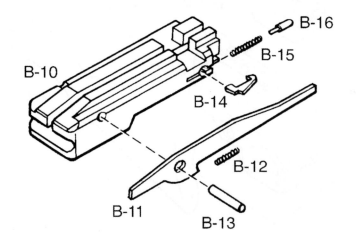

B-52 Safety
B-53 Safety Detent Plunger
B-54 Safety Detent Plunger Spring
B-23 Sear
B-24 Sear Spring

B-4-1 Stock Assembly, Complete
B-65 Take-Down Screw
B-20 Trigger
B-20D Trigger Assembly, Complete
B-2 Trigger Guard

B-2C Trigger Guard Assembly, Complete
B-21 Trigger Pivot Pin
B-39 Trigger Plunger
B-40 Trigger Plunger Spring

SPECIFICATIONS

Model: 10/22 Standard Carbine
Action: semi-automatic, blowback
Barrel: 18.5 in.
Weight Unloaded: 5.0 lb.
Caliber: .22 LR
Capacity: 10
Common Features: two position safety, open sights, detachable magazine, receiver drilled and tapped for mounting optics, hardwood or synthetic stock

BACKGROUND

The 10/22 is an iconic American rimfire rifle with a slick rotary magazine. Some five million have been manufactured since introduced in 1964. The 10/22 as is a fun plinker and small game getter. It is also highly customizable and since it is an easy rifle to work on many shooters trick out their 10/22 to suit their shooting situation or their personality.
Year Introduced: 1964
Country of Origin: USA
Current Manufacturer: Ruger (ruger.com)
Similar Models: Target (heavy barrel), Sporter (checkered stock), Tactical (flash hider), Compact (16 in. barrel, shorter stock)

REQUIRED TOOLS

Field Stripping: flat blade screwdriver, 1/8 inch punch, nylon hammer
Disassembly/Assembly: 3/32 inch punch, needle-nose pliers

FIELD STRIP

1. Close the bolt assembly (part #B-10A) and ensure the action is be cocked.
2. Using a flat blade screwdriver loosen the barrel band screw (B-69) and remove the barrel band (B-68) by sliding off the barrel toward the muzzle. Note some models do not have a barrel band so skip this step.
3. Fold the rear sight so it will not get damaged and place it top down on a padded bench surface.
4. Loosen but do not remove the take-down screw (B-65) and then center the safety button (B-52) so an equal amount of the button shows on each side of the trigger guard (B-2), Figure 1. If the safety is not positioned properly the stock (B-4-1) will be damaged when it is lifted off the barrel-receiver assembly. Lift the stock off the barrel-receiver assembly.
5. Use a 1/8 inch punch to push out the two receiver cross pins (B-5) and bolt stop pin (B-46), Figure 2. Note that these pins may fall free when the barrel-receiver

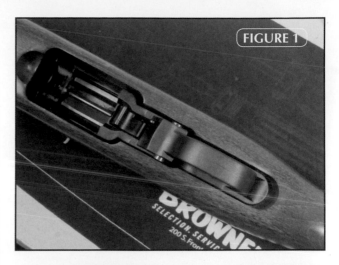

FIGURE 1

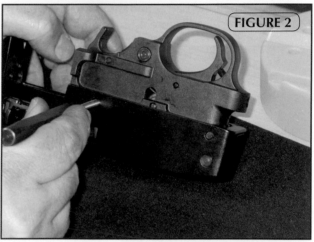

FIGURE 2

assembly is placed on its side. The trigger guard assembly (B-2C) can now be removed from the receiver (B-1).
6. To remove the bolt (B-10A), place the top side of the rifle down on a padded surface so the bolt is accessible.
7. Fully pull the bolt handle (B-48A) to the rear of the receiver with one hand and with your other hand lift up the front of the bolt until it disengages from the bolt handle, Figure 3. You may want to gently turn over the barrel/receiver assembly the bolt will drop out.
8. Remove the bolt handle assembly through the ejection port of the receiver and lift the bolt out of receiver. If it does not come out easily turn the receiver over and the bolt will drop free from the receiver.

At this point routine cleaning can be performed without further disassembly.

DETAILED DISASSEMBLY

1. To remove the barrel (B27501), unscrew the two barrel retaining screws (B-67) using a 5/32 hex or Allen

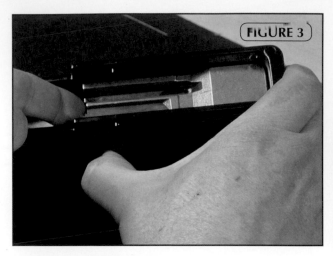
FIGURE 3

wrench and pull the barrel and the barrel retainer (B-66) from the receiver, Figure 4.

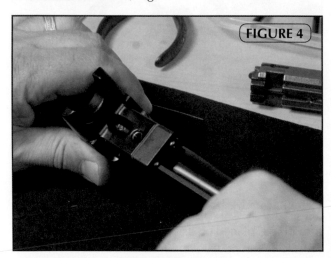
FIGURE 4

Tuning Tip: Swapping out the stock barrel can transform a 10/22's accuracy. Barrels from E.R. Shaw (ershawbarrels.com), Green Mountain (gmriflebarrel.com), Clark Custom (clarkcustomguns.com), Volquartsen (volquartsen.com) and others come in all types of configurations and materials—stainless steel, carbon fiber sleeves, muzzle brakes, straight flutes, spiral flutes.

2. To remove the hammer spring assembly, which consists of the hammer spring (B-14), hammer strut (B-18) and hammer strut washer (B-45), first decock the hammer (B01703) by pulling the trigger (B-20). You can hold the hammer down with your thumb when pulling the trigger and ease it to the fired position. Note that the hammer is under spring tension.

3. Remove the hammer spring assembly, with a pair of needle-nose pliers by pulling the top of the hammer strut out of the hammer, Figure 5.

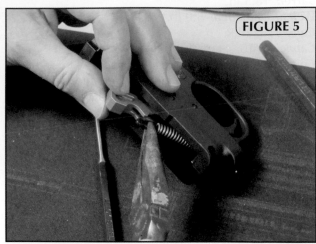
FIGURE 5

4. To remove the ejector (B-8), use a punch to drift out the magazine latch pivot and ejector pin (B-35). Note that the bolt lock spring (B-42) is held under tension by this pin but held in place by the hammer pivot pin (B-19).

5. With the pin removed pull the ejector up and out of the trigger guard.

6. Next remove the hammer assembly buy drifting out the hammer pivot pin (B-19), Figure 6. The hammer,

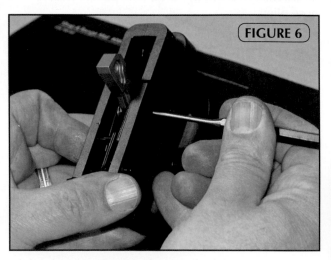
FIGURE 6

bolt lock spring and two hammer bushings (B-43), one on each side of the hammer.

7. To remove the bolt lock (B-41), use a punch to drift out the magazine latch pivot & ejector pin (B-35).

8. Pull the bolt lock up and out of the trigger guard.

9. To remove the trigger/sear assembly, which made up of the trigger, sear (B-23), sear spring (B-24), disconnector (B-25), disconnector pin (KE02800), use a punch to drive out the trigger pivot pin (B-21). You can then pull the trigger/sear assembly out of the trigger guard.

10. With the trigger assembly removed then you can remove the trigger plunger (B-39) and trigger plunger spring (B-40) by pulling them out of trigger guard with a pair of needle-nose pliers.

11. To remove the magazine catch (B00034) first depress the magazine retainer piston (B-36) your finger and then pull the magazine catch out from the bottom of the trigger guard.

Reassemble in reverse order.

> **Customization Tip:** Make your 10/22 untouchable with the "Chicago" kit from SCOTTWERX (1022fungun.com) which transforms Ruger 10/22 rifles into Tommy guns from the 1920-30's complete with wood stock and pistol grips and an optional 50-round drum magazine.

MAGAZINE DISASSEMBLY

1. Use a 9/64 inch hex or Allen wrench to loosen, but do not completely remove, the magazine screw at the front of the magazine, Figure 7.

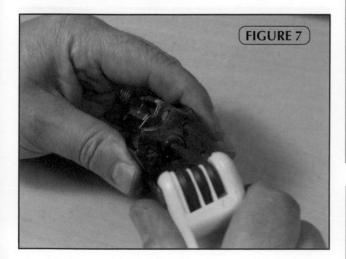

FIGURE 7

2. Push the magazine screw to pop out the magazine cap nut from the rear of the magazine.

3. Then remove the magazine screw.

4. Next remove the magazine cap from the rear of magazine shell.

5. Pull out the magazine rotor and magazine rotor spring.

6. Pull the magazine throat from the top of the magazine shell.

> **Reassembly Tip:** On either the end of the magazine throat there is either a large or small knob. The large knob is inserted into the magazine shell first. The knob fits into a large hole. Insert the magazine rotor with the magazine rotor spring end facing out and rotate it clockwise until the long vane touches the magazine throat. Replace the magazine end cap. Note the magazine rotor spring end tab fits into a small hole in the magazine cap nut. This allows tension to be placed on the spring as magazine rotor rotates when a cartridge is loaded. Rotate the magazine shall in one hand while you hold the magazine cap nut so it fits into the hexagonal hole in the magazine end cap. Hold it in place and insert the magazine screw and tighten it. Do not over tighten the screw and nut.

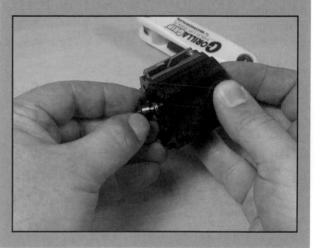

> **Maintenance Tip:** The 10/22 magazine is made of polymers that are self lubricating. Oil will only collect dust and debris and gum up the mechanism.

SPECIFICATIONS
Model: M&P15-22
Action: semi-automatic, blowback
Barrel: 16 in.
Weight Unloaded: 5.5 lb.
Caliber: .22 LR
Capacity: 10-, 25-round magazines
Common Features: polymer upper and lower, two position safety, open sights, detachable magazine, Picatinny rail, adjustable CAR stock

BACKGROUND
The popularity of AR-style rifles has spawned the desire for rimfire versions. The M&P 15-22 replicates the controls and features of its centerfire cousin closely while using inexpensive .22 rimfire ammo to really kick brass for a lot less money. The take down procedure is very similar to a centerfire AR, the difference is in the breech bolt assembly.
Year Introduced: 2009
Country of Origin: USA
Current Manufacturer: Smith & Wesson (smith-wesson.com)
Similar Models: Pink Platinum (pink camo finish upper), Performance Center (18 in. threaded barrel, fixed or adj. stock), Realtree APG HD Camo (camo finish upper/lower, fixed or adj. stock), MOE (Magpul sights, stock, grip)

REQUIRED TOOLS
Field Stripping: none
Disassembly/Assembly: paper clip, 1/8 inch punch, barrel nut wrench, adjustable wrench, vise

FIELD STRIP
1. Remove the magazine then push the bolt release to ensure that the bolt is in the forward position .
2. Next push in the take down pin which is located above the safety switch of the left side of the lower receiver and pull the pin out on the right of the lower receiver until it stops, Figure 1.
3. Now pivot lower receiver down and away from upper receiver.

FIGURE 1

4. Pull the charging handle to the rear and remove the bolt assembly, which includes charging handle and bolt assembly, Figure 2.

FIGURE 2

UPPER/LOWER DISASSEMBLY
1. To remove the upper from the lower, push out the pivot pin and the upper and lower can be separated, Figure 3.
2. The barrel is removed from the upper receiver by first removing the compensator —if so equipped—by unscrewing it using an adjustable wrench.

Performance Tip: Smith & Wesson recommends that the following brands and types of .22 LR ammunition for optimal performance in the M&P15-22 rifle:

- Aguila Super Extra High Velocity
- Aguila Super Extra Std. Velocity
- CCI Mini-Mag
- CCI Standard Velocity
- Federal American Eagle
- Federal GameShock
- Winchester Super-X High Velocity

3. Next remove the handguard spacer by pressing in the four clips, work the spacer free from the handguard and slide it off along the barrel, Figure 4.

FIGURE 3

4. You will need a barrel nut wrench like the ones manufactured by Shooboy Tools or H&W Steel, Figure

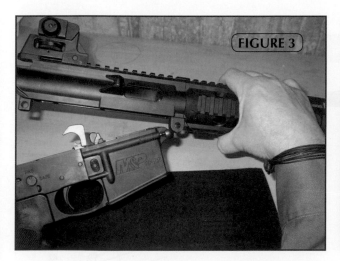

FIGURE 4

FIGURE 5

5. Slide the barrel wrench over the barrel, tabbed end first, and engage the tabs of the wrench with the slots in the barrel nut. Mount the barrel in a vise with barrel vise jaws and use an adjustable wrench on the barrel wrench to unscrew the barrel nut. Once the nut is loosened, remove the barrel from the vise and use the barrel wrench to completely unscrew the nut. Tip the barrel muzzle down and the barrel nut will slide off the barrel.

5. The handguard is removed from the receiver by pulling free and sliding it down the barrel.

6. The barrel can then be pulled through the back of the receiver.

7. The fire assembly is removed from lower assembly by drifting out the hammer pin using a 1/8 punch and removing the hammer, Figure 6.

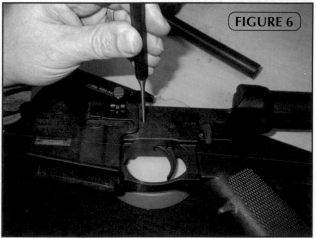

FIGURE 6

8. Next remove the safety switch by rotating it in the middle between "safe" and "fire" and then wiggle it out.

9. Then drift through the trigger pin and before removing the punch hold your hand over the top of the lower receiver to control the trigger or place the lower top side down on the bench.

10. Remove the punch and the trigger assembly—trigger and trigger spring—will fall from the lower.

BOLT DISASSEMBLY

1. To disassemble the bolt assembly remove the charging handle and then pull back on the recoil spring along the recoil spring guide rod enough to pull up on the rear portion of the recoil spring guide rod to remove it from the rear bolt assembly, Figure 7.

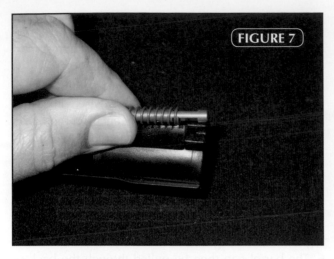

FIGURE 7

3. Remove the firing pin and firing pin spring by drifting out the firing pin retaining pin using a small roll pin punch. As you remove the punch, the firing pin will fall free and the firing pin spring can be extracted.

4. The extractor is removed by pushing the extractor plunger back into the bolt and sliding the extractor outward until it falls free. Note the extractor plunger is under tension from the extractor plunger spring so control it.

Reassemble in reverse order.

Reassembly Tip: Do not over tighten the barrel nut as the receiver is made of polymer and could strip.

2. Then slide the rear bolt assembly rearward so the two guide rods can be extracted from the bolt.

Rimfire Bolt Action

CZ 455

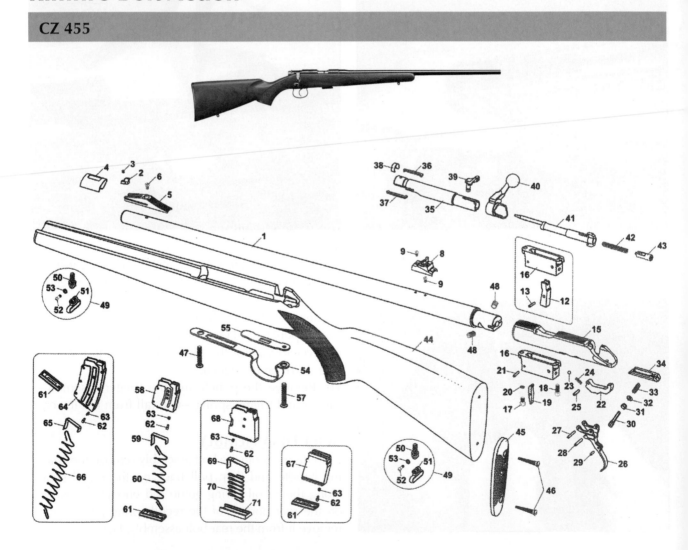

PARTS LIST

1 Barrel
2 Front Sight
3 Front Sight Screw
4 Front Sight Cover
5 Front Sight Base
6 Front Sight Base Screw
8 Rear Sight
9 Rear Sight Screw (2x)
12 Magazine Housing Insert
13 Magazine Housing Insert Pin
15 Receiver
16 Magazine Housing
17 Magazine Housing Front Screw
18 Magazine Housing Rear Screw
19 Magazine Catch
20 Magazine Catch Spring
21 Magazine Catch Pin
22 Sear
23 Sear Steel Ball
24 Sear Spring
25 Sear Pin
26 Trigger

27 Trigger Rivet
28 Trigger Pin
29 Trigger Rod Pin
30 Trigger Rod
31 Trigger Rod Nut
32 Trigger Spring Washer
33 Trigger Pull Spring
34 Bolt Guide
35 Bolt
36 Extractor
37 Holder
38 Extractor Spring
39 Safety
40 Bolt Handle
41 Striker
42 Striker Spring
43 Striker Spring Support
44 Stock
45 Butt Plate
46 Butt Plate Screw (2x)
47 Front Stock Screw
48 Barrel Screw (2x)
49 Sling Swivel Assembly (2x)

50 Sling Swivel Wood Screw
51 Sling Swivel
52 Sling Swivel Screw
53 Elastic Spacer
54 Trigger Guard
55 Trigger Guard Plate
57 Rear Stock Screw
58 Magazine Shell
59 Magazine Follower
60 Magazine Follower Spring
61 Magazine Base
62 Magazine Plunger
63 Magazine Plunger Spring
64 Magazine Shell
65 Magazine Follower
66 Magazine Follower Spring
67 Adapter Body
68 Magazine Shell
69 Magazine Follower
70 Magazine Follower Spring
71 Magazine Base

SPECIFICATIONS

Model: CZ 455
Action: bolt
Barrel: 20.5 in.
Weight Unloaded: 6.1 lb.
Caliber: .17 HMR, .22 LR, .22 WMR
Capacity: 5
Common Features: two position safety, open sights (Lux, FS models), detachable magazine, dovetailed receiver for mounting optics, adjustable trigger, cocking indicator, interchangeable barrel system, Turkish walnut stock

BACKGROUND

The CZ 455 rimfire bolt action rifle features a hammer forged barrel and adjustable trigger. The interchangeable barrel system allows shooters to quickly swap barrels and calibers with a few tools.
Year Introduced: imported since 2009
Country of Origin: Czech Republic
Current Importer: CZ-USA (cz-usa.com)
Similar Models: Lux, Varmint, American, FS (full stock/mannlicher), Varmint Evolution, Varmint Precision Trainer

REQUIRED TOOLS

Field Stripping: none
Disassembly/Assembly: large Torx wrench, small hex or Allen wrench, 1/8 in. punch

FIELD STRIP

1. Remove the bolt assembly by lift the bolt handle (part #40) and pulling it rearward while pulling the trigger (77). The bolt assemble can then be withdrawn from the receiver (15).

At this point the CZ 455 can be cleaned without further disassembly.

BOLT DISASSEMBLY

1. To disassemble the bolt assembly, remove the bolt assembly from the receiver.
2. While holding the bolt handle in your right hand, grasp the bolt (35) in your left hand and rotate the bolt handle downward the same way you would close the bolt on the rifle. This releases the striker spring (42). Note the position of the striker spring support (43).
3. Using either a dowel or the edge of the work bench, push the striker spring support into the bolt and at the same time pull the safety (39) up and out of the bolt, Figure 1. Warning the striker spring is under compression so slowly release the striker spring support.
4. The striker spring support, striker spring, striker (41) can them easily be removed from the rear of the bolt.
5. To remove the extractors (36) remove the extractor spring (38) which is similar to a spring clip.

BARREL/RECEIVER DISASSEMBLY

1. To remove the barrel (1) or adjust the trigger assembly, lay the rifle top down on a padded surface and remove the stock (44) by unscrewing two large Torx screws, the front stock screw (47) and rear stock screw (57) using a large Torx wrench.

FIGURE 1

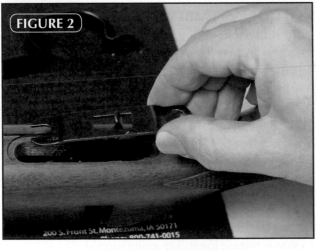

FIGURE 2

200 S. Front St. Montezuma, IA 50171

2. After the two screws are removed the trigger guard (54) and trigger guard plate (55) will easily be removed from the stock, Figure 2.

3. The barreled action can now be easily removed from the stock. Note that the magazine housing insert pin (13) may fall free from the magazine housing (16) and the magazine housing insert (12).

4. To remove the barrel, place the barreled action on a padded surface and push out magazine housing insert pin with a small punch. The magazine housing insert will fall free from the magazine housing.

Tuning Tip: To adjust the trigger, rotate the trigger rod nut (31), Figure 3.

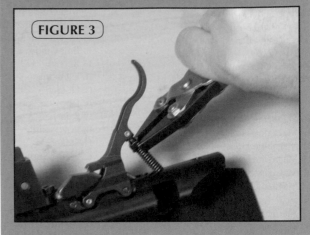

FIGURE 3

5. Loosen the magazine housing rear screw (18) one to two turns to allow the barrel to easily fit into the receiver.

6. Unscrew the two barrel screws (48) using a hex or Allen wrench, Figure 4.

7. Pull the barrel from the receiver.

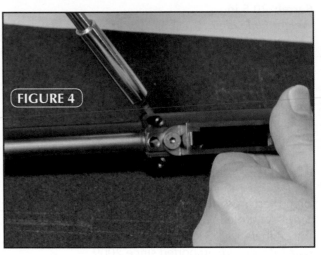

FIGURE 4

To reassemble follow the disassemble instructions in reverse order.

Reassembly Tip: Ensure the barrel screws are torque to 3.7 ft lb. If swapping barrels of different calibers you may or may not need to replace the magazine housing insert and pin. The stock screws should be torque to 4.4 ft. lb.

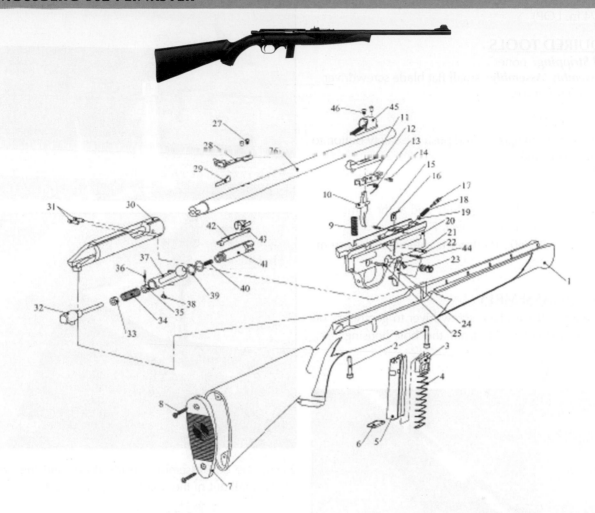

PARTS LIST

1 Stock
2 Action Screw
3 Magazine Follower
4 Magazine Spring
5 Magazine Housing
6 Magazine Base Plate
7 Butt Plate
8 Butt Plate Retaining Screw
9 Sear Spring
10 Trigger
11 Sear

12 Safety Bridge
13 Trigger Spring
14 Trigger Spring Pin
15 Ejector Pin
16 Ejector
17 Detent Plunger
18 Detent Spring
19 Detent Ball
20 Trigger Housing
21 Sear Pin
22 Magazine Release Pin
23 Safety Button

24 Magazine Release
25 Trigger Pin
26 Barrel
27 Rear Sight Screw
28 Rear Sight Assembly
29 Rear Sight Height Adjuster
30 Receiver
31 Receiver Pins
32 Striker Pin Assembly
33 Bolt Spring Rear Collar
34 Bolt Spring
35 Bolt Spring Front Collar

36 Collar Pin
37 Bolt Body Assembly
38 Collar Screw
39 Bolt Washer
40 Firing Pin Spring
41 Bolt Housing
42 Firing Pin
43 Shell Extractor
44 Receiver Screw
45 Front Sight
46 Front Sight Screw

SPECIFICATIONS

Model: 802 Plinkster
Action: bolt
Barrel: 21 in.
Weight Unloaded: 4.2 lb.
Caliber: .22 LR
Capacity: 5- and 10-round magazine
Common Features: two position safety, open sights, detachable magazine, dovetailed receiver for mounting optics, cocking indicator, synthetic thumbhole stock

BACKGROUND

The 802 Plinkster is an economical and accurate rimfire bolt action rifle and nearly perfect for the activity it is so named after. Some 25 model configurations exist.
Year Introduced: 2006
Current Manufacturer: O.F. Mossberg & Sons (mossbergs.com)
Similar Models: 802 Varmint Plinkster (21-in. bull barrel), 802 Bantam Plinkster (12-1/4 in. LOP), 817

(.17 HMR caliber), 817 Varmint (.17 HMR caliber, 21-in. bull barrel), 801 Half-Pint Plinkster (single shot, 12-1/4 in. LOP)

REQUIRED TOOLS
Field Stripping: none
Disassembly/Assembly: small flat blade screwdriver, Phillips screwdriver

FIELD STRIP
1. Remove the magazine and push the safety button to the "fire" position.
2. Lift the bolt handle and pull the bolt to the rear of the action.
3. Press back on the trigger fully and at the same time pull the bolt out of the receiver, Figure 1.
At this point the 802 Plinkster is sufficiently disassembled for cleaning.

BOLT DISASSEMBLY
1. Use a small flat blade screwdriver to gently pry off the shell extractor (43) from the bolt housing (41), Figure 2.

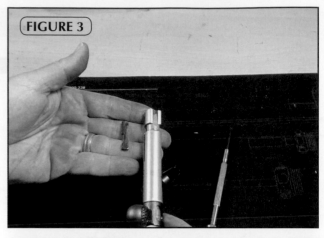

FIGURE 3

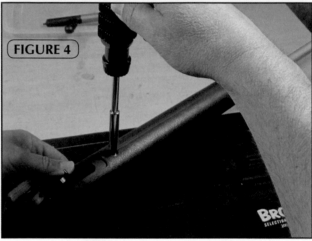

FIGURE 4

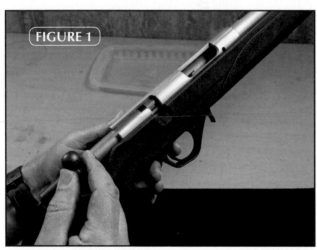

FIGURE 1

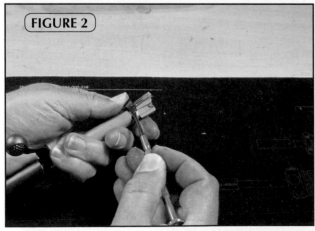

FIGURE 2

2. Flip the bolt assembly upside down and the firing pin will fall out of the bolt housing, Figure 3.

BARREL/RECEIVER DISASSEMBLY
1. Using a medium Phillips screwdriver to remove the two action screws (2) from the bottom of the stock (1), Figure 4.
2. Lift out the barrel/receiver assembly from the stock, Figure 5.
3. Unscrew and remove the two receiver screws and lift the barrel assembly from the trigger housing assembly.

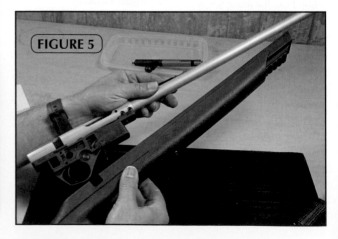

FIGURE 5

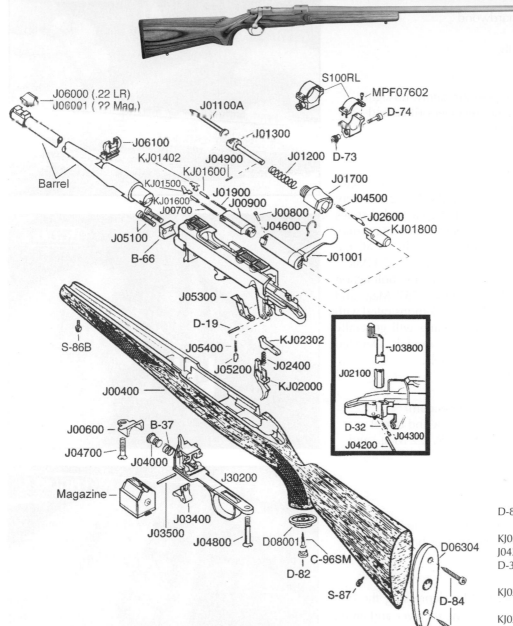

J06000 (.22 LR)
J06001 (.22 Mag.)
S100RL
MPF07602
J01100A
D-74
J06100
D-73
KJ01402
J04900
J01300
J01200
Barrel
KJ01600
J01700
KJ01500
J01900
J04500
KJ01600
J00900
J02600
J00700
J00800
KJ01800
J05100
J04600
B-66
J01001
J05300
D-19
S-86B
KJ02302
J05400
J03800
J05200
J02400
J02100
J00400
KJ02000
D-32
J04200
J04300
J00600
B-37
J04700
J04000
J30200
Magazine
J03400
J03500
J04800
D08001
D06304
C-96SM
D-82
S-87
D-84

PARTS LIST

K0J8007 Barrel
B-66 Barrel Retainer, V-Block
J05100 Barrel Retainer Screw (2 Req'd.)
KJ01001T Bolt Handle
J02600 Bolt Lock Plunger
KJ02600T Bolt Lock Plunger
J04600 Bolt Lock Plunger Retainer
J04500 Bolt Lock Plunger Spring
KJ01700T Bolt Sleeve
KJ05300T Bolt Stop

J05200 Bolt Stop Plunger
J05400 Bolt Stop Plunger Spring
KJ20901T Breech Block Assembly
J00800 Breech Block Retainer
B-91 Butt Plate Screw, 2 Req'd.
KJ01500 Cartridge Support
KJ01600 Cartridge Support Plunger
J00700 Cartridge Support Spring
KJ01800T Cocking Piece
KJ01402 Extractor
KJ01600 Extractor Plunger

J01900 Extractor Spring
J01100A Firing Pin All Models
KJ04700T Front Mounting Screw
JMX-1 Magazine Complete, 9-shot
J03402 Magazine Latch Lever
KJ03501 Magazine Latch Pivot Pin
J04000 Magazine Latch Plunger
KJ00600T Magazine Well Liner
KJ04800T Rear Mounting Screw
D06304 Recoil Pad, Black, Rubber

D-84 Recoil Pad Screw (2 Req'd.)
KJ03800 Safety Selector
J04300 Safety Selector Detent
D-32 Safety Selector Detent Spring
KJ02100 Safety Selector Retainer
KJ02303 Sear
J04200 Sear Pivot Pin
S-86B Sling Swivel Front Screw with Nut
S-87 Sling Swivel Rear Mounting Stud
J00432 Stock, Black Laminate
J01300 Striker All Models
KJ31700T Striker/Cocking Piece Assembly
J04900 Striker Cross Pin
J01200A Striker Spring
KJ02000T Trigger
KJ20201T Trigger Guard Assembly
D-19 Trigger Pivot Pin
J02400 Trigger/Sear Spring

SPECIFICATIONS

Model: K77/17-VMBBZ
Action: bolt-action
Stock: black laminate hardwood
Barrel: 24.0 in.
Weight Unloaded: 7.5 lb.
Caliber: .17 HMR
Capacity: 9
Common Features: three position safety, no sights, detachable rotary magazine, receiver drilled and tapped for mounting optics

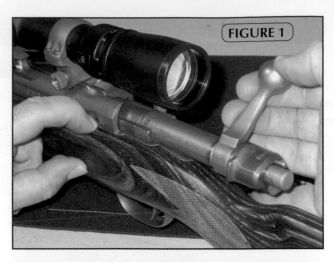

FIGURE 1

BACKGROUND

In 1983 Ruger introduced the 77/22 based on the Ruger Model 77 Mark II centerfire rifle. The 77/22 is a very popular adult-size rimfire rifle that spawned a series of bolt action rifles that use Ruger's rotary magazine. The family of rotary magazine rifle includes all the usual rimfire suspects—.22 LR, .22 Mag., .17 HMR—and relatively new to the rotary magazine, bolt action platform are two centerfire calibers—.357 Mag. and .44 Mag. The instructions below are demonstrated with a 77/17 Target rifle and field stripping will generally work for both rimfire and centerfire models. Detailed disassemble focuses on rimfire models.

Year Introduced: 1983
Country of Origin: USA
Current Manufacturer: Ruger (ruger.com)
Similar Models: 77/22 (various stock and barrel configurations, chambered for .22LR, .22 Mag., and .22 Hornet)

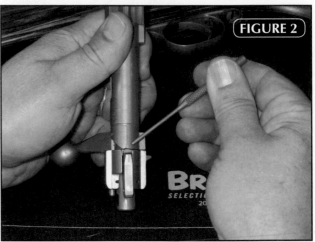

FIGURE 2

REQUIRED TOOLS

Field Stripping: none
Disassembly/Assembly: 5/64 diameter punch or nail, 1/8 inch punch, large flat blade screwdriver, brass hammer

FIELD STRIP

1. Remove the bolt assembly by depressing the bolt stop (J05300) on the left side of the receiver and lift up the bolt handle (J01001) and pull it rearward and out of the receiver, Figure 1.

At this point the rifle needs no further disassembly for cleaning.

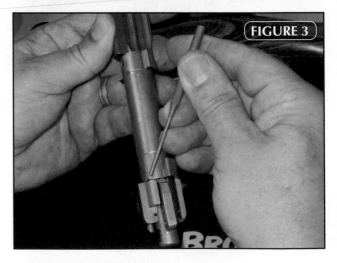

FIGURE 3

BOLT DISASSEMBLY

1. To disassemble the bolt assembly, note that the knob on the bolt sleeve is in a slight recess on the bolt, Figure 2. Hold the bolt handle and rotate the bolt sleeve (J01001) clock-wise until the striker piece knob is out of the recess in the bolt, Figure 3.

2. Next align the holes in the bolt so the breech block retaining pin (J00800) can be removed. When the holes

are aligned the breech block retaining pin may easily fall out, Figure 4. If not use a small punch to push out the breech block retaining pin from the opposite side of the bolt. Note the alignment of the holes and pin must be precise to remove the breech block retaining pin.

3. With the pin removed, Insert a 5/64 punch or a nail of the small diameter into what Ruger calls the "disassembly

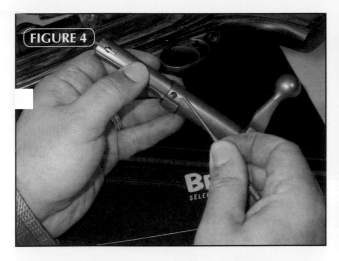

FIGURE 4

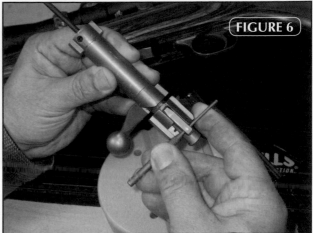

FIGURE 6

hole" in the striker/cocking piece assembly to hold it in the rear position and slide the breech block assembly (KJ20901T) forward and out of the bolt, Figure 5.

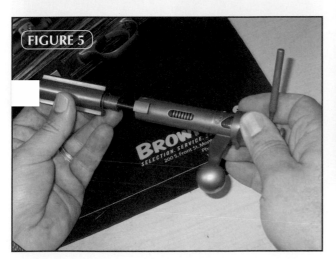

FIGURE 5

FIGURE 7

5. Gently lift the stock free from the barrel/receiver assembly.

6. To remove the trigger and sear, place the safety selector (J03800) in the "Fire" position.

7. Next drive out the trigger pivot pin (D-19), Figure 8. Note the trigger/sear spring (J02400) is under tension. Remove the trigger and trigger/sear spring.

4. Next unscrew the bolt sleeve counterclockwise and remove the bolt sleeve assembly from the bolt.

5. The firing pin (J01100A) can now be removed from the rear of the receiver, Figure 6.

BARREL/RECEIVER DISASSEMBLY

1. To remove the stock (S-87) from the barreled action, make sure the bolt and magazine have been removed. Place the rifle top-side down on a padded surface. Using a flat blade screw driver, remove the rear mounting screw (J04800) in the trigger guard (J30200).

2. Pull the rear of the trigger guard out of the stock to clear trigger (KJ02000), Figure 7.

3. Next unhook the trigger guard assembly from the receiver and remove it.

4. Next remove the front mounting screw (J04700) and magazine well liner (J00600).

FIGURE 8

8. Next remove the sear (KJ02302) by drifting out the sear pivot pin (J04200) from the side of the receiver using a small punch. Turn the receiver upside down and slide sear forward. The sear will drop out of the top of the receiver.

9. The safety assembly is removed by rotating the safety selector rearward so that the upper section is positioned fully over the center of the receiver tang. Hold the safety selector in place with your fingers thumb and forefinger and slide the safety selector retainer (J02100) up and out of receiver. Note that the safety selector is under spring tension from the safety selector detent spring (D-32). The safety selector detent spring and safety selector detent plunger need to be contained. Then lift out the safety selector, and remove the safety selector detent and safety selector detent spring.

10. To remove the bolt stop, depress the bolt stop plunger (J05400) using a small screwdriver and remove the bolt stop from the pivot. Note the bolt stop plunger spring (KJ01800) and bolt stop plunger are under tension and need to be controlled. Remove the bolt stop plunger and bolt stop plunger spring.

MAGAZINE DISASSEMBLY

For disassembling the magazine, see section for Ruger 10/22 Carbine. Rimfire and centerfire magazine are very similar.

Reassemble in reverse order.

Reassembly Tip: When reassembling the bolt, rotate the bolt sleeve assembly counterclockwise until the cocking piece engages the small notch in the bolt. Remove the nail or paperclip from the cocking piece. If the breech block does not rotate freely—about 1/16 inch is each direction—then reinsert the nail in the cocking piece disassembly hole and check that the breech block retaining pin is fully seated. When replacing the trigger guard make sure the notches on the forward on the trigger guard fir back into the tabs of the receiver. Tilt the forward end of the trigger guard into the stock first to engage the tabs and then rotate the rear of the trigger guard into the stock.

Rimfire Lever Action

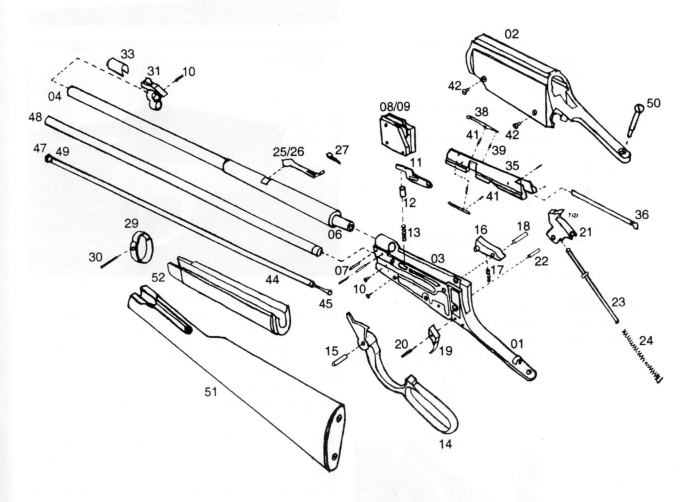

PARTS LIST

01 Receiver
02 Cover
03 Carrier Axle
04 Barrel
06 Cylinder Pin
07 Taper Pin
08/09 Carrier
10 Carrier Screw
11 Carrier Feed Lever
12 Carrier Tube

13 Carrier Spring
14 Lever
15 Lever Pin
16 Lock Bar
17 Locking Bar Spring
18 Locking Bar Pin
19 Trigger
20 Trigger Spring
21 Hammer
22 Hammer Pin
23 Hammer Guide
24 Hammer Spring

25/26 Rear Sight
27 Rear Sight Elevator
29 Barrel Band
30 Barrel Band Screw
31 Front Sight
33 Sight Cover
35 Bolt
36 Firing Pin
37 Firing Pin Spring
38 Extractor
39 Spring
40 Ejector

41 Ejector Pin
42 Cover Screw
44 Inner Mag Tube
45 Magazine Spring Guide
46 Magazine Spring
47 Magazine Button
48 Outer Tube
49 Notch Pin
50 Stock Screw
51 Buttstock Assembly
52 Fore End
54 Trigger Pin

SPECIFICATIONS

Model: Henry Lever Action .22 Model H001
Action: Lever
Barrel: 18.75 in.
Caliber: .22 Short/Long/LR
Capacity: 21 (.22 short), 17 (.22 Long), 15 (.22 LR)
Common Features: straight-grip American walnut stock, adjustable rear/fixed hooded front sight, half cock safety, grooved receiver for mounting optics

BACKGROUND

The Henry Lever Action .22 is a traditional lever action rifle with exposed hammer. The tube magazine is feed via a port in the tube. Though no direct lineage to the late 19th century Henry rifle, these modern rimfire plinkers do live up to the Henry reputation with exceptionally smooth actions.
Year Introduced: 1997
Country of Origin: USA
Current Manufacturer: Henry Repeating Arms (henryrepeating.com)
Similar Models: Lever Action Magnum (.22 Mag), Lever Action Octagon Frontier Model (.22 Short/Long/LR or .22 Mag or .17 HMR; blued finish), Carbine (16 in. barrel), Youth (13 in. length of pull)

REQUIRED TOOLS

Disassembly/Assembly: medium flat blade screwdriver, small and medium sized punches, brass/nylon hammer, vise grips, needle nose pliers

DISASSEMBLY

1. Unscrew the receiver cover tang screw (part #50) and remove the buttstock (51), Figure 1.
2. Next remove the four receiver cover screws (42), Figure 2.
3. Lift off the receiver cover (02), Figure 3.
4. Slide the bolt (35) out the rear of the receiver cover.

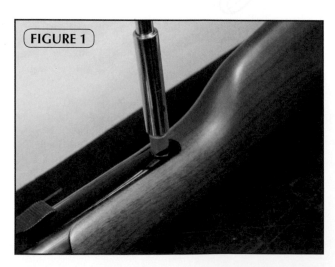

FIGURE 1

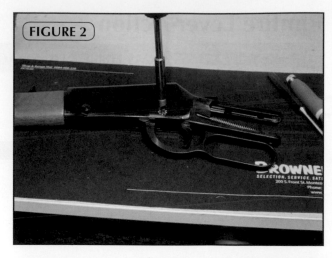

FIGURE 2

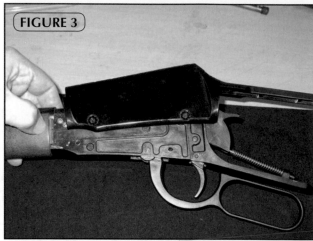

FIGURE 3

5. To remove the firing pin (36) from the bolt, drift out the firing pin retaining pin at the rear of the bolt.
6. The extractor (38) and ejector (40) are removed by drifting out the ejector pin (41) and extractor pin (41) from the bottom to the top of the bolt.
7. Next cock back the hammer (21) as far as it will go to compress the hammer spring (24) along the hammer guide (23) and capture the hammer guide with a pair of vise grips near the hammer guide support on the receiver (01), Figure 4. Note the hammer spring is under tension.
8. Next push out the hammer pin (22) using a small punch. With the hammer spring retained, the hammer will come free, Figure 5.
9. The trigger (19) is removed by drifting out the trigger pin. Remove the trigger and the trigger spring (20) through the back of the receiver.
10. The lock bar (16) is removed by drifting out the locking bar pin (18); ensure the lever (14) is closed and remove the lock bar slightly to the rear and up and out of the top of the receiver.

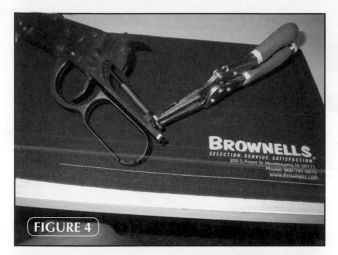

12. The lever is removed by pushing out the lever pin (15) and gently maneuvering the lever out from the bottom of the receiver.

13. Next remove the carrier (08/09) by removing the two carrier screws (10) from the left side of the receiver. Then depress downward on the carrier feed lever (11) and carrier spring (13) with a small flat blade screwdriver and remove the carrier up and out the top of the receiver.

14. Remove the carrier lever by sliding it off its receiver post on the left inside wall of the receiver.

Reassemble in reverse order.

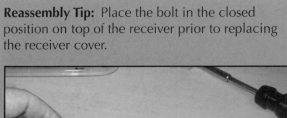

Reassembly Tip: Place the bolt in the closed position on top of the receiver prior to replacing the receiver cover.

FIGURE 5

11. The locking bar spring (17) can then be pulled out from the top of the receiver with a pair of needle nose pliers.

Rimfire Single Shot

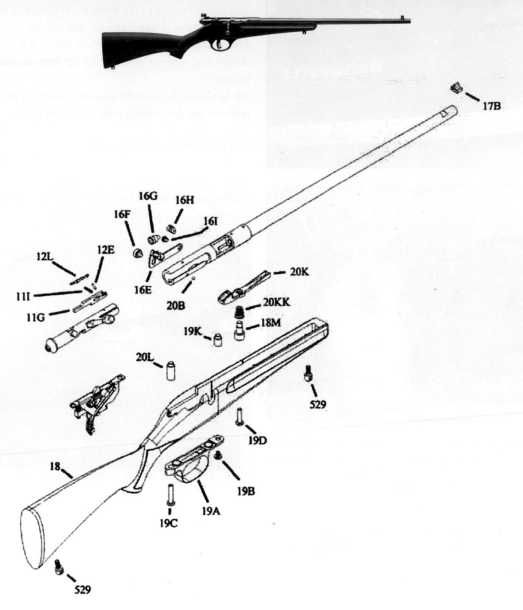

PARTS LIST

11I Firing Pin Retaining Pin
12E Extractor Pin
11G Firing Pin
12L Extractor
16E Sight Bracket
16F Rear Sight Locking Screw
16G Rear Aperture

16H Aperture Nut
16I ear Sight Pivot Screw
17B Front Sight Blade
18 Stock Assembly
18 Front Stud
19A Trigger Guard (Wood Stock)
19B Trigger Guard Screw (Wood Stock)
19C Rear Action Screw

19D Front Action Screw
19K Action stud
20B Safety Insert
20K Loading Platform/Feed Ramp
20KK Feed Ramp Spring
20L Rear Action Screw Stud
529 Swivel Stud

SPECIFICATIONS

Model: Rascal
Action: bolt
Barrel: 16.12 in.
Weight Unloaded: 2.7 lb.

Caliber: .22 LR
Capacity: 1
Common Features: two position safety, open sights, single shot, drilled and tapped for scope mounts, synthetic stock

BACKGROUND

The Rascal is Savage's latest entry in the youth rifle market. The rifle looks like it was shrunk in the dryer to fit a youngster's stature.

Year Introduced: 2012
Current Manufacturer: Savage Arms (savagearms.com)

REQUIRED TOOLS

Field Stripping: none
Disassembly/Assembly: 5/32 hex or Allen wrench, small roll pin punch, brass hammer

FIELD STRIP

1. Push the safety lever to the "fire" position.
2. Lift the bolt handle and pull the bolt to the rear of the action.
3. Press back on the trigger fully and at the same time pull the bolt out of the receiver, Figure 1.

At this point the Rascal is sufficiently disassembled for cleaning.

BOLT DISASSEMBLY

1. Use a small roll pin punch to drift out the firing pin retaining pin (11I), Figure 2. The firing pin (11G) will fall free from the bolt.
2. Use the same small punch to drift of the extractor pin (12E) and remove the extractor (12L) and extractor spring.

BARREL/RECEIVER DISASSEMBLY

1. Using a 5/32 hex or Allen wrench remove the front action screw (19D) and the rear action screw (19B) from the bottom of the stock assembly (18), Figure 3.
2. Lift out the barrel/receiver assembly from the stock, Figure 4.
5. Unscrew and remove the two trigger housing assembly screws using a hex or Allen wrench and lift the trigger housing assembly from the barrel/receiver assembly.

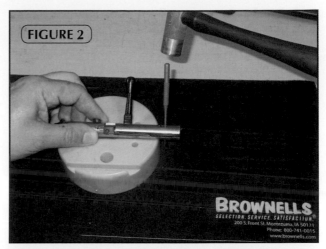
FIGURE 2

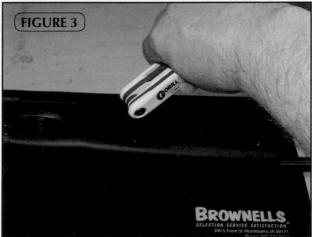
FIGURE 3

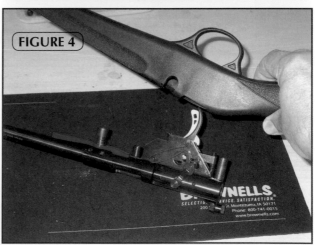
FIGURE 4

Reassemble in reverse order.

Tuning Tip: The Rascal has a similar AccuTrigger as centerfire rifles. Adjust the trigger pull weight by inserting the AccuTrigger tool into the bottom of the trigger return spring to engage the tail of the spring with the slot in the tool. Turn clockwise increase pull weight, counterclockwise to decrease pull weight.

FIGURE 1

Black Powder

Pistols

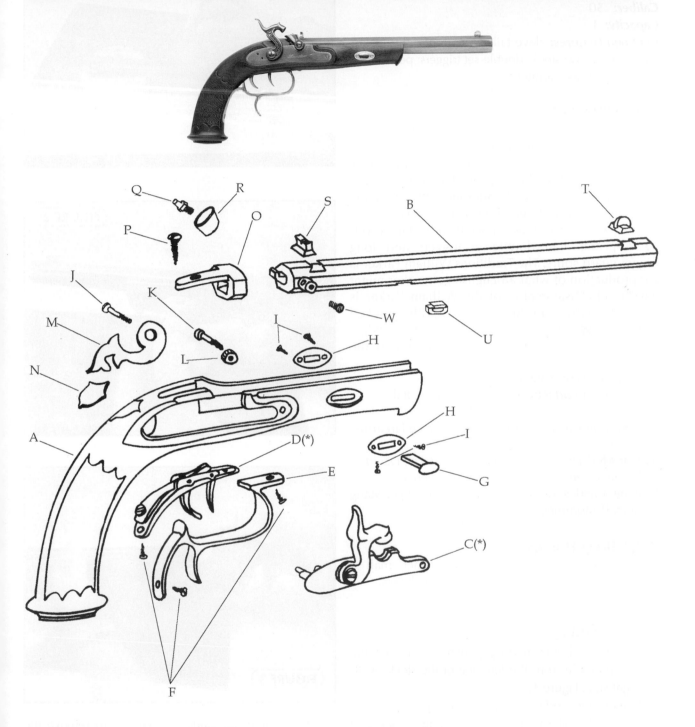

PARTS LIST

A Stock
B Barrel
C Percussion Lock
D Trigger Assembly
E Trigger Guard

F Trigger Guard Screw
  (3 Req'd.)
G Wedge
H Wedge Plate (2 Req'd.)
I Wedge Plate Screw
  (4 Req'd.)

J Rear Lock Screw
K Front Lock Screw
M Stock Plate
O Barrel Tang
P Tang Screw
Q Nipple

R Flash Cup
S Rear Sight
T Front Sight
U Barrel Tenon
W Bolster Screw

SPECIFICATIONS

Model: Traditions William Parker
Action: percussion lock ignition
Barrel: 10.375 in.
Caliber: .50
Capacity: 1
Common Features: dove-tailed rear/front sights; checkered wood stock; double-set triggers; polished steel finish; brass furniture

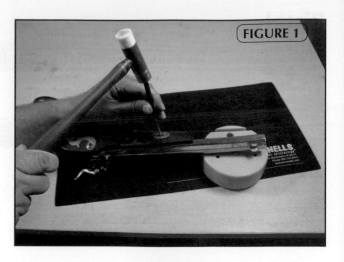

FIGURE 1

BACKGROUND

At one time dueling was an accepted method to resolve disputes among respectable gentlemen and dueling pistols were a part of many a gentlemen's accouterment. The dueling pistol was typically a large caliber and ornately adorned with engraving and select wood. A matched pairs of pistols with loading accessories were elegantly boxed in velvet. Some pistols had double-set triggers and long trigger guard spurs. The Traditions William Parker is a reproduction of what an English gun maker might have built. Disassembly of the William Parker is similar to many reproduction pistols with a hooked breech plug, percussion side lock and a wedge/tenon pin method of securing the barrel to the stock.

Year Introduced: 1800s
Country of Manufacture: England, France, Italy, Spain
Current Importer: Traditions Performance Firearms (traditionsfirearms.com)
Similar Models: Traditions: Trapper, Crocket; Davide Pedersoli (davide-pedersoli.com): Continental Dueling, Charles Moore, Kuchenreuter, Le Page, Mang in Graz, P. Mortimer,

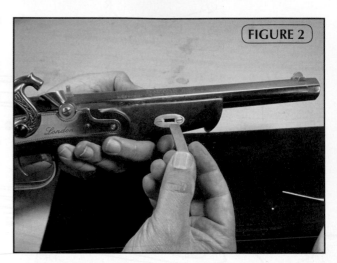

FIGURE 2

REQUIRED TOOLS

Disassembly/Assembly: nylon/brass hammer, small punch, medium and large flat blade screwdrivers, nipple wrench

DISASSEMBLY

1. Use a small non-marring punch to drift out the wedge (part #G) from the left side of the stock (A) to the right side, Figure 1.
2. Remove the wedge from the stock, Figure 2.
3. Lift the barrel (B) up and out of the stock and disengage the hook on the barrel breech plug out of the barrel tang (O), Figure 3.

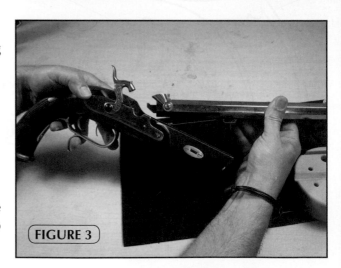

FIGURE 3

4. Use a large flat blade screwdriver to remove the bolster screw (W), Figure 4.
5. Remove the nipple (Q) using a nipple wrench.

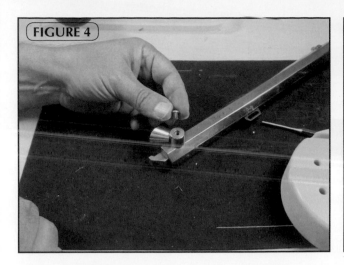

FIGURE 4

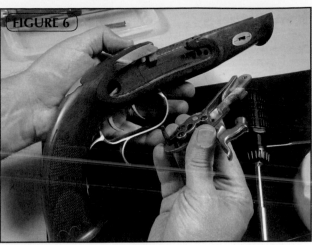

FIGURE 6

6. Use a medium flat blade screwdriver to remove the front lock screw (K) and rear lock screw (J) from the left side of the stock, Figure 5.

At this point no further disassembly is required for cleaning the barrel and lock.

Reassemble reversing the procedure.

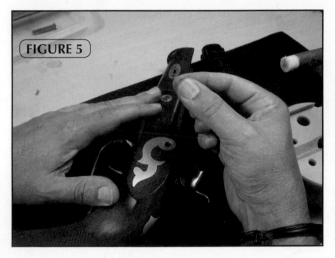

FIGURE 5

Reassembly Tip: Use a non-marring nylon hammer to drive home the wedge.

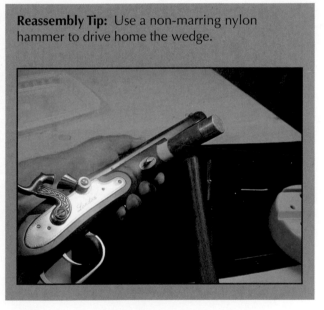

7. Gently pull the lock (C) from the right side of the stock, Figure 6.

Revolvers

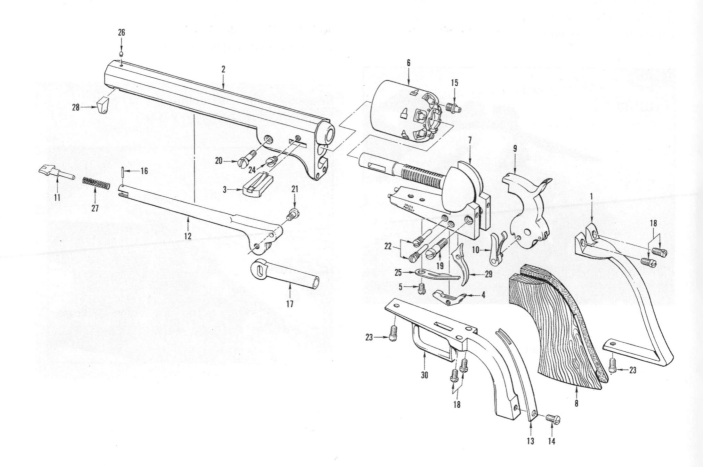

PARTS LIST

1. Backstrap
2. Barrel
3. Barrel Wedge Assembly
4. Bolt
5. Bolt Spring Screw
6. Cylinder Assembly
7. Frame
8. Grip
9. Hammer Assembly

10. Hand & Spring Assembly
11. Latch, Loading Lever
12. Lever, Loading
13. Mainspring
14. Mainspring Screw
15. Nipple
16. Pin, Latch Retaining
17. Plunger, Loading

18. Backstrap and Trigger Guard Screw
19. Hammer Screw
20. Loading Lever Screw
21. Plunger Screw
22. Trigger Bolt & Trigger Screw
23. Trigger Guard & Butt Screw

24. Wedge Screw
25. Sear and Bolt Spring
26. Sight, Front
27. Spring, Latch
28. Stud, Barrel
29. Trigger
30. Trigger Guard

SPECIFICATIONS

Model: 1851 Navy
Action: revolver; SA
Overall Length: 13 in.
Overall Height: 4.9 in.
Overall Width: 1.54 in.
Barrel: 7.5 in.
Weight Unloaded: 42.3 oz.
Caliber: .36
Capacity: 6
Common Features: case colored frame, blued octagon barrel, brass backstrap/trigger guard, notched hammer rear/brass front sight, smooth walnut grip

BACKGROUND

The Colt 1851 Navy was known in the day as the Navy Revolver for the fact that the revolver was engraved with a naval battle scene on the cylinder in appreciation for Second Texas Navy purchasing Colt's first successful revolver the Paterson. During the Civil War both sides used the Navy revolver. Robert E. Lee carried one. Perhaps the most famous gunslinger to pack a pair of Colt Navy revolvers was Wild Bill Hickok. Samuel Colt was a consummate marketer and not only was the Navy a popular gun in the cap-and-ball era it continued to be used well after metallic cartridge revolvers were introduced. They are nicely balanced and easy to carry. Navy revolvers and other Colts of the period are known as open top revolvers because they do not have a top strap like modern revolvers. The takedown for the Navy and Colt's other open-top revolvers such as the Walker, Dragoons, Army and other revolvers is very similar.

Year Introduced: 1851
Country of Origin: USA
Original Manufacturer: Colt (coltsmfg.com)
Current Manufacturers: EMF (emf-company.com), Traditions (traditionsfirearms.com), Uberti (uberti.com)
Similar Models: 1847 Walker, 1848 1st/2nd/3rd Model Dragoon, 1849 Pocket Dragoon, 1851 Navy squareback (square back trigger guard), 1860 Army, 1861 Navy (round barrel), 1862 Pocket Navy

REQUIRED TOOLS

Field Stripping: nylon hammer
Disassembly/Assembly: small flat blade screwdriver, nipple wrench

FIELD STRIP

1. Pull back the hammer (part #9) to half cock.
2. Use a nylon hammer to tap the barrel wedge pin (3) from the right side of the barrel (2), Figure 1. Note that the wedge pin for a Colt Walker is drifted from left to right.

FIGURE 1

3. Grasp the wedge pin and pull it as far as the wedge screw (24) will allow, Figure 2.

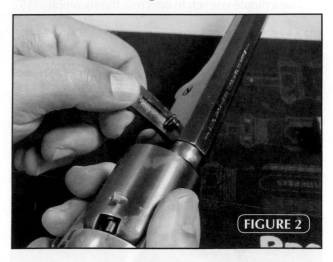

FIGURE 2

4. Pull the barrel forward from the frame (7), Figure 3.
5. Pull the cylinder (6) from the frame, Figure 4.

At this point the Navy is field stripped.

FIGURE 3

FIGURE 4

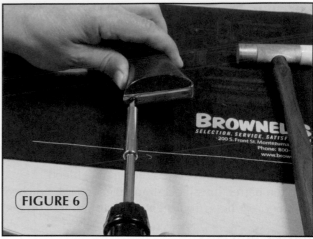

FIGURE 6

CYLINDER DISASSEMBLY

1. Use a nipple wrench to unscrew the six nipples (15).

FRAME DISASSEMBLY

1. Use a small flat blade screwdriver to remove the two backstrap screws (18), Figure 5. Remove the trigger

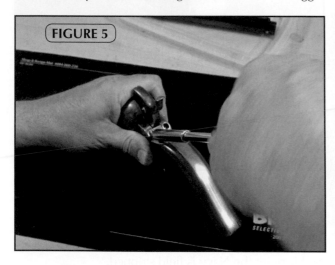

FIGURE 5

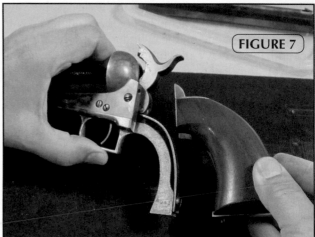

FIGURE 7

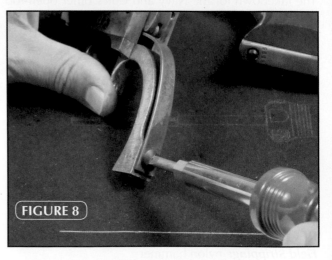

FIGURE 8

guard & butt screw (23), Figure 6. The backstrap (1) and grip (8) will come free from the frame, Figure 7.

2. Remove the mainspring screw (14), Figure 8. Then pull the mainspring (13) free from the hammer.

3. Next remove the two trigger guard screws (18) and one trigger guard & butt screw (23). The trigger guard (30) will fall free.

4. Unscrew the bolt spring screw (5) and remove the sear and bolt spring (25).

5. Remove the trigger screw (22) and pull the trigger (29) from the bottom of the frame.

6. Unscrew the bolt screw (22) and remove the bolt from the bottom of the frame.

7. Take out the hammer screw (19) and the hammer and hand & spring assembly (10) will come free as an assembly.

BARREL DISASSEMBLY

1. Use a medium flat blade screwdriver to remove the plunger screw (20) and the loading lever assembly—loading lever (12), loading lever latch (11), loading plunger (17)—will come free from the barrel, Figure 9.

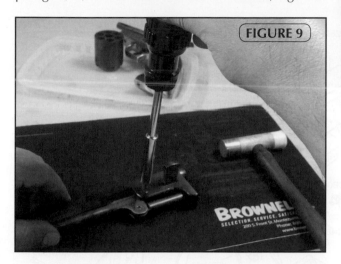

FIGURE 9

Reassemble in reverse order.

Tuning Tip: All open top Colts employ a barrel wedge to hold the barrel to the frame and cylinder. The farther in the wedge is pushed in, the tighter the barrel-to-cylinder gap. If the wedge is pushed too far inward, the barrel will bind against the face of the cylinder and jam the revolver. If the cylinder binds, slightly tap the wedge out to unbind the barrel against the cylinder.

RUGER OLD ARMY

PARTS LIST

CB-6 Barrel Assembly
CB02900 Base Pin
CB02800 Base Pin Retaining Pin Assembly
CB00900 Bullet Rammer
CB-1 Cylinder
CB04500 Cylinder Latch
CB03400 Cylinder Latch Pivot

KCB04600 Cylinder Latch Spring
CB00200 Frame
CB-36 Front Sight
CB00300 Grip
XR01700 Grip Frame Screw-A-Front
XR01800 Grip Frame Screw-B-Back (2 Req'd.)
XR01900 Grip Frame Screw-C-Bottom

XR01000 Grip Panels
KXR01400 Grip Panel Dowel
XR01200 Grip Panel Ferrule, Left
XR01100 Grip Panel Ferrule, Right
KXR01300 Grip Panel Screw
CB04000 Hammer
CB01600 Hammer Pivot
KCB04102 Hammer Plunger
KE-22 Hammer Plunger Pin

KCB04300 Hammer Plunger Spring
XR01500 Hammer Strut
CB00800 Loading
CB06700 Loading Lever Latch
CB06800 Loading Lever Latch Screw
KCB06900 Loading Lever Latch Spring
CB00400 Mainspring
XR00500 Mainspring Seat

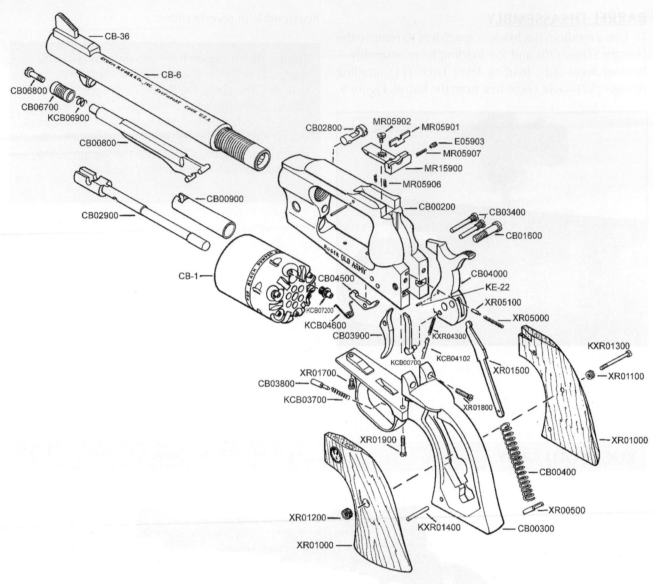

KCB07200 Nipple (6 Req'd.)
KCB00700 Pawl
XR05100 Pawl Plunger
XR05000 Pawl Plunger Spring
MR15900 Rear Sight Assembly
MR05902 Rear Sight

Elevation Screw
MR05901 Rear Sight Blade
MR05906 Rear Sight Elevation
  Spring, Adjustable
  (2 Req'd.)
MR05600 Rear Sight Pivot Pin

E05903 Rear Sight Windage
  Adjustment Screw
MR05907 Rear Sight Windage
  Spring
CB03900 Trigger
CB03400 Trigger Pivot Screw

CB03800 Trigger Plunger
KCB03700 Trigger Spring

SPECIFICATIONS

Model: Old Army
Action: revolver; SA
Overall Length: 13 in.
Overall Height: 4.9 in.
Overall Width: 1.54 in.
Barrel: 7.5 in.
Weight Unloaded: 32.8 oz.
Caliber: .45
Capacity: 6
Common Features: blued or stainless finish, adjustable
rear/fixed front sight, smooth rosewood grip

BACKGROUND

From the outside the Old Army looks similar to the
Remington 1858 revolver but inside it uses a mechanism
that is similar to Ruger Blackhawk single action revolvers.
The Old Army is thoroughly modern with coil springs
throughout, stainless steel nipples and adjustable sights.
The most recently manufactured models wore fixed sights.
Once the loading lever and cylinder are removed the frame
disassembly is similar to the New Model Blackhawk.
Year Introduced: 1972
Country of Origin: USA
Original Manufacturer: Ruger (ruger.com)

REQUIRED TOOLS

Field Stripping: medium flat blade screwdriver
Disassembly/Assembly: small flat blade screwdriver, nipple wrench, retaining pin, small flat blade screwdriver

FIELD STRIP

1. Pull back the hammer (part #CB04000) one click so the cylinder rotates.

2. Use a medium flat blade screwdriver to rotate the base pin retaining pin assembly (CB02800) counter-clockwise until it stops, Figure 1.

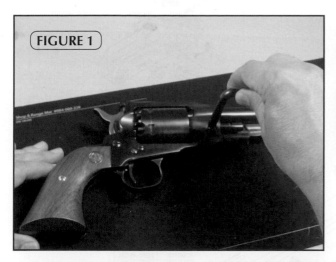

FIGURE 1

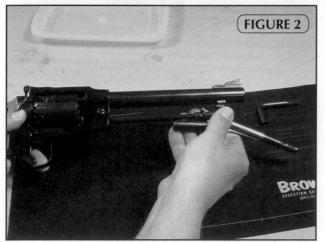

FIGURE 2

3. Pull back on the loading lever latch (CB06700) and swing the loading lever (CB00800) down from the underside of the barrel (CB-6).

4. Pull the rammer/base pin assembly toward the muzzle until it come free from the frame (CB00200), Figure 2.

5. The cylinder (CB-1) can then be removed from the right side of the frame, Figure 3.

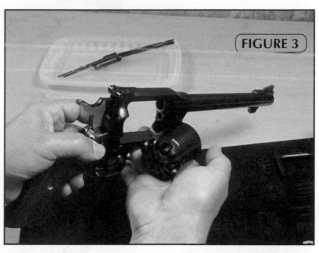

FIGURE 3

At this point the Old Army is sufficiently disassembled for cleaning.

CYLINDER DISASSEMBLY

1. Use a nipple wrench to unscrew the six nipples (KCB07200).

FRAME DISASSEMBLY

Follow the frame disassembly procedures for the Ruger New Model Blackhawk as the mechanisms are very similar.

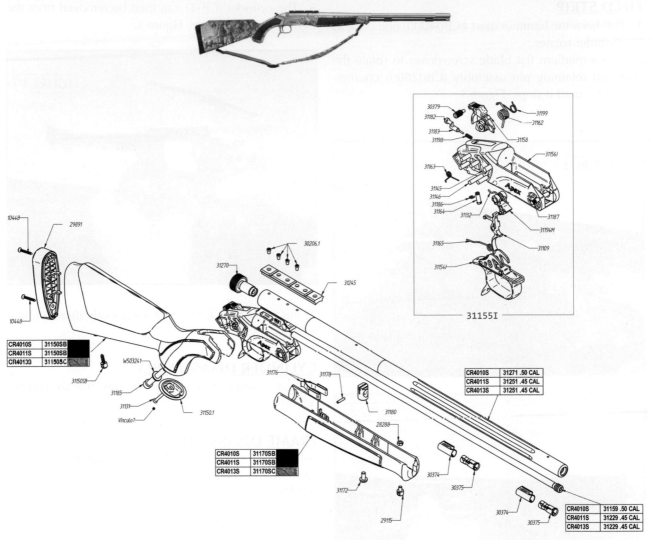

311155I

PARTS LIST

31150 Stock
10448 Recoil Pad Screw
  (2 Req'd.)
29891 Recoil Pad
31150SB Rear Sling Stud
31131 Stock Cap Screw
W503241 Stock Bolt
  washer
31185 Stock Bolt
31150.1 Stock Cap
31172 Fore end screw

30374 Ram Rod Thimble
  (2 Req'd.)
30375 Ram Rod Thimble Insert
  (2 Req'd.)
31270 Breech Plug
30206.1 Scope Mount Screw
  (4 Req'd.)
31245 Scope Mount
31178 Pin
31180 Fore End Fixture
31176 Ram Rod Retention Spring
28288 Front Sling Swivel Stud Nut

29115 Front Sling Swivel Stud
31170 Fore End
31182 Firing Pin Extension
30379 Hammer Extension
31198 Firing Pin Spring
31156I Frame
31163 Spring
31146 Pin
31145 Pin
31186 Trigger Adjustment Screw
  Retainer
31164 Trigger Adjustment Screw

31132 Barrel Catch Spring
31187 Barrel Pivot Pin
31109 Trigger
31165 Spring
31154I Trigger Guard
31155I Frame Assembly
31183 Firing Pin
31194M Barrel Catch
31199 Spring
31162 Hammer Spring
31158 Hammer

SPECIFICATIONS

Model: Apex Muzzleloader
Action: Single shot, SA, break-open, in-line ignition
Barrel: 25 in. (centerfire/rimfire calibers), 27 in.
(muzzleloader)

Caliber: .45 or .50
Capacity: 1
Common Features: scope mount; black or camo
synthetic stock; exposed hammer; stainless or blued
finish

BACKGROUND

The Apex offers the versatility of swapping barrels from centerfire to muzzleloader to rimfire. Some 14 calibers are available. The action breaks open by pulling on the trigger guard. Typically only the barrel needs to be removed for a thorough cleaning. Instructions below are for the Apex muzzleloader set-up.

Year Introduced: 2009
Country of Manufacture: Spain
Current Importer: CVA (cva.com)
Similar Models: Apex Centerfire, Apex Rimfire

REQUIRED TOOLS

Field Strip: none
Disassembly/Assembly: large flat blade screwdriver, small Phillips screwdriver, small punch, brass hammer, 6mm hex bit socket and ratchet or 6mm hex or Allen wrench

FIELD STRIP

1. Remove the ramrod (part #31159).
2. Pull the trigger guard (311541) backward to open the action, Figure 1.
3. Remove the breech plug (31270) from the breech end of the barrel (31271) using your fingers.

FIGURE 2

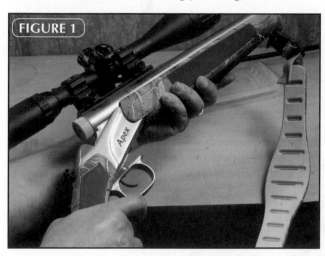

FIGURE 1

FIGURE 3

At this point no further disassembly is required for cleaning.

DETAILED DISASSEMBLY

1. Remove the fore end (31170) by unscrewing and removing the fore end screw (31172) using a large flat blade screwdriver.
2. Drift out the barrel pivot pin (31187) using small punch and brass hammer, Figure 2.
3. With the barrel pivot pin removed the barrel (31271) will pivot forward and off the frame (31156I), Figure 3.

4. To remove the stock (31150), first unscrew and remove the stock cap screw (31131) and remove the stock cap (31150.1), Figure 4. Use a 6mm hex or Allen wrench or 6mm hex bit socket and ratchet to remove the stock bolt (31185), Figure 5. Then pull the stock from the frame.

Reassemble reversing the procedure.

FIGURE 4

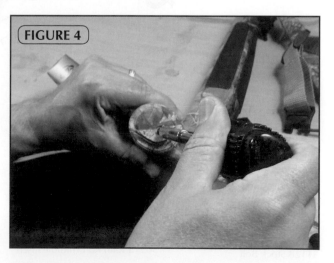

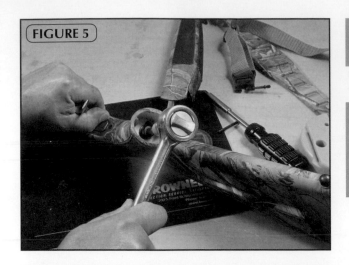

FIGURE 5

Reassembly Tip: Reinstall the barrel pivot pin with the action in the open position.

Cleaning Tip: Pull the stock off and use a solvent and dry cloth to clean the mechanism. Give the mechanism a good blast of canned air to blow out any black powder grit. Add a dab of grease on the barrel pivot pin before reassembling.

CVA OPTIMA

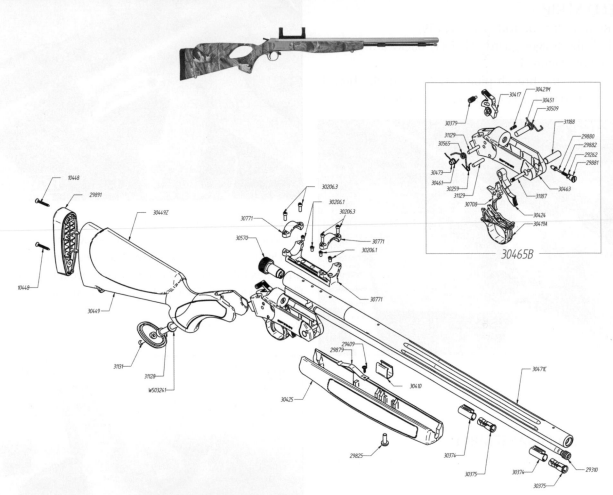

30465B

PARTS LIST

10448 Recoil Pad Screw (2 Req'd.)
29891 Recoil Pad
30449Z Stock Check Piece
31131 Stock Cap and Screw
31128 Stock Bolt

W503241 Stock Bolt Washer
29825 Fore End Screw
29879 Ram Rod Retaining Spring
30410 Ram Rod Fore End Channel
30374 Ram Rod Thimble
30375 Ram Rod Thimble Insert

29310 Ram Rod
30206.3 Scope Ring Screw (4 Req'd.)
30206.1 Scope Mount Screw (4 Req'd.)
30570 Breech Plug
29409 Ram Rod Retaining Spring

Screw
30771 Top Scope Ring (2 Req'd.)
30449 Stock
30425 Fore end
30465B Frame Assembly
30419A Trigger Guard
30424 Barrel Catch

31187 Barrel Pivot Pin	31188 Barrel Pivot Pin Bushing
30463 Frame	30509 Barrel Catch Spring
29881 Firing Pin Bushing	30451 Barrel Catch Pivot Pin
29262 Firing Pin Bushing Sleeve	30421M
29882 Firing Pin Spring	30708 Trigger
29880 Firing Pin	31129 Trigger Guard and Trigger

Pin	30565 Hammer Spring
30259 Trigger Spring	30379 Hammer Extension
30473 Ram Rod Bracket (2 Req'd.)	30417 Hammer
30461 Spring	30471C Barrel
31129 Hammer Pin	

SPECIFICATIONS

Model: Optima
Action: Single shot, SA, break-open, inline
Barrel: 26 in
Caliber: .50
Capacity: 1
Common Features: adjustable rear/fix front fiber optic sights or scope mount; black or camo synthetic traditional or thumbhole stock; .209 primer ignition; stainless, blued or stainless finishes

BACKGROUND

The Optima is an inline muzzleloader with a breech plug that can be removed by hand even after numerous shots. No wrench required. It features a break-open action and a fluted stainless steel barrel. The Optima is completely ambidextrous. The trigger mechanism is not normally disassembled for cleaning.
Year Introduced: 2003
Country of Manufacture: Spain
Current Importer: CVA (cva.com)
Similar Models: Optima Pistol

REQUIRED TOOLS

Field Strip: none
Disassembly/Assembly: medium flat blade screwdriver

FIELD STRIP

1. Remove the ramrod (part #29310).
2. Press the barrel catch (30424) to open the action.
3. Remove the breech plug (30570) from the breech end of the barrel (30471C) using your fingers, Figure 1.

FIGURE 1

At this point no further disassembly is required for cleaning.

DETAILED DISASSEMBLY

1. Close the action.
2. Use a medium flat blade screwdriver to remove the fore end screw (29825) and pull the fore end (30425) off of the barrel, Figure 2.

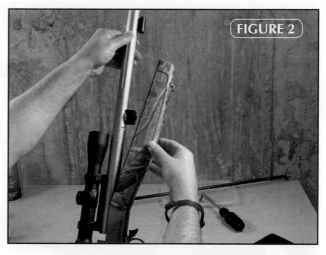

FIGURE 2

3. Press the barrel catch to open the action and the barrel will pivot forward and off of the frame (30463), Figure 3.

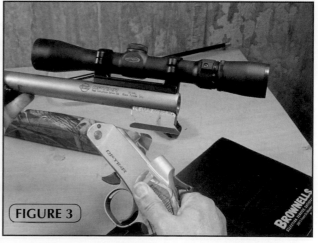

FIGURE 3

4. Using a small flat blade screwdriver remove the firing pin bushing (29881) from the breech face of the frame, Figure 4. The firing pin (29880) and firing pin spring (29882) will come out of the frame.

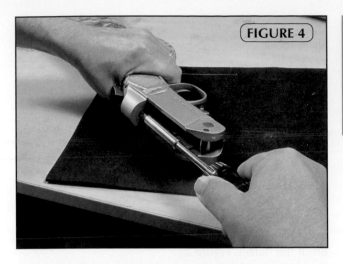

FIGURE 4

Cleaning Tip: Clean the firing pin bushing, firing pin and firing pin spring as well as the firing pin bushing hole in the frame thoroughly, then lubricate the threads on the firing pin bushing with an anti-seize compound. Apply anti-seize compound generously to the breech plug threads.

Reassemble reversing the procedure.

LYMAN MUSTANG

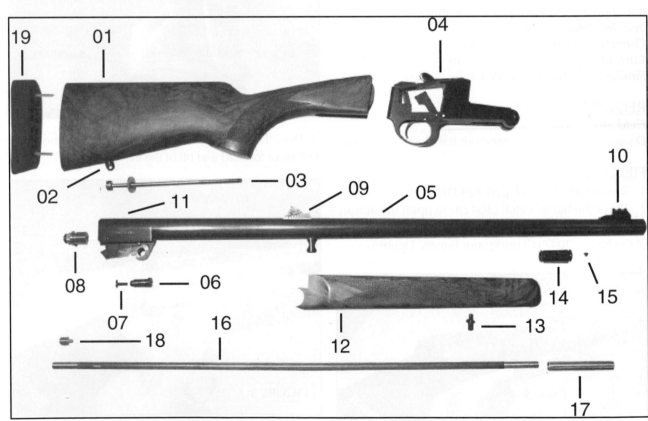

PARTS LIST

01 Stock
02 Rear Sling Swivel Stud
03 Stock Bolt
04 Receiver Assembly

05 Barrel
06 Barrel Hinge Screw
07 Barrel Hinge Stop Screw
08 Breech Plug
09 Rear Sight and Mounting Screw

10 Front Sight and Mounting Screw
11 6-48 Plug Screw (4 Req'd.)
12 Forend
13 Front Sling Swivel Stud
14 Ramrod Thimble

15 Ramrod Thimble Screw
16 Ramrod
17 Ramrod Handle Extension
18 Cleaning Jag
19 Recoil Pad and Screws (2 Req'd.)

SPECIFICATIONS

Model: Mustang Breakaway 209 Magnum
Action: Single shot, SA, break-open, inline
Barrel: 26 in.
Caliber: .50
Capacity: 1
Common Features: adjustable rear/fix front fiber optic sights; checkered wood stock; .209 primer ignition; blue finish; drilled and tapped for optics; ambidextrous safety

BACKGROUND

The Mustang Breakaway utilizes a break-open, hammerless action with a silent thumb safety. The barrel has an easily removable breech plug, is drilled and tapped for mounting a scope, and uses 209 shotgun primers for its ignition system.
Year Introduced: 2006
Country of Origin: Spain
Current Importer: Lyman Products (lymanproducts.com)

REQUIRED TOOLS

Disassembly/Assembly: 1/2 inch hex socket and ratchet, small punch, two flat blade screwdrivers, Philips screwdriver

FIELD STRIP

1. Remove the ramrod (part #16) from the ramrod thimbles (14) and open the action by pivoting the thumb lever to the right.
2. Remove the breech plug (08) from the breech end of the barrel (05) using a ½ inch socket/box end/open end wrench, Figure 1.

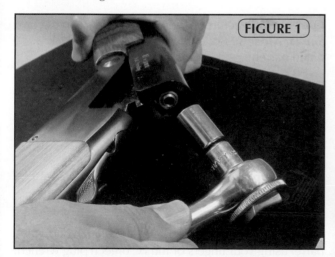

FIGURE 1

At this point the Mustang can be cleaned without further disassembly.

DETAILED DISASSEMBLY

1. Remove the forend by unscrewing the front sling swivel stud (13) with a small punch or screwdriver

inserted into the hole of the front sling swivel stud, Figure 2. Then pull down on the front of the forend and pull it from the barrel, Figure 3.

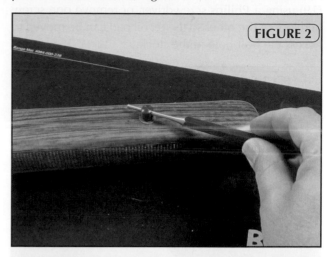

FIGURE 2

FIGURE 3

2. Use two flat blade screwdrivers to unscrew the barrel hinge stop screw (07) from the barrel hinge screw (06) and remove them from receiver assembly (04), Figure 4.

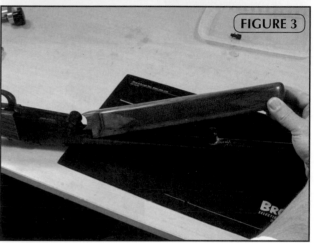

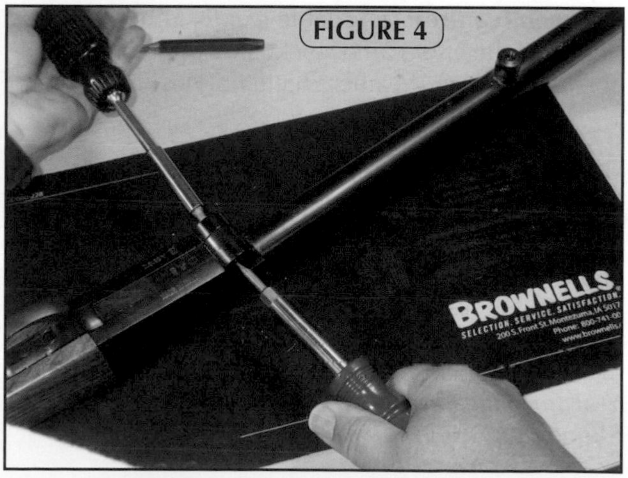

FIGURE 4

3. The barrel can now be removed from the receiver assembly.

4. Remove the two recoil pad screws and recoil pad (19) using a Philips screwdriver, or remove one screw and loosen the other so the recoil pad can be moved to access the bolt hole in the stock.

FIGURE 5

5. Next remove the stock (01) by using a long shaft flat blade screwdriver to unscrew and remove the stock bolt (03), Figure 5. With the stock bolt removed, pull the stock from the receiver assembly, Figure 6.

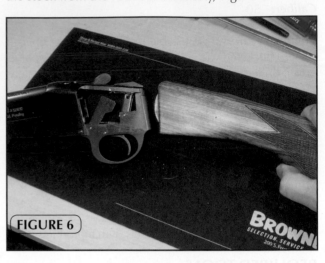

FIGURE 6

Reassemble in reverse order.

THOMPSON/CENTER TRIUMPH

SPECIFICATIONS
Model: Triumph
Action: Single shot, SA, break-open, inline
Barrel: 28 in.
Caliber: .50
Capacity: 1
Common Features: adjustable rear/fix front fiber optic sights; synthetic or camo stock; .209 primer ignition; blue, stainless or Weather Shield finishes

BACKGROUND
The Triumph is simplicity itself borrowing the fire-control system from the Omega rifle and adding a break action for easy loading and cleaning. They are known for their crisp trigger pulls. The real triumph for the Triumph is the Speed Breech XT which allows the breech plug to be removed by hand by merely rotating the breech plug a quarter turn.
Year Introduced: 2008
Country of Origin: USA

Current Manufacturer: Thompson Center (tcarms.com)
Similar Models: Bone Collector (Flex Tech stock, fluted barrel)

REQUIRED TOOLS
Field Strip: TC breech plug wrench
Disassembly/Assembly: 1/16 inch hex or Allen wrench, small punch

FIELD STRIP
1. Open the action by pivoting the trigger guard forward.

2. Remove the breech plug from the breech end of the barrel using your fingers or the TC breech plug wrench. Turn the breech plug ¼ turn counterclockwise and pull it out of the barrel, Figure 1.

At this point the Triumph can be cleaned without further disassembly.

FIGURE 1

DETAILED DISASSEMBLY

1. To further disassembly, pull the ramrod from the thimbles then unscrew the two forend screws and remove the forend from barrel.

2. Use a 1/16 inch hex or Allen wrench to loosen the pivot pin retaining screw, Figure 2. You do not have to completely remove the pivot pin retaining screw just

enough to push the trigger guard pivot pin out of the trigger guard with a punch, Figure 3.

3. Using two medium flat blade screwdrivers, remove the barrel hinge pin retaining screw and barrel pivot pin from on each side of the receiver, Figure 4.

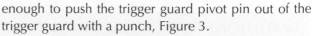
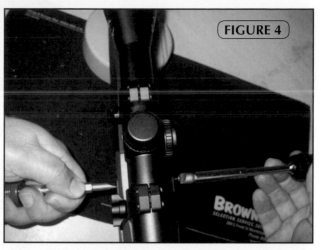
FIGURE 4

4. Push the barrel pivot pin out of the receiver and the barrel will detach from the receiver, Figure 5.

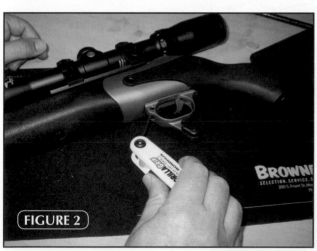
FIGURE 2

FIGURE 5

Reassemble in reverse order.

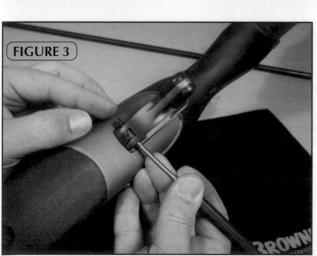
FIGURE 3

Maintenance Tip: When reinstalling the breech plug after cleaning, lubricate the threads on the breech plug and the threads inside the breech area of the barrel with an anti-seize lubricant. This will help make removing the breech plug easier after shooting.

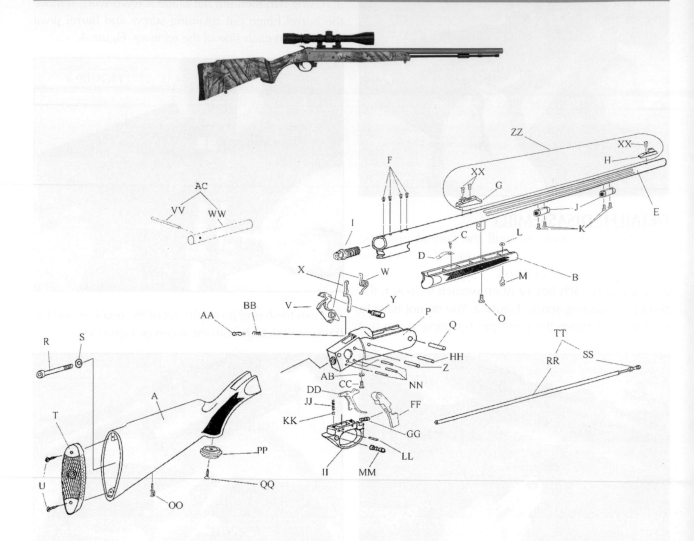

PARTS LIST

A Rear Stock
B Fore Stock
C Ramrod Retaining Screw
D Ramrod Retaining Spring
E Barrel Assembly
F Plug Screw (4 Req'd.)
G Rear Sight
H Front Sight
I Breech Plug
J Ramrod Thimble (2 Req'd.)
K Ramrod Thimble Screw
   (4 Req'd.)
L Sling Swivel Stud – Front nut

M Sling Swivel Stud – Front
O Forend Stock Screw
P Frame
Q Frame Pivot Pin
R Tang Screw
S Tang Screw Washer
T Buttpad
U Buttpad Mounting Screw (2
   Req'd.)
V Hammer
W Hammer Spring
X Transfer Bar
Z Hammer Pin
AA Firing Pin

BB Firing Pin Spring
CC Firing Pin Retaining Screw
FF Barrel Catch
GG Barrel Catch Spring
HH Barrel Catch Pin
II Trigger Guard
JJ Trigger Guard Spring
KK Ball
LL Safety Pin
MM Safety
NN Trigger Guard and Trigger
   Pin (3 Req'd.)
OO Sling Swivel Stud-Rear
PP Pistol Grip Cap

QQ Pistol grip Cap Screw
RR Ramrod
SS Ramrod Tip
TT Ramrod Assembly
VV Wrench Handle
WW Hexagonal Wrench
XX Rear and Front Sights Screw
   (3 Req'd.)
ZZ Rear and Front Sight
   Assembly
AB Firing Pin Screw Washer
AC Hexagonal Breech Plug
   Wrench

SPECIFICATIONS

Model: Pursuit Ultralight
Action: Single shot, SA, break-open, inline
Barrel: 26 in.
Caliber: .50

Capacity: 1
Common Features: adjustable rear/fix front fiber optic sights; black or camo synthetic traditional or thumbhole stock; .209 primer ignition; blued or CeraKote finishes

BACKGROUND

The Pursuit Ultralight is Traditions mid-level inline muzzleloader with a break-open action to access the proprietary Accelerator breech plug, which is removable with your fingers. In 2011 *Field and Stream* magazine awarded it the "Best of the Best" honor. The trigger and hammer mechanism is held in the frame via pins and really do not need to be nor should be removed routinely.

Year Introduced: 2009
Country of Manufacture: Spain
Current Importer: Traditions Performance Firearms (traditionsfirearms.com)
Similar Models: Pursuit Ultralight XLT (28-in. barrel)

REQUIRED TOOLS

Field Strip: Accelerator breech plug wrench
Disassembly/Assembly: 4mm and 6mm hex or Allen wrench, two small punches, brass hammer

FIELD STRIP

1. Remove the ramrod assembly (part #TT).
2. Remove the breech plug (I) from the breech end of the barrel (E) using your fingers or the Accelerator breech plug wrench. Some older models have a hexagonal breech plug that requires use of a special hexagonal breech plug wrench (AC). Turn the breech plug three full rotations and pull it out of the barrel, Figure 1.

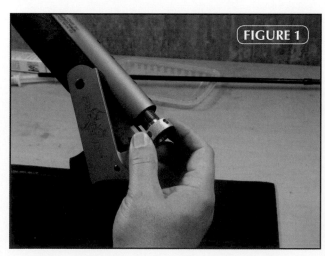

FIGURE 1

At this point no further disassembly is required for cleaning.

DETAILED DISASSEMBLY

1. Use a 4mm hex or Allen wrench to remove the fore stock screw (O) and pull fore stock (B) from the barrel (E).

2. Open the action by pressing in the barrel catch (FF) and pivoting the barrel downward and off of the frame (P), Figure 2.

FIGURE 2

3. Remove the two buttpad mounting screws (U) then remove the buttpad (T).
4. Use a 6mm hex socket, extension and ratchet to remove the tang screw (R) and tang screw washer (S), Figure 3.

FIGURE 3

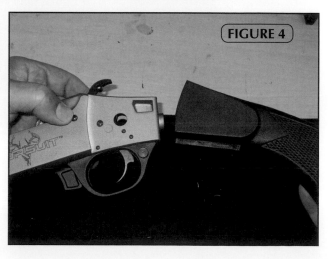

FIGURE 4

5. Pull the rear stock (A) from the frame, Figure 4.

6. Use a punch as a retaining pin and place it through the access holes in the frame (P) and under the leg of the hammer spring (W).

7. Remove the trigger guard (II) by drifting out the two trigger guard pins (NN) from either side of the frame, Figure 5.

8. Pull the rear of the trigger guard out from the frame and pivot it forward, Figure 6.

9. Drift out the trigger pin (NN) and remove the trigger (DD), Figure 7.

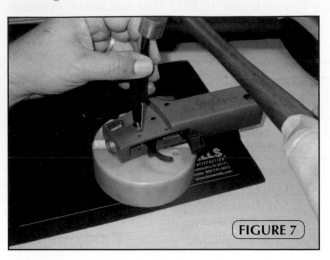

FIGURE 7

Reassemble reversing the procedure.

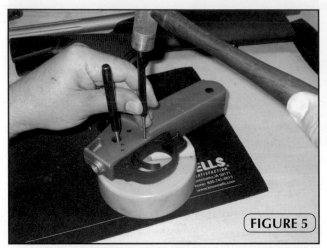

FIGURE 5

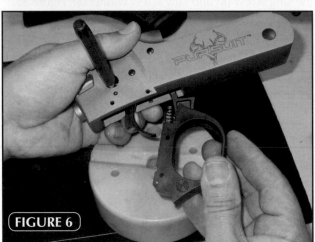

FIGURE 6

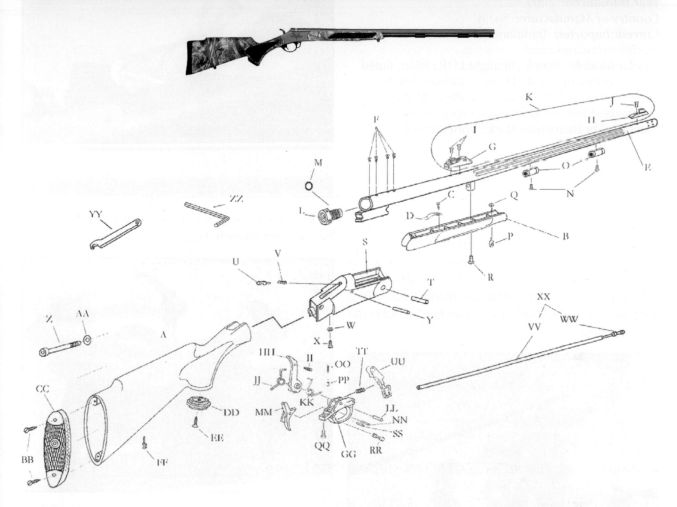

PARTS LIST

A Rear Stock
B Fore Stock
C Ramrod Retaining Screw
D Ramrod Retaining Spring
E Barrel Assembly
F Plug Screw (4 Req'd.)
G Metal Fiber Optic Rear Sight
H Metal Fiber Optic Front Sight
I Rear Sight Screw (2 Req'd.)
J Front Sight Screw
K Metal Williams Sight
   Assembly
L Accelerator Breech Plug

M Rubber O- Ring
N Ramrod Thimble (2 Req'd.)
O Ramrod Thimble Screw (2
   Req'd.)
P Sling Swivel Stud- Front
Q Sling Swivel Stud- Front Nut
R Fore Stock Screw
S Frame
T Frame Pivot Pin
U Firing Pin
V Firing Pin Spring
W Firing Pin Screw Washer
X Firing Pin Retaining Screw
Y Barrel Catch Pin

Z Tang Screw
AA Tang Screw Washer
BB Buttpad
CC Buttpad Screw (2 Req'd.)
DD Pistol Grip Cap
EE Pistol Grip Cap Screw
FF Sling Swivel Stud Rear
GG Trigger Guard
HH Hammer
II Hammer Handle
JJ Hammer Mainspring
KK Hammer Antagonist Spring
LL Hammer Pin
MM Trigger

NN Trigger Pin
OO Trigger Guard Spring
PP Pin
QQ Trigger Guard Screw
RR Safety
SS Safety Pin
TT Barrel Catch Spring
UU Barrel Catch
VV Ramrod
WW Ramrod Tip
XX Ramrod Assembly
YY Accelerator Breech Plug
   Wrench
ZZ Allen Wrench

SPECIFICATIONS

Model: Vortek Ultralight
Action: Single shot, SA, break-open, inline
Barrel: 28 in.
Caliber: .50
Capacity: 1
Common Features: adjustable rear/fix front fiber optic sights; black or camo synthetic traditional or thumbhole stock; .209 primer ignition; stainless, camo or CeraKote finishes

BACKGROUND

The Vortek is a muzzleloader for the 21st century. It features a break-open action to access the breech plug that can be unscrewed with your fingers and a drop out trigger housing for easy cleaning. The speed load system is easier to start a bullet down the barrel and ensures the bullet/sabot are centered with the barrel rifling.

Year Introduced: 2009

Country of Manufacture: Spain

Current Importer: Traditions Performance Firearms (traditionsfirearms.com)

Similar Models: Vortek Ultralight LDR (30-in. fluted barrel), Vortek (non-fluted barrel, stainless finish, traditional or thumbhole stock), Vortek Ultralight Northwest Magnum (percussion cap ignition, traditional or thumbhole stock), Vortek Pistol

REQUIRED TOOLS

Field Strip: Accelerator breech plug wrench

Disassembly/Assembly: 4mm hex or Allen wrench

FIELD STRIP

1. Remove the ramrod assembly (part #XX).

2. Remove the breech plug (L) from the breech end of the barrel (E) using your fingers or the Accelerator breech plug wrench (YY) from the manufacturer. Turn the breech plug three full rotations and pull it out of the barrel, Figure 1.

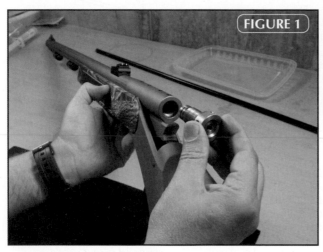

FIGURE 1

At this point no further disassembly is required for cleaning.

DETAILED DISASSEMBLY

1. Use a 4mm hex or Allen wrench to remove the fore stock screw (R) and pull fore stock (B) from the barrel, Figure 2.

2. Open the action by pressing in the barrel catch (UU) and pivoting the barrel downward and off of the frame (S).

3. If a hammer extension, Traditions calls it a hammer handle (II), unscrew and remove it from the hammer (HH).

4. Pull the hammer fully rearward in the "cocked" position and press the safety (RR) to the "safe" position.

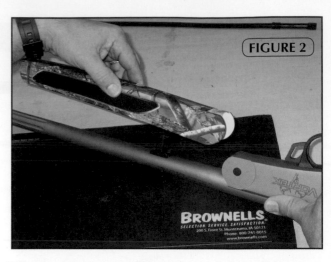

FIGURE 2

5. Remove the trigger guard screw (QQ) using a 4mm hex or Allen wrench, Figure 3.

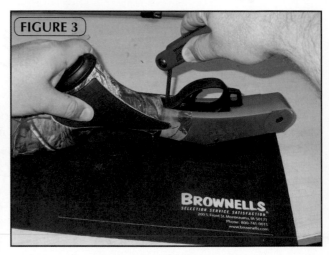

FIGURE 3

6. Pull down on the rear of trigger guard (GG) and the trigger group will come free from the bottom of the frame.

7. Remove the release lever spring from the front of the trigger assembly, Figure 4.

Reassemble reversing the procedure.

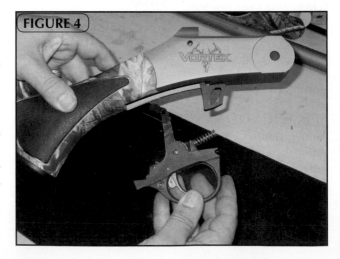

FIGURE 4

Sidelock Muzzleloaders

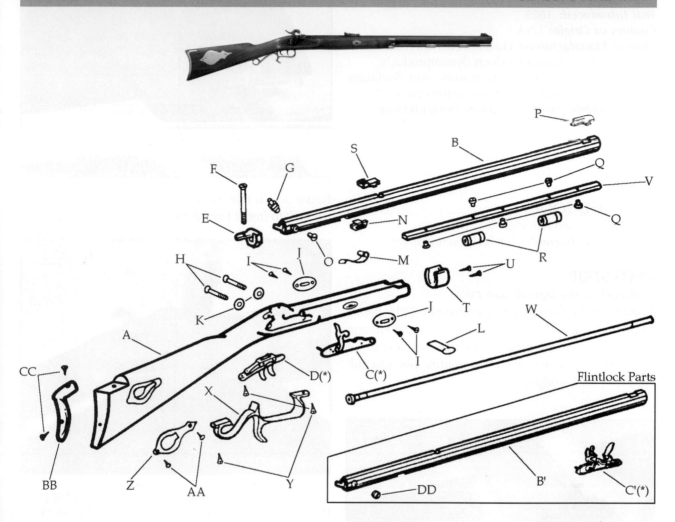

Flintlock Parts

PARTS LIST

A Stock
B Barrel
C Lock
D Trigger Assembly
E Barrel Tang
F Tang Screw
G Nipple

H Lock Plate Screw (2)
I Stock Plate Screw (4)
J Stock Plate (2)
K Lock Plate Washer (2)
L Barrel Tennon Wedge
M Ramrod Retaining Spring
N Barrel Tennon
O Bolster Screw

P Front Sight
Q Thimble/Barrel Rib Screw (5)
R Ramrod Thimble (2)
S Rear Sight
T Nose Cap
U Nose Cap Screw (2)
V Barrel Rib
W Ramrod Assembly

X Trigger Guard
Y Trigger Guard Screw (3)
Z Patchbox
AA Patchbox Screw (2)
BB Butt Plate
CC Butt Plate Screw (2)
DD Touch Hole Insert

SPECIFICATIONS

Model: Thompson/Center Arms Renegade Cap lock
Action: Single shot, SA, percussion sidelock
Barrel: 28 in.
Caliber: .50
Capacity: 1
Common Features: percussion ignition; hooked breech, blued finish octagon barrel; brass trigger guard, patch box and butt plate; set trigger; coil or leaf spring lock; American Walnut stock; brass, blued or browned hardware

BACKGROUND

Jacob and Samuel Hawken moved west to set up shop in St. Louis, Missouri. The brothers adapted the design of east coast long rifles like the Kentucky, Pennsylvania and Tennessee to better suit the needs of the western frontier. The Hawken brothers built lighter, shorter rifles in larger calibers. Mountain men like Jim Bridger and Kit Carson used Hawken rifles during their exploits in the Rockies and western plains. Today Hawken-style rifles are made with newer and stronger steels and used by traditional hunters across the country during muzzleloader season. Many Hawken-style rifles have brass hardware. Shown is a TC Renegade with blued hardware and barrel with a breech hook which makes disassembly and cleaning easier.

Year Introduced: 1823
Country of Origin: USA
Current Manufacturers: Davide Pedersoli (davide-pedersoli.com), Lyman Products (lymanproducts.com), Thompson/Center Arms (tcarms.com), Traditions Performance Firearms (traditionsfirearms.com)
Similar Models: Hawken, Country Hunter (Davide Pedersoli); Great Plains, Great Plains Hunter, Lyman Trade Rifle, Deerstalker (Lyman); Hawken, Firestorm (Thompson/Center Arms); Hawken Woodsman, Frontier Muzzleloader (Traditions Performance Firearms)

REQUIRED TOOLS

Field Strip: nylon hammer
Disassembly/Assembly: flat blade screwdriver

FIELD STRIP

1. Withdraw the ramrod (part #W).
2. Pull out the barrel tennon wedge pin (L) by gently tapped it out partially from the left side of the forearm then grasp the wedge pin from the right side and pull it out, Figure 1. You may need non-marring pliers to pull out the tennon wedge pin.

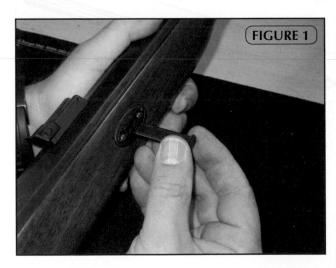

3. Cock back the hammer so it clears the nipple (G) on the barrel (B).
4. Next lift the barrel up and unhook it from the barrel tang (E), Figure 2.
At this point the Hawken can be cleaned without further disassembly.

DETAILED DISASSEMBLY

1. To remove the lock (C), unscrew the two lock plates screws (H) located on the left side of the stock (A),

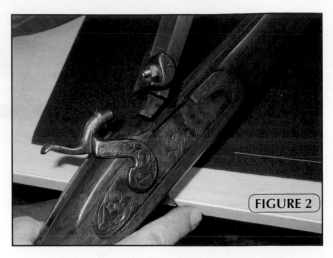

Figure 3. You may need a rubber mallet to gently tap the lock to free it from the stock.

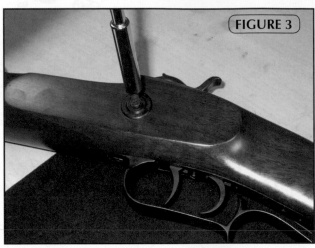

2. Remove the two trigger guard screws (Y), Figure 4. Pull the trigger guard from the bottom of the stock.
3. Remove the trigger assembly (D) by removing the one trigger guard screw to the rear of the triggers.

Reassemble in reverse order.

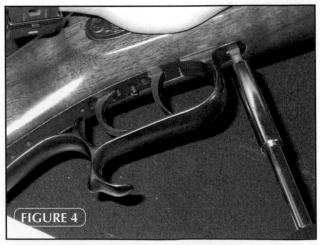

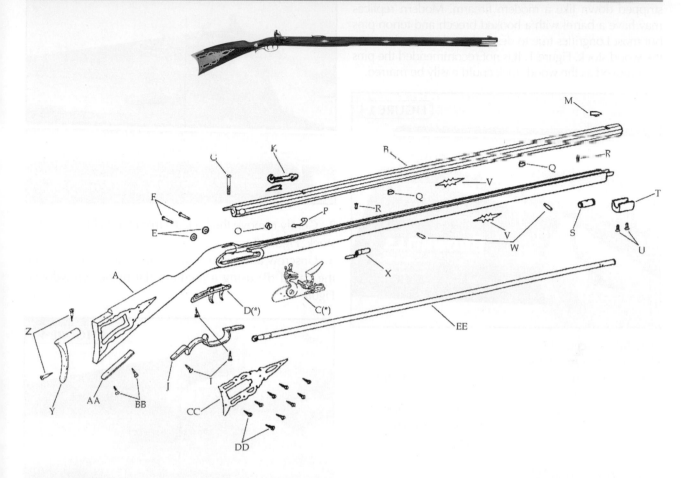

PARTS LIST

A Stock
B Barrel
C Flintlock
D Trigger Assembly
E Lock Plate Washer (2 Req'd.)
F Lock Plate Washer Screw
    (2 Req'd.)

G Tang Screw
I Trigger Guard Screw (3 Req'd.)
J Trigger Guard
K Rear Sight
M Front Sight
O Touch Hole Insert
P Ramrod Retaining Spring
Q Barrel Tenon (2 Req'd.)

R Ramrod Thimble Screw
    (2 Req'd.)
S Front Thimble
T Nose Cap
U Nose Cap Screw (2 Req'd.)
V "Hunter's Star" Small (2 Req'd.)
W Barrel Tenon Pin. (2 Req'd.)
X Rear Thimble

Y Butt Plate
Z Butt Plate Screw (2 Req'd.)
AA Toe Plate
BB Toe Plate Screw (2 Req'd.)
CC Patchbox
DD Patchbox Screw (9 Req'd.)
EE Ramrod

SPECIFICATIONS

Model: Traditions Shenandoah
Action: flintlock
Barrel: 49 in.
Caliber: .50
Capacity: 1
Common Features: dove-tailed front/adj. rear sights;
full length hardwood stock; double-set triggers; brass
furniture with patch box

BACKGROUND

The Longrifle is distinctly American tracing its roots back
to Lancaster, Pennsylvania, in the mid 18th century. The
longrifle is the stuff of legends. Daniel Boone carried a
Kentucky Longrifle. The design was produced by German
gunsmiths who immigrated to settlements in the new
world. Lineage can be traced back to the German Jaeger
rifle but the longrifle was purpose built for use in what
would become the United States. Most were stocked
in curly maple with decorative inlays of silver or brass.
Calibers were small ranging from .32 up to .45 and barrel
length ranged long from 35 inches up to 57 inches or
more. Depending on your geographic location Longrifles
were known as Tenneesse, Kentucky or Pennsylvania
Longrifles. They were initially built using flintlock ignition
and changed to percussion as that technology became
available. I can think of no better combination of accuracy,
craftsmanship and artistry than a handmade Longrifle.
Today companies like Traditions bring the classic Longrifle
to life. The procedure below shows their Shenandoah

model. Instructions are very similar for both flint lock or percussion lock ignition. Longrifles are not typically stripped down like a modern firearm. Modern replicas may have a barrel with a hooked breech and tenon pins but most Longrifles true to design have barrels pinned to the wood stock, Figure 1. It is not recommended the pins be removed as the wood stock could easily be marred.

FIGURE 1

Year Introduced: 1740s
Country of Manufacture: USA
Current Importer: Traditions Performance Firearms (traditionsfirearms.com)
Similar Models: Traditions: Pennsylvania, Tennessee, Kentucky; Davide Pedersoli (davide-pedersoli.com): Kentucky, Alamo, Cub DIXIE, Pennsylvania, Frontier, Scout

REQUIRED TOOLS
Disassembly/Assembly: medium flat blade screwdriver

DISASSEMBLY
1. Remove the two lock plate screws (part #F) and two lock plate washers (E) from the left side of the stock (A) using a medium flat blade screwdriver, Figure 2.

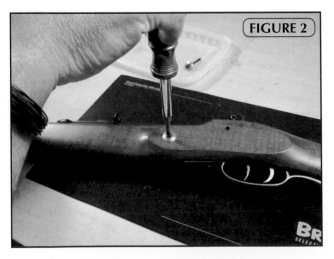

FIGURE 2

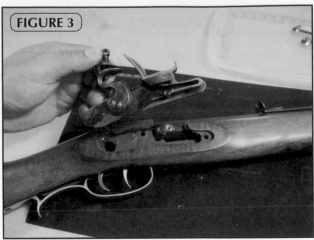

FIGURE 3

2. Gently remove the lock (C) from the right side of the stock, Figure 3.
3. Unscrew and remove the touch hole insert (O) from the barrel (B) using a medium flat blade screwdriver, Figure 4.

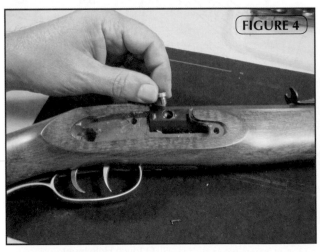

FIGURE 4

At this point no further disassembly is required for cleaning.

Reassemble reversing the procedure.

> **Cleaning Tip:** Use hot soapy water and a jag with a patch to clean the bore. With the touch hole insert removed tip the barrel so the soapy solution flows through the barrel and into a bucket. Try not to soak the wood will the solution. Work the solution until a patch comes out clean then run a light oiled patch through the bore and light oil the threads of the touch hole insert. Too much oil will cause the rifle to misfire. Brush the lock with the soapy solution or use a CLP (Clean Lubricate Protect) solution.

Shotguns

Semi-Automatic Action

BENELLI VINCI

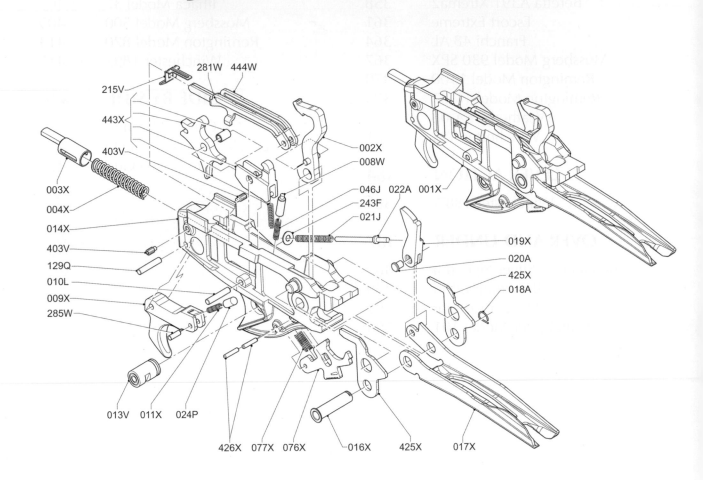

281W 444W

215V

443X

403V

003X

004X

014X

403V

129Q

010L

009X

285W

002X
008W

046J 022A 001X
243F
021J

019X
020A
425X
018A

013V 011X 024P

426X 077X 076X 016X 425X 017X

PARTS LIST

Diagram 1
001X Trigger group assembly
002X Hammer
003X Hammer spring cap
004X Hammer spring
008W Safety plunger pin
009X Trigger
010L Pin
011X Trigger spring
013V Safety button
014X Trigger guard
016X Trigger pin bush
017X Carrier
018A Trigger guard pin spring
019X Bolt stop tooth

020A Bolt stop tooth pin
021J Carrier spring
022A Bolt latch pin
024P Trigger spring bush
046J Safety spring
076X Cartridge drop lever
077X Cartridge drop lever
  spring
129Q Pin
215V Disconnector
243F Washer
281W Hammer link (R.H.)
285W Disconnector trigger
  roller

403V Stroke-end grub screw
  (hammer spring cap)
425X Carriage fixing plate
426X Cartridge drop lever
  rotating pin
443X Disconnector assembly
444W Hammer link (L.H.)
Diagram 2
024X Bolt assembly
025X Firing pin
026X Bolt assembly, partial
028A Firing pin retaining pin
030X Bolt handle
031X Locking head pin

032X Locking head
033J Extractor spring
034A Extractor
035X Extractor pin
036A Inertia spring
037A Firing pin spring
100X Bolt return spring
165X Locking head assembly
168X Ejector frame
438X Bolt spring plunger pin
439X Bolt shoulder-plate
440X Bolt stroke-end rubber
  insert
441X Full ejector guide pin

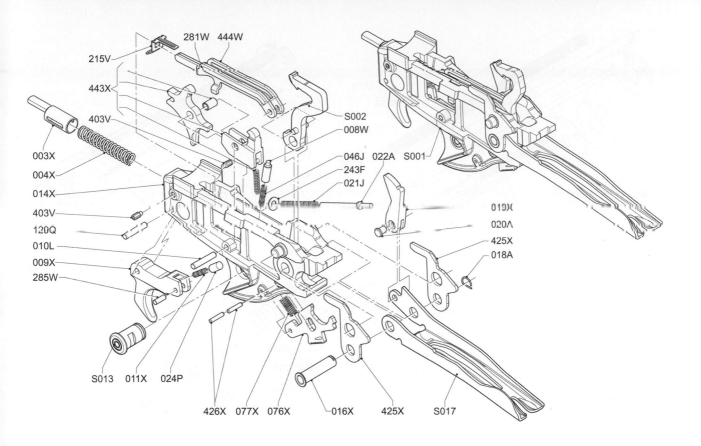

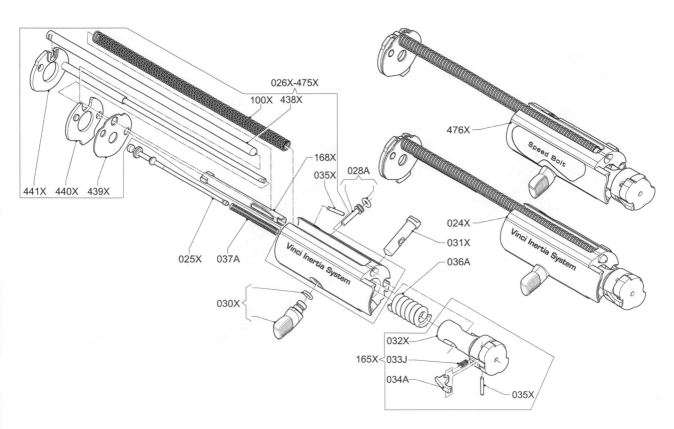

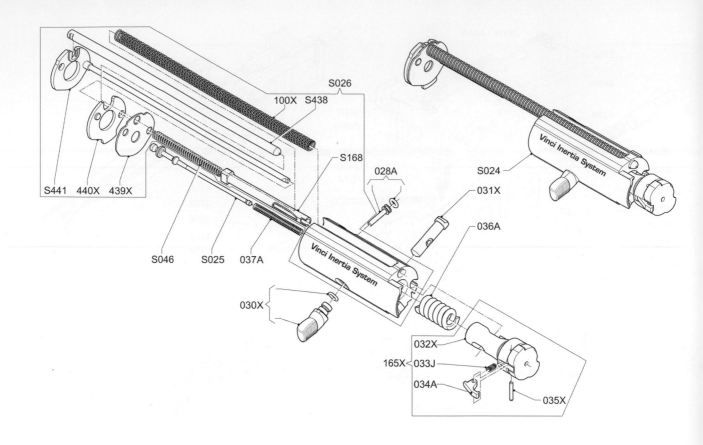

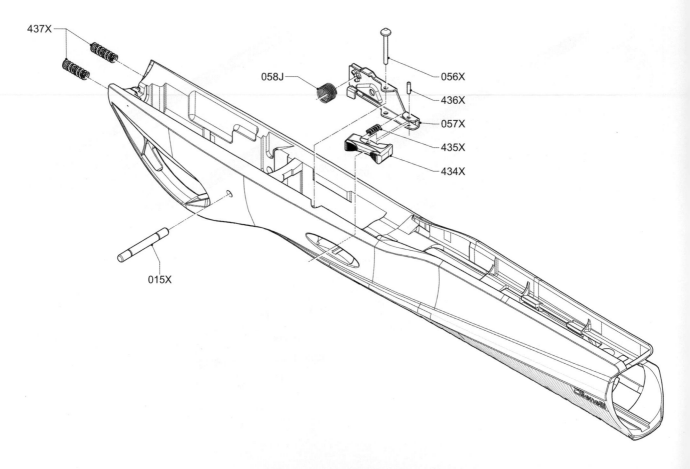

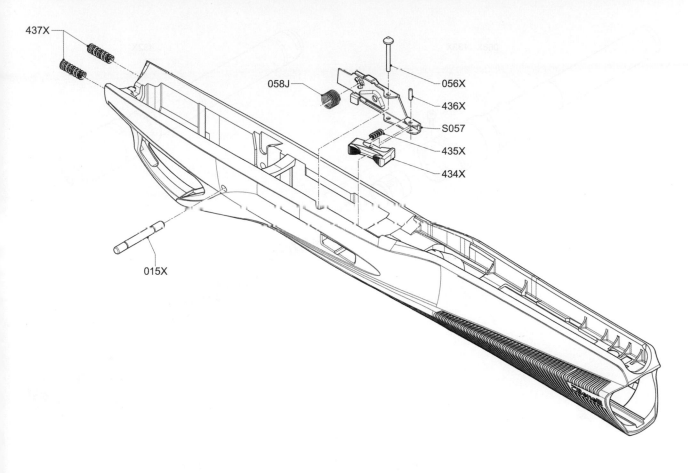

437X

056X

058J

436X

S057

435X

434X

015X

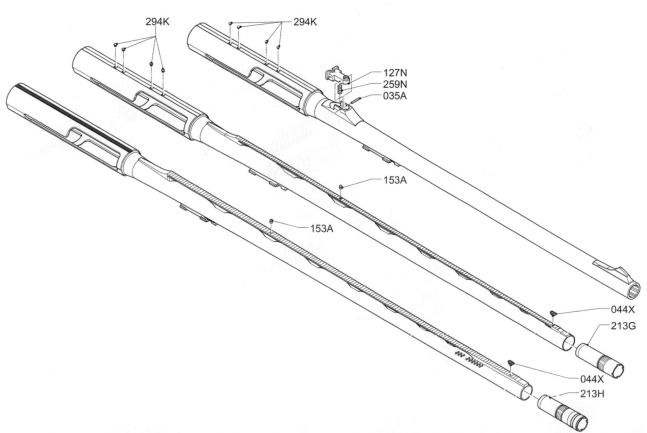

294K

294K

127N

259N

035A

153A

153A

044X

213G

044X

213H

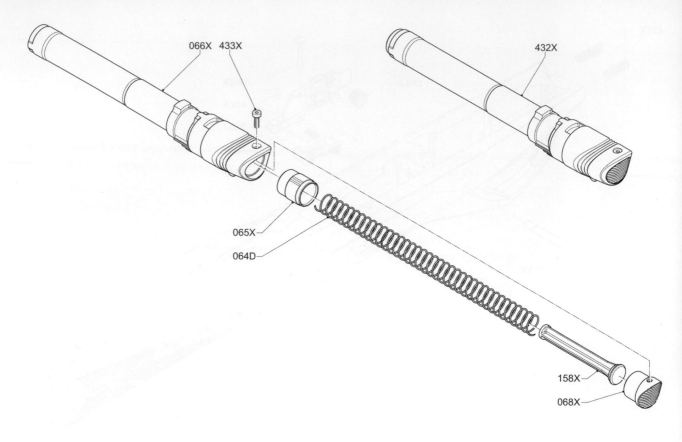

066X 433X

432X

065X

064D

158X

068X

387X - 430X

457X

388X
431X
474X

380X

445G 428X

429X

147X

473X

427X

379X

160X
460X

456X

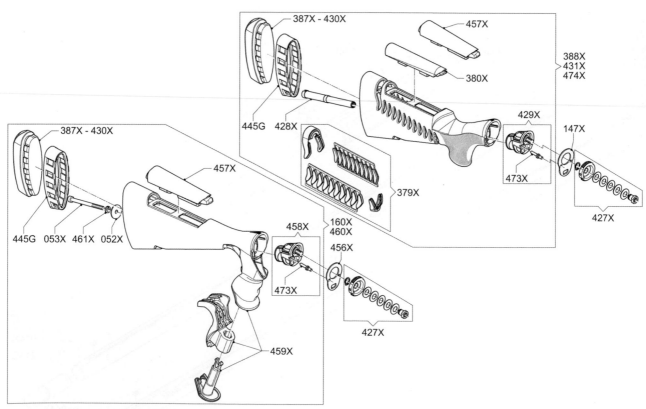

387X - 430X

457X

445G 053X 461X 052X

458X

473X

427X

459X

475X Bolt assembly, partial Vinci SuperSport - Cordoba
476X Bolt assembly Vinci SuperSport - Cordoba

Diagram 3

015X Trigger guard pin
056X Carrier latch pin
057X Carrier latch
058J Carrier latch spring
434X Carrier latch button
435X Cartridge stop latch button spring
436X Rotating pin for cartridge stop latch button
437X Carriage play recovery spring

Diagram 4

035A Pin
044X Front sight
127N Rear sight
153A Intermediate sight

213G Internal choke
213H Internal choke knurled-end
259N Rear sight spring
294K Cap/plug for cover holes

Diagram 5

064D Magazine spring
065X Magazine follower
066X Magazine tube M265, partial
068X Magazine tube plug M265
158X Shot plug (three round)
432X Magazine tube M265, assembly
433X Plug tube magazine fixing screw

Diagram 6

052X Stock fixing washer
053X Stock fixing screw

147X Drop change plate, deviation 50
147X Drop change plate, deviation 55
147X Drop change plate, deviation 60
147X Drop change plate, deviation 65
160X Complete Pistol grip stock assembly, 360 mm (R.H.)
379X Chevrons assembly, Comfort stock
380X Comb, Comfort stock
387X Butt plate (R.H.)
388X Stock assembly Comfort mm 360 (R.H.)
427X Stock locking ring nut assembly
428X Tension rod, Comfort stock

429X Front spacer Comfort stock assembly
430X Butt plate (L.H.)
431X Stock assembly Comfort mm 360 (L.H.)
445G Buttpad ring
456X Pistol grip stock front plate
457X Medium comb for Pistol grip stock
458X Front insert assembly for Pistol grip stock
459X Partial Pistol grip stock assembly
460X Complete Pistol grip stock assembly, 360 mm (L.H.)
461X Stock fixing grower washer
473X Stock retaining pin
474X Stock assembly Comfort mm 360 (R.H.) - medium comb

SPECIFICATIONS

Model: Vinci
Action: semi-automation, inertia-driven system
Barrel: 24 in., 26 in., 28 in. or 30 in.
Caliber: 12 gauge (2-3/4 and 3-in. chamber)
Capacity: 3+1
Common Features: vent rib barrel, red bar front sight, matte or camo finishes, choke tubes, manual safety, magazine cut-off, drilled and tapped for scope mounting

BACKGROUND

The Vinci uses an inertia-driven system that helps reduce felt recoil. The system actually uses nearly the entire shotgun as a component during recoil. Only the bolt remains stationary during firing. This Benelli makes liberal use of polymers in its construction and breaks down quickly—or assembles quickly—into three modules: trigger group/forearm module, barrel/receiver module and buttstock module. Leonardo would be proud.
Year Introduced: 2009
Country of Origin: Italy
Current Manufacturer: Benelli (benelliusa.com)
Similar Models: Vinci Steady Grip (pistol grip stock), Super Vinci (3.5 in. chamber)

REQUIRED TOOLS

Field Strip: none
Disassembly/Assembly: small inch punch, 13mm wrench

FIELD STRIP

1. Ensure the bolt is closed and the hammer is cocked.
2. Press the assembly/disassembly button and rotate the magazine tube plug (part #068X) counterclockwise, Figure 1.
3. Slide the trigger group/forearm module forward detaching it from the barrel/receiver module, Figure 2.
4. Grasp the barrel then rotate the stock assembly (388X) counterclockwise 90°, Figure 3. Remove the stock assembly from the barrel, Figure 4.
At this point the Vinci is broken down to its three main components.

FIGURE 1

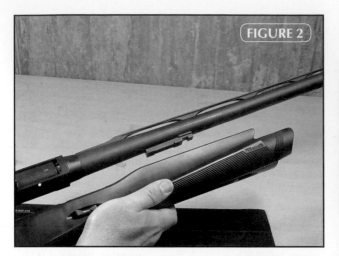
FIGURE 2

bolt assembly, Figure 6. Slide the bolt assembly from the barrel/receiver module, Figure 7.

FIGURE 5

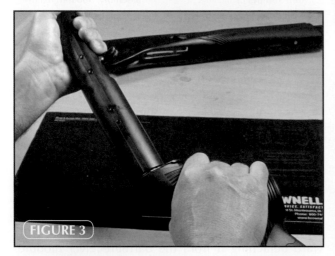
FIGURE 3

FIGURE 6

FIGURE 4

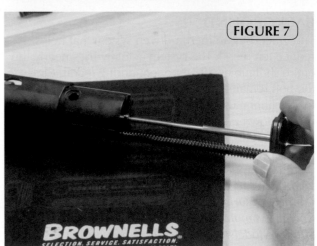
FIGURE 7

BARREL/RECEIVER MODULE DISASSEMBLY

1. Push downward on the back of the bolt assembly (024X) to disengage it from the inside of the rear of the barrel/receiver module, Figure 5.

2. Pull the bolt handle (030X) back to bring the bolt assembly rearward then pull the bolt handle from the

3. Remove the firing pin retaining pin (028A) by pulling it from the bolt assembly. Control the firing pin (025X) as it is under spring tension from the firing pin spring (037A). The firing pin and firing pin

spring can then be removed from the rear of the bolt assembly.

4. Pull out the locking head pin (031X) and slide out the locking head (032X) from the front of the bolt assembly. Then the inertia spring (036X) will fall free from the front from of the bolt assembly.

TRIGGER GROUP/FOREARM MODULE DISASSEMBLY

1. Press the safety button (S013) to the "safe" position, then using a small punch drift out the trigger guard pin (015X) from the trigger group/forearm module, Figure 8.

3. Rotate clockwise the magazine tube assembly (432X) until the assembly/disassembly button is positioned then push the assembly/disassembly button all the way down and slide the magazine tube assembly forward and out of the trigger group/forearm module.

BUTTSTOCK MODULE DISASSEMBLY

1. Use a 13mm wrench to unscrew the stock locking ring nut assembly (427X) from the stock assembly (338X), Figure 9.

2. Slide the drop change plate (147X) from the stock assembly.

2. Press the cartridge latch button (434X) and rotate the trigger group assembly (001X) upward and out of the top of the trigger group/forearm module.

Stock Fit: The Benelli Vinci features a shim kit for stock drop and cast so shooters can customize the shotgun fit to their specific body size and shooting style.

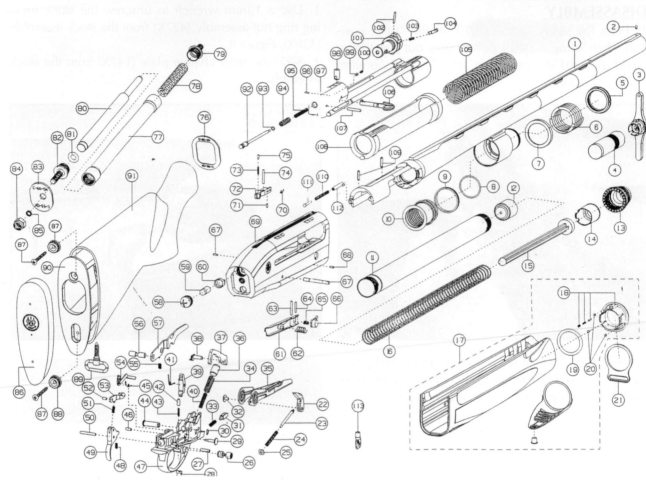

PARTS LIST

1 Barrel
2 Sight
5 Nut
6 Spring
7 Valve
8 O-Ring, Cylinder
9 Ring, Piston Elastic
10 Piston
11 Tube, Magazine
12 Flange, Mag. Tube
13 Cap, Forend
14 Cap, Magazine
15 Plug, Magazine
16 Spring, Magazine
17 Forend
18 Flange, Forend Sleeve
   Assembly
21 Swivel, Front

22 Spring, Forend
23 Magnet, F/E Sleeve
24 Swivel, Front
25 Carrier
26 Lever, Carrier
27 Guide Carrier Lever Spring
28 Spring, Carrier Lever
29 Plate, Spring Guide
30 Pin, Carrier Lever
31 Plunger, Carrier Catch
32 Spring Carrier Catch Plunger
33 Bushing, Retaining Spring
   Ring
34 Bushing, Carrier
35 Hammer Spring
36 Cap Hammer Spring
37 Hammer
38 Pin, Hammer
39 Safety

40 Spring, Safety
41 Cap, Safety Handle
42 Trigger Plate Assembly
43 Pin
44 Sear
45 Trigger
46 Trigger Lever
47 Pin, Trigger
48 Spring, Sear
49 Pin
50 Spring, Sear
51 Cartridge Latch Assembly
52 Spring Cart Latch Body
53 Pin Magazine Cut Off
54 Pin, Cart Latch
55 Spring, Cart Latch
56 Button Cart Latch
57 Pin, Trigger Plate Retaining
   Pin

58 Pin, Universal, Short
59 Pin, Universal, Short
61 Head, Shock Absorber
62 Absorber, Shock
63 Cap, Shock Absorber
64 Pin Magazine Cut Off Spring
65 Spring Magazine Cut Off
66 Lever, Magazine Cutoff
67 Spring, Safety
68 Pin Magazine Cut Off
69 Plunger Cut Off
70 Pin, Ejector Stop
71 Spring, Ejector
72 Ejector
73 Pin, Ejector
74 Stop, Piston
75 Spring, Recoil
76 Pin, Firing
77 O-Ring, Firing Pin

78 Spring, Firing Pin, External	88 Extractor	100 Cap, Stock Bolt Tube	108 Washer, Stock Bolt
79 Spring, Firing Pin, Internal	89 Handle, Cocking	101 Spring Shock Absorber	109 Swivel Assembly
80 Pin, Spring	90 Pin, Firing Pin Retaining	103 Body, Shock Absorber	110 Swivel Nuts
81 Slide Breech Bolt Assembly	93 Bushing, Butt Plate	104 Absorber, Shock, Mobile Mass	111 Swivel Nut Insert
82 Pin, Breech Bolt	94 Screw Butt Plate	105 Cap, Recoil Spring, 391/391 Xtrema	112 Kick Off System
83 Pin, Cocking Handle	96 Spacer	106 Washer, Plate, Drop	113 Receiver
84 Spring, Cocking Handle Pin	97 Stock Insert	107 Nut, Stock Bolt	
86 Pin, Extractor	98 Stock		
87 Spring, Extractor	99 Spacer, Drop		

SPECIFICATIONS

Model: A391 Xtrema2
Action: semi-automatic, gas-operated
Barrel: 26 in or 28 in.
Caliber: 12 gauge, 3.5-in. chamber
Capacity: 5 + 1 (2-3/4 in. shells), 4 + 1 (3 in. shells), 3 + 1 (3-1/2 in. shells)
Common Features: stock adj. for drop/cast, vent rib barrel, anodized aluminum receiver, magazine cut off, camo or matte black finishes, TRUGLO fiber optic front sight, excepts choke tubes, synthetic stock w/ soft touch inserts, Kick-Off recoil reduction system on some models

BACKGROUND

The Beretta A391 Xtrema2 is a beefed up waterfowl/turkey—deadly on coyotes, too—gun based on Beretta's A391 Urika line. The Xtrema2 is designed to take the pounding of heavy 3-1/2 inch, 12 gauge hunting loads without battering a shooter's shoulder. Some models include a hydraulic recoil reduction system Beretta calls Kick-Off. The Xtreme2 can also easily handle light target loads. The mechanism features a rotating bolt with two locking lugs that engage the barrel tang. The gas system has two ports that drive a piston and dual operating rods rearward to cycle the action.
Importation Began: 2002
Country of Origin: Italy
Current Manufacturer: Beretta (berettausa.com)

REQUIRED TOOLS

Field Strip: small punch
Disassembly/Assembly: stock tool or socket and extension

FIELD STRIP

1. Push the safety button (part #39) to the fire position and depress the carrier stop button (56).
2. Pull the cocking handle (89) back until the breech bolt (81) is locked back.
3. Unscrew the fore-end cap (13), Figure 1. Remove the front swivel (24) if installed.
4. Next slide the fore-end off the magazine tube (17) then pull the barrel (1) along with piston assembly and gas cylinder (10) out of the receiver.

FIGURE 1

5. You can then slide the piston out of the gas cylinder, Figure 2.

At this point the Xtrema2 is field stripped for routine cleaning.

FIGURE 2

DETAILED DISASSEMBLY

1. Disassembly of the breech bolt assembly is accomplished by holding the cocking handle with one hand then pressing the breech bolt button to allow the breech bolt to slide forward until it stops.
2. Next press the bolt until it aligns to the edge of the bolt body, Figure 3. While holding the breech bolt in this position pull the bolt handle out of the breech bolt, Figure 4.

FIGURE 3

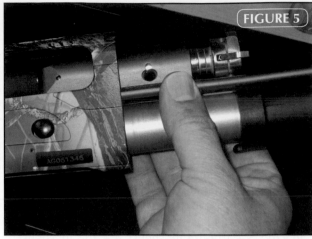

FIGURE 5

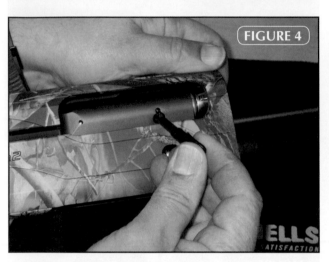

FIGURE 4

FIGURE 6

3. With the ejection port facing up slide the operating rod sleeve and breech bolt forward toward the muzzle and off the magazine tube, Figure 5.

4. The trigger assembly is removed from the receiver by first ensuring the hammer is cocked and carrier stop button is pushed.

5. Using a punch, push out the trigger plate pin (57). While pressing the breech bolt release button, pull the trigger plate by the trigger guard slightly forward then down and out of the receiver, Figure 6.

Reassemble in reverse order.

Maintenance Tip: Takedown of the breech bolt assembly and trigger is recommended after 500 to 1,000 shells fired. Heavy duty shells can produce an awful lot of residue from burning gases, so make sure to also clean the piston, the elastic seal and outside of the magazine tube.

Reassembly Tip: When reinstalling the bolt handle, first make sure the breech bolt aligns with the bolt body.

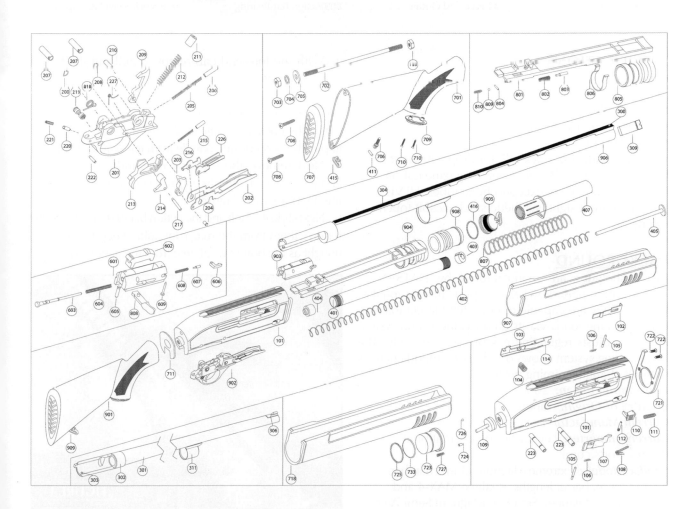

PARTS LIST

101 Receiver
102 Carrier Latch- Inner
103 Carrier Latch Rivet
104 Carrier Latch Spring
105 Carrier Latch Pin
106 Shell Latch Retaining Plug
107 Shell Latch
108 Shell Latch Spring
109 Stock Connection Plug
110 Magazine Cut-Off
111 Magazine Cut-Off Spring
112 Magazine Cut-Off Pin
114 Carrier Latch -Outer
201 Trigger Plate
202 Carrier
203 Carrier Level
204 Carrier Level Rivet

205 Carrier Spring
206 Carrier Spring Guide
207 Carrier Pin
208 Carrier Pin Retaining Plug
209 Hammer
210 Hammer Pin
211 Hammer Spring Guide
212 Hammer Spring
213 Trigger
214 Sear
215 Sear Spring Guide
216 Sear Spring
217 Sear Pin
218 Trigger Spring
219 Safety Button
220 Safety Spring Guide
221 Safety Spring
222 Safety Pin

223 Trigger Assembly Pins (2)
226 Inner-Carrier
227 Inner-Carrier Spring
301 Slug Barrel
302 Barrel Tang
303 Barrel Tang Pin
304 Ventilated Rib
306 Casted Front Sight
308 Metal Bead Front Sight
309 Inner Choke
311 Gas Cylinder
401 Magazine Tube
402 Magazine Spring
403 Magazine Spring Retaining
     Plug
404 Magazine Spring Follower
405 Magazine Plug
407 Magazine Extension Tube

411 Swivel Pin
415 Casted Swivel
416 Gas Cylinder O-Ring
601 Bolt
602 Locking Block
603 Firing Pin
604 Firing Pin Spring
605 Firing Pin Stop
606 Extractor
607 Extractor Pin
608 Extractor Spring
609 Extractor Retaining Pin
701 Stock
702 Stock Connection Rod
703 Stock Connection Rod Nut
704 Stock Connection Rod
     Spring Washer

705 Stock Connection Rod Washer	722 Fore-End Plate Screws	801 Action Bar	810 Action Bar Bearing Spring
706 Stock Swivel Screw	723 Fore-End Bushing	802 Action Bar Spring	901 Stock (Complete)
707 Butt-Plate	724 Fore-End Bushing Bearing Pin	803 Action Bar Pin	902 Trigger Group(Complete)
708 Butt-Plate Screws	725 Fore-End Bushing Retaining Plug	804 Action Bar Bearing Pin	903 Bolt(Complete)
709 Stock Plastic Cap	726 Fore-End Bushing Bearing	805 Action Bar Bushing	904 Action Bar (Complete)
710 Stock Plastic Cap Screw	727 Fore-End Bushing Bearing Spring	806 Action Bar Bushing Retaining Plug	905 Fore-End Cap(Complete)
711 Stock Drop Spacer	733 Fore-End O-Ring	807 Recoil Spring	906 Ventilated Rib Barrel
718 Plastic Fore-End		808 Cocking Handle	907 Fore-End (Complete)
721 Fore-End Plate		809 Action Bar Bearing	908 Piston (Complete)
			909 Stock Swivel (Complete)

SPECIFICATIONS

Model: Extreme S/A Camo
Action: semi-automatic, gas-operated
Barrel: 28 in.
Caliber: 12 gauge, 3.5-in. chamber
Capacity: 4+1
Common Features: stock adj. for drop/cast, vent rib barrel, aluminum alloy receiver, magazine cut off, Realtree camo finish, excepts choke tubes, Hi Vis fiber optic front sight, synthetic stock w/ soft touch inserts

BACKGROUND

Escort shotguns are manufactured by HATSAN in Turkey and imported by Legacy Sports International of Nevada. They are capable of firing light target loads to heavy hunting loads via its Smart Value Piston system that self adjusts regulating gas pressure to cycle. The Fast Loading system allows one-handed round changes without changing aiming position.

Importation Began: 2002
Country of Origin: Turkey
Current Manufacturer: Hasten Arms Co.
Current Importer: Legacy Sports International (legacysports.com)
Similar Models: Extreme Magnum (3 in. chamber, 22 and 28-in. barrel lengths, Realtree MAX-4 and AP finishes, 12 gauge), Supreme Magnum Semi-Auto (28-in. barrel, blued finish, wood stock, 12 gauge), Standard Magnum Semi-Auto (26 and 28-in. barrel lengths, blued finish, 20 and 12 gauge), Semi-Auto (22-in. barrel, blued finish, wood or synthetic stock, 20 gauge)

REQUIRED TOOLS

Field Strip: small punch, hammer
Disassembly/Assembly: stock tool or socket and extension

FIELD STRIP

1. Make sure the bolt (part #903) is in the forward position.
2. Remove the fore-end cap (905) from the magazine tube (401) by unscrewing it counter-clockwise.

3. With the fore-end cap removed pull out the barrel (906) from the receiver (101).
4. Next use your fingers to compress the bolt from the front of the receiver so the notch on the bolt aligns with the tab on the cocking handle (808) then use your other hand to pull the bolt cocking handle from the bolt, Figure 1.
5. Next remove the rubber gas cylinder 0-ring (416) and gas piston assembly off the magazine tube by sliding them forward, Figure 2.
6. Next slide the bolt and the action bar (910) forward and remove them from the magazine tube. Keep the receiver upright as the bolt may fall free from the action bar.

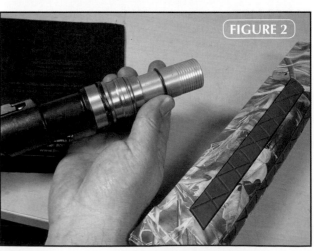

FIGURE 1

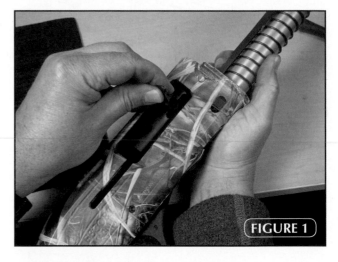

FIGURE 2

At this point the Escort is field stripped for routine cleaning.

DETAILED DISASSEMBLY

1. The trigger assembly is removed by using a small punch and hammer to drive out the two trigger assembly pins (223), Figure 3.

2. Gently pull down on the carrier (202) until the trigger assembly moves downwards then use the trigger guard (201) to pull it free from the receiver, Figure 4.

3. To remove the stock (701) or to remove/add stock drop spacers (711), unscrew the butt plate screws (708) and remove the recoil pad (707).

4. Use a stock take down tool or a socket and long extension to remove the stock connection rod nut (703), stock connection rod spring washer (704) and stock connection rod washer (705) via the hole in the rear of the stock. Then remove the stock from the stock connection rod (702).

Tuning Tip: With the stock removed the stock drop and cast can be adjusted with stock spacer shims. Place the spacer shim over the stock connection rod, replace stock over the rod and replace the butt pad.

To reassemble, reverse the disassembly procedures.

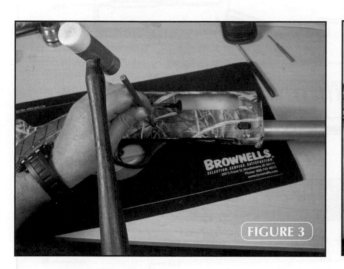

FIGURE 3

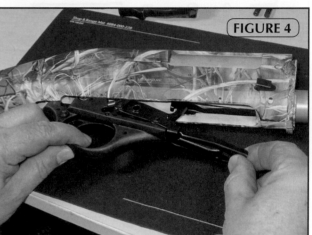

FIGURE 4

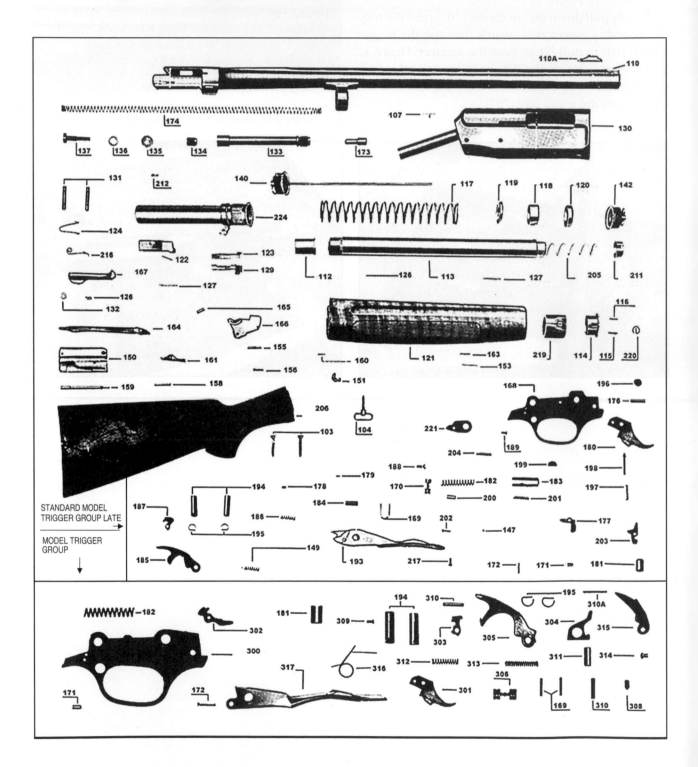

STANDARD MODEL
TRIGGER GROUP LATE

MODEL TRIGGER
GROUP

PARTS LIST

103 Buttplate Screw (2 Req'd.)
104 Swivel
107 Ejector
110 Front Sight, Silver Bead
110A Front Sight w/ Ramp
112 Magazine Follower
113 Magazine Tube
114 Nylon Ring
115 Magazine Cap Retaining Pin
116 Magazine Cap Retaining Pin Spring
117 Recoil Spring
118 Friction Ring
119 Governor Ring
120 Friction Spring
121 Forend
122 Carrier Latch
123 Auxiliary Shell Latch
124 Carrier Latch Spring
126 Detent Spring (3 Req'd.)
127 Pin (3 Req'd.)
129 Magazine Shell Latch
131 Trigger Guard Pin
132 Carrier Latch Button
133 Action Spring Tube
134 Action Spring Tube Retainer
135 Stock Fastening Eccentric Washer
136 Washer, Elastic
137 Stock Retaining Screw
140 Forend Cap
142 Forend Cap w/ Swivel
147 Trigger Lever Spring Ball
149 Trigger Lever Spring
150 Breech Block
151 Extractor
153 Extractor Plunger
155 Locking Block Lever Pin
156 Locking Block Lever Spring
158 Firing Pin Limit Stop
159 Firing Pin
160 Firing Pin Spring
161 Locking Block Lever
163 Extractor Spring
164 Link
165 Link Pin
166 Locking Block
167 Operating Handle
168 Trigger Guard
169 Hand & Auto Safety Retaining Pin
170 Hand Safety
171 Hand Safety Spring Follower
172 Hand Safety Spring
173 Action Spring Follower
174 Action Spring
176 Trigger Pin
177 Trigger Lever
178 Trigger Lever Pin
179 Trigger Lever Retaining Pin
180 Trigger
181 Hammer Spring Follower
182 Hammer Spring
183 Hammer Spring Tube
184 Hammer Pin
185 Hammer
186 Sear Spring
187 Sear
188 Sear Pin
189 Carrier Dog Pin
193 Carrier
194 Trigger Guard & Carrier Pin Bushing
195 Trigger Guard Pin Detent Spring (2 Req'd.)
196 Carrier Spring Stem Pivot Point
197 Carrier Spring
198 Carrier Spring Stem
199 Carrier Spring Detent
200 Safety Spring Plunger, Auto
201 Auto Safety Spring
202 Safety Spring Guide, Auto
203 Auto Safety
204 Auto Safety Pin
205 Magazine Spring
206 Stock
211 Magazine Spring Retaining Ring
212 Magazine Tube Blocking Spring
216 Magazine Shell & Auxiliary Shell Latch Spring
219 Nylon Ring
220 Nylon Ring Spring
300 Trigger Guard
301 Trigger, Late Model
302 Trigger Lever, Late Model
303 Sear, Late Model
304 Safety, Auto, Late Model
305 Hammer, Late Model
306 Hand Safety, Late Model
308 Trigger Stop Screw, Late Model
309 Trigger Lever Pin, Late Model
310 63370 Trigger & Sear Pin, Late Model
310A Sear Retaining Pin, Late Model
311 Carrier Spring Follower, Late Model
312 Trigger Spring, Late Model
313 Carrier Spring, Late Model
314 Carrier Dog Pin, Late Model
315 Carrier Dog, Late Model
316 Safety Spring, Auto, Late Model
317 Carrier

SPECIFICATIONS

Model: 48 AL Deluxe Prince of Wales
Action: semi-automatic, recoil-operated
Barrel: 24 in, 26 in. or 28 in.
Caliber: 28 gauge or 20 gauge
Capacity: 4+1
Common Features: satin walnut or A-grade satin walnut stock, vent rib barrel, aluminum alloy receiver, magazine cut off, blued finish, choke tubes

BACKGROUND

The Franchi 48 AL is long recoil operated shotgun. The action is very reliable and does not rely on the gas of a fired round to cycle the action. On firing, the bolt and barrel travel rearward, as pressure inside the barrel drops, the bolt and barrel unlock and the barrel returns forward under spring pressure. The bolt follows, picking up a fresh shell on its way and returns to battery. While the barrel and bolt are locked together during recoil the compressing recoil spring makes the shooter experience less felt recoil. At a little over five pounds the 48 AL is lightweight and a delight to carry all day in grouse coverts or chopped corn fields chasing pheasant. It's the last of the recoil-operating shotguns.
Importation Began: 1950
Country of Origin: Italy

Current Manufacturer: Franchi (franchiusa.com)
Similar Models: Field, Field Short Stock, Deluxe

REQUIRED TOOLS

Field Strip: none
Disassembly/Assembly: small punch, hammer, medium flat blade screwdriver

FIELD STRIP

1. Pull back the operating handle (part #167) to lock the breech bolt (150) in the rear position.
2. Slightly push the barrel into the receiver (130) and unscrew and remove the fore-end cap (140) from the magazine tube (113).
3. Slide off the fore-end (121) and barrel (110), Figure 1.
4. Remove the friction ring (118), governor ring (119), friction spring (120) and recoil spring (117), Figure 2.

At this point the 48 AL is field stripped for routine cleaning.

DETAILED DISASSEMBLY

1. Control the operating handle and press the carrier latch button (132) on the left side of the receiver so the breech bolt moves to its forward most position.

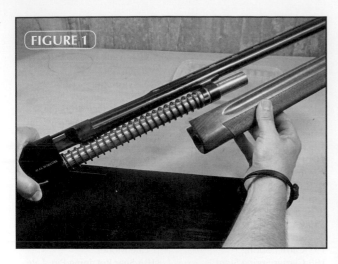

FIGURE 1

FIGURE 2

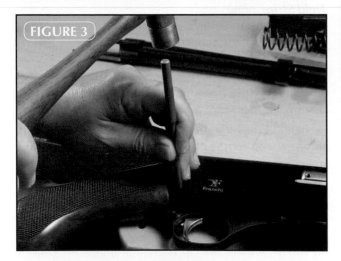

FIGURE 3

2. Use a small punch to drift out the two trigger guard pins (131), Figure 3.

3. Remove the trigger assembly from the bottom of the receiver, Figure 4.

4. Depress the action spring follower (173) with a medium screwdriver or punch to release the link (164) at the rear of the breech bolt, Figure 5.

5. Push the breech bolt forward out of the receiver while holding the operating handle. The operating handle will slip out of its slot in the breech bolt.

FIGURE 4

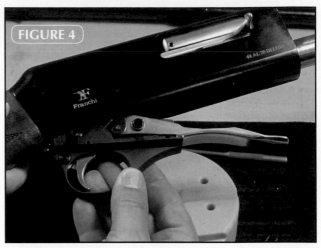

FIGURE 5

6. To remove the firing pin (159) and firing pin spring (160) use a roll-pin punch to drift out the firing pin limit stop (158) at the rear of the breech bolt.

To reassemble, reverse the disassembly procedures.

PARTS LIST

1 Barrel Assembly
2 Front Sight
3 Choke Tube
4 Sling Swivel Assembly (2 Req'd.)
5 Magazine Cap Assembly
6 Forearm
7 Receiver Assembly
8 Trigger Housing Pin
9 Stock Pin
10 Return Spring Retainer Pin
11 Return Spring Plunger
12 Return Spring
13 Return Spring Retainer

14 Trigger Housing Assembly
15 Rear Shell Stop
16 Front Shell Stop Spring
17 Front Shell Stop
18 Front Shell Stop Pin
19 Rear Shell Stop Pin
20 Shell Stop Retaining Clip
21 Rear Shell Stop Spring
22 Forearm Retainer
23 Gas System Return Spring
24 Pusher Assembly
25 Gas Piston Spacer Tube
26 Gas Piston Assembly
27 Seal Ring
28 Magazine Spring Retainer

29 Magazine Cap Detent
30 Magazine Plug
31 Magazine Spring
32 Magazine Follower
33 Slide Assembly
34 Link Pin
35 Link
36 Bolt Assembly
37 Operating Handle
38 Buttstock
39 Stock Retention Plate
40 Stock Nut Spacer
41 Stock Nut
42 Recoil Pad
43 Recoil Pad Screw (2 Req'd.)

SPECIFICATIONS
Model: Model 930 SPX Pistol Grip
Action: semi-automatic, gas-operated
Barrel: 27 in., 28 in. or 30 in.
Caliber: 410, 28, 20, or 12 gauge; 3-in. chamber
Capacity: 5+1 (2-3/4-in. shells)
Common Features: vent rib barrel, blue finish, excepts choke tubes, checkered wood stock

BACKGROUND
The Mossberg 930 is a versatile autoloader that chews through 2-3/4 and 3-inch shells. The gas system vents the excess gases from burning powder to reduce recoil. As with most Mossberg shotguns the 930 is well suited for upland birds, turkey, waterfowl and whitetail deer. The 930 High-Performance models are tricked out for 3-gun competition. Special Purpose models have pure tactical intentions.
Year Introduced: 2005
Current Manufacturer: O.F. Mossberg & Sons (mossbergs.com)
Similar Models: 930 Turkey (camo finish, 24-in. ported barrel), 930 Waterfowl (camo finish, 28-in. ported barrel), 930 Field (checkered walnut stock, blued finish), 930 Turkey – Pistol Grip (black synthetic pistol grip stock), 930 Slugster (Monte Carlo stock, rifled barrel), 930 Field/Deer Combo (two barrel set), 930 High Performance – Patrick Flannigan Rhythm Series (extended magazine, blue synthetic stock), 930 High Performance – Jerry Miculek JM Series (9- or 10-shot extended magazine, black synthetic stock), 930 SPX Pistol Grip – Blackwater Series (8-shot magazine, pistol grip stock), 930 Tactical (5-shot magazine), 930 SPX (standard synthetic stock), 930 Home Security (5-shot magazine, black synthetic stock), 930 Combo (two barrel set)

REQUIRED TOOLS
Field Strip: none
Disassembly/Assembly: small punch, brass hammer, Phillips screwdriver, small flat blade screwdriver

FIELD STRIP
1. Pull back the operating handle (part #37) to lock back the bolt assembly (36) in the fully rearward position.
2. Unscrew the magazine cap assembly (5) or, if your model has an extended magazine tube, unscrew the magazine cap/extended magazine tube and control the magazine spring (31) as it is under compression then slide the forearm (6) forward and off the receiver and magazine tube.
3. Pull the barrel assembly (1) forward to disengage it from the receiver and magazine tube. The seal ring (27)

and gas piston assembly (26) may come off with the barrel assembly, Figure 1.
4. Remove the gas piston spacer tube (25), pusher assembly (24), gas system return spring (23), and forearm retainer (22) from the magazine tube, Figure 2.

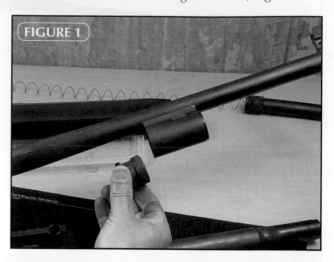

FIGURE 1

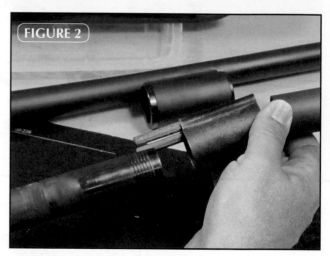

FIGURE 2

At this point the 930 is sufficiently disassembled for routine cleaning.

DETAILED DISASSEMBLY
1. Ensure the bolt assembly is in its forward most position by gasping the operating handle and pushing the bolt release button. Control the bolt assembly's forward movement.
2. Pull the bolt handle straight out of the bolt assembly, Figure 3.
3. Reach inside the receiver and depress the front shell stop the remove the bolt assembly and slide assembly (33) by sliding it forward and out from the receiver, Figure 4.
4. With the slide assembly free from the receiver, the bolt assembly can be removed from the slide assembly.

FIGURE 3

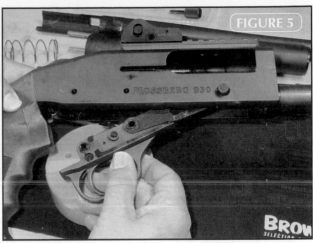

FIGURE 5

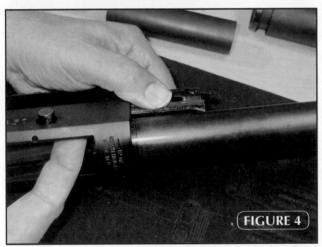

FIGURE 4

5. Remove the link (35) from the bolt assembly by pushing out the link pin (34) with a small punch and remove the link.

6. Use a small punch to drift out the firing pin retaining pin from the bolt assembly and remove the firing pin and firing pin spring from the rear of the bolt.

7. The extractor is removed by using a small flat blade screwdriver to depress the extractor plunger and extractor plunger spring then lift out the extractor from the bolt assembly.

8. Remove the trigger housing assembly (14) by drifting out the two trigger housing pins (8) from either side of the receiver.

9. Pull the trigger housing assembly straight out of the receiver, Figure 5.

10. Remove the buttstock (38) by first unscrewing and removing the two recoil pad screws (43) and the recoil pad (42). Then use a ¾ inch socket wrench to remove the stock nut (41), stock nut spacer (40), stock nut retention plate (39) and the stock.

Reassemble in reverse order.

Reassembly Tips: To ensure the tip of the link engages the return spring plunger (11) hold the receiver muzzle up when reinstalling. Look inside the receiver and position the link with a small screwdriver so it fits into the cup of the return spring plunger. The angled surface of the seal ring faces outward when reinstalled.

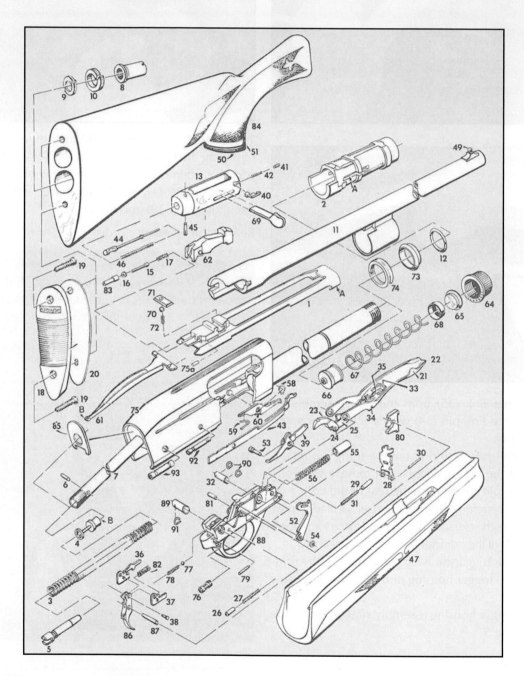

PARTS LIST

1 Action Bar Assembly
2 Action Bar Sleeve
3 Action Spring
4 Action Spring Follower
5 Action Spring Plug
6 Action Spring Plug Pin

7 Action Spring Tube
8 Action Spring Tube Nut
9 Action Spring Tube Nut
  Washer
10 Action Spring Tube Nut Lock
   Washer
11 Barrel Assembly
12 Barrel Seal

13 Breech Bolt
14 Breech Bolt Buffer
15 Breech Bolt Return Plunger
16 Breech Bolt Return Plunger
   Retaining Ring
18 Butt Plate Frame
19 Butt Plate Screw
20 Butt Plate Insert

21 Carrier
22 Carrier Assembly
23 Carrier Dog
24 Carrier Dog Pin
25 Carrier Dog Washer
26 Carrier Dog Follower
27 Carrier Dog Follower Spring
28 Carrier Latch

29 Carrier Latch Follower
30 Carrier Latch Pin
31 Carrier Latch Spring
32 Carrier Pivot Tube
33 Carrier Release
35 Carrier Release Pin
36 Carrier Release Spring
37 Connector, Left
38 Connector, Right
39 Disconnector
40 Extractor
41 Extractor Plunger
42 Extractor Spring
43 Feed Latch
44 Firing Pin
45 Firing Pin Retaining Pin
46 Firing Pin Retractor Spring
47 Fore-End Assembly

48 Fore-End Support Assembly
49 Front Sight
52 Hammer
53 Hammer Pin
54 Hammer Pin Washer
55 Hammer Plunger
56 Hammer Spring
58 Interceptor Latch Retainer
59 Interceptor Latch Spring
60 Interceptor Latch
61 Link
62 Locking Block Assembly
64 Magazine Cap
66 Magazine Follower
67 Magazine Spring
68 Magazine Spring Retainer
68 a Middle Sight
69 Operating Handle

70 Operating Handle Detent
   Ball
71 Operating Handle Plunger
   Retainer
72 Operating Handle Detent
   Spring
73 Piston
74 Piston Seal
74a Piston/Piston Seal Assembly
75 Receiver Assembly
75 a Return Plunger Retaining
   Pin
76 Safety Mechanism
77 Safety Mechanism Detent
   Plunger
78 Safety Mechanism Spring
79 Safety Mechanism Spring
   Retaining Pin

80 Sear
81 Sear Pin
82 Sear Spring
83 Slide Block Buffer
84 Stock Assembly
85 Stock Bearing Plate
86 Trigger
87 Trigger Pin
88 Trigger Plate RH Safety
   Mechanism
89 Trigger Plate Pin Bushing,
   Rear
90 Trigger Plate Pin Detent
   Spring, Front (2 Req'd.)
91 Trigger Plate Detent Spring,
   Rear
92 Trigger Plate Pin, Front
93 Trigger Plate Pin, Rear

SPECIFICATIONS

Model: Model 1100
Action: semi-automatic, gas-operated
Barrel: 27 in., 28 in. or 30 in.
Caliber: 410, 28, 20, or 12 gauge; 3-in. chamber
Capacity: 5+1 (2-3/4-in. shells)
Common Features: vent rib barrel, blue finish, excepts choke tubes, checkered wood stock

BACKGROUND

Since the introduction of the 1100 in 1963 this Remington shotgun has been popular with hunters and competition shooters. Over 4,000,000 have been produced. It uses a gas-operated system that is durable and produces noticeably less recoil than other gas-operating actions.

Year Introduced: 1963
Current Manufacturer: Remington (remington.com)
Similar Models: Competition Synthetic (adjustable synthetic stock), Classic Trap (blued finish, Monte Carlo wood stock), Competition (polished blue finish, semi-fancy walnut stock), Premier Sporting series (nickel-plated receiver, gold embellishments), Sporting Series (blued finish, wood stock), TAC 4 (22 in. barrel, magazine extension, synthetic stock)

REQUIRED TOOLS

Field Strip: none
Disassembly/Assembly: small punch, long shaft flat blade screwdriver, brass hammer, Phillips screwdriver, small flat blade screwdriver

FIELD STRIP

1. Push the safety mechanism (part #76) to the "safe" position and pull the operating handle (69) fully rearward until the breech bolt assembly is held open by the carrier latch (28).

2. Unscrew and remove the magazine cap (64) then slide the fore-end assembly (47) forward and off the magazine tube of the receiver assembly (75), Figure 1.

3. Pull the barrel assembly (11) forward from the receiver assembly, Figure 2.

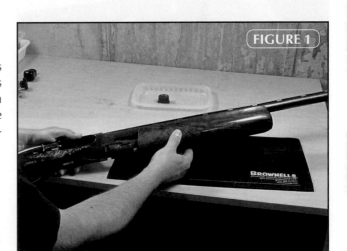

FIGURE 1

FIGURE 2

4. Slide the barrel seal (12), piston (73) and piston seal (74) forward and off the magazine tube of the receiver assembly.

At this point the shotgun is sufficiently disassembled for routine cleaning.

DETAILED DISASSEMBLY

1. Drift out the front trigger plate pin (92) and rear trigger plate pin (93), Figure 3.
2. Lift the rear of the trigger plate assembly, slide it rearward and remove it from the receiver assembly, Figure 4.

FIGURE 3

FIGURE 4

3. With the bolt assembly fully forward, pull the operating handle from the bolt (13), Figure 5.

FIGURE 5

4. Push the carrier release (33) and push upward on the carrier (21). Next reach into the bottom of the receiver and press and hold the feed latch.
5. Next pull the action bar assembly (1) from the receiver then release the feed latch.
6. Lift the breech bolt assembly from the rear of the action bar assembly.
7. Drift out the firing pin retaining pin (45) downward from the breech bolt assembly. Then remove the locking block assembly (62) from the bottom of the breech bolt assembly.
8. The firing pin (44) and firing pin retractor spring (46) can then be removed from the rear of the breech bolt assembly.
9. To remove the extractor (40) insert a small screwdriver between the extractor and extractor plunger (41) and press the extractor plunger and extractor spring rearward while pulling up on the extractor.
10. The stock (84) is removed by unscrewing the two recoil pad screws (70) and removing the recoil pad or buttplate (18) and spacer (20).
11. Use a long shaft flat blade screwdriver to remove the action spring tube nut (8) and the action spring tube nut lock washer (10) and action spring tube nut washer (9) will come free.
12. Insert a screwdriver into the hole of the magazine spring retainer (68) and place your hand over the end of the magazine tube as the magazine spring (67) is under compression then gently pry up on the magazine spring retainer. Pull the magazine spring and magazine follower (66) out.

Reassemble in reverse order.

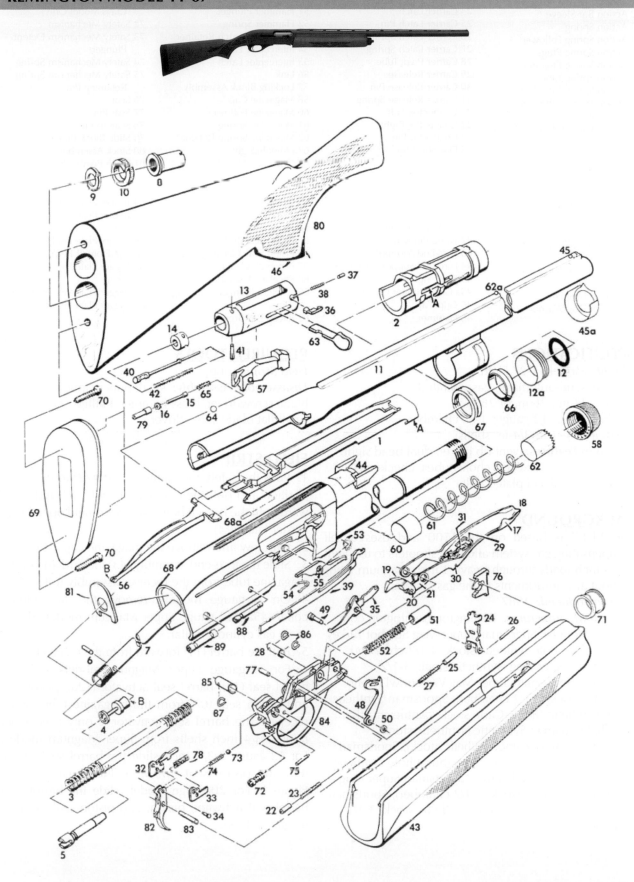

PARTS LIST

1 Action Bar Assembly
2 Action Bar Sleeve
3 Action Spring
4 Action Spring Follower
5 Action Spring Plug
6 Action Spring Plug Pin
7 Action Spring Tube
8 Action Spring Tube Nut
9 Action Spring Tube Nut
   Washer
10 Action Spring Tube Nut Lock
   Washer
11 Barrel Assembly
12 Barrel Seal
12a Barrel Seal Activator
13 Breech Bolt
14 Breech Bolt Buffer
15 Breech Bolt Return Plunger
16 Breech Bolt Return Plunger
   Retaining Ring
17 Carrier
18 Carrier Assembly
19 Carrier Dog
20 Carrier Dog Pin
21 Carrier Dog Washer
22 Carrier Dog Follower
23 Carrier Dog Follower Spring
24 Carrier Latch
25 Carrier Latch Pin
26 Carrier Latch Spring
27 Carrier Latch Spring
28 Carrier Pivot Tube
29 Carrier Release
30 Carrier Release Pin
31 Carrier Release Spring
32 Connector, Left
33 Connector, Right
34 Connector Pin
35 Disconnector
36 Extractor
37 Extractor Plunger
38 Extractor Spring
39 Feed Latch
40 Firing Pin
41 Firing Pin Retaining Pin
42 Firing Pin Retractor Spring
43 Fore-End Assembly
44 Fore-End Support Assembly
45 Front Sight
45a Gas Cylinder Collar
46 Grip Cap
48 Hammer
49 Hammer Pin
50 Hammer Pin Washer
51 Hammer Plunger
52 Hammer Spring
53 Interceptor Latch Retainer
54 Interceptor Latch Spring
55 Interceptor Latch
56 Link
57 Locking Block Assembly
58 Magazine Cap
60 Magazine Follower
61 Magazine Spring
62 Magazine Spring Retainer
62a Middle Sight
63 Operating Handle
64 Operating Handle Detent
   Ball
65 Operating Handle Detent
   Spring
66 Piston 12 Gauge
66 Piston Seal 20 Gauge
67 Piston Seal 12 Gauge
67 Piston 20 Gauge
68 Receiver Assembly
68 a Return Plunger Retaining
   Pin
69 Recoil Pad Brown
70 Recoil Pad Screw
71 Rubber Grommet (Sporting
   Clays Model Only)
72 Safety Mechanism
73 Safety Mechanism Detent
   Plunger
74 Safety Mechanism Spring
75 Safety Mechanism Spring
   Retaining Pin
76 Sear
77 Sear Pin
78 Sear Spring
79 Slide Block Buffer
80 Stock Assembly
81 Stock Bearing Plate
82 Trigger
83 Trigger Pin
84 Trigger Plate Assembly
85 Trigger Plate Pin Bushing,
   Rear
86 Trigger Plate Pin Detent
   Spring, Front (2 Req'd.)
87 Trigger Plate Detent Spring,
   Rear
88 Trigger Plate Pin, Front
89 Trigger Plate Pin, Rear

SPECIFICATIONS

Model: Model 11-87 Field
Action: semi-automatic, gas-operated
Barrel: 23 in., 26 in. or 28 in.
Caliber: 20 or 12 gauge; 3-in. chamber
Capacity: 4+1 (2-3/4-in. shells)
Common Features: vent rib barrel, dual bead sight, satin blue finish, excepts choke tubes, checkered wood stock, nickel plated bolt

BACKGROUND

The 11-87 is based on the 1100 and uses a self compensating gas system allowing shooters to use light 2-3/4 inch loads through heavy 3 inch magnum loads without any adjustments to the gas system.

Year Introduced: 1987
Current Manufacturer: Remington (remington.com)
Similar Models: Sportsman Super Mag Surshot Turkey (camo thumbhole synthetic stock, 3-1/2 chamber), Sportsman Super Mag (synthetic stock, 3-1/2 chamber), Sportsman Super Mag Waterfowl (camo synthetic stock, 3-1/2 chamber), Sportsman Synthetic Deer (synthetic Monte Carlo stock, cantilever rifled barrel), Sportsman Synthetic (synthetic stock), Sportsman Camo (camo synthetic stock), Sportsman Surshot Camo Cantilever (camo thumbhole synthetic stock cantilever rifled barrel), Sportsman Super Mag Synthetic (synthetic stock, 3-1/2 chamber), Sportsman Super Mag Waterfowl (camo synthetic stock, 3-1/2 chamber)

REQUIRED TOOLS

Field Strip: none
Disassembly/Assembly: small punch, long shaft flat blade screwdriver, brass hammer, Phillips screwdriver, small flat blade screwdriver

FIELD STRIP

1. Push the safety mechanism (part #72) to the "safe" position and pull the operating handle (63) fully rearward until the breech bolt assembly is held open by the carrier latch (24).

2. Unscrew and remove the magazine cap (58).

3. Slide the fore-end assembly (43) forward and off the magazine tube from the receiver assembly (68).

4. On 12-gauge models, remove the gas cylinder collar (45a); 12-gauge Super Magnum models do not use a gas cylinder collar.

5. Pull the barrel (11) forward from the receiver.

6. For 12-gauge Super Magnum models slide the barrel seal (12), barrel seal activator (12a), piston (66) and piston seal (67) from the magazine tube on the receiver. The barrel seal activator is only used when firing 2-3/4 inch shells from Super Magnum models. For 12-gauge 2-3/4 inch slide the barrel seal, piston (66) and piston seal (67) from the magazine tube, Figure 1. For 20-gauge models slide the barrel seal, barrel seal activator, piston, and piston seal from the magazine tube.

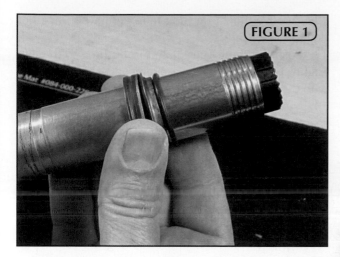

FIGURE 1

At this point the 11-87 is sufficiently disassembled for routine cleaning.

DETAILED DISASSEMBLY

1. Control the operating handle and depress the carrier release (29) to close the action.

2. Pull the operating handle from the breech bolt (13).

3. Push the carrier release and push upward on the carrier (17).

4. Reach in the bottom of the receiver and depress and hold the feed latch (39), Figure 2. Then slide the action bar assembly (1) from the receiver and magazine tube, Figure 3. The breech bolt will easily detach from the action bar assembly.

5. Drift out the firing pin retaining pin (41) downward from the breech bolt assembly, Figure 4. Then remove the firing pin (40) and firing pin retractor spring (42) can then be removed from the rear of the breech bolt assembly. The locking block assembly (57) can then be removed from the bottom of the breech bolt.

6. The extractor (36) is removed by using a small flat blade screwdriver to depress the extractor plunger (37)

and extractor spring (38), and pivoting the extractor out and out from the breech bolt. The extractor spring is under compression so control it after the extractor is removed.

7. Next drift out the front trigger plate pin (88) and rear trigger plate pin (89) from the receiver, Figure 5.

8. Lift the rear of the trigger plate assembly (84), slide it rearward and pull it out from the receiver.

FIGURE 3

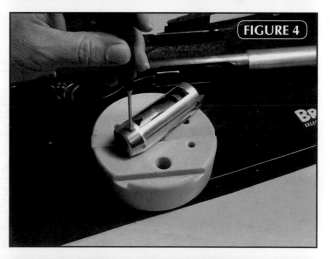

FIGURE 4

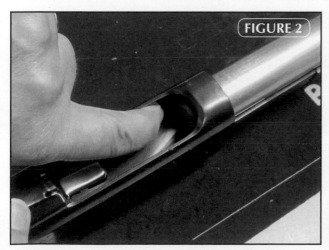

FIGURE 2

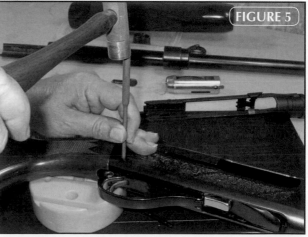

FIGURE 5

9. Remove the link (56) by sliding it forward until its two legs come free at the rear of the receiver and pull out the bottom of the receiver.

10. Hold and control the hammer (48) as you pull the trigger (82) so the hammer is in its fully forward/fire position. Then slide the front trigger plate detent spring (86) from its groove in the carrier pivot tube (28), Figure 6. Push out the carrier pivot tube.

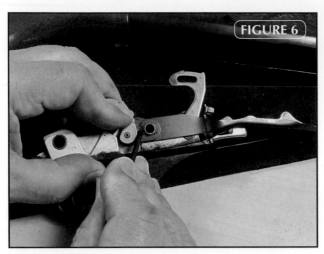

FIGURE 6

11. Next pull the carrier latch (24) to the rear to disengage it from the trigger plate.

12. Remove the carrier dog follower (22) and carrier dog follower spring (23).

13. Push out the trigger plate pin bushing to the left. Slightly pull the trigger to ease removal. It will come out with the rear trigger plate detent spring (87) attached.

14. Next disengage the sear spring (78) from the sear (76).

15. Use a small punch to drift out the trigger pin (83) from right to left. The trigger can then be pulled out from the trigger plate. The trigger will come out as an assembly with the left connector (32) and right connector (33) attached.

16. The stock (80) is removed by unscrewing the two recoil pad screws (70) and removing the recoil pad (69).

17. Use a long shaft flat blade screwdriver to remove the action spring tube nut (8) and the action spring tube nut lock washer (10) and action spring tube nut washer (9) will come free.

18. Use a screwdriver to depress and rotate the magazine spring retainer (62). The magazine spring (61) is under compression. Remove the magazine spring and magazine follower (60).

Reassemble in reverse order.

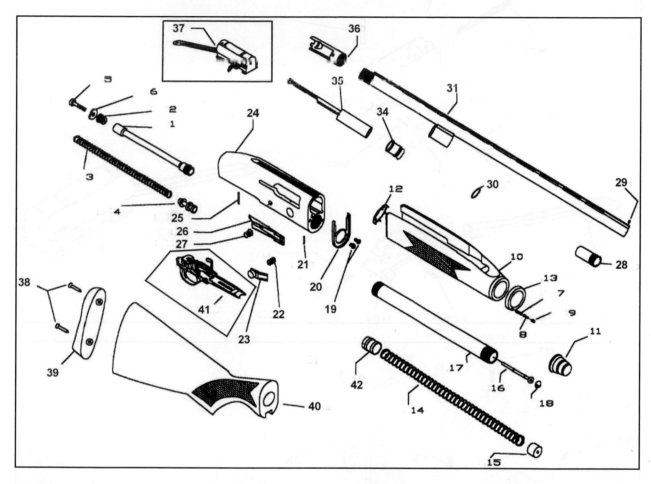

PARTS LIST

1 Recoil Spring Tube
2 Nut, Stock Retaining
3 Spring, Recoil
4 Cap, Recoil Spring
5 Screw, Stock Retaining
6 Washer, Stock Retaining
7 Spring, Cap Stop
8 Screw, Cap Stop
9 Plunger, Cap Stop
10 Forend
11 Magazine Cap
12 Forend Pinned Plate
13 Forend Plate
14 Spring, Magazine
15 Retainer, Magazine Spring
16 Magazine Plug
17 Magazine Tube
18 Magazine Plug Blocker
19 Screw, Forend Latch
20 Forend Latch
21 Pin, Cartridge Latch Button

22 Spring, Cartridge Latch
   Button
23 Bolt Release Button
24 Receiver
25 Pin, Cartridge Latch
26 Cartridge Latch
27 Spring, Cartridge Latch
28 Choke Tube
29 Front Sight
30 O-Ring, Gas Cylinder
31 Barrel
34 Piston
35 Slide Arm Assembly
36 Barrel Extension
37 Bolt Assembly
38 Screw, Recoil Pad
39 Recoil Pad
40 Stock
41 Trigger Assembly
42 Magazine Follower

Bolt Assembly
M01 Firing Pin

M02 Firing Pin Spring
M03 Bolt Handle
M04 Extractor
M05 Spring, Extractor
M06 Link
M07 Pin, Link
M08 Pin, Bolt Handle Spring
   Retaining
M09 Sliding Bar Block
M10 Pin, Bolt Handle
M11 Spring, Bolt Handle Pin
M12 Bolt
M13 Pin, Extractor
M14 Locking Block
M15 Pin, Firing Retaining
M16 Plunger, Extractor Spring

Trigger Assembly
B01 Trigger Guard
B02 Safety
B03 Pin, Safety Plunger Spring
B04 Spring, Safety Plunger
B05 Pin, Safety Spring Retaining

B06 Pin, Trigger Stop
B07 Disconnector
B09 Spring, Trigger
B10 Trigger
B11 Spring, Disconnector
B13 Pin, Disconnector
B14 Pin, Trigger Pivot
B15 Hammer
B16 Spring, Hammer
B17 Cap, Hammer Spring
B18 Carrier Latch Connector
B19 Carrier Latch
B20 Hammer Tube
B21 Hammer Tube D-Ring
B22 Spring, Carrier Lock Button
B23 Carrier Lock Button
B24 Carrier
B25 Breech Bolt Latch
B26 Pin, Breech Bolt Latch
B27 Pin, Carrier
B28 Spring, Breech Bolt Latch
B29 Breech Bolt Latch Spring Cap
B30 Pin, Receiver

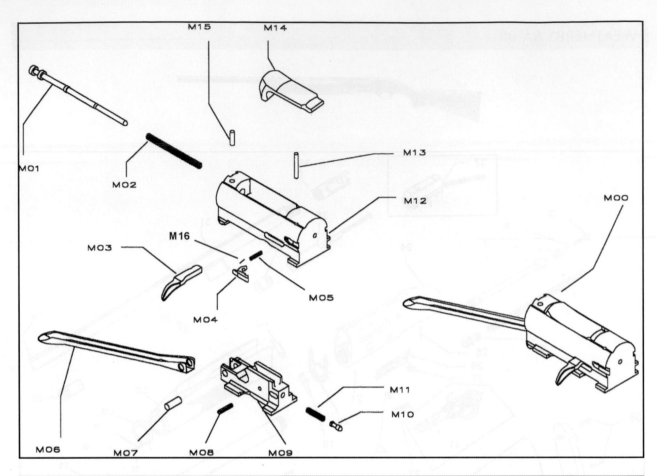

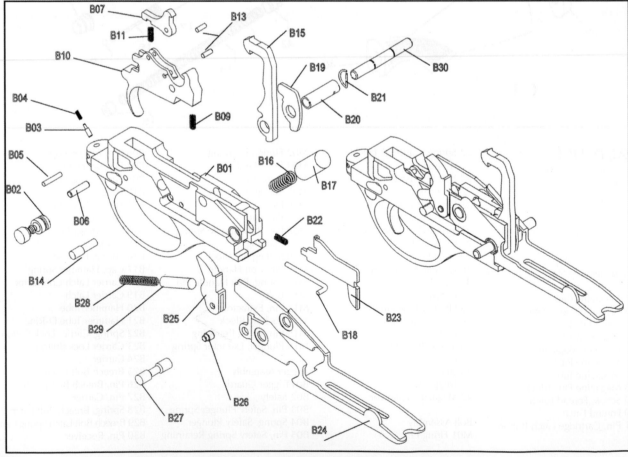

SPECIFICATIONS

Model: SA-08 Deluxe
Action: semi-automatic, gas-operated
Barrel: 26 in. or 28 in.
Caliber: 12 gauge or 20 gauge, 3-in. chamber
Capacity: 5+1 (2-3/4-in. shells)
Common Features: vent rib barrel, blue finish, excepts choke tubes, dual valve gas system, checkered wood stock, magazine cut off

BACKGROUND

The SA-08 is manufactured in Turkey for Weatherby and is chambered in either 12 or 20 gauge. The action uses a dual valve system that requires the pistons to be manually swapped out depending on loads to be fired. One piston for light target loads and the other for heavy hunting loads. The trigger assembly drops out quickly and easily from the receiver.

Year Introduced: 2008
Current Manufacturer: Weatherby (weatherby.com)
Similar Models: Deluxe (checkered wood stock, blued finish), Synthetic (blued finish, polymer stock, 12 gauge), Synthetic Youth (26 and 28-in. barrel lengths, blued finish, 20 and 12 gauge), Upland (22-in. barrel, checkered wood stock, blued finish), Synthetic Waterfowler 3.0 (camo finish, polymer stock)

REQUIRED TOOLS

Field Strip: small punch, hammer
Disassembly/Assembly: stock tool or socket and extension

FIELD STRIP

1. First cock the action by pulling the bolt assembly to the rear via the bolt handle (part #M03) and releasing it by depressing the bolt release button (23).

2. Next unscrew the magazine cap (11) counter clock-wise until it is removed from the magazine tube (17).

3. Remove the forend (10) by sliding it forward toward the muzzle until it clears of the magazine tube.

4. Next remove the barrel (31) by grasping and pulling forward out from the receiver (24).

At this point the SA-08 is disassembled for routine cleaning.

DETAILED DISASSEMBLY

1. To remove the trigger assembly, place the safety (B02) in the "safe" position. Make sure the action is cocked and bolt assembly is forward.

2. Use a small punch and hammer to drift out the receiver pin (B30) through either side of the receiver until the receiver pin can be grasped by hand then remove it from the receiver, Figure 1.

3. Next slightly push the trigger assembly forward and then pull the trigger assembly straight out from the receiver, Figure 2.

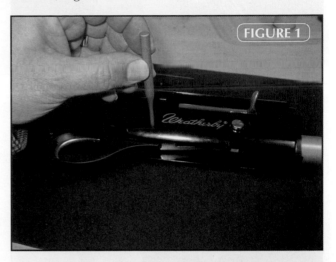

4. Remove the bolt assembly from the receiver by first remove the piston from magazine tube by sliding it forward until it is free from tube.

5. Next push the bolt assembly rearward about one inch and hold it while grasping the bolt handle and pulling it out from the bolt, Figure 3. The bolt assembly is under spring tension so make sure to control it.

6. Next remove the slide arm assembly (35) along the magazine tube until the bolt assembly is out of the receiver, Figure 4. The bolt assembly will then detach from the slide.

7. The magazine plug is removed by first detaching the magazine plug blocker (18) from the magazine tube by

FIGURE 3

pushing the magazine plug blocker into the magazine tube approximately 3/8 inch and rotating it upward until a side of the magazine plug blocker protrudes above the magazine tube.

8. Remove the magazine plug blocker and then pull the magazine plug (16) out from the magazine tube.

Reverse procedures to reassemble.

Reassembly Tip: Make sure the piston is placed back onto the magazine tube correctly by making sure the large outside diameter of the piston is placed onto the magazine tube first.

FIGURE 4

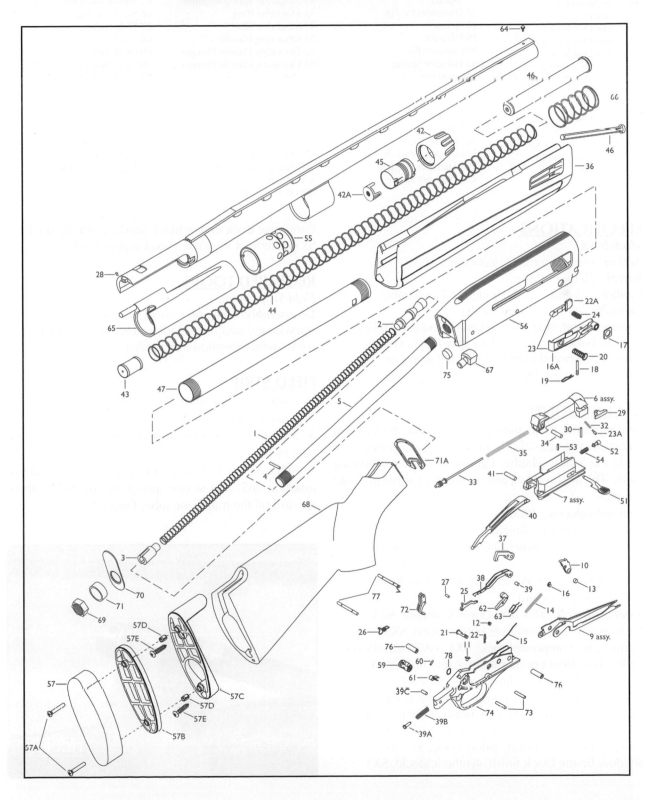

PARTS LIST

1 Action Spring
2 Action Spring Plunger
3 Action Spring Retainer
4 Action Spring Retainer Pin
5 Action Spring Tube
6 Bolt Assembly
7 Breech Block Slide
9 Carrier Assembly
10 Carrier Dog
11 Carrier Dog Buffer
12 Carrier Dog Lower Stop
13 Carrier Dog Rivet
14 Carrier Dog Spring
15 Carrier Dog Spring Guide
16 Carrier Dog Upper Stop
16A Carrier Latch
17 Carrier Latch Damper
18 Carrier Latch Pin
19 Carrier Latch Pin Clip
20 Carrier Latch Spring
21 Carrier Pin
22 Carrier Pin Retainer

22A Cartridge Stop
23 Cartridge Stop & Carrier
   Latch Assembly
23A Cartridge Stop & Extractor
   Plunger
24 Cartridge Stop Spring
25 Disconnector
26 Disconnector & Trigger
   Spring
27 Disconnector Pin
28 Ejector
29 Extractor
30 Extractor Pin
32 Extractor Spring
33 Firing Pin
34 Firing Pin Retainer Pin
35 Firing Pin Spring
36 Forearm
37 Hammer
38 Hammer Link
39 Hammer Link Pin
39A Hammer Plunger
39B Hammer Spring

39C Hammer Spring Plunger
   Pin
40 Link
41 Link Pin
42 Magazine Cap
42A Magazine Cap Retainer
43 Magazine Follower
44 Magazine Spring
45 Magazine Spring Retainer
46 Magazine Plug
47 Magazine Tube
51 Operating Handle
52 Operating Handle Plunger
53 Operating Handle Plunger
   Pin
54 Operating Handle Plunger
   Spring
55 Piston Assembly
56 Receiver
57 Recoil Pad
57A Recoil Pad Screw
57B Recoil Pad Spacer Plate
57C Recoil Pad Support
57D Recoil Pad Support Insert

57E Recoil Pad Support Screw
   (2 Req'd.)
59 Safety
60 Safety Plunger
61 Safety Spring
62 Sear
63 Sear Spring
64 Sight Front
65 Sleeve Assembly
66 Sleeve Spring
67 Slide Buffer
68 Stock
69 Stock Bolt Nut
70 Stock Bolt Plate
71 Stock Bolt Washer
71A Stock Spacer
72 Trigger
73 Trigger & Sear Pin
74 Trigger Guard
75 Trigger Guard Buffer
76 Trigger Guard Bushing
77 Trigger Guard Pin
78 Trigger Guard Pin Retainer

SPECIFICATIONS

Model: SX3
Action: semi-automatic, gas-operated
Barrel: 26 in. or 28 in.
Caliber: 12 gauge or 20 gauge, 3-in. chamber
Capacity: 4+1 (2-3/4-in. shells)
Common Features: alloy receiver/magazine tube, vent rib barrel, matte black or grey finish, choke tubes, back-bored barrel, checkered wood or composite adjustable stock

BACKGROUND

The Super X3 (SX3) uses an active value system that automatically self-adjusts the correct gas pressure to cycle the action whether light target or heavy hunting loads. The action is fast able to shoot 12 shots in 1.442 seconds.
Year Introduced: 2006
Country of Origin: Belgium
Current Manufacturer: FN (Fabrique Nationale d'Herstal)
Current Importer: Winchester Repeating Arms (winchesterguns.com)
Similar Models: SX3 Black Field Compact, SX3 Cantilever Deer (cantilever optic mount), SX3 Composire (composite stock), SX3 NWTF Cantilever Turkey (cantilever optic mount, camo finish), SX3 Sporting Adjustable (adjustable comb stock), SX3 Universal Hunter (camo finish, polymer stock), SX3 Walnut Field (matte gray finish, walnut stock), SX3Waterfowl Hunter (camo finish), SX3 Black Field (matte black finish, wood stock), SX3 Black Shadow (matte black finish, synthetic stock), SX3

Cantilever Buck (matte black finish, synthetic stock), SX3Waterfowl Realtree Max-4 (camo finish)

REQUIRED TOOLS

Field Strip: none
Disassembly/Assembly: small punch, Phillips screwdriver, small flat blade screwdriver, ½-inch socket with extension and ratchet

FIELD STRIP

1. Place the safety (part #59) in the "safe" position.
2. Unscrew and remove the magazine cap (42).
3. Slide the forearm (36) forward and off the magazine tube (47).
4. Remove the barrel, piston assembly (55), sleeve assembly (65) and sleeve spring (66) by sliding them forward off the magazine tube, Figure 1.

FIGURE 1

At this point the SX3 is disassembled for routine cleaning.

DETAILED DISASSEMBLY

1. Hold the operating handle (51) while depressing the carrier latch (16A) and control the forward moving of the bolt assembly (6).

2. Push out the two trigger guard pins (77) using a small punch from either side of the receiver (56).

3. Pull the trigger guard (74) up and out of the receiver, Figure 2.

4. Pull the operating handle out of the bolt assembly, Figure 3.

FIGURE 4

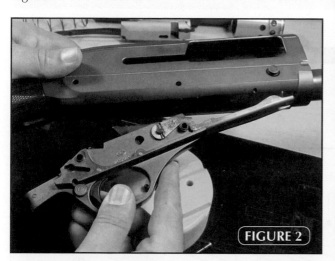
FIGURE 2

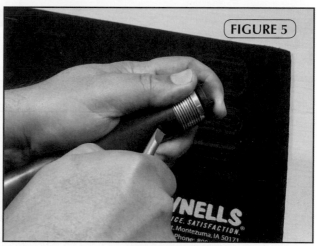
FIGURE 5

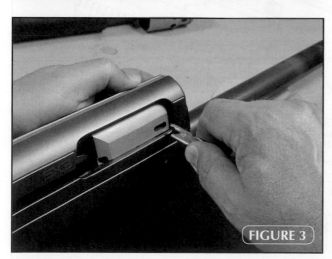
FIGURE 3

Reassemble in reverse order.

5. Slide the bolt assembly and breech block slide (7) forward and out of the front of the receiver, Figure 4. The bolt assembly and breech block slide will separate.

6. Remove the magazine plug (46) by using a small flat blade screwdriver to depress the magazine spring retainer tab in the magazine tube, Figure 5. Keep your hand over the magazine tube to control the magazine spring (44) as it comes free with the magazine plug.

Reassembly Tip: When you slide bolt assembly and breech block slide back into the receiver, make sure the link (40) at the rear of the bolt slide fits into the recess in the action spring plunger (2).

Lever Action

WINCHESTER 1887   CLASSIC FIREARM

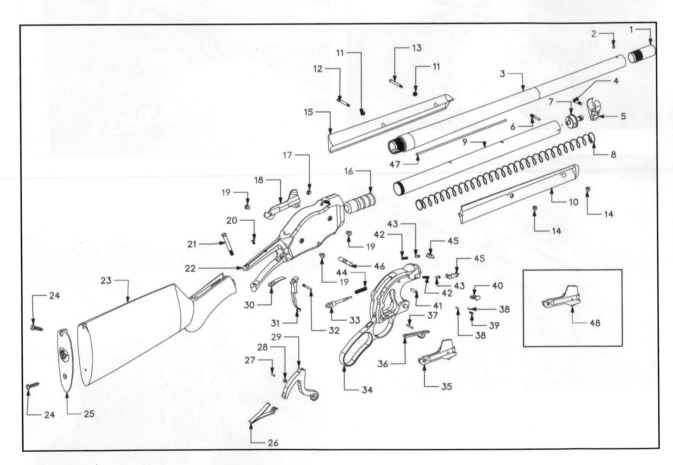

PARTS LIST

1 Choke Tube
2 Front Sight
3 Barrel
4 Barrel Band Screw
5 Barrel Band

6 Magazine Tube Locking Screw
7 Magazine Tube Plug
8 Magazine Spring
9 Magazine Tube
10 Right Forend
11 Forend Screw Washer

12 Forend Front Screw
13 Forend Rear Screw
14 Threaded Forend Washer
15 Left Forend
16 Magazine Follower
17 Shell Detent Screw

18 Left Cartridge Guide
19 Cartridge Guide Screw
20 Trigger Spring Screw
21 Tang Screw
22 Receiver
23 Stock

24 Buttplate Screw	30 Trigger Spring	36 Carrier	42 Spring
25 Buttplate	31 Trigger	37 Carrier Pin	43 Extractor Link
26 Hammer Spring	32 Trigger Screw Pin	38 Pin	44 Firing Pin Spring
27 Hammer Inner Washer Pin	33 Firing Pin	39 Camme Screw	45 Left Extractor
28 Inner Washer Pin	34 Breech Bolt	40 Camme	46 Receiver/Bolt Pin
29 Hammer	35 right cartridge guide	41 Pin	47 Magazine Reduction Rod

SPECIFICATIONS

Model: Puma M-87
Action: Lever
Barrel: 22 in. or 28 in.
Weight Unloaded: 6.75 lb.
Caliber: 12 gauge
Capacity: 5+ 1
Common Features: open sights, choke tubes, rebounding hammer, thumb safety, color case hardened receiver, blue barrel finish; smooth wood stock/forearm

BACKGROUND

The Winchester 1887 was the first successful repeating shotgun. There are subtle differences between original Winchester-made 1887s and replicas like the Puma M-87. The instructions below are specifically for the M-87 and with some subtleties will work with original Winchesters.
Year Introduced: 1887 (Puma new 2009)
Country of Origin: USA
Current Importer: Legacy Sports (legacysports.com)
Similar Models: Fast Load Shotgun (22 in. barrel; fast-load, two-round capacity), Chiappa 1887 T-Model (18.5 inch barrel, pistol grip)

REQUIRED TOOLS

Disassembly/Assembly: small and medium flat blade screwdrivers, 1/8 in. punch, nylon hammer, needle-nose pliers

DISASSEMBLY

1. Completely open the action by cycling the lever (part #34), Puma calls it the breech bolt as the lever and breech bolt are an assembly, forward. Then compress the hammer spring (26) using a pair of needle-nose pliers. Lift out the front hook of the mainspring off the receiver/bolt pin (46) and remove the main-spring back and through the slot in the breech bolt, Figure 1.

2. Push out the receiver/bolt pin from either side of the receiver (22) using a punch, Figure 2.

3. Remove the hammer (29) downward and through the slot in the breech bolt, Figure 3.

4. Remove the two cartridge guide screws (19) one on each side of the receiver (22) using a medium flat blade

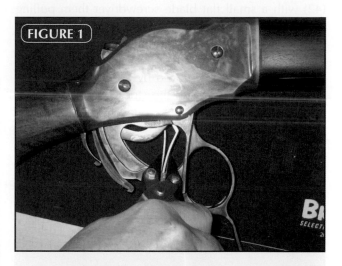

FIGURE 1

FIGURE 2

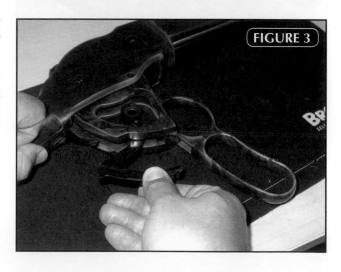

FIGURE 3

screwdriver, Figure 4. Remove the breech bolt from the bottom of the receiver along with the left cartridge guide (18) and right cartridge guide (35).

5. Remove the left extractor (45) from the breech bolt by depressing extractor link (43) and extractor spring (42) with a small flat blade screwdriver them pulling the left extractor out of the breech bolt. The extractor link and extractor spring are under tension so control them with the screwdriver as your remove the extractor.

6. The stock (23) is removed by unscrewing the tang screw (21), Figure 5. Pull the stock rearward and off the receiver.

8. Remove the magazine tube plug (7) by first removing the barrel band screw (4), Figure 6. Use a nylon hammer to gently tap the barrel band off the protrusion on the magazine tube plug. Then unscrew the magazine tube locking screw (6). With the magazine tube locking screw removed, control the magazine tube plug as the magazine spring (8) is under compression.

FIGURE 4

FIGURE 6

Reassemble in reverse order.

Reassembly Tip: Use a punch as a slave pinto align the receiver/bolt pin holes in breechblock, hammer and receiver. Then insert the receiver/bolt pin while withdrawing the punch/slave pin.

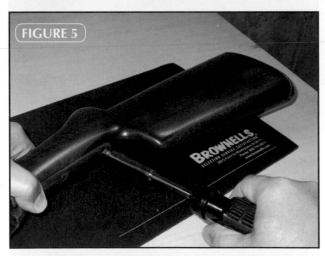

FIGURE 5

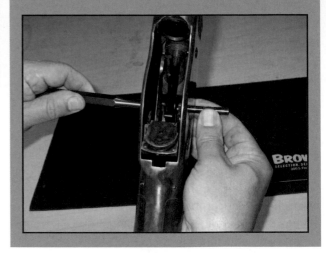

7. The left forend (15) and right forend (10) are removed by unscrewing the forend front screw (12) and forend rear screw (13) then pulling the forends toward the muzzle.

Over and Under

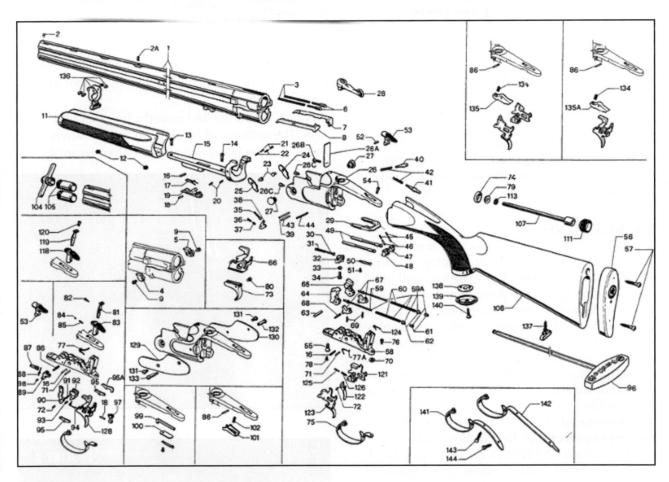

PARTS LIST

1 Barrel
2 Sight, Front
3 Spring, Ejector
4 Shoulder, LH Barrel
5 Shoulder, RH, Barrel
6 Plunger, Ejector
7 Ejector, RH
8 Ejector, LH
9 Screw, Bbl Shield
11 Forearm
12 Forearm Washer
13 Forearm Screw
14 Forearm Screw
15 Forearm WB iron Assembly
16 Forearm Pin
17 Forearm Spring
18 Pin, Spring

19 Forearm Catch
20 Forearm Screw
21 Forearm Plunger
22 Forearm Spring
23 Forearm Pin
24 Forearm Lever
25 Lever, Forearm Iron LH
26 Receiver
27 Pin, Hinge
28 Top Lever
29 Latch, Locking
30 Pin, Top Lever Spring
31 Spring, Top Lever
32 Top Lever Pin
33 Top Lever Nut
34 Screw, Top Lever
35 Plunger, Locking Latch
  Release
36 Spring, Sear

37 Plunger, Sear
38 Lever, Locking Latch Clamp
39 Pin, Lock Latch Clamp Lever
40 Pin, Firing Right Hand Lower
41 Pin, Firing, Left Hand Upper
42 Spring, Firing Pin
43 Pin, Firing Pin Stop Spring
44 Pin, Cocking Lever
45 Spring, Cocking Lever
46 Plunger, Cocking
47 Lever, RH Cocking
48 Lever, LH Cocking
49 Rod, Cocking
50 Spring, Safety
51 Screw, Safety Spring
52 Pin, Safety
53 Safety
54 Screw, Top Tang
55 Screw, Trigger

57 Screw Butt Plate
58 Plate, Trigger
59 Spring, Hammer Assembly
60 Spring, Hammer Assembly
61 Bushing, Hammer Spring
  Guide
62 Nut, Hammer Spring Guide
63 Pin, Hammer
64 Hammer, Left Hand
65 Hammer, Right Hand
66 Trigger, Adjustable, Upper
67 Sear
68 Pin, Sear
69 Spring, Sear
70 Washer, Trigger Guard Screw
71 Pin Connect Lever Trigger
  Spring
72 Pin, Inertia Block/Trigger
73 Trigger, Adjustable

73 Trigger, Canted RH	85 Spring, Selector Lever	98 Pin, Inert Lever/Ext Stop	128 Trigger, Non-Adjust
74 Washer, Concave	86 Pin, Inertia Block	99 Rod, Automatic Safety	129 Side Plate LH/RH
75 Guard, Trigger	87 Lever, Inertia Pawl	100 Washer, Auto Safety Spring	131 Screw, Front Side Plate
75 Guard, Trigger	88 Spring, Inertia Block Lever	101 Lever, Safety	132 Screw, Dummy Side Plate
76 Screw, Trigger Guard	89 Lever, Inertia Block	102 Spring, Safety Lever	(Rear)
77 Spring, St Trigger	90 Rest, Inertia Block	105 Choke Tube	133 Screw, Dummy Side Plate
78 Screw, Trigger Plate Screw	91 Pin, Universal, Long,	107 Stock Bolt	(Rear)
Lock	92 Block, Inertia	108 Stock	134 Spring, Safety Lever
79 Washer, Convex	93 Pin, Universal, Short	111 Collar Stock Support	135 Lever, Safety
80 Screw, Trigger	94 Spring, Inertia Lever	113 Washer, Spring Stock Bolt	136 Swivel, Front
81 Lever	95 Lever, Connecting	119 Lever, Selector	137 Swivel, Stock
82 Pin, Selector Lever	96 Wrench, Stock Bolt, Allen	120 Screw, Barrel Selector Lock	145 Lever, St Connecting
83 Safety	Style	121 Trigger Body	146 Bead, Mid Rib
84 Ball, Safety	97 Pawl, Selector	122 Trigger, RH	

SPECIFICATIONS

Model: 687 Silver Pigeon II
Action: break action, double barrel, over and under
Barrel: 26 in. or 28 in.
Caliber: 20 or 12 gauge
Capacity: 2
Common Features: vent rib barrel, choke tubes, barrel selector, automatic safety, single selective trigger, ejectors, oil finished walnut stock, recoil pad, engraved receiver

BACKGROUND

The Beretta 680 series of over and under shotguns are natural pointers built for hunting or targeting shooting. If your credit allows, Beretta will build an exquisite example of the shotgun maker's art. All 680 series are known for their low-profile receivers. Most over and under do not need detailed disassembly for cleaning. Occasionally or after a few hundred rounds pull the stock off and blow the mechanism with canned air to remove debris. The Beretta 680 series, like other over and unders, can be complicated to disassemble.

Year Introduced: 1999 (680 series since 1988)
Current Manufacturer: Beretta (berettausa.com)
Similar Models: 687 EELL Diamond Pigeon (hand engraved receiver and side plates, highly figured walnut stock), 687 Silver Pigeon V (pistol grip or straight English stock, engraved case-color receiver), 686 Silver Pigeon I (minimally engraved receiver), 687 Silver Pigeon III (extensively engraved receiver), 687 Ultralight Deluxe (aluminum and titanium frame), 686 White Onyx (satin nickel frame)

REQUIRED TOOLS

Field Strip: none
Disassembly: small flat blade screwdriver, long shaft flat blade screwdriver or 6mm socket and extension, rubber mallet

FIELD STRIP

1. Pull out the forearm catch (part #19) out from the forearm (11) and pivot the forearm away from the barrels (1), Figure 1.

2. Grasp the barrels and push the top lever (28) to the right. The action will break open as the barrels pivot down. Pull the barrels from the receiver, Figure 2.

FIGURE 1

FIGURE 2

DISASSEMBLY

1. Remove the stock (108) by removing two recoil pad screws (57) and removing the recoil pad (56).
2. Use a 6mm hex head socket, extension and ratchet to remove the stock bolt (107), Figure 3.

3. Pull the stock from the receiver (26), Figure 4.

Reassemble in reverse order.

FIGURE 3

FIGURE 4

BROWNING CITORI

CLASSIC FIREARM

PARTS LIST

1 Butt Plate
2 Butt Plate Screw
3 Cocking Lever
4 Cocking Lever Lifter
5 Cocking Lever Lifter Pin
7 Cocking Lever Pin
8 Connector
9 Connector Stop Pin
10 Drop Stop Adjustment Set Screw
11 Ejector Extension Lift
12 Ejector Extension Right
13 Ejector Extension Screw
14 Ejector Hammer Left
15 Ejector Hammer Pin
16 Ejector Hammer Right
17 Ejector Hammer Spring
18 Ejector Hammer Spring Guide
19 Ejector Hammer Spring Receiver

20 Ejector Hammer Spring Receiver Screw
21 Ejector Retaining Pin (Screw)
22 Ejector Right & Left
23 Ejector Sear
24 Ejector Sear Pin
25 Ejector Sear /Cocking Lever Lifter Spring
26 Ejector Trip Rod Left
27 Ejector Trip Rod Right
28 Firing Pin Over
29 Firing Pin Retaining Pin
30 Firing Pin Spring Under
31 Firing Pin Under
32 Forearm Bracket
33 Forearm Screw
34A Forearm Screw Escutcheon
34 Forearm
35 Hammer Left
36 Hammer Pin
37 Hammer Right
38 Impact Ring Retaining Woodscrew In Recoil Reducer

39 Inertia Block
39A Inertia Block Pin
40 Link
41 Link Pin Inertia Block
42 Link Pin Receiver
43 Locking Bolt
44 Mainspring
45 Mainspring Guide
46 Recoil Pad Assembly
62 Sear Left
63 Sear Pin
64 Sear Right
65 Sear Spring
66 Selector Ball Spring Type
67 Selector Ball Type
68 Selector Block Type
69 Selector Safety
70 Selector Spring
71 Selector Spring Detent Pin
71A Selector/Take Down Lever
72 Sight Bead Front
73 Sight Center
80 Stock Bolt

81 Stock Bolt Lock Washer
82 Stock Bolt Washer
83 Stock
84 Takedown Lever
85 Takedown Lever Bracket
86 Takedown Lever Bracket Screw
87 Takedown Lever Bracket Screw Rear
89 Takedown Lever Pin
90 Takedown Lever Spring
92 Top Lever
93 Top Lever Dog
94 Top Lever Dog Screw
95 Top Lever Spring
96 Top Lever Spring Retainer
97 Top Lever Spring Retainer Screw
98 Trigger
99 Trigger Guard
102 Trigger Piston
103 Trigger Piston Pin
104 Trigger Piston Spring

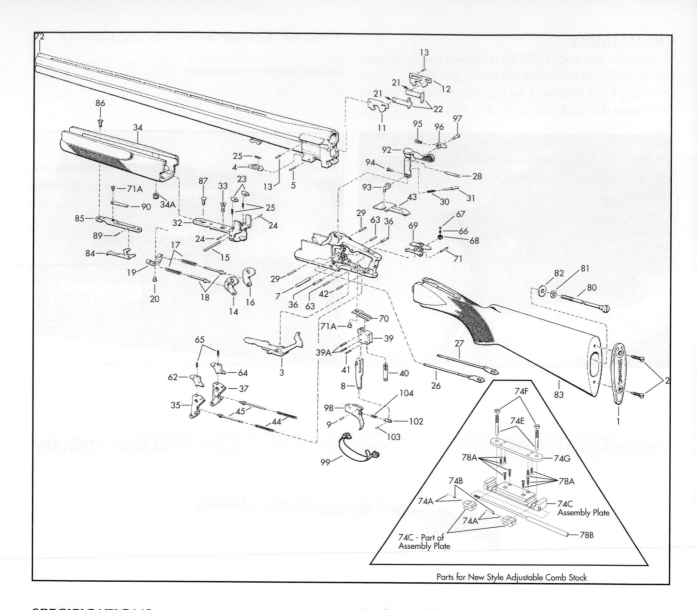

Parts for New Style Adjustable Comb Stock

SPECIFICATIONS

Model: Citori Model 425
Action: break action, double barrel, over and under
Barrel: 26 in., 28 in. or 30 in.
Caliber: 410, 28, 20, or 12 gauge; 3-in. chamber
Capacity: 2
Common Features: vent rib barrel, choke tubes, barrel selector, manual safety, mechanical triggers, hammer ejectors, adjustable trigger shoes, back bored barrels, checkered fancy black walnut stock, recoil pad, silver nitride finish steel receiver

BACKGROUND

The Citori succeeded the Browning Superposed and has a reputation as a reliable, quality over-and-under shotgun. For that reason countless Citori shotguns have been hunted hard and used effectively on clays.
Year Introduced: 1973
Current Manufacturer: Browning (browning.com)

Similar Models: 725 Field, 725 Sporting (ported barrels), 625 Feather (alloy receiver), 625 Field (steel receiver), 625 Sporting (steel receiver, ported barrels), 725 Sporting Adjustable (adjustable stock, ported barrels), Citori Feather Lightning (alloy receiver), Citori GTS Grade I, Citori Heritage (gold relief engraved side plates), Citori Lightning, Citori Midas Satin Hunter, Citori Satin Hunter, Citori Superlight Feather, Citori white Lightning, Citori XS Skeet, Citori XS Skeet Adjustable comb, Citori XS Special, Citori XS Special High Post Rib, Citori XT Trap, Citori XT Trap Gold, Citori XT Trap Unsingle, Citori XT Trap Unsingle Adjustable Comb

REQUIRED TOOLS

Field Strip: none
Disassembly: small flat blade screwdriver, long shaft flat blade screwdriver, rubber mallet (optional)

FIELD STRIP

1. Pull out the takedown lever (part #84) out from the forearm and the forearm (34) will pivot away from the barrels (72), Figure 1.

2. Grasp the barrels and push the top lever (92) to the right. The action will break open as the barrels pivot down. Pull the barrels from the receiver, Figure 2.

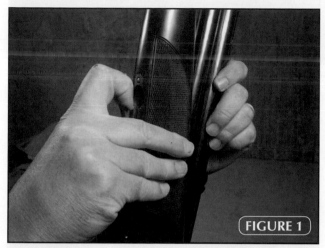

FIGURE 1

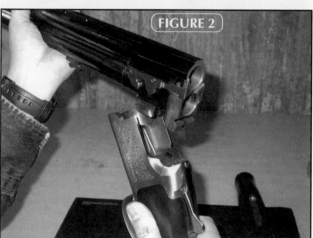

FIGURE 2

DISASSEMBLY

1. Ensure the hammers (35 and 37) are down in the fired position. Remove the stock (83) by removing two recoil pad screws (2) and removing the recoil pad (1).

Disassembly Tip: When removing rubber recoil pads use a drop Armorall on the shaft of the screwdriver so it rotates easily against the rubber.

2. Use a long shaft flat blade screwdriver or a long shaft socket extension to remove the stock bolt (80) and remove the stock from receiver, Figure 3. You may need

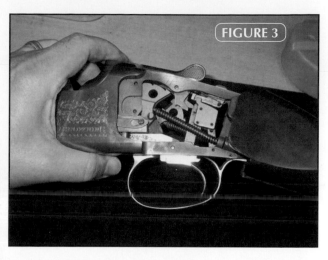

FIGURE 3

to tap the stock with the heel of your hand or a rubber mallet to free it from the receiver.

3. To remove mainsprings (44) and mainspring guides (45) use a pair of needle-nose pliers to pull the tip of the mainspring guide out of the recess in the hammer, Figure 4. Do this for both the top and bottom hammer springs. Note the hammer springs are under tension.

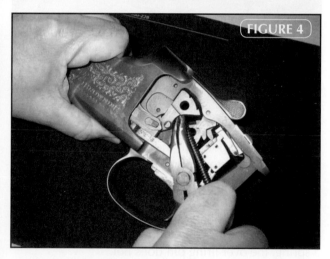

FIGURE 4

4. Next remove the hammer pins (36) by using a small flat blade screwdriver to rotate the pin so that the two flat surfaces at the top of the pin fit into the slot in the ejector trip rod, left (26) and right (27). Then use a small punch to push the ejector trip rods backward to the rear of the receiver until the hammer pin clears the slot in the ejector trip rod. Then unscrew the hammer pin and remove, Figure 5.

5. Once the hammer pins are removed the hammers can be removed, Figure 6.

6. To remove the firing pins, under (30) and over (28), use a small punch and hammer to drift the firing pin retainer pins (29). Drift out the top firing pin retainer

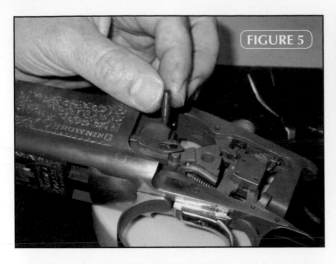

FIGURE 5

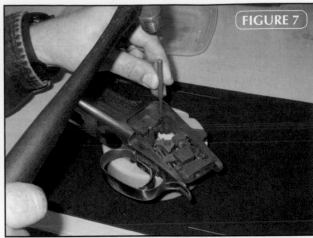

FIGURE 7

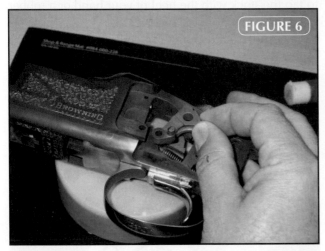

FIGURE 6

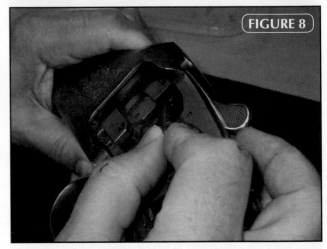

FIGURE 8

pin by driving it out from the right side of the receiver, Figure 7. The bottom firing pin retainer pin is drifted out from the left side of the receiver. The firing pins may fall free after the firing pin retainer pin is removed, Figure 8. If not push the firing pin free from the breech face using a non-marring tool. The under firing pin has a spring, the over firing pin does not.

7. Remove ejector trip rods by pulling them toward the rear of the receiver.

8. To remove the ejectors assembly unscrew the three screws (86, 87 and 33) on the inside of the forearm, with either a flat blade or Phillips screwdriver. Older

Citori have slotted screw heads, newer ones have Phillips slotted screw heads.

9. Rotate the ejector hammer, left (14) and right (16), toward the ejector hammer spring (17) to remove the ejector hammer spring. Note the spring is under tension.

Reassemble in reverse order.

Reassembly Tip: The ejector trip rods are not interchangeable. Make sure you know which is which before reassembling.

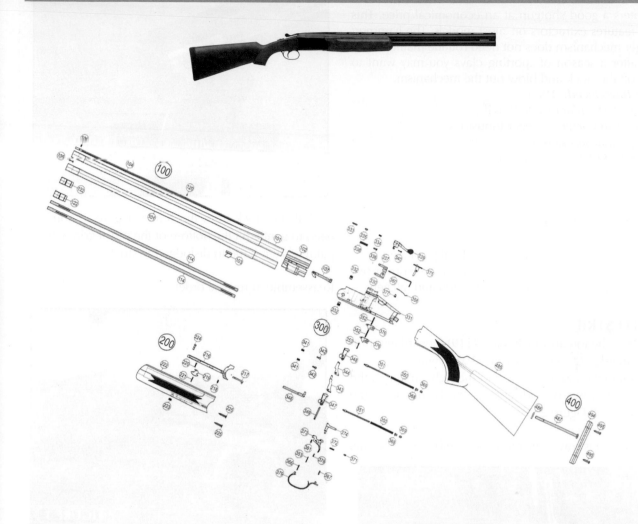

PARTS LIST

101 Barrel
102 Barrel Latch
103 Forearm Iron Catch
104 Top Rib
105 Barrel Junction Profile
106 Front Sight
107 Extractor
114 Lateral Ribs
216 Forearm/Rod Iron
217 Cocking Lever
218 Cocking Lever Pin
219 Forearm Lock
120 Intermediate Sight
122 Screw-in Choke Tubes
220 Forearm Lock Spring
221 Forearm Lock Pin

222 Wood Forend
223 Forend Washer
224 Vertical Forend Screw
225 Horizontal Forend Screw
330 Frame
331 Frame Tail
332 Trunnion Pin
333 Lever Lock Pin
334 Top Lever Spring
335 Top Lever Pin
336 Lever Lock Impeller Pin
337 Lever Lock
338 Lever Impeller Spring
339 Top Lever
340 Retainer Pin
341 Firing Pin Spring
342 Firing Pin
343 Top Firing Pin Plunger

344 Bottom Firing Pin Plunger
346 Hammer Cocking Cam
347 Hammer - Left
348 Hammer - Right
349 Hammer Pin
350 Hammer Spring
351 Hammer Impeller
352 Sear Spring
353 Sear and Trigger Pin
358 Safety Spring
360 Safety Fastening Pin
366 Trigger Guard Front
Fastening Pin
367 Trigger Guard Rear
Fastening Pin
368 Hammer Activator Guide
369 Hammer Impeller Spring
Limiter Nut

371 Equalizer Impeller Pin
372 Equalizer Impeller Spring
373 Trigger
374 Equalizer
375 Safety Catch
376 Sear
377 Safety Activating Spring
Screw
378 Equalizer Fastening Pin
379 Trigger Guard
381 Trigger Spring
485 Wood Stock
486 Stock Bolt Washer
487 Stock Bolt
494 Rubber Butt Pad
495 Butt pad Screws

SPECIFICATIONS

Model: Condor
Action: hammerless, boxlock, extractors
Barrel: 24, 26, or 28 in.
Caliber: .410, 28, 20, 16 or 12 gauge

Capacity: 2
Common Features: single trigger, thumb safety, blue finish, fixed choke or choke tubes, pistol-grip checkered walnut or synthetic stock, vent rib, auto ejectors

BACKGROUND

The Condor over and under is built in Brazil and provides shooters a good shotgun at an economical price. This gun features extractors on most models. The hammer/trigger mechanism does not need routine maintenance but after a season of sporting clays you may want to pull off the stock and blow out the mechanism.

Year Introduced: 1985

Country Manufactured: Brazil

Current Importer: Stoeger Industries (stoegerindustries.com)

Similar Models: Condor Supreme, Condor Combo, Condor Youth, Condor Competition, Condor Competition Combo, Condor Outback

REQUIRED TOOLS

Field Strip: none

Disassembly/Assembly: medium Phillips blade screwdriver, large flat blade long shaft screwdriver or a 7/16 inch socket with long extension and ratchet

FIELD STRIP

1. Press the forearm lock (part #219) forward and pull the forend (222) off the barrels (101), Figure 1.

2. Rotate the top lever (339) to the right and press the barrels downward to disengage the barrels from the frame (330), Figure 2.

The Condor is now sufficiently disassembled for cleaning.

FIGURE 2

3. Pull the stock from the frame, Figure 3. You may need to gentle hit the bottom of the pistol grip with the palm of your hand to dislodge the stock.

Reassemble in reverse order.

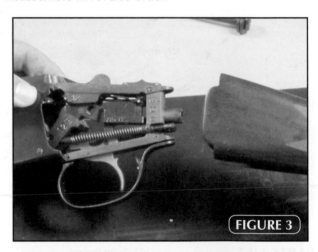

FIGURE 3

Cleaning Tip: Blow out the action. Then lightly lubricate the front of the frame where it mates with the forearm iron, pivot pins and the inside of the frame where it contacts the barrels.

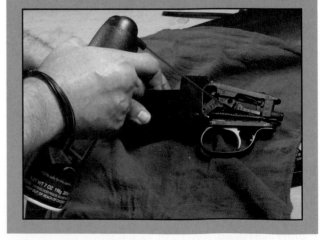

FIGURE 1

DETAILED DISASSEMBLY

1. Remove the two butt plate screws (495) using a Phillips screwdriver and remove the butt plate (494) from the stock (485).

2. Use a large flat blade long shaft screwdriver or a 7/16 inch socket with long extension and ratchet to remove the stock.

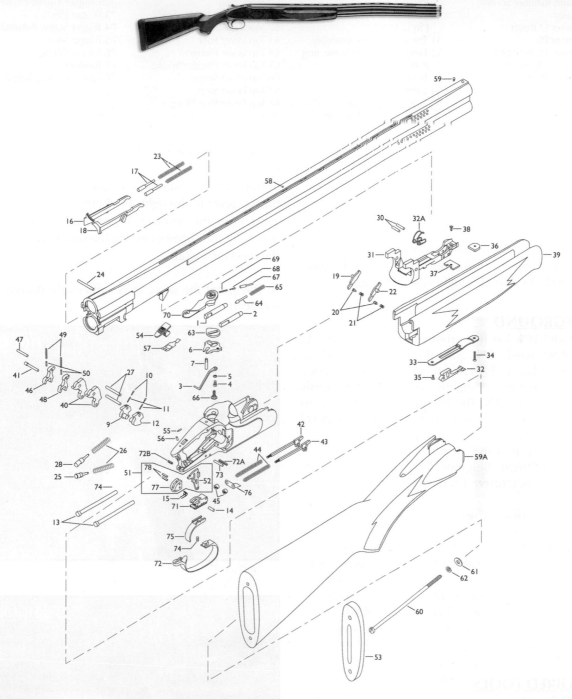

PARTS LIST

1 Barrel Bolt Left
2 Barrel Bolt Right
3 Bolt Extension
4 Bolt Extension Screw
5 Bolt Extension Washer
6 Bolt Spacer
7 Bolt Spacer Guide
9 Cocking Lever Left

10 Cocking Lever Plunger (2 Req'd.)
11 Cocking Lever Plunger Spring (2 Req'd.)
12 Cocking Lever Right
13 Cocking Rod (2 Req'd.)
14 Connecting Rod Pin
15 Connecting Rod Spring
16 Ejector Left
17 Ejector Plunger (2 Req'd.)

18 Ejector Right
19 Ejector Sear Left
20 Ejector Sear Plunger (2 Req'd.)
21 Ejector Sear Plunger Spring (2 Req'd.)
22 Ejector Sear Right
23 Ejector Spring (2 Req'd.)
24 Ejector Stop
25 Firing Pin Lower

26 Firing Pin Spring Upper & Lower
27 Firing Pin Stop Pin (2 Req'd.)
28 Firing Pin Upper
30 Forearm Bolt Pin (2 Req'd.)
31 Forearm Bracket
32 Forearm Lock
32A Forearm Lock Spring
33 Forearm Plate
34 Forearm Plate Screw Front

35 Forearm Plate Screw Rear
36 Forearm Plate Screw
   Retainer Front
37 Forearm Retainer Plate
38 Forearm Retainer Screw
39 Forearm
40 Hammer (2 Req'd.)
41 Hammer Pin
42 Hammer Plunger Left
43 Hammer Plunger Right
44 Hammer Plunger Spring (2
   Req'd.)
45 Hammer Plunger Stop (2
   Req'd.)

46 Hammer Sear Left
47 Hammer Sear Pin
48 Hammer Sear Right
49 Hammer Sear Spring (2
   Req'd.)
50 Hammer Sear Spring Guide
   Pin (2 Req'd.)
51 Percussion Sear Assembly
52 Percussion Sear Connecting
   Rod
53 Recoil Pad
54 Safety Stud
55 Safety Stud Guide
56 Safety Stud Locking Pin

57 Safety Stud Spring
58 Sight Center
59 Sight Front
59A Stock
60 Stock Bolt
61 Stock Bolt Flat Washer
62 Stock Bolt Lock Washer
63 Top Lever Foot
64 Top Lever Plunger
65 Top Lever Plunger Spring
66 Top Lever Screw
67 Top Lever Stop
68 Top Lever Stop Plunger
69 Top Lever Stop Spring

70 Top Lever
71 Trigger
72 Trigger Guard
72A Trigger Guard Pin Front
72B Trigger Guard Pin Rear
73 Trigger Pin
74 Trigger Screw Adjustable
75 Trigger Shoe
76 Trigger Spring
77 Tumbler
78 Tumbler Pin (2 Req'd.)

SPECIFICATIONS

Model: 101 Field

Action: break action, double barrel, over and under

Barrel: 26 in. or 28 in.

Caliber: 12 gauge, 3-in. chamber

Capacity: 2

Common Features: steel engraved receiver, vent rib barrel, blued finish, choke tubes, back-bored barrels, checkered wood stock, single selective trigger

BACKGROUND

The Model 101 was first produced from 1963 through 1987 and when FN and Browning licensed the Winchester brand, FN continued production in 2007. This "new" 101 differs slightly from the Olin-Kodensha 101s built prior to FN. The 101 makes use of a massive center locking lug. The steps her are for the newer FN-manufactured 101s.

Year Introduced: 1963

Country of Origin: Belgium

Current Manufacturer: FN (Fabrique Nationale d'Herstal)

Current Importer: Winchester Repeating Arms (winchesterguns.com)

Similar Models: Model 101 Pigeon Grade Trap (Monte Carlo style wood stock, 30- or 32-in. ported barrels), Model 101 Pigeon Grade Trap adjustable Comb (adjustable comb Monte Carlo style wood stock, 30- or 32-in. ported barrels), Model 101 Sporting (wood stock, 28- or 30- or 32-in. ported barrels, extended choke tubes)

REQUIRED TOOLS

Field Strip: none

Disassembly/Assembly: small punch, Phillips screwdriver, long shaft flat blade screwdriver

FIELD STRIP

1. Push the safety (part #54) in the "safe" position.
2. Remove the forearm by pulling outward on the forearm lock (32) and pushing the forearm (39) away from

the barrels, Figure 1. Pull the forearm away and off the barrels.

3. Separate the barrels from the receiver by pushing the top lever to the right. The barrels will hinge downward from the receiver. When the barrels are fully down, lift the chamber end of the barrels up and out of the receiver, Figure 2.

At this point the shotgun is sufficiently disassembled for cleaning.

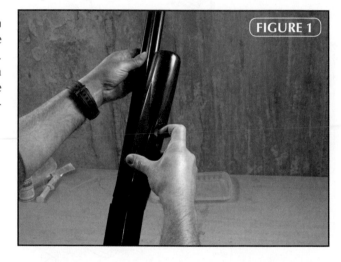

FIGURE 1

FIGURE 2

DISASSEMBLY

1. Use a Phillips screwdriver to remove the two recoil pad screws and the recoil pad (part #53).

2. Next using a long shaft flat blade screwdriver loosen and remove the stock bolt (60), stock bolt flat washer (61) and stock bolt lock washer (62), Figure 3.

3. Pull the stock (59A) from the receiver, Figure 4. You may need to use a rubber mallet to gently tap the stock free.

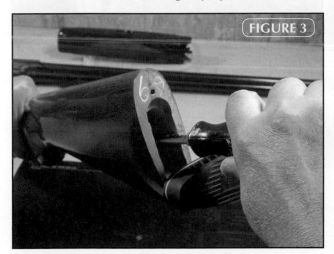

FIGURE 3

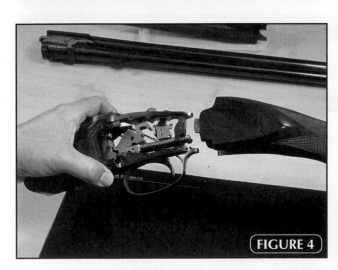

FIGURE 4

FIGURE 5

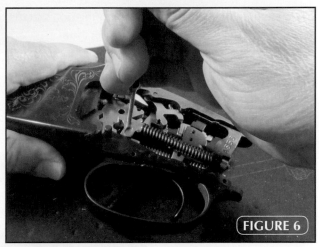

FIGURE 6

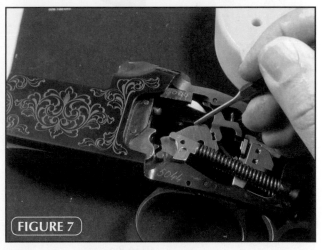

FIGURE 7

4. Remove the firing pins—lower (25) and upper (28)—by first tripping the two hammers (40) to the full forward/"fired" position by pushing up on the rear of the sears (48), Figure 5. With the hammers forward, use a small punch to pull the left hammer plunger (42) and right hammer plunger out of the recess in the back of the hammers, Figure 6. The hammer plungers are under tension from and hammer plunger springs (44). Rotate the hammers backward, Figure 7. Then drift out the firing pin stop pin (27) for the upper firing pin from either side of the receiver, Figure 8. Drifting out

the firing pin stop pin for the lower firing pin will also allow the left cocking lever (9) and right cocking lever (12) to move out of position, Figure 9.

Reassemble in reverse order.

FIGURE 8

FIGURE 9

Reassembly Tip: Make sure to align the holes in the left and right cocking levers so the firing pin stop pin can be reinstalled for the lower firing pin.

Pump Action

BENELLI NOVA

PARTS LIST

001N Trigger group assembly
002N Hammer
003A Hammer spring cap
004N Hammer spring
007A Safety plunger spring
008A Hand safety plunger
009N Trigger
010N Trigger pin
011N Trigger spring
013N Hand safety button
014N Trigger guard
016N Trigger pin bush
017N Carrier
018A Trigger guard pin spring
019N Bolt stop tooth
020A Bolt stop tooth pin
021N Carrier spring
214N L.H. carrier latch
215N Disconnector

216N Disconnector plunger
217N Disconnector hammer
218N Disconnector hammer
  spring
219N Breech bolt latch
220N Breech bolt latch spring
221N Bolt stop cap
222N R.H. carrier latch
224N Bolt assembly
025N Firing pin
028A Retaining pin
031N Locking head pin
032N Locking head
033J Extractor spring
034A Extractor
035A Pin
037N Firing pin spring
165N Locking head assembly
223N L.H. action bar
224N Action bar retaining pin
225N R.H. action bar

232N Mag-Stop button
233N Mag-Stop bush
234N Mag-Stop spring
236N Fore-end assembly
044N Front sight
045N Ejector pin
046N Ejector pin spring
047N Pin
048N Receiver
064A Magazine spring
064C Magazine spring
065N Magazine follower
067N Shot plug
068C Magazine tube plug
069N Barrel retaining cap
074J Cap retaining pin bushing
108P Cap retaining pin spring
132G Magazine spring seal
144C Magazine tube extension
  (+3 round)

144N Magazine tube extension
  (+2 round)
145C Magazine tube extension
  (+1 round)
151N Butt plate
153A Intermediate sight
196L Screw
213B Internal choke
226N Trigger guard pin (long)
227N Trigger guard pin (short)
229N Barrel retaining cap
230N Mag-Stop magazine tube
237N Recoil reducer support
  assembly
238N Recoil reducer support
239N Recoil reducer latch
240N Recoil reducer spacer
241C Barrel retaining ring
  assembly

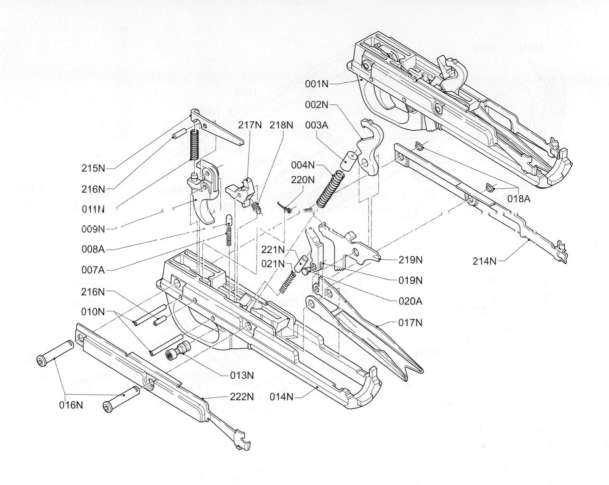

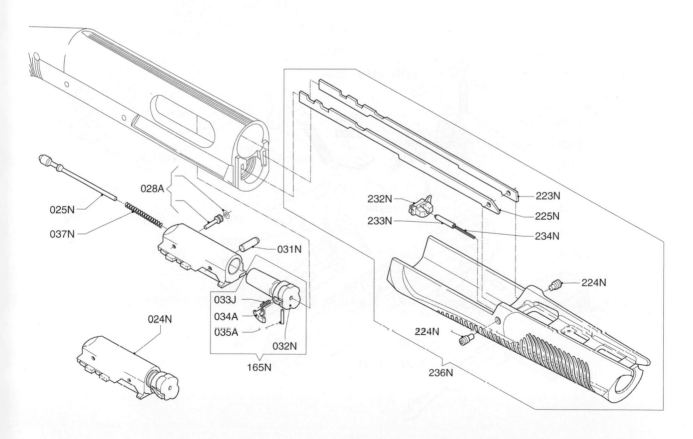

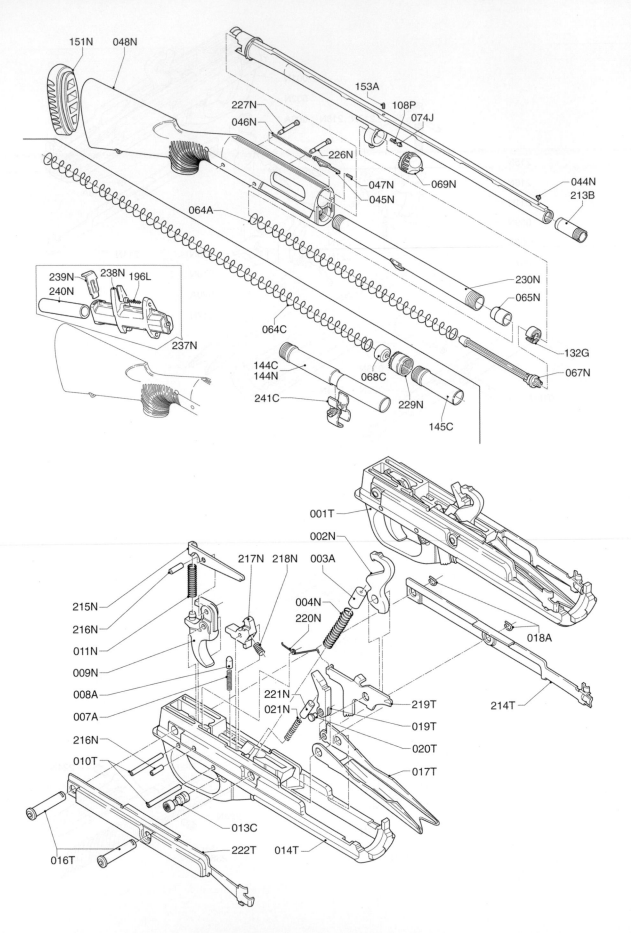

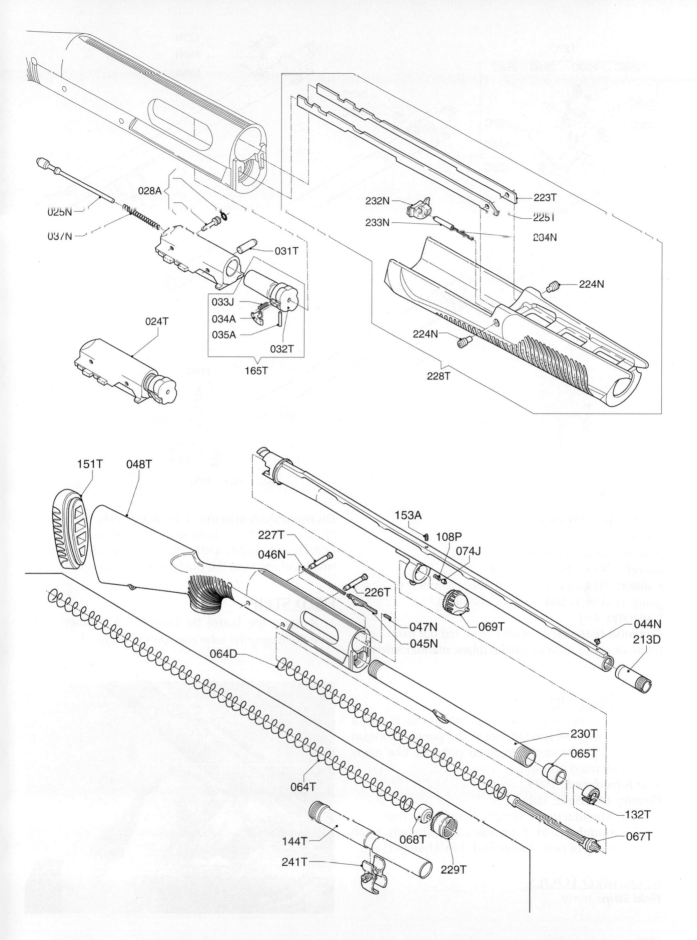

028A

025N

037N

024T

031T

033J
034A
035A
032T

165T

232N
233N

223T
225T
234N

224N

224N

228T

151T 048T

227T
046N

226T

047N
045N

064D

064T

144T
241T

068T

229T

153A
108P
074J

069T

044N
213D

230T

065T

132T

067T

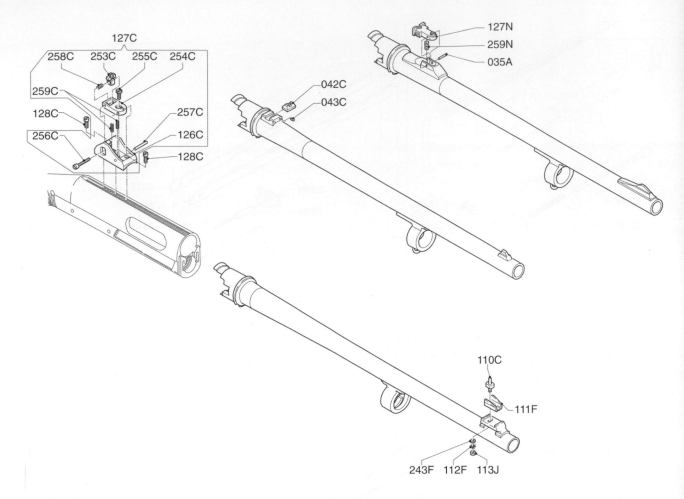

SPECIFICATIONS

Model: Nova
Action: pump action
Barrel: 24 in., 26 in., or 28 in.
Caliber: 20 gauge (2-3/4 and 3 in. chamber) or 12 gauge (2-3/4, 3, and 3-1/2 in. chamber)
Capacity: 4+1
Common Features: vent rib barrel, red bar front sight, matte or camo finishes, choke tubes, manual safety, magazine cut-off

BACKGROUND

The Nova is distinct for a pump shotgun as it uses a one-piece receiver and butt stock. This popular shotgun is constructed of steel-reinforced polymer like many polymer-framed pistols.
Year Introduced: 1999
Country of Origin: Italy
Current Manufacturer: Benelli (benelliusa.com)
Similar Models: Field (2-3/4 and 3 in. chamber), Youth (13-in. length of pull), Turkey (3-1/2 in. chamber)

REQUIRED TOOLS

Field Strip: none

Disassembly/Assembly: 3/16 inch punch, medium Phillips screwdriver, long shaft flat blade screwdriver or 7/16 inch socket with extension, nylon hammer, small and medium flat blade screwdrivers

FIELD STRIP

1. Remove the barrel by unscrewing counter-clockwise the magazine tube cap (069N), Figure 1.

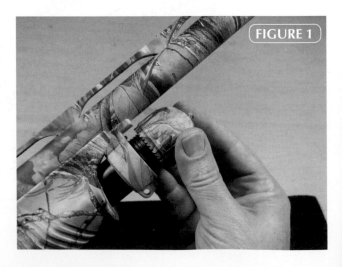

FIGURE 1

2. Depress the breech bolt latch (219N) and pull the fore-end assembly (236N) partially rearward, Figure 2.

3. Slide the barrel forward along the magazine tube (230N) until it clears the magazine tube then slightly lift the barrel up and away from the magazine tube, Figure 3.

At this point the Nova is sufficiently disassembled for cleaning.

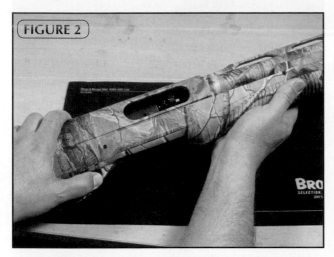

FIGURE 2

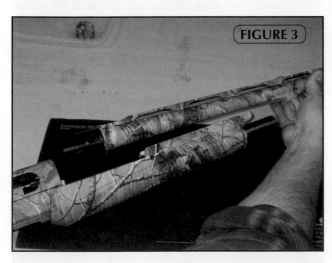

FIGURE 3

DETAILED DISASSEMBLY

1. Use the protrusion on the end of the magazine tube cap to push the two trigger guard pins—trigger guard pin long (226N) and trigger guard pin short (227N)—out from the right/ejection port side of the receiver (048T). Note the longer of the two pins fits the front hole; the smaller in the rear hole, Figure 4.

2. Then use the open inside edge of the magazine tube cap to hook the heads of the trigger guard pins from the left side of the receiver, Figure 5.

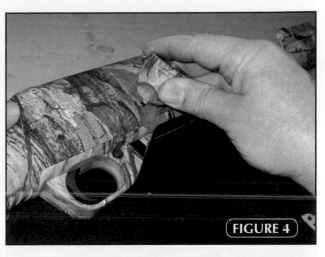

FIGURE 4

FIGURE 5

3. Place the top of the receiver down on a padded work surface so the trigger group assembly faces up and remove the trigger group assembly (001N) by pulling the trigger guard up and away from the bottom of the receiver, Figure 6.

4. While holding the Nova with bottom opening of the receiver facing downward, use your thumb to press

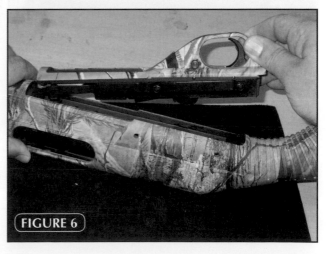

FIGURE 6

down on the bolt assembly (024T) to the inside of the receiver to separate the bolt assembly from the two action bars—L.H. action bar (223T) and R.H. action bar (225T)—on the fore-end assembly, Figure 7. Then pull the fore-end assembly forward and off the magazine tube, Figure 8.

5. Compress the bolt assembly by squeezing together the locking head assembly (165T) and bolt body and pull the bolt assembly up and out of the receiver, Figure 9.

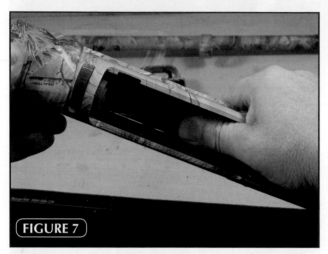

FIGURE 7

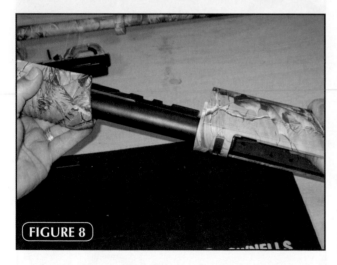

FIGURE 8

6. Slide the fore-end assembly along and off the magazine tube.

FIGURE 9

7. Press in and hold the rear of the firing pin (025N) then pull the retaining pin (028A) out from the bolt assembly, Figure 10. Note the firing pin and firing pin spring are under tension so control the firing pin and gradually release pressure until spring pressure is relieved.

8. Remove the firing pin and firing pin spring from the rear of the bolt.

9. The magazine spring (064A), magazine follower (065N) and shot plug (067N) are removed by gently prying out the magazine spring seal (132G) using a small screwdriver. Note magazine spring is under tension so control the spring once the magazine spring seal is removed.

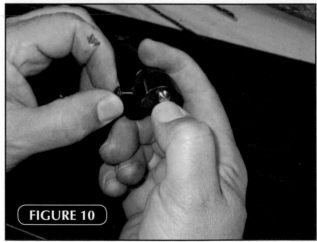

FIGURE 10

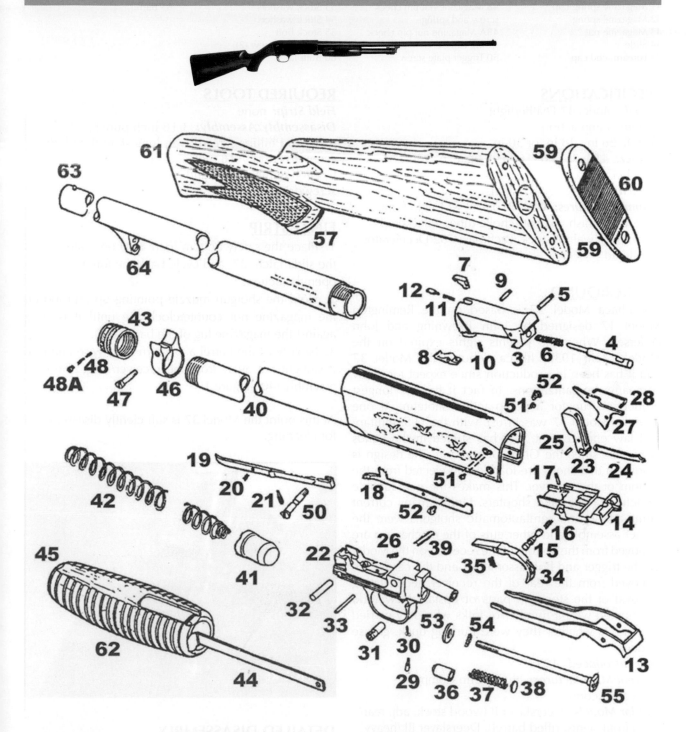

PARTS LIST

3 Breechblock
4 Firing pin
5 Firing pin check
6 Firing pin spring
7 Positive extractor
8 Bottom extractor
9 Extractor hinge pin
10 Bottom extractor spring

11 Positive extractor
12 Positive extractor
13 Carrier
14 Slide
15 Slide pin
16 Slide pin spring
17 Slide pin check pin
18 Positive shell stop (right)
19 Spring shell stop (left)

20 Spring shell stop spring
21 Spring shell stop screw
22 Trigger plate
23 Hammer bar pin
24 Hammer bar
25 Hammer
26 Slide stop spring
27 Slide stop
28 Slide stop release

29 Safety catch
30 Safety catch spring
31 Safety
32 Hammer pin
33 Trigger pin
34 Trigger
35 Trigger spring
36 Mainspring cup
37 Mainspring

SPECIFICATIONS

Model: Model 37 Featherlight
Action: pump action
Barrel: 26 in., 28 in. or 30 in.
Caliber: 410, 28, 20, 16, or 12 gauge; 3-in. chamber
Capacity: 4+1 (2-3/4-in. shells)
Common Features: vent rib barrel w/ Truglo front sight, blue finish, excepts choke tubes, checkered fancy black walnut stock, Pachmayr 752 Decelerator recoil pad

BACKGROUND

The Ithaca Model 37 is based on the Remington Model 17 designed by John Browning and John Pedersen. When the patents rights expired on the Model 17 in 1937, Ithaca debuted the Model 37 and it has been in production since expect for a few company reorganizations. In fact it has the longest production run for a pump-action shotgun. At one time the Model 37 was in use with the U.S. military and law enforcement, and has shined in the hands of hunters since the Great Depression. The design is unique in that shells are loaded and ejected from the bottom of the receiver. This makes the gun suitable for left- or right-hand shooters. Unlike many current pump-action and semiautomatic shotguns were the trigger assembly and other guts of the mechanism are removed from the bottom of the receiver, on the Model 37 the trigger and bolt assemblies and the carrier are removed from the rear of the receiver necessitating removal of the stock. In parts of upstate New York, I've hunted with a number of folks who only carried Model 37s whether they were hunting duck, grouse or deer.

Year Introduced: 1933
Current Manufacturer: Ithaca Gun Company (ithacagun.com)
Similar Models: Deerslayer II (wood stock, adj. rear/fixed front sights, rifled barrel), Deerslayer III (heavy fluted rifled barrel, Monte Carlo stock, weaver optics rail), Defense (matte finish, synthetic or wood stock, 18.5 inch barrel, 7+1 capacity), Trap (30 in. vent rib barrel, wood Monte Carlo stock), Turkey Slayer (synthetic, camo or thumbhole stock, camo or matte finish, adj. rear/fixed front sights), Waterfowler (synthetic stock, matte finish), Ladies Stock (Featherlight model with stock designed for women)

REQUIRED TOOLS

Field Strip: none
Disassembly/Assembly: 3/16 inch punch, medium Phillips screwdriver, long shaft flat blade screwdriver or 7/16 inch socket with extension, nylon hammer, small and medium flat blade screwdrivers

FIELD STRIP

1. Place the safety bottom (part #31) on "safe," press the slide latch (27) and cycle back the forearm (62) to open the action.
2. Hold the shotgun muzzle pointing up and loosen the magazine nut counterclockwise until it is snug against the magazine lug of the barrel (64).
3. Next twist the barrel a 1/4 turn clockwise and pull it straight out away from the receiver/magazine tube assembly (40), Figure 1.

At this point the Model 37 is sufficiently disassembled for cleaning.

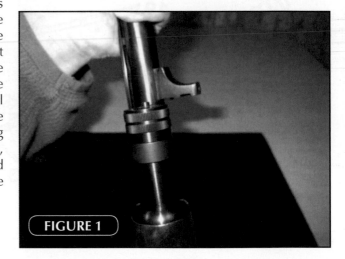

FIGURE 1

DETAILED DISASSEMBLY

1. To disassemble the magazine tube, unscrew the magazine nut (43) by turning it clockwise. Note the magazine cap is under spring tension from the magazine spring (42) so make sure you control it until tension is relieved, Figure 2.
2. Pull the magazine spring out of the magazine tube and then turn the shotgun muzzle end down so you

FIGURE 2

FIGURE 4

can push the follower (41) loose. Place your hand over magazine tube to catch the follower.

3. Next use a small flathead screw driver to remove the yoke screw (47) in the yoke at the end of the magazine tube. Gently spread the yoke apart and slide it off of the magazine tube, Figure 3.

FIGURE 3

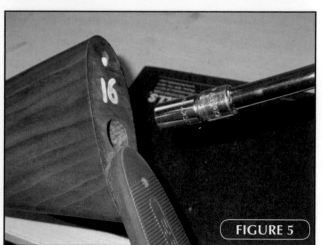

FIGURE 5

4. Next slide the forend forward until the action locks. Place the shotgun top side down and in the ejection/loading port push the slide pin 15 to the left using a flathead screw driver, Figure 4. Then pull the forend off of the magazine tube.

5. To remove the trigger assembly, first loosen and remove the recoil pad/buttplate screws (59) and remove the recoil/buttplate (60).

6. Using a long shaft large flat blade screwdriver or socket with extension, remove the stock bolt (55), Figure 5.

7. Pull the stock (61) from the receiver, Figure 6.

8. Next remove the cross screw on the left side of the receiver, Figure 7.

FIGURE 6

9. Push the safety button the "fire" position and pull the trigger to lower the hammer, now the trigger assembly can be removed down and to the rear of the receiver, Figiure 8. You may need to tap out the trigger assembly using a nylon hammer.

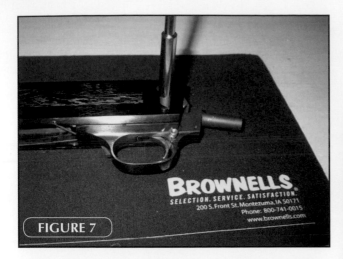

FIGURE 7

FIGURE 8

bottom of the receiver. The left shell stop can then be removed.

Reassemble in reverse order.

FIGURE 9

Reassembly Tip: Place an anti-seize compound like Birchwoods Casey Choke Tube Lube or Loctite Anti-Seize Stick, Silver Grade grease on the threads of the barrel before replacing so the next time you remove the barrel from the receiver it will easily disassemble.

10.   With the trigger assembly removed, the right shell stop (18) can be removed from beneath the receiver.
11.   To remove the bolt assembly first remove the lock screw (51) from the main carrier pivot screw (52) on the left side of the receiver, Figure 9. Then unscrew the main carrier screw and the carrier (13) and bolt assembly can now be removed from the rear of the receiver.
12. The left shell stop (19) is removed by partially unscrewing the spring shell stop screw (21) at the

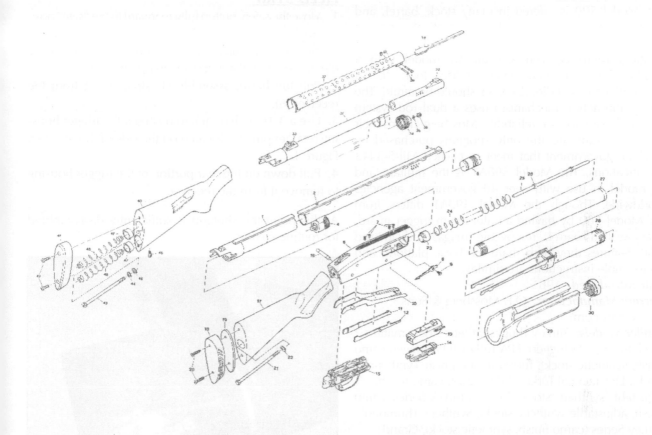

PARTS LIST

1 Barrel Assembly
2 Mid-Point Bead
3 Front Sight
4 Takedown Screw
5 Choke Tube
6 Receiver
7 Scope Mount Dummy Screws
8 Ejector
9 Ejector Screw
10 Elevator
11 Cartridge Stop

12 Cartridge Interrupter
13 Bolt Assembly
14 Bolt Slide
15 Trigger Housing Assembly
16 Trigger Housing Pin
17 Stock
18 Recoil Pad
19 Spacer
20 Recoil Pad Screw
21 Stock Bolt
22 Lock Washer
23 Ejector Follower
24 Magazine Spring

25 Limiting Plug
26 Retaining O-Ring
27 Magazine Tube
28 Action Slide Assembly
29 Forearm
30 Action Slide Tube Nut
31 Rifled Barrel
32 Front Sight Assembly
33 Rear Rifle Sight Assembly
34 Magazine Cap
35 Retaining Washer
36 Front Swivel Stud
37 Heat Shield

38 Heat Shield Spacer
39 Heat Shield Screw/Nuts
40 Speedfeed Stock
41 Speedfeed Recoil Pad
42 Speedfeed Recoil Pad
   Screws
43 Speedfeed Stock Bolt
44 Lock Washer
45 Flat Washer
46 Stock Swivel Q.D. Post
47 Speedfeed Followers
48 Speedfeed Springs

SPECIFICATIONS

Model: Model 500 All Purpose Field
Action: pump action
Barrel: 14 in. to 30 in.
Caliber: 410, 20, or 12 gauge; 3-in. chamber
Capacity: 5+1 (2-3/4-in. shells)
Common Features: vent rib barrel, blue finish, excepts choke tubes, checkered wood stock

BACKGROUND

The Model 500 is offered in many stock, barrel, and finish configurations, from full on tactical weapons to turkey hunting guns and slugster models for deer hunting. There is even a chainsaw model with a combination carry handle/forearm that looks like a chainsaw carry handle. Zombies should be afraid. The 500 pump action mechanism uses a dual rod system and dual extractors for reliability. Mossberg claims their pump shotguns are the only shotguns purchased by the U.S. government that meet or exceed Mil-S-3443 specifications. The Model 590A1 is the military and LE model in use with over 40 government agencies worldwide. Though the Model 590A1 differs from the Model 500 by having an aluminum trigger guard, heavy-walled barrel, removable magazine cap and other features they both share the basic platform and disassemble instructions are similar.

Year Introduced: 1961
Current Manufacturer: O.F. Mossberg & Sons (mossbergs.com)
Similar Models: Turkey Thug (synthetic stock, matte black finish, LPA trigger), LPA Turkey (LPA trigger, camo finish, synthetic stock), Turkey (camo finish, synthetic stock), LPA Tactical Turkey (LPA trigger, camo finish, adjustable synthetic stock), Tactical Turkey Series (camo finish, adjustable synthetic stock), Synthetic Thumbhole Turkey Series (camo finish, synthetic stock), Grand slam Series – Turkey (synthetic stock, camo finish, X-Factor ported choke tube), Waterfowl (synthetic stock, camo finish), Flyway Series – Waterfowl (synthetic stock, camo finish, X-Factor ported choke tube), LPA Slugster (LPA trigger, blued or camo finish, synthetic or wood stock, rifled bore), Slugster (blued or camo finish, synthetic or wood stock, rifled bore), LPA Combo (LPA trigger, camo finish, synthetic stock, two barrel set), Combos (blued or camo finish, wood or synthetic stock, two barrel set), Bantam (13 in. LOP), Super Bantam (13 in. LOP, adjustable synthetic stock), Just In Case (pistol grip, 18.5 in, barrel), Tactical Tri-Rail (tactical tri-rail forend), Blackwater Series (stand-off barrel), Chainsaw (integrated carry handle, stand-off barrel, tactical tri-rail forend), SPX (adj. stock, Picatinny rail), Road Blocker (heavy-walled barrel w/ muzzle brake), Persuader/Cruiser (pistol grip, heavy-walled barrel w/ muzzle brake), Tactical (6- or 8-shot

capacity), HS410 Home Security (spreader choke), Mariner (Maronite finish, pistol grip)

REQUIRED TOOLS

Field Strip: none
Disassembly/Assembly: 3/16 inch punch, medium Phillips screwdriver, long shaft flat blade screwdriver or ½ inch socket and extension

FIELD STRIP

1. Move the safety button fully rearward to the "safe" position then loosen the takedown screw (part #4) by turning it counterclockwise until the screw threads are completely disengaged from the end of the magazine tube.
2. Pull the barrel assembly (1) straight out from the receiver (6).
3. Use a 3/16 inch punch to push out the trigger housing retainer pin (16) located on the side of the receiver, Figure 1.
4. Pull down on the rear portion of the trigger housing to remove it from the receiver.

At this point the shotgun is sufficiently disassembled for routine cleaning.

FIGURE 1

DETAILED DISASSEMBLY

1. The receiver is further disassembled by removing the cartridge stop (11), which may fall free once the trigger housing is removed.
2. Then remove the cartridge interrupter (12). It is held to the inside receiver wall by a post, Figure 2.
3. Next move the forearm (29) and action slide assembly rearward so that the bolt assembly (13) and bolt slide (14) is aligned with the grooves inside of the receiver then lift the bolt slide upward and out of the receiver, Figure 3.

FIGURE 2

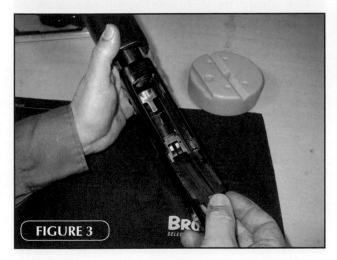

FIGURE 3

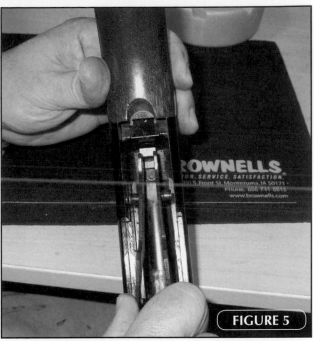

FIGURE 5

4. Remove the bolt assembly by sliding it forward and out at the front of the receiver, Figure 4.

5. Remove the elevator (10) by pivoting the front portion up and out of the receiver then squeeze the two elevator arms together sufficiently to disengage and remove the elevator from the receiver, Figure 5.

6. Remove the forearm/action slide assembly by sliding it forward and off the magazine tube (27), Figure 6.

7. The firing pin is removed by drifting out the firing pin retaining pin with a small punch from the bottom of the bolt to the top, Figure 7. The firing pin can then be extracted from the rear of the bolt.

8. The extractors are removed by drifting out the extractor retaining pin from the bottom of the bolt to the top of the bolt, Figure 8.

9. To remove the stock (17) loosen the two recoil pad screws (20) using a Phillips screwdriver and remove recoil pad (18).

10. Access the stock bolt (21) via the hole in the stock and use either a large, long shaft screwdriver or a 1/2 inch socket and extension. The stock can now be removed from the receiver.

FIGURE 4

FIGURE 6

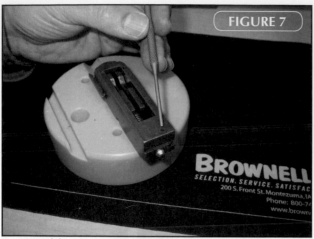

FIGURE 7

Reassemble in reverse order.

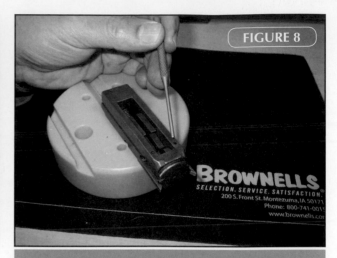

FIGURE 8

Reassembly Tip: Make sure the guide rod tab fit into the notches of the bolt slide.

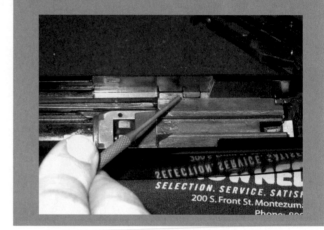

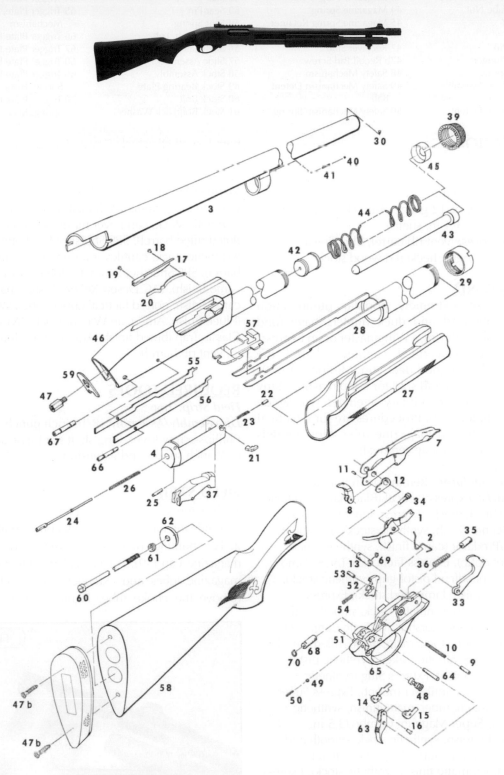

26 Firing Pin Retractor Spring
27 Fore-end Assembly
28 Fore-end Tube Assembly
29 Fore-end Tube Nut
30 Front Sight
33 Hammer
34 Hammer Pin
35 Hammer Plunger
36 Hammer Spring
37 Locking Block Assembly
39 Magazine Cap
40 Magazine Cap Detent

41 Magazine Cap Detent Spring
42 Magazine Follower
43 Magazine Plug, 3-Shot
44 Magazine Spring
45 Magazine Spring Retainer
46 Receiver Assembly
47 Receiver Stud
47b Recoil Pad Screw
48 Safety Mechanism
49 Safety Mechanism Detent
   Ball
50 Safety Mechanism Spring

51 Safety Mechanism Spring
   Retaining Pin
52 Sear
53 Sear Pin
54 Sear Spring
55 Shell Latch, Left
56 Shell Latch, Right
57 Slide Assembly
58 Stock Assembly
59 Stock Bearing Plate
60 Stock Bolt
61 Stock Bolt Lock Washer

62 Stock Bolt Washer
63 Trigger Assembly
64 Trigger Pin
65 Trigger Plate, R.H. Safety
   Mechanism
66 Trigger Plate Pin, Front
67 Trigger Plate Pin, Rear
68 Trigger Plate Pin Bushing
69 Trigger Plate Pin Detent
   Spring, Front
70 Trigger Plate Pin Detent
   Spring, Rear

SPECIFICATIONS

Model: Model 870 Tactical
Action: pump
Barrel: 14 in. to 30 in.
Caliber: 410, 20, or 12 gauge; 3-in. chamber
Capacity: 5+1 (2-3/4-in. shells)
Common Features: vent rib barrel, blue finish, excepts choke tubes, checkered wood stock

BACKGROUND

The 870 is an extremely popular pump-action shotgun. Many bird and duck hunters have fond memories of shouldering a Wingmaster or an Express, respectively. With a rifled cantilever barrel the shotgun becomes a good deer gun. Millions of 870s have been produced and sold for good reason. Many law enforcement and military agencies worldwide use the Remington 870. Procedures are for a tactical variant with extented magazine tube. Most models will start at magazine cap removal.

Year Introduced: 1950
Current Manufacturer: Remington (remington.com)
Similar Models: Express Tactical (Blackhawk synthetic stock, matte black finish), Express Super Mag Turkey/Waterfowl (camo finish, synthetic stock), SPS Super Mag Turkey/Predator (camo finish, synthetic stock, red/green dot optic), Express Tactical A-TACS Camo (camo finish, speedfeed pistol-grip synthetic stock), Express (matte finish, laminated stock), Express Combo (matte finish, synthetic stock, smooth and rifled barrel), Express Shurshot Synthetic Cantilever (synthetic pistol-grip stock, matte finish, rifled barrel), Express Shurshot Synthetic Turkey (synthetic pistol-grip stock, camo finish), Express Slug (synthetic stock, matte finish, cantilever mount), Express Super Magnum (3.5 in. chamber, matte finish, synthetic stock), Express Super Magnum Combo (3.5 in. chamber, matte finish, synthetic stock, smooth and rifled barrels), Express Super Magnum Synthetic (3.5 in. chamber, matte finish, synthetic stock), Express Super Magnum Turkey Camo (3.5 in. chamber, camo finish, synthetic stock), Express Super Magnum Waterfowl Camo (3.5 in. chamber, camo finish, synthetic stock), Express Synthetic 18" (18 in. barrel, synthetic stock), Express Synthetic 7-Round (18 in.
barrel, synthetic stock, 7-round magazine), Express Synthetic Deer (rifled barrel, synthetic stock), Express Turkey (matte finish, synthetic stock), Special Purpose Marine Magnum (nickel-plated finish, synthetic stock, 6-round magazine), SPS Shurshot Synthetic Super Slug (synthetic stock, cantilever mount with scope, heavy fluted rifled barrel), SPS Shurshot Synthetic Cantilever (synthetic stock, cantilever mount, heavy fluted rifled barrel), SPS Shurshot Synthetic Turkey (pistol grip, camo finish), TAC Desert Recon (7-shot magazine, camo finish, ported tactical choke tube), Wingmaster (blued finish, American Walnut stock), Wingmaster Classic Trap (blued finish, American Walnut stock, 30 in. vent rib barrel)

REQUIRED TOOLS

Field Strip: none
Disassembly/Assembly: 3/16 inch punch, medium Phillips screwdriver, long shaft flat blade screwdriver or ½ inch socket and extension

FIELD STRIP

1. Push the safety button (part #48) in the "safe" position and slide the fore-end (27) back approximately halfway.
2. For hunting models, unscrew and remove the magazine cap (39). For tactical models with extended magazine tubes and extended tactical chokes tubes, remove the choke tube, Figure 1. Next remove the

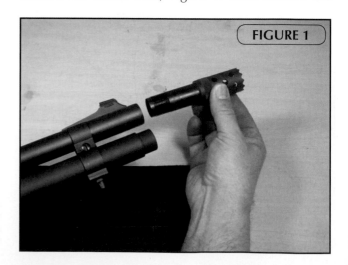

FIGURE 1

coupler screw to loosen and remove the coupler, Figure 2. Then remove the magazine cap and control the magazine spring until it is fully extended. This spring is long and under tension, Figure 3.

3. Slightly slide the forearm back and the pull the barrel (3) from the receiver (46), Figure 4.

4. Push the carrier (7) upward then depress and hold the left shell latch (55), Figure 5.

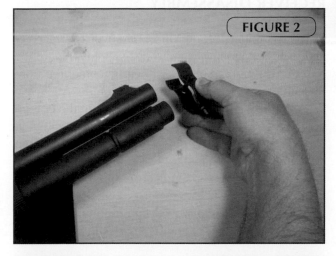

FIGURE 2

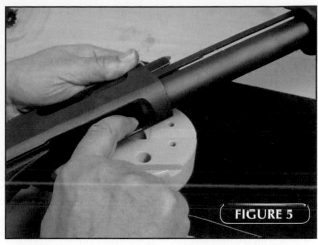

FIGURE 5

5. Slide the fore-end forward and off of the magazine tube.

6. Lift the breech bolt assembly and slide assembly from the rear of the action bars (28).

7. Using a punch, drift out the front and rear trigger plate pins (66 and 67), Figure 6.

8. Lift the rear of the trigger plate assembly, then slide it rearward and remove it from the receiver, Figure 7.

FIGURE 3

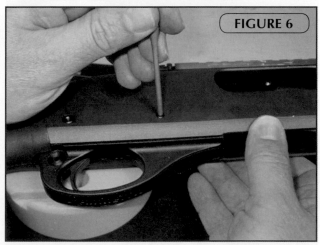

FIGURE 6

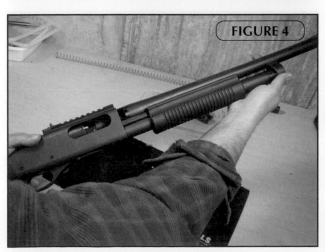

FIGURE 4

FIGURE 7

At this point the 870 is sufficiently disassembled for routine cleaning.

TRIGGER GROUP DISASSEMBLY

1. Hold the hammer (33) with your thumb, push the safety to the "fire" position and pull the trigger to release the hammer.

2. Push out the trigger plate pin bushing (68) from right to left using a punch, Figure 8.

3. Remove the sear spring (54), Figure 9.

4. Hold the carrier (7) in place and remove the carrier pivot tube (13) from left to right using a punch. Control the carrier and remove it up from the trigger plate. The carrier dog (8) and carrier dog washer (12) are attached to the carrier via the carrier dog pin (11).

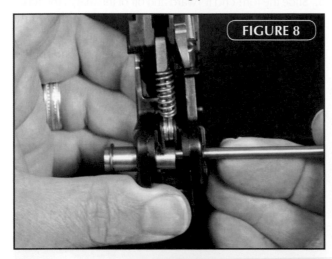

FIGURE 8

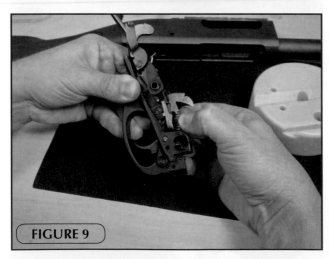

FIGURE 9

5. Next drift out the trigger pin (64) and remove upward the trigger and attached left connector (14) and right connector (15).

6. Remove the sear (52) by drifting out the sear pin (53) from right to left. The sear will come free.

Tuning Tip: Timney Triggers (timneytriggers.com) has a Trigger Fix kit that will change the factory trigger pull of the 870. The kit contains a replacement sear and sear springs in 4-, 3- and 2-lb. weights. Follow the manufacturer's installation instruction.

RECEIVER DISASSEMBLY

1. The remove the forend, press the left shell stop () with your finger through the bottom of the receiver and slide bolt assembly and slide assembly toward the muzzle. The bolt assembly will easily come free from the guide bars of the slide once clear of the receiver.

2. Pull the locking block retainer (37) from the bottom of the breech bolt (4), Figure 10.

3. To remove the firing pin (24) drift out the firing pin retaining pin (25), Figure 11. Remove the firing pin and firing pin retractor spring (26) from the rear of the breech bolt.

4. The stock (58) is removed by unscrewing the two recoil pad screws (47b) and removing the recoil pad.

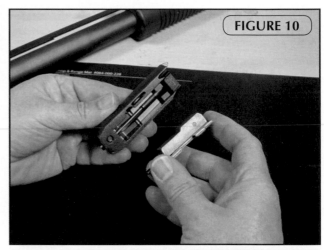

FIGURE 10

FIGURE 11

5. Use a long shaft flat blade screwdriver to remove   Reassemble in reverse order.
the stock bolt (60) and stock bolt lock washer (61).

Stock Tip: The 870 is compatible with numerous aftermarket stocks from Hogue (getgrip.com), MagPul (magpul.com), Mesa Tactical (mesatactical.com), Advanced Technology (atigunstocks.com) and others. The Pachmayr (pachmayr.com) Vindicator pistol grip and forend in checkered black rubber along with BATF-legal shortened barrel can turn your old bird gun into a home defender in 15 minutes or less.

WINCHESTER 1897

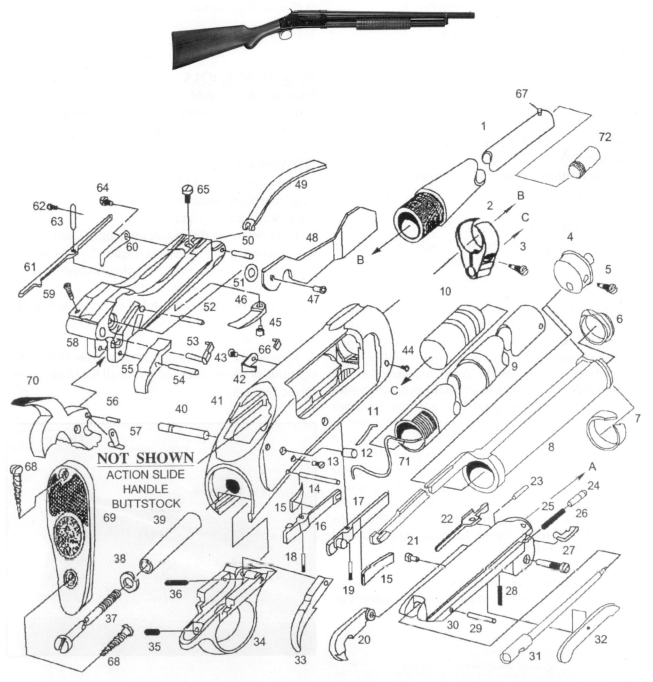

NOT SHOWN
ACTION SLIDE
HANDLE
BUTTSTOCK

PARTS LIST

1 Barrel
2 Magazine Band
3 Magazine Band Bushing Screw
4 Magazine Plug
5 Magazine Plug Screw
6 Action Slide Sleeve Screw Stop
7 Action Slide Spring
8 Action Slide
9 Magazine Tube
10 Magazine Follower
11 Action Slide Lock Release Plunger Pin Spring
12 Action Slide Lock Release Plunger Pin
13 Cartridge Guide Stop Screw
14 Trigger Pin
15 Cartridge Stop Spring (2 Req'd.)
16 Left Cartridge Stop
17 Right Cartridge Stop
18 Cartridge Stop Screw, left
19 Cartridge Stop Screw, Right
20 Action Slide Hook
21 Firing Pin Lock Screw
22 Extractor, Left
23 Extractor Pin, Left
24 Extractor Plunger, Right
25 Extractor Plunger Spring, Right
26 Extractor, Right
27 Action Slide Hook Screw
28 Firing Pin Lock Spring
29 Firing Pin Stop Pin
30 Breech Bolt
31 Firing Pin
32 Firing Pin Lock
33 Trigger
34 Trigger Bow
35 Trigger Stop Screw
36 Trigger Spring
37 Buttstock Bolt
38 Buttstock Bolt Washer
39 Receiver Shank
40 Carrier Pin
41 Receiver
42 Ejector Spring
43 Ejector Spring Screw
44 Magazine Tube Retaining Screw Stop Screw
45 Sear Spring Screw
46 Sear Spring
47 Cartridge Guide Rivet Screw
48 Cartridge Guide
49 Main Spring
50 Mainspring Pin
51 Cartridge Guide Friction Spring
52 Hammer Pin
53 Action Slide Lock Release Plunger
54 Sear Pin
55 Sear
56 Hammer Stirrup Pin
57 Hammer Stirrup
58 Carrier
59 Carrier Pin Stop Screw
60 Action Slide Lock Spring
61 Action Slide Lock
62 Action Slide Lock Joint Pin
63 Action Slide Lock Joint Pin
64 Action Slide Lock Spring
65 Main Spring Strain Screw
66 Ejector Pin
67 Front sight
68 Buttplate Screw (2 Req'd.)
69 Buttplate
70 Hammer
71 Magazine spring
72 Choke Tube

SPECIFICATIONS

Model: Model 1897
Action: pump
Barrel: 20 in.
Caliber: 12 gauge; 2-3/4-in. chamber
Capacity: 5+1
Common Features: blued finish, smooth wood stock/grooved forend

BACKGROUND

The original Winchester 1897 was available in numerous barrel lengths and shooters had a choice of either 12 or 16 gauge and solid frame or takedown. Over one million of these shotguns were manufactured, some old timers affectionately or not call them "thumb busters" as the slide protrudes from the rear of the frame upon pumping the action and if your grip is too high—well you get the picture. During World War I a trench version of the Model '97 with a heat shield over the barrel and bayonet lug was used to clean the trenches and was called a "trench sweeper." Today many of these old '97s have had their barrels cut down to compete in cowboy action shooting. I call that a great retirement for these old shotguns. If the trigger is pressed while the forearm is pumped the gun will fire. Compared to modern pump action shotguns the Model '97 is a complicated mechanism. The steps below use a solid frame Chinese-manufactured clone of Model '97.
Year Introduced: 1897–1957
Original Manufacturer: Winchester
Similar Models: Trench Gun (heat shield, bayonet lug)

REQUIRED TOOLS

Disassembly/Assembly: small punch, small and medium flat blade screwdriver, nylon hammer, wooden dowel or small block of wood

DISASSEMBLY

1. Use a medium flat blade screwdriver to remove the magazine band bushing screw (part #3) and loosen the magazine band (2), Figure 1.
2. Hold down on the magazine plug (4) and remove the magazine plug screw (5), Figure 2. Then remove the magazine band, magazine plug, magazine spring (71) and magazine follower (19).
3. Remove the magazine tube retaining screw (44) on the right side of the receiver (41) then unscrew the magazine tube (9).
4. Remove the cartridge guide stop screw (13) on the right side of the receiver using a small flat blade screwdriver, Figure 3.

FIGURE 1

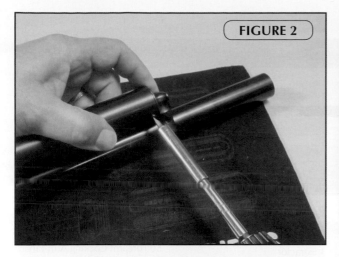

FIGURE 2

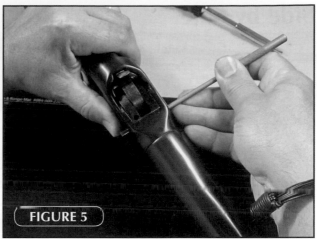

FIGURE 5

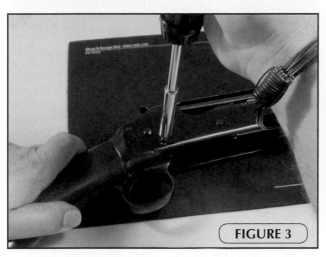

FIGURE 3

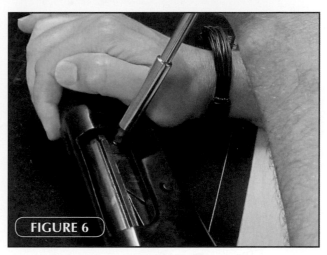

FIGURE 6

5. Using a small flat blade screwdriver remove carrier pin stop screw (69), Figure 4. Then drift out carrier pin (50) using a small punch, Figure 5.

6. Next remove the buttstock by first remove the two buttplate screws (68) and butt plate (69) then use a long shaft flat blade screwdriver to loosen and remove the buttstock bolt (37).

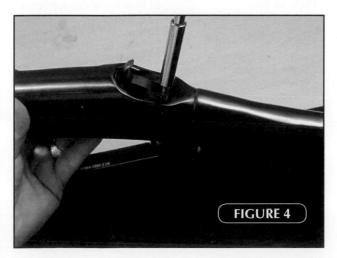

FIGURE 4

7. Pull the buttstock rearward off the receiver shank (39).

8. Cock back the hammer fully rearward and push the right cartridge stop button (17) on the right side of the receiver. Through the ejection port insert a small wood block or dowel or non-marring tool between the breech bolt (30) and carrier (58) so the carrier comes free through the bottom of the receiver.

9. Unscrew action slide hook screw (27), Figure 6. Then separate the action slide hook (20) from the breech bolt using a small flat blade screwdriver and remove the action slide hook from the bottom of the receiver.

10. Slide the breech bolt to the rear and pull it free from the receiver.

11. Drift out the trigger cross pin (14). Then use a nylon hammer to gently tap the trigger bow (34) to the rear of the receiver.

Reassemble in reverse order.

Side by Side

CZ CLASSIC HAMMER

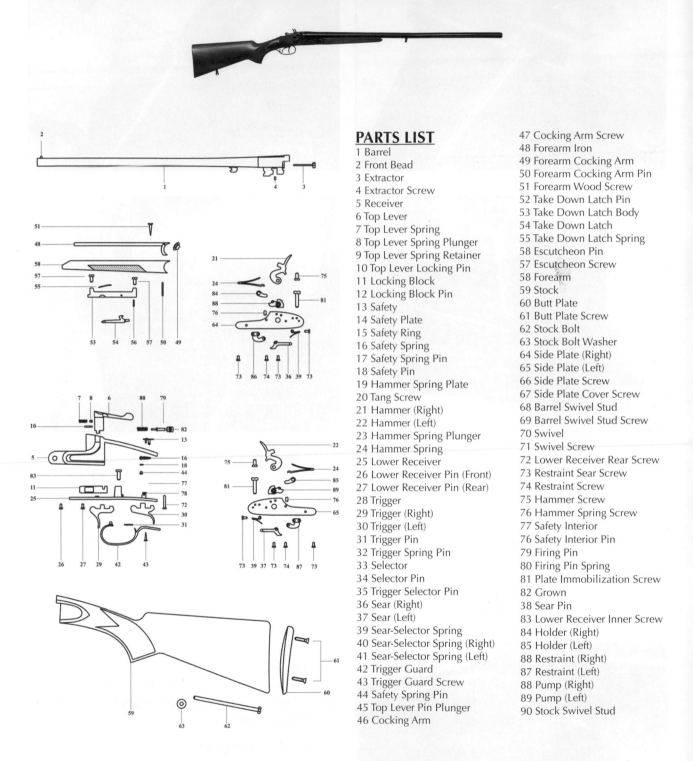

PARTS LIST

1 Barrel
2 Front Bead
3 Extractor
4 Extractor Screw
5 Receiver
6 Top Lever
7 Top Lever Spring
8 Top Lever Spring Plunger
9 Top Lever Spring Retainer
10 Top Lever Locking Pin
11 Locking Block
12 Locking Block Pin
13 Safety
14 Safety Plate
15 Safety Ring
16 Safety Spring
17 Safety Spring Pin
18 Safety Pin
19 Hammer Spring Plate
20 Tang Screw
21 Hammer (Right)
22 Hammer (Left)
23 Hammer Spring Plunger
24 Hammer Spring
25 Lower Receiver
26 Lower Receiver Pin (Front)
27 Lower Receiver Pin (Rear)
28 Trigger
29 Trigger (Right)
30 Trigger (Left)
31 Trigger Pin
32 Trigger Spring Pin
33 Selector
34 Selector Pin
35 Trigger Selector Pin
36 Sear (Right)
37 Sear (Left)
39 Sear-Selector Spring
40 Sear-Selector Spring (Right)
41 Sear-Selector Spring (Left)
42 Trigger Guard
43 Trigger Guard Screw
44 Safety Spring Pin
45 Top Lever Pin Plunger
46 Cocking Arm

47 Cocking Arm Screw
48 Forearm Iron
49 Forearm Cocking Arm
50 Forearm Cocking Arm Pin
51 Forearm Wood Screw
52 Take Down Latch Pin
53 Take Down Latch Body
54 Take Down Latch
55 Take Down Latch Spring
58 Escutcheon Pin
57 Escutcheon Screw
58 Forearm
59 Stock
60 Butt Plate
61 Butt Plate Screw
62 Stock Bolt
63 Stock Bolt Washer
64 Side Plate (Right)
65 Side Plate (Left)
66 Side Plate Screw
67 Side Plate Cover Screw
68 Barrel Swivel Stud
69 Barrel Swivel Stud Screw
70 Swivel
71 Swivel Screw
72 Lower Receiver Rear Screw
73 Restraint Sear Screw
74 Restraint Screw
75 Hammer Screw
76 Hammer Spring Screw
77 Safety Interior
76 Safety Interior Pin
79 Firing Pin
80 Firing Pin Spring
81 Plate Immobilization Screw
82 Grown
38 Sear Pin
83 Lower Receiver Inner Screw
84 Holder (Right)
85 Holder (Left)
88 Restraint (Right)
87 Restraint (Left)
88 Pump (Right)
89 Pump (Left)
90 Stock Swivel Stud

SPECIFICATIONS

Model: Classic Hammer
Action: side locks, extractors
Barrel: 30 in.
Caliber: 12 gauge
Capacity: 2
Common Features: double mechanical triggers, manual tang safety, color casehardened engraved action, blue finish, choke tubes, checkered Turkish walnut stock with pistol grip and splinter forend, rebounding hammers

BACKGROUND

Do not believe the hype some firearm brands say about guns that won the west. The common side-by-side shotgun was used by countless settlers in the westward expansion of the U.S. It filled the cooking pot and protected the family. The CZ Classic Hammer is similar to many double-barrel shotguns from the last 19th century and early 20th century. The Classic Hammer has updated the design with a thumb safety and choke tubes.

Year Introduced: 2010
Current Manufacturer: CZ (CZ-usa.com)
Similar Models: Hammer Coach (20 inch barrel)

REQUIRED TOOLS

Field Strip: none
Disassembly/Assembly: medium flat blade screwdriver with thin blade

FIELD STRIP

1. Pull the take down latch (part #54) on the forearm (58), Figure 1.
2. Pivot the forearm assembly away and up from the barrels (2) and receiver (5).

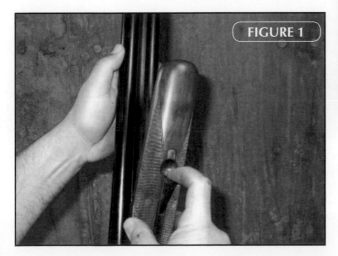

FIGURE 1

3. Hold the barrels in your left hand and grip the stock in your right; push the top lever (6) to the right. Use your left hand to push the barrels down. The barrels will then disengage from the receiver, Figure 2.

The shotgun is now sufficiently disassembled for cleaning.

FIGURE 2

DISASSEMBLY

1. To remove the side locks, first unscrew the plate immobilization screw (81) using a medium flat blade screwdriver on the left side plate (65), Figure 3. You may need to gently tap the locks with a rubber mallet to free them from the stock (59) and receiver, Figure 4.

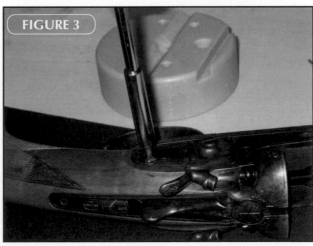

FIGURE 3

2. To remove the trigger guard (42), unscrew the rear trigger guard screw (43) using a medium flat blade screwdriver, Figure 5. Then unscrew the trigger guard from the receiver, Figure 6.

Reassemble in reverse order.

FIGURE 4

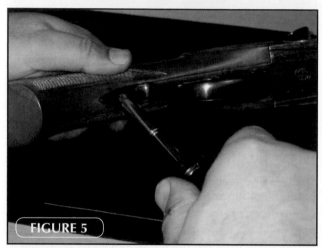

FIGURE 5

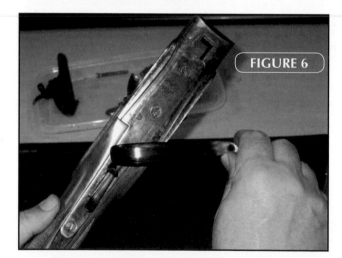

FIGURE 6

Reassembly Tip: The side lock have a tab at the forward most edge, Figure 7. Make sure you insert this tab into the receiver first when replacing the side locks, Figure 8. Also make sure the triggers are fully forward so they are below the side lock trigger bar.

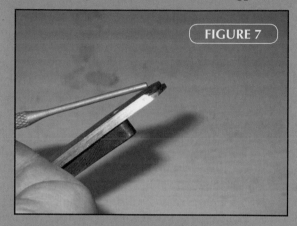

FIGURE 7

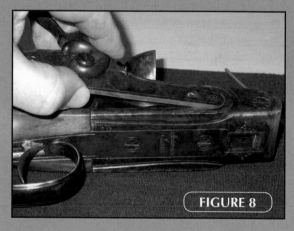

FIGURE 8

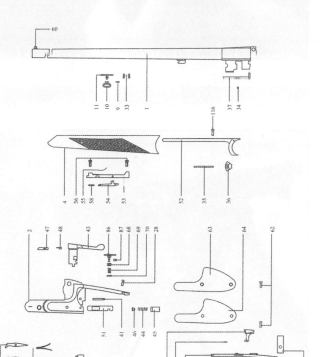

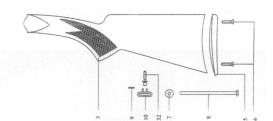

PARTS LIST

1 Barrel
2 Front Bead
3 Extractor
4 Extractor Screw
5 Receiver
6 Top Lever
7 Top Lever Spring
8 Top Lever Spring Plunger
9 Top Lever Spring Retainer
10 Top Lever Locking Pin
11 Locking Block
12 Locking Block Pin
13 Safety
14 Safety Plate
15 Safety Ring
16 Safety Spring
17 Safety Spring Pin
18 Safety Pin
19 Hammer Spring Plate
20 Tang Screw
21 Hammer (Right)
22 Hammer (Left)
23 Hammer Spring plunger
24 Hammer Spring
25 Lower Receiver
26 Lower Receiver Pin (Front)
27 Lower Receiver Pin (Rear)
28 Trigger
29 Trigger (Right)
30 Trigger (Left)
31 Trigger Pin
32 Trigger Spring Pin
33 Selector
34 Selector Pin
35 Trigger Selector Pin
36 Sear (Right)
37 Sear (Left)
39 Sear-Selector Spring
40 Sear-Selector Spring (Right)
41 Sear-Selector Spring (Left)
42 Trigger Guard
43 Trigger Guard Screw
44 Safety Spring Pin
45 Top Lever Pin plunger
46 Cocking Arm

47 Cocking Arm Screw
48 Forearm Iron
49 Forearm Cocking Arm
50 Forearm Cocking Arm Pin
51 Forearm Wood Screw
52 Take Down Latch Pin
53 Take Down Latch Body
54 Take Down Latch
55 Take Down Latch Spring
58 Escutcheon Pin
57 Escutcheon Screw
58 Forearm
59 Stock
60 Butt Plate
61 Butt Plate Screw
62 Stock Bolt
63 Stock Bolt Washer
64 Side Plate (Right)
65 Side Plate (Left)
66 Side Plate Screw
67 Side Plate cover Screw
68 Barrel Swivel Stud
69 Barrel Swivel Stud Screw
70 Swivel
71 Swivel Screw
72 Lower Receiver Rear Screw
73 Restraint Sear Screw
74 Restraint Screw
75 Hammer Screw
76 Hammer Spring Contra
   Screw
77 Safety Interior
76 Safety Interior Pin
79 Firing Pin
80 Firing Pin spring
81 Plate Immobilization Screw
82 Grown
38 Sear Pin
83 Lower Receiver Inner Screw
84 Holder (Right)
85 Holder (Left)
88 Restraint (Right)
87 Restraint (Left)
88 Pump (Right)
89 Pump (Left)
90 Stock Swivel Stud

SPECIFICATIONS

Model: Ringneck 201A Mini Single
Action: hammerless, boxlock, extractors
Barrel: 26 in. or 28 in.
Caliber: 410 or 28 gauge
Capacity: 2

Common Features: single mechanical trigger, selective safety, proportional frame to gauge, color casehardened engraved action with side plates, blue finish, choke tubes, checkered Turkish walnut stock with Prince of Wales pistol grip and splinter forend

BACKGROUND

The frame of the Ringneck 201A Mini Single is scaled down for 28-gauge shells. At six pounds the Ringneck is a delight to carry in field. It utilizes a single selective trigger and choke tubes. The Ringneck, like many side-by-sides and over-and unders, can be complicated to completely disassemble. The fact is most of these doubles don't need the detail strip of other firearms to keep them functioning for generations.

Year Introduced: 2005
Current Manufacturer: CZ (CZ-usa.com)
Similar Models: Ringneck 201A Single (20, 16 and 12 gauge; Prince of Wales grip stock), Ringneck Target (pistol grip stock, 30 inch barrels), Ringneck Straight Grip (20 gauge; English-style straight grip stock)

REQUIRED TOOLS

Field Strip: none
Disassembly/Assembly: medium flat blade screwdriver, 12mm socket with long extension

FIELD STRIP

1. Pull the take down latch (part #54) on the forearm (58), Figure 1.
2. Pivot the forearm assembly away and up from the barrels (2) and receiver (5), Figure 2.

FIGURE 1

3. Hold the barrels in your left hand and grip the stock in your right; push the top lever (6) to the right. With your left hand push the barrel down. The barrels will then disengage from the receiver, Figure 3.

The shotgun is now sufficiently disassembled for cleaning.

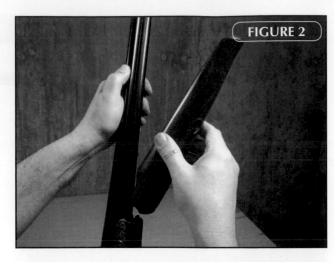

FIGURE 2

FIGURE 3

DETAILED DISASSEMBLY

1. To remove the stock (59) first unscrew the two recoil pad screws (61) using a medium Phillips screwdriver and remove the recoil pad (60).
2. Then use a 12mm socket on a long extension to remove the stock bolt (62), Figure 4.

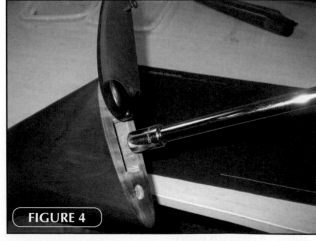

FIGURE 4

3. Next unscrew the four side plate screws; one side plate screw (66) and one Side plate cover screw (67) for each side plate, Figure 5. You may need to gently tap the receiver with a rubber mallet to dislodge the side plates. Remove side plates, Figure 6.

4. Next remove the rear trigger guard screw (43), Figure 7.

5. Pull the stock rearward and off the receiver, Figure 8. You may need to gently tap the stock with a rubber mallet to dislodge it.

6. The trigger guard (42) is removed from the receiver by unscrewing it, Figure 9.

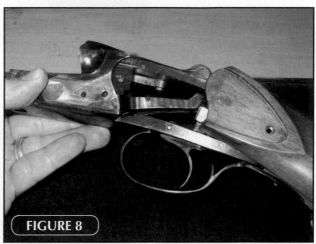

FIGURE 8

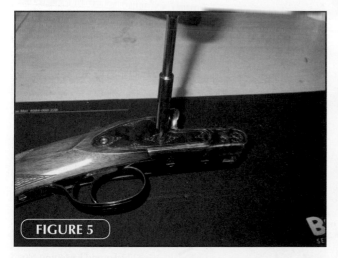

FIGURE 5

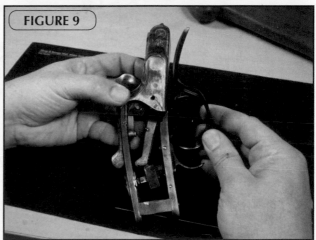

FIGURE 9

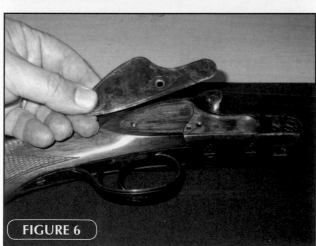

FIGURE 6

Disassembly Tip: When removing the stock on a shotgun, instead of removing the recoil pad from the stock just remove one recoil pad screw and loosen the other. Then you can swing the recoil pad which is still attached to the stock out of the way so you can access the stock bolt through the stock butt hole.

Reassemble in reverse order.

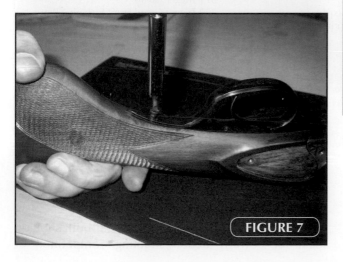

FIGURE 7

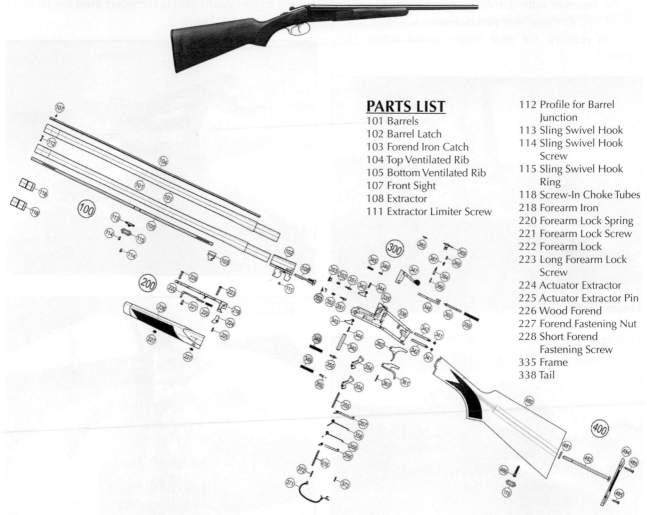

PARTS LIST

101 Barrels
102 Barrel Latch
103 Forend Iron Catch
104 Top Ventilated Rib
105 Bottom Ventilated Rib
107 Front Sight
108 Extractor
111 Extractor Limiter Screw

112 Profile for Barrel Junction
113 Sling Swivel Hook
114 Sling Swivel Hook Screw
115 Sling Swivel Hook Ring
118 Screw-In Choke Tubes
218 Forearm Iron
220 Forearm Lock Spring
221 Forearm Lock Screw
222 Forearm Lock
223 Long Forearm Lock Screw
224 Actuator Extractor
225 Actuator Extractor Pin
226 Wood Forend
227 Forend Fastening Nut
228 Short Forend Fastening Screw
335 Frame
338 Tail

340 Trunnion Pin
341 Cocking Pin Ring (2 Req'd.)
342 Hammer Cocking Pin (2 Req'd.)
343 Cocking Levers (2 Req'd.)
344 Actuator Fastening Pins (2 Req'd.)
345 Lever Lock Spring
346 Lever Spring Pin
347 Top Lever
348 Lever Lock
349 Hammer Impeller Spring (2 Req'd.)
350 Hammer Impeller (2 Req'd.)
351 Firing Pin (2 Req'd.)
352 Firing Pin Spring (2 Req'd.)

353 Firing Pin Fastening Nut (2 Req'd.)
354 Hammer (2 Req'd.)
355 Hammer and Sears Pin (2 Req'd.)
356 Left Sear
357 Right Sear
358 Sear Spring (2 Req'd.)
359 Lock Impeller Spring
360 Lock Impeller
361 Left Trigger
362 Right Trigger
363 Trigger Pin
364 Trigger Lock Lever
365 Trigger Lock Lever Pin

366 ever Fastening Pin
367 Trigger Lock Spring
368 Trigger Lock Spherical Pin
369 Trigger Lock
371 Trigger Guard
372 Trigger Guard Front Fastening Pin
373 Trigger Guard Rear Fastening Pin
480 Stock
481 Washer
482 Stock Fastening Screw
484 Butt Plate
485 Butt Plate Screw (2 Req'd.)
486 Sling Swivel Screw

SPECIFICATIONS

Model: Coach Gun
Action: hammerless, boxlock, extractors
Barrel: 20 in.
Caliber: .410, 20 gauge or 12 gauge
Capacity: 2
Common Features: double mechanical trigger, thumb safety, blue or nickel finish, fixed choke or choke tubes, pistol-grip or straight checkered walnut or synthetic stock

BACKGROUND

The Stoeger Coach Gun is a sturdy, well-built shotgun ideal for cowboy action shooting competition or

home defense. This short-barreled scatter gun features extractors and a relatively simple boxlock mechanism.
Year Introduced: 1991
Country Manufactured: Brazil
Current Importer: Stoeger Industries (stoegerindustries.com)
Similar Models: Coach Gun Supreme, Silverado, Silverado with English Stock

REQUIRED TOOLS

Field Strip: none
Disassembly/Assembly: medium Phillips screwdriver, large flat blade long shaft screwdriver

FIELD STRIP

1. Press the forearm lock (part #222) rearward and pull the forend (226) off the barrels (101), Figure 1.
2. Rotate the top lever (347) to the right and press the barrels downward to disengage the barrels from the frame (335), Figure 2.

The shotgun is now sufficiently disassembled for cleaning.

DETAILED DISASSEMBLY

1. Remove the long forearm lock screw (233) and short forearm screw (228) and remove the forearm latch assembly from the forend.
2. Unscrew and remove the two butt plate screws (485) and remove the butt plate (484) from the stock (480).
3. Use a large flat blade long shaft screwdriver to remove the stock, Figure 3.

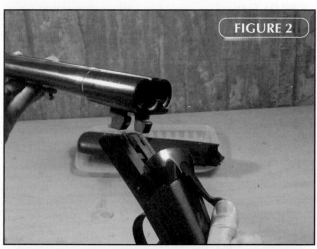

FIGURE 2

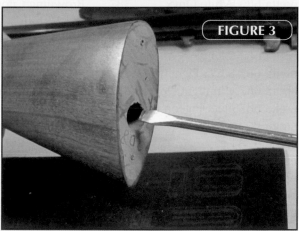

FIGURE 3

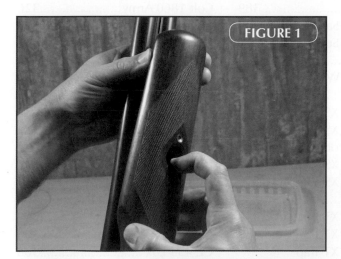

FIGURE 1

Reassemble in reverse order.

Cleaning Tip: Keep the breech faces clean and dirt free. If too much burned powder residue accumulates the action may not close and prevent the shotgun from firing. With the stock off blow out any grit. Typically the stock does not need to be removed for routine cleaning. Grease the lug areas liberally.

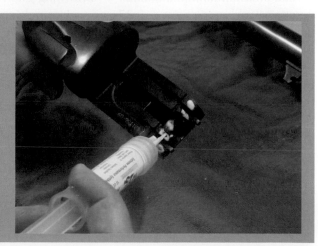

Cross Reference